"The sheer abundance of scholarship in this book makes it well worth reading. But Father Dale Launderville has not only gathered and digested the traditions surrounding celibacy in Greece, Mesopotamia, and ancient Israel. His insights and interpretations are compelling and often inspiring. Father Launderville writes well and helps the reader with frequent summaries and conclusions. A must-read book!"

—Irene Nowell, OSB
Author of *Women in the Old Testament*
(Liturgical Press)

"This wide-ranging book situates virginity, chastity, and celibacy within the larger social structure of the patriarchal household in Mesopotamia, Israel, and Greece. Drawing out the understandings of human sexuality in these three pre-Hellenistic cultures, this probing study examines sexual 'outliers,' such as the celibate prophet, Jeremiah. In this study, celibacy emerges as an effort to separate from customary social-sexual relations with a human partner in order to connect with the divine in a manner that would transcend death; it is, in other words, 'a proleptic death and a quest for transcendence.' The result is an understanding—and a concrete rationale for—the symbolic value of celibacy in the modern world: 'For one committed to a celibate life such sexual discipline is a fundamental means of shaping the ascetic body into a symbol of enduring life in the cosmic community.' The result of this challenging book is a rethinking of sexual 'outliers,' based on a learned examination of the very societies of antiquity that influenced Christian traditions of celibacy."

—Mark S. Smith
Skirball Professor of Bible
and Ancient Near Eastern Studies
New York University

"This volume provides a masterful treatment of celibacy in the ancient world. Dale Launderville discusses the topic in relationship to inner-household relationships, intermarriage, virginity and chastity, relationships with the divine, and transcending death's limitations. Skillfully utilizing vastly diverse material from ancient Israel, Mesopotamia, and Greece, he illuminates how celibacy was understood within each society while also illustrating how the parallels mutually inform our understanding of celibacy in the ancient world."

—John L. McLaughlin
Associate Professor of
Old Testament/Hebrew Bible
Director of Advanced Degree Programs
Faculty of Theology
University of St. Michael's College,
Toronto, Ontario

Dale Launderville, OSB

CELIBACY in the Ancient World

Its Ideal and Practice in Pre-Hellenistic Israel, Mesopotamia, and Greece

M G

A Michael Glazier Book

LITURGICAL PRESS
Collegeville, Minnesota

www.litpress.org

A Michael Glazier Book published by Liturgical Press

Cover design by David Manahan, OSB. Cover photo: Bronze sculpture, *Visionary Man*, © Gautier Willaume and istockphoto.com

1 2 3 4 5 6 7 8 9

Library of Congress Cataloging-in-Publication Data

Launderville, Dale.
Celibacy in the ancient world : its ideal and practice in pre-hellenistic Israel, Mesopotamia, and Greece / Dale Launderville.
p. cm.
"A Michael Glazier book."
Includes bibliographical references and index.
ISBN 978-0-8146-5697-6 — ISBN 978-0-8146-5734-8 (e-book)
1. Jeremiah (Biblical prophet) 2. Celibacy—History.
3. Chastity—History. I. Title.

BS580.J4L38 2010
204'.47—dc22 2010016697

Dedicated to my grandparents Edwin and Marie Madsen and Vincent and Marie Launderville for their profound love of family life.

Contents

Preface

Is celibacy possible? Does it play a socially constructive role for the communities in which it is practiced? These two questions have guided my investigation of the traditions of ancient Israel, Mesopotamia, and Greece in identifying those instances in which authoritatively endorsed celibacy occurred and to explain the contextual factors supporting such a way of life. Many of the texts dealing with this way of life in which sexual renunciation plays a fundamental role have strongly influenced the development of attitudes toward family life and sexual morality in the traditions of the Western world. To see how the celibate way of life was possible in these three ancient cultures prior to the Hellenistic age and the rise of Christianity helps us to understand those human and natural factors within contemporary communities that call forth the practice of celibacy.

In the abstract, celibacy is a cold, unappealing way of life. But I contend in this study that the celibate way of life is compelling in the context of a particular set of nurturing relationships. These vital, nurturing relationships that endure and extend through more than one generation are familial in character. Such relationships are formed not only in a nuclear family but also in the extended family and in those communities that work to make visible the cosmic destiny of such familial relationships. Celibates wager their lives on the matrix of relationships of love that constitute a family and thereby help to fashion a cosmic scope to the potential of earthly life. The outlook, attitude, and discipline of the celibate overlaps and complements in significant ways that of the married members of a household. Thus attention to how to live as a celibate can be beneficial to both married and unmarried members of a household.

Close attention to the context and the particularities of the practice of celibacy and sexual renunciation is based on the conviction that insight on how to live this way of life can be gained by entering into dialogue with these ancient voices. By trying to re-create the ways the ancients thought about these practices, the modern reader can come to a better understanding of how to carry them out in the present era. It is through attention to a particular set of circumstances that one can gain insights on how to live the celibate way of life. An underlying goal of this study is to provoke such reflection that leads individuals to new insights on particular ways to live the celibate life.

I have dedicated this work to my maternal and paternal grandparents. They created a matrix of meaning through their devotion to family life that has guided and sustained me through my first fifty-eight years. Their love and attention to a good larger than themselves lives on in my memory and in relationships that sustain me.

I am indebted to Abbot John Klassen and my brothers in my monastic community for their support and their witness to the familial life of Christians. They know only too well that the present writer is the one who has the most to learn from these voices from the past.

I wish to acknowledge the careful, meticulous copyediting provided by Dr. Linda Maloney. Her numerous recommendations have enhanced the final version.

I am grateful to my colleagues in the Department of Theology of the College of Saint Benedict and Saint John's University and in the School of Theology/Seminary for their insightful discussion of the thesis and argument of this work. In particular, I am indebted to the following colleagues and confrères for reading and criticizing one or more chapters of this work: William Cahoy, Charles Bobertz, Anna Mercedes, Rene McGraw OSB, and Roman Paur OSB. Also members of the Old Testament Colloquium and the Seminar on Divinity in Ancient Israel of the Catholic Biblical Association provided valuable direction on individual chapters.

I am greatly indebted to Janine Lortz of the interlibrary loan department of our Alcuin Library at Saint John's University. Her ability to obtain even the most obscure titles and to do so expeditiously was indispensable for keeping this research project on track.

Finally, I am most grateful to more than twenty undergraduate theology majors at the College of Saint Benedict and Saint John's University who read and commented on this book in manuscript form and on a number of occasions advanced the argument in significant ways. Their courage and insightfulness in engaging this challenging area of personal and communal life is a gift not to be underestimated.

The translations of editions of the Hebrew, Greek, and Akkadian texts are my own unless otherwise indicated. The chronologies followed in this book are based on the following sources: Jacques Brunschwig and G. E. R. Lloyd, *Greek Thought: A Guide to Classical Knowledge* (Cambridge, MA: Belknap Press of Harvard University Press, 2000), 999–1005; E. J. Bickerman, *Chronology of the Ancient World* (London: Thames and Hudson, 1968), 197–213; John Bright, *A History of Israel* (Philadelphia: Westminster, 1981), 465–74; Dominique Charpin, "The History of Ancient Mesopotamia: An Overview," *Civilizations of the Ancient Near East*, ed. Jack Sasson (New York: Scribners, 1995), 807–29.

Dale Launderville, OSB
Saint John's University School of Theology/Seminary
Collegeville, Minnesota
September 2009

Introduction

> "The one who is not able to live in community or who has no need to be part of the city because he is self-sufficient must either be a beast or a god."
>
> Aristotle, *Politics*, Book 1.2, 1253a 28-30

The practice of celibacy places one in a liminal state. To commit to remain unmarried (Latin *caelebs*, "unmarried, single") for a lifetime or an extended period places one outside the mainstream of human society. Celibacy is a form of withdrawal from human society that seems at odds with human nature. The solitary character of this way of life positions the celibate, as Aristotle's words in the masthead indicate, to participate in the spheres of the gods and of the beasts. The celibate, it is presumed, refrains from sexual relations; otherwise there would be little difference between the unmarried state of the celibate and that of the prostitute. The unusual or extraordinary character of the celibate way of life arises from making a liminal state permanent. The potency of the liminal state of the unmarried in terms of sexuality and youth aims to sustain itself—albeit in transmuted forms—over the duration of one's existence. This condition of delayed fulfillment can be experienced as one of hopeful anticipation or as one of frustrated absence. To sustain this way of life seems to be the prerogative of deities like Hestia, Artemis, or Athena; humans would seem to be tempting fate by laying claim to the potency of a liminal state for a lifetime.

The extraordinary, if not abnormal character of the celibate way of life, is attested only sporadically in the cultures of ancient Israel, Mesopotamia, and Greece, yet these exceptional occurrences afford the opportunity to examine the social, economic, political, and religious circumstances that have allowed the celibate way of life to become visible and be remembered. An ongoing concern of this study will be to uncover the continuities between the normal practices of sexual renunciation (e.g., avoiding adultery) and the more extreme form entailed by celibacy. So, for example, there should be similarities in the skills required to resist extramarital affairs and those required to live as a celibate; the continuity becomes a bit clearer if one pictures the married person as exclusively devoted to a spouse and the celibate as exclusively devoted to a deity. In the case of the celibate, however, the erotic dimension of the personal relationship to a deity would be expressed in a more spiritual and less carnal way than that typical of a husband and wife.[1] This question of spiritualizing the erotic is directly engaged by Plato in his *Symposium* and indirectly in prophetic, literary, and ritual texts in the Israelite and Mesopotamian traditions. This issue of the place of the erotic in the celibate way of life is continuous with the perennial human concern for the integration of sexuality in a healthy human life.

Within social and political dynamics, the way a phenomenon behaves in extreme circumstances can shed new light on how it behaves under normal conditions.[2] A recurring factor among those giving rise to celibacy is a social or political crisis. To gain one's bearings in the rapidly shifting circumstances of a crisis, one needs to find a fixed point. The magnitude of the forces of disintegration in this crisis reveal that this experience is a form of confrontation with death. To find a way of domesticating death or bringing death within the dynamics of the cosmic household—i.e., one spanning the spheres of heaven, earth, and the netherworld—is the quest that brings coherence to the celibate way of life. Celibacy makes sense only when the dynamics of the human household are placed within those of the cosmic household. In the process, however, the danger of spiritualizing the carnal into oblivion or of defiling the spiritual through the carnal is ever present. How these three ancient cultures wrestled with the challenge of integrating the spiritual with the carnal in a human existence faced with death is an ongoing concern of this study.

1. Cf. Pirjo Lapinkivi, "The Sumerian Sacred Marriage and Its Aftermath," in *Sacred Marriages: The Divine-Human Sexual Metaphor from Sumer to Early Christianity*, ed. Martti Nissinen and Risto Uro, 7–41 (Winona Lake, IN: Eisenbrauns, 2008), at 33.

2. Mary Douglas, *Purity and Danger* (London: Routledge & Kegan Paul, 1966), 4; Carl Schmitt, *Political Theology: Four Chapters on the Concept of Sovereignty* (Cambridge, MA: Massachusetts Institute of Technology Press, 1985), 5, 13, 33, 36, defines the sovereign as "the one who decides on the exception"; thus in a time of crisis the qualities of both the leader and the community can be seen more clearly.

A key question in assessing the practice of celibacy is the context in which it occurs. As a form of sexual renunciation, celibacy requires that its proponents shape their bodies into living symbols of a reality that goes beyond appearances. On the surface, lifelong celibacy appears to be a form of suicide. But within the web of relationships spanning the cosmic household, the sacrificial element of celibacy aims to strengthen vertical relationships (human to divine) at the expense of horizontal ones (human to human). The countercultural character of the celibate witness has as its immediate goal the triggering of reflection, within a community in crisis, on the transcendent matrix that alone can bring coherence to an existence beset by death.

The renunciation of sexuality required by celibacy is a moment of negativity that can unfold deeper levels of one's identity. Hegel claimed that the essence of a thing has a "negative self-relation": i.e., a thing is defined by what it is not and so a thing effects a more refined statement of what it is through comparison with other things by which it defines itself over against them.[3] In other words, a comparative dynamic is inherent in the very nature of an entity. In light of this negative self-relation of a thing to itself, one could argue that the renunciation or negativity inherent in the celibate state is a striving for a deeper dimension of life, one that goes beyond death.

A recurrent way of imagining the transcendent destiny of humans within the texts of the traditions of Israel, Mesopotamia, and Greece is the construction of a web of relationships extending beyond the earthly household to the cosmic one. The practice of burying one's ancestors within the household or on the ancestral land is attested in all three cultures. These people would give food and drink offerings to their ancestors with the conviction that their ancestors were still present with them.[4] Even though life in the netherworld was a gloomy existence, the attention to this sphere testified to a desire for transcendence. Even if meaningful life for the individual after death was muted in the pre-Hellenistic period, many Israelites, Mesopotamians, and Greeks had a clear sense that the individual lived on in the ancestors. When Jeremiah refrained from marrying and having a family to concretize his message of the end of Judah and Jerusalem (Jer 16:1-4), he was both affirming and

3. Georg W. F. Hegel, *The Encyclopaedia Logic (with the Zusätze)*, Part I of the *Encyclopaedia of Philosophical Sciences with the Zusätze*, trans. T. F. Geraets, W. A. Suchting, and H. S. Harris (Indianapolis: Hackett, 1991), §114, pp. 178–79.

4. 1 Sam 28:13; Ps 106:28; Isa 8:19-20; Theodore Lewis, "The Ancestral Estate (*naḥălat ʾelōhîm*) in 2 Samuel 14:16," *JBL* 110 (1991): 597–612, at 602–3, 607–8.

challenging this cosmic household model. On the one hand, he was claiming that the land would be devastated and that there would be no remaining descendants to keep alive the memory of the deceased ancestors (Jer 16:3-4). On the other hand, he was placing his hope in YHWH that, as the ultimate agent of doom, he would provide a way out for those who repented. This way out would be a form of communion with the divine that would transcend death (cf. Jer 17:8). Analogously, Plato imagined a form of communion with the good by the soul's efforts to behold the good (*Rep.* 508e). Even though this striving of the soul to behold the good seems to spiritualize the human person out of his or her carnality, there is still a sense of individual consciousness or personhood in this act of beholding. This surviving individual identity in communion with a transcendent agent suggests that a form of community—capable of developing into a matrix of relationships like that of a household—will be operative in the transcendent sphere.

Proponents of the practice of celibacy support the view of a meaningful afterlife not only because of the hope it offers but also because of the equilibrium it can bring into conflicted relationships within a community. A meaningful afterlife validates forms of extreme sacrifice for the common good that would otherwise appear to be mindlessly suicidal. However, critics of this practice brand this "pie in the sky" strategy as an instance of using a symbol to exploit the people.[5] They claim that those Judahites who affirm the authenticity of Jeremiah's celibate lifestyle as a judgment decreeing the imminent end of their nation will be stepping back from the existing sociopolitical structures in Judah and foregoing their immediate concrete benefits with the vague expectation that some future form of compensation will be offered them.

An analogy might be drawn from the example of the Homeric hero Achilles. As a heroic warrior he was ready to lose his life in battle at an early age with the prospect that he would be honored in the community in coming generations by the bards' singing his exploits (Il. 9.410-16).[6] Achilles became angrily skeptical of the community's commitment to

5. Pierre Bourdieu, "The Production and Reproduction of Legitimate Language," in *Language and Symbolic Power*, ed. John B. Thompson (Cambridge, MA: Harvard University Press, 1991), 51; Roy Rappaport, *Ritual and Religion in the Making of Humanity* (Cambridge: Cambridge University Press, 1999), 55; Zdzislaw Mach, *Symbols, Conflict, and Identity. Essays in Political Anthropology* (New York: SUNY Press, 1993), 108, 268–69; Jonathan Hart, *Northrop Frye: The Theoretical Imagination* (New York: Routledge, 1994), 241.

6. Charles Segal, *Singers, Heroes, and Gods in the Odyssey* (Ithaca, NY: Cornell University Press, 1994), 140–41.

this heroic code when Agamemnon confiscated his war trophy (*Il.* 9.315-22). It was Achilles' devotion to his friend Patroclus, whose death he would avenge at the cost of his own life, that moved him to reenter the war (*Il.* 18.1-34, 215-29). For Achilles the community's former promise of glorifying its fallen warriors through the songs of the bards was replaced with the love he had for his friend. This love transcended death, even if Achilles did not explicitly articulate that transcendence in terms of the friend's future existence in the netherworld.

In Jeremiah's case, even if he did not describe the form individual existence would take after death in communion with YHWH, he does suggest that there will be some form of postmortem existence of the individual. Perhaps the enduring communion gained through devotion to the Torah can be seen as a form of love. The depth of meaning in such a relationship of love can overpower a human's fear of death. Thus, in Jeremiah's embattled existence in the last days of Judah in which he gave witness by his celibate way of life to YHWH's intervention as a judge in the affairs of Judah, he was somehow strengthened so that his devotion to YHWH won out over his fear for his own survival. Abstracting from Jeremiah's personal sacrifice in his relationship to YHWH and from Achilles' avenging the death of Patroclus, one can see that in a relationship of love the individual dies to self but lives on by focusing on the other. Celibacy receives its ultimate justification on the basis of love, a form of sacrificial love that is preeminently exemplified in the relationships that bind together husband and wife and parent and child.

The primary arena in which celibate love had to work in order to realize itself in the pre-Hellenistic cultures of Israel, Mesopotamia, and Greece was the patriarchal household.[7] When a young woman is asked by her father to maintain her virginity until marriage and at the time of her arranged marriage to relinquish her virginity, a post-Enlightenment observer would probably regard such control of a daughter's sexuality as tyrannical.[8] Most young women in Greece and Mesopotamia were probably not much older than fourteen at the time they were given in marriage. So the requirement of sexual sacrifices on behalf of a patriarchal

7. On the 19th-century CE focus on the family as the locus of sexuality see Michel Foucault, *The History of Sexuality*, vol. 1: *An Introduction*, trans. Robert Hurley (New York: Pantheon, 1978), 108–11.

8. Cf. Jerrold S. Cooper, "Virginity in Ancient Mesopotamia," in *Sex and Gender in the Ancient Near East: Proceedings of the 47th Rencontre Assyriologique Internationale, Helsinki, July 2–6, 2001*, CRRAI 47, ed. Simo Parpola and Robert M. Whiting, 91–112 (Helsinki: The Neo-Assyrian Text Corpus Project, 2002), at 105.

household raises the issue of the way in which power shapes the interpretation of sexual desire and its expression. Foucault has argued that sexual desire in all its diversity should be given the space to express itself.[9] He is pessimistic about the potential of liberation movements to effect needed change and instead appeals to individuals to be skeptical of cultural constraints on sexual expression.[10]

The channeling of sex as a powerful drive is a perennial concern of the cultures of Israel, Mesopotamia, and Greece. Is it simply that the regulation of sex is an effective tool for hegemonic forces to sustain their power? Or is there a legitimate concern for the common good and social order that calls for such regulation by the heads of households? In the pre-Hellenistic era in these three cultures, the need for the regulation of sexuality was largely unquestioned, and the responsibility rested not only upon the households but also on the city or state.[11] The regulation of sexuality is seen in the Holiness Code in Israel (Leviticus 18–20), in the *Code of Hammurapi* and other Mesopotamian collections of laws, and in Solon's laws in sixth-century Greece. Various legal cases show that this was a matter of serious concern for a stable sociopolitical order.[12] In all three cultures sexual transgression was regarded as a defiling force that undermined the integrity of the community as a whole.[13] The public sensibility that certain sexual improprieties are harmful to the common

9. Foucault, *The History of Sexuality*, vol. 1: *An Introduction*, 103; Anthony Giddens, *The Transformation of Intimacy: Sexuality, Love and Eroticism in Modern Societies* (Stanford, CA: Stanford University Press, 1992), 33.

10. Foucault, *Introduction*, 92–95, 123.

11. Lev 20:10; Deut 22:22; Prov 6:29-35; Daniel Block, "Marriage and Family in Ancient Israel," in *Marriage and Family in the Biblical World*, ed. Ken M. Campbell, 33–102 (Downers Grove, IL: InterVarsity Press, 2003), at 63; *CH* 129; 131-32; Victor Matthews, "Marriage and Family in the Ancient Near East," 1–32, at 27, in *Marriage and Family in the Biblical World*; Raymond Westbrook, *Old Babylonian Marriage Law*, AfO Beiheft 23 (Horn, Austria: F. Berger, 1988), 75; Cynthia B. Patterson, *The Family in Greek History* (Cambridge, MA: Harvard University Press, 1998), 145; Elizabeth Meier Tetlow, *Women, Crime, and Punishment in Ancient Law and Society* (New York: Continuum, 2004), 51–52.

12. Martha T. Roth, *Law Collections from Mesopotamia and Asia Minor*, SBL Writings from the Ancient Word Series 6, 2d ed. (Atlanta: Scholars Press, 1995), 71–142; for Solon's laws see, e.g., *Solon of Athens: New Historical and Philological Approaches*, ed. Josine H. Blok and André P. M. H. Lardinois (Leiden: Brill, 2006); Demosthenes, "Theomnestus and Apollodorus Against Naeara," 59:16, 52 in *Demosthenes: Private Orations*, vol. 3, *Orations L–LIX*, trans. A. T. Murray (Cambridge, MA: Harvard University Press, 1939).

13. Block, "Marriage and Family in Ancient Israel," 63; Westbrook, *Old Babylonian Marriage Law*, 75; Patterson, *The Family in Greek History*, 145.

good is still operative in American society, as evidenced by the public's reaction to President Clinton's affair with Monica Lewinsky.

The laws, customs, and teachings of these three ancient cultures in the pre-Hellenistic era are characterized by mediating positions between Foucault's call for nonregulation of sexual expression by direct and indirect cultural agents and the later Hellenistic Stoic strategy of channeling sexual desire.[14] When political leaders implement measures that intrude into the private sphere of the household, they mount a defense based on the plight of the common good. Ezra breaks up mixed marriages in fifth-century Yehud to stave off assimilation of the Yahwistic community into the local culture (Ezra 10:1-12).[15] A Middle Assyrian Law (§55) dictates that if a married man rapes a young woman, his wife shall be raped and replaced with the young woman whom he has raped.[16] In Athens in 451 BCE, Pericles championed the enactment of a citizenship law requiring that for a newborn to be a citizen both parents must be Athenian citizens.[17] These state intrusions into the private realm of the household indicate that the private and public realms in a community overlapped.[18] The key question was the extent to which the oversight of authority figures in the lives of ordinary people was vitalizing or oppressive. In the midst of the ambiguity and indirection of sexual dynamics, the particular judgments of authorities are of greater import than general principles.

For equilibrium to be maintained in individual and collective bodies fueled by desire, it was essential that authorities and individuals alike foster a discipline (ascesis) attentive to competing forces. Geoffrey Harpham has argued that such discipline is essential to the vitality of sexual desire, for he claims that repression arose in consciousness

14. Michel Foucault, *The History of Sexuality*, vol. 2: *The Use of Pleasure*, trans. Robert Hurley (New York: Pantheon, 1985), 25–32; Margaret R. Graver, *Stoicism and Emotion* (Chicago: University of Chicago Press, 2007), 185–89.

15. Sara Japhet, "People and Land in the Restoration Period," 96–116, in eadem, *From the Rivers of Babylon to the Highlands of Judah: Collected Studies on the Restoration Period* (Winona Lake, IN: Eisenbrauns, 2006), at 99, 115; Daniel L. Smith, *The Religion of the Landless: The Social Context of the Babylonian Exile* (Bloomington, IN: Meyer-Stone Books, 1989), 197; Daniel Smith-Christopher, "The Mixed Marriage Crisis in Ezra 9–10 and Nehemiah 13: A Study of the Sociology of the Post-Exilic Judaean Community," in *Second Temple Studies. 2. Temple and Community in the Persian Period*, *JSOTSup* 175, ed. Tamara Eskenazi and Kent Richards, 243–65 (Sheffield: Sheffield Academic Press, 1994).

16. Roth, *Law Collections from Mesopotamia and Asia Minor*, 174–75.

17. Demosthenes, "Against Naeara," 59:16.

18. David Cohen, *Law, Sexuality, and Society: The Enforcement of Morals in Classical Athens* (Cambridge: Cambridge University Press, 1994), 74.

simultaneously with desire.[19] They function coordinately, as do the opposite forces of a bowstring; it is the simultaneous movement in opposite directions that creates the requisite tension in the bowstring. To fail to channel sexual desire is to slide toward dissipation, where sexual desire has diminished—a movement toward death. By contrast, the repressed state of a virgin carries the aura of an untapped potency in the estimation of the household or community, even if such repression is experienced as stultifying by the individual. This repressed state symbolizes an enduring relationship with the divine that transcends death (cf. Gen 39:9; Prov 1:20-33; 7:4-5; 8:1-36).[20] The various types of sexual renunciation enjoined by the codes of these three cultures—e.g., refraining from premarital and extramarital sex, monitoring genital emissions—are form-producing activities.[21] They are the sexual calisthenics by which the disciplined body is shaped into an exemplary artifact. For one committed to a celibate way of life such sexual discipline is a fundamental means of shaping the ascetic body into a symbol of enduring life in the cosmic community. Since descriptions of the celibate life are only sporadically attested in the records of these three ancient cultures, most of the practices of sexual renunciation are associated with the patriarchal household and not with those more radical measures guided by devotion to a transcendent reality.

Disciplinary measures that try to sculpt sexual desire are not only physical but also linguistic in character. Foucault strongly objected to the Christian church's use of auricular confession to shape the landscape of legitimate sexual desire.[22] He protested that this technique focused attention on desire rather than on objective acts and thus led to the repression of sexual desires essential to human flourishing. He argues that these excessively intrusive measures enhanced the power and identity of the Christian establishment at the expense of human vitality.[23] For

19. Geoffrey Galt Harpham, *The Ascetic Imperative in Culture and Criticism* (Chicago and London: University of Chicago Press, 1987), 52, 54; Alexandre Leupin, *Lacan Today: Psychoanalysis, Science, Religion* (New York: Other Press, 2004), 4.

20. Cf. Foucault, *Use of Pleasure*, 20, 243.

21. Harpham, *The Ascetic Imperative*, xiv.

22. Foucault, *Introduction*, 57–66.

23. Ibid., 12; Foucault, *Use of Pleasure*, 20; Bernard Reginster, *The Affirmation of Life: Nietzsche on Overcoming Nihilism* (Cambridge, MA: Harvard University Press, 2006), 45. Charles Taylor (*A Secular Age* [Cambridge, MA: Belknap Press, 2007], 18) explains a fundamental tension in Christian life as follows: "Flourishing is good, nevertheless, seeking it is not our ultimate goal. But even where we renounce it, we re-affirm it, because we follow God's will in being a channel for it to others, and ultimately to all."

Foucault, as for Nietzsche before him, the ascetic body was a sign of alienation from life rather than a symbol of a deeper life beyond appearances. Nietzsche had charged that the Israelite priests of the Persian era stood reality on its head; in his view the vibrant sensuality and violence of the earlier Old Testament period gave way to the anemic, world-denying program of the disenfranchised priests.[24]

So the important question remains: what constitutes a constructive way of transmuting sexual desire so that the community as well as the individual flourishes? The fear of the sexual drive, because of its tendency to go to excess, tends to give rise to measures that try to exert excessive control and usually become counterproductive. For example, to categorize sensual desire as polluting can stifle personal expression. By contrast, contemplative activity can allow the realities of beauty and truth to attract and shape sexual desire.[25] The impact of language on sexual desire is a matter of great concern, for both sexual desire and the capacity to speak are primordial human functions that decisively shape individuals and communities.

The experience of alienation is as primordial to the human condition as the capacity to speak. The psychoanalyst Jacques Lacan explains that the infant learns how to form sentences by becoming aware of itself apart from its mother.[26] The separation of the subject from the predicate of a sentence manifests the "over-againstness" of the subject and its environment. When the infant was joined to its mother, the otherness of the mother was part of the infant. But when the infant came to birth and began to speak, the otherness of the mother separated from the infant. An important point to be drawn from this effort to describe the birth of language is that alienation is integral to the human that speaks and should not be squelched.[27] The strategy for maturation and growth must address the way to balance alienation with constructive forms of union.

24. Friedrich Nietzsche, "Genealogy of Morals," in idem, *Birth of Tragedy and the Genealogy of Morals*, trans. Francis Golffing (Garden City, NY: Doubleday, 1956), §6, pp. 165–66; idem, *Beyond Good and Evil*, trans. Marianne Cowan (Chicago: Henry Regnery, 1955), §62, pp. 70–71.

25. Foucault, *Use of Pleasure*, 243.

26. Jacques Lacan, "The Mirror Stage as Formative of the Function of the I as Revealed in Psychoanalytic Experience," 1–7, and "The Signification of the Phallus," 281–91, at 289–90, in idem, *Écrits: A Selection* (New York and London: W. W. Norton, 1977).

27. Bruce Fink, *The Lacanian Subject: Between Language and Jouissance* (Princeton: Princeton University Press, 1997), 51–52; Colette Soler, *What Lacan Said About Women: A Psychoanalytic Study*, trans. John Holland (New York: Other Press, 2006), 31.

It is in this separation of the subject from "the other" that distinctive human characteristics of love and trust take shape.

Harpham argues that along with the capacity to speak comes the experience of temptation.[28] Eve's dialogue with the serpent is the first instance of human speech in the Old Testament, but it is also, according to Harpham, an illustration of the fact that temptation is inherent in language.[29] He extends his argument further to state that temptation is a sign of repression. Thus he sees the desire for the forbidden fruit as an awareness equiprimordial with the inner movement to counter this desire.[30] The upshot of this explanation is that efforts to eradicate all forms of repression as cultural constructions that give rise to alienation are misguided. The strategy is to seek a balance between desire and repression that is attentive to the life of the individual within a human and cosmic community.

The balancing act toward sexual desire is part and parcel of the human need to engage the world in order to realize the life offered to one. Hannah Arendt contended that life is not simply handed to one but must be realized not only through ongoing questioning of the meaning of life but also through acting to manifest one's identity as an agent in the world.[31] But such an engagement with the world cannot overlook the fact that life is a gift. This bestowal of life on the individual summons one to recognize the transcendent origin of life. The appeal of the transcendent to the human questioner places one in the situation in which receptivity, rather than skepticism, is the starting point for getting one's bearings on life. To doubt everything in order to find an indubitable starting point fails to appreciate the bond with the other that has been established by the donation of life itself. Jean-Luc Marion argues that the question "does anyone out there love me?" opens up a dimension of existence that eludes the thinking ego in its quest for indubitable knowledge.[32] The knowing that comes from loving is more primordial than that which comes from questioning.

28. Harpham, *The Ascetic Imperative*, 49, 61.

29. Ibid., 49.

30. Ibid., 54.

31. Hannah Arendt, *The Human Condition* (Chicago: University of Chicago Press, 1958), 168–74.

32. Jean-Luc Marion, *The Erotic Phenomenon*, trans. Stephen Lewis (Chicago: University of Chicago Press, 2007), 46. For a critique of the Enlightenment view of the essential self see Mary Midgley, "The Soul's Successors: Philosophy and the 'Body,'" in *Religion and the Body*, ed. Sarah Coakley, 53–68 (Cambridge: Cambridge University Press, 1997), at 56.

Arendt claims that love (*agapē*) is antipolitical, for it distances itself from the good and bad qualities of the one who is loved.[33] She defines the political sphere as one in which the judgment of the thinking individual interacts with the judgment of the community. Thus in her view the good of the community calls upon the individual thinker to move from solitude into the political sphere by the act of judging.[34] The celibate Jeremiah is an example of one who enters into judgment with the people of Judah and Jerusalem both by his words and by his way of life. His embodied existence becomes a symbol of impending judgment on Jerusalem. The receptivity that characterizes love must adapt to the reality of the political sphere in which judging is indispensable. The meditation on the Torah that would sustain a celibate like Jeremiah would seem to communicate this kind of love (*ḥesed*) that allows for judging. The polyvalence of the concept of love reveals its integrative potential, which stems from a kind of knowing that arises from the heart and not simply from the head.

The integrative power of love is diminished if erotic love is repressed out of fear of its potential to go to excess. Marion counsels that the individual must set as a goal to be the first one to love and to do so without fear of rejection.[35] The goal of such a lover is to love. Even when the lover's love is rejected, the lover can be assured that he or she has loved.[36] Such love is always directed toward the face of another, which demands respect for the boundaries that person sets. Marion's exhortation is designed to open the way for love to wield its power in transforming relationships and moving them onto new ground. The lack at the heart of erotic love need not be exploitative but rather a force that moves an individual to reach out to others. In contrast to Arendt, Marion can be seen as regarding love as political in the sense that the individual is called into meaningful existence by the Other: i.e., reality outside of one's ego.[37]

This study assesses the traditions of ancient Israel, Mesopotamia, and Greece according to the form they manifested in the Axial Age (sixth to fourth centuries BCE).[38] What characterizes this age is its quest to find

33. Hannah Arendt, *The Human Condition*, 242; Julia Kristeva, *Hannah Arendt* (New York: Columbia University Press, 2001), 107.

34. Hannah Arendt, *The Life of the Mind*, vol. 1: *Thinking* (New York: Harcourt, 1977), 215–16; Kristeva, *Hannah Arendt*, 153, 215.

35. Marion, *The Erotic Phenomenon*, 71.

36. Ibid., 71–72.

37. Ibid., 26–27, 88.

38. Karl Jaspers, *The Origin and Goal of History*, trans. Michael Bullock (London: Routledge & Kegan Paul, 1953), 1–2.

a transcendent principle of order: In Israel, YHWH was worshiped as the only God who exists; in Mesopotamia, Persian devotion to Ahura Mazda built on the centralization achieved by the Marduk religion in the first millennium BCE; in Greece, Heraclitus's Logos and Plato's "the Good" were proposed as transcendent principles ruling the cosmic order. This centralized view of a benevolent cosmos promoted an attitude of trust and receptivity in contrast to the ambivalence arising from a polycentric view.[39] A key characteristic of this transcendent ruling principle is that it made an appeal through its beauty, goodness, and truth to those who would listen. The goal of listening to the transcendent is to maximize human flourishing and to enhance the relationships of humans with one another.[40] However, Martha Nussbaum has criticized Plato's appeal to transcendent principles as importing standards alien to the human order and thus creating disequilibrium by championing ideals inattentive to the particularities of the human contexts.[41] Thus erotic love stirred by the transcendent can become a force of disintegration if it is not attentive to the face of the other. The danger of the disequilibrium posed by erotic love led the Stoics to try to control sexual desire so that reason might operate with greater clarity and consistency.

A Comparative-Thematic Approach to the Topic of Celibacy

The comparative character of this study aims to bring the voices of these three traditions from the pre-Hellenistic era into conversation on a topic that admits of no definitive solution but demands ongoing engagement.[42] Even though most of the speakers called upon in this study did not engage in a dialogue with one another, their voices were authoritative in their cultures in the sixth to fourth centuries BCE. Some of these voices speak out of the past as traditional authorities (e.g., the Old Babylonian *Code of Hammurapi)*.[43] The purpose of creating a dialogue among their

39. Jaspers, *The Origin and Goal of History*, 2–3; Steven G. Smith, *Appeal and Attitude: Prospects for Ultimate Meaning* (Bloomington: Indiana University Press, 2005), 13–14.

40. Smith, *Appeal and Attitude*, 17–18.

41. Martha Nussbaum, *The Fragility of Goodness: Luck and Ethics in Greek Tragedy and Philosophy*, rev. ed. (Cambridge: Cambridge University Press, 2001), 8.

42. For additional discussion of the comparative method I employ, see also my *Piety and Politics: The Dynamics of Royal Authority in Homeric Greece, Biblical Israel, and Old Babylonian Mesopotamia* (Grand Rapids: Eerdmans, 2003), 7–10, and *Spirit and Reason: The Embodied Character of Ezekiel's Symbolic Thinking* (Waco, TX: Baylor University Press, 2007), 17–28.

43. Even if the Mesopotamian law "codes" do not represent a system of specific, enforceable laws they concretely map out a vision of a just social order that was educative

views on selected topics is to gain new insights on how celibacy and sexual renunciation can be practiced constructively. Because the voices of these three traditions can only be understood properly by situating them within their historical contexts, a sustained effort will be made to reconstruct the historical contexts for the speakers and their issues so that they are not mistaken for disembodied voices purveying timeless truths. Inevitably there is a subjective, constructive dimension to the organization of a thematic study of this nature, but such an acknowledgment must be accompanied by a renewed effort to listen faithfully to what these voices were trying to say to their original audiences and to respect the fact that they were not addressing these questions from a twenty-first-century CE perspective and were often silent on aspects of issues of greatest concern to an audience in contemporary America.

Since the evidence for the practice of celibacy in these three cultures is limited, it is necessary to assemble all references to celibacy as a practice or an ideal in their traditions. Since celibacy is the renunciation of marriage, it is a relational reality that is a variation within the matrix of relationships of a household. The abundant evidence on household relationships within the three cultures provides the means for reconstructing their understanding of marriage and family relationships. As a practice defining itself over against the institutions of marriage and family, celibacy in these three ancient cultures can be better understood with a clearer picture of the structure and dynamics of the patriarchal household in that period.

This study is organized thematically. Each chapter addresses a particular theme. The material from the Israelite tradition is presented first. The materials from Mesopotamia and Greece have usually been selected to respond to the theme of the chapter, but some materials from these two traditions have been included to respond to the material in the Israelite tradition. Thus two factors govern the selection of materials for comparison: the theme of the chapter and the picture of the Israelite tradition's treatment of this theme. In other words, the Israelite tradition's understanding of household relationships and their renunciation is a privileged source in this comparative project. Nevertheless, roughly equal attention is given to the understanding of these relationships in the Mesopotamian and Greek traditions. Within each chapter the material

---

and widely disseminated: the building blocks of the ancient Near Eastern legal culture (see David M. Carr and Colleen M. Conway, "The Divine-Human Marriage Matrix and Constructions of Gender and 'Bodies' in the Christian Bible," 275–303 in *Sacred Marriages* [2008], at 279).

from each tradition on the designated theme is presented as a continuous narrative; at the conclusion of the chapter the comparisons and contrasts among the three traditions are drawn. Insofar as possible, primary texts set the agenda for the discussion of each tradition. But some topics demand a more synthetic approach: i.e., drawing on secondary sources that have addressed an issue too complex to be treated on the basis of one or two primary texts (e.g., the Athenian citizenship law of 451 BC or the development of the Mesopotamian scribal profession). The discussion of each tradition's response to the theme of the chapter is presented on the basis of materials available in the sixth to the fourth centuries BCE: the exilic and Persian periods in Israel; the Neo-Babylonian and Late-Babylonian periods in Mesopotamia; and the Archaic and Classical Ages in Greece. Many of the materials will have been composed much earlier (e.g., in the Old Babylonian or Neo-Assyrian periods in Mesopotamia) and were handed on as part of the stream of tradition; other materials were stored in palace, temple, or personal archives and were known to the scribes of the sixth to the fourth centuries who maintained them.

The main texts selected to address the themes of each chapter are outlined as follows:

Chapter One. Theme: sexual restraint within the context of a cosmic household.

a. Israelite tradition: Ezekiel 16 portrays collective Jerusalem as the adulterous wife of YHWH who will be subjected to severe punishment. This text emphasizes the exclusive character of this divine-human marriage and thus indicates on a human level that collective Jerusalem was not allowed to marry or have sexual relations with a human partner.
b. Mesopotamian tradition: The theme of permitted sexual expression by a representative of a collective entity is addressed by the following:
    i. Sumerian texts: "The Song of the Hoe," "Enlil and Ninlil," "Dumuzi and Enkimdu," *The Curse of Agade*, and the balag "Uru-amirabi."
    ii. Akkadian texts: *Atrahasis*, the *Epic of Gilgamesh*, "The Birth Legend of Sargon," and an Old Akkadian royal inscription of Naram-Sin.
c. Greek tradition: The theme of the violation of sacred relationships within the human and cosmic households with serious repercus-

sions in the collective entity. The Greek texts include Aeschylus's *Eumenides*; Sophocles' *Antigone, Oedipus Tyrannus*, and *Oedipus Colonus*; and Euripides' *Ion* and *Bacchae*.

Chapter Two. Theme: the understanding of marriage and the integrity of relationships of a household within a political community.

a. Israelite tradition: Ezra 9–10 describes the reform of Yehud in which Ezra takes steps to dissolve mixed marriages. Selected texts on the character of Israelite marriage or the threat of apostasy posed by marriage practices are Hos 2:24; Deut 7:1-4; 13:6-10; 22:23-29; 24:1-4; Mal 2:15//Gen 2:24; Prov 6:29-35; Judges 19.
b. Mesopotamian tradition: Akkadian texts on marriage practices are taken from "The Marriage of Martu," the *Enūma Elish*, the *Code of Hammurapi*, and a contract from the Murashû Archive.
c. Greek tradition: texts on marriage practices are drawn from Homer's *Odyssey*, Aeschylus's *Eumenides*, Sophocles' *Trachiniae* and *Antigone*, Aristotle's *Politics*, and the orations of Isaeus.

Chapter Three. Theme: the place of the erotic in the divine-human relationship.

a. Israelite tradition: the marital and familial metaphors applied to the divine-human relationship are illustrated in Hosea 2, 4, 11, and Genesis 2–3. Texts on same-sex erotic relationships are taken from 2 Samuel 1, Leviticus 19, Genesis 19, and Judges 19.
b. Mesopotamian tradition: texts on erotic relationships among the gods and between gods and humans have been selected from the following:
    i. Sumerian texts: excerpts from hymns concerning Inanna and Dumuzi are drawn from "The Sacred Marriage of Iddin-Dagan and Inanna," "Enki and Ninhursaga," "Nergal and Ereshkigal," and *The Descent of Inanna*.
    ii. Akkadian texts: excerpts are taken from the *Enūma Elish*, the *Epic of Gilgamesh*, the *Descent of Ishtar*, and *Erra and Ishum*.
c. Greek tradition: the main text drawn upon for illustrating the role of the erotic in the quest for the transcendent is Plato's *Symposium*; this text is supplemented with excerpts from Homer's *Iliad*, Hesiod's *Theogony*, and texts from Parmenides.

Chapter Four. Theme: the integrity or bodily wholeness symbolized by virginity and sexual restraint.

a. Israelite tradition: the topic of female virginity is addressed in Deuteronomy 22, Genesis 34, and Judges 11. Texts on sexual restraint illustrating the discipline that would be needed for male virginity are drawn from Genesis 39 and Proverbs 7. Texts on practices of sexual restraint that promote physical wholeness are provided in Leviticus 15, 18–20.
b. Mesopotamian tradition: texts on female virginity are taken from:
    i. Sumerian text: "Enlil and Ninlil."
    ii. Akkadian texts: the *Laws of Lipit-Ishtar*, letters from Mari and the OB period, the *Middle Assyrian Laws*, the *Epic of Gilgamesh*, an OB legal text, and the omen collection of *Šumma ālu*.
c. Greek tradition: texts that address the topic of female virginity are selected from Homer's *Iliad* and *Odyssey*, the *Homeric Hymn to Aphrodite*, Aeschylus's *Eumenides*, Sophocles' *Antigone*, Plato's *Laws*, and the Hippocratic writer. The main text selected for addressing the topic of male virginity is Euripides' *Hippolytus*.

Chapter Five. Theme: the mediating role of composite figures at the cosmic junctures of heaven, earth, and netherworld.

a. Israelite tradition: texts on primal composite figures charged with responsibilities related to cosmic balance are Ezekiel 28 and Genesis 2. A form of spiritual or noncorporeal divine androgyny may be suggested by Gen 1:26-28.
b. Mesopotamian tradition: texts on divine and human composite figures are drawn from:
    i. Sumerian texts: "The Sacred Marriage of Iddin-Dagan and Inanna" and the balag "Uru-amirabi."
    ii. Akkadian texts: *Atrahasis*, *Šumma ālu*, *Epic of Gilgamesh*, *Adapa*, an Assyrian state ritual, *The Descent of Ishtar*, *Erra and Ishum*, *Maqlû*, an Assyrian contract, and an excerpt from the *Middle Assyrian Palace Discipline*.
c. Greek tradition: the text selected for addressing divine and human composite figures is Euripides' *Bacchae*.

Chapter Six. Theme: celibacy as a confrontation with death and a quest for transcendence.

a. Israelite tradition: the sole Israelite text enjoining the practice of celibacy for an individual is Jer 16:1-4. Texts to contextualize this call to celibacy are Jer 14:1-22; 15:10-21; 16:5-9; 17:14-18; 18:21-23;

20:7-9. Texts on the quest for transcendence by means of meditation on the Torah are Jer 17:7-8; 31:31-34; Deut 6:6-9; Ezek 36:26-27; Psalms 19 and 119.

b. Mesopotamian tradition: an Akkadian text on a personal crisis that moves the speaker to reimagine the transcendent is *Ludlul bēl nēmeqi*. Other Akkadian texts on the quest for transcendence via wisdom communicated in oral and written form are *Adapa, Enūma Anu Enlil*, a letter of an Assyrian scholar, a ritual prayer from the *bīt rīmki* ritual.

c. Greek tradition: the main text addressing the quest for transcendence as a way of overcoming death is Plato's *Republic*. Other texts selected as relating to the quest for transcendence are taken from Plato's *Phaedrus* and *Philebus* and Aristotle's *Nicomachean Ethics*.

Chapter Seven. Theme: the sacramental potential of the erotic love of man and woman.

a. Israelite tradition: Song of Songs; Genesis 2.
b. Mesopotamian tradition: a love song of Dumuzi and Inanna entitled "The Women's Oath"; the *Epic of Gilgamesh* OB VA + BM, ii 2'-13', Standard Babylonian version, I:188-94.
c. Greek tradition: Homer's *Iliad* 14.314-17; *Odyssey* 5.204-13; 6.149-61, 239-45; 23:300-9; Sappho 31:7-16; and a selection from the blame poetry of Archilochus.

Overview of the Study

Chapter One: "Sexual Restraint Within the Context of a Cosmic Household." On the basis of Ezekiel 16, sexual integration for a Jerusalemite is possible only by an exclusive commitment to YHWH—as if the Jerusalemites collectively were YHWH's wife. Infidelity deprives one of a fixed point necessary for balancing the multiple relationships constitutive of communal life and creates an unbounded neediness. Since his household is undermined by such promiscuous behavior, YHWH acts decisively to correct it. In Mesopotamia, exclusive commitment to one deity is not the typical practice, yet the households individually and collectively as part of the state regulate forms of sexual expression integral to their well-being (e.g., premarital sex, adultery). Ishtar as the personification of sex is both honored and feared; her capacity to go to excess demands circumspectness. In Greece, Athena extends special protection to the Athenians but does not prohibit the worship of other Olympian deities. The violation of the sacred in terms of space and relationships is a serious collective concern in all three cultures, because God or the gods will not allow such transgressions to go uncorrected. Divine punishment of a collective entity usually takes the form of a historical crisis in which the irrational breaks forth into daily life and shows how individual bodily integrity is fundamental to collective wholeness. The contrasting visions of the structure and expectations of the divine world among the three cultures call forth different strategies for maintaining collective and individual integrity.

Chapter Two: "Intermarriage: A Threat to the Household as the Enduring Matrix of Personal Identity?" The household embodied in its people and property is the locus of immortality in the popular culture of these three traditions. Remnants of the ancestral cult are evident in the literary and archaeological remains. A compelling explanation of the ancients' concern over patriarchal lineage may be the consistency of inheritance practices. However, at issue is not only property but also biological continuity, which is articulated by claiming commonality of bloodline. The woman is the key player in maintaining the boundaries and the intergenerational continuity of the household. She not only gives birth to but also socializes the young. She becomes a wife at an early age and potentially lives to an old age such that her life spans three generations. This key household role of the wife offers an explanation of Ezra's radical measure of breaking up mixed marriages in fifth-century Yehud. He feared the loss of Israelite identity through assimilation of the household—the immortal core of the Israelite community—into the surrounding cultures. In Mesopotamia the tension between herders and city-dwellers and, in Greece, the Athenian predilection for endogamy manifests a similar concern for a closed society and a clear identity.

Because the integrity of the household is vitally important to the state, its officials began to intrude into the affairs of the household in each of these cultures. Within the framework of the earthly household, celibacy would be equivalent to suicide. But within the framework of the cosmic household the virgin Antigone is ready to join her family in the tomb rather than have her family members compromised by the demands of the state. She laments not having offspring but does not see herself sliding into oblivion by not having them. As an alternative, Gilgamesh exemplifies one who tries to find immortality beyond the household as he searches into the far reaches of the cosmos for an escape from death. He fails but returns instead with an enduring wisdom that can strengthen both the household and the state.

Chapter Three: "Sex and the Holy: Erotic Synergy or Warfare?" Erotic energies must be sustained rather than suppressed because they build bridges to others and show that vitality inheres in communion with others. *Erōs* may be defined as a need; its energy may be seen as taking the form of reaching out to others to satisfy this need. *Erōs* has a propensity to go to excess and to transgress against the boundaries of the other. Hungry *erōs* may even dare to take what is sacred to the identity of the other. This obliviousness to what is sacred falls under Hosea's charge that the people lack knowledge because the priests fail to instruct them (4:6). Their misguided worship takes the form of mechanical sacrifices and participation in Baalistic practices. Through improper attention to the otherness of YHWH the Israelites defile the holy, especially through sexual activity within the sphere of the cult according to Hos 4:14. To what extent such sexual activity carried religious significance for the idolaters is not clear in this text, but as a general principle the fiery desire of *erōs* is good, but the self-indulgent exploitation of the other to satisfy this desire is bad. Negotiating this ambiguity demands knowledge of the other and of the communal context. In Mesopotamia the sacred marriage ritual, whether enacted physically with human participants or abstractly with statues of gods, aimed to revitalize nature and culture within the community for the coming year. In this ritual the relation of sex to the holy was regarded as synergistic. In Plato's *Symposium*, Diotima describes *erōs* as an intermediary between gods and humans. In the *Phaedrus*, *erōs* is an essential energy propelling the soul in its quest for the beautiful and the good. Nevertheless, reason (*nous*) stands in tension with *erōs* as it tries to contain the potentially transgressive energy of *erōs*.

Chapter Four: "Virginity and Chastity: Feminine Ideals Integral to the Patriarchal Household." Premarital virginity for women did not become an ascetical practice since most women were married at around the age of fourteen. One reason for insisting that a daughter not have sexual intercourse prior to marriage was the purity of the paternal line of her future husband's household. Another reason—although increasingly questioned by scholars—was the ideal of female bodily wholeness as a symbol of the honor of the household. The intactness of the woman's body, a pristine state undefiled by semen, was believed to be an index of the honor of the patriarchal household. Thus Jacob's sons reacted violently to Shechem's having intercourse with their sister Dinah, an action they regarded as defiling their household (Genesis 34). Some argue that the daughter's virginal state signaled that her relationship with her father was still intact. The account of Jephthah's sacrifice of his daughter in Judges 11 highlights the trauma a daughter could experience either in the loss of her virginity in a marriage arranged by her father or in her father's dedicating her to a life of perpetual virginity. In Mesopotamia a form of lifelong celibacy—presumably free from sexual relations—was practiced in the Old Babylonian period (2003–1595 BCE) by cloistered *nadiātum* (= *nadītum*-women) dedicated by their fathers to the temples of Shamash in Sippar and Ninurta in Nippur. Their primary religious role was to serve as intercessors for their families. In other words, their ties to the natal household remained strong when they transferred to the household of the cloister, an adjunct to the temple household.

Male virginity is rarely evidenced in the literature of these three cultures. Wherever men embodied this feminine ideal, their example was countercultural. When Joseph resists the advances of Potiphar's wife (Gen 39:8-12) he exercises the discipline necessary to avoid adultery. Furthermore, this form of sexual restraint stands in continuity with that expected of a virgin, even though Joseph's abstinence from sexual relations is contextual and particular rather than absolute and lifelong. Nevertheless, his appeal to his indebtedness to his master and to his fear of YHWH illustrates the kind of awareness necessary for a virgin to refrain from sexual relations: i.e., an awareness showing an individual's commitment to a larger web of communal relationships. In Mesopotamian literature Enkidu was portrayed as a virgin during his time of roaming with gazelles prior to his encounter with Shamhat. In the Greek tradition the tragedian Euripides created the character Hippolytus as a male virgin. The pride Hippolytus takes in his abstinence from sexual relations incites the ire of the goddess Aphrodite, who takes steps to make him aware of her presence. Aphrodite causes Hippolytus's mother-in-law to fall madly in love with him. The tragic end of the upright Hippolytus raises questions about the extent to which lifelong virginity is an ideal appropriate for humans; the demands of such a way of life may perhaps only be met by deities like Artemis, Athena, and Hestia.

Chapter Five: "Composite Guardian Figures: Tension at the Cosmic Junctures." In times of crisis in which the death-dealing forces of the netherworld make inroads into the earthly sphere, individuals who can navigate in the sphere of the netherworld are highly valued. The cherub figure in Ezek 28:11-18 is a composite figure who seems to have been identified with the royal priestly figure in vv. 12-13 as a primal human. The harmony envisioned in this Eden on the mountain of God is a promise contingent on the cherub's functioning as a guardian of YHWH's sovereignty rather than as a usurper. His transgression leads to his expulsion from the garden. He has used his wisdom to promote his own autonomy and self-absorption. This obliviousness to the other and forgetfulness of one's context dissolves the necessary tension between the divine, the human, and the bestial in the cherub figure. Thus, in pretending to be God, the cherub becomes bestial, a perpetrator of violence. He inverts his potential as a bulwark against hostile forces. In the Mesopotamian tradition, as a response to the crisis of the flood, the primeval sages known as *apkallū*, "fish-men," brought civilization back to the land. Thereafter, when trouble irrupted in the cities of Mesopotamia, the sages were called upon to bring about a solution. These sages appear in the Greek tradition; one named Epimetheus was summoned to Athens to dispel a plague triggered by the Cylonian affair in the late seventh century BCE. In Mesopotamia androgynous cultic figures associated with Ishtar, known as *kurgarrû* and *assinnu*, were both respected and feared for their excess of sexual power. Their wild antics in the rituals of Ishtar earned them disdain, but their social value rose in times of crisis when some uncanny force from the netherworld was believed to have invaded the land.

In these ancient cultures the presence of male and female sex and masculine and feminine gender in the same human being was anomalous and usually regarded as ominous. However, in the divine sphere or in the mythical atmosphere of the primeval age such androgynous hermaphrodites illustrated the complete or perfect being in which opposites were united in one person. For the typical human the tension between these opposites of sex and gender would be so strong that a human could hold them together only temporarily. Nevertheless, to reduce the tension by taking the extreme step of eliminating one of the countervailing forces of gender or sex could lead to the opposite result of ramping up the tension. The dynamic in the polarities of male/female and masculine/feminine resembles that of a bowstring: the appropriate force in opposite directions makes the bowstring operational. In Euripides' *Bacchae* the character Pentheus tries to control the behavior of the women of Thebes and to contain the feminine element in his own person. Dionysus, the androgynous deity identified with the amoral life force, thwarts Pentheus's efforts to maintain a rational civic order divorced from the irrational. Other figures with an ambiguous sex and gender identity were the eunuchs in the royal governments of the ancient Near East. However, their profile as members of a marginalized group associated with the palace rather than with the sanctuary rendered them less ominous than androgynous cultic officials like the *kurgarrû* and *assinnu*. In Israel anyone who became a eunuch was to be excommunicated; however, the royal governments in Israel and Judah employed eunuchs (e.g., 2 Kgs 9:32; Jer 38:7). The number of eunuchs in the Assyrian government grew during the eighth and seventh centuries BCE as the Assyrian royal power increased.

Chapter Six: "Celibacy as a Proleptic Death and a Quest for Transcendence." Celibacy begins with a confrontation and acceptance of death in order to transcend death. Jeremiah figuratively met death in the form of the message of doom for Jerusalem and the resulting hostility from the condemned Jerusalemites. The intensity of this deathlike experience stripped him of all human and material support and left him crying out to YHWH, whose ways confused him. In 399 BCE in Athens, Socrates analogously experienced hostility from his compatriots that ended in his execution. As a gadfly, Socrates challenged those around him to live uncompromisingly according to the truth. He created enemies by the questions he posed to others, not only concerning their blind spots but also about the gods and civic religion. Socrates believed that his soul was immortal and that humans could not harm someone who was good. His trust in the power of truth made him uncompromising in the face of death. Socrates' connection with the true, the beautiful, and the good revealed a pathway toward immortality that transcended the household, the traditional locus of immortality. However, the enlightened one was obliged to return to the city and its households to educate its citizens. In the Mesopotamian tradition, the *Myth of Adapa* and the *Epic of Gilgamesh* relate how heroic individuals come close to gaining immortality but return to the earthly sphere equipped with divine-like wisdom. Their quest was complemented by the theologians of the Mesopotamian royal court who aimed to create a sacred canopy around the king and the nation. The Jeremiah presented in the book of Jeremiah survives the opposition of the Jerusalemites through trust in YHWH, an experience to be sustained through attentiveness to the word of God imparted to him. Although Jeremiah's relationship with YHWH was anguished, it was concrete and vibrant. This connection with the divine was the pathway on which celibacy could play a constructive, meaningful role. The pursuit of wisdom by Jeremiah and Israelite teachers, by Gilgamesh and Mesopotamian intellectuals, and by Socrates and Greek thinkers created the context in which celibacy could contribute by opening up interior space and intensifying desire for transcendent, enduring reality.

Chapter Seven: "Communion with the Real: The Goal of Celibacy." The relentless force of erotic energy can bring humans into communion with one another and the divine. According to Song of Songs 8:6, "love is as strong as death." The celebration of erotic love and the creation of erotic desire in the Song of Songs are unique in the Old Testament, which usually is cautious about the excesses to which erotic love is prone rather than extolling its potential for communion with others and with God.

Love songs and mythical texts in the Mesopotamian and Greek traditions describe erotic experience but are not as evocative as the dialogue of the Song of Songs, which invites the readers to imagine the experience of the lovers. The sacramental potential of erotic love is a reality that one who embraces celibacy must acknowledge. The death to erotic sexual expression is a turning away from an embodied to a more contemplative means of communion with the divine, in which *erōs* is transmuted into a less carnal and more spiritualized form of union with the transcendent through beauty, truth, and goodness. Celibacy that includes only dying to carnal sexual expression is suicidal. Such asceticism makes sense only if it creates a deep longing for beauty and truth that is fed and sustained on the pathway toward the transcendent.

After this overview of celibacy as a discipline within the relationships of a cosmic household, we are ready to compare and contrast the voices of these three traditions on central aspects of this divinely influenced discipline.

Chapter One

Sexual Restraint Within the Context of a Cosmic Household

The sexual drive is a persistent force that reminds an individual that he or she is inextricably part of a larger physical and cultural world. As vulnerable infants, humans depend on their parents for sustenance and direction. Infants not only inherit physical characteristics from their parents but also imbibe customary ways of interacting with other humans and the environment that have shaped the identity of their parents and their communities. This larger relational web is the context within which the birth of an individual human marks the beginning of something new. The exercise of the individual's capacity to choose realizes a freedom that is uniquely human. The choices this individual makes take the form of a dialectic with an environment that shapes and, in turn, is shaped by the individuals who act within it. This mutual exchange, even though the individual is not equal to the collective entity in size and strength, highlights the power and novelty of individual choice.

The genetic constitution of the individual and the cultural heritage bestowed at birth and in the initial formative years of life shape the preverbal and verbal components of a person's consciousness. An individual never starts from zero but is thrust into the middle of a living web of relationships within the physical and cultural spheres. The sexual drive reminds the individual agent of his or her belonging to the physical and cultural spheres but also challenges the individual to stand back from these spheres and forge her or his unique place within this larger collective environment. The sexual drive will absorb, overwhelm, and disperse the individual if it is not resisted, just as it will rise up in revolt if it is ignored or denied through repression. This sexual balancing act is a vital component in the formation of the identity of individuals and their communities.

This chapter will examine how the covenantal relationship with YHWH provides a living cultural web within which the sexual drive is to be negotiated. The integration of this drive within the embodied character of the individual requires that one have at hand a constructive vision that shows how the individual and collective energies of a community can converge. Ezekiel 16 will be the primary text for the comparative examination of this topic. This chapter, of which at least the core was composed by the prophet Ezekiel at some point between 593 and 587 BCE, is the first of three history-like narratives (Ezekiel 16, 20, 23) in which he describes how Jerusalem has committed abominations, calling for the purging and destruction of the city.[1] Echoing the larger structure of the book of Ezekiel, chapter 16 ends with the confirmation that YHWH's covenant with Jerusalem is "everlasting" (*ʿōlām*, 16:60). But Jerusalem's reception of the grace of this covenant will be marked by a sense of shame and renewed self-examination as it struggles with the help of YHWH's Spirit to integrate its sexual drive within the larger web of relationships that constitute it (Ezek 16:61-63; 36:31-32).

The vision and the pointers provided by Ezekiel 16 for sexual integration will first be examined and then compared and contrasted with texts representing the Mesopotamian and Greek traditions on this issue. The texts of each tradition will be organized according to the following four subtopics: (1) the expression of collective identity and the maintenance of integrity; (2) the sexual drive as a form of physical and cultural power; (3) the requirement of sexual constraint in the encounter with the holy; (4) the dynamics of boundary formation in the forging of sexual identity.

Israel: A Summons to Covenantal Fidelity for Collective Integrity in Ezekiel 16

Ezekiel 16, the longest literary unit in the book, is a judgment narrative relating a dispute between YHWH and Jerusalem in which Jerusa-

1. Walther Zimmerli, *Ezekiel 1: A Commentary on the Book of the Prophet Ezekiel, Chapters 1–24* (Philadelphia: Fortress Press, 1979), 333–35, 348; Daniel Block, *The Book of Ezekiel* (2 vols.; Grand Rapids: Eerdmans, 1997, 1998), 1.460.

lem's role is to listen and understand the charges brought against her. Ezekiel is instructed to "make Jerusalem know her abominations" (*tôʿăbōtêhā*, 16:2). The root *tʿb* occurs sixteen times in Ezekiel 16, indicating that the actions Jerusalem is carrying out are incompatible with the holiness of YHWH.[2] Therefore Ezekiel must cut through all the defenses Jerusalem has constructed to legitimate her behavior.

The emphatic language that punctuates the entire narrative consists not only of "pornoprophetic" phrases but also traditional markers for divine speech.[3] Examples of such pornoprophetic phrases are: "you spread your legs to everyone who was passing by" (16:25); "you acted promiscuously with the Egyptians, your neighbors, the ones with the large male organs" (v. 26); "because your genital flow was poured out and your nakedness was revealed (v. 36). Ezekiel's repeated use of the phrase "oracle of the Lord" (*nĕum YHWH*, vv. 8, 14, 19, 23, 30, 43, 58) seems to be designed to impress on a resistant audience that certain statements in the narrative are indeed from YHWH and are not products of Ezekiel's imagination.[4] In addition, Ezekiel refers to YHWH's use of the oath formula, "as I live" (v. 48), in order to drive home a troubling point about Jerusalem as more corrupt than Sodom—a contention Jerusalem was sure to deny.[5] These and other instances (vv. 20, 23, 30, 35) of Ezekiel's emphatic rhetoric combine to make this a passage judicious translators render with less directness.[6]

2. Block, *Ezekiel*, 1.571.

3. Athalya Brenner, "On Prophetic Propaganda and the Politics of 'Love': The Case of Jeremiah," in *A Feminist Companion to the Latter Prophets*, ed. Athalya Brenner, 256–74 (Sheffield: Sheffield Academic Press, 1995), at 259–61, 266; eadem, *The Intercourse of Knowledge: On Gendering Desire and 'Sexuality' in the Hebrew Bible*, Biblical Interpretation 26 (Leiden: Brill, 1997), 166–67. Robert Carroll, "Desire Under the Terebinths: On Pornographic Representation in the Prophets: a Response," in *A Feminist Companion to the Latter Prophets*, 275–307, at 286, 296–97, 301; idem, "Whorusalamin: A Tale of Three Cities As Three Sisters," in *On Reading Prophet Texts: Gender-Specific and Related Studies in Memory of Fokkelien Van Dijk-Hemmes*, Biblical Interpretation 18, ed. Bob Becking and Meindert Dijkstra, 62–82 (Leiden: Brill, 1996) at 75–78; Carol Dempsey, "The 'Whore' of Ezekiel 16: The Impact and Ramifications of Gender-Specific Metaphors in Light of Biblical Law and Divine Judgment," in *Gender and Law in the Hebrew Bible and the Ancient Near East*, *JSOTSup* 262, ed. Victor Matthews, Bernard Levinson, and Tikva Frymer-Kensky, 57–78 (Sheffield: Sheffield Academic Press, 1998), at 58 n. 4, 61; Gale Yee, *Poor Banished Children of Eve: Woman as Evil in the Hebrew Bible* (Minneapolis: Fortress Press, 2003), 120–22.

4. Block, *Ezekiel*, 1.472–73.

5. Carroll,"Whorusalamin," 81, notes the strangeness and subversive character of Ezekiel's claim that sister Sodom is saved by the promiscuity of sister Jerusalem!

6. Block, *Ezekiel*, 1.467.

According to v. 42, YHWH admits that he is furious with Jerusalem for her adulterous, promiscuous behavior.[7] Thus the tenor of the narrative seems to be one of increasing anger until it reaches a climax in the judgment speech of vv. 35-43. In the book of Ezekiel it is typical that there is no recorded response of the audience to YHWH's statements; however, in the case of the delivery of the judgment narrative of Ezekiel 16 the audience would probably have been stunned into silence.[8]

Ezekiel's strong language was a response to the crisis that beset Jerusalem in 597 and increased until the destruction of the city in 586. Those who denied the severity of the crisis, or alternatively those who regarded the troubles as an indicator of YHWH's indifference or lack of power, were individuals who refused to share in the collective responsibility of the Jerusalemites for their situation.[9] Ezekiel, communicating from his location in Babylon not only to the exiles but also to those who remained in Jerusalem, showed no tolerance for the confusion of the lamenters. He insisted that they face the facts and acknowledge the enormity of their wrongdoing. Hence the use of the traditional metaphor of adultery to describe transgressions against the covenant offered a level of emotional intensity that could communicate the seriousness of Jerusalem's acts of infidelity.[10] The anger of a cuckolded husband would have been apparent to Ezekiel's audience, yet it appears that the intensity of this emotion needed to be heightened by describing the infidelities of

7. S. Tamar Kamionkowski, *Gender Reversal and Cosmic Chaos: A Study of the Book of Ezekiel*, *JSOTSup* 368 (Sheffield: Sheffield Academic Press, 2003), 41, claims that feminist interpreters of the marital metaphor texts switch the emphasis from God's perspective in the narrative to that of the woman, which she identifies as two sides of the same model of the relationship rather than offering a new model. Block (*Ezekiel*, 1.469) replies to feminist criticism of the offensive imagery of Ezekiel by noting that the problem addressed in the chapter is the infidelity of the Jerusalemites. He argues that it is "hubristic to sit in judgment of God" by assessing the expression of intense divine anger as inappropriate.

8. Dale Launderville, *Spirit and Reason: The Embodied Character of Ezekiel's Symbolic Thinking* (Waco, TX: Baylor University Press, 2007), 191. Thomas Renz, *The Rhetorical Function of the Book of Ezekiel*, *VTSup* 76 (Leiden: Brill, 1999), 17 notes that the book of Ezekiel reports the words of Ezekiel's audience only once, at 24:17.

9. Joel S. Kaminsky, *Corporate Responsibility in the Hebrew Bible*, *JSOTSup* 196 (Sheffield: Sheffield Academic Press, 1995), 176–78, 185; Paul Joyce, *Divine Initiative and Human Response in Ezekiel*, *JSOTSup* 51 (Sheffield: JSOT Press, 1989), 146; Gordon Matties, *Ezekiel 18 and the Rhetoric of Moral Discourse*, SBLDS 126 (Atlanta: Scholars Press, 1990), 191–92.

10. Julie Galambush, *Jerusalem in the Book of Ezekiel*, SBLDS 130 (Atlanta: Scholars Press, 1992), 37; Peggy L. Day, "Yahweh's Broken Marriages as Metaphoric Vehicle," in *Sacred Marriages: The Divine-Human Sexual Metaphor from Sumer to Early Christianity*, ed. Martti Nissinen and Risto Uro, 219–41 (Winona Lake, IN: Eisenbrauns, 2008), at 232–33.

Jerusalem as having multiplied far beyond the breaking point.[11] Ezekiel makes the point that the punishment Jerusalem is undergoing is a consequence of YHWH's justified anger against faithless Jerusalem.

This narrative, written in highly stylized prose, can be read as a unit. However, as Walther Zimmerli notes, the theme of vv. 44-58, which compare Jerusalem's behavior with that of her sisters Samaria and Sodom, has a different focus from that of vv. 1-43, which tells the story of adulterous Jerusalem from the time of her birth to the present.[12] Verses 59-63 address the theme of the everlasting covenant and so can be demarcated from the preceding 58 verses. On the basis of catchwords and continuities in content, Zimmerli argues that Ezekiel 16 grew by a process of supplementation: i.e., vv. 44-58 were composed in light of vv. 1-43, and then vv. 59-63 were composed in light of vv. 1-58.[13] Moshe Greenberg claims that the entire narrative is a composition by Ezekiel in which the prophet once again uses a particular stylistic technique, which Greenberg labels "halving": theme A (Jerusalem as YHWH's wife, vv. 3-43) is repeated but varied in theme B (Jerusalem as sister of Sodom and Samaria in vv. 44-58); in the conclusion (vv. 59-63) themes A and B are fused.[14] In theme B the three sisters Samaria, Sodom, and Jerusalem are the focus, and of these sisters, Sodom was never the wife of YHWH; thus the motif of Jerusalem as YHWH's wife fades into the background in theme B.[15] Arguing also for the unity of Ezekiel 16, Block contends that the retrospective section in vv. 1-43 is joined by the prospective section in vv. 44-58 to make the point that the exile is not the last word on Jerusalem's fate. The covenant stands in suspension during the exile, but its everlasting character will reemerge in the restoration of the exiles to the land (vv. 59-63). He notes that chapter 16 mirrors the larger movement of the book of Ezekiel from judgment (chaps. 1–32) to restoration (chaps. 33–48), a transition that is not a return to a previous status quo but rather includes the people's growth in self-awareness, repentance, and shame over past conduct.[16]

The narrative of Ezekiel 16 can be outlined as follows:[17]

11. Block, *Ezekiel*, 1.464–67; Galambush, *Jerusalem in the Book of Ezekiel*, 102.

12. Zimmerli, *Ezekiel 1*, 333–34.

13. Ibid., 334.

14. Moshe Greenberg, *Ezekiel 1–20*, AB 22 (Garden City, NY: Doubleday, 1983), 297.

15. Ibid., 303.

16. Block, *Ezekiel*, 1.463.

17. Dempsey, "The 'Whore' of Ezekiel 16," 59, demarcates the structure according to the genres incorporated into this passage: Part I: vv. 3-43bα, a judgment speech: A. vv. 3-14, description of Jerusalem's origin and growth; B. vv. 15-34, series of accusations; C.

I. Verses 1-2: Ezekiel is charged to make Jerusalem know her abominations.
II. Verses 3-5: Jerusalem's non-Israelite parents exposed her at her birth.
III. Verses 6-14: YHWH adopted and married her, elevating her to royal status.
IV. Verses 15-22: Jerusalem trusted in her beauty and spent herself on passersby.
V. Verses 23-30: Jerusalem prostituted herself in public and extended her services to Egyptians, Assyrians, and Chaldeans.
VI. Verses 31-34: Autonomous Jerusalem became addicted to sex.
VII. Verses 35-43: YHWH will punish adulterous Jerusalem by exposing her before all her lovers, who will deal with her in anger and jealousy.
VIII. Verses 44-58: Jerusalem's reputation for infidelity becomes proverbial and exceeds that of her sisters Sodom and Samaria.
IX. Verses 59-63: YHWH will remember his covenant with Jerusalem, which in turn will lead Jerusalem to remember with shame her infidelity.

In this story of YHWH's intense involvement with Jerusalem, the generative power of sexuality transmutes into a destructive power that controls the life of wife Jerusalem. Sexual power loses its proper context and becomes an idolatrous force that leads to the disintegration of wife Jerusalem. How the metaphors of this narrative explain sociopolitical realities and how those realities in turn shed light on the larger relational context in which the balancing act of sexual integration can be negotiated will be issues of particular concern in the following reading of Ezekiel 16.

Collective Jerusalem:
From Canaanite Foundling to Royal Wife of YHWH

To address the sociopolitical dynamics of Jerusalem's relationship with YHWH, Ezekiel draws on two traditional metaphors: the city as woman and the city as wife. Although the metaphor of the city as wife has been subsumed by some scholars under the more inclusive metaphor

---

vv. 35-43bα, proclamation of punishment to come. Part II: vv. 43bβ-58, a diatribe: A. vv. 43bβ-52 comparison; vv. 53-58, promise of restoration. Part III: vv. 59-63, salvation oracle.

of the city as woman,[18] the identification of these metaphors as forming two separate metaphoric traditions reflects more accurately the cross-cultural data and that of Hosea, where the adulterous wife is the people (Hos 2:2-23) and not a city.[19] A longstanding view has been that the metaphor of the city as woman arose in the West Semitic world in pre-historical times.[20] An alternative proposal has been that the metaphor of the city as woman was communicated to the Israelite tradition by the Mesopotamian lamentations (balag and ershemma), whose composers in the second and first millennia BCE had received the motif of the destroyed city as a weeping goddess from the Sumerian city-laments (ca. 2000–1925 BCE).[21] The goddess in the five extant Sumerian city-laments who wails over the destruction of Ur, Uruk, Eridu, and Nippur is Inanna (or a local manifestation of this goddess).[22] Common to both the West Semitic and East Semitic explanations for the origin of the metaphor of the city as woman is the "deeply rooted" perception that the city has feminine functional or structural characteristics: e.g., the companionship, protection, and nurturing a city provides for its inhabitants.[23]

18. Aloysius Fitzgerald, "The Mythological Background for the Presentation of Jerusalem as a Queen and False Worship as Adultery in the OT," *CBQ* 34 (1972): 403–16, at 403–4; F. W. Dobbs-Allsopp, *Weep, O Daughter of Zion: A Study of the City-Lament Genre in the Hebrew Bible*, Biblica et Orientalia 44 (Rome: Pontifical Biblical Institute, 1993), 85–87; Galambush, *Jerusalem in the Book of Ezekiel*, 22–23; Mark Biddle, "The Figure of Lady Jerusalem: Identification, Deification and Personification of Cities in the Ancient Near East," in *The Biblical Canon in Comparative Perspective: Scripture in Context IV*, Ancient Near Eastern Texts and Studies 11, ed. K. Lawson Younger, Jr., William W. Hallo, and Bernard F. Batto, 173–94 (Lewiston, NY: Edwin Mellen, 1991), at 186–87.

19. Kamionkowski, *Gender Reversal and Cosmic Chaos*, 24.

20. Fitzgerald, "Mythological Background," 405; for a critical analysis of the argument and data supplied by Fitzgerald for an early West Semitic origin of the idea of the city as a goddess married to its patron deity see Peggy L. Day, "The Personification of Cities as Female in the Hebrew Bible: The Thesis of Aloysius Fitzgerald, F.S.C.," in *Reading from This Place*, vol. 2: *Social Location and Biblical Interpretation in Global Perspective*, ed. Fernando F. Segovia and Mary Ann Tolbert, 283–302 (Minneapolis: Fortress Press, 1995).

21. F. W. Dobbs-Allsopp, "Darwinism, Genre Theory, and City Laments," *JAOS* 120 (2000): 625–30, at 626–27; Walter C. Bouzard, Jr., *We Have Heard With Our Ears, O God: Sources of the Communal Laments in the Psalms*, SBLDS 159 (Atlanta: Scholars Press, 1997), 45; Tikva Frymer-Kensky, *In the Wake of the Goddesses: Women, Culture, and the Biblical Transformation of Pagan Myth* (New York: The Free Press, 1992), 41.

22. Bouzard, *We Have Heard*, 54–55; Biddle, "The Figure of Lady Jerusalem," 176, 181–82.

23. Galambush, *Jerusalem in the Book of Ezekiel*, 7, maintains that "while 'city' is a relatively sophisticated concept, the metaphoric designation of the city as female, and thus as mother, wife, and especially, within a patriarchal culture, as 'other,' plays on basic male-

According to the story line in Ezekiel 16, Jerusalem is imagined to be a girl in the land of Canaan who was cast off (*tušlĕkî*, v. 5) by her Amorite father and Hittite mother (v. 3). Jerusalem was abandoned immediately on the day of her birth, as Ezekiel makes known to her: "Your navel cord was not cut, nor were you washed with water and anointed, nor were you rubbed down with salt and wrapped in swaddling clothes" (v. 4).[24] Through this action (or rather, inaction) the parents severed all ties with the child physically and symbolically.[25] She was left to die, for no one cared for her or had compassion on her. The root *gʿl*, "abhor, neglect" (v. 5), which describes infant Jerusalem's abandoned condition, is also used in an active sense to identify a family trait that Jerusalem and her two sisters Samaria and Sodom will inherit from their mother (v. 45).[26] Thus it seems that in Ezekiel's view this cruel practice of child exposure was endemic to the Canaanite city-state, which would call into question the claim of such a city to be called a "mother."[27]

YHWH recounts for Jerusalem how he rescued her: "I passed by (*wāʾeʿebōr*) and saw you kicking about in your blood and said to you, 'Live in your blood'"[28] (v. 6). This condition of an abandoned infant swimming in its amniotic fluid was regarded in Mesopotamian law (*CH* §185) as one in which the infant could be adopted immediately by the one who found it.[29] In the Mesopotamian legal tradition the casting off

---

female, self-other dualities, and so the metaphor may be expected to be deeply rooted and persistent."

24. Greenberg, *Ezekiel 1–20*, 274, notes that in this Middle Eastern region the newborn are typically rubbed with salt for seven days to toughen the skin and then wrapped in cloths from forty days to six months in order to straighten the limbs.

25. Meir Malul, "Adoption of Foundlings in the Bible and Mesopotamian Documents: A Study of Some Legal Metaphors in Ezekiel 16.1-7," *JSOT* 46 (1990): 97–126, at 101, 105.

26. Dempsey, "The 'Whore' of Ezekiel 16," 61, claims that this view of the handing on of a corrupt state from the Canaanite mother to her three daughters betrays "the assumption that the seeds of corruption are rooted in and flow from the female gender." It is revealing that in Ezekiel's rejection of the intergenerational transfer of guilt in Ezek 18:5-21 he uses the imagery of father and son and not that of mother and daughter. See further Aelred Cody, *Ezekiel* (Wilmington, DE: Michael Glazier, 1984), 79, 87; Keith W. Carley, *Ezekiel* (Cambridge: Cambridge University Press, 1974), 96.

27. On the issue of exposure of children as a form of birth control or abortion see Joseph Blenkinsopp, *Ezekiel* (Louisville: John Knox, 1990), 77; Carley, *Ezekiel*, 96. On female infanticide in eighth-century Israel and seventh-/sixth-century Judah see Beth Alpert Nakhai, "Female Infanticide in Iron II Israel and Judah," in *Sacred History, Sacred Literature: Essays on Ancient Israel, the Bible, and Religion in Honor of R. E. Friedman on His Sixtieth Birthday*, ed. Shawna Dolansky, 257–72 (Winona Lake, IN: Eisenbrauns, 2008), at 265–66.

28. Omit *wāʾōmar lāk bĕdāmayik ḥăyî*.

29. Malul, "Adoption of Foundlings," 106–7.

of a newborn without washing, cleansing, and clothing it was a sign by the parents that they were relinquishing all legal rights to the newborn.[30] YHWH's statement "live in your blood" appears to be "a formal declaration of adoption."[31] The infant then appears to have been raised under YHWH's care for the next twelve to fourteen years; the narrative briefly describes how the young girl was allowed to grow "like a plant of the field" (v. 7) until she reached puberty. But in this condition of sexual maturity she is described as "undressed and naked" (*ʿērōm wĕʿeryâ*, v. 7). This condition of unclothed vulnerability may allude to the Garden of Eden story (Gen 3:7, 10-11, 21), where the consciousness of nakedness carries with it a sense of shame and humiliation.[32]

YHWH then passed by (*waʾeʿebōr*, v. 8) once again to elevate the young woman Jerusalem in status. His first action was to spread the edge of his garment (*wāʾeprōś kĕnāpî)* over her. In Ruth 3:9 this refers to sexual intercourse. Such an action is to be understood at the metaphorical rather than the literal level. Yet it is a daring anthropomorphism on the part of Ezekiel; nowhere else do we have an Old Testament story that speaks of YHWH engaging in sexual intercourse with a human, analogous to the actions of Apollo (Euripides, *Ion*, 338-66, 965). But Ezekiel, who regards humans as radically lower in status than YHWH, also dares to give an anthropomorphic description of YHWH enthroned on the cherubim in his inaugural vision (1:26-28). The significance of imagining YHWH as having intercourse with woman Jerusalem as part of the act of marrying her is to emphasize the reality of the committed relationship between YHWH and wife Jerusalem.[33] However, the defiling character of sexual intercourse from the priestly perspective (Lev 15:18) would seem to be a barrier the priest-prophet Ezekiel would be reluctant to cross. But just as Ezekiel dared to describe metaphorically the enthroned YHWH in human form to emphasize that he had not abandoned his sovereign rule

30. Ibid., 109; Raymond Westbrook, "The Character of Ancient Near Eastern Law," in *A History of Ancient Near Eastern Law*, 2 vols., ed. Raymond Westbrook, 1:1–90 (Leiden: Brill, 2003), at 1:53, §5.3.2.

31. Malul, "Adoption of Foundlings," 111. Galambush, *Jerusalem in the Book of Ezekiel*, 81, 92, claims that the phrase "live in your blood" indicates that adopted Jerusalem is still in a state of ritual defilement.

32. Dempsey, "The 'Whore' of Ezekiel 16," 65–66, 72; Claus Westermann, *Genesis 1–11* (Minneapolis: Augsburg Press, 1984), 236; Bill T. Arnold, *Genesis* (Cambridge: Cambridge University Press, 2009), 66.

33. See chap. 2 on the rituals of marital commitment. Raymond Westbrook, *Old Babylonian Marriage Law*, AfO Beiheft 23 (Horn, Austria: F. Berger, 1988), 58, 60, points out the analogous elements of the rituals of adoption and marriage.

in the time of the Babylonian exile, so also he may have dared to describe metaphorically the husband YHWH consummating his marriage with wife Jerusalem by having intercourse with her.[34] On a literal level YHWH transcends sexuality. But on a metaphorical level the description in v. 8 of YHWH spreading his cloak over wife Jerusalem alludes to sexual intercourse to emphasize the exclusive character of YHWH's relationship with Jerusalem, a fact Jerusalem could not have misunderstood.[35] The metaphorical truth communicated by YHWH's "spreading the corner of his garment over" Jerusalem indicates that the capacity of sexual intercourse to create an enduring, intimate bond between two persons is also that of an action YHWH carries out with humans, but not in the same way that two humans do in the act of sexual intercourse.[36]

With the marriage bond in place at the time of the sexual union of the couple, the remaining two statements in v. 8 build upon rather than effect that bond.[37] The statement that YHWH swore and entered into covenant with woman Jerusalem may be an allusion to the patriarchal promise, for as Greenberg points out: "nowhere is marriage expressly called a covenant or the husband charged with an oath."[38] YHWH's statement, "You became mine," expresses a fundamental theme of the narrative: a wife is under the authority of her husband. Rather than regarding a wife as if she were mere property, this statement of possession emphasizes that the relationship between a husband and a wife is unique and cannot be compromised.[39] When it is, it means that the wife no longer belongs to the husband (cf. 16:15, 16, 19) and this is a mark of dishonor for the husband.[40]

34. Kamionkowski, *Gender Reversal and Cosmic Chaos*, 104–9.

35. Marvin Pope, "Mixed Marriage Metaphor in Ezekiel 16," in *Fortunate the Eyes That See: Essays in Honor of David Noel Freedman in Celebration of His Seventieth Birthday*, ed. Astrid Beck, et al., 384–99 (Grand Rapids: Eerdmans, 1995), at 393.

36. On YHWH's role in the sexual union of male and female see Robin H. Jarrell, "The Birth Narrative as Female Counterpart to Covenant," *JSOT* 97 (2002): 3–18, at 4. On the understanding of the encounter with the holy as an experience on the continuum between the literal and the figurative see Marcel J. H. M. Poorthuis, "Introduction," in *Purity and Holiness: The Heritage of Leviticus*, ed. Marcel J. H. M. Poorthuis and Joshua Schwartz, 3–26 (Leiden: Brill, 2000), at 5, 9.

37. Block, *Ezekiel*, 1.482-84.

38. Greenberg, *Ezekiel 1–20*, 277.

39. For a critique of Koschaker's interpretation of the *terḫatum* ("brideprice / bridewealth") in Mesopotamia as a purchase price, see Westbrook, *Old Babylonian Marriage Law*, 54.

40. Galambush, *Jerusalem in the Book of Ezekiel*, 34, n. 30.

After the marriage bond has been sealed by the symbolic actions described in v. 8, further symbolic actions of washing, purifying, anointing, clothing, and feeding wife Jerusalem in vv. 9-13 indicate that she has undergone a rite of passage.[41] The quality of the clothing and jewelry signal that she has been raised to royal status, a fact the final phrase of v. 13 explicitly affirms: "you enjoyed royal status (*mĕlûkâ*)." This change in status is an event within the social and political spheres, since her reputation for the perfection of her beauty had spread throughout the nations (v. 14; cf. 28:12; Isa 62:2-5).[42] But YHWH makes clear to her that this came about "through my splendor which I had set upon you" (v. 14).[43]

Up to this point in the narrative YHWH has been the actor; Jerusalem has been the passive recipient.[44] Kamionkowski argues that the image of the woman as weak is fundamental to the dominant metaphors of Ezekiel 16: a weak man is a woman and a strong woman is a man.[45] If the masculinity and femininity of the actors in this narrative are compromised, the gender identity of the members of the community is also compromised, and ambiguity begins to efface distinctions foundational to Ezekiel's priestly vision of community.[46]

The personification of Jerusalem as a woman communicates the understanding that the common life of the city has a life of its own that comes into being through the action of human beings (i.e., the birth of the girl Jerusalem from a Hittite mother and an Amorite father), but this common life can only survive through intimate union with YHWH, who has rescued this common life and joined it to himself. This common life can also be identified as the body politic of the city of Jerusalem, but this colder expression of the web of human relationships that binds together human beings who live in a particular place does not capture the dynamism and vitality of that milieu as well as the relationship between

41. Block, *Ezekiel*, 1.484.

42. A phenomenon analogous to that of Princess Diana in twentieth-century England.

43. Block, *Ezekiel*, 1.485–86.

44. Ibid., 1.486. On distortions in the imagination of the marriage relationship spawned by the patron/client model see Dempsey, "The 'Whore' of Ezekiel 16," 66.

45. Kamionkowski, *Gender Reversal and Cosmic Chaos*, 92. Note the following Mesopotamian treaty curse: "May they treat you like a woman in the presence of your enemy," line 617, in Donald J. Wiseman, *The Vassal-Treaties of Esarhaddon* (London: The British School of Archaeology in Iraq, 1958), 75–76.

46. Kamionkowski, *Gender Reversal and Cosmic Chaos*, 7–8, 132; Galambush, *Jerusalem in the Book of Ezekiel*, 101–2; cf. David Carr, "Gender and the Shaping of Desire in the Song of Songs and its Interpretation," *JBL* 119 (2000): 233–48, at 239–40.

husband and wife. The sense of place emanating from one's hometown captures well the living reality of the common life that suffuses yet transcends the individuals within it. It is the feeling that moves the psalmist to cry out: "If I forget you, Jerusalem, let my right hand be forgotten" (Ps 137:5).[47] This common life of Jerusalem was exceptionally beautiful and attractive to the nations on the day of YHWH's wedding with her (Ezek 16:14). But YHWH makes clear that her beauty is a consequence of the gifts he has bestowed upon her since the day of her birth. Ezekiel's judgment of Jerusalem focuses on Jerusalem's failure to be mindful of the fundamental role YHWH plays in her life.

Adulterous Jerusalem: Narcissistic Autonomy and an Excessive Sex Drive

Beauty is a dangerous reality for a human being. The acclaim it generates can distort the perception of the beautiful person. This was the fatal misstep of wife Jerusalem that undermined her relationship with YHWH. Her action as described in Ezek 16:15 finds an echo in that of the king of Tyre in Ezek 28:11-17 who became enamored of his own beauty and wisdom and began to exploit others through it. According to Ezek 16:15, YHWH charges wife Jerusalem with trusting in her own beauty, so that she began to prostitute herself because of the acclaim her beauty had generated. The precipitous fall of wife Jerusalem and of the king of Tyre are presented by Ezekiel as a consequence of an unreflective narcissism.[48] Because Jerusalem's narcissism undermines her marriage, the wrath and jealousy fueling YHWH's words of condemnation increase as he confronts wife Jerusalem with a series of her infidelities.[49]

YHWH accuses wife Jerusalem, saying: "You poured out your promiscuity on everyone who passed by" (16:15). This radical shift from trusting in her beauty to indiscriminate offers to give her beautiful body to any passerby is shocking. Wife Jerusalem is not forced to sell her body due to desperate economic circumstances. She seems to be driven by a form of sexual desire in which unconscious physical forces are gaining ascendancy over cultural concerns, i.e., how she fits into the web of re-

47. Read *tiššākaḥ* with LXX.

48. Launderville, *Spirit and Reason*, 45–46, 180–81. Daniel Bodi, *The Book of Ezekiel and the Poem of Erra*, OBO 104 (Fribourg: Universitätsverlag, 1991), 158–59, notes that Ezekiel is unique in linking hubris with *hāmôn* (Ezek 23:42; cf. 7:11, 13–14).

49. Dempsey, "The 'Whore' of Ezekiel 16," 63, 70, 71, evaluates the offensive character of the imagery of Ezekiel 16 and finds the divine response to wife Jerusalem's abominations not only excessive but also in contradiction to divine law. See also Kamionkowski, *Gender Reversal and Cosmic Chaos*, 38.

lationships among cities and nations.[50] This imbalance in her body manifests itself in a voracious need to be shown affection. She will take the clothing, which YHWH gave her to symbolize her royal status, and use it to construct shrines where she acts as a prostitute (*wattiznî*, v. 16).[51] The logic of her action seems to be that she wants to create a sacred space in which she can offer access to her private parts. Galambush has argued that the body of wife Jerusalem symbolizes the temple within which the holy of holies is her womb.[52] By building these sacred spaces alternative to the temple, in which her body lies at the center of the activities of the shrine, wife Jerusalem has thrown off the constraints of limited access to the holy of holies in the temple. She uses sacred space and its activities to supply her with sexual partners.

She also takes the beautiful gold and silver jewelry given to her by YHWH and melts it down to form male images (*ṣalmê zākār*) with which she prostitutes herself (v. 17). How she is using these male images remains a matter of speculation,[53] but it is clear that she is setting up an alternative sacred site where she is at the center of the activities rather than YHWH. Therefore she is taking all the clothing and food YHWH has given her and using it to beautify and feed these male images; in other

50. Day, "Yahweh's Broken Marriages," 235, argues that the description of this unnatural behavior by wife Jerusalem is driven by the tenor of the marriage metaphor, that is, the covenant relationship as undermined by treaties with foreign nations that require punishment. Kamionkowski, *Gender Reversal and Cosmic Chaos*, 113–17, emphasizes that in vv. 15-42 wife Jerusalem becomes assertive and begins to act; she does not hold fast to the days of her nakedness and vulnerability. Concerning the anxiety over guarding a woman's sexual expression in terms of honor and shame in village life in contemporary Turkey see Carol Delaney, "Seeds of Honor and Fields of Shame," in *Honor and Shame and the Unity of the Mediterranean*, ed. David D. Gilmore, 35–48 (Washington, DC: American Anthropological Association, 1987), at 41-43.

51. Block, *Ezekiel*, 464, 466, notes that the root *znh*, "to act as a prostitute," occurs twenty-one times in Ezekiel 16 and serves as the leitmotif of the chapter. He speculates that the abstract formation *taznût*, which occurs only in Ezekiel 16 and 23, was an invention by Ezekiel.

52. Galambush, *Jerusalem in the Book of Ezekiel*, 87. Tikva Frymer-Kensky, *In the Wake of the Goddesses*, 57, claims that "in ancient Sumer, divine vaginas bring birth and renewal. When, as in the Bible, the divine has no vagina, how can the world be renewed? Clearly, the entire conceptualization of nature has to undergo fundamental change." On temple entrances and fertility figures see William P. Brown, *Seeing the Psalms* (Grand Rapids: Eerdmans, 2002), 63–67.

53. Kamionkowski, *Gender Reversal and Cosmic Chaos*, 121–22, suggests that she used them as dildoes. However, Margaret Odell, in a review of Kamionkowski's *Gender Reversal and Cosmic Chaos* in *CBQ* 67 (2005): 321, regards this interpretation of Ezek 16:17 as going beyond the evidence of the text.

words, she uses these gifts from YHWH to attract clients to her shrines. Wife Jerusalem redistributes the gifts of YHWH in order to enhance the kind of cultic establishment that serves her needs.

The primary transgression at the heart of idol-making is that the idol-maker aims to replace YHWH with herself/himself as the center of attention.[54] Jerusalem's all-consuming focus on maintaining the shrines that served her sexual needs is evident in her sacrificing her children to these idols (v. 20). On the metaphorical level of the story it must be that these children were born to her through her union with YHWH,[55] for YHWH says: "You slaughtered my children (*bānâ*) and donated them by making them cross over to them (*bĕhaʿăbîr*, v. 21). Such "crossing over" is usually interpreted as burning.[56] In a sacrifice, the offerer gives what is valuable and identifies with the victim that is about to be transferred into the realm of the holy through burning.[57] But in normative Yahwistic practice with regard to firstborn humans (Exod 13:15), a substitute was supplied rather than actually burning a human being. Here wife Jerusalem, the mother of the inhabitants of the city, ignores the practice of substitution and mindlessly disposes of her children (cf. Ezek 20:25-26).[58] So strong is her need to make her own shrine functional. The irony in Jerusalem's behavior is that she disposes of her children with the same lack of compassion as shown by her parents in exposing her.[59] Thus YHWH confronts her: "In all of your abominations and promiscuous acts, you did not remember the days of your youth when you were undressed,

54. Block, *Ezekiel*, 1.488.

55. Ibid., 1.489–90.

56. Greenberg, *Ezekiel 1–20*, 369–70; Block, *Ezekiel*, 1.636; Zimmerli, *Ezekiel 1*, 411–12; Day, *Molech*, 65–71.

57. Maurice Bloch, *Prey into Hunter: The Politics of Religious Experience* (Cambridge and New York: Cambridge University Press, 1992), 31–34; Jean-Pierre Vernant, "A General Theory of Sacrifice and the Slaying of the Victim in the Greek *Thusia*," in *Mortals and Immortals: Collected Essays*, ed. Froma Zeitlin, 290–302 (Princeton: Princeton University Press, 1991), at 293. As a critique of the masculine character of traditional sacrificial practice, Julia Kristeva, in Catherine Clement and Julia Kristeva, *The Feminine and the Sacred* (New York: Columbia University Press, 2001), 15, counters that "the sadomasochism of the sacred connection (body/meaning) seems more obvious to a woman, more operative in a woman."

58. Launderville, *Spirit and Reason*, 270–71. For a view of this as a punishment in which YHWH set the Jerusalemites up for failure see Corrine Patton, "'I Myself Gave Them Laws That Were Not Good': Ezekiel 20 and the Exodus Traditions," *JSOT* 69 (1996): 73–90, at 79; Jon D. Levenson, *The Death and Resurrection of the Beloved Son: The Transformation of Child Sacrifice in Judaism and Christianity* (New Haven: Yale University Press, 1993), 7.

59. Cf. Dempsey, "The 'Whore' of Ezekiel 16," 61.

naked, and kicking about in your blood" (v. 22). If she had been mindful of her origins she would have recognized that her survival depended on her being rescued from the sphere of Canaanite culture to take up residence in the sphere of Yahwistic culture; instead, she realizes the proverb, "like mother, like daughter" (v. 44).

When YHWH introduces the topic of Jerusalem's practice of child sacrifice, he interjects, "as if your promiscuous acts were not enough" (v. 20b). He also begins the next section (vv. 23-30) on a note of frustration: "Woe, woe to you" (v. 23). Jerusalem shows that her sexual appetite has grown stronger. Now she has built a platform and an elevated place in every square and at every street corner. Ezekiel's narrative then begins to ratchet up the intensity of the rhetoric with the addition of pornoprophetic phrases.[60] He says that wife Jerusalem has taken her station on these elevated places. YHWH confronts her with the charge: "You spread your legs to everyone who was passing by; you multiplied (*wattarbî*) your promiscuous acts" (v. 25). This phrase "multiplying your promiscuous acts" occurs three times in this section with reference to passersby, the Egyptians, and the Chaldeans (vv. 25, 26, 29). Between the Egyptians and the Chaldeans is a reference to the Assyrians in which YHWH charges Jerusalem: "You acted promiscuously toward the Assyrians without finding satisfaction" (v. 28).[61] This notion of multiplying promiscuous acts in a desperate effort to respond to the signals of her body is the converse of YHWH's granting increase (*rbh*, v. 7) to the girl Jerusalem during her formative years. When YHWH plays a formative role in her life, woman Jerusalem increases in vitality and beauty. When she tries to be autonomous and to structure her life apart from YHWH she becomes fragmented and incapable of finding peace.[62] YHWH concludes this section with another interjection: "How feverish (*ʾămulâ*) was your heart" (v. 30). The center of Jerusalem's person, which coordinates one's thinking and feeling, was parched and burning with a fever.

The cause of Jerusalem's disorientation was her acting like "a domineering prostitute" (*ʾiššâ-zônâ šallāṭet*), v. 30. Ezekiel's diagnosis of the ills of Jerusalem concludes that the primary sin of Jerusalem is her desire to be autonomous and to construct a world of her own in which she is

60. Greenberg, *Ezekiel 1–20*, 296–97.

61. Jacqueline Lapsley, *Can These Bones Live? The Problem of the Moral Self in the Book of Ezekiel*, BZAW 301 (Berlin and New York: de Gruyter, 2000), 85, notes that in Israelite society prostitutes were believed to be motivated by lust as well as by economic reasons.

62. Cf. Block, *Ezekiel*, 1.498. On wife Jerusalem's abnormal lust see Galambush, *Jerusalem in the Book of Ezekiel*, 117.

in charge. Kamionkowski identifies such behavior as gender reversal: a woman is taking on a man's role when she becomes the active agent rather than the passive one.[63] Ezekiel certainly condemns wife Jerusalem for refusing to remain as YHWH's wife and for forgetting all that he has done for her. But these initiatives by wife Jerusalem are radical instances of being an active agent. There are multiple ways of being an active agent and still understanding oneself to belong to a larger web of relationships of family and city. The reversals that wife Jerusalem's actions mirror are those of the first couple in the Garden of Eden, where their choice of breaking the taboo forbidding the eating of the fruit of the tree of good and evil was, in effect, an effort to replace God as the ruler over the Garden.[64] Their action set them on the path where they would be repeatedly tempted to be autonomous rather than heteronomous. Wife Jerusalem likewise loses focus when YHWH is no longer her husband in practice; she becomes fragmented by insatiable desire. The demand to focus on YHWH alone is a theological question that goes beyond the dichotomy of male versus female to the more fundamental distinction of God versus human. Wife Jerusalem does not simply want to act as a male; she wants to act as God.

The radical disorientation arising from her desire to be autonomous is highlighted in the final section of YHWH's accusation (vv. 31-34), where she is described as one whose desire for sexual satisfaction drives her to behavior untypical of a prostitute. Most prostitutes serve their clients for a fee. Adulterous Jerusalem not only refuses payment but even bribes potential clients. The phrase at the beginning and end of this section describes Jerusalem: "It was different (*hēpek*) with you . . . . You were different (*hepek*)" (v. 34).[65] Wife Jerusalem is driven by a strong addiction to sex. The psychophysical dimension of sex for her has completely

63. Kamionkowski, *Gender Reversal and Cosmic Chaos*, 127–28. David Carr, "Gender and the Shaping of Desire," 244, claims that in ancient Israel "many understood divine-human love to be male-female love *governed by much the same principles as male-female love on the human level*."

64. Walter Brueggemann, *Genesis* (Atlanta: John Knox, 1982), 48; cf. Westermann, *Genesis 1–11*, 248.

65. Kamionkowski, *Gender Reversal and Cosmic Chaos*, 127, notes that *hāpak*, "overturn," refers not merely to physical objects but also to cosmic categories. Therefore the woman who acts as a man and thus inverts the natural order is playing the role of God. Carr, "Gender and the Shaping of Desire," 233–48, at 240, points out that a woman who seeks out another lover calls into question the social hierarchy in which a woman's place is to submit to her husband; because the divine-human relationship was conceived in terms of the marital metaphor, such rebellion had cosmic ramifications.

overwhelmed its cultural components. Her move toward autonomy brings her chaos.

The Punishment and Purgation of Defiled Jerusalem

In Israel, the holy is a dangerous reality. Those who encounter the holy are those who fear for their lives; those who treat lightly the presence of the holy lose their lives.[66] Wife Jerusalem has sinned against YHWH by setting up alternative sanctuaries and engaging in promiscuous acts that negate her exclusive loyalty to YHWH in sexual matters. From a priestly perspective she has polluted the temple and the city by bringing the impure into contact with the holy.[67] Such defilement is sure to call forth a response from YHWH.

In response to the indictment of wife Jerusalem in vv. 15-34, YHWH delivers his judgment against Jerusalem in vv. 35-41. He begins by addressing her: "Prostitute, hear the word of the Lord" (v. 35). He summarizes her sins as acts of prostitution and child sacrifice (v. 36). In the spirit of reciprocity or talion, YHWH decrees that for her sins of uncovering her nakedness to her lovers he will gather all her lovers, including those she liked and those she hated, and he will uncover her nakedness for all of them to see (v. 37).[68] This action, which is repeated in v. 39 when the group strips her clothes from her, reduces her to the state Adam and Eve were in after eating the forbidden fruit.[69] Perhaps wife Jerusalem, with the collective gaze of her lovers upon her, would feel that sense of shame at nakedness that is normal for humans in the post-Eden context. This feeling of shame may remind her then of the alienation with which

66. Baruch Schwartz, "Israel's Holiness: The Torah Traditions," in *Purity and Holiness*, 47–59, at 53; Jan Joosten, *People and Land in the Holiness Code: An Exegetical Study of the Ideational Framework of the Law in Leviticus 17–26*, VTSup 67 (Leiden: Brill, 1996), 123; Jacob Milgrom, *Leviticus 1–16*, AB 3 (New York: Doubleday, 1994), 73.

67. Galambush, *Jerusalem in the Book of Ezekiel*, 78, 81, 87–88.

68. Day, "Yahweh's Broken Marriages," 231, 235–41, points out how this punishment does not conform to the laws of Deut 22:22 and Lev 20:10 in which both the adulteress and her lover are to be put to death; therefore the need to account for the rape and abuse visited upon Jerusalem by Babylonian invaders (the tenor of the metaphor) drives the description of punishment for adulterous Jerusalem (the vehicle of the metaphor).

69. Jacqueline Lapsley, "Shame and Self-Knowledge: The Positive Role of Shame in Ezekiel's View of the Moral Self," in *The Book of Ezekiel: Theological and Anthropological Perspectives*, SBL Symposium Series 9, ed. Margaret Odell and John Strong, 143–73 (Atlanta: Scholars Press, 2000), at 161–62; Westermann, *Genesis 1–11*, 250–51. Zimmerli, *Ezekiel 1*, 346, notes that this nakedness returns her to the status she had as a foundling.

all humans must wrestle in dealing with their sexuality.[70] The urges and desires need to be channeled rather than followed impulsively.

In her promiscuous acts wife Jerusalem had no difficulty in showing her nakedness to her lovers individually, but to do so with them all gathered together changes the experience. This group, some of whom had copulated with her on the platforms or elevated places (vv. 24, 31), are to render judgment on her, treating her as an adulteress and murderer deserving of capital punishment (v. 38; cf. Lev 20:10; 24:17; Exod 21:12).[71] They are to demolish her platforms and elevated places and to strip her clothes from her; these actions would be taking away the gifts YHWH had given her. Then they are to bring up an "assembly" (*qāhāl*, v. 40) against her to stone her. The rationale for stoning is that the offender has polluted the community and rendered it vulnerable.[72] The removal of the adulteress is not only punishment of the offender but a purging of the community from impurity. The splitting apart of her body with swords and the burning of her house likewise have as a goal the elimination of defilement from the community.[73]

All these judgments are to be carried out in the view of many women in the community (v. 41). Is this action meant to be a deterrent to the observing women so that they do not engage in fornication? Or is it a strategy aimed at heightening the sense of shame at sinful sexual acts? The purpose of these public humiliations and punishments seems to have been to create a stronger sense of guilt over those sins that polluted the community and undermined the body politic.[74] Lapsley contends that the feminine form of shame described in Ezekiel 16 is one that a female audience could understand most fully; therefore, women would be able to get a message across to wife Jerusalem more so than a mixed

70. Gerhard von Rad, *Genesis*, rev. ed., trans. J. H. Marks, OTL (Philadelphia: Westminster, 1972), 85, 91; Lapsley, "Shame and Self-Knowledge," 149–50, 152.

71. Block, *Ezekiel*, 1.502.

72. Galambush, *Jerusalem in the Book of Ezekiel*, 102–4.

73. Ibid., 108–9. On the purging of Jerusalem see Ezek 24:6-13, in which the pieces of meat (i.e., the defiled inhabitants of Jerusalem) are taken one by one from the cauldron (Jerusalem) and then placed back in it only to be boiled away so that the city might be cleansed.

74. Lapsley, "Shame and Self-Knowledge," 144, 159. Karel van der Toorn, *Scribal Culture and the Making of the Hebrew Bible* (Cambridge, MA: Harvard University Press, 2007), 46, claims: "In ancient civilizations, such as Mesopotamia and Israel, the human person is understood as a character (*personnage*) rather than as a personality (*personne*). The individual is indistinguishable from his or her social role and social status."

audience of men and women.[75] She notes, however, that this strategy of increasing a sense of disgrace within wife Jerusalem by public humiliation did not work; public shaming did not provide her with new self-knowledge and a new capacity to feel shame appropriately. Wife Jerusalem would be able to feel this positive, constructive form of shame only when YHWH intervened to transform her moral capacity.[76]

YHWH notes that once this punishment is carried out he will let go of his wrath and jealousy (v. 42). He says to wife Jerusalem: "Because you did not remember the days of your youth, you enraged me on account of all these things. So I will bring your ways back on yourself" (v. 43). Abominable and polluting actions are incompatible with YHWH. If they build up in the land, he must act to purge them even if this means destroying Jerusalem itself.[77] For Ezekiel, Jerusalem dies at the time of its destruction in 586 by the Babylonians. He does not mention the name "Jerusalem" in his restoration oracles.[78] So if woman Jerusalem was to be the wife of YHWH, it was imperative that she not compromise the exclusive character of their relationship.[79]

The intimacy of the marriage relationship serves as a metaphor for the relationship between YHWH and the people of Jerusalem. Despite Ezekiel's claim that guilt from one generation does not pass to the next and that each individual is accountable for his or her own sins (Ezek 18:20), he does not do away with the sense that people are responsible for one another.[80] When impurities enter the community through idolatry and cultic or ethical sins, it is imperative to expiate these sins and purge their defilement. If impurities are allowed to remain in the community, they will eventually drive YHWH out. Then YHWH will bring destroyers against the defiled city so that the land itself might be purged and so be able to have a new start. Ezekiel 8–11 describes how the temple and the

75. Lapsley, "Shame and Self-Knowledge," 162.

76. Ibid., 156, 165; eadem, *Can These Bones Live?* 110–12.

77. Galambush, *Jerusalem in the Book of Ezekiel*, 79–80, 88, 104.

78. Lawrence Boadt, "Rhetorical Strategies in Ezekiel's Oracles of Judgment," in *Ezekiel and His Book: Textual and Literary Criticism and Their Interrelation*, BETL 74, ed. Johan Lust, 182–200 (Leuven: Leuven University/Peeters, 1986), at 193; Margaret Odell, "The City of Hamonah in Ezekiel 39:11-16: The Tumultuous City of Jerusalem," *CBQ* 56 (1994): 479–89, at 486–89.

79. J. N. Postgate, *Early Mesopotamia: Society and Economy at the Dawn of History* (London: Routledge, 1992), 130, notes with regard to the cloistered EN-priestesses at Ur: "the gods were presumably as jealous of their spouses as their human counterparts, so that we need not be surprised that the *entum* was protected from the outside world."

80. Lapsley, *Can These Bones Live?* 25, 33.

city of Jerusalem were destroyed under YHWH's direction. According to Ezekiel, this catastrophe did not happen by chance nor was it carried out under the direction of the Babylonian god Marduk. This watershed event in Israel's history was YHWH's response to defilement of the land and the temple.[81] A primary purpose for the strong rhetoric of Ezekiel 16 was to explain the severity of the punishment visited upon Jerusalem in 586. Ezekiel's position is clear: the punishment fits the crime. He exhorts his audience to accept responsibility and to repent. By getting a new heart and a new spirit they will be able to have a new future in the land (Ezek 18:31; 36:26).

Restored Jerusalem: Shame over Past Infidelities

What angers YHWH about the adulterous actions of wife Jerusalem is that she has treated lightly what is sacred to their relationship. She has given away this intimate core to numerous lovers. The betrayal in an adulterous action undermines the trust that is constitutive of the core relationship in a nuclear family (cf. Ezek 22:3-12). Such an action reverberates from the nuclear to the extended family, to the clan, and eventually to the people as a whole. This boundary violation makes a mockery of the sacrifices required to sustain the common life of the family and the nation. This tear in the fabric of the common life is a question of the integrity of the family, which bears the name of the father.[82] The center that plays a key role in holding together and nurturing the diverse relationships within the family or community is impaired by an adulterous relationship. This integrity of the family among the peoples of the ancient Near East and the ancient Mediterranean world was also identified as its honor.[83] When this integrity was violated, the destructive action did

81. Galambush, *Jerusalem in the Book of Ezekiel*, 88; Launderville, *Spirit and Reason*, 95–96, 106–9, 118–20, 131–33.

82. Galambush, *Jerusalem in the Book of Ezekiel*, 102–3; Kamionkowski, *Gender Reversal and Cosmic Chaos*, 92; Launderville, *Spirit and Reason*, 257–58.

83. Delaney, "Seeds of Honor and Fields of Shame," 40, argues that "paternity is overdetermined"; so much emphasis is placed on legitimacy of offspring that abusive measures (infibulation, clitoridectomy) and excessive restrictions have been inflicted on women. Gale Yee, *Poor Banished Children of Eve*, 42, states that "biblical notions of honor and shame are (re)productions of an established male ideology. They do *not* indicate how women evaluate themselves or their men." Lapsley, "Shame and Self-Knowledge," 150, notes: "The behaviors constituting shame for women in the bible include deference and submission to male authority, a certain passivity in behavior, covering nakedness, sexual exclusiveness, a lack of sexual desire, and modesty in attire and deportment." However, applied to men, these are negatives.

not violate the individual honor of the father as much as it did the collective honor of the family.

Ezekiel explains that wife Jerusalem, by abandoning her exclusive relationship with YHWH, has reverted to the Canaanite ways of her original family. Her behavior confirms the proverb: "Like mother, like daughter" (Ezek 16:44). The Canaanite pattern of the mother and her daughters spurning their husbands and children extends linearly from the Canaanite matriarch not only to woman Jerusalem but also to Jerusalem's sisters Samaria and Sodom. Within the frame of the narrative of Ezekiel 16 it appears that the sisters Samaria and Sodom were raised in the context of Canaanite culture; they were not cast off at birth like Jerusalem. Jerusalem's adoption of Canaanite ways suggests that her genetic constitution or blood relationship with her Canaanite parents was an inheritance that remained with her and could not be easily changed.[84] Jerusalem's living within the context of Yahwistic culture from the day of her birth until shortly after her marriage with YHWH did not transform her sufficiently to do away with her attachments to Canaanite ways, even though she would have been in a more favorable position than her sisters for giving up those ways.

The narrative focuses on the puzzling behavior of wife Jerusalem. Why would the lure of Canaanite culture be so strong? Wife Jerusalem had previously scorned her sister Sodom as one who was debased. But YHWH emphatically testifies: "As I live—oracle of the Lord God—your sister Sodom and her daughters have not acted as you and your daughters have done" (v. 48). Jerusalem, as privileged recipient of YHWH's special favor since the day of her birth, finds herself in a much more debased condition than her sister Sodom because she has treated lightly the relationship YHWH extended to her. By ignoring the exclusive character of this relationship she has unleashed within herself desires that result in lewd behavior for which even her Philistine neighbors ("daughters of the Philistines," v. 27) feel shame on her behalf. [85]

In the days of Jerusalem's pride (*gāʾôn*, v. 56), she had regarded Sodom as the proverbial desolate one whom YHWH had removed from the land (v. 50). According to Ezekiel the sins of Sodom were pride (*gāʾôn*, v. 49), sufficiency of food, quiet ease, and indifference toward the poor and the needy.[86] Such haughty behavior indicated that Sodom was

84. Pope, "Mixed Marriage Metaphor in Ezekiel 16," 395.

85. Block, *Ezekiel*, 1.496.

86. Zimmerli, *Ezekiel 1*, 350, regards these sins as an adaptation of Sodom's reputation in Genesis in the direction of "typical social conditions in Israel."

unmindful of YHWH.[87] But YHWH pointed out to Jerusalem that Sodom and her daughters—the city of Sodom and the villages around her—did not commit half the abominations Jerusalem did. YHWH then emphasizes to Jerusalem: "You made your sister look more upright than you through all the abominations that you have done" (v. 51). The point of such a comparison is to try to get Jerusalem to feel shame at her actions.[88] By calling to her attention the inconsistency of her behavior—regarding Sodom as debased but acting more abominably than she—YHWH tried to get Jerusalem to feel shame. He even tried to make her feel jealous of her sisters in that she has given them the consolation that they are more upright than she is (vv. 54, 62) and that they will be restored to their homelands ahead of her (v. 55).[89] But even these tactics failed.

The only way to save Jerusalem from herself is through the intervention of YHWH, who would take her out of the land and then restore her. When she comes back, according to Ezekiel's restoration oracles (chaps. 34–48), she would not be named Jerusalem; however, those who had the mark placed on their forehead (Ezek 9:4) or who had gone into exile would be the thread of continuity between preexilic Jerusalem and the postexilic community. On the basis of the dying and rising experience of exile and restoration, wife Jerusalem would be purged of all her defilements and so be in a position to remember and feel shame at her past sins. This moral capacity to feel constructive shame is essential to the integrity of the covenant relationship (v. 60).[90] YHWH's gracious actions saved the foundling Jerusalem; adulterous Jerusalem will also be saved and transformed by the gracious intervention of YHWH.[91] Woman Jerusalem will come to true self-knowledge: that her identity is founded on being faithful to YHWH her husband. The story of woman Jerusalem in Ezekiel 16 is the story of YHWH's grace.

87. Block, *Ezekiel*, 1.509.

88. Margaret Odell, "An Exploratory Study of Shame and Dependence in the Bible and Selected Near Eastern Parallels," in *The Biblical Canon in Comparative Perspective*, 217–29, at 228–29, argues that the prophets took the experience of shame that the people felt at divine abandonment—a sense of shame arising from a failed relationship—and turned it on its head by claiming that the people were responsible for this divine withdrawal.

89. Block, *Ezekiel*, 1.510, 513–14.

90. Lapsley, "Shame and Self-Knowledge," 153–54.

91. In Gen 3:8-11, God questions and punishes the first human couple but is merciful in not subjecting them to the death penalty: i.e., God's actions heighten the sense of shame (see Arnold, *Genesis*, 66–67).

Summary

Ezekiel draws on the Semitic practice of personifying a city both as a woman and as a wife in order to convey the dynamic relational character of collective and individual responsibility. Within the judgment narrative of Ezekiel 16, Ezekiel surfaces the affective logic of the covenant relationship through the marriage metaphor; the angry response of YHWH to adulterous Jerusalem's promiscuous behavior emphasizes that this exclusive relationship stands at the center of a web of relationships that extends not only vertically to heaven but also horizontally within Jerusalem and to the ends of the earth. Wife Jerusalem's Canaanite origins seem to be a factor in her promiscuous ways, but her Yahwistic upbringing holds her to a higher standard and puts greater pressure on her to live in right relationship with YHWH. Her disordered sexuality not only undermines her intimate relationship with YHWH but also leads her to sacrifice her children to secure the favor of her lovers (i.e., treaty partners). Remembering the gracious actions of YHWH in adopting and marrying her are vital to wife Jerusalem's integrity and well-being. When YHWH punishes her through her lovers, she will recognize how her misplaced love and trust were shameful deeds that compromised her person. Ezekiel communicates his message of the necessity of covenantal fidelity for the integration of sexuality within communal relationships. Unfortunately, the metaphor of the unfaithful wife rhetorically communicates to the unreflective listener an image of woman as the cause of evil in the community. Attentiveness to the dynamic of this metaphor is indispensable to properly understanding the challenges inherent in covenantal fidelity and the process of integrating sexuality with spirituality.

Mesopotamia: A Vision for Communal Integrity in a Mythical Tradition

Institutions that persist through time are those that effectively serve the needs of the people who invest in them. The more effective institutions are typically those of moderate size that are mindful of the need to keep their vision responsive to the vital needs of the people they serve. Mythmaking is an ongoing activity in which a people engage one another through narrative to be attentive to fundamental existential questions. At the beginning of the Mesopotamian tradition the Sumerian people created stories about the gods that reflected their collective concerns: i.e., relational issues that were constitutive of their community. These stories were written down after generations of storytelling had refined and adapted them for particular audiences. The imagining or visioning promoted by these stories helps individuals find their place in a community and assists a community to be faithful to its traditioning process: i.e., to continue the content of the tradition while adapting it to new circumstances.

In continuity with the four major topics addressed in our interpretation of Ezekiel 16, this section will address how the following four issues are illustrated by selected texts from the Mesopotamian tradition: (1) how gender functions in the construction of collective identity; (2) how discretion can channel the sex drive toward the creation of community; (3) how the interplay between nature, culture, and gender shape authority in a community; and (4) how the formation of boundaries within a polytheistic world differs from such formation in a monotheistic one.

Gender and Collective Identity: Hierarchy versus Partnership

The place one calls home consists not only of its natural, physical aspects but also of its cultural artifacts. The sense of belonging that arises from interacting with a group of people in the same place over a number of years has a fragile stability that inspires gratitude and cautions against complacency. Although home provides a shelter against a competitive world, it is also a dynamic environment that can slip away if it is taken for granted. Friends who are neglected will find new friends; objects or activities that lie dormant may be taken over by others searching for new opportunities. However, there are forces in the collective environment that can shift and so diminish an individual's sense of belonging to a place despite that individual's best efforts. In these times of displacement or alienation we try to understand the sociopolitical structures of which we are a part. We may then draw on the resources with which our elders and our culture have equipped us.

In a Sumerian song that seems to have been preserved as a school exercise from the Isin period (2017–1793 BCE), "The Song of the Hoe," the composer presents an account of the creation of the world and of humans that indirectly privileges the male role in reproduction. Even though the composer may have had a humorous purpose in mind for this text, he was ignoring the full significance of the role of "mother earth" as a partner in the reproductive process:[92]

> Not only did the lord who never changes his promises for the future make the world appear in its correct form—Enlil who will make the seed of mankind rise from the earth—not only did he hasten to

92. Frymer-Kensky, *In the Wake of the Goddesses*, 46.

> separate heaven from earth . . . and earth from heaven, but, in order to make it possible for humans to grow "where the flesh sprouts," he first affixed the axis of the world in Duranki. (ll. 1-7)[93]

Enlil, "Lord Wind," is the true executive power.[94] The earth is not imagined here as the goddess KI in sexual union with the sky-god AN; rather, earth and heaven are demythologized and regarded as locations to be separated. Then the seed (i.e., the male contribution to reproduction) will sprout human flesh from the earth. Removing personal qualities from the earth and leaving it simply as a receptacle for incubating the seed diminishes the female role in the reproductive process. Even though the role of Mother Earth is muted in extant Sumerian works, there are myths that celebrate the fundamental role of the feminine in the generation of the gods.[95] For example, in the myth "Enki and Ninmaḫ" the goddess Nammu is described as "the primeval mother" who gave birth to the first generation of the gods (l. 17).[96] In this myth she not only creates humankind but also is the first to have the idea; however, this myth shows Enki approving the idea, reflecting his authority over the functions of the mother goddess.[97] This myth is then echoed in the genealogy at the beginning of the *Enūma Elish* in the late second millennium, which speaks of Apsû and Tiāmat giving birth to Lahmu and Lahamu who in turn give birth to Anshar and Kishar who in turn become the parents of Anu.[98]

93. *COS* 1.157.

94. Thorkild Jacobsen, "The lil$_2$ of ^{d}En-lil$_2$," in *DUMU-E$_2$-DUB-BA-A: Studies in Honor of Åge W. Sjöberg*, Occasional Publications of the Samuel Noah Kramer Fund 11 (Philadelphia: University Museum, 1989), 267–76, at 270–71; idem, *Treasures of Darkness* (New Haven: Yale University Press, 1976), 98–104.

95. Wilfred G. Lambert, "Ancient Mesopotamian Gods: Superstition, Philosophy, Theology," *Revue de l'Histoire des Religions* 207 (1990): 115–30, at 122, identifies the mother goddess as Ninhursag, who held a position on a committee of three (with An and Enlil) who governed the pantheon from the end of the third to the end of the second millennium. The mother goddess was alternatively named Nintu, Arūru, or Bēlet-ilī.

96. In *COS* 1.159, Jacob Klein notes that "elsewhere, Nammu . . . is called "the Bearer (birthgiver) of Heaven and Earth." Her logogram ENGUR, "subterranean (sweet) water," locates her in the same domain as her son Enki.

97. Frymer-Kensky, *In the Wake of the Goddesses*, 72–73.

98. Wilfred G. Lambert, "Kosmogonie," *RlA* 6 (1980/83): 218–22, at 220; Manfred Hutter, "Earth," *DDD*, 272.

The process by which humans sprouted from the earth and then were able to reproduce is described as the "Song of the Hoe" continues:[99]

> Here, "where the flesh sprouts," he [Enlil] set this very hoe to work: he had it place the first model of mankind in the brickmold. And (according to this model) his people started to break through the soil towards Enlil, and he looked approvingly at his "blackheaded people." Now the Anuna-gods stepped up to him: . . . they wanted to demand the "blackheaded people" from him. The lady who (once upon a time) had given birth to the ruler, who had given birth to the king, Ninmena now set the human reproduction going. (ll. 18-27)[100]

The brickmold, which apparently elaborates upon an earlier metaphorical reference to "seed," describes the governing portion of the reproductive process in terms of fabrication. Perhaps this fabrication model explains how the first human was created when there was no possibility of a man having sexual intercourse with a woman. However, unlike Gen 2:18-23, the text does not describe how the first woman was created. The text simply turns the matter of reproduction over to the goddess Ninmena, who presumably then works through the sexual union of man and woman to produce offspring.[101] Thus "The Song of the Hoe" reinforces the foundational power of the male god Enlil in the creation of humans and promotes hierarchy rather than partnership in the way men relate to women.

This same sequence in the creation of humans of an initial, foundational contribution by a male god followed by the work of the mother goddess is related at greater length in the OB Akkadian poem of *Atraḫasīs*. The lower-ranking Igigi gods who were constructing canals as directed by the higher-ranking Anuna gods protested and called upon the divine midwife Bēlet-ilī to create humans to take their place. But Bēlet-ilī, also known as "the wise Mami" (l. 193) and as Nintu (l. 198), responded that Enki first had to provide her with clay. Enki then proposed before the great gods that the following process be followed:

> On the first, seventh, and fifteenth days of the month, I will establish a purifying bath. Let one god be slaughtered so that the gods may

99. Gertrud Farber, *COS* 1.157, p. 511, notes that in this "satirical school text" from the Isin period the parts of the composition are only loosely connected by the theme of the "hoe."

100. *COS* 1.157.

101. Jacobsen, *Treasures of Darkness*, 109, refers to Ninmena (= Ninhursag) as the one who gives birth to kings and gives them the insignia of their office.

> be purified by immersion. Let Nintu mix clay with his flesh and blood. Let that god and the human be completely mixed in the clay. May we hear the drum for the rest of time. (I:206-14)[102]

Here the mother goddess is pictured as a fabricator. She is not a force working within nature as much as she is a craftsperson who shapes raw material. Here she resembles the goddess Ninurra, the patron of pottery-makers.[103] The assembled Anuna gods approved the process and thus humans began to exist as beings whose source of life was the blood of a rebellious god and who were appointed to carry on the work that had weighed down the gods. Thus male deities—Enki and the Anuna gods—are thoroughly in charge of the process for creating humans.

The normal human reproductive process shows that women are closely tied to nature.[104] By contrast, men with their agricultural hoes or other tools relate to nature as fabricators, taking in hand raw materials that need to be shaped. As these myths show, the female role in reproduction is essential and can hardly be denied. So it is only in the misty past of primordial times in which the origin of the first human is at issue that the male mythmakers could make the case that a female fabricator at the behest of a male god initiated the creation of humans. However, these Sumerian and Akkadian myths do not presume that primordial reality transcended gender. Rather, as Tikva Frymer-Kensky claims, "all reality and all power are gender-structured."[105] What the comparison of the Sumerian myths cited here with the poem *Atra-ḫasīs* reveals is that a process of marginalizing feminine deities is underway in Mesopotamia from the third millennium onward. As Frymer-Kensky explains, there was a gradual erosion of the feminine role in maintaining the cosmos: e.g., the goddess Nammu originally was the divine power in the subterranean sweet waters before this role was ceded to Enki/Ea; the goddess Damu who assisted the goddess Gula in healing was originally the

102. Edition: Wilfred G. Lambert and Alan R. Millard, eds., *Atra-Ḫasīs: The Babylonian Story of the Flood* (Winona Lake, IN: Eisenbrauns, 1999), 56, 58.

103. Frymer-Kensky, *In the Wake of the Goddesses*, 32–33, notes that Ninurra, the wife of Shara at Umma, later was transformed into a male god and was eventually absorbed into the figure of Enki/Ea.

104. Ibid., 47. On a family-centered versus a clinically-centered birthing system see George W. Lowis and Peter G. McCaffery, "Sociological Factors Affecting the Medicalization of Midwifery," in *Midwifery and the Medicalization of Childbirth: Comparative Perspectives*, ed. Edwin R. van Teijlingen, et al., 5–41 (Huntington, NY: Nova Science Publishers, Inc., 2000), esp. 8, 12.

105. Frymer-Kensky, *In the Wake of the Goddesses*, 45.

daughter of Ninisinna and then of Gula before she was transformed into Gula's son.[106] This evidence contributes to the picture in Mesopotamia that hierarchy gradually displaces partnership in gender relationships. However, this shift cannot eliminate the fundamental perception that the web of relationships binding the members of the community together at the level of their identity has a pronounced feminine character, as illustrated in the Sumerian city-laments where Inanna weeps over her city as if she were a mother bereft of her children.[107]

Channeling the Sex Drive Toward the Creation of Community

The characters in Sumerian myths are gods whose narrated experience offers guidance to humans on how to navigate persistent tensions or contradictions in their lives. On the basis of its myths, it appears that Sumerian society prohibited premarital sex.[108] Yet the story form of the myth "Enlil and Ninlil" recognizes the positive dimension of sexual attraction for the vitality and maintenance of society and its households. Set in the prehistory of Nippur when Enlil and Ninlil were the only two young people in the town, the action begins with a warning from Ninlil's mother to her daughter:

> May you not, o woman, bathe in the pure canal, in the pure canal, may you not, o Ninlil, come stepping (back) unto the bank of Nunbirdu! He who is all bright eyes, the master, who is all bright eyes, will be laying eyes upon you, the great mountain, father Enlil, who is all bright eyes, will be laying eyes upon you, the shepherd, the decision maker, who is all bright eyes, will be laying eyes upon you. Forthwith that cock will come burgeoning, he will be kissing you, and, happy, will gladly leave with you the glorious sperm filled into the womb. (ll. 15-21)[109]

The youthful Enlil described here will later become a father and a decision maker. But here his attraction to Ninlil is emphasized by the light in his eyes; in looking at Ninlil he is irresistibly drawn to her and will

106. Ibid., 43, 46.

107. J. J. M. Roberts, "The Motif of the Weeping God in Jeremiah and Its Background in the Lament Tradition of the Ancient Near East," *Old Testament Essays* 5 (1992): 361–74, at 364–66.

108. Gwendolyn Leick, *Sex and Eroticism in Mesopotamian Literature* (London and New York: Routledge, 1994), 90. On virginity in Mesopotamia see chap. 4, pp. 31–32.

109. Thorkild Jacobsen, *The Harps That Once . . . Sumerian Poetry in Translation* (New Haven: Yale University Press, 1987), 171–72.

not stop until he has had sexual relations with her. The narrative suggests that the mother's warning is pro forma or has not the slightest chance of deterring the mating of the two young deities. With no hint that Ninlil wrestled with acting contrary to the warning of her mother, the narrative states that she immediately went to the canal and bathed. Enlil, standing on the opposite side of the canal, sees her and propositions her. She resists by saying:

> My parts are little, know not how to stretch, my lips are little, know not how to kiss! If my mother learned about it she would be slapping my hand, if my father learned about it he would be grabbing hold of me (harshly), and it would not be for me, now to tell my girlfriend, I should be drying up on her! (ll. 30-36)[110]

Honoring the reality of sexual attraction between the two young gods, the narrative nevertheless indicates that the young woman's relationship with her parents and with her girlfriend should make her hesitate about engaging in premarital sex. But Ninlil's words of protest not only do not deter Enlil, they also do not seem to heighten her resistance to him.[111]

In the next part of the narrative of "Enlil and Ninlil," Enlil is convicted of "statutory rape" and banished from the city (ll. 56-60). He is regarded as permanently defiled for this sexual offense and so is extirpated from the community.[112] As Enlil leaves the town for the netherworld, Ninlil, having given birth to the moon god Suen (l. 55), pursues him. In her search for him she encounters the man of the city gate who serves as Enlil's mouthpiece (ll. 75-77, 87-90). When she enters the inner chamber to have sexual relations with him, the text identifies her partner as Enlil. She becomes pregnant with Nergal, a ruling god in the netherworld (l. 90). Next she encounters Enlil in the person of the man next to the river of the mountains. Here she becomes pregnant with Ninazu, the goddess of grain (l. 118). Finally, Ninlil encounters Enlil in the person of Silulim the ferryman. As a result of her relations with the ferryman Ninlil becomes pregnant with Enbilulu, the god of irrigation (l. 141). These illicit premarital sexual encounters result in the birth of four deities typically active in city life in Mesopotamia: (1) the moon god was regarded as rejuvenating living things; (2) Nergal was associated occasionally with agricultural growth but more often with plague, pestilence, famine, and sudden death; (3) Ninazu and (4) Enbilulu were forces that ensured

110. Ibid., 172.

111. Ibid., 167.

112. Ibid., 174, n. 18.

successful agriculture.[113] The narratives describe the condemnation of Enlil for his initial intercourse with Ninlil (ll. 55-62),[114] but the subsequent narrative (ll. 63-64) seems to exonerate Enlil and indicates that nature will have its way even in those places where societal conventions try to contain or channel sexual desire in contrary ways.

One notable instance in the Mesopotamian tradition in which a sexual impropriety resulted in unwanted pregnancy is related in "The Birth Legend of Sargon of Akkad." The genre of the extant initial twenty-two lines of the text is a *narû*-text: i.e., it is a pseudo-autobiographical narrative with a prologue, narrative, and epilogue that looks back on the accomplishments of a king and exhorts those who would come after him to follow his example in order to be blessed.[115] The short narrative preserved resembles that found on royal inscriptions.[116] The initial four lines describe his origins:

> I am Sargon the mighty king, the king of Agade. My mother was a high priestess (*entu*), I did not know my father. My father's relatives reside in the mountains. My city Azupiranu is located on the bank of the Euphrates.[117]

Most scholars believe that this work was initially composed for Sargon of Akkad/Agade (2334–2279 BCE), whose drive toward territorial expansion evidenced an incipient imperialism.[118] He was a usurper of the throne of Agade, and so he needed to make the case that he had legiti-

113. Ibid., 170.

114. Jerrold Cooper, "Review of *Enlil und Ninlil: Ein sumerischer Mythos aus Nippur* by Hermann Behrens," *JCS* 32 (1980): 175–88, at 182, notes that Enlil violated the command prohibiting premarital sex that he himself had promulgated, and so is banished from the city in ll. 55-62.

115. Tremper Longman III, *Fictional Akkadian Autobiography: A Generic and Comparative Study* (Winona Lake, IN: Eisenbrauns, 1991), 47–48; Joan Goodnick Westenholz, "Heroes of Akkad," *Studies in Literature from the Ancient Near East Dedicated to Samuel Noah Kramer*, AOS 65, ed. Jack M. Sasson, 327–36 (New Haven: American Oriental Society, 1984), at 327–28; eadem, *Legends of the Kings of Akkade* (Winona Lake, IN: Eisenbrauns, 1997), 264–66.

116. Brian Lewis, *The Sargon Legend: A Study of the Akkadian Text and the Tale of the Hero Who Was Exposed at Birth*, ASOR Dissertation Series 4 (Cambridge, MA: American Schools of Oriental Research, 1980), 91.

117. Edition: Lewis, *The Sargon Legend*, 24.

118. William W. Hallo, "The Birth of Kings," in *Love and Death in the Ancient Near East*, ed. John H. Marks and Robert M. Good, 42–52 (Guilford, CT: Four Quarters Publishing Co., 1987), at 47–48. Lewis, *Sargon Legend*, 104, argues that it refers to Sargon II of Assyria (709–705 BCE).

mately taken over this position. He did not know who his father was but generally located his ancestral people in a mountainous region near the Euphrates. But his mother seems to have been of noble status as an *entu*-priestess.[119] She was forbidden to have children and was probably expected to remain chaste except for the times when she participated in the sacred marriage ritual.[120] If she had been impregnated by the king in the context of the sacred marriage, it would seem unlikely that she would have had to hide her pregnancy and giving birth.[121] So it would seem that the father was an outsider—just as the text says.

The middle section of this *narû*-text speaks of how Sargon's mother placed him in a reed basket and secured it before sending it down the river. The danger to an infant in such a place is apparent. But the river brought him to the point where he was discovered by Aqqi, the water-drawer (ll. 8-11). This laborer on the irrigation works rescued the child and adopted him. Because the parents were unknown to Aqqi he seems to have adopted the child by the very fact of rescuing him and then taking care of him.[122] There was no need for a contractual statement from the natural parents in order for a foundling to be adopted.[123] One of the rights of an adopted son was that he be trained in the occupation of his adopted father.[124] So it appears that Sargon was a gardener in his early years. It was in this occupation that Sargon met the goddess Ishtar. The text says: "When I was gardening, Ishtar loved me. For fifty-five years I exercised royal rule

119. *Laws of Lipit-Ishtar* 22; *CH* 110, 181. Richard A. Henshaw, *Female and Male: The Cultic Personnel, The Bible and the Rest of the Ancient Near East*, Princeton Theological Monograph Series 31 (Allison Park, PA: Pickwick, 1994), 204, 208, 234.

120. Lewis, *The Sargon Legend*, 37–38; Henshaw, *Female and Male*, 194. For a summary of views on setting and actors for the Mesopotamian sacred marriage see Pirjo Lapinkivi, "The Sumerian Sacred Marriage and Its Aftermath," in *Sacred Marriages* (2008), 7–41, at 22–23; idem, *The Sumerian Sacred Marriage in Light of the Comparative Evidence*, SAAS 15 (Helsinki: Neo-Assyrian Text Corpus Project, 2004), 8–11; Leick, *Sex and Eroticism in Mesopotamian Literature*, 108–10.

121. Lewis, *The Sargon Legend*, 38, 42.

122. See Westbrook, "The Character of Ancient Near Eastern Law," in *A History of Ancient Near Eastern Law*, 1–90, at 1:53, §5.3.2; Muhammed A. Dandamaev, *Slavery in Babylonia: From Nabopolassar to Alexander the Great (626–331 BC)*, rev. ed., trans. Victoria Powell, ed. Marvin Powell and David Weisberg (DeKalb, IL: Northern Illinois University Press, 1984), 103, notes that abandoned infants were raised by those who found them either to be slaves or adopted children.

123. Lewis, *The Sargon Legend*, 50.

124. Ibid., 51.

(ll. 12-13)." Sargon attributes his rise to power and his success during a lengthy reign to the protection and assistance that Ishtar offered him.[125]

This rags-to-riches story of Sargon shows how his banishment as a child became the occasion for his success. From Sargon's perspective looking back on the sexual transgression of his mother, this action could be labeled "a happy fault." It created the opportunity for him to rise in status and then to enjoy the love Ishtar showed him. It seems that the community's expectations for Sargon's mother, the *entu*-priestess, put intense pressure on her and led her to the coldly cruel act of exposing her infant son Sargon. The pressure of public opinion would seem to have been a major factor in the exposure of Sargon by his mother but, in light of the belief in divine sovereignty over history, the human community did not have the final say on Sargon's fate. The mythical narratives "Ninlil and Enlil" and "The Birth Legend of Sargon" reveal that the community had rules on premarital sex for women in general and on chastity for women occupying particular cultic positions. But at the same time these narratives indicate that the rules needed to be interpreted within a larger web of cosmic relationships because the particularities of certain cases might call for the transgression of these rules for a higher good.

The Holiness of Inanna/Ishtar: The Fixed Point for a Paradoxical Deity

The early days and months of a child's life have a profound influence on the formation of his or her character. The mother who nurses the child provides a sense of security and orientation to the world that the child has newly entered. In terms of the spheres of nature and culture, the mother occupies a strategic position. It is in these areas of nurture and upbringing that the Mesopotamian mother goddess extends her assistance.[126] If a person is denied this motherly care, he or she must search elsewhere for the means to cultivate this underlying sense of security.

Unlike the infant Moses who is rescued by Egyptian royalty and nursed by his own mother (Exod 2:7-9), Sargon appears to have been bereft of an important mother figure in his upbringing. The legend of Sargon's birth does not mention an adoptive mother as a wisdom figure who instructs him in the language and customs of the household. Instead, this legend emphasizes the next stage in his upbringing by noting that he served as a gardener. It is in the garden, in his work with plants that

125. Ibid., 59.

126. Frymer-Kensky, *In the Wake of the Goddesses*, 15–19, 40, 92.

germinate and grow, that he meets Ishtar/Inanna. She seems to have a special predilection for gardeners, which would connect with the side of her character as a goddess of sex.[127] In a Sumerian myth ("Dumuzi and Enkimdu") in which the shepherd Dumuzi and the farmer Enkimdu are set in competition for gaining Inanna as a wife, Inanna indicates initially that she is drawn to the farmer Enkimdu: "I, the maiden, let the farmer marry me! The farmer who grows multicolored flax; the farmer who grows multicolored barley" (ll. 23-25).[128] In the *Gilgamesh Epic*, Gilgamesh gives a list of those Ishtar has loved, among whom is a gardener named Ishullanu. Gilgamesh notes:

> You loved Ishullanu, your father's gardener, who continually carried a basket of dates to you, day after day brightening your table. When you coveted him, you approached him, saying: "O my Ishullanu, let us absorb your power! Put out your hand and touch our vulva." (*Gilg*. VI:64-69)

According to Gilgamesh, when Ishullanu turned down Ishtar's proposition she turned him into a dwarf.[129] The ambiguity associated with the sexual power of Ishtar comes to the fore in the differing fates of Sargon and Ishullanu. Because Sargon became a powerful political figure, it appears that Ishtar's presence in his life manifested itself more in his ruling activities than in terms of love making.[130]

In her role as protector of Sargon and the dynasty of Akkad, Ishtar became a figure on whom the Sargonic kings increasingly came to rely.[131] This focus on Ishtar, which diminished attention to the other gods, was particularly the case with Naram-Sin (2254–2218), who began the practice of writing his name with the divine determinative, a practice that was

127. Leick, *Sex and Eroticism in Mesopotamian Literature*, 52–53.

128. Translation: Yitschak Sefati, "The Shepherd and the Farmer: Suitors' Rivalry," in *Love Songs in Sumerian Literature: Critical Edition of the Dumuzi-Inanna Songs*, 324–43 (Ramat Gan: Bar-Ilan University, 1998), at 326, 332.

129. Rivkah Harris, *Gender and Aging in Mesopotamia* (Norman: University of Oklahoma Press, 2000), 126, interprets Gilgamesh's brash dismissal of the goddess Ishtar as status inversion and Ishtar's proposal of marriage as role inversion since she assumes the male role in this action.

130. Leick, *Sex and Eroticism in Mesopotamian Literature*, 56–57; Lewis, *Sargon Legend*, 59.

131. Barbara Böck, "Überlegungen zu einem Kultfest der altmesopotamischen Göttin Inanna," *Numen* 51 (2004): 20–46, at 23; Claus Wilcke, "Politik im Spiegel der Literatur, Literatur als Mittel der Politik im älteren Babylonien," in *Anfänge politischen Denkens in der Antike: Die nahöstlichen Kulturen und die Griechen*, ed. Kurt Raaflaub and Elisabeth Müller-Luckner, 29–75 (Munich: Oldenbourg, 1993), at 45–58.

to continue in Mesopotamia for the next five hundred years until the time of Hammurapi (1792–1750).[132] One of Naram-Sin's inscriptions, highlighting the way he has been empowered by Ishtar, reports that citizens from Akkad requested from the protector gods of several cities that he be made the protector god of Akkad:[133]

> Naram-Sin, the powerful one, king of Agade: When the four world regions fought together against him, he won nine battles in only one year through the love Ishtar showed to him. He captured the kings who lifted themselves against him. Because he had made firm the foundations of his city in distress, (the citizens of) his city requested from Ishtar in E'anna, from Enlil in Nippur, from Dagan in Tuttul, from Ninhursag in Kesh, from Ea in Eridu, from Sin in Ur, from Shamash in Sippar (and) from Nergal in Kutha that he become like a god for their city. They built a temple for him in the middle of Agade. (RIME E2.1.4.10, ll. 1-56)[134]

In his suppression of this widespread revolt by what seem to have been coalitions of Babylonian cities and external foes including Amorites and Gutians, Naram-Sin reasserted his power in the region.[135] He refers to himself as "ruler of the four quarters" rather than simply as "ruler of Kish," which signals his aspiration for universal rule.[136] He exalts himself as an incomparable ruler and attempts to have the peoples of Mesopotamia regard him as a god.[137] Franke notes that in making this claim to

132. William W. Hallo, *Origins: The Ancient Near Eastern Background of Some Modern Western Institutions* (Leiden and New York: Brill, 1996), 152; Wolfram von Soden, *The Ancient Orient: An Introduction to the Study of the Ancient Near East* (Grand Rapids: Eerdmans, 1994), 67–69; Henri Frankfort, *Kingship and the Gods* (Chicago: University of Chicago Press, 1948), 224–26.

133. Sabina Franke, "Kings of Akkad: Sargon and Naram-Sin," *CANE*, 834; Von Soden, *The Ancient Orient*, 67–69.

134. Edition: Douglas Frayne, *Sargonic and Gutian Periods (2334–2113 BC)*, RIME 2 (Toronto: University of Toronto Press, 1993), 113–14. This inscription was located on a socle of a copper statue depicting a crouching male figure of a *laḫmu*-monster.

135. Marc van de Mieroop, *A History of the Ancient Near East, ca. 3000–323 BC* (Malden, MA: Blackwell, 2004), 66–67.

136. William W. Hallo, *Early Mesopotamian Royal Titles, A Philologic and Historical Analysis*, AOS 43 (New Haven: Yale University Press, 1957), 49, notes that Naram-Sin introduced the title "ruler of the four world quarters" into the Mesopotamian royal titulary; see also Sabina Franke, *Königsinschriften und Königsideologie: Die Könige von Akkade zwischen Tradition und Neuerung* (Münster: LIT Verlag, 1995), 193.

137. William W. Hallo, "Sumerian Religion," in *Kinattūtu ša darāti*, ed. A. F. Rainey, 15–35 (Tel Aviv: University of Tel Aviv Press, 1993), at 24–25, claims that that only Shu-Sin (2037–2029 BCE) among the Mesopotamian divinized kings appears to have demanded

be divine, Naram-Sin came to rely increasingly on Ishtar, a move that would make his dynasty particularly vulnerable when hard times came upon Akkad.[138]

With the collapse of the Old Akkadian empire under Sharkalisharra in 2193 BCE, the city of Akkad was destroyed and never rebuilt. The total elimination of this "imperial" state—whose kings Sargon and Naram-Sin had made a lasting impression on the imaginations of the peoples of the region by their military and political accomplishments—was a reality that haunted the later kings of the Ur III dynasty and kept some of them from claiming continuity with the Old Akkadian dynasty.[139] Cooper explains that the kings of Ur III modeled their organizational structures on those created by the Akkadian king but validated their authority by claiming continuity with legendary rulers of Uruk of the distant past like Lugalbanda and Gilgamesh.[140]

A text composed in the Ur III period that aimed to account for the sudden demise of the Old Akkadian empire was the *Curse of Agade*.[141] This text explains how Enlil, the king of the gods ruling from Nippur, had taken rule from Kish and Uruk and given it to Sargon. With this development Inanna allied with Sargon and had her temple Ulmash built in Akkad (ll. 1-9). She was energetic and persistent in the construction and provisioning of this temple (ll. 10-15). The festivals were joyful and unique (ll. 16-24). The storehouses were full (ll. 25-29). There was harmony in the city and prosperity that was augmented by abundant foreign trade (ll. 29-57). But then for some unexplained reason Enlil denied the Akkadian dynasty permission to rebuild Ekur, Enlil's temple in Nippur, a sign indicating that the dynasty was out of favor with

---

that a sanctuary and offerings be established for him during his lifetime; however, ll. 54-57 of RIME E2.1.4.10 claims that the citizens of Akkad built a temple for Naram-Sin.

138. Franke, *Königsinschriften und Königsideologie*, 191–98. This focus on Ishtar as a mother-figure in whom a king placed his trust occurs in the prophecies and inscriptions of Esarhaddon and Ashurbanipal; see Jacobsen, *Treasures of Darkness*, 237–38.

139. Piotr Michalowski, "Memory and Deed: The Historiography of the Political Expansion of the Akkad State," in *Akkad: The First World Empire: Structure, Ideology, Traditions*, History of the Ancient Near East 5, ed. Mario Liverani, 69–90 (Padova: Tipografia Poligrafica Moderna, 1993), at 89, notes that there was a cult of Sargon and Naram-Sin at Mari in the Ur III period and that later Assyrian monarchs took their names. Yet the swift demise of Akkad merited it only a brief mention in many scribal lists.

140. Jerrold S. Cooper, "Paradigm and Propaganda: The Dynasty of Akkade in the 21st Century," in *Akkad: The First World Empire*, 11-23, at 15.

141. Jerrold S. Cooper, *The Curse of Agade* (Baltimore and London: Johns Hopkins University Press, 1983), 11–12, dates this composition between 2150 and 2000 and notes that there is insufficient data to give a precise date.

Enlil.[142] Inanna's reaction reveals much about her character and her position within the Mesopotamian pantheon of the time:

> Akkade became to her fraught with shuddering, fear befell her in Ulmash, she took her seat out of the city. Like a maiden who decides to abandon home holy Inanna abandoned Akkade's temple close, like a warrior going up against armed might, she brought (the forces for) fight and battle out of the city, confronted them with murderous foes. (ll. 58-66)[143]

Inanna acknowledged the sovereign authority of Enlil, but she immediately abandoned the Akkadian dynasty. Naram-Sin had devoted his attention primarily to her and so was now at a loss. He tried desperately to regain Enlil's favor, but to no avail (ll. 89-93). He then decided to dismantle Ekur without Enlil's permission (ll. 93-148), a hubristic act that Enlil countered by bringing Gutian invaders from the Zagros mountains against the Akkadian kingdom (ll. 149-93).[144] Why did Inanna not intercede with Enlil on behalf of Akkad? Why such a precipitous cutting of ties?[145]

Inanna is the one goddess of the Mesopotamian pantheon who remained an active deity throughout the third millennium BCE and later. Her powers were not co-opted by male deities, as happened to most female deities in Mesopotamia.[146] But to remain active she had to engage in activities that were typically male, especially those connected with war. Tzvi Abusch claims that a type of earth goddess lies behind the profile of Inanna.[147] As this notion of an earth goddess lost credibility in the third millennium, Inanna retained functions that related to the various parts of the spectrum of natural and social reality. Abusch speculates that these retained functions became configured as polarities: "love/

142. Cooper, *The Curse of Agade*, 5, speculates that the temple Naram-Sin sought permission to construct was one for Inanna; thus Enlil's denial leads to Inanna's withdrawal from Naram-Sin.

143. Translation in Jacobsen, *The Harps That Once*, 363–64.

144. Cooper, *The Curse of Agade*, 5, claims that in response to unfavorable omens from Enlil, Naram-Sin hubristically plundered Enlil's sanctuary of Ekur, which then led to Enlil's bringing the Gutians against Akkade/Agade. The great gods try to pacify Enlil by the unusual act of reciting a lengthy curse against Akkade/Agade.

145. Frymer-Kensky, *In the Wake of the Goddesses*, 65; Rivkah Harris, "Inanna-Ishtar as Paradox and a Coincidence of Opposites," *History of Religions* 30 (1991): 261–78, at 265–67.

146. Frymer-Kensky, *In the Wake of the Goddesses*, 27.

147. Tzvi Abusch, "Ishtar," *DDD*, 452–56, at 455.

death, sex/war, male/female, upper class establishment/social fringe, opponent of convention."[148] Thus Inanna appears as a conflicted personality who can turn from one extreme to the other with little warning. But as a deity addressing many of the concerns of an earth goddess in a culture that has marginalized this goddess, Inanna keeps these feminine concerns alive, even if she must do so at the expense of functioning as if she were an androgynous deity.[149] As Rivkah Harris explains at length, "Inanna-Ishtar is ambiguity incarnate."[150] She not only embodies opposites; she sets them against one another to create a paradoxical figure that calls the entire structure of the Mesopotamian pantheon into question. Through her androgyny she relativizes gender distinctions and then reinforces them: a sequence manifest in the carnivalesque dimension of her festivals.[151] She is a threat to the entire cultural order by her combining "male aggressiveness with the force of a superabundance of female sexuality."[152] As a deity whose sphere of influence is the entire natural and cultural order, she embodies many other polarities that both support the existing order and reveal its limitations.

This paradoxical Inanna-Ishtar who is portrayed in the *Curse of Agade* as abandoning the Akkadian dynasty without a word of protest is the same deity who weeps at great length over the destruction of Akkad in the balag-lamentation "Uru-amirabi: The City Which Has Been Pillaged!"

> Oh city (and) house! Oh city (and) house!" she says. The hierodule of heaven, Inanna, the destroyer of the mountain, the lady of the Eanna, she who causes the heavens to rumble, the lady of the gipar, Lillaenna, the lady of the cattle pen and sheepfold, says, "My house!"

148. Abusch, "Ishtar," 455; see also Lapinkivi, "The Sumerian Sacred Marriage and Its Aftermath," 34.

149. Böck, "Überlegungen zu einem Kultfest," 24. Brigitte Groneberg, "Der sumerisch-akkadische Inanna/Ištar: Hermaphroditos?" *WO* 17 (1986): 25–46, at 44, notes that Inanna/Ishtar is a goddess with masculine power. Leick, *Sex and Eroticism in Mesopotamian Literature*, 157, claims that Inanna is not androgynous but is always portrayed as a woman. With regard to a conflicted divine personality, Jacobsen, *Treasures of Darkness*, 187–90, notes that another earth goddess figure challenged by competing loyalties is Tiāmat, as portrayed toward the beginning of the *Enūma Elish*: as a mother she wants to protect the young gods begotten by her and Apsû; then she is portrayed as the chaotic sea at war against the active pantheon headed by Marduk. However, Frymer-Kensky, *In the Wake of the Goddesses*, 17, claims that Tiāmat only became aggressive against the pantheon after Apsû was slain.

150. Harris, "Inanna-Ishtar as Paradox," 266.

151. Ibid., 270, 273.

152. Ibid., 270.

> She says, "My city!" She says, "My spouse!" She says, "My child!" "Oh, I want to stand up! My standing place!" she says. "Oh, I want to sit down. My sitting place!" she says. "Wherever I walk, it is as if (I have) no strength!" she says. Thus does my good spouse utter. My house has been destroyed like (any other) established house. My city has been destroyed like (any other) established city. Those men have plundered your dwelling places like (all the other) settlements. Those Anunna-gods who sit (in counsel) have forgotten me. (ll. 62-76)[153]

Inanna/Ishtar is a protector deity of Uruk (a role she shares with Anu), Akkad, and Kish in the third millennium. In the Assyrian empire of the first millennium her cult is prominent in Nineveh and Arbela.[154] In "Uru-amirabi," rather than turning away as if unattached to any particular place,[155] Inanna acts like an anguished mother who has lost her husband, children, and home to a disaster. She takes up the centuries-old feminine practice of voicing lamentations and so becomes a weeping goddess—a standard motif in the balags.[156] The balag, which builds on the city laments from the twentieth century BCE, was a communal lament sung by the GALA-priests in a tradition spanning the second and first millennia BCE and with roots in the ritual laments sung by women for funerals and other occasions from the earliest times to the present.[157] Whereas the city laments were composed to be performed on the single occasion of the petition to the city deity for permission to rebuild her or his temple, the balags were designed to address ongoing communal issues regarding which the gods were praised and petitioned so that they might be favorably disposed.[158]

Despite Inanna's characteristic of challenging and transgressing boundaries, she defends the traditional sacral order of her temple at Uruk. In an edition of "Uru-amirabi" from the first millennium BCE,

153. Mark E. Cohen, *The Canonical Lamentations of Ancient Mesopotamia*, 2 vols. (Potomac, MD: Capital Decisions Limited, 1988), 2:588–89.

154. Wilfred G. Lambert, "Ištar of Nineveh," in *Nineveh: Papers of the XLIXe Rencontre Assyriologique Internationale, London, 7–11 July 2003*, 2 vols. (London: The British School of Archaeology in Iraq, 2005), 1:35–39; Biddle, "The Figure of Lady Jerusalem," 175–76.

155. On Inanna's unmarried and uncommitted lifestyle predominant in Sumerian myths see Jacobsen, *Treasures of Darkness*, 141. However, here her mourning testifies to long-lasting love and devotion; see Frymer-Kensky, *In the Wake of the Goddesses*, 36.

156. Bouzard, *We Have Heard*, 64–65; Biddle, "The Figure of Lady Jerusalem," 181.

157. Jerrold Cooper, "Genre, Gender, and the Sumerian Lamentation," *JCS* 58 (2006): 39–47, at 44.

158. Bouzard, *We Have Heard*, 67–68; Cohen, *Canonical Lamentations*, 22; Dobbs-Allsopp, *Weep, O Daughter of Zion*, 162.

Inanna is portrayed as one who is violently angry against a temple servant who seems to have engaged in a sacred marriage ritual within the Eanna temple. The transgression is described as follows:

> She goes wild. Ecstasy! She goes wild! Ecstasy! She has intercourse. The young girl, the maidservant has done the forbidden. The maidservant, the "mother-of-sin," has done the forbidden. The "mother-of-sin," she of a bitter fate, she of a bitter fate, eyes blurred with tears, she who sat upon the holy throne, who had lain upon the holy bed, the resting place, has experienced both intercourse and fellatio. . . . [For this transgression, Inanna] looks at her with death (in her) eye. The lady shouts; it is a sinful cry. She grabs her by her forelocks. And the girl, the "mother-of-sin," is thrown from the wall. Let the shepherd kill her with his staff! Let the GALA-priest kill her with his drum! Let the potter kill her with his pitcher! Let the cult dancer kill her with his dagger and knife![159]

A young woman, dubbed the "mother of sin," took a seat on the holy or pure throne and then lay on the holy/pure bed where she experienced intercourse and "kisses." Scholars have speculated on the basis of parallels with *The Descent of Inanna* ("shepherd," ll. 333-37) that the young woman's partner in the Kulaba sanctuary within the Enamtila temple at Uruk was Dumuzi, but he is not explicitly named.[160] When Inanna, who was away from Uruk at Zabalam, heard of the transgression, she sent her vizier Ninshubur to pronounce judgment on the young woman. She was then eliminated—perhaps ritually—by a shepherd, a GALA-priest, a potter, and a *kurgarrû*-priest. Volk speculates that this episode was perhaps recited at the beginning of each month to temple servants

159. Cohen, *Canonical Lamentations*, 2:592–93; see also Konrad Volk, *Die Balag-Komposition Uru-Àm-ma-ir-ra-bi: Rekonstruktion und Bearbeitung der Tafeln 18 (19'ff), 19, 20 und 21 der späten, kanonischen Version*, Freiburger Altorientalische Studien 18 (Stuttgart: Franz Steiner Verlag, 1989), tablet 18:19'-27', pp. 57, 60; tablet 19:12-18, pp. 77–79, 90.

160. Volk, *Die Balag-Komposition Uru-Àm-ma-ir-ra*-bi, 52–53. John Maier, "Gender Differences in the First Millennium: Additions to a Canonical Lamentation," in *Sex and Gender in the Ancient Near East: Proceedings of the 47th Rencontre Assyriologique Internationale, Helsinki, July 2–6, 2001*, ed. Simo Parpola and Robert M. Whiting, 345–54 (Helsinki: Neo-Assyrian Text Corpus Project, 2002), at 348–51, describes the transgressing young temple servant as Inanna's alter ego who violates two central symbols of Inanna's power: her throne and her bed. Therefore the young woman must be purged from the sanctuary in a form of capital punishment. The removal of the young woman here and that of Dumuzi in *The Descent of Inanna* (ll. 284-90) are both instances of an individual suffering for the community, i.e., their sacrifices release tension and restore harmony to the community.

to make them aware of the consequences of transgressing the prohibitions of Inanna.[161]

Throughout the third millennium and into the Isin-Larsa period (2017–1763), the sacred marriage ritual at Uruk in which the EN-priest or the king would engage in sexual congress with Inanna (i.e., her representative from the ranks of the *entu*-priestesses) occurred at least annually, sometimes more frequently.[162] This ritual has been interpreted by many scholars as the occasion on which the divine and human came together harmoniously and so renewed the cosmos for another year. Tikva Frymer-Kensky explains that in this ritual "male and female appear as the interlocking pieces which combine to open the riches of the universe."[163] It was an occasion for the king to gain unique access to the divine realm and for the divine-human partnership to be renewed, an arrangement in which the gods bestow favor on humans and humans labor to put the divine gifts into action. The synergy between the two parties was believed to be essential to the vitality of the realm.[164] Inanna's violent reaction to the transgression of the maidservant makes clear that the distinction between sacred and profane is important to her. Where the separateness of the sacred is ignored, she sees defilement happening—a condition that demands a purging of the defilement, primarily against those parties who have committed the transgression.[165]

From the early third millennium onward in Mesopotamia, a male deity or council of male deities exercising sovereignty over the cosmos was the dominant model of authority.[166] The partnership between male and female evident in many natural processes was subordinated to this hierarchical cultural model. The inadequacies of this model are addressed by the paradoxical figure of Inanna, who participates actively in the male

161. Volk, *Die Balag-Komposition Uru-Àm-ma-ir-ra-bi*, 54.

162. Jacob Klein, "Sacred Marriage," *ABD* 5:867–68; Zainab Bahrani, *Women of Babylon: Gender and Representation in Mesopotamia* (London: Routledge, 2001), 137–38. Lapinkivi, "The Sumerian Sacred Marriage and Its Aftermath," 27, judges the evidence for copulation in the ritual to be insufficient; idem, *The Sumerian Sacred Marriage*, 243–45.

163. Frymer-Kensky, *In the Wake of the Goddesses*, 56. Lapinkivi, "The Sumerian Sacred Marriage and Its Aftermath," 10–11, notes that even though the view of the sacred marriage as a ritual aiming to induce fertility is "outdated," it is a claim that led to viewing these texts in other categories: e.g., legitimation of the king, secular love song, religious duties of a priest. What Lapinkivi claims to be outdated appears to be the linking of sexual congress in the ritual with renewal of reproductive forces in nature.

164. Frymer-Kensky, *In the Wake of the Goddesses*, 57.

165. Cohen, *Canonical Lamentations*, 32.

166. Lambert, "Ancient Mesopotamian Gods, 122.

world yet brings to the fore a superabundance of female sexuality that is essential to the functioning of the cosmos.[167] But Inanna, for all her transgressive behavior, is committed to the separation of the sacred from the impure in her temple. Her paradoxical behavior indicates that maintenance of the boundaries of the cosmic community is a tensive process that does not conform to clearly stated formulas but rather demands an ongoing attentiveness to multiple forces that contribute to cosmic equilibrium.

The Dynamics of Boundary Formation in the Forging of Sexual Identity

Walled cities with their rulers and citizens began to assume increasing importance in the rhetoric about political boundaries in the Sargonic royal inscriptions (ca. 2350–2193).[168] In the previous millennium, urban as well as rural residents devoted considerable attention to the issue of fertility, that is, finding enough to eat and gaining offspring to sustain the family into the next generation.[169] The complications for settled life arising from raids from armed outsiders raised the value of the heroic warrior, whose charisma was imagined to be a divine gift bestowed by a warrior god.[170] Thus the Mesopotamian pantheon developed, as Jacobsen has explained, beyond the concerns with fertility toward issues of security provided by the state.[171] The cosmos became a state in which the gods ruled the spheres of heaven, earth, and netherworld.

167. Leick, *Sex and Eroticism in Mesopotamian Literature*, 109.

168. Cf. Seth Richardson, "The World of Babylonian Countrysides," in *The Babylonian World*, ed. Gwendolyn Leick, 13–38 (London and New York: Routledge, 2007), at 22; Postgate, *Early Mesopotamia*, 75–76; Marc van de Mieroop, *The Ancient Mesopotamian City* (Oxford and New York: Oxford University Press, 1999), 73.

169. Jacobsen, *Treasures of Darkness*, 25–27; cf. Robert McCormick Adams, *The Evolution of Urban Society: Early Mesopotamia and Prehispanic Mexico* (Chicago: Aldine, 1966), 45–47, 51; idem, *Heartland of Cities: Surveys of Ancient Settlement and Land Use on the Central Floodplain of the Euphrates* (Chicago: University of Chicago Press, 1981), 78–81, 86–87; Postgate, *Early Mesopotamia*, 83.

170. A. Leo Oppenheim, *Ancient Mesopotamia: A Portrait of a Dead Civilization* (Chicago: University of Chicago Press, 1964), 82–83; Adams, *The Evolution of Urban Society*, 59–61.

171. Jacobsen, *Treasures of Darkness*, 9–11, 73–78, describes the powers of nature in myths that seem to reflect Mesopotamian society of the fourth millennium as "intransitive" numinous power. Such powers are named and treated as deities, but their character is defined by the natural power they represent. This minimally anthropomorphized picture of these "nature" gods is countered by Lambert, "Ancient Mesopotamia," 123, who argues that there is no evidence of a "pre-anthropomorphic stage of religion" in Mesopotamia.

In this context of the cosmos as state, the value of the warrior increased dramatically. The hierarchy in the pantheon adjusted to reflect the increase in power devoted to male activities, a consequence of which was that female power began to be marginalized. However, Inanna/Ishtar increased her role in the pantheon, covering not only matters of war and sex but also rain, the power of the storehouse, harlotry, and various other concerns.[172] She grew in influence not only by taking on roles typically carried out by males but also by representing those forces in the environment that cannot be completely managed by human institutions. She was a threatening paradox that had to be honored.[173]

Ishtar was particularly important to Sargon and Naram-Sin in the latter part of the third millennium, but also to the Assyrian kings Esarhaddon and Ashurbanipal in the seventh century BCE.[174] The increasing reliance of Naram-Sin on Ishtar resembled a monolatrous relationship.[175] Even though each Mesopotamian city had only one patron deity, several other deities could reside within the temple of the patron deity.[176] The gods of the temple household were organized as a family.[177] The hierarchy in this temple family had a structural unity that could evolve into a monarchical system: the members of the family could metaphorically be seen to be parts of the body of the father.[178] In this move toward centralization, the differences between the gods could be flattened out as the functions and identities of various gods were assimilated by the main

172. Jacobsen, *Treasures of Darkness*, 135–43; Frymer-Kensky, *In the Wake of the Goddesses*, 58, 65; Harris, "Inanna-Ishtar as Paradox," 261–64.

173. Ibid., 263.

174. Simo Parpola, *Letters from Assyrian and Babylonian Scholars*, SAA 10 (Helsinki: Helsinki University Press, 1993), 8; idem, *Assyrian Prophecies*, SAA 9 (Helsinki: Helsinki University Press, 1997), LIII, 7–8; Martti Nissinen, *References to Prophecy in Neo-Assyrian Sources*, SAAS 7 (Helsinki: Neo-Assyrian Text Corpus Project, 1998), 101, 170–71; idem, "The Socioreligious Role of the Neo-Assyrian Prophets," in *Prophecy in Its Ancient Near Eastern Context: Mesopotamian, Biblical, and Arabian Perspectives*, SBL Symposium Series 13, ed. Martti Nissinen, 89–114 (Atlanta: Society of Biblical Literature, 2000), at 105.

175. Cf. Wilfred G. Lambert, "The Historical Development of the Mesopotamian Pantheon: A Study in Sophisticated Polytheism," in *Unity and Diversity: Essays in the History, Literature, and Religion of the Ancient Near East*, ed. Hans Goedicke and J. J. M. Roberts, 191–99 (Baltimore: Johns Hopkins University Press, 1975), at 198.

176. Ibid., 192.

177. Ibid., 192, 197; Hans Nissen, *The Early History of the Ancient Near East, 9000–2000 B.C.* (Chicago: University of Chicago Press, 1988), 143.

178. Lambert, "The Historical Development of the Mesopotamian Pantheon," 195, 197–98; idem, "The Pantheon of Mari," *MARI* 4 (1985): 525–39, at 527–30

god of the polity.[179] So instead of trying to balance the interests of several gods and making their diverse contributions harmonize within the polity, the monolatrous, henotheistic approach wagers that one deity will take care of the polity's diverse needs.[180]

Ishtar was portrayed as a goddess who not only carried out male functions such as protecting kings in battle but was also the patroness of prostitutes and was endowed with "a superabundance of female sexuality."[181] This juxtaposition of sex and violence positioned Ishtar as the embodiment of powerful forces that break into everyday life either from without or from within to upset the balance within the routines of individuals, families, and nations.[182] In a religio-political system aiming to be monotheistic, Ishtar could, in her paradoxical way, be seen to transcend gender. However, she remained a goddess; thus the divinity she communicated in its paradoxical otherness was anchored in the feminine.[183] For Ishtar to be the primary deity of the Mesopotamian pantheon would have required that she displace Enlil, Aššur, and Marduk, a change the conservative religious system would have resisted, as later exemplified in the failure of Nabonidus to advance the status of the moon god Sin in sixth-century Babylonia.[184]

The boundary between the sacred and the impure is highly charged. When the temple servant played the role of the wife in a sacred marriage ritual, Inanna/Ishtar had her killed and eliminated from the temple compound. She regarded the usurpation of this sacred role as defiling. Female roles as well as male ones needed to be respected within the cult. The holy character of the deity emanated from the deity herself or himself to transform the temple and its furnishings into the holy. This divine presence was a source of blessing to the community.[185] However, the dynamic by which these boundaries were maintained was a matter not

179. Lambert, "The Historical Development of the Mesopotamian Pantheon," 197.

180. Jean Bottéro, *Religion in Ancient Mesopotamia*, trans. Teresa L. Fagan (Chicago: University of Chicago Press, 2001), 41–42.

181. Harris, "Inanna-Ishtar as Paradox," 264.

182. Ibid.; Frymer-Kensky, *In the Wake of the Goddesses*, 68.

183. Leick, *Sex and Eroticism in Mesopotamian Literature*, 157; Frymer-Kensky, *In the Wake of the Goddesses*, 27, 46.

184. Leick, *Sex and Eroticism in Mesopotamian Literature*, 59–60, notes that in the Enheduanna composition in-nin ša-gur$_4$-ra from the late second millennium BCE Inanna tries to take over Enlil's position in the pantheon. On the cult of Sin during the reign of Nabonidus see Paul-Alain Beaulieu, "King Nabonidus and the Neo-Babylonian Empire," *CANE* 1:969–79, at 975.

185. Jacobsen, *Treasures of Darkness*, 16, 39.

simply of keeping everything in its proper place but rather of recognizing that many of these dynamic realities can be kept in order only through the coincidence of opposites.[186]

Summary

Just as Jerusalem was imaged as a woman, so also were Mesopotamian cities, as shown in the weeping mother motif in city laments. Even though the collective bonds of the city were often imagined to be feminine in Mesopotamia, the masculine role in reproducing the community or body politic began to dominate in the evolving tradition of myths. Even though the mother goddess played a key role in the creation of humans, her work as fabricator was often directed by Enki or Enlil. In the processes of reproduction and maturation the female role was reduced in visibility in favor of the directive role of male deities. Just as wife Jerusalem in Ezekiel 16 was expected to have been formed by YHWH's care for her from adoption to adulthood, so also was the birth and development of the Mesopotamian citizenry believed to have been governed by male deities. Partnership between male and female deities gave way to hierarchy in the ongoing process of making and remaking communal bonds.

The ambiguous power of sexual attraction for the reproduction of the community is acknowledged in myths such as "Enlil and Ninlil" and "The Birth of Sargon." Even though the sexual drive can act out in ways contrary to social norms, these transgressions can later be paradoxically valued as having given birth to heroic individuals or significant social practices. Sargon was conceived as a consequence of a breach in his mother's obligation to remain chaste, but his subsequent good fortune argues that such a breach was a "happy fault." As a foundling who later came under the protection of Ishtar, Sargon rose in fortune, whereas wife Jerusalem slid toward ruin as she embraced a promiscuous way of life, one that the Mesopotamian tradition would perhaps have seen as infused with the power of Ishtar. Sargon's association with Ishtar was primarily in the sphere of war rather than of sex, although the latter is not to be excluded, as suggested by his encounter with her in a garden ("Birth Legend of Sargon," 12–13). Ishtar became the primary deity of the Sargonic dynasty, yet the level of protection she provided was limited by the leading male deities of the pantheon.

186. Harris, "Coincidence of Opposites," 263–64.

Ishtar was a paradoxical deity who called into question distinctions between male and female, violence and love, the established and the marginalized, and other polarities in a community. But she suspended or transgressed these distinctions only to reestablish them so that they were perceived as differences within a larger unity. She would punish a human who profaned her holiness, that is, her distinct identity within the cosmic community. Thus Ishtar's characteristic fluidity required a fixed point.

Greece: Engaging Shared Emotion to Foster Wholeness Within the Polis

To be present in an assembly in which a prophetic judgment is pronounced is a different experience from participating in a group that is being instructed in the myths of a community. Both of these forms of communal engagement also feel much different from attending a theater in which the imaginary world of the play becomes one's own world. The thread that connects these three forms of shared experience is the participants' formative engagement with the tradition of their community. Shared emotions in a community cultivate a sense of belonging or a sense of place continuous with that underlying sense of security provided by a sound upbringing by family and community.

Facing the Irrational Within Collective Existence

A distinctive feature of the culture of fifth-century Athens was the staging of tragic plays.[187] During each day of the festival of the Great Dionysia (five to six days in late March), the Athenian audience would attend twelve plays at which three tragedians would each present a trilogy and a satyr play. The top three plays were selected by a panel of judges and awarded prizes.[188] Most tragedies were designed to engage the audience to experience the emotions of fear and pity as the characters

187. Joel D. Schwartz, "Human Action and Political Action in *Oedipus Tyrannos*," in *Greek Tragedy and Political Theory*, ed. J. Peter Euben, 183–209 (Berkeley: University of California Press, 1986), at 204–5, notes that tragic characters who dramatize figures like Achilles or Odysseus begin to appear shortly after Homeric rhapsodes began competing at the Panathenaic festivals in the mid-sixth century BCE.

188. Charles Segal, *Oedipus Tyrannus: Tragic Heroism and the Limits of Knowledge* (New York: Twayne Publishers, 1993), 36; Bernhard Zimmermann, *Greek Tragedy: An Introduction* (Baltimore and London: Johns Hopkins University Press, 1991), 9.

suffered a terrible fate.[189] By empathizing with characters who suffered major setbacks the audience collectively acknowledged the fragility of human life and thereby developed a means of coming to terms with setbacks in order to move beyond them. Plato rejected this acquiescence to the irrational element of life as promoted by the tragic poets and urged the Athenians to increase their knowledge of the rational, ethical order of the world (*Rep.* 607b-c).[190] For Plato the catharsis an audience experienced at a tragic performance took place within an imaginary world that gratified the lowest part of the soul and diverted one's attention from the pursuit of truth.[191] Although the creative period of tragic drama did not continue much beyond the end of the fifth century BCE, the capacity of these ancient productions to illuminate aspects of the irrational dimension of life continues to the present.[192]

The subject matter and characters of these plays were drawn from the myths and epic narratives of the Greek tradition.[193] Agamemnon, Clytemnestra, Ajax, Menelaus, Helen, and other characters from Homer's *Iliad* are major figures in a number of the plays of Aeschylus, Sophocles, and Euripides. Myths about the city of Thebes, most notably that of Oedipus, form an imaginary landscape on which the city of Athens could view its shadow side and thus help it find ways to come to terms with

189. Martha Nussbaum, "Introduction," vii–xliv, in Charles K. Williams, *The Bacchae of Euripides* (New York: Farrar Strauss & Giroux, 1990), at xxxix.

190. Martha Nussbaum, *The Fragility of Goodness: Luck and Ethics in Greek Tragedy and Philosophy*, rev. ed. (Cambridge: Cambridge University Press, 2001), 51, notes that moderns respond to the dilemmas of Greek tragedy as situations a person should take steps to avoid; there is little appreciation for the fact of the tragic character's getting caught in this situation.

191. Thomas Gould, *The Ancient Quarrel between Poetry and Philosophy* (Princeton: Princeton University Press, 1990), xvi–xx, 5. Schwartz, "Human Action and Political Action in *Oedipus Tyrannos*," 187, notes that the gnomic saying "know thyself" in the Archaic period referred to restraint and piety: i.e., one did not overstep one's limits, especially with reference to the gods. But the inverse meaning was in vogue among the sophists and humanists of the latter part of the fifth century BCE: use your power to examine the human condition and improve it.

192. Jean-Pierre Vernant, "The Historical Moment of Tragedy in Greece: Some of the Social and Psychological Conditions," in idem and Pierre Vidal-Naquet, *Myth and Tragedy in Ancient Greece*, 23–28 (New York: Zone Books, 1988), at 25; Paula Debnar, "Fifth-Century Athenian History and Tragedy," in *A Companion to Greek Tragedy*, ed. Justina Gregory, 3–37 (Malden, MA: Blackwell, 2005), at 13, notes that tragedy did not begin in 478 with the victories at Salamis and Plataea and did not end in 404 with Athens' defeat by Sparta; however, during this time period it appears that more than 900 plays were performed at the City Dionysia.

193. Zimmermann, *Greek Tragedy*, 14.

problems threatening its collective existence.[194] At the conclusion of Sophocles' *Oedipus Colonus*, the aged Oedipus, exiled king of Thebes, finds a home in a suburb of Athens where he will be buried (*OC* 1518-33); the oracles indicate that this accursed king will become a source of blessing to Athens (*OC* 90).[195] Because Oedipus had unknowingly killed his father Laius and fathered two sons (Eteocles and Polyneices) and two daughters (Antigone and Ismene) with his mother Jocasta, he was a source of pollution to the city of Thebes. Although both of these crimes of parricide and incest were committed without his knowledge, his actions had created a dissonance with the land of Thebes that made exile the only situation from which he could pass on to others the learning he had gained from his tragic experience.[196] Oedipus will become a blessing to Athens by illuminating them on those tensions that lie below the surface in the city of Athens and could erupt as they did in Thebes. Oedipus's contribution would not simply be catharsis for the Athenians but also a catalyst for reflection on the power of the irrational in their collective existence.[197]

For Sophocles the irrational is not to be located in the unconscious of an individual. It is an external reality that exists in the relationships between gods, humans, and beasts.[198] It emerges in the interactions of beings inhabiting the tripartite cosmos of heaven, earth, and netherworld. For example, the sphinx, the man-eating composite being guarding the border between the territories of Minyan Orchomenos and Thebes, proposes a riddle to the Thebans that Oedipus solves by reasoning rather than by divination (*OT* 35-39, 390-98; Aesch., *Seven against Thebes* 772-77).[199] This salvific act elevates Oedipus to the kingship of

194. Froma Zeitlin, "Thebes: Theater of Self and Society in Athenian Drama," in *Greek Tragedy and Political Theory* (1986), 101–41, at 102.

195. Laura Slatkin, "*Oedipus at Colonus*: Exile and Integration," in *Greek Tragedy and Political Theory* (1986), 210–21, at 210–11, refers to Pindar's celebration of Oedipus's sacrifice of self as a gift to the household and polis in *Pythian* 4.261-69.

196. When the Athenian elders (i.e., the chorus) learn of Oedipus's identity, they are afraid that he will communicate a curse to the city and insist that he depart (*Oedipus at Colonus* 226, 234-36); see Slatkin, "*Oedipus at Colonus*: Exile and Integration," 213–14.

197. Vernant, "The Historical Moment of Tragedy in Greece," 26–27.

198. Charles Segal, *Oedipus Tyrannus*, 63.

199. Segal, *Oedipus Tyrannus*, 52, notes that the riddle of the Sphinx is essential to the Oedipus myth for Aeschylus and Sophocles; however, in the version of the myth in Hesiod, *Theogony* 326-32, there is no riddle and Heracles is the one who subdues the Sphinx. Schwartz, "Human Action and Political Action in *Oedipus Tyrannos*," 198, notes that the Sphinx, in contrast to the Gorgons and Harpies, is a monster that overcomes its victims with logic; like Apollo, she poses a riddle and afflicts with a plague until it is solved.

Thebes, but it sets the stage for his crimes of parricide and incest. These intrafamilial crimes not only cause the house of Laius to implode but also send negative reverberations throughout the kingdom.

The plague that initiates the action of *Oedipus Tyrannus* is a consequence of the bloodguilt for the murdered Laius (*OT* 100, 136).[200] A priest pleads with Oedipus to take steps to save the city:

> For as you yourself see, the city is already shaking and is still not able to lift its head from the depths, from the bloody commotion. Decay is on the fruit-bearing plants; decay is on the pasturing herds and on the women unable to give birth. On the city, a fire-bearing god has fallen heavily, a most hated plague strikes. Through it, the house of Cadmus is left empty, while black Death becomes wealthy through groaning and weeping. (ll. 22-30)

The city of Thebes is pictured here both as a ship and as a household—that of Cadmus, its legendary Phoenician founder. As a collective entity Thebes is on the verge of collapse. So the priest hopes that Oedipus might take steps to save the city. Oedipus responds that he has sent his nephew Creon to Apollo's oracle at Delphi to find an answer. When Apollo reveals that the plague is caused by bloodguilt, Oedipus pledges to remove the polluter from the land (*OT* 100, 136).[201] The challenge before him is to identify the murderer, for the report of the killing at the crossroads is that all the members of the group were killed except one and that the murderers were many. This search for the "one" and the "many" will eventually lead to Oedipus, who as the royal leader of the city is "the one and the many."[202] Oedipus's search for self-knowledge constitutes the central action of the play. The outcome of this action is foreordained, but the process of getting to this knowledge illuminates the power of the irrational in collective experience.[203]

200. Segal, *Oedipus Tyrannus*, 8–9, 52, 72.

201. Marcel Detienne, "Forgetting Delphi between Apollo and Dionysus," *Classical Philology* 96 (2001): 147–58, at 156–57. Schwartz, "Human Action and Political Action in *Oedipus Tyrannos*," 196, states: "Apollo enters the drama with the plague and the oracle not to manipulate Oedipus so much as to spur him on, to commission his search for knowledge." See *OT* 255, 469–70.

202. Segal, *Oedipus Tyrannus*, 11; idem, "Greek Tragedy and Society: a Structuralist Perspective," in *Greek Tragedy and Political Theory* (1986), 51–52; cf. Jean-Pierre Vernant, "Ambiguity and Reversal: On the Enigmatic Structure of Oedipus Rex," in *Myth and Tragedy in Ancient Greece* (1988), 122, 132, 139.

203. Segal, *Oedipus Tyrannus*, 71.

The chorus, echoing at points the words of the priest's plea to Oedipus to take action (*OT* 23-30), makes intercession with the gods Apollo, Athena, Artemis, and Dionysus to assist the city of Thebes (*OT* 151-215). The chorus is always present on the stage and can interact with the main actors. It represents the voice of the collective entity of which the Athenian audience is a part.[204] It is the voice of the common good, not just of mythical Thebes but much more importantly of fifth-century Athens. So when the chorus in the 420s says: "Alas, I suffer woes without number. My entire fleet is diseased. Merely paying heed is no weapon for driving it away" (*OT* 167-71), the audience is led to think about the plague that ravaged Athens in 430. It was a devastating event that claimed among its victims Pericles, a leader whom Oedipus seems to represent.[205] The chorus makes clear that the solution to the plague is not a matter of thinking; as the chorus demonstrates by its actions, it is a matter of prayer.

One of the gods with whom the chorus intercedes is Dionysus. One of their number voices the following intercession:

> I invoke the golden-girdled god whose name is upon this land, the ruddy-faced Bacchic god, the Evian one, in company with the maenads, to fight against the god, dishonored among the gods, who burns us with a pine torch. (*OT* 210-15)

Dionysus is the patron god of Thebes. He is the son of Zeus and of Semele, a daughter of Cadmus. Historically, Dionysus was a god worshiped in Greece in the second millennium,[206] but in Euripides' *Bacchae*, Dionysus is regarded as born in Thebes (ll. 1-2) but raised in Asia Minor (l. 13).[207] He describes his journeys that eventually led him back to Greece as follows:

> Departing from the gold-rich lands of Lydia and Phrygia, over the sun-stricken landscape of Persia, by the fortifications of Bactria, over the wintry ground of Medea, I traversed rich Arabia and all of Asia that lies along the salty sea, filled with beautifully-towered cities where Greeks and foreigners mingle together. I entered this first

204. Ibid., 39.

205. Ibid., 9. Schwartz, "Human Action and Political Action in *Oedipus Tyrannos*," 192–93, notes how Oedipus is a strong agent on behalf of the polis Thebes; of 199 questions posed in *Oedipus Tyrannus*, 123 are stated by Oedipus; he is "the cause of the action of the play."

206. Burkert, *Greek Religion*, 162.

207. Charles Segal, *Dionysiac Poetics and Euripides' Bacchae* (Princeton: Princeton University Press, 1982), 10.

> Greek city and taught my dances and established my rites so that I might be manifest to humans as a god (*daimōn*). (*Bacchae* 13-22)

According to this play dating to around 396 BCE, Dionysus is a god from Asia Minor who has gained a following in cities throughout the Persian Empire.[208] So while he represents "the Other" or the outsider, he is also the insider since he was born from the line of Cadmus. He notes how he has been present in cities with mixed populations of Greeks and foreigners. This practice of incorporating foreigners into Athens was one that met with much opposition. In 451, Pericles enacted a law that forbade Athenians to marry foreign women.[209] Yet this capacity to diversify through immigration was necessary for the vitality of Athens, a point made by Sophocles in his portrayal of Thebes as a closed, inwardly turned society that is diminishing through such rigidity.[210]

Dionysus primarily presents himself in human form throughout the *Bacchae*.[211] This identification with humans then challenges Dionysus to manifest his divinity. The characteristic mark of his presence is "frenzy," which he most often bestows on women to make them rush out of the domestic sphere and engage in ecstatic behavior in the mountains.[212] This retreat of the women to the mountains to celebrate rituals in which no males were allowed to participate was typically followed by a renewed commitment to family life within the city.[213] In the *Bacchae*, however, this frenzied behavior is taken to the extreme when Dionysus as a god and Dionysus as a beast merge in the participants' violent behavior of tearing apart an animal (*sparagmos*; *Bacchae* 1114-36).[214] Here Dionysus manifests his presence in both ecstasy and violence in order to prove that he is actually a god.[215] He indicates at the beginning of the *Bacchae* that he made the women flee to the mountains in a frenzy because they had questioned his credentials as a god:

208. Zimmermann, *Greek Tragedy*, 88.

209. Sarah C. Humphreys, *Anthropology and the Greeks* (London: Routledge & Kegan Paul, 1978), 137; Josiah Ober, *Political Dissent in Democratic Athens: Intellectual Critics of Popular Rule* (Princeton: Princeton University Press, 1998), 19–20.

210. Zeitlin, "Thebes: Theater of Self and Society," 121.

211. Segal, *Dionysiac Poetics and Euripides' Bacchae*, 28.

212. Ibid., 14; Richard Seaford, "Dionysus as Destroyer of the Household: Homer, Tragedy, and the Polis," in *Masks of Dionysus*, ed. Thomas H. Carpenter and Christopher A. Faraone, 115–46 (Ithaca, NY: Cornell University Press, 1993), at 115–16.

213. Seaford, "Dionysus as Destroyer of the Household," 122–23.

214. There is no consumption of Pentheus's flesh raw (*ōmophagos*) narrated here.

215. Detienne, "Forgetting Delphi between Apollo and Dionysus," 156–57.

> They were saying that Dionysus was not begotten by Zeus but rather that Semele had slept with another man and then attributed the sexual transgression to Zeus. A clever deception by Cadmus, they sneered, that he might falsify matters related to marriage. On account of this, Zeus killed her. (*Bacchae* 28-33)

This same skepticism toward the claim of divine parentage occurs in Euripides' play *Ion* when Ion's mother Creusa claims that she was made pregnant by Apollo (*Ion* 338-66, 965).[216]

The collective identity of Thebes—and thus, by implication, of Athens—is expressed by the interplay between Oedipus and Dionysus. The plague that besets the city is an illness that ravages Oedipus's body. This view of the body politic as the other body of the king is an inherent characteristic of the monarchical model of rule.[217] The suffering Oedipus shows that he is much more than an abstract "principle of community."[218] As king of Thebes, he bears in his body the brunt of the irrational fate that has descended upon this city. The collective identity of the city points to the web of relationships that is maintained only if individuals are ready to forego personal gain when the common good demands it. This "polis principle" was modeled by Solon in the early sixth century and was personified as Lady Justice (*Dikē*, Solon, frgs. 4.14–16; 13.7–8).[219] The principle received a more abstract, geometric formulation on the cosmic level by Anaximander when he imagined the cosmos attaining order as a tensive form of equilibrium between relatively equal competing forces

216. Stanley Hoffer, "Violence, Culture, and the Workings of Ideology in Euripides' 'Ion,'" *Classical Antiquity* 15 (1996): 289–318, at 307, notes that Creusa has no means to call Apollo to account for raping her and looks for a way to get redress (*Ion* 433–51, 974–75, 1557–58).

217. Jean-Pierre Vernant, "Oedipus Without the Complex," in *Myth and Tragedy in Ancient Greece* (1988), 85–111, at 106. Although Sophocles does not explicitly state that the king's body is an analogy for the body politic, such language of European medieval political theology is implicit in the political rhetoric of these ancient cultures; cf. Ernst Kantorowitz, *The King's Two Bodies: A Study in Mediaeval Political Theology* (Princeton: Princeton University Press, 1957), 3–6.

218. Marcus I. Finley, *The World of Odysseus* (New York: Viking, 1965), 106.

219. Joseph Almeida, *Justice as an Aspect of the Polis Idea in Solon's Political Poems* (Leiden: Brill, 2003), 77–79; Jean-Pierre Vernant, *The Origins of Greek Thought* (Ithaca, NY: Cornell University Press, 1982), 76; Elizabeth Irwin, *Solon and Early Greek Poetry* (Cambridge: Cambridge University Press, 2005), 175, 178, 180–82. On the divine character of the polis in the Greek tradition see Werner Jaeger, *Paideia*, 2 vols. (New York: Oxford University Press, 1939), 1:110.

(DK 12A9 lines 7–8 + B1).[220] But the common good symbolized in Oedipus's person is much more concrete and opaque than a geometric model.[221] The messiness of the competing forces—divine, human, bestial—that tear apart Oedipus's life show that the irrational will have its say in cultural structures and processes. If Dionysus is not acknowledged, he will make his presence known in painful disorder.

The Sex Drive Within the Cosmic Household as an Ambiguous Generative Force

The sex drive is essential not only for procreation but also for the generativity of personal relationships. The power of sex appeal in influencing the course of events is illustrated in the episode in Homer's *Iliad* where Hera comes to the aid of the Achaeans when she diverts Zeus's attention away from the battlefield by making love with him and luring him to sleep (*Il.* 14.153-340). Hera is able to do so with the aid of Aphrodite, who supplies Hera with a talisman upon which were "set all kinds of enchantment: on it were affection, yearning, and sweet talk that strongly beguiles the mind of the circumspect" (*Il.* 14.215-17). When Hera has worked her magic on Zeus so that he insists on going to bed with her, the impact of their union on nature is emphasized:

> Then the son of Cronus took his wife in his arms and under them the god-like earth made fresh grass grow and dewy lotus and crocus and hyacinth, thick and soft, so as to keep them high above the ground. They lay down on this and covered themselves with a beautiful, golden cloud, and glistening dew fell from it. (*Il.* 14.346-51)

The imagery, particularly the final statement on the dew descending, gives the impression that the terrestrial realm below is receiving rain that will make the earthly vegetation grow in imitation of that which is under Hera and Zeus.[222] This enactment of the sacred marriage, or the joining together of Zeus and Hera, of male and female to renew the natu-

220. Vernant, *The Origins of Greek Thought* (1982), 92; Charles Kahn, *Anaximander and the Origins of Greek Cosmology* (New York: Columbia University Press, 1960), 237; W. K. C. Guthrie, "Milesians," in his *A History of Greek Philosophy*, 4 vols. (Cambridge: Cambridge University Press, 1962–1981), 1:39–145, at 99.

221. Schwartz, "Human Action and Political Action in *Oedipus Tyrannos*," 207–8, notes that the citizen in Sophocles' plays is both ruler and ruled, one who takes action and is shaped by the polis, which has a quasi-divine status.

222. Richard Janko, *The Iliad: A Commentary*, vol. 4: *Books 13–16* (Cambridge: Cambridge University Press, 1992), 171–72, 206.

ral realm is regarded by some as a more effective means of bringing order to the cosmos than the battles a warrior god wages against rebellious forces.[223]

The union of the three cosmic spheres of heaven, earth, and underworld to make them into a family is a project at which women are adept.[224] In Greek myth women are more strongly associated with nature than with culture and are located on the periphery in darkness rather than at the center in light.[225] From this position at the margin, women tend to mediate between the spheres of nature, humans, and the gods.[226]

The Demeter cult at Eleusis honored the grain goddess who not only embodied and governed the annual cycle of grain growing but also stood at the center of the mystery cult at Eleusis that arose in the late seventh century BCE to offer the option of life after death to initiates from any social class. Thus the Eleusinian mysteries came to play an important role in linking the local family cults with the civic ones.[227] The myth central to the identity of the Demeter cult is the story of Hades' rape and abduction of Persephone and of her mother Demeter's mournful search to find her, which is recounted in the *Homeric Hymn to Demeter*.[228] Here Persephone is playing in the meadow with the daughters of Ocean when the earth opens and Hades in his chariot seizes her as she cries out (ll. 16-20). Only Hecate hears her, and then makes this known to Helios (ll. 24-27). But the sun god does nothing, because it is Zeus's plan to give Persephone to Hades as a wife (ll. 28-32), a plan Zeus had not communicated to her mother Demeter. By continually crying out, Persephone is finally heard by Demeter (ll. 38-39), but Demeter cannot locate her (ll. 44-49). Hecate leads Demeter to Helios (ll. 60-62), who tells her of Zeus's plan and

223. Robert Parker, *Polytheism and Society at Athens* (Oxford: Oxford University Press, 2005), 76–77, notes that the *hieros gamos* was a local or household ritual celebrated not only in the city of Athens but also in its demes. Aphrodite A. Avagianou, "*Hieros Gamos* in Ancient Greek Religion: The Human Aspect of a Sacralized Ritual," in *Sacred Marriages* (2008), 148–50, 171, contends that the *hieros gamos* applies only to the divine couples Zeus/Hera and Hades/Kore-Persephone, who provide a model for legitimate marriage but do not bring fertility to the human realm in the process.

224. Helene P. Foley, *Homeric Hymn to Demeter* (Princeton: Princeton University Press, 1994), 115.

225. Anne Carson, "Dirt and Desire: The Phenomenology of Female Pollution in Antiquity," in *Constructions of the Classical Body*, ed. James I. Porter, 77–100 (Ann Arbor: University of Michigan Press, 1999), at 79–80.

226. Foley, *Homeric Hymn to Demeter*, 139–40.

227. Ibid., 140–45.

228. Michael Crudden, trans., *The Homeric Hymns* (Oxford: Oxford University Press, 2001), 4–22.

counsels her to give up her lamentation (ll. 78-82). Helios notes that Hades is a suitable husband for her daughter since he rules over one of the three cosmic spheres distributed to the sons of Cronus (ll. 83-88): Hades over the netherworld, Poseidon over the sea, and Zeus over the heavens (*Il.* 15.185-93). But Demeter refuses to be consoled (l. 90). She withdraws from Olympus (l. 94) and wanders about through human cities and then resides at Eleusis (ll. 94-95, 356). She refuses to support the growth of grain (ll. 306-7). Thus a famine ravages the earth, which forces Zeus to intervene (l. 313). He first sends Iris, but Demeter ignores her (ll. 316-29). Next he sends Hermes to bring Persephone back to Demeter (ll. 335-56). As Persephone is leaving the netherworld, Hades offers her some pomegranate to eat (ll. 373). Eating it obliges Persephone to return to the netherworld and spend one-third of the year there (ll. 398-400).

This myth makes the claim that Demeter controls the earth. Zeus must respond to her demand for the return of Persephone or famine will extinguish the living and deprive the Olympians of their sacrificial offerings. Once Persephone has been returned, Demeter is reconciled and is willing to take her place once again among the Olympians. Yet because of Persephone's eating of the pomegranate she must return to Hades for one-third of every year.[229] Thus through the women Demeter and Persephone there is a uniting of the three cosmic spheres, which nevertheless retain their distinctness. This approach to cosmic order is the opposite of that of the sons of Cronus, who fight to maintain strict boundaries between their spheres and so to maintain a hierarchy among them.[230]

The propensity of males to maintain clear distinctions and to view a world with excessive fluidity as chaotic does not mean that males do not cross boundaries. The famous "ode to man" in Sophocles' *Antigone* celebrates the aggressive character of the man:

> Many the marvels but nothing is more marvelous than man (*anthrōpos*). He crosses the grey sea in the midst of winter storms, passing

229. Christiane Sourvinou-Inwood, "Festivals and Mysteries: Aspects of the Eleusinian Cult," in *Greek Mysteries: The Archaeology and Ritual of Ancient Greek Secret Cults*, ed. Michael B. Cosmopoulos, 25–49 (London and New York: Routledge, 2003), at 39, notes that Persephone/Kore resided in the netherworld for one-third of the year according to the Athenian calendar, but it seems that in the Syracusan calendar she stayed there for half of the year. Nevertheless, there was probably not a major divergence in the rites of this cult in the Mediterranean region. Walter Burkert, *Greek Religion* (1985), 160–61, argues that the Demeter/Persephone myth does not aim to explain the phases of the agricultural cycle but rather how death entered into the earthly sphere.

230. Foley, *Homeric Hymn to Demeter*, 82, 111, 115.

> through the surging waves. The earth, the most exalted of the deities, imperishable and untiring, he wears her away by rolling her over with ploughs year after year, turning the soil with a mule. (*Antigone*, 332-41)

Farming, which was essential to city life, and seafaring, which made possible the securing of goods through war or trade, were occupations in which men created an environment in which they could live. But this ode indicates how these occupations have a transgressive character: farming churns up the earth year after year and tries to draw a livelihood from it; seafaring dares to challenge the dangers of the watery abyss in order to reach distant places. These actions, like that of Hades' abduction of Persephone, are aimed at drawing goods from other spheres in order to enhance the world that the man has fashioned.[231] The question becomes whether the exchange among the spheres of the cosmos promotes life or death.

The sexual union of Hades with Persephone was not for the purpose of procreation. The inhabitants of the netherworld are the dead; they arrive there from the earth on a regular basis. Hades' desire to marry Persephone seems to have been for the purpose of acquiring a fulfilling personal relationship.[232] He does not seem to have been scheming to increase the population of his sphere by triggering a famine on earth. Thus Hades' desire to find fulfillment in marriage in the sterile environment of the netherworld is focused on the unitive rather than the procreative aspect of his relationship with Persephone. This unitive or relational dimension of life in Hades is also accented in Sophocles' *Antigone*. When Antigone performs burial rites for her brother Polyneices and is punished by Creon by being entombed alive, she states: "Neither having had a share in wedding songs nor a song for brides sung for me up to this point, I will marry Acheron [i.e., Hades]" (*Antigone*, 813-16). Antigone does not envision her marriage with the netherworld to be a sinking into nothingness. Rather she claims that there she will be able

231. Ruth Scodel, "Sophoclean Tragedy," in *A Companion to Greek Tragedy*, ed. Justina Gregory, 233–50 (Malden, MA: Blackwell, 2005), at 237. On the positive portrayal of the anthropocentric character of this "Ode to Man" see Gregory Crane, "Creon and the 'Ode to Man' in Sophocles' *Antigone*," *Harvard Studies in Classical Philology* 92 (1989): 103–16, at 106–7.

232. H. J. Rose, "The Bride of Hades," *Classical Philology* 25 (1925): 238–42, at 239, speculates that the entry of a virgin into the netherworld would be a gift of the virgin's unspent fertility to a chthonic deity.

to reestablish her relationship with her natal family (*Antigone*, 890-912). For Antigone, family relationships are stronger than death.[233]

Antigone's father Oedipus also struggled throughout his life to find the right balance in his relationships with family. The primary blind spot in Oedipus's relationship with his family was his not knowing the identity of his parents, for he had been cast out at birth (*OT* 717-20). Oracles from Apollo at Delphi make known to him the urgency of his finding out who his parents are (*OT* 790-94). Toward the beginning of *Oedipus Tyrannus*, an oracle makes known that the plague ravaging Thebes is due to bloodguilt from the murder of Laius (*OT* 95-98). Oedipus vows to discover this murderer, whom the oracle says is still within the land of Thebes (*OT* 110, 135-40). When he seeks further information on the identity of the murderer from the seer Teiresias, the seer reluctantly tells Oedipus that Oedipus himself is the murderer, information Oedipus angrily rejects (ll. 350-78).

Teiresias then explains further to Oedipus what is in store for him:

> Then do you know from whom you are? You, although being an enemy to your own below the earth and above it, have gone unnoticed. A terribly mobile curse, striking from both father and mother, is set to drive you at some time from this land. Now you see visible things, but, at that time, darkness. (*OT* 415-19)

Oedipus does not flee from this threat but seeks all the more urgently to find out who the murderer is. Oedipus tries to undercut Teiresias's threatening prophecy by accusing Creon of plotting to take over the throne. But Jocasta intervenes and tries to get Oedipus to dismiss Teiresias's warning as a false prophecy. She compares this prophecy with one she and Laius received long ago:

> An oracle once came to Laius—I will not say it came from Phoebus himself but rather from his servants—how a fate would come that he would die at the hands of a son to be born from Laius and me. But as the report says, foreign robbers killed him at the intersection of three roads. [As for the son's birth] before three days had passed, Laius pierced the ankles of his son's feet and had him cast by the hands of others on an inaccessible mountain. At that time, Apollo did not fulfill (the oracle) that the son would murder his father, nor did the terrible thing that he feared—that the son should kill his

233. Seaford, "Dionysus as Destroyer of the Household," 120–21; Jean-Pierre Vernant, "Tensions and Ambiguities in Greek Tragedy," in *Myth and Tragedy in Ancient Greece* (1988), 29–48, at 41.

> father—materialize. So the oracles speaking of these matters did not materialize and so you should not pay heed to them. Whatever a god finds he has need of, he himself easily reveals it. (*OT* 711-25)

When Oedipus hears that Laius was killed at a crossroads, he recalls that he had killed a man at such a place (*OT* 729-38).

Jocasta then tells Oedipus that one servant survived the incident and is a shepherd (*OT* 756, 760-62).[234] He would be able to say whether there were one or several robbers who had murdered Laius. Before the shepherd arrives at court, a messenger comes from Corinth who makes known to Oedipus that Polybus, the king of Corinth and his adopted father, has died (*OT* 943). The messenger recalls that he had brought the infant Oedipus from the slopes of Cithaeron, where he was about to be exposed by a shepherd (*OT* 1026-29). The tendons of the feet of the infant Oedipus had been pierced (*OT* 1033-34). Oedipus wants to search out the shepherd who had brought the infant to the mountain (*OT* 1049-51). Jocasta tried to dissuade him from pursuing this knowledge (*OT* 1060-61). But the shepherd eventually arrives and confirms that he had taken the infant Oedipus to the mountain. The infant had been given to him by his mother Jocasta (*OT* 1171-74).[235]

This convergence of the stories of the messenger and the shepherd makes it known that Oedipus was a child who had been exposed and rescued and then adopted and raised in the royal house of Corinth. But when Oedipus had received an oracle from Apollo at Delphi predicting that he would kill his father and marry his mother, he had fled, only to meet Laius at the crossroads and kill him. The unspeakable oracle was confirmed.

Another story of the exposure of an infant concerns Ion, who was of the line of Erichthonius, the founder of Athens. At the beginning of Euripides' *Ion*, Hermes states:

> In the not insignificant Greek city named after Pallas of the Golden Lance, Phoebus forced Creusa, the daughter of Erechtheus, to join together with him as married persons do, there at the northern-exposed rocks below the Hill of Pallas in Athens, which the lords of Attica call the Long Lands. Not knowing the father, which was the

234. On the link between the Theban shepherd and Apollo, see Schwartz, "Human Action and Political Action in *Oedipus Tyrannos*," 197.

235. On exposure as the opposite of *amphidromia*, the rite of integrating a newborn into the family and the paternal line of descent, see Jean-Pierre Vernant, *Myth and Thought Among the Greeks* (London: Routledge & Kegan Paul, 1983), 155.

> desire of the god, she carried the burden in her womb. But when the time arrived, Creusa gave birth to a child within the chambers and then carried the infant to the same cave where she had lain with the god. She left it there to die in a hollow cradle with running wheels. (*Ion* 8-20)

At a point in the narrative many years later an old man questions her on how she could possibly have abandoned her child like this (*Ion* 954-64). Such an action would go against normal motherly feeling. Creusa responds that she did so with the expectation "that the god might save his own child" (*Ion* 965). She has been doubted by others, including her son Ion, that Apollo had fathered the child (*Ion* 338-66), but despite Hermes' statement in line 14 that she did not know the father, she has no doubt. In fact, her son had been rescued by Apollo, who had Hermes bring the child in its cradle and place it before Apollo's temple in Delphi. A prophetess there discovered him and raised him within the precincts of the temple (*Ion* 28-57). Thus Apollo arranges for a woman to raise his son within his own household.[236]

Before knowing Creusa's identity as his mother, Ion questions her about her earlier ancestor Erichthonius. She confirms the story that claims that Erichthonius had sprouted from the earth (*Ion* 267). The fuller mythical account in the tradition states that Hephaestus had tried to rape Athena but only was able to spill his semen on her thigh, which she then wiped off and cast onto the ground.[237] This soil served as the womb from which Erichthonius was born. The reason for championing the view that the city's ancestors sprang from the soil rather than from a heterosexual union was to promote undivided devotion to the place.[238] The proponents of the autochthonous origin of Athenian citizens believed that a citizen's attachment to the city needed to be so strong that he would offer his child for it. The story that Erechtheus had sacrificed his daughters for the deliverance of Athens is one that Creusa confirms for Ion (ll. 277-

236. Froma Zeitlin, "Mysteries of Identity and Designs of the Self in Euripides' *Ion*," in her *Playing the Other: Gender and Society in Classical Greek Literature*, 285–338 (Chicago: University of Chicago Press, 1996), at 335. Saxonhouse, "Myths and the Origins of Cities," 260, notes that Euripides allows the myth of autochthony to live on in the *Ion* but introduces the female role into the origin of the city since the child stands in need of nurture.

237. Zeitlin, "Mysteries of Identity," 325–26.

238. Arlene W. Saxonhouse, *Fear of Diversity: The Birth of Political Science in Ancient Greek Thought* (Chicago: University of Chicago Press, 1992), 82; Nicole Loraux, *Born of the Earth: Myth and Politics in Athens* (Ithaca, NY: Cornell University Press, 2000) 16-17, 30-31.

78).[239] She says that she had escaped this sacrifice because she was only an infant at that time (ll. 278-80).

Arlene Saxonhouse argues that the myth of autochthony exalts the male role at the expense of the female in procreation—an argument resembling that of Apollo in Aeschylus's *Eumenides* in which he aims to lower the severity of Orestes' crime of matricide:[240]

> A mother is not a begetter of what is called a child, but rather a nurse of the newly-sown foetus. The begetter is he who breeds. But the stranger as a stranger preserves the young shoot, provided that a god does not hinder it. I will show you a sure sign of what I am saying. There can be a father without a mother. Right here is a witness, the daughter of Olympian Zeus. She was not nurtured in the dark places of the womb, for such a young shoot no goddess could bring forth. (*Eum.* 658-66)

Athena was born from the head of Zeus after he had swallowed her pregnant mother Metis (Hesiod, *Theog.* 880-929). Metis was essential for the conception and growth of Athena as a foetus, but Zeus gave birth to her. Here in Euripides' *Ion*, Hephaestus is not celebrated as the progenitor of Athens. Rather, Euripides emphasizes that the soil is the locus for the origin of the Athenians. Their primordial ancestor, the infant Erichthonius, needed a woman to nurture him.[241]

According to Greek myths, the sex drive is persistent, powerful, and pervasive. Its unruly force is evident in the rapes perpetrated by the gods Hades, Apollo, and Hephaestus. The unwanted pregnancies that resulted

239. Zeitlin, "Mysteries of Identity," 292, 294, 296–97, 298; Jon D. Mikalson, "Erechtheus and the Panathaneia," *American Journal of Philology* 97 (1976): 141–53, at 143. Stanley Rosen, *Plato's Symposium*, 2d ed. (New Haven: Yale University Press, 1987), 224, notes with respect to Diotima in the *Symposium* and to Aspasia, the concubine of Pericles, that "Peace, and therefore justice, is impossible without the mediation of the female element. In the political context woman is connected with the mother-earth; in the theoretical context she mediates between man and the heavens."

240. Saxonhouse, *Fear of Diversity*, 79, 83; eadem, "Myths and the Origins of Cities," 257.

241. Saxonhouse, "Myths and the Origins of Cities," 257, notes that Euripides' emphasis on the female role in the origin of cities moves away from the myth of autochthony towards the view of Aspasia in Plato's *Menexenus* (237b-c, 238a) in which the earth is described as mother. Zeitlin, "Mysteries of Identity," 336–37, acknowledges that Creusa must act within a structure of gender relations that are dominated by the masculine, but she criticizes Saxonhouse for oversimplifying Euripides' play by not paying attention to the following facts: (1) that Creusa exposed her child and did not nurture him as mothers typically do, and (2) that Creusa is needed as *epiklēros* for her family, since it has no male heir.

from these divine actions brought great distress upon the women and their families. The mythical tradition upheld the reality of the gods' role in these pregnancies but also presented the opportunity for the hearers to reflect on the ambiguity of the situation and the distress that the mother had to undergo. The strength of the sex drive is evident in Hades' desire to have sexual experience be part of his realm of death and sterility. The pleasurable relationship epitomized in the sexual joining of Zeus and Hera on Mt. Ida is one that Hades wants to share with Persephone in the netherworld. But Hades' aggression causes distress to Demeter and the natural world: i.e., death obstructs natural processes. In Sophocles' *Oedipus Tyrannus*, the omen about strife in the royal house leads Laius and Jocasta to expose the infant Oedipus. Although it may appear to be a self-serving action on the part of Laius and Jocasta, this form of infant sacrifice was also intended to keep peace within the city and kingdom of Thebes. Creusa's exposure of her infant was a means of protecting her and her family from an unwanted pregnancy, but she explains her action as a challenge to Apollo to take responsibility for fathering the child.[242]

The story of the autochthonous origin of Athens's ruling family is a "noble lie" (cf. *Rep*. 389b-c).[243] The story, which sidesteps the reality of heterosexual union as essential to the birth of the ruling family, tries to promote an extreme devotion to the soil of Athens and to exclude foreigners from citizenship.[244] The exaltation of the male role in procreation and the marginalization of the female role is a tactic focused on maintaining the hierarchy of categories favorable to men. This male drive to construct a world that men will regard as inhabitable is celebrated in Sophocles' "Ode to Man" (*Antigone* 332-72). By contrast, as seen in the way Persephone and Demeter unite the three cosmic spheres, the female role tries to create continuities across boundaries so that the integrity of the whole is fostered. In the coincidence of opposites, the male and female roles are upheld as complementary.

242. Hoffer, "Violence, Culture, and the Workings of Ideology in Euripides' 'Ion,'" 296, refers to the societal "double standard" that caused Creusa to expose her child as an illustration of the violence involved in founding civilization and maintaining the boundary between the sacred and the profane.

243. Saxonhouse, "Myths and the Origins of Cities," 252–53.

244. On Euripides' efforts to balance autochthony with receptivity to outsiders (*philoxenia*), see Zeitlin, "Mysteries of Identity," 331–32.

The Sacred Character of Family Relationships

Oedipus's crimes of incest and parricide brought disease and famine on the land of Thebes. He was subjectively innocent (*OC* 538), but objectively guilty (*OT* 739, 745, 1011, 1183-85). Pollution of the land happened through objective responsibility for the deeds. The defilement is so great that Oedipus cannot bear to look upon himself. He uses the brooches fastening the robe of Jocasta, who has hanged herself, to dash out his eyes (*OT* 1267-78). When the chorus challenges him that he would be better dead than blind, he responds:

> It was best done this way and not otherwise. Do not instruct me or advise me further. I do not know with what eyes I might ever look upon my father or my suffering mother when I enter Hades—those two to whom I did things meriting consequences worse than hanging. But would the sight of children, begotten as I begot them, be a delight for me to look at? Certainly not! Never for these eyes of mine! For I, most wretched man raised in Thebes, robbed myself of city, tower, and honored holy places of the gods when I told everyone of the expulsion of the impious one, whom the gods have revealed to be defiled and of the family of Laius. Having made known my defilement, could I look directly on these people with eyes? (*OT* 1369-85)

The objective character of what Oedipus has done is too much for him to look upon. His crimes of parricide and incest have disrupted a relational reality fundamental to existence.[245] The transgression of these intimate bonds causes disorientation that is almost insurmountable. Oedipus feels that he cannot face his parents, his children, or the people of his city. Even to go to the netherworld with his eyes intact would not spare him from seeing his parents. So Oedipus chooses the path of blindness as a way of purging himself and the land of Thebes of the pollution of his crime.

Where he is to reside in order to carry out further purification is a matter with which he needs assistance. Claiming that his pollution is not contagious, he appeals to the chorus:

> I pray to the gods that as soon as possible you hide me somewhere outside the land or that you kill me or that you cast me into the sea where you will no longer look on me. Come, see fit to touch a

245. Segal, *Oedipus Rex*, 73–74, 76, notes that more than 300 lines of the play remain after the self-blinding of Oedipus; in the latter section of the play Oedipus meets citizen-subjects, Creon, and his two daughters and shows that he has gained a deeper vision of life through suffering.

> miserable man. Be persuaded. Do not be afraid. No mortal besides me can bear my evils. (*OT* 1410-15)

Then he asks Creon: "Let me dwell in the mountains where my mountain called Cithaeron is, which my mother and father, if living, would have designated as my tomb" (*OT* 1451-53). But Creon and the others in the city do not drive him out at that point. As Oedipus relates later in *Oedipus at Colonus* (440-45), it is only when Oedipus has calmed down and regained his senses that his ambitious sons Eteocles and Polyneices and the city of Thebes decide to expel him. He is sent forth to wander like a beggar with only his daughters Antigone and Ismene to assist him.

At the beginning of *Oedipus at Colonus*, Oedipus and Antigone come to a suburb of Athens known as Colonus. They find a shaded garden area that seems like a good place to rest, but a stranger informs them that it is a sacred place to which no one is allowed entry (*OC* 36-37). Here, as Segal explains, the grove associated with feminine divinity symbolizes the two faces of woman: the generosity and destructiveness of the mother.[246] But Oedipus has been informed by an oracle from Apollo that he is to find rest in a place near the Furies (*OC* 86-90). So he addresses them in prayer and communicates the content of the oracle:

> After a long time, I choose this resting place, coming to the last land where I might receive a seat and lodging place among the revered goddesses, here to round out my miserable life, giving gain to those who have received me and a curse to those who have sent me away. (*OC* 89-93)

The chorus then regards Oedipus as a blasphemous vagabond who has dared to transgress the sacred space of the Furies. It appears that Oedipus had entered the sacred thicket as a place of sanctuary so that he might not be driven from the place (*OC* 174-77). When he tells them that he is Oedipus, the chorus says: "Out! Move on! Get out of the land!" (*OC* 226). But Oedipus pleads with them to be true to the reputation of Athens for receiving strangers. He asks that one of the leaders of Athens be summoned so that he may make his plea for asylum.[247] Theseus arrives, is sympathetic to Oedipus (*OC* 550, 560), and grants him citizenship (*OC* 636). Thereafter Creon arrives with an armed guard to bring Oedipus

246. Charles Segal, "Greek Tragedy and Society," 53.

247. Slatkin, "*Oedipus at Colonus*: Exile and Integration," 214–15, notes that Oedipus warns the Athenians that excluding him—an innocent victim of circumstances—from their society would be "irreligious" (*asebēs*, *OC* 284).

back to Thebes for eventual burial (*OC* 735-39). However, Ismene had earlier informed Oedipus that Creon would not risk burying him on Theban land itself, but only somewhere near the border.[248] Although the Thebans know of the oracle that spoke of a blessing to be conferred by the deceased Oedipus, they fear that his remains might instead bring a curse on their land (*OC* 404-5). Throughout this episode Theseus protects Oedipus. Eventually Oedipus is taken by a thunderous divine intervention to be buried in the area of the sacred place of the Furies at Colonus, but no one knows the exact location (*OC* 1517-33).

In Euripides' *Ion*, when the infant born from Apollo and Creusa was taken by Hermes to the sanctuary of Apollo at Delphi and raised within the sanctuary (ll. 29-49), Ion lived, so to speak, with his father. But his mother he did not know (*Ion* 325). Hermes reports: "When he [Ion] had physically reached manhood, the Delphians installed him as treasurer of the god, the trusted distributor of all. In the god's temple, he has lived to the present a holy life" (*Ion* 54-57). This life in the sanctuary has agreed with Ion (ll. 149-52). He identifies himself as Apollo's slave (*Ion* 305) and notes that "the whole house of Apollo is mine, in whatever part I might sleep" (*Ion* 315).[249] When Xuthus, the husband of Creusa, receives an oracle at Delphi that Ion is his son, he invites Ion to return with him to Athens. But Ion is reluctant because he feels he will be an outsider in Athens, even to the point that the women of Xuthus's house will try to eliminate him (*Ion* 589-620).

Ion's forebodings are on target, because Creusa does not want the line of the Athenian ruling family going back to Erichthonius through her to be broken, so she plots to have Ion killed (*Ion* 1003-38).[250] But when the plot becomes known to the authorities at Delphi (*Ion* 1186-1215), Creusa is convicted of trying to kill "a holy one inside the temple precincts" (*Ion* 1224-25). The penalty is execution by being "thrown off a cliff" (*Ion* 1223).[251] Creusa is saved from this fate when she proves that she is Ion's mother (*Ion* 1402-1511). Athena appears as a *dea ex machina*

248. Zeitlin, "Thebes: Theater of Self and Society," 105.

249. Hoffer, "Violence, Culture, and the Workings of Ideology in Euripides' 'Ion,'" 294, notes, however, that in lines 1373, 1382 Ion shows some resentment over his life as a temple slave, yet in this earlier speech Ion seems to perceive his status as higher than that of slave since he is linked to the sanctuary of Apollo.

250. In *Ion* 1473, Ion refers to himself as "the *nothos* (i.e., bastard) child of an unmarried woman." See Daniel Ogden, *Greek Bastardy in the Classical and Hellenistic Periods* (Oxford: Clarendon Press, 1996), 16.

251. On Ion's virginal status and his role in keeping the sanctuary precincts pure from the defilements of the profane world (e.g., birds, *Ion* 154-80), even to the extent of purging

to move the action forward; thus Creusa is freed, and Ion is appointed to the throne in Athens with the people of the region thereafter bearing his name as "Ionians" (*Ion* 1554-92).[252]

Common to the pollution threatened by Oedipus and by Ion as a presumed outsider to the ruling house of Athens is the potential of these contagions to defile the sacred character of the core relationships of the family. The crimes of incest and parricide universally undermine family relationships, whereas the incorporation of an outsider into the royal line of Athens was a particular issue of purity linked to that time and place. But the presence of Oedipus and Ion raised the issue of how to protect a community from individuals who were regarded as carrying within them the defilement arising from illegitimate sexual actions.

With regard to Oedipus's trespassing in the sacred grove of the Furies and Creusa's plot to poison Ion, the territory and belongings of deities were threatened by humans. Such actions would have defiled sacred space. But in the case of Oedipus's entry into the female space of the Furies there is the added dimension of an "entering the dark forbidden place of the mother, connected with her mysterious power of creating life."[253]

Overcoming Tragedy Through Compassion and Commitment

The aged Oedipus in his final resting place near the Furies at Colonus stands on the margin of the city of Athens and supports its life—analogous to the ways the Furies do by mediating the chthonic powers of the earth for the support of the city with its system of justice, one that goes beyond that of the family. Here the female principle of the earth is brought together with the male principle of the structured polis in ways that are compatible and at times synergistic.[254] The pattern at Thebes of tying civil authority and the distinction between insider and outsider to the family model has changed on the basis of what Oedipus learned through his

---

Creusa from the community for her alleged sacrilegious act, see Hoffer, "Violence, Culture, and the Workings of Ideology in Euripides' 'Ion,'" 298, 300.

252. Hoffer, "Violence, Culture, and the Workings of Ideology in Euripides' 'Ion,'" 313–14, argues that this link between Athens and the Ionians mystifies Athenian imperialism in the fifth century.

253. Segal, "Greek Tragedy and Society," 53.

254. Zeitlin, "Thebes: Theater of Self and Society," 135; cf. Rush Rehm, *Marriage to Death: The Conflation of Wedding and Funeral Rituals in Greek Tragedy* (Princeton: Princeton University Press, 1994), 56–57.

experience.[255] It is no longer sufficient to support a member of the family simply on the basis of genes. The family member must also make choices that demonstrate his or her commitment to be a member of the family: e.g., the sons Eteocles and Polyneices choose not to care for their father Oedipus in his time of distress and so disqualify themselves from the family.[256] Antigone remains in the previous pattern of Thebes, where a member of the family is accorded full acceptance regardless of behavior; she treats Polyneices as her brother and tries to bury him at the risk of her own life, even though he has been indifferent to his father Oedipus. By contrast, Oedipus disowns his two sons for their lack of love but shows great affection for Antigone and Ismene because of their care for him. Having endured the ill effects of the curse of his ancestral house of Laius, Oedipus follows the advice of an oracle to situate himself near the boundary of Athens so that the blessings of his hero cult will be mediated to Athens, where the family structure is expected to support the bonds among the citizenry, or the well-being of the state.[257]

After Oedipus recovers from the initial horror of what he has unknowingly done he maintains that he is innocent (*OC* 270, 538, 547). He recognizes the pollution caused by his actions, but he is no longer ready to allow it to have the last word. He is deeply concerned that his actions will taint the reputation of his daughters Antigone and Ismene (*OC* 1120-31). Yet he insists from the time right after his blinding that his misfortune is his own and is not contagious (*OC* 1409-15). Nevertheless, Oedipus's incest and parricide within the royal house of Thebes were deeply disruptive of the kingdom of Thebes, as it suffered not only from a deadly plague but also from political upheavals caused by the fraternal strife of Eteocles and Polyneices. However, what Oedipus suffers within his person as a result of his incest and parricide is a reality he wishes would elicit compassion rather than shunning, since he was an unknowing victim of circumstances (*OC* 277-91).[258]

In spite of these more rational approaches toward personal and national misfortune that are articulated toward the end of the later plays

255. Zeitlin, "Staging Dionysus Between Athens and Thebes," in *Masks of Dionysus* (1993), 147–82, at 150.

256. Zeitlin, "Thebes: Theater of Self and Society," 132–33.

257. Slatkin, "*Oedipus at Colonus*: Exile and Integration," 220–21, argues that the community principle operative in the polis shows itself more inclusive and adaptable than that of the family; the bonds of the family and the political power of the polis show themselves in the experience of Oedipus to be incompatible.

258. Ibid., 216–17.

about Oedipus, the dominant picture of Oedipus in Sophocles' plays is that of a man torn apart by forces and circumstances beyond his control. There is much skepticism about oracles by the characters in *Oedipus Tyrannus*, but the oracles govern the action of the play. They decree a fate from which Oedipus cannot escape. The gods direct a sequence of events in which the irrational element is shocking. There is no way to deny its force. Therefore the audience viewing this play is moved to see that the way to negotiate polarities within human experience that create tensions and wrenching problems is not by offering facile solutions but by staying with the particular people who suffer tragedies and showing them compassion and pity.[259] One might argue that the tragic play's capacity to promote the emotional response of love to irresolvable sociopolitical problems is a far greater ethical advance than the creation of a court system to replace blood vengeance. The tragic performance evokes a collective feeling of pity for unwitting victims, which offers a way for the citizenry to deal with the irrational. As Dionysus, the god of the theater, makes clear, the sphere of the irrational will have its say, particularly if it is denied or repressed.

Summary

Oedipus solved the riddle of the Sphinx by rational logic (*OT* 35-39, 391), only to become the king of Thebes in which he would unwittingly become guilty of incest in addition to a previously unknown act of parricide. The cause of these objective transgressions in the myth of Oedipus is the curse on the house of Laius. The punishment for errors of an earlier generation is believed to be visited on the members of a later one. As a royal representative of the community of Thebes, Oedipus experiences the alienation of exile within his own land until eventually, when he is old, his ambitious sons drive him from the kingdom of Thebes. An oracle directs him to Colonus, where he tries to find the spot in which he will be buried. It is located near a sacred grove of the Furies. His entry into their sacred space poses the question of how to incorporate immigrants and at the same time sustain the rootedness of the citizens in the polis. This interplay between traditional ways and rational planning unfolds in the tension between Oedipus transgressing the boundary of the sacred grove and the Furies defending their sacred space. Ultimately, Oedipus's grave and hero cult are in the vicinity of the Furies' sacred grove in Colo-

259. On the moral challenge the living Oedipus poses to the Athenians in *Oedipus at Colonus* and to the audience see ibid., 218.

nus; both Oedipus and the Furies adapt to one another's roles in sustaining the common good of Athens. Masculine and feminine agents are necessary for the well-being of the polis. Although masculine and feminine agents define themselves over against one another according to their natural endowments and distinctive functions, they do so on the foundation of a common nature and shared life. For the Athenian community the process of defining and redefining masculine and feminine roles unfolds in the conflicts of the tragic performances. Dionysus, the god of the inside and the outside with masculine and feminine characteristics, was revered as the life force infusing and guiding the tragic performances. Efforts at restoring communal equilibrium required appeals to him.

The waxing and waning of the life force regularly unfolded within the agricultural cycle. The sacred marriage rite of the Anthesteria festival (March/April) recognized the regenerative force of sexuality as a fundamental cosmic force. Hades' abduction of Persephone testifies to the yearning of the realm of the dead for the unitive love epitomized by the sexual union of Zeus and Hera. Her abduction leads to famine on the earth, whereas the sexual union of Zeus and Hera rejuvenates nature. Persephone's annual return to be with Hades for part of the year testifies that death has made its way into the natural sphere and must be acknowledged. Dionysus moves between heaven, earth, and the netherworld. His embodiment in the tragic performance helps the members of the polis community be mindful of the experiences of dying and rising that are vital to their communal well-being.

The sex drive is present in the gods of heaven and the netherworld as well as in humans. In light of a human's capacity to be godlike or beastlike, an individual may be seen as a microcosm of the macrocosm spanning heaven, earth, and the netherworld. The integration or disintegration of the sex drive in an individual is potentially influenced by forces from the three cosmic spheres. For example, Creusa's unwanted pregnancy leads to child exposure. This brush with death is a response to Apollo's aggressive entry into Creusa's life. In the mythical foundation of Athens, Athena spurned the sexual aggression of Hephaestus and the royal line and citizenry of Athens is born from the seed of a god in the soil of Athens. As protector of the polis, Athena honors the soil as the womb of the populace. The feminine nurturance of polis life is honored, even though the masculine oversight of this common life is given priority. Within the action of the tragic performance, masculine and feminine aspects of life stand in a tensive unity, the coincidence of opposites. Sexuality is a primary manifestation of the life force that traverses the three cosmic spheres and makes its ambiguous reality known most forcefully within embodied human life.

Synthesis: Bodily Integrity in a Monolatrous Model Contrasted with That in a Polytheistic Model

In the judgment narrative of Ezekiel 16, the prophet marshals his rhetorical resources to shock his exilic audience into believing that Jerusalem's behavior toward YHWH and others has been that of a sex addict. Such adulterous behavior typically calls for capital punishment (Lev 20:10). The catastrophic destruction about to come upon Jerusalem was triggered by Jerusalem and not by YHWH or by cosmic chance. The chaotic irrationality that irrupts in Jerusalem's history can be explained. By contrast, in the Mesopotamian *Curse of Agade*, the fall of Akkad is attributed to Enlil's inscrutability and Ishtar's changeability. The human actors do not bear the blame for this catastrophe. In fifth-century Athens, the audience of Sophocles' play *Oedipus Tyrranus* would have been moved to pity for Oedipus, who is unknowingly guilty of incest with his mother and of parricide. The cause of these particular crimes is a curse on the royal household of Laius, which, according to Euripides' lost *Chrysippos*, was caused by Laius's homosexual abduction of the boy Chrysippus, the son of Pelops.[260] The Mesopotamian traditionists and the Greek tragedians spent considerable time puzzling over the irrational component of human experience as triggered by the gods. The monotheist Ezekiel refused to be confused by Jerusalem's destruction; the puzzling, irrational element in this catastrophe was Jerusalem's infidelity to YHWH. This prophet gave the individuals of his audience no room to blame the evil on an outside force.

The Expression of Collective Identity and the Maintenance of Integrity

Ezekiel describes Jerusalem as YHWH's wife who had earlier been adopted by YHWH as a foundling after birth. There are two metaphors operative here: Jerusalem is a woman, and Jerusalem is a wife. It is the former metaphor that is paralleled in the image of the Mesopotamian goddess Inanna/Ishtar weeping over the destruction of Uruk in the balag "Uru-amirabi." Here Inanna is the protector deity who regards the inhabitants and the institutions of Uruk as constituting her own household. In sixth-century Greece, Solon refers to the bonds that form the social fabric of the community as the goddess *Dikē*, but the city of Athens in the tragedies of Aeschylus and Sophocles appears as a male rational construction under

260. Timothy Gantz, *Early Greek Myth: A Guide to Literary and Artistic Sources* (Baltimore: Johns Hopkins University Press, 1993), 490–91. For Aeschylus's version of the troubles of the house of Laius with no mention of Chrysippus see his *Seven Against Thebes*, 742-91.

the sponsorship of Athena and Apollo built in coordination with the Furies (who function also as the residual voice of the mother goddess). This move toward abstraction in Greece will not be able to account for human agency by completely divorcing itself from metaphorical language. The tragic performance keeps this metaphorical dimension intact as it explores the possibility of a more rational system for securing justice beyond that of blood vengeance. The metaphor of the city as woman plays an important role in the rhetoric of each tradition for evoking collective identity.

For the vision and vitality of a collective entity like a city, the people need to have a picture of how their collective life participates in and is influenced by the divine realm. Jerusalem was born of foreign parents and then adopted by YHWH. Mesopotamian cities were built by kings with the permission of the gods. The Mesopotamians regarded the first human either as sprouting from the earth like a plant from a germinating seed or as fashioned from clay according to a model mapped out on a brick; in either case, the Mesopotamian mother goddess was imagined to be a builder rather than one who gives birth. In light of the myths incorporated into Greek tragedy the city of Athens was constructed by the citizens as an ongoing project of attending both to the initiative of its autochthonous ancestors and to its need to incorporate new immigrants. In Athens the original inhabitants were said to have sprung from the soil into which the seed of Hephaestus had fallen; their mother was the soil of Athens. Ezekiel 16 stands apart from the examples from Mesopotamia and Greece discussed earlier by locating the origin of the collective entity Jerusalem in foreign parentage that carries an ominous note for attentiveness to the collective good of Jerusalem; by contrast, for the Mesopotamian and Greek examples the origin of the inhabitants of the collective entity emphasizes their predilection for the collective good of their respective cities. The need for singleheartedness is imperative for the Jerusalemites addressed in Ezekiel 16. But numerous gods are involved, along with the protector deity, in producing the autochthonous landscape promoted by Mesopotamian and Greek cities; they thus divide the attention of the inhabitants.

Ezekiel claims that YHWH married the young woman Jerusalem by passing the corner of his cloak over her. The metaphor for sexual intercourse between divine and human partners is mirrored (a) in the *Gilgamesh Epic* in Ishtar's encounter with the gardener Ishullanu and her attempted liaison with Gilgamesh (VI:7-21, 64-69), and (b) in Euripides' *Ion* and *Bacchae*, in the reports of the sexual union of Apollo with Creusa (*Ion* 338-66, 965) and of Zeus with Semele (*Bacchae* 28-33). For Ezekiel this daring metaphor of sexual union with the divine is intended to accent the exclusive character of Jerusalem's relationship with YHWH. It is the opposite with Inanna/Ishtar, for it accents her superabundant female sexuality that is not tied down to a single divine or human partner. As the superior partner in this relationship with a human, Ishtar is not constricted by the regulations on female sexual practice in the patriarchal household. Ishtar is free to have sexual relations with those she chooses. With the Greek gods Apollo and Zeus, the rationale for intercourse appears to be primarily sexual attraction. The metaphor of marriage of a human to God provides a practical model for the ongoing task of an embodied human trying to achieve wholeness or live with integrity through close association with the divine. The marriage metaphor provides a productive way to speak about the dynamics involved in the integration of sexuality with spirituality.

The Sex Drive as a Form of Physical and Cultural Power

Ezekiel indicts wife Jerusalem as an adulteress whose multiple liaisons are driven by excessive sexual desire. Although the book of Ezekiel does not explicitly say it this way, one can make the case that in Ezekiel 16 wife Jerusalem imitates Ishtar, the Mesopotamian patroness of prostitutes. Ezekiel describes the extreme character of her sexual desire as disqualifying her even as a prostitute: she bribes her potential lovers rather than receiving payment for her services. In the Mesopotamian and Greek contexts prostitution has its place as a legitimate profession, but adultery is condemned. In the Mesopotamian and Greek texts under consideration the adultery metaphor is not applied to relationships in which one of the parties is a collective entity.

The prohibitions against sex outside of marriage are evident in the stories of the exposure of infants found in all three traditions—a way of responding to unwanted pregnancies. The infant girl Jerusalem, Sargon, and Oedipus are each cast out by the parents shortly after birth. No reason is given for the exposure of infant Jerusalem except for hints at the hardheartedness of the mother of Jerusalem, Samaria, and Sodom (Ezek 16:45). Sargon's mother is an *entu*-priestess who was forbidden to bear children. Creusa cast out her infant son Ion in the hope that Apollo would rescue him and take responsibility for fathering him.

In times of national crisis, kings in Israel such as Ahaz (2 Kgs 16:3) and in Greece such as Agamemnon (cf. Soph. *Agam.* 146–55, 228–47) are reported to have taken the step of offering their offspring to appease the anger of the protector deity who had withdrawn his favor. But wife Jerusalem has created a crisis by her promiscuity and uses child sacrifice as a way to respond to her need for more lovers (16:20). YHWH accuses wife Jerusalem of sacrificing his children to other deities. Here the metaphor of divine parentage applied to YHWH accents a sense of belonging or ownership rather than physical begetting. In Athens, Erechtheus is said to have sacrificed his daughters in order to save the city; thus the attitude the citizens are encouraged to adopt is that their love of the soil of the city is to be so strong that they will make extreme sacrifices for its well-being. Child sacrifice is not documented in Mesopotamia.

Ezekiel indicts Jerusalem for forgetting how she was rescued and raised in her youth. This obligation to seek self-knowledge by trying to find one's true parents is the main concern of Oedipus. In the story of Sargon's origins—a rags-to-riches story whose upbeat tone reflects its difference in genre from the prophetic judgment of Ezekiel 16 and the tragedy of *Oedipus Tyrranus*—Sargon marvels at the good fortune visited on him and recalls his origins with gratitude, particularly the divine favor shown him by Ishtar.

When Jerusalem is forgetful of her marriage to YHWH, Ezekiel calls her to task for acting as if she were autonomous. In the *Curse of Agade* it is reported that Sargon became frustrated by Enlil's silence and began removing parts of Enlil's temple without his approval. Such independent, autonomous action was hubristic. In *Oedipus Tyrannus*, Jocasta tries to convince Oedipus to regard the dire oracles about him from Apollo as false. But her skepticism seems to have been driven by the fear that the truth about Oedipus's exposure as an infant might be made known.

The sexual drive manifests itself as a passionate force shaping personal and cultural relationships. It is a constructive force when it operates within the web of relationships constituting the household and the community. When it transgresses against this web of relationships it can spin out of control, as in the case of wife Jerusalem, or it can become a bad memory that comes back to haunt one as in the case of Jocasta, the mother and wife of Oedipus. Mindfulness and the search for self-knowledge are activities that create a constructive context within which the sex drive can promote human flourishing.

The Requirement of Sexual Constraint in the Encounter with the Holy

The body is an apt analogue to the temple or the sanctuary. Its different parts form an organic whole, and yet some parts are more vital to life and other parts are regarded as off-limits or of limited access. Transgression of the boundaries of the body causes disequilibrium or defilement. The same is true for the temple or sanctuary. Ezekiel condemns

Jerusalem for her abominations and announces that she will be judged collectively by her lovers. They will execute her as an adulteress and murderer (16:38). Oedipus pollutes the land of Thebes by murdering his father and having sexual relations with his mother (*OT* 350-78, 1171-74). Oedipus has done these actions unknowingly and blinds himself when they become known to him—so great is his shame. YHWH tries to get Jerusalem to feel shame for her deeds through collective punishment, but such shame will only arise for her after she has been destroyed and rebuilt; only when she "dies and rises" will she have the moral capacity to perceive the full extent of the corruption to which her sexual addiction and forgetfulness of YHWH have led her. Her actions defile the innermost parts of the sacred space of Jerusalem (16:36). Ishtar also is outraged when the innermost parts of her temple in the form of a sacred marriage ritual are defiled by a temple servant; this woman is executed by being thrown from the temple—an act of purgation. Sexual transgressions introduce a potent disequilibrium into a system, particularly when they impinge upon the most important dimensions of individual and communal identity.

The Dynamics of Boundary Formation in the Forging of Sexual Identity

The maintenance of good boundaries depends largely on how well one knows oneself. Jerusalem is enamored with her own beauty and falls into a self-destructive pattern of trying to secure the love and adulation of all who pass by. This narcissistic choice deprives her of perspective, and she stumbles headlong into an addictive pattern of behavior. She is not the victim of an ancestral curse, although the loose behavior of Sodom and Samaria and their indifference toward their children suggest that wife Jerusalem's genetic makeup may have something to do with her self-centeredness. Because of the ancestral curse on the house of Laius, Oedipus and his household elicit the pity of all onlookers—those in Thebes and Athens and in the audience. The curse that came upon Akkad as a result of Sargon's hubris led the later kings of Ur III, who adopted many of Sargon's organizational structures, to steer away from associating their rule with that of the Sargonic kings. The inner dynamic that fuels narcissism and the force that drives an intergenerational curse are psychosocial realities that take on a life of their own and can burgeon into a monstrous force capable of consuming an individual or a community.

The countervailing force that restores and maintains equilibrium must be attached to a fixed point. An individual and a community require a focus in which each invests and so finds common ground. Ezekiel insists that Jerusalem was capable of choosing to remain faithful to YHWH. She was not controlled by an ancestral curse. YHWH was there to assist her; her challenge was to love YHWH alone. In the case of keeping personal and communal boundaries intact in Mesopotamia and Greece, the irrational element in human experience was given greater credence. The goddess Ishtar and the god Dionysus were both feminine and masculine. Polarities characterize the personality profiles of these deities. Thus the maintenance of boundaries where these gods were acknowledged meant trying to maintain equilibrium in one's environment through the balancing of countervailing forces: love versus hate, masculine versus feminine, life versus death.

Marriage to God is a metaphor capable of guiding a lifelong commitment to celibacy. Ezekiel 16 personifies the city Jerusalem as a woman and wife. An individual like Jeremiah can symbolize this city in such a way that his renunciation of marriage and family can point to the dying experience of the Jerusalemite community. But his positive oracles on Jerusalem's future indicate that he symbolizes not merely the dying of Jerusalem but also its rising. This hope for the future is grounded in wholehearted trust in YHWH, a movement of the heart based on an intimate relationship or strong attraction (cf. Song 1:15-17; 3:1-5; 4:1-15). The marriage of Jerusalem to YHWH, which an individual like Jeremiah can concretize in his own way of life, is, in terms of horizontal human relationships, a celibate way of life. The commitment to direct one's sexual energies toward the divine raises the issue of how these energies find their place within the divine-human relationship, one in which there are places and times in which sex and the sacred are incompatible. The roadmap for integrating sexuality and spirituality is filled with diverse pathways, some of which lead to dead ends and others to more engaging complexity. A version of this roadmap will be traced out and discussed in the following chapters.

Chapter Two

Intermarriage: A Threat to the Household as the Enduring Matrix of Personal Identity?

When one feels like an alien in one's own home, that person is compelled to find out why he or she feels like "a fish out of water" in order to find a remedy. There are many ways one may delude oneself or refuse to acknowledge key factors that have led to this alienation. But if pain compels one to find a way out, how one defines the problem and identifies the causes will be key steps in whether or not a new equilibrium can be reached. This rational approach to navigating a personal crisis aims to integrate reason and emotion. In times when the causes are elusive, intuition or feeling may be more effective than analytical reason. In any case, reason and emotion must collaborate in restoring a sense of being at home in one's living situation.

The experience of alienation is one of confronting the reality of limits. It is a foretaste of death. When and where these limits show up may seem arbitrary and so one may fight against them. When faced with the loss of his friend Enkidu, Gilgamesh is confronted with the reality of his own death. He refuses to accept this and fights against it by undertaking a journey to the ends of the earth to find a way to escape death. It is a heroic quest in which Gilgamesh will not leave the liminal state of mourning to return to ordinary life after the traditional seven-day period. As he reaches the outer edges of the world, before he crosses the waters of death, he meets the wise barmaid Shiduri, who gives him this advice:

> When the gods created humankind, they placed death upon humankind and retained life for themselves. You, Gilgamesh, should let your stomach be full. Day and night you should enjoy yourself. Have fun each day. Dance and play day and night. Let your clothes be clean and your head washed; may you bathe in water. Attend to the child that grasps your hand. Let your wife enjoy herself in your embrace. (OB VA+BM iii 3-13)

Shiduri's nonheroic stance counsels a form of resignation Gilgamesh is not prepared to accept. He presses on. One is left with the question of whether Gilgamesh is wasting his life in trying to gain immortality. Shiduri tells him that his quest for immortality is futile and he should enjoy life, particularly life within the context of the nuclear family.[1] If the normal, as opposed to the heroic approach to finding an answer to death lies within the family, what are the factors that make the family a solution to the problem of mortality? Shiduri points to pleasures that come from the family. But is this a sufficient basis? Gilgamesh tries to find wholeness in life by reaching beyond the confines of the domestic sphere: his oppressive use of force in Uruk in his early years, his friendship and adventures with Enkidu, and now his efforts to transcend death. How could the family, founded on the marriage relationship, provide a way to deal with human mortality? That is the central question of this chapter. It will be posed to materials from the Israelite, Mesopotamian, and Greek traditions according to the following three topics: (1) efforts of a heroic leader to reform the family and maintain the traditional culture; (2) the household as a hereditary socioeconomic unit that functions like an organism by preserving property and the relationships attached to it; (3) the relationship of the family to the clan and the state, which illustrates the tension between heteronomy and autonomy.

Israel: Intermarriage as the Clash of Religious Cultures in Yehud

The sense of dislocation arising from the Babylonian exile led to increased questioning by individuals of how they fit within the Judahite community and its covenantal traditions (Ezek 11:14-16; 33:23-29; Jer 29:4-14; Ps 74:1-11). When things were going well for Judahite individuals in the land before the exile, their sense of being part of a family, a clan, and a nation would have provided a context in which individual agency

1. OB VA+BM iii 1–15 (cf. Eccl 9:7-9); A. R. George, *The Babylonian Gilgamesh Epic*, 2 vols. (Oxford and New York: Oxford University Press, 2003), 275.

had a place.[2] But with the loss of land, occupation, and status, the exiles would have wondered whether their covenantal traditions were still valid. The covenant model, which gave them a sense of how they as individuals fit into the social and political fabric of the Judahite nation, had been seriously called into question in the exilic context. How the individual fit within the family and bore corporate responsibility for it would need to be scrutinized more carefully (Ezek 18:20; Jer 31:29-30).[3]

The experience of exile was not simply that of an individual, but of a community. The dialectic of competing voices over how to make sense of this traumatic event made the exiles aware of how they were embedded within a larger network of national and international forces. How these competing forces influenced one another would have an impact on how the individual defined himself. He could negotiate those limits that gave definition to his life only by wrestling with the ways the family, clan, and nation referenced embodied experience in their communities. Personal identity is forged in the interplay of individual and communal, human and divine, material and spiritual, national and international forces. The lines drawn between these forces have a relative, dynamic character; in other words, identity is a relational rather than a reified reality. The dialectic of these forces shows that the private sphere of the household and the public sphere of the state are intertwined; the qualities of each sphere will have an impact on the others.

2. According to Daniel L. Smith, *The Religion of the Landless: The Social Context of the Babylonian Exile* (Bloomington, IN: Meyer-Stone Books, 1989), 98–99, 102, 115, 120, the ties fostered through blood relationship and residence in the same place seem to have been extended to a larger group as a survival strategy in the exile. The solidarity characteristic of the *bêt ʾāb* was regarded as extending to their combination into larger units known in the exile as *bêt ʾābôt*—which in preexilic terminology would have been identified as *mišpĕḥôt*, "clans"; see also Rainer Albertz, "The Thwarted Restoration," in *Yahwism After the Exile: Perspectives on Israelite Religion in the Persian Era*, ed. idem and Bob Becking, 1–17 (Assen: Van Gorcum, 2003), at 13. However, Gale Yee, *Poor Banished Children of Eve* (Minneapolis: Fortress Press, 2003), 35, notes that *bêt ʾāb* can refer to the nuclear family or to the extended family or to the lineage; the *mišpāḥâ* overlaps with the *bêt ʾāb* but usually refers to larger units such as the extended family or the clan; see also Roland de Vaux, *Ancient Israel*, vol. 1: *Social Institutions* (New York: McGraw-Hill, 1965), 20–21.

3. Gordon Matties, *Ezekiel 18 and the Rhetoric of Moral Discourse*, SBLDS 126 (Atlanta: Scholars Press, 1990), 218–22. On the exilic or postexilic dating of the "sour grapes" passage see William Holladay, *Jeremiah 2* (Minneapolis: Fortress Press, 1989), 163; Walther Zimmerli, *Ezekiel 1* (Philadelphia: Fortress Press, 1979), 377–78; Daniel Block, *The Book of Ezekiel: Chapters 1–24* (Grand Rapids: Eerdmans, 1997), 558–61.

Ezra's Intrusive Leadership: A Paradoxical Form of Heroism

Ezra takes a heroic stance against the marriage practices of the Yehud community in 458 BCE that is antiheroic in its profile. His paradoxical way of being a hero lies in his humble confession of communal sin, an antiheroic way of behaving that has as its ambitious goal a drastic alteration in the practices of the community.[4] He champions the highly controversial proposal that households in Yehud having a non-Jewish wife and mother were to dismiss the wife with her children. Ezra claims that the practice of intermarriage in Yehud is an abomination (*tôʿēbâ*, Ezra 9:1-2, 14); it is a type of transgression incompatible with the holiness of YHWH and will eventually result in the expulsion of the entire people from the land. So Ezra argues that the Yehud community within scarcely more than fifty years after its return to the land is on a trajectory that will lead to the loss of the land.[5]

Ezra fights against the corruption of intermarriage by identifying himself with the community in which it occurs. Although Ezra was recently commissioned by the Persian king and sent from his home in Babylonia (Ezra 7:12-26), he makes clear by his distress and mourning that he himself is part of this community he believes is headed for serious trouble. When leaders of the community inform him of the problem of intermarriage, he reports: "I ripped my clothes and my robe; I pulled out hair from my head and beard and sat down, quite overcome" (Ezra 9:3). This way of responding to a covenantal violation mirrors that of Josiah in 622 BCE when he realized that the Judahites had broken the covenant (2 Kgs 22:11). So the action of Ezra, like that of Josiah before him, is to implore YHWH to counter the curses that are expected to come upon those who violate the covenant. Ezra's response is regarded, in light of the deuteronomic tradition, as the mark of a pious leader.[6]

4. On Ezra's public mourning as a way of shaping communal opinion see Joseph Blenkinsopp, *Ezra–Nehemiah*, OTL (Philadelphia: Westminster, 1988), 177.

5. Rainer Albertz, *A History of Israelite Religion in the Old Testament Period*, vol. 2: *From the Exile to the Maccabees*, OTL (Louisville: Westminster John Knox, 1994), 372, suggests that the exile may have improved the lot of the lower classes in Judah while under Babylonian administration. Also Tamara Eskenazi, "Out of the Shadows: Biblical Women in the Postexilic Era," *JSOT* 54 (1992): 25–43, claims that socioeconomic circumstances in the pre-state and postexilic eras promoted equality between men and women.

6. Lester Grabbe, *Ezra–Nehemiah* (London: Routledge, 1998), 142, 150. On the righteous reforming king who humbles himself in 2 Kgs 22:19 and delays the punishment against Jerusalem see Marvin Sweeney, *King Josiah of Judah: The Lost Messiah of Israel* (New York: Oxford University Press, 2001), 49–51.

Ezra notes that he remained immobilized in his position of mourning until the evening oblation.[7] Such inactivity, although exemplary for a religious hero standing before a transcendent deity, is the opposite of the approach of a military hero in the ancient Near East, who would draw on all of his physical and mental resources to win his way.[8] Even though such military heroes called upon and gave thanks to their protector deities, they promoted themselves as the agents who had carried out the victory. Here Ezra's heroism lies in his calling the Yehud community to reform in ways they are sure to resist. His mourning draws attention to the seriousness of the problem of intermarriage for the integrity of the Jewish community. By the humble stance Ezra takes before YHWH he aims both to judge the Yehud community for their disobedient neglect of YHWH and to show that he himself shares in the fate of the community. Responsibility for abominations committed in the community rests not simply on the violators but also on the entire community (Ezra 9:2).

Ezra does not act alone. He is the spokesperson for a group in the community that opposes intermarriage. Members of this group are characterized as "leaders" (*śārîm*) who bring the problem of intermarriage to Ezra's attention (9:1). When Ezra dramatizes the seriousness of this transgression through mourning and immobility, it is members of this group identified as "tremblers" (*ḥărēdîm*, 10:3) who step forward and propose measures that can perhaps provide a way forward.[9] Shecaniah (10:2) recommends that the community make a solemn pact to banish their foreign wives with their children. His concrete proposal fits the profile of a political man of action in contrast to the pious intercessory action of Ezra.[10]

7. Saul Olyan, *Biblical Mourning: Ritual and Social Dimensions* (New York: Oxford University Press, 2004), 68–69.

8. Ehud ben Zvi, "What Is New in Yehud? Some Considerations," in *Yahwism After the Exile* (2003), 32–48, at 41, 46, claims that the literati of fifth-century Jerusalem were self-effacing individuals with meager resources who glorified revered figures from the foundational period.

9. Joseph Blenkinsopp, "A Jewish Sect of the Persian Period," *CBQ* 52 (1990): 5–20, esp. 17–18; idem, *Ezra–Nehemiah*, 178–79, has argued that these "tremblers" are part of a prophetic-eschatological group who are also mentioned in Third Isaiah (Isa 65:8-16; 66:2, 5; cf. Mal 3:13-21); cf. Shemaryahu Talmon, "The Emergence of Jewish Sectarianism in the Early Second Temple Period," in his *King, Cult and Calendar in Ancient Israel: Collected Studies*, 165–201 (Leiden: Brill; Jerusalem: Magnes, 1986), at 188. Grabbe, *Ezra–Nehemiah*, 147, claims that more information is needed to establish that these "tremblers" are a prophetic-eschatological group who make up Ezra's supporters.

10. Grabbe, *Ezra–Nehemiah*, 142.

The actual number of households with foreign wives was, on the basis of the list in Ezra 10:18-44, relatively small.[11] Among these households were some high-ranking priests and aristocrats, which suggests that Ezra's tactic is aimed in part at those households that had considerable material resources.[12] Those who had returned from exile in the late sixth and early fifth centuries found that they had come back to an ancestral land that was not empty.[13] They had to compete with others to find their place in the land. One way to increase one's material resources was to "marry up," i.e., to gain a wife from the landed class.[14] But Ezra and his group of tremblers regarded such a way of gaining power in the community as undercutting the identity and fabric of the Yahwistic community and threatening to land them back in exile.[15]

In this intracommunity conflict Ezra makes clear that marriage practices are not simply the preserve of the *paterfamilias* and his family. These relationships have a defining effect on the character of the entire community of Yehud. So, like the Deuteronomic reformers before him, Ezra insists that the practices of the individual households be in accord with the covenant with YHWH that distinguishes Israel from the nations (cf. Deut 7:1-6).[16] As a leader of the Jewish community as a whole, Ezra

11. The number of marriages dissolved as a result of the work of the tribunal appointed by Ezra to examine all the cases was moderate: seventeen priests, six Levites, one singer, and three gatekeepers; the remaining mixed marriages of the total of sixty-six were from the community (Ezra 10:18-44). Grabbe, *Ezra–Nehemiah*, 35–36, questions why there was such a fuss over so small a number of mixed marriages.

12. Blenkinsopp, *Ezra–Nehemiah*, 189–90.

13. Grabbe, *Ezra–Nehemiah*, 136, argues that on the basis of 2 Kings and the book of Jeremiah only a minority were deported to Babylon; those remaining in Judah consisted of nobles, military men, and priests as well as the poor. Second Chronicles gives the picture that the land was empty and thus experiencing a sabbatical.

14. Daniel Smith-Christopher, "The Mixed Marriage Crisis in Ezra 9–10 and Nehemiah 13: A Study of the Sociology of the Post-Exilic Judaean Community," in *Second Temple Studies. 2. Temple and Community in the Persian Period, JSOTSup* 175, ed. Tamara Eskenazi and Kent Richards, 243–65 (Sheffield: Sheffield Academic Press, 1994), at 260.

15. The criteria for membership in the Jewish community of the fifth century BCE were a matter of dispute; the community in Yehud consisted of descendants of the indigenous inhabitants of Judah, the returned exiles from Babylon, Mesopotamians exiled by the Assyrians, Mesopotamians who returned with the exiles, and proto-Samaritans; see Bob Becking, "Law as Expression of Religion (Ezra 7–10)," in *Yahwism After the Exile* (2003), 18–31, at 19; Sara Japhet, "People and Land in the Restoration Period," in her *From the Rivers of Babylon to the Highlands of Judah: Collected Studies on the Restoration Period*, 96–116 (Winona Lake, IN: Eisenbrauns, 2006), at 99.

16. Blenkinsopp, *Ezra–Nehemiah*, 189; Albertz, *A History of Israelite Religion*, 2:390. Gary Knoppers, "An Achaemenid Imperial Authorization of Torah in Yehud," in *Persia and Torah:*

believes he must take intrusive measures to ensure that deficiencies in religious and social relationships within the individual households do not endanger the entire community of Yehud. The public realm of politics is tied to the private realm of the household.

The Organic Character of the Israelite Household

The household is a fundamental unit in the covenant community of Israel.[17] The Decalogue—even though its imperatives are stated in the second person masculine singular— addresses everyone in the household.[18] These imperatives provide the basic, minimum expectations for those who would be part of the covenant community in whose midst YHWH dwells.[19] The first three imperatives deal with the vertical relation of the community members with YHWH; the next seven imperatives address the horizontal relations of the community members with one another. The women and children are also expected to obey these imperatives, but the focus here is on the father of the family as embodying the whole unit. If these households are to exist together as part of a community, the members of the individual households must respect the life and property of the other members of the community. It is the integrity of these relationships that provides a grounding and an orientation for the members of the community.[20] If these fundamental relationships are violated, the ripple effect of the injured parties trying to reestablish these relationships can disrupt the entire community. Blood vengeance

The Theory of Imperial Authorization of the Pentateuch, SBL Symposium 17, ed. James W. Watts, 116–34 (Atlanta: Society of Biblical Literature, 2001), at 133, notes that as a local official Ezra could have promoted his prohibition on intermarriage quite apart from imperial backing.

17. Leo Perdue, "The Israelite and Early Jewish Family: Summary and Conclusions," in Leo Perdue, Joseph Blenkinsopp, John J. Collins, and Carol Meyers, *Families in Ancient Israel*, 163–222 (Louisville: Westminster John Knox, 1997), at 168, states that in the Second Temple period, in contrast to the monarchical period, "the family household regained its prominent place as the center of Jewish social life." See also Albertz, *A History of Israelite Religion*, 2:375.

18. Carol Meyers, *Exodus* (Cambridge: Cambridge University Press, 2005), 165. Brevard Childs, *Exodus* (Louisville: Westminster, 1976), 400, claims that the Decalogue is not addressed to "a specific segment of the population . . . but to every man." However, Joseph Blenkinsopp, "The Family in First Temple Israel," in *Families in Ancient Israel* (1997), 48–103, at 54, notes how the Decalogue is aimed at landowners and slaveowners and is concerned about the protection of their property.

19. Childs, *Exodus*, 398.

20. Meyers, *Exodus*, 165–66.

as well as compensation for adultery, theft, and slander can break a community apart.

According to the Decalogue, the Israelite household is founded on its relationship with YHWH. Exclusive fidelity to YHWH and upholding and honoring this relationship undergird the relationships in the household.[21] The parents hold an honored position as those who work together with YHWH in begetting and raising the members of the household. Their role is critical to the integrity of the household, particularly as a hereditary unit that passes on the traditions and property of earlier generations.[22] It is the composition of this fundamental relationship of husband and wife that becomes an issue for Ezra and his supporters.[23]

Ezra argues that the wife and mother of an Israelite household must be Jewish (Ezra 9:2; 10:2, 10, 14, 17, 18).[24] The Ezra-group appeals to laws against intermarrying with the seven nations in the land in Deut 7:1-6 but substitutes for three of the nations the prohibitions against intermarrying with the Ammonites, Moabites, and Egyptians as stated in Deut 23:3-6. Perhaps it is the number seven as a symbol of totality that moves Ezra to expand this prohibition into an unqualified ban on intermarriage with all foreign wives. Ezra's interpretation builds on the earlier Deuteronomic laws that aim to stop the drift of the Israelite community toward assimilation with surrounding cultures but goes beyond the letter of these earlier laws and becomes a form of lawmaking for the situation in fifth-century Yehud.[25]

21. Childs, *Exodus*, 398, 403; Meyers, *Exodus*, 169–70.

22. Meyers, *Exodus*, 173–74, 192, 265; eadem, "Daughters of the Inhabitants of the Land as Marriage Partners (Exod 34:16; Gen 24:3; 27:46; 28:1, 6, 8; Deut 7:3; Josh 23:12-13; Judg 3:5-6)," in *Women in Scripture*, ed. Carol Meyers, Toni Craven, and Ross Shepard Kraemer, 200–1 (Boston: Houghton Mifflin, 2000); Childs, *Exodus*, 418–19.

23. Ezra's exilic, imperially backed religion clashed with the family religion of those who remained in the land; see Albertz, *A History of Israelite Religion*, 2:407, 461.

24. Saul M. Olyan, *Rites and Rank: Hierarchy in Biblical Representations of Cult* (Princeton: Princeton University Press, 2000), 88, 101, points out that with Ezra–Nehemiah the mother's status becomes determinative for the child's status as an Israelite; previously only the father had to be an Israelite for the child to be an Israelite. Now both parents need to be Israelites. Helena Zlotnick-Sivan, "The Silent Women of Yehud: Notes on Ezra 9–10," *Journal of Jewish Studies* 51 (2000): 3–18, at 9, 16, contends that Ezra excludes foreign wives for economic reasons. Mary Douglas, "Responding to Ezra: The Priests and the Foreign Wives," *Biblical Interpretation* 10 (2002): 1–23, at 11–12, argues that there were (1) not enough wives in a system that allowed polygamy and (2) some of the returned exiles were marrying into local families in order to gain property so that they might enter the farming economy.

25. Yonina Dor, "The Composition of the Episode of the Foreign Women in Ezra IX–X," *VT* 53 (2003): 26–47, at 28, 46, notes how Ezra 10 refers only to women (vv. 2, 3, 10, 11, 14,

Ezra does not allow for foreign wives and their children to convert.[26] Many of these families would have been formed for some time when Ezra delivered the proclamation that these relationships must be dissolved. The issue for Ezra must have been the culture of the families, for the wife-mother would have held a strategic position in raising the children.[27] In these programmatic years of personal development the basic loyalties of the children are shaped. Since conversion was allowed in the subsequent centuries leading up to the Common Era, it must be that Ezra judged that the level of assimilation to surrounding cultures had progressed so far that an emergency measure was necessary.[28] Thus he decreed that the families with foreign wives and children had to dismiss them.

Ezra came to Yehud from Babylon with the authority to evaluate how the Torah of the God of Israel was being observed (Ezra 7:12) and to appoint magistrates to see to the implementation of that law (Ezra 7:25). The law that is implemented appears to be a version of the Pentateuch.[29] The calling of the assembly in Nehemiah 8 appears to have been

---

17, 18, 19, 44), whereas Ezra 9 refers to a mixing of men and women of the nations (vv. 1, 2, 11, 12, 14). She argues that Ezra 10 was an earlier, more extreme view on breaking up mixed marriages, whereas Ezra 9 is more moderate in including both men and women in its censure and anchoring this reform in the traditions of the Torah. However, Eskenazi, "Out of the Shadows," 36, contends that the author of Ezra–Nehemiah is as much opposed to foreign husbands as to foreign wives.

26. Sara Japhet, "People and Land in the Restoration Period," 115, notes that the only evidence of converts in Ezra–Nehemiah is in Ezra 6:21 and Neh 10:29.

27. Carol Meyers, "The Family in Early Israel," in *Families in Ancient Israel* (1997), 1–47, at 28–32; Olyan, *Rites and Rank*, 85–86.

28. Smith, *The Religion of the Landless*, 197, notes that from a sociological perspective Ezra's strategy of exclusivism was "a creative response to the threat of domination and minority existence." Becking, "Law as Expression of Religion," 30, defines religion as "a symbol system [that] offers a pattern of language and rituals for group internal communication about the basics of life." Ezra seems to have judged that the Israelite symbol system was on the verge of being silenced. Albertz, *A History of Israelite Religion*, 2:375, 449, notes the increased importance of religious confession for maintaining identity in a land populated by substantial numbers of foreigners and observes with reference to Ezra 6:21 and Neh 10:29 that foreigners could become part of the Israelite community in Yehud.

29. Blenkinsopp, *Ezra–Nehemiah*, 66, 153–55, says that this law "cannot simply be equated with the Pentateuch." He identifies this law primarily as the laws of Deuteronomy along with some ritual legislation from the Priestly source and the Holiness Code. The traditional view in Judaism is that this law was the Pentateuch. Meindert Dijkstra, "The Law of Moses: The Memory of Mosaic Religion in and after the Exile," in *Yahwism After the Exile* (2003), 70–98, at 91–92, contends that the author of the Ezra tradition in Ezra 7–10, Nehemiah 8, has the Pentateuch in mind when he refers to Torah; he notes that the law of

one of the initial actions by Ezra on his return in 458.[30] With the entire community—men, women, and children—present at the Water Gate on the feast of Tabernacles, Ezra reads the Law from early morning until noon. He reads and translates the text throughout the seven days of the feast and has Levites instruct the people from the first to the last day (vv. 10, 13) on the meaning of this Law.[31]

The issue of intermarriage, adjudicated on the twentieth day of the ninth month (Ezra 10:9), appears to have been a test case for the observance of Ezra's newly promulgated Torah. The Law promulgated by Ezra was probably already present in its essentials as customary law among the community of Yehud.[32] The Law brought by Ezra was a scribal version of the law that had been in preparation by the priestly groups exiled to Babylon in the sixth century BCE. The key point in Ezra's proclamation of the Law to the community at the feast of Tabernacles was the elevation of the written law to normative status. The written word gained authority over the oral tradition. The community of Yehud became a people of the book. Ezra based his authority not only on his lineage—which he traced back to Aaron—but also on his commission from the Persian king.[33]

Moses, which would have functioned as a rule of faith for the Pentateuch, was still in a fluid form in the Persian Period. Albertz, *A History of Israelite Religion*, 2:470, draws on the work of Erhard Blum and argues that the Deuteronomic edition of the Pentateuch (K^d) would have been completed by the end of the sixth century and available by the mid-fifth century for Nehemiah.

30. Blenkinsopp, *Ezra–Nehemiah*, 60, 65–66. However, Rainer Albertz, "The Thwarted Restoration," 13, dates Ezra's return to 398 BCE in the aftermath of Persia's loss of control over Egypt in 406 when the Persian king would have been ready to grant special privileges to the Jews (i.e., money for temple maintenance, tax exemption for cultic personnel) to secure their loyalty. Sara Japhet, "Composition and Chronology in the Book of Ezra–Nehemiah," in *From the Rivers of Babylon to the Highlands of Judah* (2006), 245–67, at 251, who argues that the author of the book of Ezra is different from the author of the book of Nehemiah, says that Nehemiah 8 seems to belong to Ezra 7–10 but that the link is at the level of sources. By contrast, Blenkinsopp, *Ezra–Nehemiah*, 45, 53–54, contends that the Chronicler is the author of both Ezra and Nehemiah and transferred Nehemiah 8 from its earlier position before Ezra 9.

31. Antje Labahn, "Antitheocratic Tendencies in Chronicles," in *Yahwism After the Exile* (2003), 115–35, at 121–25; see also ben Zvi, "What Is New in Yehud?" 45.

32. Blenkinsopp, *Ezra–Nehemiah*, 152. Ezra's midrashic method shares with the customary law of the ancient Near East the *modus operandi* that certain principles and frames of reference are established in the traditions of the community, and in turn are in conversation with the legal traditions of the ancient Near East. These principles and frames of reference are authoritative guides rather than elements of a code; see Grabbe, *Ezra–Nehemiah*, 144, 148.

33. In his commissioning by Artaxerxes, Ezra was instructed to enforce "the law (*dātāʾ*) of your God and the law (*dātāʾ*) of the king" (7:26). Grabbe, *Ezra–Nehemiah*, 26, 140, notes

Ezra's group consisted of those who had returned from exile. Those who remained in the land and could not trace their genealogy back to those who had been exiles were regarded as outsiders to the Ezra-group.[34] Therefore the battle over who was within the authentic Yehud community and those who were outside it was one that concerned not only culture but also property. The wives who came from families apart from those who had returned from exile may well have belonged to families who possessed property in the land. A number of those returning from exile probably tried to improve their status by marrying into these families and positioning themselves to profit from the higher economic status of the wife's family.[35] Even though ancient Near Eastern marriages were patrilocal—i.e., the wife transferred from her father's house to that of her husband—the wife could become the heir to more of her father's patrimony than her dowry if she had no brothers (cf. *CH* 181-82).[36] But the association with the landed families would in any case have offered economic advantages to the family. Ezra's law on intermarriage disallowed such an advantage.

In ancient Israel marriages were arranged by the father or brother of the bride (cf. Gen 24:50-51). The groom honored the father and his household for the gift of his daughter by paying the bridewealth (*mōhar*).[37] The texts are for the most part silent about the intimacy between the couple about to be married. What is accented in the texts is that a marriage was an exchange between two households.[38] The bride, who was expected to be a virgin (Deut 22:13-19), was transferred from her father's house to that of her husband. The husband probably was still living within his father's house. In preexilic times the typical Israelite family compound housed three to four generations: grandparents, parents, their adult offspring, and their offspring's children. The houses for the nuclear

that Ezra seems to have been instructed to teach the law to everyone in the province of Ebir-nari, including those who were not Jews.

34. Blenkinsopp, *Ezra–Nehemiah*, 83–84, 175–76; Talmon, "The Emergence of Jewish Sectarianism in the Early Second Temple Period," 185–87.

35. Smith-Christopher, "The Mixed Marriage Crisis," 260; Blenkinsopp, *Ezra–Nehemiah*, 176.

36. In Num 27:1-11, Moses legislates that the daughters of Zelophehad can inherit the paternal property if there are no living male heirs; however, Num 36:1-9 qualifies this inheritance practice by decreeing that the daughters must marry within the clan. The daughter who inherits in *CH* 181-82 is a *nadītum*; see Raymond Westbrook, ed., *A History of Ancient Near Eastern Law*, 2 vols. (Leiden: Brill, 2003), §6.2.5.1, 1:60.

37. Meyers, *Exodus*, 197.

38. Ibid., 196.

families within the extended family would be arranged around a courtyard to form a compound. According to Lawrence Stager these extended families would range from ten to thirty individuals. This extended family of three to four generations was known as the *bêt ʾāb*, "the house of the father."[39] In postexilic times the *bêt ʾāb* became much larger in size—sometimes with as many as two hundred individuals—and seems to have been equivalent to the *mišpāḥâ*, "clan."[40]

The marriages within a *bêt ʾāb* were typically monogamous (Gen 2:24; Mal 2:14-16).[41] According to the Mishnah a man could have as many as five wives; if he were a king, he could have up to eighteen.[42] The Roman emperor Theodosius outlawed polygamy among the Jews in 393 CE.[43] It was not until the eleventh century CE that the Jewish tradition prohibited a Jewish man from having more than one wife.[44] In the Israelite tradition, unless a man were a king or the possessor of substantial wealth, the primary reason for having more than one wife seems to have been to secure the male offspring needed to keep his name alive.[45] In the time of the Judges, Elkanah had two wives, Hannah and Peninnah (1 Sam 1:2). Earlier, the patriarch Jacob had married both Leah and Rachel (Gen 29:15-30). The tradition is more concerned with the issue of legitimate offspring to carry on the father's name than it is with the intimacy of the relationship between husband and wife.[46] Surely intimacy was a factor in these relationships: for example, the husband of Michal weeps bitterly when David takes her away from him to include her in his royal harem (2 Sam 3:16); also the regulation against a husband turning away a woman whom he has married because he did not like her must have something

39. Lawrence Stager, "The Archaeology of the Family in Ancient Israel," *BASOR* 260 (1985): 1–35, at 20.

40. Smith, *The Religion of the Landless*, 98–99, 102, 115.

41. Leo Perdue, "The Israelite and Early Jewish Family: Summary and Conclusions," in *Families in Ancient Israel* (1997), 163–222, at 185; Meyers, *Exodus*, 199.

42. Blenkinsopp, "The Family in First Temple Israel," 64.

43. John J. Collins, "Marriage, Divorce, and Family in Second Temple Judaism," in *Families in Ancient Israel* (1997), 104–61, at 122.

44. Since the tenth century CE the rabbis have prohibited bigamy or polygamy under pain of excommunication (based on the *takkanah* of Rabbi Gershon b. Judah of Metz); see Menachem Elon, "Bigamy and Polygamy," *Encyclopedia Judaica*, 2d ed. (Detroit: Macmillan/Keter, 2007), 3:691–94, at 691.

45. Perdue, "Israelite and Early Jewish Family," 185.

46. Meyers, *Exodus*, 195–99; Jon Levenson, *Resurrection and the Restoration of Israel: The Ultimate Victory of the God of Life* (New Haven: Yale, 2006), 78–79.

to do with compatibility and intimacy (Deut 22:13; 24:1-4; Hos 2:14).[47] But the priority given to the question of legitimate offspring shows that the issue of immortality through perpetuation of the father's line was a greater concern in the tradition than the quality of the relationship between husband and wife.

If a husband and wife did not produce a male offspring, the biblical tradition seems to encourage means other than adoption for securing an heir.[48] In Gen 15:2-4 Abraham was resigned to adopting his household slave Eliezer as his heir. But as an alternative, Sarah gave Abraham her maidservant Hagar as a concubine who then gave birth to Ishmael as his son and heir (Gen 16:1-6, 15).[49] Another means to keep a man's name alive was to have a brother or male relative of a deceased man without a son have relations with the deceased man's wife in order to secure a male heir for him (Gen 38:6-11; Deut 25:5-10).[50] The importance of living on in one's own family was a vital concern in the Israelite tradition.

47. Richard Nelson, *Deuteronomy*, OTL (Louisville: Westminster John Knox, 2002), 287; Graham I. Davies, *Hosea* (Grand Rapids: Eerdmans, 1995), 78–79. Athalya Brenner, *The Intercourse of Knowledge: On Gendering Desire and 'Sexuality' in the Hebrew Bible*, Biblical Interpretation Series 26 (Leiden: Brill, 1997), 18, 29–30, 178, notes how, outside of the Song of Songs, reciprocity in married love is rarely expressed in the Hebrew Bible. On the intimacy in relationship of future brides and grooms in Sumer see Gwendolyn Leick, *Sex and Eroticism in Mesopotamian Literature* (London and New York: Routledge, 1994), 70–71.

48. Tikva Frymer-Kensky, "Israel," in *A History of Ancient Near Eastern Law* (2003), 2:975–1046, at 1015 [§5.2.4.4], notes that no laws or narratives describe an actual adoption in the OT. Jacob Milgrom, *Leviticus 17–22*, AB 3A (New York: Doubleday, 2000), 1787, says there was no institution of adoption in ancient Israel. However, Gen 48:5-6; Exod 2:10; Ruth 4:16-17 seem to refer to adoption (see Godfrey R. Driver and John C. Miles, *The Babylonian Laws*, vol. 1: *Legal Commentary* [Oxford: Clarendon Press, 1952], 384). In effect, adoption would genealogize an outsider into the family as if he or she were a blood relative; see Blenkinsopp, "The Family in First Temple Israel," 53.

49. Jon Berquist, *Controlling Corporeality: The Body and the Household in Ancient Israel* (New Brunswick, NJ: Rutgers University Press, 2002), 65, refrains from using terms like "polygamy, polyandry" in an effort to see the ancient Israelite household apart from modern models or preconceptions. He notes: "The dominant [Israelite] male had sexual access to the women of his household, and the household itself depended upon the sexual activities that would lead to procreation; otherwise the household could not keep up its numbers and thus guarantee its vitality as an economic and social unit. Thus, sexuality was constructed as the male's activity within the household, designed to maximize the household's fertility. A good head of household would father children with several women in the house, creating a household of increasing numbers and growing strength."

50. Perdue, "Israelite and Early Jewish Family," 187–88.

In premonarchic Israel the eldest son seems to have been charged with maintaining the ancestral cult.[51] The deceased ancestors were, as Karel van der Toorn puts it, "semigods."[52] However, from the Deuteronomic perspective the Israelites were not allowed to give offerings to their ancestors in return for favors (cf. Deut 18:9-14).[53] Certainly the male offspring was responsible for caring for his aged parents and for their burial. But once they had passed away it would appear that the proponents of the Deuteronomic code were trying to keep the Yahwistic worshipers from bringing them monthly offerings or performing other cultic actions designed to increase their happiness in the netherworld or to win their favor toward their living descendants (Deut 18:9-14).[54] Apart from Deuteronomy's strictures against communicating with the dead, the male heir was responsible for keeping the name of the father and his line alive. This notion of immortality by way of the family is persistent within the tradition and is consistent with the view of the identity of the individual as inseparable from that of the family. Even though the consciousness of the individual as a separate agent receives more attention in exilic times (Ezek 18:20; cf. Deut 24:16), the dominant picture is that an individual's identity is tied to that of his or her family.

With the emphasis on the father's line, the wife is regarded as an outsider who is brought into the patriarchal household.[55] It seems—if the viewpoint of the priestly circles toward the burial of the immediate family is taken into account—that this outsider status is never completely overcome. The priestly law dictates that a priest may participate in the funeral for his nuclear family: father, mother, brothers, and sisters, but

51. 1 Sam 28:13; Ps 106:28; Num 25:2; Isa 8:19-20; Theodore Lewis, "The Ancestral Estate (*naḥălat ʾelōhîm*) in 2 Samuel 14:16," *JBL* 110 (1991): 597–612, at 602–3, 607–8; Perdue, "Israelite and Early Jewish Family," 205–6.

52. Karel van der Toorn, "The Nature of the Biblical Teraphim in the Light of the Cuneiform Evidence," *CBQ* 52 (1990): 203–22, at 211.

53. Joseph Blenkinsopp, "Deuteronomy and the Politics of Post-Mortem Existence," *VT* 45 (1995): 1–16, esp. 7–10; van der Toorn, "The Nature of the Biblical Teraphim," 215–16. For a contrasting viewpoint on the status of the deceased ancestors as merely dead see Brian Schmidt, "Afterlife Beliefs: Memory as Immortality," *Near Eastern Archaeology* 63 (2000): 236–39; idem, *Israel's Beneficent Dead: Ancestor Cult and Necromancy in Ancient Israelite Religion and Tradition* (Winona Lake, IN: Eisenbrauns, 1996), 275, 286–87. Levenson, *Resurrection and the Restoration of Israel*, 62, states that there are no narratives describing the "legitimate feeding of the dead or sacrificing" to the ancestors in the Hebrew Bible and sees no evidence for this practice outside of Deut 26:14.

54. Blenkinsopp, "Deuteronomy and the Politics of Post-Mortem Existence," 10–15.

55. Joseph Blenkinsopp, "The Family in First Temple Israel," 59; see also Meyers, "The Family in Early Israel," 33–34; Berquist, *Controlling Corporeality*, 70.

not for his wife (Lev 21:1-4). When Ezekiel's wife dies he is instructed not to mourn for her (Ezek 24:15-18). Here this command promotes dissociation, since Ezekiel's wife stands as a symbolic parallel for the city of Jerusalem; however, this command is also in line with priestly practice, which keeps the wife removed by a degree from the rest of the nuclear family.

Ezra's prohibition of intermarriage points, however, to the strategic position the wife and mother holds in the nuclear family.[56] Her exclusive fidelity to her husband guarantees the legitimacy of her children as patrilineal offspring. Her fidelity to her husband's household would also be reflected in the way that she raised her children. It is this nurturing function that seems central to Ezra's concern about intermarriage (cf. Prov 1:8; 6:20; 23:22-25; 31:8-9).[57] If the mother is from a non-Jewish culture she will inevitably pass on to her children values from her own culture. If this happens consistently among a number of households, these households will remain Jewish in name only. Ezra took the drastic step of disbanding established marriages in the mid-fifth century BCE because he and his supporters regarded the level of assimilation of the Yehud community to the surrounding cultures to have passed the point at which Jewish identity could be maintained.[58]

One might wonder what happened in the marriage ritual that positioned the wife as one who had transferred from her father's house but yet was not completely assimilated into the house of her husband. The ritual appears to have been more a process than a legal event.[59] There was a period of betrothal in which the wife-to-be was treated as if she were off-limits to any other suitor (Deut 22:23-29). The marital union of the couple was not consummated until their sexual union.[60] The transfer of the bride from the father's house to the house of the groom was the

56. On woman as an ambiguous figure and mediating category in Genesis 2–3 see Yee, *Poor Banished Children of Eve*, 72.

57. Blenkinsopp, "The Family in First Temple Israel," 78; Olyan, *Rites and Rank*, 88, 101.

58. Zlotnick-Sivan, "The Silent Women of Yehud," 12–13.

59. Meyers, *Exodus*, 196; Victor P. Hamilton, "Marriage (OT and ANE)," *ABD* 4:566, notes that only in Ezek 16:8 and Mal 2:14 is marriage referred to as a covenant.

60. On sexual union as bonding man and woman into a unit see Berquist, *Controlling Corporeality*, 59–60. Blenkinsopp, "The Family in First Temple Israel," 59–60, notes that Deut 22:28-29 updates Exod 22:16-17 such that a father loses his discretionary power on whether to have his daughter marry one who has seduced or raped her, thus indicating, from the Deuteronomic perspective, that an irrevocable bonding has occurred through sexual union.

public ceremony that marked the time at which the marriage was about to be consummated. The notion of a marriage contract may have taken the form of a pledge between the couple; this can be inferred from YHWH's words to the nation of Israel as his spouse in Hosea 2:21: "I will betroth you to myself forever, I will betroth you with integrity and justice and with tenderness and love." This initial step in the marriage process would have involved the payment of the bridewealth (*mōhar*).[61] Then later YHWH says: "I will say to No-People-of-Mine, 'You are my people,' and he [Israel] will answer, 'You are my God'" (Hos 2:24). These declarations by YHWH and Israel reflect the pledges made in "adoption, marriage, and covenant-making in general."[62] The recording of the marriage contract in the Aramaic texts from Elephantine in the fifth century BCE shows that the legal dimension of the marriage ritual was particularly important with regard to the dowry,[63] which was the wife's form of social security in the event the marriage failed. If she were returned to her father's house, the dowry was to go along with her. If her father had passed away and the wife was at the point of death, her dowry could be inherited by her children.[64] However, in the biblical texts the dowry is rarely mentioned.[65]

Divorce was the act of reversing the marriage ritual. Deuteronomy 24:1-4 indicates that a document was issued, apparently stipulating the grounds on which the divorce occurred and so dealing with the issues of dowry and bridewealth (*mōhar*).[66] If an *ʿerwat dābār*, "an impurity" (Deut 24:1) could be stipulated, the husband could dismiss his wife without returning her dowry to her. If he divorced her simply because he hated her, then presumably he would have had to return her dowry.[67] The law states that the husband cannot remarry his first wife if she has contracted a second marriage. Carolyn Pressler argues that this Deuteronomic stance regards "the purity and integrity of the family" as more important than "male prerogative."[68]

61. Francis I. Anderson and David Noel Freedman, *Hosea*, AB 24 (Garden City, NY: Doubleday, 1980), 283; Blenkinsopp, "The Family in First Temple Israel," 59.

62. Anderson and Freedman, *Hosea*, 289.

63. Collins, "Marriage, Divorce, and Family in Second Temple Judaism," 109–10.

64. Ibid., 114–15.

65. Blenkinsopp, "The Family in First Temple Israel," 59.

66. Ibid., 64–65; Nelson, *Deuteronomy*, 287.

67. Frymer-Kensky, "Israel," 2:1010 [§5.1.4.1]; Nelson, *Deuteronomy*, 287–88.

68. Carolyn Pressler, *The View of Women Found in the Deuteronomic Family Laws*, BZAW 216 (Berlin and New York: de Gruyter, 1993), 46.

The prophet Malachi in the first half of the fifth century BCE proclaims that YHWH hates divorce (Mal 2:16).[69] Collins notes that Malachi departs from the Israelite tradition in condemning the husband for breaking the marriage covenant with his wife.[70] The unity of the marriage relationship is understood here on the basis of Genesis 2:24, in which the husband and wife become one flesh (Mal 2:15). The goal of this union is the production of "God-given offspring" (*zeraʿ ʾĕlōhîm*, Mal 2:15). But within Yehud there apparently are those who are divorcing their wives and marrying foreign wives (Mal 2:11). Malachi condemns such a practice as an abomination (*tôʿēbâ*, Mal 2:11). He characterizes the foreign wife as "a daughter of an alien god" (*bat ʾēl nēkār*, Mal 2:11). Thus the threat that the foreign wife poses is that she will introduce the worship of a foreign deity into the household (cf. 1 Kgs 11:1-8; Neh 13:26).[71] However, unlike Ezra, Malachi does not call for the dismissal of the foreign wife. Instead, he focuses on the indissolubility of the marriage bond, a stance unique within the Israelite tradition.[72]

The pivotal position of the wife within the family is reflected in the laws of adultery. If the wife is unfaithful, the paternity of the children in the family will be unknown. Thus adultery is a direct attack on those relationships that are fundamental to the household and to the entire social order of Israel.[73] Therefore adultery was regarded as a capital crime in which the offenders must be removed from the community (Lev 20:10; Deut 22:22); if the offender was a betrothed virgin she was to be stoned by the community (Deut 22:20-21).[74] From the perspective of the *paterfamilias* toward the male adulterer, this transgression was a form of theft that cut deeply into his life. Thus Prov 6:29-35 warns young men to steer clear of such a transgression:

> So it is with the man who cohabits with his neighbor's wife: no one who touches her will escape punishment. People do not show contempt for the thief when in hunger he steals to revive himself. But

69. Andrew E. Hill, *Malachi*, AB 25D (New York: Doubleday, 1998), 221–23; Daniel Block, "Marriage and Family in Ancient Israel," in *Marriage and Family in the Biblical World*, ed. Ken M. Campbell, 33–102 (Downers Grove, IL: InterVarsity Press, 2003), at 51–52.

70. Collins, "Marriage, Divorce, and Family in Second Temple Judaism," 124.

71. Ibid., 123–24; Gary N. Knoppers, "Sex, Religion, and Politics: The Deuteronomist on Intermarriage," *HAR* 14 (1994): 121–41, at 134–35.

72. Collins, "Marriage, Divorce, and Family in Second Temple Judaism," 125; Hill, *Malachi*, 223.

73. Berquist, *Controlling Corporeality*, 45, 71, 78, 80.

74. Pressler, *The View of Women Found in the Deuteronomic Family Laws*, 30.

> when he is caught, he must repay seven times the amount and give up all his household possessions. But the man who commits adultery lacks intelligence; the one who does this destroys himself. He will receive a humiliating beating and his disgrace will not be wiped away. Indeed, jealousy incites the husband such that he shows no pity on the day of vengeance. He will not consider any compensation and does not want a larger gift.

The fact that the husband will accept no compensation for such a transgression indicates that the wife holds a key position within the relationships in the household, one that goes far beyond what the category of property signifies.[75]

The Pressure of the State System on the Household

Ezra was concerned about the integrity of the community of Yehud, "the men of Benjamin and Judah" (Ezra 10:9). These were heads of the households whose lineage could be traced through the genealogy of Ezra 2; Nehemiah 7. The individuals of these households or their ancestors had been through the experience of the exile and so were among those qualified to be part of the restored community of Yehud.[76] But intermarriage with foreign women and mixing with the people of the land diluted the community and undermined its focus. Thus these heads of households in Yehud were summoned to Jerusalem. Anyone who did not appear within three days was presumed guilty of violating Ezra's decree against intermarriage and thus his movable property (*rĕkûš*, 10:8) was to be confiscated. When they had assembled on the twentieth day of the ninth month Ezra decreed that the foreign wives and their children were to be expelled (10:10-11). But since it was a large assembly and cold rain was falling on them in the temple square, it was proposed that a tribunal be appointed to adjudicate which families had foreign wives (10:12-14). A group of four named individuals protested—it appears they believed

75. Block, "Marriage and Family in Ancient Israel," 63. On the injury to "self" (*nepeš*) that a man suffers by committing adultery see Richard Clifford, *Proverbs*, OTL (Louisville: Westminster John Knox, 1999), 81.

76. Japhet, "People and Land in the Restoration Period," 111; Grabbe, *Ezra–Nehemiah*, 137. Charles E. Carter, "The Province of Yehud in the Post-Exilic Period: Soundings in Site Distribution and Demography," in *Second Temple Studies 2* (1994), 106–45, at 109–10, notes that there is little difference between the Golah lists in Ezra 2:1-67, which gives for Yehud a population total of 7,273, and Neh 7:4-69, which gives a population total of 7,430.

this proposal was simply a stalling tactic (10:15).[77] Yet Ezra accepted the proposal and appointed the magistrates who would form the tribunal (10:16). The tribunal completed its work by the first day of the first month (10:17) and reported the households with foreign wives in the list in Ezra 10:18-44.

The intrusiveness of Ezra and his supporters into the households of the people of Yehud subordinates the family to the state in a way that calls into question the integrity of the family. These families, in which the foreign wives were mothers of children, were to be broken apart. Nowhere in the Pentateuchal traditions was a law against intermarriage universalized. Ezra was not allowing these foreign women and their children to convert; he was treating them as if they were members of the nations that had been placed under the ban in Deut 7:1-4. There the argument was that intermarrying would lead to syncretism—a blending of cultures as well as of religious practices (Exod 34:16; Deut 7:3-4; Proverbs 1–9). Here the rationale seems to be the same.[78] The removal of the foreign wives and their children is the elimination from the community of foreign elements that are regarded as dangerous to the integrity of the Yahwistic community.[79] In the eyes of Ezra's supporters these women and children were never members of the covenant community, so the juridical action by Ezra's tribunal can be more appropriately labeled an annulment of marriages rather than an excommunication of covenant violators.[80] Nevertheless, the action of the husbands in marrying foreign wives is labeled a *maʿal*, "apostasy" (Ezra 9:2, 4; cf. Ezek 14:13; 15:8; 17:20; 18:24; 20:27; 39:26), which highlights the danger such marriages pose, from Ezra's perspective, to the covenant relationship.[81]

A precedent for the intrusion of the state into the affairs of the family occurred within the Josianic reform. At the time of the centralization of

77. Dor, "The Composition of the Episode of the Foreign Women in Ezra IX–X," 35–36.

78. Japhet, "People and Land in the Restoration Period, " 113; Blenkinsopp, "The Family in First Temple Israel," 78.

79. On the *ʾiššâ zārâ* of Prov 7:5 as an unmarried "foreign woman" who will dilute the social cohesion of Yehudite society see Herbert Marbury, "The Strange Woman in Persian Yehud: A Reading of Proverbs 7," in *Approaching Yehud: New Approaches to the Study of the Persian Period*, ed. Jon L. Berquist, 167–82 (Atlanta: Society of Biblical Literature, 2007); see especially 175–76.

80. Cf. Japhet, "Law and 'the Law' in Ezra–Nehemiah," in her *From the Rivers of Babylon* (2006), 137–68, at 147.

81. Becking, "Law as Expression of Religion," 29, states that *maʿal* implies that "human conduct is assessed as a transgression of a divinely given moral code."

the cult in Jerusalem and the elimination of other cultic sites in the land (Deut 12:2-7; 2 Kgs 23:4-20), the members of families were exhorted to be on their guard against any sign of apostasy among the people of Judah:

> If your brother—the son of your father or[82] of your mother—or your son or daughter, or your beloved wife, or your close friend secretly tries to entice you, saying: "Come, let us serve other gods" . . . you must not give way to him, nor listen to him. You must show him no pity nor spare him. Do not conceal him. Instead you must kill him. Let your hand be the first against him in putting him to death, followed by the hand of all the people. You must stone him to death. (Deut 13:7-11)

The severity of this command belongs to the order of hyperbole. As such the exhortation has as its objective to make the point that worship of deities other than YHWH cannot be tolerated in the land. Members of households must be committed to exclusive worship of YHWH such that they would be willing to eliminate members of their nuclear family who are non-observant.[83] The second round of execution by communal stoning shows that such false worship defiles the entire community and renders it vulnerable to punishment by YHWH. Nevertheless, one wonders how such a militant approach to maintaining the purity of the community might have arisen. Its locus appears to be the YHWH-alone worshipers within the Deuteronomic circles, militants who later can trace their roots to Elijah (1 Kgs 18:40).[84]

Such intolerance prioritizes the purity of the communal environment over the freedom of the individual conscience. Respect for individual choice is shown in a number of key passages in the Deuteronomic corpus: the Decalogue (Deut 5:6-21), the Shema (Deut 6:4-5), the commitment to the covenant (Josh 24:16-24). Yet the individual in the Deuteronomic corpus is never conceived as autonomous, but always as heteronomous.[85] The question before the individual is which external law he or she will

82. With the Samaritan Pentateuch and LXX add *ben ʾābîkā ʾô*.

83. Nelson, *Deuteronomy*, 165, 171–72. Albertz, *A History of Israelite Religion*, 2:411, notes that the Deuteronomic reform recognized the crucial role the family plays in sustaining the religious traditions.

84. Bernhard Lang, *Monotheism and the Prophetic Minority* (Sheffield: Almond Press, 1983), 29–30. Nelson, *Deuteronomy*, 168, describes the mind-set of Deuteronomy 13 as paralleling that of the Assyrian treaty documents that called for absolute loyalty of the subjects to the overlord.

85. Ibid., 11–12.

obey. The choices an individual makes within a community are not isolated and self-contained; they have an impact on other members within the community. It is this sense that human lives are intertwined that spurs on an attitude of intolerance within the YHWH-alone circles. They commit to a clear standard of worshiping YHWH alone and hold one another accountable for it.[86]

Ezra and "the tremblers" are worshipers of YHWH-alone. However, the community of Yehud in the fifth century does not seem to have committed to the same strict standard of behavior in worship of YHWH-alone. They appear to allow for a measure of pluralism in the manifestation of their religious beliefs. They have compromised on the exclusive worship of YHWH in order to adapt to the social and political realities of a land in which other peoples reside.[87] But Ezra, with the authorization of the Persian emperor, intends to shift the communal environment so that the worshipers of YHWH alone can form a distinctive community in the land. One of the first actions he takes after promulgating his version of the Torah is to call for the purge of the foreign wives and their children: he aims to change the environment in which the Yahwistic community lives and worships.[88]

The families with foreign wives and children seem to be asked to make an impossible sacrifice. In the Genesis narrative Sarah drives out Hagar and Ishmael (Gen 16:6; 21:10-14). Divorce, although infrequently attested, was an option for marriages that had been corrupted or were no longer working (Deut 24:1-4). But this large-scale dismissal of wives and children by a state official seems to be a serious infringement on the freedom of the *paterfamilias* to govern his household. Even in pre-state tribal Israel the family was part of a larger network of clans and tribes. The *paterfamilias* with his household was not an autonomous unit. When the Israelite elders opted to have a king and his state apparatus govern them (1 Sam 8:4-9), they opened the door to the possibility of oppressive measures by the state. Now in the postexilic world in which the government of Yehud is a unit within the larger Persian empire, the family is subject to the intrusive authority of a foreign monarchy.[89]

86. Ibid., 10.

87. William Horbury, "Extirpation and Excommunication," *VT* 35 (1985): 13–38, at 20, 26–27.

88. Bob Becking, "Law as Expression of Religion," 31; idem, "Continuity and Community: The Belief System of the Book of Ezra," in *The Crisis of Israelite Religion: Transformation of Religious Tradition in Exilic and Post-exilic Times*, ed. Bob Becking and Marjo Korpel, 256–75 (Leiden: Brill, 1999), at 270–71.

89. Rainer Albertz, "The Thwarted Restoration," 13–14; Smith-Christopher, "The Mixed Marriage Crisis," 245.

In his communal confession of sin in Ezra 9:3-15, Ezra makes clear that he regards the Persian government as an instrument of YHWH (v. 9). Ezra acknowledges that Israel's ancestors have been disobedient to YHWH from the earliest times; eventually this led to the removal of Israel and Judah from their land (v. 7). Against this history of infidelity, Ezra proclaims:

> But now, recently, there is mercy from the Lord our God who has left us a remnant and given us a holding in his holy place so as to revive us and give us some relief in our servitude. For we are servants, but our God has not abandoned us in our servitude. He has shown loyal love to us in the presence of the Persian kings in giving us the opportunity to rebuild the house of our God and restore its ruins and in giving us a stone wall in Judah and Jerusalem. (Ezra 9:8-9)

By Ezra's stance of acknowledging his solidarity in sin with the Israelites throughout the generations and praising YHWH for giving them another chance through the assistance of the Persian government he appears to try to build a bridge to those *patresfamiliae* from whom he is asking a tremendous sacrifice: the expulsion of their wives and children. This harsh, intrusive measure would seem to be a deathblow to most of these households. Yet Ezra does not seem to want to drive away these *patresfamiliae*, but rather to encourage them to follow his example of repentance, which in turn is an imitation of the example of Moses (Exod 32:30-34; 33:12-17).[90]

The renunciation of family relationships that Ezra asks of these *patresfamiliae* in what Ezra frames as a time of emergency in the Yahwistic community seems extreme. If they accede to Ezra's request, many of them will forfeit not only their intimate relationships but also their hope for the future. Some of them could probably start another family, but for many of them this renunciation probably meant an end to their family and to the expectation of living on in their descendants indefinitely. For these latter, Ezra's request amounted to a life of celibacy lived for the sake of the purity and integrity of the Yahwistic community.

Even though Ezra had the backing of the Persian government in 458 BCE, he was expected to interact with the Yehud community in a constructive way. Rebellion in Egypt and many years of war with Greece made the region of the eastern Mediterranean a buffer zone between

90. On the self-effacing profile of the literati of fifth-century Jerusalem who glorified revered figures from the foundational period see Ehud ben Zvi, "What Is New in Yehud?" 41, 46.

Persia and its foes.[91] It may be that Ezra's mission lasted only for one year because he stirred up so much opposition that the imperial authorities recalled him.[92]

Summary

The issue of intermarriage struck at the heart of the Israelite household. Ezra aimed to reform marriage practices in Yehud in order to reinstate the centrality of the command that worship of YHWH alone cannot be compromised in the community of Yehud. The problem of mixed marriages was primarily an issue of the clash of religious cultures. The Yahwistic ethos was intolerant of the worship of other deities, whereas henotheistic communities tolerated the worship of other deities as long as their chief deity received primary attention.[93] Ezra fought against the syncretistic attitude that was seeping into the community of Yehud via the foreign wives and mothers who were the primary formators of the children.

Ezra is a paradoxical hero in fifth-century Yehud. He takes a hard line and an aggressive stance in favor of the dissolution of mixed marriages, yet he does so by identifying himself as a sinner along with his ancestors and the *patresfamiliae* with foreign wives. He is uncompromising on the importance of purifying the community of influences that erode the ethos of worship of YHWH alone. Although property and space are essential for the embodied character of the household, even more important for the viability of the household is its culture.[94]

Ezra persists in fighting this uphill, seemingly no-win battle because it is vital to the Yahwistic community. His role as an agent of the central government making demands on the culture of the Israelite households is in line with the centralizing program of the Deuteronomic movement. The intrusion of the state into the affairs of the household was feared at the time the monarchy was inaugurated in Israel (1 Sam 8:11-18). At that time, according to 1 Samuel 8, a primary reason offered by the elders for requesting the king was the problem of corruption in the existing tribal government (1 Sam 8:3). A royal government was put forward as offering a corrective to such corruption. Ezra draws on the authority of the central

91. Albertz, "The Thwarted Restoration," 14.

92. Blenkinsopp, *Ezra–Nehemiah*, 179.

93. Mark S. Smith, *The Origins of Biblical Monotheism: Israel's Polytheistic Background and the Ugaritic Texts* (New York: Oxford University Press, 2001), 78.

94. Becking, "Continuity and Community," 256–58.

government to bring about reform in the households of Yehud. The actual numbers of households that followed through on Ezra's directions are not recorded. What is more important, though, is his championing of the principle of worship of YHWH-alone as an indispensable element of the Yahwistic culture of the household.[95] The individual decision to worship YHWH is crucial, but this decision is made on the basis of the formative environment of the household from which the individual emerges. The *patresfamiliae* who acceded to Ezra's demands undertook a path of sexual renunciation and distancing from household relationships that bears some analogies with that of a life of celibacy: a sacrifice made for the integrity of the relationships in social units centered on YHWH.

Mesopotamia: Intermarriage as an Element in the Evolution of Urban Culture

In Babylonia in the fifth century BCE under Persian rule there were a number of ethnic enclaves, including the Jews, the Tyrians, the Greeks, and the Egyptians. Some of these foreign communities began as a result of trade, others as a consequence of deportation by the Assyrians or Babylonians, and still others through migration or the slave trade.[96] The general policy of the Persian emperors to tolerate diversity and encourage the development of local laws and customs laid the groundwork for Babylonians and other ethnic groups to cooperate with the Persians.[97] Babylonian enclaves sprang up in Persepolis and other Persian cities; they were granted considerable freedom to pursue commercial and artistic opportunities. An examination of patronymics seems to show that intermarriage took place between a number of Persians and Babylonians.

95. Ibid., 270–71.

96. Matthew W. Stolper, "Archive of Murashû," *ABD* 4:927–28.

97. Jon Berquist, *Judaism in Persia's Shadow* (Minneapolis: Fortress Press, 1995), 53–55, 57. Paul-Alain Beaulieu, "A Finger in Every Pie: The Institutional Connections of a Family of Entrepreneurs in Neo-Babylonian Larsa," in *Interdependency of Institutions and Private Entrepreneurs*, MOS Studies 2, ed. A. C. V. M. Bongenaar, 43–72 (Leiden and Istanbul: Nederlands Historisch-Archaeologisch Instituut te Istanbul, 2000), at 63–64, claims that the archives of Itti-Šamaš-balāṭu of Larsa reveal that the business activities of his son Arad-Šamaš dropped precipitously with Cyrus's conquest of Babylon in 539 BCE. However, Larsa was a marginal area in the sixth century BCE and the general picture, according to Muhammed Dandamayev, "An Age of Privatization in Ancient Mesopotamia," in *Privatization in the Ancient Near East and Classical World*, ed. Michael Hudson and Baruch A. Levine, 197–210 (Cambridge, MA: Peabody Museum of Archaeology and Ethnology, Harvard University, 1996), at 198, is that private and temple households played leading roles in the sixth-century economy and not the Persian emperor.

Even though it is debated whether patronymics provide a reliable indicator of ethnicity,[98] it would seem possible that some of the Babylonian individuals with Persian elements in their names married into Persian households to advance their interests.[99]

Intermarriage between various ethnic and cultural groups regularly occurred throughout Mesopotamian history, even though endogamy was the more common practice.[100] In the third millennium a text known as "The Marriage of Martu" symbolizes a political alliance between the seminomadic herders and the citizens of the Sumerian city of Ninab as a marriage proposal from the herder Martu to a certain Numushda for the hand of his daughter Adnigkidu.[101] The characters in this myth are gods of the tribal group and of the city dwellers. After the god Martu requests from his mother that she find him a wife (ll. 42-43), she advises him to follow his heart (ll. 47-48). So he goes to a beer festival in Ninab and participates in wrestling matches in which he vanquishes his opponents, to the delight of the god Numushda (ll. 65-76). In choosing a prize for his victory, Martu turns down presents of silver and gold and instead requests the hand of Numushda's daughter Adnigkidu in marriage (ll. 81-82). Numushda agrees; however, a friend of Adnigkidu protests about the uncivilized ways of the herder: "He eats uncooked food; he has no house while he lives; he is not interred when he dies; my friend—how is it that you would marry Martu!" (ll. 136-39).[102] This marriage points to the tensions that accompanied the ongoing interactions between city-dwellers and herders in Mesopotamian society, a dynamic important to the dimorphic society of Mesopotamian cities.[103]

98. Pierre Briant, *From Cyrus to Alexander: A History of the Persian Empire*, trans. Peter T. Daniels (Winona Lake, IN: Eisenbrauns, 2002), 83, 724.

99. Briant, *From Cyrus to Alexander*, 334, 724, notes that Xenophon reported that the Spartan king Agesilaus persuaded the Paphlygonian king Otys to marry the daughter of the Persian Spithridates because of her noble pedigree and not for her beauty (*Hellenica* VI.1.6-7).

100. Karel van der Toorn, *Family Religion in Babylonia, Syria and Israel: Continuity and Change in the Forms of Religious Life*, Studies in the History and Culture of the Ancient Near East 7 (Leiden: Brill, 1996), 22, 24–26.

101. Samuel Noah Kramer, "The Marriage of Martu," in *Bar-Ilan Studies in Assyriology: Dedicated to Pinhas Artzi*, ed. Jacob Klein and Aaron Skaist, 11–27 (Ramat Gan: Bar-Ilan University Press, 1990), at 11.

102. Translation from Kramer, "The Marriage of Martu," 11–27, at 20–21.

103. Michael B. Rowton, "Enclosed Nomadism," *JESHO* 17 (1974): 1–30, at 3, 7–8, 17, 22, 27–30; Anne Porter, "The Dynamics of Death: Ancestors, Pastoralism, and the Origins of a Third-Millennium City in Syria," *BASOR* 325 (2002): 1–36, at 6. Van der Toorn, *Family Religion in Babylonia*, 38, states that city-dwellers tended to characterize the Amorites as

In the seventh century BCE, Babylonian society consisted of urban residents, rural farmers, pastoralists on the inland steppe, and inhabitants of southern marshes. The urban residents were the longstanding inhabitants known as Akkadians; they would identify themselves by their family and town. But the tribal people who inhabited the steppe and the marshes would identify themselves by the tribe to which they belonged, of which the main groups were the Chaldeans and the Arameans.[104] The Akkadians were the bearers of the ancient culture and had formed a society over the generations that can be described as a melting pot.[105] However, the tribal groups, whose genealogies highlight blood relationship, were the restive element within the society in the seventh century that resisted the efforts of the Assyrians to subdue Babylon and eventually produced the leaders of the powerful NB kingdom—Nabopolassar (625–605) and Nebuchadrezzar II (604–562). This creative tension between tribal and urban culture in the seventh century mirrors a number of the dynamics of the herder/urban-dweller relationship in the third and second millennia, which are succinctly captured in the myth of "The Marriage of Martu."[106]

The Persian government does not seem to have promoted the intermarriage of its officials with influential local inhabitants. Briant notes that there is a surprising absence of intermarriages of Persians of any rank with individuals of other ethnic groups.[107] Where marriage plays a significant role in Persian politics is in the impact it has on the ranking of Persian aristocrats vis-à-vis one another. If a high-ranking aristocrat is permitted to marry a daughter of the king, his rank rises noticeably. However, such marriages with the royal family did not grant an individual any claim on the throne.[108] Succession struggles in Persia were not so readily resolved by an appeal to genealogies or marital privileges.

---

uncivilized as a way of using them as an antitype that helped the city-dwellers define themselves. On the marriage of the shepherd Dumuzi to the city-dweller Inanna in the love songs of Dumuzi and Inanna see Leick, *Sex and Eroticism in Mesopotamian Literature*, 82–83.

104. Grant Frame, *Babylonia 689–627 B.C.: A Political History* (Istanbul: Nederlands Historisch-Archaeologisch Instituut te Istanbul, 1992), 32.

105. Ibid., 34.

106. Rowton, "Enclosed Nomadism," 29–30; idem, "Urban Autonomy in a Nomadic Environment," *JNES* 32 (1973): 201–15, at 202–3, 210.

107. Briant, *From Cyrus to Alexander*, 83, 501; Frame, *Babylonia 689–627 B.C.*, 34–35; John A. Brinkman, *Prelude to Empire: Babylonian Society and Politics, 747–726 B.C.* (Philadelphia: University Museum, 1984), 53, 95.

108. Briant, *From Cyrus to Alexander*, 309.

The Hero's Battle to Bring Genealogy and Local Tradition to a New Synthesis

Within Babylonia during the Persian period (538–333 BCE), the canonical cosmogonic myth *Enūma Elish* appears to have been recited regularly at the New Year's festival in the Esagila in Babylon and at Eanna in Uruk.[109] This myth narrates how intergenerational struggles among the family of the gods lead to a reconfiguration of the hierarchy among the gods.[110] The vibrant, dynamic components of the divine family are the younger gods, but their "noise" disturbs the couple Apsu and Tiāmat.[111] When Apsu, with the assistance of his vizier Mummu, persuades Tiāmat that they should do away with the younger gods, Ea intervenes and by means of a magical spell subdues Apsu and kills him. But such a measure is only provisional, for Tiāmat is now without a spouse and is troubled by the activities of the younger gods. Later, when the young hero Marduk, son of Ea and Damkina, confronts Tiāmat in battle and counters the deceptive magic of her spells, he says to her:

> Why are you friendly outwardly, while inwardly plotting to go war? Although the sons made demands and showed disrespect to their fathers, should you, who bore them, refuse to be merciful? You named Kingu your partner. You established sovereign authority for him, even though not destined for him. Against Anshar, the king of the gods, you sought to do evil. And against the gods of my fathers, you have been determined to do evil. (*EE* IV:77-84)

In his rhetoric Marduk categorizes Tiāmat as a threat against his ancestral house. He regards this "feminine other" as a threat to the viability of his divine household, whose generations are traced from (1) Lahmu and Lahamu to (2) Anshar and Kishar to (3) Anu/Anshar to (4) Ea and Damkina to (5) Marduk. Marduk defeats Tiāmat and saves his ancestral

109. Mark E. Cohen, *Cultic Calendars* (Bethesda, MD: Capital Decisions Limited, 1993), 440; Beate Pongratz-Leisten, *Ina Šulmi Irub: Die kulttopographische und ideologische Programmatik der akītu-Prozession in Babylonien und Assyrien im 1. Jahrtausend v. Chr.* (Mainz: Philipp von Zabern, 1994), 11; Julye Bidmead, *The Akītu Festival: Religious Continuity and Royal Legitimation in Mesopotamia* (Piscataway, NJ: Gorgias, 2002), 94–96; Jacob Klein, "Akitu," *ABD* 1:138–39.

110. Rivkah Harris, "The Conflict of Generations in Ancient Mesopotamian Myths," *Comparative Studies in Society and History* 34 (1992): 621–35, at 630–31; eadem, *Gender and Aging in Mesopotamia* (Norman: University of Oklahoma Press, 2000), 74–75; F. A. M. Wiggermann, "Theologies, Priests, and Worship in Ancient Mesopotamia," *CANE*, 1857–70, at 1868–69.

111. Harris, *Gender and Aging in Mesopotamia*, 84–85, describes Tiāmat as a young woman in childbearing years when the scheme to eliminate the younger gods was first proposed, and so she opposed it; later as she grew older, she sought to avenge the death of Apsu.

household.[112] Subsequently Marduk secures concessions from the other gods so that he will be able to wield sovereign power independent of the assembly of the gods. The justification for such a rise in power among the gods is the high-risk action he undertakes on behalf of his ancestral household. Without such a sacrifice for the common good, Marduk seems to fight merely to gain political power.[113]

Ea and Marduk respond to the threat to the community posed by the marriage alliances of Tiāmat with Apsu and Kingu. Tiāmat has given birth to numerous composite creatures to be fierce fighters in her army, which she places under the command of her husband/lover Kingu. Her "marriages" (or liaisons with her lovers) are an important component in her drive for power, whereas for Marduk marriage plays no strategic role in his rise to earthly power—other than the fact that he was born from the union of Ea and Damkina.[114] Marduk's attention is focused on defending against the wiles of the "feminine other" and securing the well-being of the patriarchal household of the gods. Marduk reconfigures political power within the household of the gods with the rationale that he is preserving the household (*EE* IV:81-85).[115] His revolutionary political and military actions are intended to be seen as maintaining the age-old order by securing control over "destinies" (*šīmātu*) in his role as patron of magic.[116]

The Organic Character of the Hereditary Mesopotamian Household

The household was a basic socioeconomic unit in Mesopotamian society.[117] Because humans are constrained by their basic bodily needs

112. Kai Alexander Metzler, "Tod, Weiblichkeit und Ästhetik im Mesopotamischen Weltschöpfungsepos *Enūma elîš*, " in *Sex and Gender in the Ancient Near East: Proceedings of the 47th Rencontre Assyriologique Internationale, Helsinki, July 2–6, 2001*, ed. Simo Parpola and Robert M. Whiting, 393–411 (Helsinki: Neo-Assyrian Text Corpus Project, 2002), at 395–96, 406.

113. Wim van Binsbergen and Frans Wiggermann, "Magic in History: A Theoretical Perspective, and Its Application to Ancient Mesopotamia," in *Mesopotamian Magic: Textual, Historical, and Interpretative Perspectives*, Ancient Magic and Divination 1, ed. Tzvi Abusch and Karel van der Toorn, 3–34 (Groningen: Styx, 1999), at 23; note how Marduk's success in gaining the Tablets of Destiny will enable him to alter destinies and so to keep the cosmos configured in a way favorable to the Mesopotamians and their gods.

114. Metzler, "Tod, Weiblichkeit und Ästhetik," 398.

115. Richard Clifford, *Creation Accounts in the Ancient Near East and in the Bible*, CBQMS 26 (Washington, DC: Catholic Biblical Association of America, 1994), 91, 93.

116. Binsbergen and Wiggermann, "Magic in History," 28–29.

117. Van der Toorn, *Family Religion in Babylonia*, 20. A. Leo Oppenheim, *Ancient Mesopotamia: Portrait of a Dead Civilization*, rev. ed. (Chicago: University of Chicago Press, 1977),

for food, clothing, and shelter, they typically secure these necessities within the cooperative context of a household. Property is an essential component of a household. Its fundamental character is revealed in the practice of debt slavery as described in the *Code of Hammurapi* (*CH*):[118]

> If an obligation seizes a man with the result that he sells his wife, his son, and his daughter or gives them into debt-slavery, they shall work in the house of their buyer or master for three years. In the fourth year, their release is to be carried out. (§117)

In times of financial crisis the head of the household sells his labor resource in order to pay his indebtedness.[119] Economically this is logical. Nevertheless, it reveals the vulnerability of humans in that the relationships of the household are not an absolute guarantee that one will be able to remain within that household. The demands of physical necessity must be met, even if this calls for the absence of wife and children from the home to work in another context. The sacrifice of three years of their lives from the family shows how the material dimension of life intrudes into the relational context of the family and shapes the identity of the family in significant ways. The limitation of debt slavery to three years, which seems generous in contrast to the limit of six years in ancient Israel (Exod 21:2), indicates how the tradition informing the *CH* wanted to minimize this intrusion into the relationships of the household.[120]

Debt slavery treats the members of the household as if they were atoms, that is, units that retain their identity and worth if detached from

---

113–14, reconstructs the place of the household in the ancient Mesopotamian city as analogous to that of the household in the Greek cities of the fifth and fourth centuries BCE; see also Marc van de Mieroop, *The Ancient Mesopotamian City* (Oxford and New York: Oxford University Press, 1999), 109–13.

118. Muhammed A. Dandamaev, *Slavery in Babylonia: From Nabopolassar to Alexander the Great (626–331 BC)*, rev. ed., trans. Victoria Powell; ed. Marvin Powell and David Weisberg (DeKalb, IL: Northern Illinois University Press, 1984), 103, 157–60, notes that debt slavery diminished markedly in the NB period vis-à-vis the OB and OA periods; if a debtor was not able to settle with his creditor he was subject to a workhouse or prison maintained by temples or wealthy households.

119. Driver and Miles, *The Babylonian Laws*, 1:217, state that the sale of a wife or child in *CH* 117 can be negotiated either *ana kaspim* (i.e., as a sale for silver) or *ana kiššātim* (i.e., as a pledge that can be redeemed).

120. Ibid., 1:221. Samuel Greengus, "Legal and Social Institutions of Ancient Mesopotamia," *CANE*, 469–84, at 478, notes that there is "no evidence that this law was observed" in Hammurapi's reign or thereafter. With regard to Israel, Étan Levine, "Biblical Women's Marital Rights," *Proceedings of the American Academy for Jewish Research* 63 (1997–2001): 87–135, at 89–90, notes that the Israelite wife was never sold into slavery.

their original context and transferred into a new one.[121] However, the typical individual in Mesopotamian society was not imagined apart from the family; his or her identity was bound to the family and could not be detached from this relational context without diminishing it.[122] From conception to birth to the time of weaning to young adulthood the child depends on the parents and is nurtured not only physically but also socially and psychologically. What seems so obvious, yet bears repeated attention, is the way physical reality challenges the members of the family to care for one another and to make sacrifices that shape the tone and texture of their household environment.

In Mesopotamia there was typically a sizeable disparity between the ages of the two spouses. Women frequently married at the age of fourteen to nineteen, whereas men waited until they were nearly thirty.[123] Marriage was a relational concern of the household much more so than of the individual. The father or brother of the bride would negotiate with the father of the groom or with the groom himself.[124] In terms of social status and economics, marriage was a significant event between two households.[125] The bride would leave her father's household to become a resident of her husband's or father-in-law's household. The *terḫatum* ("bridewealth") paid by the groom can be seen as a symbolic sum that honored the sacrifice

121. Driver and Miles, *The Babylonian Laws*, 1:219–20, seem to regard the wife and children of a family as the property of the householder, for they say that "it is indeed remarkable that in the Laws there is no explicit provision making the debtor liable in his own person but only in his property"; in *CH* 53-54 the enslaved one is punished for negligence and not as a way of repaying a debt.

122. Van der Toorn, *Family Religion in Babylonia*, 26. Van de Mieroop, *The Ancient Mesopotamian City*, 107, notes that first-millennium Babylonian texts consistently identify every person with the following three elements: "personal name 1, son of personal name 2, descendant of personal name 3; for instance Iddin-Marduk, son of Iqīsha, descendant of Nūr-Sin." He argues that this genealogical data is not based on blood-ties but rather on professions. See also Karen Rhea Nemet-Nejat, *Daily Life in Ancient Mesopotamia* (Peabody, MA: Hendrickson, 1998), 127.

123. Martha T. Roth, "Age at Marriage and the Household: A Study of Neo-Babylonian and Neo-Assyrian Forms," *Comparative Studies in Society and History* 29 (1987): 715–47, at 747.

124. On the role of the brother in arranged marriages see Leick, *Sex and Eroticism in Mesopotamian Literature*, 84. Cornelia Wunsch, "The Egibi Family," in *The Babylonian World*, ed. Gwendolyn Leick, 236–47 (London and New York: Routledge, 2007), 244, notes that in the sixth century BCE the father or both parents arranged the marriages of daughters, while sons could not marry without their father's approval.

125. Raymond Westbrook, *Old Babylonian Marriage Law*, AfO Beiheft 23 (Horn, Austria: F. Berger, 1988), 11, 12, 14; Nemet-Nejat, *Daily Life in Ancient Mesopotamia*, 135.

made by the bride's household in surrendering her to her husband.[126] The marital property (*nudunnûm*) would be at the disposal of the husband, but in the event of a divorce the dowry (*šeriktum*) would usually travel with the wife as a form of security for her (*CH* §137-38, 149).[127] Thus there was an economic or material dimension to the monetary transaction of the bridewealth/dowry exchange. However, the symbolic dimension of the exchange communicated that a relationship between the two households was at stake as well as the particular relationship between the husband and wife as individuals. From this union, legitimate children would be born in accordance with the honor of the husband's household.[128] This notion of honor is vital to the integrity of the household, for it signifies the relational reality that holds it together—a reality created and sustained by the sacrifices of the members of the household.[129] When these sacrificial contributions—which are encouraged by an accompanying sense of honor—diminish, the household weakens. The integrity of the relationship between the husband and wife had to be upheld not only internally in the household but also in the eyes of the community. If a woman was accused of adultery by a member of the community, she was expected to submit to the river ordeal in order to vindicate the honor of the household that was threatened by such a charge (*CH* §132; cf. 129, 133b).[130] But if the accusation of adultery came from her husband, the wife was only expected to take an oath before the household god (*CH* §131; cf. Num 5:11-31).[131] Thus the reality of public scandal carried a more severe penalty. Through their attention to honor the Mesopotamians made known their conviction that a household can navigate the controversies that beset it only if its members commit to a basic framework of values and rules.[132]

126. Westbrook, *Old Babylonian Marriage Law*, 54, notes that Koschaker regarded OB marriage as the groom's purchase of the bride, with the *terḫatum* being the purchase price.

127. Westbrook, *Old Babylonian Marriage Law*, 25, explains that the *nudunnûm* consists of the dowry given by the bride's family (*šeriktum* in *CH*) and gifts from her husband. See also Wunsch, "The Egibi Family," 245.

128. On the defining power of publicly observable behavior in Mesopotamian society see van der Toorn, *Family Religion in Babylonia*, 117.

129. Ibid., 140–41.

130. Marten Stol, "Women in Mesopotamia," *JESHO* 38 (1995): 123–44, at 132, points out that the *ius talionis* of the false accuser was not operative in a false charge that a woman had committed adultery. By contrast in ancient Israel, Levine, "Biblical Women's Marital Rights," 90, notes that Israelite women suspected of adultery were not subjected to the river ordeal. They were, however, threatened with the ritual of the *śōṭāh* (Num 5:11-31).

131. Westbrook, *Old Babylonian Marriage Law*, 75.

132. Van der Toorn, *Family Religion in Babylonia*, 141–42.

Marriage in the Mesopotamian tradition is more properly categorized as a social process than as a legal event.[133] Westbrook points to adoption as an analogue for marriage, that is, there is a change in status through the transfer of the woman from the parents' house to that of the groom just as a child becomes a son or daughter by way of adoption. Contractual relations between the groom and the bride's parents precede the marriage proper rather than constitute it.[134] Four key moments in the process are (1) the engagement, (2) the payment of the bridewealth and dowry by the two households, (3) the transfer of the bride from her father's house to that of the groom, and (4) the sexual union of the couple (cf. *CH* 155-56).[135] Once the process begins, there are consequences for the groom or bride should either decide to stop the process. If the groom should decide to back out, the following was legislated by the *CH*:

> If a man, who has brought the marriage gift to the house of his father-in-law and has given the bridewealth, fixes his eyes on another woman and says to his father-in-law, "I will not marry your daughter," the father of the girl may take away whatever was brought to him. (§159)[136]

Here the groom has allowed the process to advance through the first two stages. He is free to back out, but at the cost of the bridewealth. On the other hand, if the father-in-law should decide after stage two that he does not want to give his daughter to the groom, then he must pay the groom twice the amount of the bridewealth that has been given him by the groom (*CH* §160).[137] If an associate (*ibrum*) of the groom slanders the

133. Driver and Miles, *The Babylonian Laws*, 1:249–50; Westbrook, *Old Babylonian Marriage Law*, 31–32, 60.

134. Westbrook, *Old Babylonian Marriage Law*, 58, 60. He associates the *kirrum* (i.e., the sealing of the contract between groom and bride's parents by drinking beer) with this premarriage contract rather than with a meal on the wedding day (pp. 29–31); cf. Matthews, "Marriage and Family in the Ancient Near East," 1–32, at 8, 11. For the view that the *kirrum* is on the wedding day see Benno Landsberger, "Jungfräulichkeit: Ein Beitrag zum Thema 'Beilage und Eheschliessung,'" in *Symbolae Iuridicae et Historicae Martino David Dedicatae*, 2 vols., ed. J. A. Ankum, Robert Feenstra, and William F. Leemans, 2:41–105 (Leiden: Brill, 1968), at 2:78–79.

135. Nemet-Nejat, *Daily Life in Ancient Mesopotamia*, 133; Driver and Miles, *The Babylonian Laws*, 1:322–24. Westbrook, *Old Babylonian Marriage Law*, 52, 53, claims that *copula carnalis* "need not be vital" to the formation of a marriage: "the marriage is *prima facie* complete . . . although there may be the possibility of subsequent annulment for non-consummation."

136. Borger, *BAL*, 31.

137. Driver and Miles, *The Babylonian Laws*, 1:323; Westbrook, *Old Babylonian Marriage Law*, 42.

groom with the result that the father-in-law decides to end the proposed marriage, the father-in-law must pay double the bridewealth (*terḫatum*) and gift (*biblum*) to the groom (*CH* §161).[138] If the bride in an inchoate marriage wants to terminate the marriage and is found by the court to be without fault and her husband to be "wayward" (*wāṣû*), she may take her dowry and depart (*CH* §142). Westbrook argues, however, that if no fault is found in her husband and yet the inchoate wife wishes to leave, she may do so, but with the penalty of forfeiting her dowry.[139]

Virginity of the bride seems to have been an expectation in Mesopotamia.[140] Stol notes that a group of "best men" of the bride were to watch over her. They presented the "bloody sheet" after the wedding night.[141] Meir Malul has argued that an official known as the *susapinnu* was charged with being with the married couple in the bridal chamber on the wedding night in order to attest to the wife's virginity and to obtain the evidence to defend her later if the need should arise.[142] He was perhaps also expected on the wedding night to bring the couple gifts to help defray their expenses and to defend the couple against evil spirits.[143]

The wedding party itself could extend over days or even weeks among the wealthy.[144] It was a time in which the groom and his family typically brought gifts to the bride and her family: e.g., food for the wedding festivities, clothing, and jewelry. On the wedding day the bride was bathed and anointed with oil; then she was dressed with a wedding dress and veil.[145] Once the bride was transferred to the house of the groom, there may have been an oral statement between the couple making clear their commitment to one another.[146] The wedding ritual also

138. Ibid., 42–43. Driver and Miles, *The Babylonian Laws*, 1:324, note that this law "prevents one suitor from slandering another by prohibiting his marriage with the girl."

139. Westbrook, *Old Babylonian Marriage Law*, 46.

140. Nemet-Nejat, *Daily Life in Ancient Mesopotamia*, 135–36. See chap. 4 below.

141. Stol, "Private Life in Ancient Mesopotamia," *CANE* 489; Nemet-Nejat, *Daily Life in Ancient Mesopotamia*, 135.

142. Meir Malul, "The Mesopotamian *Susapinnu*: The Mesopotamian Paranymph and His Role," *JESHO* 32 (1989): 241–78, at 278.

143. Ibid., 259, 263, 268, 271; cf. Tobit 7–8.

144. Nemet-Nejat, *Daily Life in Ancient Mesopotamia*, 135.

145. Victor H. Matthews, "Marriage and Family in the Ancient Near East," in *Marriage and Family in the Biblical World* (2003), 1–32, at 11.

146. Van der Toorn, *Family Religion in Babylonia*, 40. Westbrook, *Old Babylonian Marriage Law*, 49–50, notes, with reference to Samuel Greengus, "The Old Babylonian Marriage Contract," *JAOS* 89 (1969): 505–32, at 517, that the strongest evidence for words of solemn commitment by bride and groom are inferred from divorce texts that quote the words for dissolving the marital union: "You are not my wife (or husband)" (see, e.g., BIN 7 173:16–29;

seems to have had a segment known as the groom's veiling of the bride. The bride would come to the ceremony veiled, but the groom would remove this veil, symbolizing chastity, and replace it with one symbolizing "belonging," which also implied that the groom was committed to clothe the bride thereafter.[147] In the *Middle Assyrian Laws* (§41), a husband who wished to elevate one of his concubines to the status of a legal wife would veil her (*pussumu*) in the presence of five or six witnesses, while making a public declaration that she was his wife.[148]

A primary goal of marriage from the perspective of the household was procreation.[149] If a wife was unable to bear children, it could be grounds for divorce, as the following law from the *CH* indicates:

> If a man is about to divorce his upper-class wife who has not borne him children, he must give her silver equivalent to her bridewealth and give back to her the dowry that she brought from her father's house. Then he can divorce her. (§138)[150]

If she had no bridewealth the husband must not dismiss her without funds but is expected to give an upper-class wife sixty shekels of silver (§139) and a middle- or lower-class wife twenty shekels of silver (§140). Infertility and illness were also grounds for a man to search for a second wife (cf. *CH* §144, 148, 149).[151] Although the marriage appears to have been consummated with the sexual joining of the couple, a case could be made that the marriage *per se* was not fully in place until the birth of the first child.[152] According to *CH* §163, if a wife has died without having given birth to children her dowry is to be returned to her father and the father will return the bridewealth to the husband—actions that seem equivalent to an annulment of the marriage.[153]

CT 2 44:6–16; YOS 12 371:6–15). But Westbrook examines letters and literary works regarding *verba solemnis* in marriage and concludes that such words were operative only in the elevation of a concubine to the status of a wife.

147. Van der Toorn, *Family Religion in Babylonia*, 44, 45.

148. Godfrey R. Driver and John C. Miles, *The Assyrian Laws* (Oxford: Clarendon Press, 1935), 126–30.

149. Matthews, "Marriage and Family in the Ancient Near East," 16.

150. Borger, *BAL*, 28.

151. Westbrook, *Old Babylonian Marriage Law*, 71–72; Matthews, "Marriage and Family in the Ancient Near East," 15.

152. Karel van der Toorn, *From Her Cradle to Her Grave: The Role of Religion in the Life of the Israelite and the Babylonian Woman*, trans. Sara J. Denning-Bolle (Sheffield: JSOT Press, 1994), 73–74.

153. Westbrook, *Old Babylonian Marriage Law*, 71–72.

If a marriage were childless, a couple could adopt. They might do so in order to have an heir or to have someone who would care for them in their old age.[154] For the Mesopotamians it was vital to carry on the patrilineal line and so to honor the ancestors.[155] But it was also of more immediate practical concern for an aging couple to have a son to manage their estate and make sure that they were provided for in their declining years, including provision for an honorable burial.[156] Old age is a time of great vulnerability as the following exhortation in the poem *Erra and Ishum*, in which the Sebetti try to rouse the warrior Erra into action, makes clear: "Rise up! Take a stand! Why do you sit in the city like a weary old man? Why do you sit at home like a powerless child?" (*Erra* I:46-48).[157] If a couple did adopt and then happened to have a child, the parents had to provide for the adopted son if they decided to disinherit him:

> If a man builds his household by adopting a young child and raising him but subsequently has (his own) children and decides to send away his adopted child, that son shall not go forth with empty-hands. The father who raised him shall give as his property one-third of his share of his inheritance and then he shall go forth. He shall not give to him a share of the field, orchard, or house. (*CH* §191)[158]

The husband has wide-ranging authority over the disposition of his estate, but it is not absolute according to the *CH*.[159] If a man has children by a first-ranking wife and by a slave wife, he has the authority to elevate the children of the slave wife to the status of coheirs to his estate along with the children of the first wife; the only stipulation is that the preferred son must be allowed to take his share first (*CH* §170). Also, if he remarries and has children by two successive wives, the children of both wives,

154. Harris, *Gender and Aging in Mesopotamia*, 66; Elizabeth C. Stone, "Adoption in Old Babylonian Nippur," in eadem and David I. Owen, *Adoption in Old Babylonian Nippur and the Archive of Mannum-mešu-liṣṣur* (Winona Lake, IN: Eisenbrauns, 1991), 1–33, at 11, 18.

155. Driver and Miles, *The Babylonian Laws*, 1:383; Karel van der Toorn, "The Domestic Cult at Emar," *JCS* 47 (1995): 35–49, at 47; Nemet-Nejat, *Daily Life in Ancient Mesopotamia*, 143.

156. Driver and Miles, *The Babylonian Laws*, 1:384–85; Matthews, "Marriage and Family in the Ancient Near East," 18–20.

157. Harris, "Conflict of Generations," 628; eadem, *Gender and Aging in Mesopotamia*, 65.

158. Borger, *BAL*, 37.

159. Driver and Miles, *The Babylonian Laws*, 1:386–87.

after the dowry of each has been deducted, are to receive equal shares of the patrimonial estate (*CH* §167).[160]

The family (*bīt ʾabim*) consisting of a husband and wife and two or three children was "the social and emotional centre in the life of the Babylonians."[161] This centrality of the nuclear and extended family persisted throughout the first two millennia BCE.[162] The following Sumerian proverbs offer counsel on how to promote harmony in the family:

> (1) One should pay attention to a father's words. One should submit oneself to his protection. (2) A child should behave with modesty toward his mother. He should take the older generation into consideration. (3) No matter how much wisdom exerts itself, you, fool, achieve what you need. (4) A younger brother should honor an older brother. He should treat him with human dignity.[163]

So that the father keeps his place within the household in perspective, the following proverb reminds him of how the various members of the household wield authority in their roles: "The waterskin is a man's life. The sandals are a man's eye. A spouse is a man's supervisor. A son is a man's shade. A daughter is a man's favored (?) female servant (?). A daughter-in-law is a man's gendarme" (§24.8).[164] The following proverbs recognize how laziness on the part of any member of the household can make life burdensome: "In marrying a thriftless wife, in begetting a thriftless son, (an unhappy heart was assigned to me)."[165] There are also proverbs offering counsel regarding the tensions that can arise between in-laws: from the perspective of the husband's household, "The pleasure of the daughter-in-law is anger" (§3.44); from the perspective of the bride's household, "sons-in-law, what have they brought! Fathers-in-law, what have they disposed of! (i.e., a meager bridewealth)."[166]

160. Driver and Miles, *The Babylonian Laws*, 1:347–48, note that upon the death of each mother, her children would inherit her dowry (*šeriktum*).

161. Van der Toorn, *Family Religion in Babylonia*, 20. Harris, *Gender and Aging in Mesopotamia*, 144, notes that in Mesopotamia "the woman's erotic feelings were regarded as the basis for strong nuptial ties."

162. Matthews, "Marriage and Family in the Ancient Near East," 3–4; Nemet-Nejat, *Daily Life in Ancient Mesopotamia*, 126–27.

163. Translation: Bendt Alster, ed., *Proverbs of Ancient Sumer: The World's Earliest Proverb Collections* (Bethesda, MD: Capital Decisions Limited, 1997), 324–35; *UET* 6/2, 371.

164. Translation: Alster, *Proverbs of Ancient Sumer*, 274.

165. Translation: Ibid., 219, §14.40; see also Harris, *Gender and Aging in Mesopotamia*, 72.

166. Translation: *Proverbs of Ancient Sumer*, 34, 89; see also Harris, *Gender and Aging in Mesopotamia*, 116–17.

Disharmony in the household can spiral into major disputes between a father and a son. *CH* §195 states that if a son strikes his father, his father may cut off the son's hand. This penalty seems harsh until it is compared with Exod 21:15 where the consequence for striking a parent is death. The shocking severity of these penalties is rendered more comprehensible in light of the fact that the offspring in these cases are most likely adults who are living at home rather than children or adolescents.[167] If a son becomes rebellious on more than one occasion a father may decide to disinherit him upon the second offense (*CH* §169). However, according to *CH* §168 the father cannot do so unilaterally; he must get permission from the judges—that is, the elders of the neighborhood or village.[168] Because sons marry at the advanced age of thirty, they may well be anxious to gain authority over their own property. Harris speculates that such a son may long for the imminent death of his father in order to inherit his portion of the patrimony.[169] Another context in which parricide threatened was in the high-stakes battle over the throne. In Assyria in the early seventh century Sennacherib designated his son Esarhaddon to succeed him, but Sennacherib's older sons did not accept this and plotted to kill him.[170]

Incest was explicitly outlawed between (1) a father and a daughter (*CH* §154) and (2) a son and a mother (*CH* §157). The penalty in the first case was exile for the father, which probably entailed loss of family, property, and citizenship.[171] In the second case both the mother and the son were to be burned (cf. *CH* §110; Lev 20:14; 21:9). In both scenarios there is a sense that the community needs to be purged of the transgressors and the consequences of their action. *CH* §158 states that a man who lies with his father's principal wife after his father dies is to be disinherited. Here the penalty is much less severe, since presumably the wife is not

167. Driver and Miles, *The Babylonian Laws*, 1:411.

168. See also *CH* §202-8 for limitations on the parental power to punish by the local judges. However, Karen Radner, "Neo-Assyrian Period," in *A History of Ancient Near Eastern Law* (2003), 883–910, at 892 (§4.2.2), notes that the power of the *paterfamilias* in the NA kingdom was absolute over the members of the household.

169. Harris, "Conflict of Generations," 625; eadem, *Gender and Aging in Mesopotamia*, 70.

170. Earl Leichty, "Esarhaddon, King of Assyria," *CANE*, 949–58, at 951; A. K. Grayson, "Assyria: Sennacherib and Esarhaddon (704–669 BC)," CAH, vol. 3, part 2: *The Assyrian and Babylonian Empires and Other States of the Near East, from the Eighth to the Sixth Centuries B.C.*, ed. John Boardman et al., 103–41 (Cambridge: Cambridge University Press, 1982), at 120.

171. Driver and Miles, *The Babylonian Laws*, 1:318.

related by blood to the son. A factor that may have contributed to this latter form of incest between a stepmother and a son was the age disparity between the husband and the wife, for the son and the stepmother may have been closer in age than the father and the stepmother.[172]

Disruption in the relationship between husband and wife could advance to the point of divorce. A divorce could theoretically have been initiated by either the husband or the wife (*CH* §136, 142), but it was practically unlikely that the wife could have secured a workable settlement.[173] According to *CH* §141, if a wife became rebellious or difficult the husband might divorce her without returning her dowry or giving her a monetary settlement; he could also decide to keep her in the household while demoting her in status (*CH* §141). In this law the disaffected wife gathered funds for herself and then blamed her husband for their marital problems; thus her misdeeds were primarily financial in character. However, in the subsequent laws the rebellious wife seems to be scrutinized for sexual misconduct.[174] *CH* §142 says that if a wife refused marital relations with her husband, the matter was to be investigated by city authorities. If she proved to be "chaste (*naṣrat*) and without fault," she might take her dowry and return to her father's house. However, if she was at fault she was to be thrown into the river (*CH* §143).

Adultery was a clear ground for divorce, but the penalty was usually execution of the guilty parties, since this misconduct was regarded as corrupting the society and angering the gods.[175] According to *CH* §131-32, if a wife was accused of adultery she had to submit to the river ordeal. However, if she and her partner were caught committing adultery they were both to be thrown into the river (CH §129).[176] According to the *Laws of Ur-Nammu* §7, the woman caught in adultery was to be executed, but her partner was to be released. According to the *Laws of Eshnunna* §27, a wife caught in adultery was to be executed. According to *CH* §153, if a wife who was having an affair with another man made arrangements to have her husband eliminated, she was to be impaled.

172. Roth, "Age at Marriage and the Household," 737. Driver and Miles, *The Babylonian Laws*, 1:321, argue on the basis of *MAL* A46 that a son cannot marry his father's chief wife (*rabītum*) after his father's death, but he can marry a secondary wife (*urkittu*) of his father (cf. Gen 49:4).

173. Westbrook, *Old Babylonian Marriage Law*, 84.

174. Ibid., 76–77.

175. Matthews, "Marriage and Family in the Ancient Near East," 27; Westbrook, *Old Babylonian Marriage Law*, 75.

176. Ibid., 75–76.

The embodied character of the relationships within the Mesopotamian household was addressed pragmatically in their laws, customs, and rituals. They realized that there were situations in which these relationships would not work. Although the father had considerable authority in deciding what kind of sacrifices the members of the household would be asked to make to keep the household intact, his authority was not absolute but was shared in day-to-day interactions with the members of the household. If tensions between the husband and wife could not be worked out, divorce was an option, with provisions made for the welfare of the wife who would leave the household. If major transgressions like incest or adultery occurred, the offenders were simply purged from the household with no thought of providing for them. The household was a reality bigger than husband, wife, and children; it was an intergenerational phenomenon. The honor attaching to a household reflected on the ancestors as well as the current generation. This sense of honor had an almost tangible character to it. It was not simply a metaphor for the glue that held the members of the household together through the generations; there was a sense that this metaphysical dimension to the household relations was objective and made its claim on the current generation. In this respect honor functioned much like "the holy," that is, it made the metaphysical tangible. The honor attached to marriage and the birth and raising of children celebrated the centrality of the household in Mesopotamian society.[177]

Imperial Pressure on the Mesopotamian Household in the Neo-Babylonian and Persian Periods

The identity of the Mesopotamian individual was linked with his family and clan. Van der Toorn argues that in OB times an individual's identity was tied more closely to the clan than to the household, for the clan held title to the land.[178] In sales of parcels of land the contracts typically had the names of numerous sellers, which points to clan rather than household ownership of the parcel.[179] If someone outside the clan wished to buy a parcel, there would be a communal meal in the course of the contractual dealings that served to incorporate the buyer symbolically into the clan. This adoption of the buyer into the clan kept alive the com-

177. For an interpretation of honor as an ideological reality see Yee, *Poor Banished Children of Eve*, 45–46.

178. Van der Toorn, *Family Religion in Babylonia*, 26.

179. Ibid., 25.

mitment to keep the land within the clan.[180] The identity of the members of the clan was tied not only to the property but also to the ancestors who were buried there.[181] The clan and family were building blocks of the OB urban social structure. Clan solidarity was essential to the Babylonian way of life; internal strife was the worst form of chaos (cf. *Erra* IIC 33-34).[182] Van der Toorn describes the city in terms of the following concentric circles: at the circumference is the city, next is the neighborhood (= the clan), then the compound of houses, and finally the individual household.[183]

In the course of the OB period, the model of clan ownership of property began to give way to a commercial model in which land is readily bought and sold.[184] This shift would have a significant impact on the forms of social organization intermediate between the nuclear household and the state: viz., the clan, village, or neighborhood. The documentation for these intermediate forms of social organization is limited after the OB period, although Van de Mieroop notes that the topic of extended families in the first millennium is yet to be studied.[185] By the sixth century in Babylonia, fields and gardens were readily exchanged as a commercial commodity.[186] The temple household was dependent on free laborers and tenant farmers for working its date groves, grain fields, and flocks and herds. The marketing of the products tied it into the local, regional, and international economies.[187] Prebendary families carried out particular functions in the temple from generation to generation; their income was relatively stable and secure. Independent entrepreneurs such as the Egibi and Murashu houses managed a wide range of activities from the level just above cultivation to high levels of land and canal management.[188] Even when a Babylonian city enjoyed a high degree of autonomy it had to negotiate larger regional, national, and international networks

180. Ibid., 25–26; Driver and Miles, *The Assyrian Laws*, 67.

181. Greengus, "Legal and Social Institutions of Ancient Mesopotamia," 479; Jo Ann Scurlock, "Death and the Afterlife in Ancient Mesopotamian Thought," *CANE*, 1883–93, at 1888–89.

182. Van der Toorn, *Family Religion in Babylonia*, 23, 26.

183. Ibid., 26.

184. Van de Mieroop, *The Ancient Mesopotamian City*, 104–5; see chap. 4 on the real estate dealings of the *nadītu* of Nippur.

185. Ibid., 106–7.

186. Michael Jursa, "The Babylonian Economy in the First Millennium BC," in *The Babylonian World* (2007), 224–35, at 227.

187. Ibid., 229.

188. Ibid., 230–31.

of power, which made demands on the household units through taxation, conscription, and contrasting cultural values.[189]

According to the "Cyrus Cylinder," the Persian emperor Cyrus was welcomed into Babylon in order to restore the proper worship of Marduk (ll. 11-19). As the patron deity of Babylon, Marduk owned the city and the surrounding territories. The viewpoint of the "Cyrus Cylinder" that Marduk was fully in charge of the transfer of sovereign rule from the Babylonian king Nabonidus to the Persian king Cyrus is fully in keeping with the traditional territorial understanding of the power of deities in the ancient Near East (ll. 11-17).[190] This propagandistic document portrays Cyrus's intervention as liberation from the blasphemous indifference of Nabonidus toward the cult of Marduk (ll. 3-10).[191] This negative portrait reflects the anger of the Marduk priesthood toward Nabonidus for his attention to the cult of the moon god Sin in Haran and Ur.[192] Amélie Kuhrt claims that the charge that Nabonidus tried to elevate Sin to rulership over Babylon in place of Marduk was probably fabricated.[193]

189. G. van Driel, "Landless and Hungry? An Assessment," in *Landless and Hungry? Access to Land in Early and Traditional Societies*, ed. Bernhard Häring and R. de Maaijer, 190–98 (Leiden: Research School CNWS, School of Asian, African, and Amerindian Studies, 1998), at 197.

190. Daniel Block, *The Gods of the Nations: Studies in Ancient Near Eastern National Theology*, 2d ed. (Grand Rapids: Baker, 2000), 130–31.

191. Paul-Richard Berger, "Der Kyros-Zylinder mit dem Zusatzfragment BIN II Nr. 32 und die akkadischen Personennamen im Danielbuch," *ZA* 64 (1975): 192–234, at 195–96. Piotr Michalowski, "The Cyrus Cylinder," in *The Ancient Near East: Historical Sources in Translation*, ed. Mark Chavalas, 426–430 (Malden, MA: Blackwell, 2006), at 427, notes that the first few lines of the cylinder have been translated in two different ways: (1) Cyrus criticizes Nabonidus for elevating his daughter to be the high priestess of the moon-god; (2) the sentence describes Nabonidus as "an incompetent" who has usurped power in the land.

192. Paul-Alain Beaulieu, "King Nabonidus and the Neo-Babylonian Empire," *CANE* 1:975, notes that the inscriptions of Nabonidus can be divided into three groups on the basis of Nabonidus's attention to Marduk and Sin: (1) before Teima, he poured lavish praise on Sin and was restrained in praising Marduk; (2) during Teima, he paid no attention to Sin but lavishly praised Marduk; (3) after Teima, he ignored Marduk and praised Sin beyond all previous practice. Amélie Kuhrt, "Nabonidus and the Babylonian Priesthood," in *Pagan Priests: Religion and Power in the Ancient World*, ed. Mary Beard and John North, 119–55 (Ithaca, NY: Cornell University Press, 1990), at 149, notes that there is almost no information currently available on how the Marduk priesthood interacted with the king and his cultic experts.

193. Kuhrt, "Nabonidus and the Babylonian Priesthood," 141, 143, doubts the claim of the "Persian Verse Account" that Nabonidus declared Sin to be the owner of Marduk's temple in Babylon (column V; ANET 314).

Elevated to the kingship by a group of palace supporters at an advanced age, the learned Nabonidus seems to have been an outsider to the political machinations of the capital city.[194] He withdrew to the Arabian oasis of Teima in the summer of 552 for ten years and returned to Babylon only as the Persian threat increased.[195] He seems to have mounted substantial resistance against Cyrus's forces at Opsis to the northeast of Babylon in 539. But when this effort failed, there was no further fighting against Cyrus on his way to Babylon.[196] Cyrus's Gutian governor Ugbaru was the first to enter Babylon; he died eight days later, which suggests that divine punishment for desecrating the city was visited on Ugbaru instead of Cyrus.[197]

The "Cyrus Cylinder," drawing on the language of Assurbanipal's inscriptions and a foundation cylinder of Nabopolassar marking the rebuilding of the wall Imgur-Enlil (l. 38),[198] describes Cyrus's entrance into Babylon as noncombative (l. 22). Its endorsement of the rule of Cyrus fits together with the religio-political propaganda of Darius I, who sought to win the cooperation of subject peoples by supporting their local cults (ll. 25, 33-34).[199] Such benign imperial rule masked the demands of heavy

194. Beaulieu, "King Nabonidus and the Neo-Babylonian Empire," *CANE* 1:973. David B. Weisberg, "Polytheism and Politics: Some Comments on Nabonidus' Foreign Policy," in *Crossing Boundaries and Linking Horizons: Studies in Honor of Michael C. Astour on His 80th Birthday*, ed. Gordon D. Young, Mark W. Chavalas, and Richard E. Averbeck, 547–56 (Bethesda, MD: Capital Decisions Limited, 1997), at 554, contends that Nabonidus's withdrawal to Teima indicates that he was on good terms with the power elites of Babylon and did not need to be present to counter their machinations.

195. Beaulieu, "King Nabonidus and the Neo-Babylonian Empire," *CANE* 1:975, argues that Nabonidus withdrew from Babylon because of a political crisis precipitated by theological controversy.

196. *Chronicle* 7.iii.12–17 in A. K. Grayson, *Assyrian and Babylonian Chronicles*, Texts from Cuneiform Sources 5 (Winona Lake, IN: Eisenbrauns, 2000), 109–10; Beaulieu, "King Nabonidus and the Neo-Babylonian Empire," *CANE* 1:977; Kuhrt, "Nabonidus and the Babylonian Priesthood," 133–34; David Vanderhooft, "Cyrus II, Liberator or Conqueror? Ancient Historiography concerning Cyrus in Babylon," in *Judah and the Judeans in the Persian Period*, ed. Oded Lipschits and Manfred Oeming, 351–72 (Winona Lake, IN: Eisenbrauns, 2006), at 353–54. Michalowski, "The Cyrus Cylinder," 426–27, notes that there is no contemporary evidence that Babylon fell without a battle; extant information is mediated via the ideologically charged texts of "The Nabonidus Chronicle," "The Persian Verse Account," and the "Cyrus Cylinder."

197. *Chronicle* 109 iii.12–14; cf. Jeremiah 50–51; Vanderhooft, "Cyrus II, Liberator or Conqueror?" 362.

198. Michalowski, "The Cyrus Cylinder," 427.

199. Muhammed A. Dandamayev, "Neo-Babylonian and Achaemenid State Administration in Mesopotamia," in *Judah and the Judeans in the Persian Period* (2006), 373–98, at 394–95; Briant, *From Cyrus to Alexander*, 67–70, 105–6, 313, 346–47, 388–94.

taxation that would descend on the peoples, a burden that eventually made its way into the individual households and led to the collapse of many through debt slavery.[200] The voracious appetite of the imperial war machine had to be fed by the subject peoples, for Darius knew well that the heavy taxation on the Persians during the reigns of Cyrus and Cambyses had only fueled the fires of revolution on the home front.[201]

The collection of taxes and tribute over a far-flung empire required a system.[202] The Persians' pragmatic approach to local religions was also reflected in their administration of the economy of the provinces. Unlike the Babylonian rulers before them who tried to drain the resources from the periphery to the center of their empire, the Persians aimed to support the periphery in being productive so that its surplus might then be directed toward the center.[203] This policy, which promoted long-term stability in the empire, masked the oppressive weight of imperial rule on the local communities and households.

After the successful revolt of Egypt in 464–454 BCE and the Peace of Callias in 449 with Greece, Persia was intent on stabilizing its hold on Syro-Palestine as a buffer against both Greece and Egypt.[204] The Persian economy and military seem to have remained strong throughout the fifth and fourth centuries. It was the military acumen and luck of Alexander the Great at the battles of Granicus (334 BCE) and Issus (333 BCE) that turned the tide in his favor against a formidable Persian foe.[205] The fact that Persia was able to sustain its military machine and imperial projects over more than two centuries attests to its enlightened form of

200. Ibid., 399–400, 401; Dandamayev, "An Age of Privatization in Ancient Mesopotamia," 207; idem, *Slavery in Babylonia*, 178. On the shift in land ownership through the business activities of the Egibi family see Michael Jursa, *Neo-Babylonian Legal and Administrative Documents: Typology, Contents and Archives*, Guides to the Mesopotamia Textual Record, 1 (Münster: Ugarit-Verlag, 2005), 66; Cornelia Wunsch, "The Egibi Family," 240, 246. For the view that scholarly reconstructions following A. T. Olmstead, *History of the Persian Empire* (Chicago: University of Chicago Press, 1948), 293, 297–99, tend to exaggerate the Persian tax burden in the late sixth century, see Matthew Stolper, *Entrepreneurs and Empire: The Murašû Archive, the Murašû Firm, and Persian Rule in Babylonia* (Leiden and Istanbul: Nederlands Historisch-Archaeologisch Instituut te Istanbul, 1985), 144.

201. Berquist, *Judaism in Persia's Shadow*, 47, 62; Briant, *From Cyrus to Alexander*, 120–21.

202. Berquist, *Judaism in Persia's Shadow*, 54; Briant, *From Cyrus to Alexander*, 388–94.

203. Xenophon, *Oeconomicus* IV.8; Briant, *From Cyrus to Alexander*, 75–76, 805–9; Berquist, *Judaism in Persia's Shadow*, 16, 105.

204. Ibid., 111; Briant, *From Cyrus to Alexander*, 582.

205. Josef Wiesehöfer, "The Achaemenid Empire in the Fourth Century BCE: A Period of Decline?" in *Judah and the Judeans in the Fourth Century BCE* (2007), 24, 28.

provincial administration. Darius's division of the empire into twenty satrapies staffed in the upper positions only by Persians kept the decision-making power in the hands of the Achaemenid clan and those Persians who swore absolute loyalty to the ruling regime.[206] At the same time, the satrapal organization drew on and adapted to the local forms of government and economic organization.[207]

In fifth-century Babylonia the imperial government worked together with local entrepreneurial families to manage extensive lands and to draw off substantial surpluses. The records of one such family located primarily in Nippur during the reigns of Artaxerxes I, Darius II, and Artaxerxes II are known as the Murashû archives.[208] This family engaged in agricultural contracting and supplying short-term credit. They were neither tax farmers nor bankers, but specialized in leasing land and providing equipment and venture capital for exploiting it.[209] Their efforts secured substantial tax monies for the Persian government but also seem to have garnered sizeable earnings for the Murashû family.[210] Two-thirds of the names mentioned in the Murashû archives are Babylonian; the rest are Persian, Anatolian, Egyptian, Jewish, or from other Western Semitic groups.[211]

The entrepreneurial household of the Murashû differed dramatically from the *bīt ʾabim* of the NB period. The impact of these imperially backed commercial households on local households can be seen in the following contract for the leasing of a plot of land:

206. Ibid., 20; Stolper, *Entrepreneurs and Empire*, 9–10.

207. Briant, *From Cyrus to Alexander*, 394.

208. Matthew Stolper, "Archive of Murashû," *ABD* 4:927–28; idem, "Fifth Century Nippur: Texts of the Murašûs and from Their Surroundings," *JCS* 53 (2001): 83–132, at 83–84; Dandamayev, "An Age of Privatization in Ancient Mesopotamia," 202–3, 207. Stolper, *Entrepreneurs and Empire*, 1, 10, notes that 3,300 texts are known from the reigns of Cyrus II to Darius I, but only about 1,000 for the last 150 years of Persian rule, and of these more than 600 are from the Murashû archive. G. van Driel, "The Murašûs in Context," *JESHO* 32 (1989): 203–29, at 203–4, 223–26, argued that this archive—as known in the late 1980s—consisted of dated materials that were to be disposed of (e.g., promissory notes that had run their course) and so the abrupt end of the archive (ca. 414 BCE) was not a consequence of royal intervention to inhibit the firm's activities.

209. Stolper, *Entrepreneurs and Empire*, 27–28.

210. Stolper, "Archive of Murashû." Van Driel, "The Murašûs in Context," 204–5, 217, claims that the Murashû family was only one of many firms that operated within a system for exploiting land and water through farming—a system operating prior to the arrival of the Persians.

211. Stolper, "Archive of Murashû"; Dandamaev, *Slavery in Babylonia*, 66.

> Qarhānu, servant of Enlil-šum-iddin, in the joy of his heart said this to Enlil-šum-iddin, son of Murašû: "Lease me land for cultivating cereals: the field of Bēl-uballit and Ukittu, the crown land and that of the *gardu*-workers bordering the canal (but not the plots of land bordering the canal irrigated by buckets), the crown land, the land of Ahhē-iddin and the land of Itti-Enlil-balātu bordering the Sahīdu canal, and also one plow, 34 gur of barley for seed, 1 gur of wheat, 7 gur of emmer, 4 *sūtu* of sesame, [x] chickpeas, 1 2/3 *pānu* of lentils, 1 *pānu* of millet, and I will give you annually 280 gur of barley, 7 gur of wheat, 70 gur of emmer, 12 gur of chickpeas, 1 gur of lentils, 20 gur of millet, 10 gur of *kašû*, 2 gur of sesame, for a total of 400 gur of foodstuff."[212]

A typical contract to a renter included not simply land but also water rights, equipment, draft animals, and seed. The land here will be watered by direct flow rather than by bucket, which typically meant that a third of the crop rather than a fourth had to be paid for the water.[213] After the quoted section above, the contract goes on to indicate that Enlil-šum-iddin agreed to the terms of the request and laid down a timetable for repayment. The document was then attested by seven witnesses and signed and dated by the scribe and bore the fingernail mark of Qarhānu. In this contract the initiative comes from the local level. Even though the rent was high, this system encouraged local farmers to be productive. The farmers must have secured a harvest large enough to make their own investment reasonable.[214] Most of the land transactions preserved in the legal documents of the Murashû archive deal with leases or secondary titles to the land, for the lands dealt with in these documents were either inalienable or state-owned. The Murashû texts provide significant data on those farmers who wanted to work more land than was under their control.[215] Thus they provide a picture of those Mesopotamians who did not own sufficient land and were trying to sustain their families and households through the use of land they only held temporarily.[216]

212. Edition: Stolper, "Fifth Century Nippur," 95.

213. Stolper, *Entrepreneurs and Empire*, 50.

214. Van Driel, "The Murašûs in Context," 218, 223; Francis Joannès, "Private Commerce and Banking in Achaemenid Babylon," *CANE*, 1475–85, at 1477–78.

215. Stolper, *Entrepreneurs and Empire*, 34–37, 44, remarks that water and equipment were expensive, but land was relatively cheap.

216. Stolper, *Entrepreneurs and Empire*, 29, 34, 151, notes with regard to mortgages in the Murashû archives that there was "a sharp rise in the indebtedness of Babylonian feudatories" with "some inequity and inelasticity in the situation of Babylonian smallholders." On the long-standing practice of Mesopotamian temple estates leasing their lands to

Throughout Mesopotamian history the class of non-landholding free laborers was sizeable.[217] The temple was a major player in the economy that contracted the services of free laborers as well as entrepreneurs who would manage its lands and its participation in the regional, national, and international markets.[218] The mobility of these laborers and the leasing practices of the entrepreneurs indicate that the ties of these laborers and the tenant farmers for whom they worked to particular plots of land were tenuous or nonexistent. The place the families of these laborers would call home was not protected with the aura of inalienability as an ancestral inheritance (cf. 1 Kgs 21:3). It was a long-standing practice in Mesopotamian cities to buy and sell homes. The parental home could be divided among the sons at the time of their inheritance so that some of them would sell their portion and move elsewhere.[219] In good economic times this practice of buying and selling homes may well have fit the lifestyle of these free laborers. But in times of turmoil—such as the palace revolt that brought Darius II to power in 423—the burden of producing more and cutting back on consumption fell disproportionately on these laborers and their employers at the lower levels of the economy.[220]

One wonders what happened to the OB type of family religion in fifth-century Babylonia. Because family religion responds to the pressing needs of daily life that transcend particular times and places—e.g., birth, death, infertility, and pregnancy—there is a measure of commonality to rituals in family religion cross-culturally in the first two millennia BCE.[221]

---

free tenants see Dandamayev, "An Age of Privatization in Ancient Mesopotamia," 199, 201. Albertz, *A History of Israelite Religion*, 2:447, points out how the crushing burden of Persian taxation widened the gap between the rich and the poor in Yehud: the wealthy estates that engaged in trade and making loans profited from the Persian system, but the smallholders were driven further into misery.

217. Michael Jursa, "The Babylonian Economy in the First Millennium BC," in *The Babylonian World* (2007), 224–35, at 232; Oppenheim, *Ancient Mesopotamia*, 85; Dandamayev, *Slavery in Babylonia*, 645, 656.

218. Peter Bedford, "The Economy of the Near East in the First Millennium," in *Trade and Finance in Ancient Mesopotamia*, MOS Studies 1, ed. Jan G. Dercksen, 58–88 (Leiden: Nederlands Historisch-Archaeologisch Instituut, 1999), at 68, notes that I. M. Diakonoff sees the similarities between household economies of Mesopotamia and Greece but emphasizes that the temple economy in Mesopotamia made it into a two-sector economy rather than the single sector private/communal economy of a state.

219. Van de Mieroop, *The Ancient Mesopotamian City*, 106.

220. Stolper, *Entrepreneurs and Empire*, 29, 34, 151.

221. Rainer Albertz, "Family Religion in Ancient Israel and its Surroundings," in *Household and Family Religion in Antiquity*, ed. John Bodel and Saul M. Olyan, 89–112 (Malden, MA: Blackwell, 2008), at 92–93.

Since the religious system in Babylonia was polytheistic, there would have been the possibility of paying attention to one's household deities at the same time that one was acknowledging the great gods of the Babylonian and Persian pantheons.[222] So while exclusivity of worship would not have been the driving issue in Babylon as it was in Yehud, the question of the amount of attention paid to the household deities would be a point of friction. Just as Nabonidus was condemned by the Marduk priesthood for paying attention to the moon god Sin at the expense of Marduk,[223] so also it would seem that the local householders would be challenged to shift their resources from their family deities to the national and international deities. To the extent that a family lost title to its property it would seem that the perceived power wielded by the family deities would have diminished, since the main function of these deities was to protect and sustain the family.[224]

Among the deities attended to in the household cult in the OB period were not only the clan deity (*ʾil kimtim / ʾil bītim*) but also the deified ancestors.[225] The clan deity was a true divinity; this protector may have been imagined, particularly among tribal groups, as linked with the bloodline of the household and clan. Thus the characteristics belonging to a clan that became manifest in those sharing the same bloodline may have been seen as an embodiment of the clan deity.[226] This clan deity would have been served either in the neighborhood cult or in the domestic

222. Van der Toorn, *Family Religion in Babylonia*, 57, 66, notes that a Babylonian usually paid attention primarily to one god: i.e., one's personal god who was regarded as part of one's identity, as seen in the introductions to prayer formularies such as: "I am A, son of B, whose god is C and whose goddess is D."

223. Paul-Alain Beaulieu, "King Nabonidus and the Neo-Babylonian Empire," *CANE* 1:975.

224. Albertz, "Family Religion in Ancient Israel and its Surroundings," 92, 98; idem, *A History of Israelite Religion*, 2:447.

225. Karel van der Toorn, "Family Religion in Second Millennium West Asia (Mesopotamia, Emar, Nuzi)," in *Household and Family Religion in Antiquity* (2008), 20–36, at 21; Daniel E. Fleming, "The Integration of Household and Community Religion in Ancient Syria," in ibid., 37–59, at 52–53.

226. Zvi Abusch, "Sacrifice in Mesopotamia," in *Sacrifice in Religious Experience*, Studies in the History of Religions 97, ed. Albert I. Baumgarten, 39–48 (Leiden: Brill, 2002), at 45; idem, "Etemmu," in *DDD*, 309–12, at 309; Jacobsen, *Treasures of Darkness*, 159. However, Van der Toorn, *Family Religion in Babylonia*, 57, counters that "this does not mean that the family god was incarnate in the father and passed from his body to the bodies of his children, as has sometimes been claimed."

cult.[227] In addition to the clan deity, deceased ancestors up to the fourth generation were invoked.[228] These deified ancestors were the human individuals who had lived in the household and then died. Their presence was not that of ghosts but rather of lower-ranking deities who could have an impact on the well-being and decision making of the household. The association of a custom or practice with a particular ancestor would lend it an authority that was not abstract but concrete by virtue of the presence of that ancestor, particularly at the monthly banquet known as the *kispum*. This banquet was sponsored by the eldest son; at this banquet the names of the various ancestors were mentioned.[229] This regular remembering was tied to the space of the household and the genealogy of its members. If one of these components was removed it would have been difficult for the other to sustain this ancestor cult.[230]

The practice of honoring the clan deity and the ancestral deities seems to have persisted over time. Because honoring the dead would have been incumbent on the families of the free laborers as well as the nobles both in the OB and Persian periods, the issue of maintaining a domestic space would have been important for the celebration of these family rituals. In times of social dislocation such as those in the latter part of the fifth century the households of Babylonians at the lower level of the socioeconomic spectrum would have been challenged in sustaining the domestic cult. However, Dandamayev claims that conditions were so unstable that even powerful families were vulnerable to economic ruin.[231]

In the contract of Qarhānu quoted earlier it seems that he is making an honest effort to adapt to the Persian imperial system that has been ruling in Babylonia for more than a century. Dandamayev notes that many households were not able to bear the burden of such an imperial overlay and not only lost their property but were also forced to sell members of their family into debt slavery.[232] However, he claims that in

227. Van der Toorn, "Family Religion in Second Millennium West Asia," 24, 27; Albertz, "Family Religion in Ancient Israel and Its Surroundings," 100.

228. Van der Toorn, "Family Religion in Second Millennium West Asia," 27–28; idem, *Family Religion in Babylonia*, 55; Fleming, "The Integration of Household and Community Religion" 42.

229. Van der Toorn, *Family Religion in Babylonia*, 49–50, 52, 64; T. J. Lewis, "Dead," in *DDD*, 223–31, at 225.

230. Cf. Baruch A. Levine and Jean-Michel de Terragon, "Dead Kings and Rephaim: Patrons of the Ugaritic Dynasty," *JAOS* 104 (1984): 649–59, at 654, 656.

231. Dandamayev, "An Age of Privatization," 207.

232. Ibid.

the sixth to the fourth centuries BCE economic conditions in Mesopotamia were favorable, so that even those who lost their property ended up functioning as if they were free laborers.[233] Nevertheless, the loss of the ancestral land would have reshaped the self-understanding of these laborers and their relationship to their families.[234] The land on which the ancestors had lived and labored functioned as a material substratum that facilitated family relationships taking on a corporate immortality. Even though tribal and clan dynamics were constitutive of the royal family of the Achaemenids, the welfare of the innumerable households at the base of the power pyramid was sacrificed to the larger imperial mechanism.[235] So many sacrificed the household, with its relationships in the here and now and hereafter, to the larger political and social structure of the empire.

Summary

The Mesopotamian tradition gives priority to urban culture over that of the herders, yet there is a strong measure of symbiosis between these two components of the dimorphic society in Mesopotamia from the third to the first millennium BCE. The urban dwellers anchored their culture in one place whereas the tribal elements found their fixed point in kinship. The migration of ethnic groups in and out of Mesopotamia is attested in every period. Thus the cities became melting pots that incorporated tribal elements, yet the tribal way of life persisted even though the names and numbers of their ranks shifted. The world foundational effort of Marduk celebrated in the *Enūma Elish* cloaks a revolutionary cultural and political development in traditional rhetoric. The movement to concentrate political power in the hands of the king of Babylon, who acts as Marduk's viceroy, is justified because Marduk and his king will protect the traditional patriarchal royal household of the gods. Esagila in Babylon rather than Ekur in Nippur becomes the seat

233. Dandamayev, *Slavery in Babylonia*, 649–50; idem, "An Age of Privatization," 208.

234. On increasing taxation during the reign of Darius I that culminated in revolts (484 BCE) led by the local Babylonian elites who were being displaced see Michael Jursa, "The Transition of Babylonia from the Neo-Babylonian Empire to Achaemenid Rule," in *Regime Change in the Ancient Near East and Egypt: From Sargon of Agade to Saddam Hussein*, Proceedings of the British Academy 136, ed. Harriet Crawford, 73–94 (Oxford: Clarendon Press, 2007), at 89–91; idem, *Neo-Babylonian Legal and Administrative Documents*, 17–18; Erica Ehrenberg, "Persian Conquerors, Babylonian Captivators," in *Regime Change*, 95–103, at 102.

235. Stolper, *Entrepreneurs and Empire*, 123; Dandamayev, *Slavery in Babylonia*, 54, 62–63.

of divine sovereignty. The threat to this transfer of political power comes not from Nippur or another city but from "fluidity" or chaos as symbolized by Tiāmat. Marduk is victorious and forges a new synthesis between the genealogy of ancestral gods and the new capital of Babylon.

The Mesopotamian household functioned within the structure of a clan that held title to the property. Land was regarded as inalienable, yet such sales regularly occurred by genealogizing the buyer into the clan. The re-creation of the household through marriage and childbirth was a primary, ongoing concern of the *paterfamilias*. The material substratum of the household was indispensable to its viability. The linking of two households through marriage took into account the costs and benefits to each party to the marriage not only by the exchange of materials but also by attention to the honor of each party. The Mesopotamian household was worried more about its integrity than its wealth, as evidenced by its concern about premarital virginity, adultery, and incest.

The Mesopotamian household came under stress through the burden of Persian taxation. The weight of this burden fell on the small landholders, while the entrepreneurial households found ways to capitalize on the growing number of free laborers who had lost their ancestral property through foreclosure. The records of the house of Murashu show how a firm could lease property at a high rate and provide venture capital yielding strong returns. The free laborers agreed to these contractual terms as a way to move forward, even though the major portion of the productivity went to the Murashû house as lending agent and the Persian government as recipient of taxes. This erosion of the material substratum of the Mesopotamian household would probably have weakened the traditional domestic cult that honored the ancestors through the generations. The tribal clan could survive by transferring to new ground, but the Mesopotamian dimorphic society was anchored in the patrimony of the household and the clan. The culture of a clan is more resilient than that of an individual household. The impoverished Mesopotamian household diminished with the loss of ancestral property.

Greece: Intermarriage as a Threat to Democratic Development in Athens

Marriage between aristocratic families of different city-states was a long-standing practice in Archaic Greece. The networks among aristocrats of the various city-states is enshrined in the epic narratives of Homer. However, this practice stood in tension with the practice of most Greeks of finding a wife or husband within the local area. The Athenian myth of autochthony, as related in Euripides' *Ion*, celebrates the ties of the Athenians to the soil as a patriotic force central to the web of relationships constituting the polis.[236] The rapid population growth in Athens in the fifth century testifies to its prosperity as a leading Greek city, but it also threatened to weaken the voice of the long-standing residents in the governance of the city.[237] Wealth could empower one in the political arena even if the city assembly were large, but native birth diminished in value as one's voice became one in a sea of relatively equal voices. Democrats were in favor of restricting citizenship to the native born in order to counter the tide of immigrants in imperial Athens in the fifth century. Tying citizenship to marriage practices, as intrusive as it appeared to many households, became an important issue in the ongoing task of defining the relationship between the household and the polis.

Pericles: A Champion of Democratic Athens on the Basis of Its Imperial Power

In 451 BCE, Pericles legislated that the only males who would qualify to be citizens of Athens were those who had both an Athenian father and mother. This principle, though controversial, lasted throughout most of the Classical and Hellenistic periods.[238] In 445 BCE, with a gift of grain from Psammetichus of Egypt, the citizen lists in the *demes* were examined and nearly five thousand were deleted because they were regarded as

236. Froma Zeitlin, "Mysteries of Identity and Designs of the Self in Euripides' *Ion*," in her *Playing the Other: Gender and Society in Classical Greek Literature* (Chicago: University of Chicago Press, 1996), 285–338, at 336–37; Stephanie Budin, *The Myth of Sacred Prostitution* (Cambridge: Cambridge University Press, 2008), 78.

237. Margaret C. Miller, *Athens and Persia in the Fifth Century BC: A Study in Cultural Receptivity* (Cambridge: Cambridge University Press, 1997), 250–51; J. K. Davies, "Economy and Society," in CAH, 2d ed., vol. 5, *The Fifth Century B.C.*, ed. by D. M. Lewis, John Boardman, and J. K. Davies, 287–305 (Cambridge: Cambridge University Press, 1992), at 296–301; cf. Barry S. Strauss, "On Aristotle's Critique of Athenian Democracy," in *Essays on the Foundations of Aristotelian Political Science*, ed. Carnes Lord and David K. O'Connor, 212–33 (Berkeley: University of California Press, 1991), at 227.

238. John K. Davies, "Athenian Citizenship: The Descent Group and the Alternatives," *Classical Journal* 73 (1978): 105–21, at 105. Sarah B. Pomeroy, *Families in Classical and Hellenistic Greece: Representations and Realities* (Oxford: Clarendon Press, 1997), 33–34, 39, describes the exogamous marriage practices of aristocratic families in the archaic period up to the endogamous practices of the fifth century BCE and also the reality of population growth and its curtailment by Pericles' citizenship law. Concerning the laws on illegitimate children see Cheryl Ann Cox, *Household Interests: Property, Marriage Strategies, and Family Dynamics in Ancient Athens* (Princeton: Princeton University Press, 1998), 172–73.

wrongly registered.[239] Perhaps this purge was not directly connected with the citizenship law;[240] however, there were occasions when purges (*diapsēphismos*) were ordered. In 346/5 a decree was issued by one Demophilos who had the citizen lists in all the *demes* examined; as a result many were disenfranchised.[241] This inward-looking, xenophobic practice seems contradictory for an imperial sea power, which Athens had become by the middle of the fifth century. But, as Charles Fornara and Loren Samons have argued, the tribute the Athenians extracted from their dependent states provided the funds to reimburse the Athenian citizens who sat on juries, served in the army and navy, attended the citizen assembly, and other public service jobs.[242] Such reimbursement made it possible for the entire socioeconomic spectrum of male citizens in Athens to participate in the government of the city. Thus Pericles put in place the law limiting citizenship to those with both parents as citizens in order to define who could participate in the governing tasks and be reimbursed. It was no longer necessary for an aspiring civil official to be a wealthy aristocrat for whom reimbursement was not an issue.[243]

Pericles issued his citizenship law and his law on reimbursing civil servants in the early years of his public life. These pragmatic steps made it possible for popular sovereignty to be exercised. These laws, following upon the reforms of Ephialtes in 461/460 that had limited the duties of the aristocratic court on the Areopagus to cases of blood vengeance and called for the creation of popular juries, were revolutionary in clearing the way for participation in the government of the city by all the male citizens: this was a fundamental step in the creation of democracy in Athens.[244] Earlier reforms by Cleisthenes in 508/7 had led to the registration of the citizens in newly redrawn tribal configurations, but Cleisthenes'

239. Philochorus, in Felix Jacoby et al., *Fragmente der griechischen Historiker* (FGrHist), 328 F 119; Plutarch, "Pericles," 37.2; Frank E. Adcock, "The Breakdown of the Thirty Years Peace B.C. 445–431," CAH, 1st ed., vol. 5, *Athens 478–401 B.C.*, ed. J. B. Bury, S. A. Cook, and F. E. Adcock, 165–92 (Cambridge: Cambridge University Press, 1927) at 167–68; Davies, "Athenian Citizenship," 107, 111–12.

240. P. J. Rhodes, *A History of the Classical Greek World, 478–323 BC* (Malden, MA: Blackwell, 2006), 56.

241. Davies, "Athenian Citizenship," 112.

242. Charles W. Fornara and Loren J. Samons II, *Athens from Cleisthenes to Pericles* (Berkeley: University of California Press, 1991), 66–74.

243. Josiah Ober, *Political Dissent in Democratic Athens: Intellectual Critics of Popular Rule* (Princeton: Princeton University Press, 1998), 19–20; cf. Ian Morris, *Archaeology as Cultural History* (Oxford: Blackwell, 2000), 189–90.

244. Rhodes, *History of the Classical Greek World*. E. M. Walker, "The Periclean Democracy," CAH, vol. 5: *Athens 478–401 B.C.*, 98–112, at 98–101.

moves left the aristocratic power base intact. It was not until the legislation of Ephialtes and Pericles that the wide-ranging citizen base began to express its voice.[245]

By stating that both parents must be Athenian citizens, Pericles's law on citizenship had the effect of banning intermarriage. This law is spelled out further by a set of marriage laws Apollodorus cites in the trial of the ex-prostitute Neaira around 340 BCE.[246] She had been cohabiting with an Athenian citizen named Stephanus and had given birth to children whom she then claimed were Athenian citizens. The law Apollodorus cites indicates that any Athenian citizen who becomes aware of such fraudulent claims to citizenship is to bring this matter before the *thesmothetai*, "legislators." A person who is found guilty is to be sold along with his or her property. One-third of the property is to be awarded to the citizen who brought the charge.[247] In another law cited by Apollodorus it is decreed that any citizen who arranges the marriage of a foreign woman with a citizen while presenting her as if she were a citizen shall be stripped of his rights as a citizen and shall forfeit his property. Once again the person who brings the charge against the offender is to be awarded one-third of the property.[248] The framers of such laws could defend their stance by claiming that if the *demos* of Athens were to maintain their position within the government they had to uphold the criterion of birth for citizenship.[249]

Pericles, whose mother was an Alcmeonid, championed his democratic reforms in the face of strong opposition from conservative aristocratic groups.[250] Cimon, who had visions of an imperial Greece based on an alliance between Athens and Sparta, had influenced Athens in promoting the development of the economic potential of the Delian league.

245. Fornara and Samons, *Athens from Cleisthenes to Pericles*, 25–26.

246. Demosthenes, "Theomnestus and Apollodorus against Neiara" 59:52, in *Demosthenes Private Orations:* Volume III, *Orations L–LIX*, trans. A. T. Murray (Cambridge, MA: Harvard University Press, 1939), 111–13; Davies, "Athenian Citizenship," 112–13; Cynthia B. Patterson, *The Family in Greek History* (Cambridge, MA: Harvard University Press, 1998), 111; Daniel Ogden, *Greek Bastardy in the Classical and Hellenistic Periods* (Oxford: Clarendon Press, 1996), 65–66.

247. Demosthenes, "Theomnestus and Apollodorus against Neaera," 16; Patterson, *The Family in Greek History*, 111.

248. Demosthenes, "Theomnestus and Apollodorus against Neaera," 52; Patterson, *The Family in Greek History*, 111.

249. Aristotle, *Athenian Constitution* 26.3; Fornara and Samons, *Athens from Cleisthenes to Pericles*, 74; Rhodes, *History of the Classical Greek World*, 55.

250. Fornara and Samons, *Athens from Cleisthenes to Pericles*, 1, 24, 33.

This initiative brought wealth from dependent allies into Athens. Paradoxically, Cimon prepared the way for his alienation from the Athenian democrats and for his expulsion from the city in 452 through the wealth that came to Athens. This imperial money strengthened the voice of the average Athenian citizen in the civic assembly, who then expelled those powerful individuals who were perceived to be potential tyrants, which was the rationale undergirding the Athenian practice of ostracism.[251]

The collaborative relationships between Athenian aristocrats and Spartan nobles later led the Spartans in 431 to call upon the Athenians to expel Pericles from Athens as an accursed one.[252] In this time of crisis at the beginning of the second Peloponnesian War (431–404), the Spartans were using a political ploy from which the Athenians of the sixth–fifth centuries had apparently agreed to refrain: claiming that the ancestral curse of the Alcmeonid clan from the latter part of the seventh century still tainted the offspring of this line.[253] The Alcmeonids were allegedly banished from Athens around 630 BCE for having slaughtered the men associated with Cylon after promising that they would not be killed. This sacrilegious action in the environs of the sanctuary of Apollo Patroos called for the expulsion of the members of the clan and the disinterment of their ancestral remains; shortly thereafter, according to the account in Diogenes Laertius 1.109–14, the city was purified by Epimenides from Crete.[254] Nevertheless, it appears that Alcmeon was back in Athens by the beginning of the sixth century, for he is reported to have been a participant on Athens' behalf in the First Sacred War in 595–585 BCE. It is surmised that the Alcmeonids were given amnesty in the reforms of Solon in 594.[255] Thus the presence of the Alcmeonids in Athenian politics can be traced at various points throughout the sixth–fifth centuries; there is no evidence that an Athenian used this ancestral curse as a disqualifier of the Alcmeonids. But the Spartans raised the issue in 431, which indicates that even if many of

251. Ibid., 1–2; Rhodes, *History of the Classical Greek World*, 62. Sarah Kofman, "Socrates and His Twins (The Socrates[es] of Plato's *Symposium*)," in *Feminism and the History of Philosophy*, ed. Genevieve Lloyd, 41–67 (New York: Oxford University Press, 2002), at 57, notes that Athenian democracy was "unable to tolerate exceptional human beings" and thus condemned Socrates to death—"one form of ostracism."

252. Such collaboration between certain aristocrats and Spartans had been happening in the fifth century (Thucydides, 1.107).

253. Fornara and Samons, *Athens from Cleisthenes to Pericles*, 12.

254. John Pairman Brown, *Israel and Hellas*, 3 vols., BZAW 231, 276, 299 (Berlin: de Gruyter, 1995–2001), 2:179; Martin L. West, *The Orphic Poems* (Oxford: Clarendon Press, 1983), 45–53.

255. Fornara and Samons, *Athens from Cleisthenes to Pericles*, 7.

the Athenians regarded this curse as a superstition it still lived on in the popular imagination.[256]

Pericles perished in the plague that struck Athens in 429. He appears to be the political figure behind Oedipus in Sophocles' *Oedipus Tyrannus*.[257] He was not only a leader in political reform, he was also responsible for major building projects in Athens such as the Parthenon and was a strong patron of the arts and of intellectual discussion.[258] He paved the way for democratic government in Athens; his vision and expertise encouraged popular participation.[259] With his untimely death Athens was sent into a declining spiral in which internal discord and missteps in its battles with Sparta put Athens in dire straits by the last decade of the fifth century. Athens ended by losing the Peloponnesian war with Sparta but surprised onlookers by its resilience in the face of almost certain defeat in the last years of the war.[260]

Pericles's law on citizenship built on the Athenian predilection for endogamy.[261] The region of Attica—i.e., Athens and its surrounding region—had been functioning as a unit for some time. Mythically it traced this unity to the *synoikismos* of Theseus, the founding hero whose efforts to unify Attica at the expense of the aristocrats reflects the historical accomplishments of Peisistratus and Cleisthenes in the sixth century BCE.[262] But it seems that foreign craftsmen and other metics (i.e., resident aliens)

256. Ibid., 12.

257. Charles Segal, *Oedipus Tyrannus: Tragic Heroism and the Limits of Knowledge* (New York: Twayne Publishers, 1993), 9.

258. E. M. Walker, "Athens and the Greek Powers, 462–445 B.C.," *CAH*, 1st ed., vol. 5: *Athens 478–401 B.C.*, ed. J. B. Bury, S. A. Cook, and F. E. Adcock, 68–97 (Cambridge: Cambridge University Press, 1927), at 72–74; Rhodes, *History of the Classical Greek World*, 62–65.

259. Ober, *Political Dissent in Democratic Athens*, 88–89.

260. Cf. Robert B. Strassler, *The Landmark Thucydides* (New York: Touchstone, 1996), 549; Antony Andrewes, "The Spartan Resurgence," in CAH, 2d ed., vol. 5, *The Fifth Century B.C.*, 464–98, at 496–98.

261. Ober, *Political Dissent in Democratic Athens*, 89, states that in his Funeral Oration in 430 BCE Pericles claims that "the individual's identification with the state must take priority over all other loyalties and allegiances." Richard Seaford, "Dionysus as Destroyer of the Household: Homer, Tragedy, and the Polis," in *Masks of Dionysus*, ed. Thomas H. Carpenter and Christopher A. Faraone, 115–46 (Ithaca, NY: Cornell University Press, 1993), 138, notes, however, that Dionysus is the enemy of endogamy.

262. Isocrates, *Helen*, 35; Plutarch, *Theseus*, 32; Fornara and Samons, *Athens from Cleisthenes to Pericles*, 4, 52–55; Sophie Mills, *Theseus, Tragedy, and Athenian Empire* (Oxford: Clarendon Press, 1997), 12–13, 24–25.

had been granted citizenship in the time of Solon.[263] As in the case of Neaira referred to earlier,[264] many seemed to think that there were ways to massage this law so as to incorporate outsiders into the polis community. In Sophocles' *Oedipus Colonus,* when Oedipus in his old age requests to be buried in a suburb of Athens he makes the claim that Athens is known for its openness to exiles and outcasts (*OC* 260-64)—a way that is supposed to stand in contrast to Thebes, from which he had been banished. Nevertheless, the myths of autochthony, in which the original Athenians claimed to have been born from the soil, point to a strong underlying agreement of the Athenians with Pericles's law.[265] So if one were to characterize Pericles as a heroic figure in his political reforms in the mid-fifth century, it would not seem to be on the basis of his overcoming strong opposition from the Athenians but rather of his doggedly pursuing his vision of an imperial, democratic Athens.[266]

Property, Inheritance, and Intimacy Within the Greek Household

The Alcmeonid clan to which Pericles was related was a wealthy family competing with other aristocratic families for power and influence in Athens.[267] A legendary account in Herodotus (6.125.1-5) relates in a humorous way how Alcmeon gained wealth from Croesus of Lydia. In return for Alcmeon's assistance to a Lydian delegation to the Delphic oracle, Croesus invited Alcmeon to take as much gold as he could carry on his person. Alcmeon loaded his clothing and filled his mouth and hair with gold so that he was hardly able to move—a sight Croesus found entertaining, and so he gave him that gold and much more. The substantial influence of the Alcmeonids in the politics of Athens in the sixth–fifth centuries would hardly have been possible if the family had not possessed substantial wealth. The traditional source of wealth for a household was land, but trade and the role of the merchant became increasingly important in Athens with the commercial revolution of the seventh century.[268]

263. Pomeroy, *Families in Classical and Hellenistic Greece,* 37; Davies, "Athenian Citizenship," 115.

264. See n. 242 above.

265. Vincent J. Rosivach, "Autochthony and the Athenians," *Classical Quarterly* n.s. 37 (1987): 294–306, at 303, 305.

266. Fornara and Samons, *Athens from Cleisthenes to Pericles,* 149–50.

267. Ibid., 4, 39.

268. David W. Tandy, *Warriors into Traders: The Power of the Market in Early Greece* (Berkeley: University of California Press, 1997), 136.

The anti-merchant rhetoric that surfaces on occasion in Homer's *Odyssey* (*Od*. 6.273; 7.30; 8.442; 14:285-97) may well be a mask for the aristocrats' realization that trade rather than agriculture would be the source of new wealth driving key activities in the Greek city-state.[269] The aristocratic model of the landed estate is Homer's preoccupation as he describes the turmoil that arises when the head of the household is absent due to extended military service. Over the course of Odysseus's twenty-year absence Penelope was left to manage the household and raise their infant son Telemachus. The greedy suitors were diminishing the substance of Odysseus's household for the ostensible purpose of winning the hand of Penelope in marriage (*Od*. 16.383-92). Athena, the divine protector of Odysseus's household, advises Telemachus, who is coming of age as heir, what he should urge Penelope to do: "As for your mother, if her heart urges her to marry, let her return to the house of her very powerful father. There they will arrange a wedding for her and prepare a large number of gifts, as many as are fitting to accompany a beloved daughter" (*Od*. 1.275-78). Penelope had wielded authority over the household for the past twenty years and was surprised when the heir Telemachus took steps to assume greater authority in the house (*Od*. 1.345-59).[270] Since Penelope appears to be a widow, she may remarry, but the only wealth she is allowed to remove from the household is her dowry, which she would then take with her on her return to her father's house.[271] Then the father's house would make arrangements with the household of the suitor for the transfer of Penelope to her new home.[272]

The suitors' ongoing consumption of Telemachus's household threatened to undermine his political potential as the future ruler of Ithaca.

269. Ibid., 4–5, 123–26; William Thalmann, "Review of Carol Dougherty, *The Raft of Odysseus: Ethnographic Imagination of Homer's Odyssey*," *Classical Journal* 98 (2002): 221–24, at 223. Oswyn Murray, *Early Greece* (Atlantic Heights, NJ: Humanities Press, 1980), 64, claims that "some features of the Homeric poems point to an earlier state; but as far as social and political organizations are concerned, despite the importance of the *genos* and the *oikos*, Homer and Hesiod show that the polis already existed in all essential aspects by the end of the Dark Age."

270. Froma Zeitlin, "Figuring Fidelity in Homer's *Odyssey*," in *Playing the Other*, 19–52, at 25, notes that the issue of Penelope's fidelity to Odysseus "is the principal anxiety that hovers over the whole poem."

271. Raymond Westbrook, "Penelope's Dowry and Odysseus' Kingship," in http://chs.harvard.edu/chs/files/women_property_westbrook.pdf, accessed June 24, 2009, 1–18, at 11, argues that the kingship of Ithaca was part of Penelope's dowry; thus the suitors coveting the kingship of Ithaca sought to marry her (cf. 1 Kgs 9:16; *Il*. 6.191–94; 9.147–56).

272. Cox, *Household Interests*,105.

There were no other male siblings with whom Telemachus would have been obliged to share his inheritance, but he needed this wealth in order to be able to support the members of his family, his activities, and the various servants. Servants who loyally served for many years became influential in the affairs of the household.[273] Eumaeus, the royal swineherd, seems to have taken over many of the functions of a father for Telemachus in Odysseus's absence and appears to have had a solid, close relationship with Penelope (*Od.* 15.364-79). The elderly servant Eurycleia was fully aware of the operations of the household and had gained the confidence of Penelope (*Od.* 19.466-508). This web of relationships within the aristocratic Homeric household presents a model of household relationships that shaped the imaginations of generations of Greeks in the Archaic and Classical periods. These relationships were created and sustained by the loyalty and sacrifices of the family and its servants. If the material basis of the household weakened, its embodied relationships were endangered. The presence of beggars like the disguised Odysseus and the fall from fortune of Eumaeus, who had been abducted from a noble Phoenician household as a child and sold as a slave, accent the importance of the security and material substance provided by the hereditary household.[274]

Slaves continued to play important roles in the Athenian *oikos* throughout the Archaic and Classical periods. Some slaves performed menial, thankless tasks such as working in the silver mines at Laurium; others were artisans and domestic workers; still others worked in positions in the public realm. In the household it was often difficult to distinguish a slave from a free person when they engaged in similar tasks.[275]

Competition among aristocratic houses was a hallmark of the politics of Archaic and Classical Greece. In Homer's *Odyssey* the suitors from the aristocratic families of Ithaca had a range of goals in mind in seeking the hand of Penelope. Antinous wanted a share of the property of Odysseus's household, but primarily he wanted the right of succession to the

273. For the influential roles of slaves and others in the *oikos* of the Classical period see ibid., 198.

274. Walter Donlan, "Reciprocities in Homer," *Classical World* 75 (1982): 137–75, at 155, 157; Dale Launderville, *Piety and Politics: The Dynamics of Royal Authority in Homeric Greece, Biblical Israel, and Old Babylonian Mesopotamia* (Grand Rapids: Eerdmans, 2003), 120–21, 263–64; William G. Thalmann, *The Swineherd and the Bow: Representations of Class in the Odyssey* (Ithaca, NY: Cornell University Press, 1998) 17, 20, argues that slavery was submerged in the *Odyssey*, with the hierarchical relation between the head of the household (Penelope/Telemachus) and the dependent (Eumaeus) framed in a positive manner.

275. Cox, *Household Interests*, 190, 198.

kingship of Ithaca (*Od.* 16.384-86; 22:53).[276] Others were wastrels who simply wanted to have a good time at the expense of Odysseus's household (*Od.* 6.680-95; 14.83). The aristocrats were not engaged in a war of all against all in their competition with one another, as shown by the importance they placed on alliance making.[277] The Alcmeonids were destined to be outsiders to the aristocrats in sixth-century Athens.[278] When around 575 BCE the Alcmeonid Megacles II married Agariste, the daughter of the tyrant of Sicyon, Cleisthenes the Orthagorid, he took a major step toward the rehabilitation of the Alcmeonid family in the region. He seems to have won her hand despite fierce competition from other Greek nobles (Herodotus 6.126-30).[279] The bond forged between two households brought economic benefits but, much more so, prestige and influence.[280]

Because marriages were primarily transactions between two households rather than between a man and a woman, the father of the bride played a strategic role in choosing the groom. When Nausicaa meets Odysseus on the beach and assists him with her attendants she gives him directions on how to reach her father's palace in the midst of the city, but she will not accompany him for fear of gossip by the men who have been seeking to marry her (*Od.* 6.274-84). For a young woman to meet a stranger and bring him home as a suitor was against the customs of the Greek household. Thus Nausicaa remarks, "I also would be upset with a girl who would act in this way: she, contrary to the wishes of her beloved father and mother, associates with men prior to entering into public marriage" (*Od.* 6.286-89). But when Alcinous meets Odysseus and hears part of his story, he expresses the wish that Odysseus might be his son-in-law (*Od.* 7.311-15).

Marriage was a social process rather than a legal act in Archaic and Classical Greece.[281] A marriage was validated by a series of events over time that were publicly witnessed: (1) formal betrothal and the designation of the bride as the future mother of legitimate children (*engyan*), (2) a public wedding procession and a feast on the wedding day (*gamein*),

276. Westbrook, "Penelope's Dowry and Odysseus' Kingship," 13.

277. Thalmann, The Swineherd and the Bow, 261.

278. Fornara and Samons, *Athens from Cleisthenes to Pericles*, 12; P. J. Rhodes, "The Athenian Revolution," in CAH, 2d ed., vol. 5, *The Fifth Century B.C.*, 95, at 63, 73.

279. Fornara and Samons, *Athens from Cleisthenes to Pericles*, 7–8.

280. Patterson, *The Family in Greek History*, 57–58. On the "in-class marriage system" see Ian Morris, "The Use and Abuse of Homer," *Classical Antiquity* 5 (1986): 81–138, at 113–14.

281. Patterson, *The Family in Greek History*, 108–9.

(3) the setting up of a new household (*synoikein*), and (4) the birth and recognition of children (*paidopoiein*).[282] There was no marriage contract. The events of the wedding day in item (2) would have been the key public ceremonies; however, the total process was constitutive of the marriage.[283]

Procreation was the primary goal of marriage in the Greek city-state.[284] Girls typically married at age 14, whereas men did so at age 30. The choice of the young age for the bride seems to have been aimed at increasing her years of childbearing. The practice at Sparta departed from that of the rest of Greece, for it delayed the childbearing tasks of its young women by a few years.[285] Guided by legislation attributed to their historical founder Lycurgus (Herodotus 1.65-66), the Spartans believed that the young couple, both man and woman, should be in top physical condition in order to beget the best offspring. Therefore young women undertook a program of physical exercise and conditioning that would prepare them to maximize their procreative potential. This practice of delayed childbearing came under pressure in those times when the number of war dead was high and the city needed to rebuild its population quickly.[286] Plato, whose view of the ideal city is modeled in many ways after Sparta, believes that it is a man's duty to his city and the gods to marry and produce offspring who are beneficial to the state. If he fails to marry by the age of thirty-five, a man should pay a yearly

282. Ibid., 109; Rush Rehm, *Marriage to Death: The Conflation of Wedding and Funeral Rituals in Greek Tragedy* (Princeton: Princeton University Press, 1994), 11–18; William D. Furley, *Studies in the Use of Fire in Ancient Greek Religion* (New York: Arno Press, 1981), 183–88. Aphrodite A. Avagianou, "*Hieros Gamos* in Ancient Greek Religion: The Human Aspect of a Sacralized Ritual," in *Sacred Marriages: The Divine-Human Sexual Metaphor from Sumer to Early Christianity*, ed. Martti Nissinen and Risto Uro, 145–71 (Winona Lake, IN: Eisenbrauns, 2008), at 150–56, divides the wedding ceremony into three temporal stages: (1) the day before the wedding, including sacrifices and dedications to Artemis and Hera; (2) the day of the wedding, including the nuptial bath, wedding feast, procession, and evening in the bridal chamber; (3) the day after the wedding, including the maidens' waking song and the presentation of gifts. Pomeroy, *Families in Classical and Hellenistic Greece*, 71, notes that no complete description of a Greek wedding in the Classical period is available.

283. Patterson, *The Family in Greek History*, 109; Aphrodite Avagianou, *Sacred Marriage in the Rituals of Greek Religion*, European University Studies, Classics XV (New York: Peter Lang, 1991), 1–18.

284. Walter K. Lacey, *The Family in Classical Greece* (London: Thames and Hudson, 1968), 110–11; cf. Patterson, *The Family in Greek History*, 133.

285. Ibid., 78.

286. Pomeroy, *Families in Classical and Hellenistic Greece*, 57.

fine and be deprived of the honor the elders typically receive from the young (*Laws* 6.774a-c).[287]

There was a family ceremony on the fifth, seventh, or tenth day after birth known as the *amphidromia*, "the running around." The newborn child would be carried in a circle around the hearth, the seat of the guardian goddess Hestia.[288] The father would then declare that the child was a full member of the household and a legitimate heir.[289] In Athenian law the sons shared equally in their father's estate. If the daughters received dowries, they were usually excluded from any further portion of the father's estate.[290] If the family had no sons, the daughters of the same father inherited.[291] If a family had neither sons nor daughters, then the members of the father's family would be first in line to inherit his estate. If this should fail, then the members of the mother's family were considered.[292] This web of relationships between brothers and sisters and then between paternal and maternal relatives was labeled the *anchisteia*.[293] Patterson highlights this web of relationships as the driving force in families toward sustaining the memory of the father and apportioning his estate. She argues that it is this web of relationships that guides the

287. Patterson, *The Family in Greek History*, 133–34.

288. Robert Parker, *Miasma: Pollution and Purification in Early Greek Religion* (Oxford: Clarendon Press, 1983), 51. Parker, *Polytheism and Society at Athens* (Oxford: Oxford University Press, 2005), 9, claims that Hestia was a symbol of the household and its cults since the Athenians did not have a household cult. In a similar vein, Patterson, *The Family in Greek History*, 65, argues that the hearth is a place of purity but has nothing to do with an ancestor or a god. However, Christopher A. Faraone, "Household Religion in Ancient Greece," in *Household and Family Religion in Antiquity*, 210–28, at 210–11, finds that scholarly skepticism over the existence of household cults overlooks data on gatherings of the members of the household in worship. With regard to the purity of the hearth and respect for Hestia see Susan Guettel Cole, *Landscapes, Gender, and Ritual Space: The Ancient Greek Experience* (Berkeley: University of California Press, 2004), 31–34. She interprets a passage such as Hesiod, *Op.* 733–34 as an illustration of how prohibitions that keep human physical processes separate from the divine are concerned with proper etiquette before the gods.

289. Jean-Pierre Vernant, *Myth and Thought among the Greeks* (London: Routledge & Kegan Paul, 1983), 153, 155; Louise Bruit Zaidman and Pauline Schmitt Pantel, *Religion in the Ancient Greek City* (Cambridge: Cambridge University Press, 1989), 64; Cox, *Household Interests*, 82.

290. Ibid., 105, 117.

291. Ibid., 109. Patterson, *The Family in Greek History*, 92–93, 104, notes that the legal *persona* of the heiress (*epiklēros*) is created by the polis in its concern to establish rules for the transfer of property (e.g., Arete of Phaeacia, *Od.* 7.54–66; Sophocles' Antigone).

292. Cox, *Household Interests*, 125.

293. Pomeroy, *Families in Classical and Hellenistic Greece*, 19; Patterson, *The Family in Greek History*, 58, 88–89; Lacey, *The Family in Classical Greece*, 28–29.

concern of the family members rather than a commitment to honor the deceased ancestors of the father's line.[294]

If a brother did not have a son or daughter to inherit his estate, his sister was under a strong obligation to secure an adopted son for him.[295] The emotional bonds between brother and sister were often stronger than those between husband and wife. The brother would show intense concern about a sister's dowry, her childlessness, and her potential divorce.[296] The sister's concern for her brother is illustrated in Sophocles' *Antigone* by Oedipus's daughter Antigone through her devotion to her brother Polyneices.[297] After the brothers Polyneices and Eteocles have killed one another, Antigone focuses on providing an honorable burial for both brothers. Such respect for relatives is an obligation of those who are part of the *anchisteia* of the deceased. In Sophocles' *Antigone* the new ruler of Thebes is Creon, who refuses to allow Polyneices to be buried since he has been a traitor and an aggressor against his homeland of Thebes (*Antig*. 21-39). Yet Creon is the paternal uncle of Polyneices and so is a member of his *anchisteia*. Antigone foregoes marriage and the chance for offspring out of her devotion to her brother and her family.[298] She makes known her priorities:

> But Hades, the lord of the place where all must sleep, leads me alive to the banks of Acheron. I am one who has had no share in the wedding song, nor has a nuptial song ever been sung for me. But I shall wed Acheron . . . . You have touched upon my most painful thought: the thrice-repeated fate of my father and of the destiny of the well-known house of Labdacus. Alas, for the ruin of my mother's marriage-bed and the ill-fated mother's sleeping with her own son, my father. From such ones was my wretched being begotten. I, already accursed and unwed, go to dwell with them. Alas, my brother,

294. Patterson, *The Family in Greek History*, 97–98, 144.

295. Cox, *Household Interests*, 126.

296. Ibid., 114–15.

297. Patterson, *The Family in Greek History*, 113–14. Richard Seaford, "Dionysus as Destroyer of the Household," 120–21, notes that Antigone will not marry on account of the death of her kin (Soph. *Antig*. 891–904).

298. Froma Zeitlin, "Thebes: Theater of Self and Society in Athenian Drama," in *Greek Tragedy and Political Theory*, ed. J. Peter Euben, 101–41 (Berkeley: University of California Press, 1986), at 125. Clifford Orwin, "Feminine Justice: The End of the Seven against Thebes," *Classical Philology* 75 (1980): 187–96, at 195, notes that in Aeschylus's *Seven against Thebes*, Eteocles tries to resolve the tension between family and city by regarding the city itself as a family; he understands autochthony as a claim that the city is a family.

> you came upon an ill-fate in marriage. In your being already dead,
> you kill me. (*Antig.* 810-16, 858-71)

The web of relationships Antigone shares with her family extends into the netherworld. Her devotion to her family is not simply to keep their memory alive and to honor them in the equitable distribution of their patrimony. She desires to be with them even if this means death for her.[299] This yearning to be with the ancestors reflects the piety of the family that was expressed through the family cult, as seen in the rites of the Genesia festival celebrated on Boedromium 5 (24 August).[300]

Adultery was defined as the violation of the exclusive sexual relationship of a wife with her husband. The wife needed to limit her sexual relations to her husband if the paternity of her children was to be known. The honor of the family was called into question by adulterous actions.[301] In the Homeric epics the abduction of Helen by Paris of Troy led to the ten-year Trojan war between the Achaean coalition and the allied forces of Troy. The crime of adultery went beyond an offense to the family and involved the larger community. In Aeschylus's *Oresteia*, Clytemnestra's affair with Aegisthus is not only aggression against the household of Agamemnon but also an act of corruption. Orestes defends his act of matricide before the chorus by claiming that "[Clytemnestra] is tainted with a double defilement . . . . When she killed her husband, she killed my father" (Aesch. *Eum.* 600, 602). Her crime was not simply against Agamemnon and his patriline but also against the living household as a whole.[302] Thus, as Patterson argues, when the Furies agree to a jury trial for a murder rather than exacting blood vengeance they position themselves to become "the public defenders of marriage and marital fertility."[303] In the early sixth century Solon's laws mandated that a woman caught in adultery had to be divorced and returned to her natal

299. Patterson, *The Family in Greek History*, 114, regards Antigone as "an isolated heroic figure, persevering in a courageous but limited vision of family and polis responsibility."

300. Robert Parker, *Polytheism and Society at Athens*, 20–31. Faraone, "Household Religion in Ancient Greece," 212, distinguishes worship practices identified with the *oikos* ("house, household") as location and those identified with the *genos* ("family") as genetic relations or ones based on reproduction; he argues for "household religion" (or "oikic-cult" as he terms it) by disagreeing with the dominant scholarly view that piety within the household was individually rather than communally expressed.

301. Seaford, "Dionysus as Destroyer of the Household," 135, notes that Dionysus and Hera are natural enemies.

302. Patterson, *The Family in Greek History*, 142–43.

303. Ibid., 145.

household. Thus adultery was an offense not only against the family to which the wife belonged but also against the city.[304] With the gradual rise in power of the middle class in Athens, and particularly with the revolution in civic decision making at the time of Ephialtes and Pericles, the well-being of these middle-class households was fundamental to the quality of life in the city-state.

The pragmatic concern over the right of inheritance is a serious issue that frequently sets family members at odds. Full brothers and half-brothers would battle over paternal wealth. When a sister became eligible to inherit portions beyond her dowry she could begin to act like an inheriting male.[305] In Sparta the Lycurgan system for creating an equal class of hoplite soldiers left intact the traditional family practice of inheritance. Since many men perished in battles, the women in the household were often the offspring who inherited the family estate. Aristotle reports that in the fourth century BCE women owned two-fifths of all Spartan land.[306]

The relationship between the husband and the wife lay at the center of the household. Even though marriages were arranged between households, the intimacy of the husband/wife relationship was an important concern of the household and was a matter to which the couple paid much attention. The orations of Isaeus (early fourth century BCE) emphasize this effort of the husband and wife to make the relationship work. Yet within these orations the competing viewpoints over the place of affection in marriage come to expression: some promote the ideal that a husband be romantically and sexually intimate with his wife; however, others say that such behavior is in poor taste and will lead to gossip that the woman is the man's *hetaira* ("concubine, prostitute") and not his wife (Isaeus 3.13-14).[307] If a husband in fifth/fourth-century Athens had an affair with another woman, it seems that he was expected not to bring that woman into his house.[308]

304. David Cohen, *Law, Sexuality, Society: The Enforcement of Morals in Classical Athens* (Cambridge: Cambridge University Press, 1994), 124; Elizabeth Meier Tetlow, *Women, Crime, and Punishment in Ancient Law and Society*, 2 vols. (New York: Continuum, 2004, 2005), vol. 2, *Ancient Greece*, 51–52.

305. Cox, *Household Interests*, 113; Patterson, *The Family in Greek History*, 92–93, 104.

306. Aristotle, *Politics* 1270a.23-28; Patterson, *The Family in Greek History*, 76; Pomeroy, *Families in Classical and Hellenistic Greece*, 54–56.

307. Cox, *Household Interests*, 72.

308. Patterson, *The Family in Greek History*, 137; Charles Segal, "Trachiniae," in *Tragedy and Civilization: An Interpretation of Sophocles* (Cambridge, MA: Published for Oberlin

Nevertheless, *hetairai* were a common sight in the classical *oikoi*.[309] These *hetairai*, frequently from the lower class or foreign peoples, were diverse: some were the intellectual equals of men; others were concubines; still others were residents in brothels.[310] Prostitution was a more lucrative form of work than woolworking and other occupations open to lower-class free women and slaves.[311] If a *hetaira* established a semi-permanent relationship with a male householder she gained access to his wealth.[312] Pericles divorced his wife and began a relationship with Aspasia, a *hetaira*.[313] She was revered by Socrates for her intelligence and rhetorical ability.[314] Pericles had a son by Aspasia and gained permission from the city assembly to enroll this son as a citizen. This action strengthened the right of the father of the house to designate his heir, but it undermined the wife's role in defining who was legitimate or not.[315] So Pericles seems to contradict himself by championing this right to make his own son legitimate whereas previously he had enacted the citizenship law in 451 that prohibited sons not born of Athenian wives from being counted as citizens.[316]

In Sophocles' *Trachiniae*, Deianira looks anxiously for the return of her husband Heracles from an extended military campaign. She knows that he has engaged in numerous extramarital affairs (*Trach*. 460, 545-51),[317] so initially she is not disturbed by reports that Heracles is bringing a young slave woman home with him. But the messenger imparting this news tries to prepare Deianira for the unwelcome reality that Heracles is passionately drawn to this slave woman (*Trach*. 357-73). He has brought within his

College by Harvard University Press, 1981), 60–108, at 79. Plato (*Laws*, 6.841) claims that it is dishonorable for a man to fail to keep an extramarital affair quiet.

309. Cox, *Household Interests*, 173; Edward E. Cohen, "Free and Unfree Sexual Work: An Economic Analysis of Athenian Prostitution," in *Prostitutes and Courtesans in the Ancient World*, ed. Christopher Faraone and Laura McClure, 95–124 (Madison, WI: University of Wisconsin Press, 2006), at 102.

310. Cox, *Household Interests*, 173–75; Kathleen Wider, "Women Philosophers in the Greek World: Donning the Mantle," *Hypatia* 1 (1986): 21–62, at 25, 42.

311. Cohen, "Free and Unfree Sexual Work," 106–7.

312. Cox, *Household Interests*, 188; cf. Cohen, "Free and Unfree Sexual Work," 109–10, 113.

313. Cox, *Household Interests*, 185; Wider, "Women Philosophers in the Greek World," 40–41; Elisabeth Meier Tetlow, *Women, Crime, and Punishment*, 2: 66.

314. Plato, *Menexenes*, 235e-236c; 249d; Wider, "Women Philosophers in the Greek World," 42–43.

315. Cox, *Household Interests*, 185.

316. Wider, "Women Philosophers in the Greek World," 40–41.

317. Segal, "Trachiniae," 74.

house a type of sexuality that should have remained outside; the boundary between human and bestial sexuality has been breached.[318] At this news Deianira responds: "Oh no! How has this ever happened to me? What secret calamity have I allowed under my roof? I am distressed! She is nameless just as the one who brought her here has sworn—yet she is extremely striking in her appearance and pedigree" (ll. 375-79). Heracles' passion for the slave woman Iole changes the situation for Deianira:[319]

> For I think she is no longer a maiden but a wife. I have taken on freight like a seaman, merchandise that troubles my heart. And now the two of us must stay under one cover waiting for the beloved one. Of such a kind is the gift that Heracles, the trusted one called good by us, sent back to me for maintaining the household for a long time. I do not know how to be angry with him for he is often sick with this same illness. But to live in the same house with her and to share the same marriage—what woman could do this? (*Trach.* 536-46)

It is at this point that Deianira devises her plan to afflict Heracles with the love potion given her by the centaur. She hopes it will excite his passion for her, but instead it brings him to his death (*Trach.* 1138-42). When she realizes the powers unleashed against Heracles by the centaur's potion, she takes her own life (*Trach.* 718-19, 919-30).[320] Charles Segal notes that "in the symbolism of the play erotic desire is a black poison that clouds the mind and brutalizes the soul."[321]

City-State and Household: Synergy or Compromise?

The aristocratic households of the archaic age had to face new constraints on their autonomy with the emergence of the city-state. Solon enacted legislation that limited public display at funerals.[322] These legal measures were directed at aristocratic households that championed their identity through elaborate funerals for their deceased family members. Solon also exhorted the residents of Athens to be mindful of their interdependence in the polis; they could not afford to amass wealth without taking into account the ways self-seeking competition undermined the social fabric

318. Ibid., 75–76; Rehm, *Marriage to Death*, 82.

319. Charles Segal, *Sophocles' Tragic World: Divinity, Nature, Society* (Cambridge, MA: Harvard University Press, 1995), 84.

320. Segal, "Trachiniae," 77.

321. Ibid., 94.

322. Sarah C. Humphreys, "Family Tombs and Tomb Cult in Ancient Athens," *JHS* 100 (1980): 96–126, at 99, 101; Rehm, *Marriage to Death*, 26–27.

(Solon, fr. 13, lines 7–16).[323] Such greed was probably not limited to the trading entrepreneurs but also characterized many of the landed aristocratic families that had branched out and become involved in commercial enterprises.[324] A view of the autonomous household that makes strategic alliances with other households to advance its interests would need to factor in the ways its actions influence the quality of life in the polis.[325]

Aristocratic families continued to be the major players in Athenian politics until well into the first half of the fifth century. As noted earlier, the reforms of Ephialtes marked the sharp curtailment of aristocratic power and opened the way for participation in decision making by the citizen body at large. Since the population of Athens grew during the fifth century BCE at an annual rate of one percent and reached 60,000 by 432 BCE, the Athenians began to guard their privileges as citizens more jealously. In a time of abundant population the criteria for citizenship are more closely defined than in a time of population decline.[326] So the requirement of the citizenship law of 451 BCE that both father and mother be Athenians was enforced more rigorously in times of abundant population. This law seems to have been aimed not only at limiting the number of qualified participants in the governing process but also at curbing upstarts who might wield a disproportionate amount of influence.[327] One area from which these dangerous individuals could arise was the colonies. Athenian citizens who resided in these areas capitalized on the commercial opportunities there and made agreements with the people of the region. Thus foreign influence, like alliances between aristocratic households in the past, was elevating some colonists and making it possible for them to wield a disproportionate amount of influence in the government.[328] Many of these colonists married local women in the

323. *Iambi et Elegi Graeci ante Alexandrum Cantati*, vol, 2, ed. Martin L. West (Oxford: Clarendon Press, 1972), 127.

324. Tandy, *Warriors into Traders*, 135–38.

325. Seaford, "Dionysus as Destroyer of the Household," 137, notes that "in embodying the communal principle of the polis Dionysus is a potential destroyer of the household, presenting a latent threat to the tendency of the household to autonomy."

326. Robin Osborne, "Law, the Democratic Citizen and the Representation of Women in Classical Athens," *Past and Present* 155 (1997): 3–33, at 5; Davies, "Athenian Citizenship," 110–11.

327. Osborne, "Law, the Democratic Citizen and the Representation of Women in Classical Athens," 7.

328. Sarah C. Humphreys, "The *Nothoi* of Kynosarges," *JHS* 94 (1974): 88–95, at 93–94; cf. Philip Brook Manville, "Toward a New Paradigm of Athenian Citizenship," in *Athenian Identity and Civic Ideology*, ed. Alan L. Boegehold and Adele C. Scafuro, 21–33 (Baltimore: Johns Hopkins University Press, 1994), at 27.

colony who were not Athenian. The requirement that the mother of Athenian citizens be an Athenian would thus curtail the power of some of the colonists. In the practice of ostracism, which lasted from 487 to 417 BCE, common charges scribbled on the ostraca by the members of the citizen assembly were foreign birth and treachery.[329]

The polis needed the quality of the relationships within and between households to be healthy and productive. Where these relationships broke down, constructive means of restoring them had to be developed. When Odysseus purged his house of the corruption visited upon it by the suitors by killing them he incited blood vengeance from their families (*Od.* 24.463-71). The *Odyssey* ends with the intervention of Zeus and Athena to stay the vengeful actions of the suitors' families against Odysseus, Telemachus, and Laertes (*Od.* 24.528-32). The cycle of blood vengeance demanded a more rational form of adjudication, which the court procedure introduced by Apollo and Athena in Aeschylus's *Eumenides* supplies (ll. 470-565). However, for the householders the question remains whether their security was reduced by this change to a court system. This alteration in judicial procedure reflects the curtailment of aristocratic power introduced by Ephialtes's reforms in 462. The curses that weighed upon the house of Atreus in the *Oresteia* and the house of Laius in the Oedipus plays are a dramatically heightened form of the curse that weighed upon the Alcmeonid household.[330] The charge of the intergenerational transfer of the guilt of the early Alcmeonids to later generations was judged to be excessive and distorting by the Athenians, who chose to have the Alcmeonids in their midst as contributors to the polis community. The plots of the various tragic plays of the fifth century tended to highlight contradictions and dilemmas in the royal family and other powerful families in the community.[331] These plays emphasized the importance of healthy family relations and often showed how devotion to the state and its institutions can help the family maintain its equilibrium.

Aristotle makes a clearer distinction between the private realm of the household and the public sphere of the state than does Plato (*Politics* 1261a10-24).[332] Aristotle notes that the polis is naturally prior to the *oikoi* that comprise it, "since it is necessary that the whole be prior to its parts"

329. Osborne, "Law, the Democratic Citizen and the Representation of Women in Classical Athens," 7; Patterson, *The Family in Greek History*, 160.

330. Segal, *Oedipus Tyrannus*, 9–11.

331. Zeitlin, "Thebes: Theater of Self and Society in Athenian Drama," 132.

332. Patterson, *The Family in Greek History*, 175

(*Politics* 1253a20).[333] He notes that "the city consists not only of many humans but also of diverse ones, for a city does not arise from humans who are all alike" (*Politics* 1261a24). Aristotle's respect for diversity unfolds in the context of the priority of the whole to the parts. Individual households are not autonomous; only states are autonomous (*Politics* 1261b14). Households will need to make appropriate sacrifices to the common good. For Aristotle the state is the larger sphere within which households can develop; he does not see the state as an institution that by its very nature is inimical to the household.[334]

In his *La cité antique*, Fustel de Coulanges gave priority to the household over the state. He identified devotion to the ancestors as symbolized by attention to the hearth fire as the unifying dynamic of the family.[335] "Every family, having its gods and its worship, was required to have its particular place on the soil, its isolated domicile, its property."[336] Likewise, every family was to have its own tomb.[337] The ancestral line was the reality by which the members of the family transcended death; it was their way to find immortality. So the gatherings of the family around the hearth fire were intended to keep the memory and presence of the ancestors alive; worship of the family gods and ancestors was inseparable from the property.[338] In Fustel's model the names remembered in the family cult were those of the fathers; "the domestic religion was transmitted by blood from male to male."[339] He claimed that this devotion to the ancestors persisted in the early evolution of the state when families

333. Cox, *Household Interests*, 132; Patterson, *The Family in Greek History*, 44.

334. Carnes Lord, "Aristotle's Anthropology," in *Essays on the Foundations of Aristotelian Political Science*, 49–73, at 57, 69.

335. Numa Denis Fustel de Coulanges, *The Ancient City* (New York: Doubleday, 1956 [first published 1864]), 86. On the hearth cult see Sophocles' *Trachiniae*, 606. On the defilement of the altar of Zeus Herkeios by Eurydice, marking the death of her family in Sophocles' *Antigone* 1301–5, see Rehm, *Marriage to Death*, 66–67.

336. Fustel de Coulanges, *The Ancient City*, 63, 67. See Plato, *Laws* 729c; Pomeroy, *Families in Classical and Hellenistic Greece*, 70.

337. Fustel de Coulanges, *The Ancient City*, 64–65.

338. Ibid., 34–35, 40, 73, 146.

339. Ibid., 74, 78. He claimed (p. 86) that "the wife will not become an ancestor . . . . In death as in life, she counts only as a part of her husband." However, Humphreys, "Family Tombs and Tomb Cult in Ancient Athens," 112, 114, notes that sculptured grave monuments after the plague of 430 show domestic scenes in which husband, wife, and children are displayed, emphasizing intimate domestic relationships rather than piety to dead ancestors and remembrance of lineage. Osborne, "Law, the Democratic Citizen and the Representation of Women in Classical Athens," 29–30, argues that the sculptured grave monuments point to a rise in women's status in fifth-century Athens.

joined together in a confederation to form phratries and then tribes and finally the city.[340] In Fustel's view there was no individual liberty in the city-state: this organization, which was reinforced by the civic religion, controlled the body and soul of its citizens.[341] He concluded that the family (*gens*) and the city were structurally at odds with one another and eventually the right of primogeniture was undermined by the state; this led to the desacralization of the family's property in which it was treated as a commodity to be exchanged.[342]

Fustel's model of the early family as held together by patrilineal inheritance and ancestor worship still wields considerable influence, though he has been criticized, for example, for insufficient use of source criticism, overemphasis on the religious dimension of the evidence,[343] equating family with lineage, and giving historical priority to agnatic lineage.[344] Patterson argues that blood ties were not the distinguishing mark of the relationships in the ancient Greek family; instead "the most important family interests in early Greece were those of the *oikos* and of its members bound together in the central relationships of husband/wife, parent/child, and master/slave."[345] Through these relationships the members produced and reproduced the household. It seems, though, that while Fustel de Coulanges overemphasized the role of religion in the family, Patterson understates it. The domestic ancestor cult—whether located in the nuclear family of the *oikos* or the extended family of the *deme*—offers a way of understanding how the early Greeks viewed life after death and the desire for immortality.[346] For a people whose average

340. Fustel de Coulanges, *The Ancient City*, 127; Lacey, *The Family in Classical Greece*, 28–29; Faraone, "Household Religion in Ancient Greece," 212.

341. Fustel de Coulanges, *The Ancient City*, 220.

342. Ibid., 61–62, 65, 70, 86, 101, 132, 252–54.

343. Moses I. Finley, "The Ancient City: From Fustel de Coulanges to Max Weber and Beyond," *Comparative Studies in Society and History* 19 (1977): 305–27, at 311–12, 314, finds Fustel's emphasis on family religion as the glue of the ancient society to be overstated and uncritical.

344. Patterson, *The Family in Greek History*, 15. Humphreys, "Family Tombs and Tomb Cult in Ancient Athens," 123, claims that Fustel's explanation that the state undermined the family practice of the commemorative cult is too simplistic; she proposes instead that there was "a dialectical interaction between the expression of the feelings of the bereaved, the socially accepted channels and the material resources available for this expression, the standards of ostentation felt appropriate by different classes, and the other functions which such ostentation accumulated."

345. Patterson, *The Family in Greek History*, 67.

346. Parker, *Polytheism and Society at Athens*, 20–31; Faraone, "Household Religion in Ancient Greece," 213, 217.

lifespan was less than fifty years this concern for life after death would seem to have been important.

Summary

Use of property is not only essential for human life; it is also a means by which humans symbolize what they value. Archaic and Classical Athens struggled with trying to keep the social and economic strata of their community engaged in a working harmony: the rich and the powerful needed to be countered so that they did not undermine the livelihood of others and disenfranchise them, while the majority of the citizens needed to participate in the city assembly. The fifth century was a time of rapid growth in population and wealth in Athens, but also a time of war, plague, and internal strife. In the wake of the Persian Wars (490–479 BCE), the Athenians established a maritime empire. Pericles championed democratic and imperial development as he built Athens into the dominant Greek city-state. But the Persian threat remained alongside that of Sparta during the Peloponnesian War (431–404 BCE).

The battles in the public arena had an impact on the private affairs of the household and vice versa. Therefore marriage and inheritance practices had an impact on the well-being of the polis just as citizenship laws and colonial enterprises made their presence felt in the households of Athens. The lawful presence of a *hetaira* in a household and the disclosure of an illegal adulterous affair showed how intimate relationships in the household had a ripple effect throughout the polis. Legitimate offspring were important not only for reasons of inheritance but also for fulfilling familial obligations toward deceased ancestors and living family members. Thus the relationships that constituted the household were formed in concert with other households and the entire polis and were attentive not only to the here and now but also to the past and future. Ideally the relationship between polis and *oikos* was synergistic, but realistically there were tensions and trade-offs that called for each to be vigilant of the other. The living household was the matrix of relationships within which Greeks created lives with lasting meaning.

Synthesis: Maintaining the Cultural Integrity of the Household in Times of Transition

When a community is in crisis, the practice of intermarriage can be divisive. The entry of a new wife from outside the community who brings her dowry, her connections, and her culture with her can upset the fragile equilibrium of a vulnerable community. In the ancient societies of Israel, Mesopotamia, and Greece, marriage was a process that was typically overseen by the father of the bride. Because marriages were a traditional way in which royal or aristocratic households in one polity made alliances with foreign households, the state became involved in setting criteria for marriages when it judged that the culture and composition of the polity demanded it.

Purging a Community to Maintain Traditional Values: A Manipulative Ideology or a Heroic Vision?

Ezra's decree on the dismissal of foreign wives and their children and Pericles's law that Athenian citizens would have to demonstrate that both their mother and father were Athenians are two examples of how foreigners could no longer marry into a polity. Intermarriage between seminomadic herders and sedentary agriculturalists typically raised tensions in Mesopotamia because of the clash of cultures, but these tensions are remembered as an undercurrent in the dominant pattern of the assimilation of diverse cultures into that of Babylonia. Although Persian rulers capitalized on the diversity of peoples and cultures in their empire in the sixth to the fourth centuries BCE, they did not allow anyone but those from aristocratic Persian families to hold key administrative positions in their empire. They regarded bloodlines as a reliable indicator of loyalty. On the mythical level in the Mesopotamian tradition, concern over preserving the integrity of a household against perceived outside threats was spelled out in the widely known narrative of the *Enūma Elish*. In this world-creating account Marduk vanquishes Tiāmat and her allies in order to preserve the household of gods descended from Anu/Anshan; it is a political battle with cosmic significance. Just as Ezra's efforts to prohibit intermarriage created intercommunity conflict in Yehud, so also did Pericles's efforts in limiting citizenship to individuals with both an Athenian father and an Athenian mother curtail the efforts of aristocrats and powerful entrepreneurs in using marriage with foreigners as a way of increasing their wealth and influence. Closing ranks and defining more closely who is in and who is out is a predictable reaction of a community under threat.

The culture of a household and of a community is generated through the matrix of relationships among the individuals who comprise these social units. Ezra is fighting for a culture focused on worship of YHWH alone; Pericles fights for a culture that gives a share in decision making to the full socioeconomic range of Athenian citizens; Marduk fights for a cosmic community organized under his rule that is committed first of all to the maintenance of the sanctuaries of the gods. Where this matrix of relationships has been corrupted, a purge may be required. Ezra judges that Yehud is in crisis; Pericles seems content to let his citizenship law take effect over the course of the coming generations, although there may have been a purge of citizen lists in 445 in determining who qualified to receive a portion of a gift of grain from the Egyptian king Psammetichus; Marduk's banishing of Tiāmat, Kingu, and their armies constitutes a purge of the cosmic community and the establishment of new boundaries.

Property and Relationships: Two Constitutive Elements of the Embodied Character of the Household

The property of the household is a necessary substratum for its personal relationships. Without the requisite property the embodied members of this social unit must go elsewhere. Therefore the processes by which property is gained and handed on are key concerns to these households and to the surrounding communities of which they are a part. The tangible, measurable power of a household typically resides in the physical objects it possesses, either in the objects themselves or in what they symbolize. Cultural power is not the same as material power, but there is an interplay between the two types of power as the household seeks to find its place and establish its identity in the field of competing households. Adultery, divorce, and inheritance battles were three recurrent areas of vulnerability in the web of relationships that constituted the household in ancient Israel, Mesopotamia, and Greece. In each of these cultures the marriage relationship was patrilocal and patrilineal. Although the authority of the father was supreme in the households of each of these cultures, rarely could it be labeled absolute since the household was not autonomous but part of a larger confederation of households and clans.

In a marriage, the woman transfers from the house of her father to that of the groom. In a divorce she returns to her father's house with her dowry. One might argue then that the wife remains an outsider in the household of her husband. On the other hand, the laws prohibiting intermarriage and promoting endogamy point to the crucial character of the position of the wife and mother within the household. Her fidelity is critical to the legitimacy of the children.[347] Her role as educator of the

347. Patterson, *The Family in Greek History*, 27, notes that this view of a woman's position has raised the ire of a number of contemporary critics, who see it as a denial of the full moral personhood of women.

children is fundamental to the values that will reside in their bones. Ezra and Pericles recognized this fundamental role of the wife and mother within the private sphere of the household and the public sphere of the state. Attentiveness to the role of the wife and mother in the Mesopotamian tradition is also apparent in a number of the laws of the *CH*, particularly those that deal with adultery and the rights of inheritance.

At the time of marriage, the women, who were frequently only fourteen years of age, were expected to be virgins. The parents in Israel and the *susapinnu* (the observer in the bridal chamber) in Mesopotamia were expected to testify to the virginity of the bride if the need should arise. In Greece, girls were under the protection of the goddess Artemis, who was believed to jealously protect their virginity until the time of marriage. In cases of rape, provision needed to be made both to the woman and to her household for the loss of her virginal status (Deut 22:25-29; *Laws of Lipit-Ishtar* 33). From the time of betrothal onward the young woman was to be regarded as pledged exclusively to her husband-to-be, and sexual relations outside that pledged relationship were adulterous.

Procreation was the primary goal of marriage. Pleasure and intimacy were secondary to this primary focus of re-creating and sustaining the household, which in turn formed an indispensable building block for the state. If children were not begotten in a marriage in Mesopotamia, this was grounds for a divorce. In ancient Greece, Mesopotamia, and Israel, if a marriage was childless, other measures needed to be taken to secure an heir to the household and find a way to keep the patrilineal line intact: adoption, levirate marriage, a second wife.

A male heir would not only receive special attention in the division of the property; he was also charged with honoring the parents and ancestors. In Israel the firstborn son received a double portion of the inheritance (Deut 21:17); in Mesopotamia and Greece equal shares were given to all the sons, but the firstborn son was allowed to choose his portion first. In Mesopotamia a number of letters speak of the obligation of the firstborn son to carry out the monthly offering to the ancestors. This ritual is not mentioned in the Israelite texts, but there are residues of such a ritual in certain texts (e.g., 1 Sam 20:6). In ancient Greece there was a domestic ancestor cult.[348] Such attention to the ancestors was an extension of the honor children were expected to pay to their parents while alive. The identity of the household was embedded in the honor shown to the parents and ancestors.

348. Parker, *Polytheism and Society at Athens*, 9–36; Burkert, Greek Religion, 191, 194.

Inheritance practices were directed at handing on not merely the property of the family but also its name. When both the name and the property were handed on together, the stability or longevity of the name was enhanced. The property would provide the space for the family to reproduce not only physically but also culturally. Where this nexus between property and inhabitants was severed, the members of the family were dispersed into other households and locations and were assimilated into the culture of the new location. Aristocratic families grounded their name in the property that had been passed on through the generations. Burying the ancestors in the inner room of the house (*išertum*) in Mesopotamia ensured that the living members of the family would recognize the separate or sacred character of this place. Keeping the name of the family alive is more than simply sustaining a label; it is remembering, invoking, and presencing the ancestors within the activities of the living household. The community of the household extends vertically through the generations and horizontally across its living members.

The Incorporation of the Household into the City-State: A Pathway to Death or to Life After Death?

Because the average lifespan of the members of the ancient communities of Israel, Mesopotamia, and Greece was short, there was considerable pressure for each member to contribute to reproducing the community. Plato recommended a law that would levy a stiff fine on every male over thirty-five who had not married and produced offspring (*Laws* 774a-e). The same sentiment surfaces in the traditions of Mesopotamia and Israel. An individual who did not marry remained in the household of his or her origin or was dedicated to the household of a deity. Immortality was tied to the matrix of relationships of the household. This way of overcoming death was common to the cultures of Israel, Mesopotamia, and Greece. Gilgamesh's heroic effort to gain immortality outside the household ended in failure.

The vitality of the web of relationships of the household was important to the well-being of the state. Laws against adultery in all three ancient cultures testify to the ways in which intimate relationships in the privacy of the household have an impact on the state. Yet the state was interested in having various households fit into the larger configuration of relationships that constituted a city or a region;[349] therefore the inalienability of property that promoted the longevity of the particular

349. Seaford, "Dionysus as Destroyer of the Household," 134.

households was too rigid for the needs of a state. The capacity for households to incorporate foreigners and for individuals to change locations was important for the development of the state. Here the piety of the household and the clan, centered on reverence for the ancestors and its own traditions, would clash with the sociology and economics of the state. The traditional way of responding to the reality of death provided by the family and its ancestor cult would be absent to the person who identified himself or herself primarily as a citizen of a state. Such exposure to the power of death would contribute to the rise of mystery cults in Greece in the early sixth century BCE.

Chapter Three

Sex and the Holy: Erotic Synergy or Warfare?

The erotic dimension of human life can be both energizing and distressing. This passionate aspect of human experience is most properly at home within the sphere of personal relationships. The intensity of this passion can range from that expressed between good friends to that of lovers who unite sexually.[1] How this erotic dimension unfolds depends on the concrete, particular circumstances of the individuals involved. Can this erotic passion be legitimately extended to invisible deities or to ideas such as truth, wisdom, or goodness? Can it also be applied to objects like money and property, to activities like working or eating? Mapping out the terrain of erotic passion can produce at best tentative results because the common experience of *erōs* is configured according to the unique circumstances of individuals. This particularity raises questions of how the embodied character of *erōs* can be part of a relationship an individual has with an invisible deity or an abstract idea.[2] If the deity has a body, it would seem necessary to embrace that body and not merely to imagine it. To love an abstract idea like goodness would seem to require embracing particular people or things that participate in this goodness rather than encountering the essence of goodness in some disembodied way.

1. Frisbee C. C. Sheffield, *Plato's Symposium: The Ethics of Desire* (Oxford: Oxford University Press, 2006), 77; Guilia Sissa, "Sexual Bodybuilding: Aeschines against Timarchus," in *Constructions of the Classical Body*, ed. James I. Porter, 147–68 (Ann Arbor: University of Michigan Press, 1999), at 162.

2. H. J. Rose, "The Bride of Hades," *Classical Philology* 25 (1925): 238–42, at 239, notes that "ordinary people do not marry deities, or have any sort of sexual connection with them, in normal Greek cult."

The experience of the holy puts one in contact with a reality that transcends ordinary human experience. If one uses the language of metaphor to describe the holy as a state somewhere between the literal and the figurative, one gets the sense that the intangible is in some way tangible and the visible in some way becomes visible. If a key attribute of the divine is love, then this divine form of love will be perceptible as a reality resembling human love but not constrained in the same way. There is an in-betweenness about the holy in which human perception must take into account both the otherness and the ontological reality of the holy.[3] The way in which human *erōs* encounters divine *erōs* has a determining influence on the shape of a community and its members.

Erōs is a powerful passion that can build up and tear down. The Israelites of the Exodus generation were condemned for the wild festival they celebrated in honor of Yhwh: "Aaron constructed an altar in front of the calf and proclaimed, 'Tomorrow shall be a feast for the Lord.' Early the next day they offered burnt offerings and brought communion offerings. The people sat down to eat and drink, and then stood up to play (*lĕṣaḥēq*)" (Exod 32:5-6). The term *lĕṣaḥēq*, "to play," has often been understood to refer to sexual or erotically charged activities.[4] Subsequently their boisterous behavior is described as: they "have acted corruptly (*šiḥēt*)" (32:7); they have given voice to what seem to be drinking songs (*qôl ʿannôt*, v. 18);[5] they were dancing (*mĕḥōlōt*, v. 19) before the calf; they were "running wild" (*pāruaʿ*, v. 25). Perhaps the negative judgment on the people is focused on their idolatrous exuberance before the bull-calf.[6] Even if sexual activity in sacred space is not explicitly stated here, a key element in the judgment against the Israelites is their mistaken understanding of how to connect with the holiness of Yhwh. They try to overcome their feelings of anxious emptiness through highly charged, unrestrained activities whose dynamic of striving and release resembles that characteristic of the erotic. Yhwh condemns their worship as idolatrous: i.e., they have allowed too much of themselves to become part of the object of worship.[7] The restraint Yhwh expects from them has been

3. Marcel J. H. M. Poorthuis, "Introduction," in *Purity and Holiness: The Heritage of Leviticus*, ed. idem and Joshua Schwartz, 3–26 (Leiden: Brill, 2000), at 5, 9.

4. Martin Noth, *Exodus* (Philadelphia: Westminster, 1962), 248; Brevard Childs, *The Book of Exodus*, OTL (Louisville: Westminster, 1974), 566.

5. LXX adds *oinou*.

6. Cornelis Houtman, *Exodus: Volume 3, Chapters 20–40* (Leuven: Peeters, 2000), 643, translates *lĕṣaḥēq* as "to dance" and interprets the occasion as a joyous festival before a bull-calf rather than as an orgy.

7. Childs, *The Book of Exodus*, 564–67.

articulated in Moses' command that they were to wait until he returned (Exod 24:14). But the weight of this command was too much for them to bear (32:1).

Rituals among the neighboring peoples seem to have allowed a significant measure of the erotic to enter into their rituals. The Mesopotamian sacred marriage ritual, which was celebrated at Ur, Isin, and Larsa during the period 2100–1800 BCE, involved the sexual union of the king with a priestess representing Inanna.[8] Although there is no sure evidence that this ritual was practiced in this carnal form after 1800 BCE, the ritual did continue in a form in which the statues of the city deity and his/her consort were regarded as uniting sexually in order to renew the fertility of the realm.[9] By replacing the human participants in the ritual with statues, the ritual-makers removed sexual activity from the sanctuary and added a degree of abstraction to the way human *erōs* is understood to affect the workings of divine *erōs*. In the Greek tradition maenads celebrate the presence of the god Dionysus through ecstatic rituals.[10] In the *Bacchae*, Euripides portrays the communing of the women with nature on the mountains by having snakes fasten their garments and lick their faces, by their suckling fawns and wolf cubs and by wearing wreaths of ivy (ll. 693-702). While Pentheus suspects that they are guilty of sexual improprieties, the women seem to have held themselves to the ideal of chaste behavior during this annual three-day retreat from their homes to the hillside assemblies where they honored Dionysus.[11] When placed alongside the golden calf story (Exodus 32), these examples of rituals from Mesopotamia and Greece raise the question of how the erotic dimension of experience can be properly incorporated into wor-

8. Pirjo Lapinkivi, "The Sumerian Sacred Marriage and its Aftermath," in *Sacred Marriages: The Divine-Human Sexual Metaphor from Sumer to Early Christianity* (Winona Lake, IN: Eisenbrauns, 2008), 7–41, at 20–21; idem, *The Sumerian Sacred Marriage in Light of the Comparative Evidence*, SAAS 15 (Helsinki: Neo-Assyrian Text Corpus Project, 2004), 14; Jerrold Cooper, "Sacred Marriage and Popular Cult in Early Mesopotamia," in *Official Cult and Popular Religion in the Ancient Near East*, ed. Eiko Matsushima, 81–96 (Heidelberg: C. Winter, 1993), at 83.

9. Jacob Klein, "Sacred Marriage," *ABD* 5:867.

10. Walter Burkert, *Greek Religion* (Cambridge, MA: Harvard University Press, 1985), 223.

11. Martha Nussbaum, "Introduction," in Charles K. Williams, *The Bacchae of Euripides: A New Version* (New York: Farrar, Strauss, and Giroux, 1990), vii–xliv, at xiv. However, Richard Seaford, "Dionysus as Destroyer of the Household: Homer, Tragedy, and the Polis," in *Masks of Dionysus*, ed. Thomas H. Carpenter and Christopher A. Faraone, 115–46 (Ithaca, NY: Cornell University Press, 1993), at 122, interprets this scene as one in which the maenads have sexual relations with the animals.

ship. Too little *erōs* will leave one disconnected from the deity; too much *erōs* will dishonor the otherness of the deity. How to negotiate this ambiguity is fundamental to the vitality of individual and communal life.

If raw sensuality and explicit sexual expression are to be kept out of the sanctuary, these erotic energies essential to life must be repressed, channeled, or transmuted in order for proper etiquette to be displayed before the deities. How to understand these three options of repression, channeling, and transmuting will be examined according to the following three topics in texts drawn from the traditions of ancient Israel, Mesopotamia, and Greece: (1) the presence and function of the erotic within the divine realm; (2) the relationship between sex and knowledge; and (3) the impact of *erōs* on the sociopolitical structure. A preliminary step necessary for this examination will be to clarify and compare the terminology used for erotic experience in each of these three cultural traditions.

Erotic Experience: Its Basic Terminology in Ancient Israel, Mesopotamia, and Greece

A common way to try to provide guideposts for navigating erotic experience is to distinguish between the Greek terms *erōs*, *agapē*, and *philia*.[12] *Erōs* is defined as a strong attraction toward a desired object; the lack of such an object drives one through self-interest to try to acquire it.[13] *Philia* is the desire to be with another because one likes the other person; *philia* is aptly translated as "friendship."[14] *Agapē* is concern for another person for his/her sake; the element of self-interest in the relationship is minimized for the sake of the other person and the common good.[15] *Agapē* (*agapaō*) is the term the LXX uses to translate Hebrew *ʾāhēb*, "love," but is otherwise infrequently attested in prebiblical Greek sources.[16] *Erōs* is the typical Greek term for love, which Plato examines at length in the *Symposium* and the *Phaedrus*.[17] *Philia* receives an extended

12. Gottfried Quell and Ethelbert Stauffer, *agapaō*, *TDNT* 1:21–55.

13. Stauffer, *agapaō*, 35–36. Sex as a persistent drive that seeks to fill a lack shows the ancient Greeks' concern for the dynamics of desire; see Sissa, "Sexual Bodybuilding," 152; contra Michel Foucault, *The History of Sexuality*, vol. 1: *An Introduction*; vol. 2: *The Use of Pleasure*, trans. Robert Hurley (New York: Pantheon, 1978, 1985), 1:19–20; 2:26–27, 43, 50.

14. Stauffer, *agapaō*, 36–37.

15. Ibid., 37.

16. Quell, *agapaō*, 22.

17. Stauffer, *agapaō*, 35.

treatment by Aristotle in Books 8–10 of his *Nicomachean Ethics*.[18] The primary voice for the Greek understanding of the erotic experience in this chapter will be Plato.

In Mesopotamia the term that most frequently refers to the erotic experience is *râmu*.[19] It is used to describe the emotional dimension of relationships ranging from the political to the intimate. It is used to describe relations between gods, humans, animals, treaty partners, and various combinations of these groups. *Râmu* denotes sexual attraction as well as love of a protégé, favorite place, prayer, or virtue. Another important use is to refer to the loyalty one owes to a god or a superior.[20] Other Akkadian terms for intimate love are *dādu*, "love-making, darling" and *habābu*, "to caress."[21]

In Israel the primary term for love was *ʾāhēb*. Gerhard Wallis defines it as "the passionate desire to be intimately united with a person (in all of life's relationships, not only inwardly but also outwardly) with whom one feels himself united in his affections."[22] The scope of this term is broad; it covers relationships with God, humans, family members, friends, neighbors, strangers, and enemies. Originally *ʾāhēb* may have referred to sexual relations.[23] But the meaning of the term was widened to apply to relations between siblings, parents and children, and members of the community. The extent to which *ʾāhēb* accents sensual desire or embraced commitment must be determined by the context. The command in Lev 19:18, "Love your neighbor as yourself," moves in the direction of altruism even though it measures this love for the other according to the standard of self-love.[24] Deuteronomy accents the gifts God gives to Israel as signs of the divine love (e.g., Deut 7:9; 10:15; 11:2-6). This type of parental love from a superior to a servant is one that calls forth a corresponding obedience and sense of devotion. The sensual dimension of the marriage relationship is usually overshadowed in liter-

18. Gustav Stählin, *philos*, *TDNT* 9:152–53; Martha Nussbaum, *The Fragility of Goodness: Luck and Ethics in Greek Tragedy and Philosophy*, rev. ed. (Cambridge: Cambridge University Press, [1986], 2001), 343–69.

19. Gerhard Wallis, *ʾāhēb*, "love," *TDOT* 1:101–18.

20. *CAD* R, "*râmu*," 137–45.

21. *CAD* D, "dādu A," 20; CAD Ḫ, "ḫabābu B," 2–3.

22. Wallis, *ʾāhēb*, "love," 103.

23. Ibid., 107; Ernst Jenni, "*ʾhb* lieben," *ThWAT* 1: 64; Athalya Brenner, *The Intercourse of Knowledge: On Gendering Desire and 'Sexuality' in the Hebrew Bible* (Biblical Interpretation Series 26; Leiden: Brill, 1997) 13–18.

24. Wallis, *ʾāhēb*, "love," 111; Jacob Milgrom, *Leviticus 17–22*, AB 3A (New York: Doubleday, 2000), 1653–56.

ary accounts by the call to loyalty and commitment.[25] Nevertheless, a sense of intimacy is implied in the command: "you shall love (*wĕʾāhabtā*) the Lord your God with all your heart, and with all your soul, and with all your power" (Deut 6:5).

If the erotic dimension of human experience is a place in which individuals move beyond themselves to connect with other humans and the world around them and if sexual actions are to be kept out of the cultic sphere, then the sphere of ordinary life is the place in which erotic forms of encounter with the divine can occur. What these forms of erotic encounter would look like and what limits were placed on their expression are the primary concerns of this chapter.

Israel: The Challenge of Searching for the Source of Life in the Right Place

In an investigation, how the basic question is framed will shape the outcome in a fundamental way. If Israel reduces the symbolic dimension of its rituals to their tangible, visible components it runs the risk of conflating its perception of YHWH with that of Baal. Symbols have a material component that points beyond itself to an invisible reality. The material dimension is indispensable to this ritual way of knowing the divine but cannot replace the dialogue with the divine that the symbol tries to foster. Hosea charges Israel with reducing this symbolic dimension of its life with YHWH to a mechanical exchange. The longing for life at the heart of the erotic is a positive, divinely given impulse. The challenge before Israel is to choose the source of life (YHWH) rather than an illusion (Baal). This challenge will be addressed in material drawn from the books of Hosea and Genesis by (1) developing a profile of YHWH as a husband and father, i.e., a household deity; (2) examining language about erotic, sexual experience to see whether this can lead to a deeper, more intimate knowledge of YHWH or must be screened out of the divine-human relationship; and (3) describing how the channeling of erotic, sexual experience influences the integrity and vitality of the household and larger community.

YHWH as the Divine Husband and Father

Hosea 11:1-11 is a divine speech summarizing Israel's history (vv. 1-4) and stating what will happen to Israel in the future (vv. 5-11). If this

25. Wallis, *ʾāhēb*, "love," *TDOT* 1:115; Moshe Weinfeld, *Deuteronomy 1–11*, AB 5 (New York: Doubleday, 1991), 351–52.

divine speech was read as part of the book of Hosea by the literati of Yehud in the postexilic period they would be challenged to identify with the "trans-temporal Israel" referred to in this oracle.[26] As Ehud Ben-Zvi argues, such an Israel is not confined to the events of the eighth century BCE, even though it is an heir to such experiences.[27] Rather, the literati of Yehud, viewing the events from the Exodus through the exile, would get an image of YHWH as a parent who exercised tough love toward a rebellious child. Israel went after the baals (v. 2), indicating that its people did not know how to give expression to their erotic desire for the divine. Israel invested in an alternative belief system that undercut its obligation to worship YHWH alone. Such an expectation of exclusive fidelity was probably brought into sharper focus by Israel's acquaintance with the form of ancient Near Eastern suzerain/vassal treaties in which the vassal was prohibited from making alliances with any other political power.[28]

The highlight of Hos 11:1-9 is the window it provides into the divine interior. YHWH is a parent who cannot abandon his child. Like a parent YHWH called Israel out of Egypt as a son. Like a mother, YHWH taught Israel/Ephraim to walk, sustained them "with cords of love (*ʾahăbâ*)," and lifted them to the breast as if to nurse them (vv. 3-4).[29] But when Israel rebelled it underwent the destruction of exile. Historically the ten northern tribes were assimilated into the culture of their land of exile. But the audience in Yehud, many of whom experienced the later Babylonian exile, would have resonated with the message of hope stemming from the anguish of YHWH expressed in vv. 8-9: "My heart has turned around on me; my compassion is stirred up completely. I will not act on

26. Ehud Ben Zvi, *Hosea*, FOTL 21, A1 (Grand Rapids: Eerdmans, 2005), 12, 16. Helen Schüngel-Straumann, "God as Mother in Hosea 11," in *A Feminist Companion to the Latter Prophets*, ed. Athalya Brenner, 194–218 (Sheffield: Sheffield Academic Press 1993), at 197, identifies the genre of Hos 11:1–11 as a "historical-theological lament."

27. Ben Zvi, *Hosea*, 19; Philip R. Davies, "The Wilderness Years: Utopia and Dystopia in the Book of Hosea," in *Utopia and Dystopia in Prophetic Literature*, Publications of the Finnish Exegetical Society 92, ed. Ehud Ben Zvi, 160–74 (Helsinki: Finnish Exegetical Society; Göttingen: Vandenhoeck & Ruprecht, 2006), at 161–62, 166, 174.

28. For the loyalty oaths embedded in Esarhaddon's Succession Treaty of 672 BCE see Donald J. Wiseman, *Vassal Treaties of Esarhaddon* (London: British School of Archaeology, 1958), ll. 55–82, 108–22, 162–72, 212–13, 308–14.

29. Joy Philip Kakkanattu, *God's Enduring Love in the Book of Hosea*, FAT 14, 2d ser. (Tübingen: Mohr Siebeck, 2006), 128, contends that the parental imagery here, in the absence of the terms "father" and "mother," depicts YHWH as a father with motherly characteristics. Alternatively, Schüngel-Straumann, "God as Mother in Hosea 11," 203–4, emphasizes that the imagery of nursing depicts YHWH as a mother and criticizes commentators for reading the father-image into the text.

my burning anger, I will not wipe out Ephraim again. For I am God and not man." This text emphasizes that YHWH's love transcends that of human parents toward their children.[30] The return from Babylonian exile would have served for the literati of Yehud as confirmation of YHWH's character as a God who would not abandon his people, even though he might punish them severely.[31] YHWH's parental *erōs*, especially as communicated through the striking maternal imagery ascribed to YHWH here, applies to transtemporal Israel, that is, Israel as it perdures through the generations while undergoing change. Such passionate parental love serves as a living promise for the readers of the book of Hosea.[32]

The transtemporal Israel envisioned by the book of Hosea is a child of YHWH. This familial imagery is commonly employed in the descriptions of ancient Near Eastern pantheons.[33] Some scholars regard Deut 32:8-9 as testimony to an early stage of Israelite religion in which El was the sovereign deity and YHWH was a loyal subordinate like the other national deities of the region:[34]

> When Elyon apportioned the nations their lands and divided up the human race, he established boundaries for the peoples according to the number of the sons of God;[35] indeed YHWH's own portion was his people; his inherited portion was Jacob.

If this passage reflects the hierarchy of the Canaanite pantheon, El is the father figure who wields authority over a family of male and female

30. Carole R. Fontaine, "Hosea," in *Feminist Companion to the Latter Prophets*, 40–59, at 58.

31. James M. Trotter, *Reading Hosea in Achaemenid Yehud*, *JSOTSup* 328 (Sheffield: Sheffield Academic Press, 2001), 184–85, 204–5, 219.

32. Macintosh, *Hosea*, 437–38, 448, 465; Kakkanattu, *God's Enduring Love*, 131. Fontaine, "Hosea," 54, contends that the parent-child relationship is a better analogy for the divine-human covenantal relationship than that of husband-wife, for the latter is more like a master-slave relationship.

33. Lowell K. Handy, *Among the Host of Heaven: The Syro-Palestinian Pantheon as Bureaucracy* (Winona Lake, IN: Eisenbrauns, 1994), 6–7; Thorkild Jacobsen, *Treasures of Darkness* (New Haven: Yale University Press, 1976), 160–64; Mark S. Smith, *The Origins of Biblical Monotheism: Israel's Polytheistic Background and the Ugaritic Texts* (New York: Oxford University Press, 2001), 27, 55–60, 78–79.

34. Smith, *The Origins of Biblical Monotheism*, 48–49; Kakkanattu, *God's Enduring Love*, 130; David Noel Freedman, "The Real Formal Full Personal Name of the God of Israel," in *Sacred History, Sacred Literature: Essays on Ancient Israel, the Bible, and Religion in Honor of R. E. Friedman on His Sixtieth Birthday*, ed. Shawna Dolansky, 81–89 (Winona Lake, IN: Eisenbrauns, 2008), at 88.

35. Read *běnê ʾēl* with Qumran, LXX.

deities. Mark Smith contends that this family of gods in Israel would have communicated a sense of oneness or coherence in the divine realm through the care and concern constitutive of a family unit.[36] He speculates that this divine family form evolved toward a bureaucratic structure from the eighth to the sixth centuries under the pressure of the deportations that altered the structure of the traditional Israelite *bêt ʾāb*.[37] He claims that "biblical Israel has been shorn of such a divine family, leaving divinity to be imaged largely in terms of a streamlined bureaucracy headed by an absolute monarch."[38] According to Smith's reconstruction neither monolatry nor monotheism would have been an expectation to which the original eighth-century audience of Hosea would have held one another accountable. Only the pressure of sociopolitical events over the next two centuries would move the Israelite community to assess the ups and downs of its fortunes on the basis of an exclusive fidelity to YHWH. However, if Israel was expected to see its relationship with YHWH from the perspective of his wife, then exclusive fidelity to YHWH would be essential to this marriage. Thus it seems that the marital metaphor and familial imagery of Hosea 2 indicate that monolatrous worship was an expectation of the eighth-century Israelite community.[39]

In Hosea 2, Israel is identified not only as the promiscuous Gomer but also as the three children that have been born to her during her time of promiscuity.[40] Therefore the children are identified as "children of

36. Smith, *The Origins of Biblical Monotheism*, 53; see also J. David Schloen, *The House of the Father as Fact and Symbol: Patrimonialism in Ugarit and the Ancient Near East*, Studies in the Archaeology and History of the Levant, 2 (Winona Lake, IN: Eisenbrauns, 2001), 353–56.

37. Smith, *The Origins of Biblical Monotheism*, 79; Handy, *Among the Host of Heaven*, 12–13.

38. Smith, *The Origins of Biblical Monotheism*, 78; cf. Handy, *Among the Host of Heaven*, 39.

39. Gale Yee, "'She Is Not My Wife and I Am Not Her Husband': A Materialist Analysis of Hosea 1–2," *Biblical Interpretation* 9 (2001): 345–83, at 351, 357; Alice A. Keefe, *Woman's Body and the Social Body in Hosea*, *JSOTSup* 338 (Sheffield: Sheffield Academic Press, 2001), 83, 118; Robert Gnuse, *No Other Gods: Emergent Monotheism in Israel*, *JSOTSup* 241 (Sheffield: Sheffield Academic Press, 1997), 202–3. Jeffrey Tigay, *You Shall Have No Other Gods: Israelite Religion in the Light of Hebrew Inscriptions*, HSS 31 (Atlanta: Scholars Press, 1986) 65–66, notes that only six of 1,200 names on the Samarian ostraca from the eighth century have the name Baal. Brad E. Kelle, *Hosea 2: Metaphor and Rhetoric in Historical Perspective* (Atlanta: Society of Biblical Literature, 2005), 147–48, concludes on the basis of onomastic and iconographical data that in Hosea's time "there was no officially established or widespread worship of other gods."

40. Laurie J. Braaten, "God Sows: Hosea's Land Theme in the Book of the Twelve," in *Thematic Threads in the Book of the Twelve*, BZAW 325 (New York: de Gruyter, 2003), 104–32,

promiscuity" (*bĕnê zĕnûnîm*, v. 6), which means that they are not legitimate heirs to YHWH's patrimony.[41] At the beginning of the divine monologue in 2:3-25 YHWH urges Hosea's children Jezreel, Lo-Ammi, and Lo-ruhama to try to persuade their mother Gomer to end her promiscuity. YHWH advocates this family quarrel in order to move Gomer/Israel to realize that she owes exclusive fidelity to YHWH (2:4-7). In light of the death penalty for adultery (Lev 20:10; Deut 22:22), YHWH can be said to act with restraint toward Gomer/Israel here.[42] A cuckolded husband would be expected to react with rage such as YHWH shows in Ezekiel 16, where he arranges for a deadly punishment for Jerusalem as his promiscuous wife (Ezek 16:37-41).[43]

In Hosea 2, YHWH is portrayed as the loving, generous husband who wishes to go to some length in order to get his wayward wife to reform. But even then he must punish her (2:12-15).[44] The description of this punishment resembles that meted out to wayward cities that were personified as wives (cf. Jer 2:2-3, 20-30, 33-37; Ezekiel 16 and 23).[45] But immediately this punishment, which seems to be a form of divine abandonment, is countered by YHWH's steps to hedge in her pathways by which she goes to her lovers and make her see that she was better off when she was with YHWH as her husband.[46] When Israel comes into such a state of desperation, YHWH says:

---

at 107–8, argues that in Hosea 2 the wife/mother is the land and the children are Israel and that only in Hosea 3 is the wife identified as Israel.

41. Keefe, *Woman's Body and the Social Body in Hosea*, 205; Adrian Schenker, "Kinder der Prostitution, Kinder ohne Familie und ohne soziale Stellung: Ein freundschaftliches *Sed contra* für Lothar Ruppert und eine These zu Hos 1," in "*Ich bewirke das Heil und erschaffe das Unheil (Jesaja 45,7): Studien zur Botschaft der Propheten: Festschrift für Lothar Ruppert* (Würzburg: Echter Verlag, 1998), 355–69, at 359, 361.

42. Gale Yee, *Poor Banished Children of Eve* (Minneapolis: Fortress Press, 2001), 99–100. However, on the harsh treatment threatened by YHWH against Gomer as abusive see Naomi Graetz, "God Is To Israel as Husband Is To Wife: The Metaphoric Battering of Hosea's Wife," in *A Feminist Companion to the Latter Prophets*, 126–45, at 131–32, 139–40. Francis Landy, "Fantasy and Displacement of Pleasure: Hosea 2:4-17," in ibid., 146–60, at 150, sees YHWH's stripping naked and abandoning the wife/mother (Hos 2:3) and his exposure of her to her lovers (2:10) as a vindictive aggressiveness indicative of frustrated fantasies.

43. Keefe, *Woman's Body and the Social Body in Hosea*, 188–89.

44. Graetz, "God Is To Israel as Husband Is To Wife," 139, 141–42, has strong reservations about the requirement that one suffer in order to enter into or remain in a marriage relationship; for her this requirement appears to sanction abusive treatment.

45. Kelle, *Hosea 2*, 119–22; Yee, *Poor Banished Children of Eve*, 81.

46. Landy, "Fantasy and Displacement of Pleasure," 157, interprets the return to the wilderness as a harsh requirement in which the wife is stripped of her land and her history in the land to go to a place of barrenness and death.

> I will persuade her (*mĕpattêhā*); I will bring her to the desert and speak to her heart. I will give her from there her vineyards and the valley of Achor as an entryway of hope, and she will answer there as she did in her youth when she ascended from the land of Egypt. On that day—oracle of the Lord— she will call me "my husband," and never again "my baal." I will remove the names of the baals from her mouth, and they will no longer be recalled. (Hos 2:16-19)

YHWH uses the language of intimacy to try to reach Israel's heart, the locus of her thinking and feeling (cf. Song 2:14; 8:1-7).[47] It is from this locus that choices are made and monitored. So even though the typical ancient Israelite marriage was arranged, the bond of love was still an integral component of the marriage relationship.[48] What the Israelites would experience as an erotic dimension to the relationship between husband and wife was somehow to be experienced in their relationship with YHWH.[49] YHWH does not have a body, yet he interacts with collective Israel in such a way that he is pictured as an embodied husband and she as an embodied wife with children representing the land and its inhabitants. This imagery suggests that the divine-human erotic experience lies somewhere between the figurative and the literal; it is an experience of the holy within the profane.[50] How was the sexual dimension of this experience addressed? Was it suspended? transmuted? what?

47. Kakkanattu, *God's Enduring Love in the Book of Hosea*, 135, describes YHWH's approach as one of unconditional love and forgiveness. Landy, "Fantasy and Displacement of Pleasure," 159–60, notes YHWH's reversal of attitude and tactics in giving space for the wife in terms of her body and capacity to speak.

48. Susan Ackerman, "The Personal Is Political: Covenantal and Affectionate Love (ʾAHĒB, ʾAHABÂ) in the Hebrew Bible," *VT* 52 (2002): 437–58, at 442–43, 447; Daniel Boyarin, *Carnal Israel: Reading Sex in Talmudic Culture* (Berkeley: University of California Press, 1993), 53. Graetz, "God Is To Israel as Husband Is To Wife," 142, wonders what it means for men to identify with the wife in the metaphorical marriage relationship, an action Jewish males carry out every morning as they pray Hos 2:21-22.

49. John Goldingay, "Hosea 1–3, Genesis 1–4 and Masculist Interpretation," in *A Feminist Companion to the Latter Prophets*, 161–68, at 165–67.

50. Keefe, *Woman's Body and the Social Body in Hosea*, 215–19, emphasizes that the procreative power of woman is "hierophanic." She contends that female sexuality was regarded in the eighth century, contrary to attitudes in postexilic times, as a sacral power through which life was continually created. Pirjo Lapinkivi, "The Sumerian Sacred Marriage and Its Aftermath," 38–39, argues that in the Sumerian sacred marriage ritual Inanna can be identified as the human soul that united with Dumuzi to gain well-being for the land and personal salvation. By contrast, Beate Pongratz-Leisten, "Sacred Marriage and the Transfer of Divine Knowledge," in *Sacred Marriages*, 43–73, at 68, argues that theogamy

Clues about the proper way to relate intimately to YHWH may reside in understanding what is to be avoided in relating to Baal. It may be that relating to Baal, because it is reliance on another deity, is itself a sufficient explanation for the prohibition of this relationship. The danger of Baalism may have arisen more from its potential to corrupt Israel's understanding of YHWH and its worship practices (i.e., through syncretism) than in the defection of Israelites to the Canaanite cults (apostasy).[51] More specifics of this baalistic relationship that render it incompatible with a relationship with YHWH can be gleaned from the book of Hosea. Two primary deficiencies for the Yahwistic worshiper that result from relating to Baal have been identified in Hosea's oracles: Baalism maintains (1) that fertility for all living things issues from Baal and his consort, which requires that cultic ritual appeal concretely to these deities in whom divine power is equated with sexual potency (Hos 2:5-13; 7:14) and (2) that economic and political power can be advanced by a baalistic system that sanctions the production of cash crops to the detriment of the quality of life in the local community (Hos 2:8, 12-13; 8:8-10).[52]

Scholarly reconstructions of the fertility cult of Baal have been criticized for portraying this cult as promoting sexually degenerate and magical rituals. The data for these activities is fragmentary.[53] The reconstructions, which fill in the gaps, have been criticized for trying to make Baalism a negative foil for an ethically superior Yahwism.[54] The problem of reconstructing the activities of the Baal cult from Hosea's oracles can

---

(union between a goddess and a king) elevated the status of the king to a place within the divine family but did not effect a spiritual union of the king with the goddess.

51. Kakkanattu, *God's Enduring Love*, 112–13.

52. Yee, *Poor Banished Children of Eve*, 96, 99.

53. Phyllis Bird, "Prostitution in the Social World and the Religious Rhetoric of Ancient Israel," in *Prostitutes and Courtesans in the Ancient World*, ed. Christopher Faraone and Laura McClure, 40–58 (Madison: University of Wisconsin Press, 2006), at 49–52; Martti Nissinen, "Song of Songs and Sacred Marriage," in *Sacred Marriages*, 173–218, at 188; Keefe, *Woman's Body and the Social Body in Hosea*, 54 (11, 50–65; 89–103); Kelle, *Hosea 2*, 126. Stephanie Lynn Budin, *The Myth of Sacred Prostitution in Antiquity* (Cambridge: Cambridge University Press, 2008), 17, 47, defines prostitution as involving the exchange of sex for something else and so places sacred marriage outside the sphere of prostitution; she then reviews the textual evidence and concludes that there was no sacred prostitution in the ancient Near East. For a defense of the scholarly interpretation that cultic prostitution was practiced in the ancient Near East see Richard M. Davidson, *Flame of Yahweh: Sexuality in the Old Testament* (Peabody, MA: Hendrickson, 2007), 88–89.

54. Delbert Hillers, "Analyzing the Abominable: Our Understanding of Canaanite Religion," *JQR* 75 (1985): 253–69, at 257–58; Keefe, *Woman's Body and the Social Body in Hosea*, 64; Kelle, *Hosea 2*, 127.

be illustrated in the following: "Yes, their mother [Israel] has acted promiscuously; the one who conceived them has acted shamelessly, thinking, 'I will go after my lovers,' she said, 'who provide me with my bread and my water, my wool and my flax, my oil and my drink'" (Hos 2:7). If such promiscuity is more than a metaphor for paying allegiance to Baal, then it would seem to involve sexual activities. Those who contend that Baalism was a fertility religion describe the promiscuous rituals as involving copulation between male and female cultic personnel in order to trigger an analogous coupling of Baal and his consort, i.e., sex in the sanctuary.[55] Therefore human sexual relations in the sphere of the holy would have been essential to the maintenance of fertility in the cosmos. Alternatively, the language of promiscuity may be more figurative than literal and thus refer to selling out to the royal economic system in which tribute was paid to the king and his overlords.[56] The goods of bread, wool, flax, and oil would be trade goods received in exchange for services. If so, the Israelites designated as "promiscuous wife" would be urban dwellers associated with the royal government,[57] whereas the agricultural workers constituting the majority of the Israelite people would receive these agricultural goods from the soil and not from the market.[58] The infidelity of the royal urbanites would be their devotion to a hierarchical arrangement that enabled Israel to participate in a politico-economic system that exploited the peasants for the sake of the aggrandizement of the upper class.[59] The question then is whether Hosea indicts (1) the people at large who strive for successful agriculture through rituals with a sexual component or (2) the upper-class urbanites for imposing a foreign-style commercial system on an egalitarian agricultural community. But even if the language of sexual promiscuity used for devotion to a foreign economic system is figurative, this language of devotion is communicated by Hosea's use of sexual imagery, which indicates that there are important traces of the erotic and sexual in the divine-human relationship. Hosea does not condemn erotic sexual experience *per se*,

55. James Luther Mays, *Hosea*, OTL (London: SCM, 1969), 8; cf. Kelle, *Hosea* 2, 124.

56. Yee, "She Is Not My Wife and I Am Not Her Husband," 345–83, at 347; Keefe, *Woman's Body and the Social Body in Hosea*, 12, 197.

57. Yee, "She Is Not My Wife and I Am Not Her Husband," 368, 376; Keefe, *Woman's Body and the Social Body in Hosea*, 31.

58. Francis I. Anderson and David Noel Freedman, *Hosea*, AB 24 (Garden City, NY: Doubleday, 1980), 324–25; see also 166 (Hos 1:2), 232 (Hos 2:7), 242 (Hos 2:10), 244–45 (Hos 2:11), 256–58 (Hos 2:15).

59. Yee, "She Is Not My Wife and I Am Not Her Husband," 346–47, 368; eadem, *Poor Banished Children of Eve*, 33, 106 (Hos 2:13).

but rather judges those syncretists and apostates who seem to have made sexual potency into a sovereign divine force by devotion to their lovers (Hos 2:7).

In Hosea 2 the battle over which deity controls the fertility of the land is reflected in the following verses: "it was I who provided her with the grain, the wine, and the oil" (v. 10); "on that day, I will reply—oracle of the Lord—I will reply to the heavens, and they will reply to the earth; the earth will reply to the grain, and wine, and oil; and they will reply to Jezreel" (vv. 23-24). YHWH's control over the rain and the fertility of the soil determines whether or not there is a successful crop in the valley of Jezreel.[60] Hosea claims that it is YHWH and not Baal who brings about agricultural success.[61] From a politico-economic perspective one could argue that YHWH rather than Baal is the one enthroned in heaven who controls the production and distribution of agricultural goods and determines whether or not a political arrangement that supports a king's expropriation of peasant land in Jezreel (1 Kgs 21:1-24; 2 Kgs 9:4-37) can succeed.[62] Yet the picture of a chain of command in 2:23-24—extending from YHWH to the heavens to the earth to the grain, wine, and oil—portrays the divine word as the life-force that makes the food chain possible. The growing of the grain from the earth is emphasized here in such a way that the grain, wine, and oil are seen to come from the soil rather than from a marketplace in the city. The agricultural imagery in this passage, with its emphasis on fertility, should not be reduced to politico-economic processes.

The politico-economic model of a baalistic tributary economic system does not need to displace the fertility dimension of the baalistic system.

60. Braaten, "God Sows: Hosea's Land Theme in the Book of the Twelve," 109, notes that Jezreel ("God sows") is the place in which both crops and the Israelites are to take root and grow (Hos 2:2, 23-25); otherwise they will be judged (Hos 2:1).

61. John Day, "Yahweh and the Gods and Goddesses of Canaan," in *Ein Gott allein? JHWH-Verehrung und biblischer Monotheismus im Kontext der Israelitischen und altorientalischen Religionsgeschichte*, OBO 139, ed. Walter Dietrich and Martin A. Klopfenstein, 181–96 (Fribourg: Universitätsverlag; Göttingen: Vandenhoeck & Ruprecht, 1994), at 185–87, argues that Hosea tried to eliminate the use of *baʿal* as an epithet for YHWH in eighth-century Israel (cf. Hos 2:18); see also Kelle, *Hosea 2*, 142–43. Yehezkel Kaufmann, *The Religion of Israel: From Its Beginnings to the Babylonian Exile*, trans. Moshe Greenberg (Chicago: University of Chicago Press, 1960), 140, argues that baalistic worship was widespread in Israel only during the time of the Omrides (868–854 BCE).

62. Kelle, *Hosea 2*, 152–66; Keefe, *Woman's Body and the Social Body in Hosea*, 24, 191–92. Yee, "She Is Not My Wife and I Am Not Her Husband," 366, contends that while Hosea condemned the cultic pluralism of the state that undergirded agricultural exploitation, he did not set a male God YHWH over against female fertility deities.

One could argue that there is a complementarity between the two models: Hosea has a message both for the general populace who engage in worship at baalistic shrines and for the upper-class urbanites who are invested in commercial exchange and the standard of living it offers.[63] The one Hosea condemns for engaging in orgiastic fertility rites (4:13-14) could be the same person he condemns for uttering false oaths to defraud a fellow Israelite (10:4). The crimes for which the "land mourns" (Hos 4:3) are false swearing, dishonesty, murder, theft, and adultery (4:2)—a combination of sexual and social sins.[64] Therefore what is needed is further data on the character of sexual activity in the baalistic cult and an examination of how Hosea thought such baalistic sexual activity, if practiced by the Israelites, separated them from participation in YHWH's divine life.

Sex and Knowledge of the Divine: Compatible or Incompatible?

Of the 134 occurrences of the root *znh* in the OT, twelve are in Hosea 4 (vv. 10, 11, 12 [2x], 13 [2x], 14 [3x], 15, 18 [2x]). *Znh* refers to a range of prohibited sexual liaisons including fornication, adultery, and prostitution.[65] Hosea indicts the Israelites for offering sacrifices and incense at hilltop shrines (4:13; cf. 2:13). He claims that such ritual forms of acknowledging baalistic deities (cf. 2:19) have upset family relationships to such a degree that daughters fornicate and daughters-in-law commit adultery (4:13).[66] But Hosea says that YHWH will not punish these daughters and daughters-in-law—although their actions call into question the legitimacy of their offspring—because their fathers go aside with "prostitutes" (*zōnôt*) and offer sacrifice with "women dedicated to the deities"

63. Yee, *Poor Banished Children of Eve*, 189–90; Keefe, *Woman's Body and the Social Body in Hosea*, 140, 199.

64. Katherine M. Hayes, *"The Earth Mourns." Prophetic Metaphor and Oral Aesthetic*, Academia Biblica (Boston and Leiden: Brill, 2002), 2–3; Anderson and Freedman, *Hosea*, 336–37.

65. Kelle, *Hosea 2*, 100; Bird, "Prostitution in the Social World," 42–44. Keefe, *Woman's Body and the Social Body in Hosea*, 20, 203, agrees with Bird that *znh* refers to "fornication" rather than to "prostitution" since the transgression of compromising the exclusive relationship of the wife to the husband in the patriarchal system is more adequately conveyed by the more inclusive term "fornication" than by "prostitution," which was a legitimate action when respectful of the marriage relationship.

66. Jacob Milgrom, "The Nature and Extent of Idolatry in Eighth-Seventh Century Judah," *HUCA* 69 (1998): 1–13, at 1, n. 1, claims that biblical texts accuse Israel of idolatry only fifteen times in contrast to 166 times against Judah (Lev 19:4; 26:1; Amos 5:26; Hos 5:3b-4; 6:10; Isa 2:8, 18, 20; 10:11; 17:8; 27:9; 30:22; 31:7; Mic 1:7; 5:12-13a).

(*qĕdēšôt*) of these hilltop shrines (4:14). Toward the end of this section Hosea indicts the Israelites for idolatry: "Ephraim has hooked up with idols; leave him. In their carousing, they have strayed; they have acted promiscuously; in their arrogance,[67] they love (*ʾāhăbû*)[68] shame (*qālôn*)" (4:17-18). Hosea charges the Israelites with participating in illicit sexual activities in the context of these mountaintop shrines.[69]

Prostitutes are part of these activities. Many interpreters have taken the *qĕdēšôt* as parallel to the *zōnôt* in 4:14 (cf. Gen 38:21-24; Deut 23:18-19), with the result that the *qĕdēšôt* are considered to be "temple prostitutes" (see NRSV). However, critics have emphasized that there is no clear statement that the *qĕdēšôt* engaged in sex as part of fertility rituals at these mountaintop shrines.[70] Some critics allow for the fact that prostitution may have been a service administered by these shrines, since ancient Near Eastern temple establishments have commonly been regarded as having done so.[71] The significance of the critics' objection is that if these *qĕdēšôt* engaged in sex for hire apart from religious rituals, the sexual activity condemned by Hosea would have had no meaningful role in

67. Read *miggĕʾônām*.

68. Delete *hēbû*.

69. Braaten, "God Sows," 114, and Anderson and Freedman, *Hosea*, 324–25, argue that *rûaḥ zĕnûnîm* (4:12; 5:4) is an allusion to a goddess (4:12, 19) who deludes the Israelites and makes them go astray. Ackerman, "The Personal Is the Political," 451, states with regard to the use of *ʾāhēb* and *ʾāhăbâ* that "a male Israel can be described, as in [Hos] iii 1; ix 1; and ix 10, as loving other gods, but a female Israel can be described only as the object of other gods' love." Karel van der Toorn, *From Her Cradle to Her Grave: The Role of Religion in the Life of the Israelite and the Babylonian Woman*, trans. Sara J. Denning-Bolle (Sheffield: JSOT Press, 1994), 108, regards these orgiastic rituals as merely bacchanalia and not aimed at promoting fertility.

70. Phyllis Bird, "To Play the Harlot: An Inquiry into an Old Testament Metaphor," in *Gender and Difference in Ancient Israel*, ed. Peggy L. Day, 21–38 (Minneapolis: Fortress Press, 1989), at 85–88; Keefe, *Woman's Body and the Social Body in Hosea*, 100–1; Kelle, *Hosea 2*, 123–32; Mayer Gruber, "The Hebrew *qĕdēšāh* and Her Canaanite and Akkadian Cognates," in *The Motherhood of God and Other Studies*, South Florida Studies in the History of Judaism 57 (Atlanta: Scholars Press, 1992), 17–47, at 28.

71. Macintosh, *Hosea*, 158–59; Keefe, *Woman's Body and the Social Body in Hosea*, 101; Karel van der Toorn, "Cultic Prostitution," *ABD* 5:510; Kelle, *Hosea 2*, 129. However, Julia Assante, "From Whores to Hierodules: The Historiographic Invention of Mesopotamian Female Sex Professionals," in *Ancient Art and Its Historiography* , ed. A. A. Donohue and Mark D. Fullerton, 13–47 (Cambridge: Cambridge University Press, 2003), at 33, argues that *ḫarimtu*/KAR.KID, "prostitute," was a term designating women who were independent of a patriarchal household and not necessarily engaged in prostitution as a profession; see also Budin, *The Myth of Sacred Prostitution in Antiquity*, 26–27.

connecting the worshipers with the divine.[72] In that case Hosea would be indicting the men of the Israelite households for engaging in sex outside of marriage and thus providing a bad example for their daughters and daughters-in-law whose illicit sexual activity, in turn, would undermine the social fabric of their households and the Israelite community.[73] However, the evidence in 4:14 strongly suggests that sexual activity was part of the worship; this point is reinforced by 4:18, which speaks of their love of "shame." If *qālôn* is a metaphor for Baal (cf. 4:7; Nah 3:5; Jer 13:26),[74] this phrase would also suggest that there was a sense that union with the gods (*ḥăbûr ʿăṣabbîm*, v. 17) occurred through sexual joining in these rituals.[75] However, Kakkanattu interprets *ḥăbûr* as joining an alliance committed to false gods (*ʿăṣabbîm*).[76] Thus the options of both a political and a fertility-generating relationship are possible understandings of 4:17.

Hosea charges that the illicit rituals practiced by the people on the mountaintop shrines were complemented by mindless, mechanical rituals carried out by the priests in Yahwistic sanctuaries. Thus YHWH says: "The priests are like the people. I will punish them for their ways; I will make their actions come back upon them" (4:9). The greed of the priests to increase the number of sacrificial offerings and thereby augment their wealth did not merely result in a shift in the material wealth of the community; it also brought about a diminishment in the people's knowledge of YHWH since the symbolic character of the offerings was short-circuited.[77] So YHWH confronts the priests:

> Through lack of knowledge my people perish. Because you have rejected this knowledge, I will reject you as my priest. Because you

72. Bird, "Prostitution in the Social World," 50–52; Keefe, *Woman's Body and the Social Body in Hosea*, 101.

73. Macintosh, *Hosea*, 159–60; Bird, "Prostitution in the Social World," 49.

74. Kelle, *Hosea 2*, 137, notes that the only passages describing sexual activity between Baal and Anat are KTU 1.96; KTU 1.10; KTU 1.11. See Keefe, *Woman's Body and the Social Body in Hosea*, 51, n. 14.

75. Anderson and Freedman, *Hosea*, 354–55, 376, 378, note that the root *ḥbr* might be taken as referring to "weaving" (cf. Deut 18:11; Ps 58:6) in which the idols captivate and entrap the Israelites in their "weavings." Kelle, *Hosea 2*, 136, states with reference to Deut 23:18-19, Hos 4:13-14, and Isa 57:3-10, "one cannot take these texts simply at face value as a testimony to general sex any more than as a testimony to cultic prostitution. The possibility remains that the descriptions represent only accusations and rhetorical indictments."

76. Kakkanattu, *God's Enduring Love in the Book of Hosea*, 114.

77. Macintosh, *Hosea*, 144.

> have forgotten the instruction of your God (*tôrat ʾelōhîm*), I too will forget your children." (Hos 4:6)

The torah imparted by priests typically deals with the obligations and prohibitions of the sanctuary so that the demarcation between sacred and profane can be maintained.[78] These action-oriented teachings strive to honor YHWH as the incomprehensible, free deity who resides in the sanctuary but cannot be contained by it.[79] Such pragmatic priestly knowledge aims to engage the worshipers so that they come to know YHWH by investing in the rituals of the sanctuary. This participatory knowledge tries to create a space cultically and interiorly in which YHWH can manifest his glory to the people.[80] But this knowledge (*daʿat*) of YHWH may be the memory of YHWH's great saving deeds in the Exodus; by forgetting this knowledge the Israelites would slide into syncretism by adopting Canaanite and other foreign practices.[81] Thus there is an objective as well as a subjective dimension to the obligation to know YHWH.[82]

This lack of knowledge has led to a diminishment of the social fabric: the people are guilty of breaking five of the seven commands of the Decalogue aimed at horizontal relationships in the community (4:2).[83] Hosea further claims that this impaired relationship with YHWH results not only in chaotic social conditions but also in a serious decline in the vitality of the natural realm (v. 3). The chain effect of a lack of knowledge of YHWH through the social and natural spheres reveals that this knowledge

78. Frank Crüsemann, *The Torah: Theology and Social History of Old Testament Law*, trans. A. W. Mahnke (Minneapolis: Fortress Press, 1996), 19.

79. Samuel Balentine, *The Torah's Vision of Worship* (Minneapolis: Fortress Press, 1999), 24.

80. On the performative character of animal sacrifice from an anthropological perspective see Maurice Bloch, *Prey into Hunter: The Politics of Religious Experience* (Cambridge and New York: Cambridge University Press, 1992), 33–34, 37; see also Jean-Pierre Vernant, "A General Theory of Sacrifice and the Slaying of the Victim in the Greek *Thusia*," in idem, *Mortals and Immortals: Collected Essays*, ed. Froma Zeitlin, 290–302 (Princeton: Princeton University Press, 1991), at 293.

81. Margaret S. Odell, "I Will Destroy Your Mother: The Obliteration of a Cultic Role in Hosea 4.4-6," in *A Feminist Companion to the Latter Prophets*, 180–93, at 189–90, proposes that the "mother" condemned along with the priests in Hos 4:5 was originally a cultic figure in the Aaronide tradition who specialized in leading praise of YHWH in the cult, but who has stumbled into syncretism according to Hosea (cf. Numbers 12).

82. Kakkanattu, *God's Enduring Love*, 124–26.

83. Even if the Decalogue was not arranged in its canonical form in the eighth century BCE, the tradition behind it was clearly known to Hosea; see Anderson and Freedman, *Hosea*, 337.

of YHWH is more than mere information; it is a kind of knowledge that leads to a close familial relationship with YHWH.[84]

In Hebrew the term that typically refers to sexual intercourse is "know (*yādāʿ*) a person."[85] In the story of the Garden of Eden the first human couple was commanded not to eat the fruit of the tree of the knowledge of good and evil (Gen 2:16-17). When they transgressed this taboo they became aware that they were naked (Gen 3:7). This awareness of the first man and woman of their sexual difference causes them shame (Gen 2:25; 3:7).[86] The challenge to their relationship is complicated further by the punishment visited on the woman: "I will greatly increase your toil and your pregnancies; (along) with travail you shall beget children.[87] Yet your inclination (*tĕšûqātēk*) shall be toward your husband, and he shall rule over you (*yimšol-bāk*)" (Gen 3:16). Once they have eaten the fruit of this tree, there is no turning back. They will now bear the burden of a desire for a divine form of knowledge, one that potentially covers the full range of reality—the merism "good and evil" points to the totalization of knowledge promised by this fruit.[88] Human experience testifies that we are left with this desire to know as much as possible but lack the time and the resources needed to satisfy our desire.[89] Thus the fruit of the tree of knowledge has conferred on humans an endless desire to know that brings both vitality and anxiety, benefits and dangers.

The knowledge the first couple gained marks a point of transition, of exile from paradise and entry into civilization. There would seem to be no reason to deny that the first couple had sexual relations in the Garden prior to their transgression, even though the text makes no mention of such relations.[90] At any rate, sexual relations after the transgression become a different experience since knowledge becomes part of the

84. Anderson and Freedman, *Hosea*, 265; Keefe, *Woman's Body and the Social Body in Hosea*, 118.

85. Meir Malul, *Knowledge, Control, and Sex: Studies in Biblical Thought, Culture, and Worldview* (Tel-Aviv and Jaffa: Archaeological Center Publication, 2002), 233, lists the following passages as using the sexual sense of *yādāʿ*: Gen 4:1, 17, 25; 19:5, 8; 24:16; 38:26; Num 31:17, 18, 35; Judg 11:39; 19:22, 25; 21:11, 12; 1 Sam 1:19; 1 Kgs 1:4.

86. Yee, *Poor Banished Children of Eve*, 69–70, 74.

87. Translation of Gen 3:16a from Carol Meyers, *Discovering Eve: Ancient Israelite Women in Context* (Oxford and New York: Oxford University Press, 1988), 105, 108.

88. Malul, *Knowledge, Control, and Sex*, 441; Claus Westermann, *Genesis 1–11: A Commentary*, trans. John J. Scullion (Minneapolis: Augsburg, 1984), 243.

89. Westermann, *Genesis 1–11*, 249.

90. David P. Wright, "Holiness, Sex, and Death in the Garden of Eden," *Bib* 77 (1996): 305–29, at 315; Gary Anderson, "Celibacy or Consummation in the Garden? Reflections on Early Jewish and Christian Interpretations of the Garden of Eden," *HTR* 82 (1989):

equation.[91] This new awareness and potential for gaining more information about one another and their environment makes the coupling of the man and woman a struggle as well as a fulfillment of desire. This knowledge can either increase or decrease the level of communion between the couple. The quality of their union depends on the level of mutual awareness and communication.[92] There is an ambiguity in this communing with one another, for their awareness of their nakedness moves them to cloak their private parts (Gen 3:7).[93] Now it seems that right relationship with one another demands a form of immediate, direct self-disclosure that cannot be borne. The couple will need to work together to reach the point where direct disclosure to one another is productive of a stronger relationship.[94]

The knowledge constitutive of intimate personal relationships has an element that is bigger than either of the human partners. This knowledge has a divine element (cf. Song 8:6).[95] The act of childbearing highlights the creative component of their relationship that is bigger than either of them. Their cooperation with God and nature in bringing new life into the world communicates to them a knowledge and awareness of one another, of the world, and of God that could not be gained otherwise (Gen 4:1; 5:1-3).[96] The beauty of bringing new life into the world would seem to provide much joy and pleasure to counteract the distress and pain of childbearing (Isa 66:7). Although the woman bears the burden of childbirth and experiences it more directly, it would seem that the man who communicates well with the woman would also experience a strong measure of pain and pleasure in the process of childbirth.[97] The

---

121–48, at 123, 129, 148. Meyers, *Discovering Eve*, 87, notes that the language of sin is absent from Genesis 3.

91. Westermann, *Genesis 1–11*, 251; Bill T. Arnold, *Genesis* (Cambridge: Cambridge University Press, 2008), 63. Ackerman, "The Personal Is Political," 442, claims that the Bible—with the exception of the Song of Songs—will speak of a woman's love for another when the context is not sexual; otherwise, sexual love is spoken about from the man's perspective.

92. Westermann, *Genesis 1–11*, 250; Meyers, *Discovering Eve*, 110. On the ambiguity of the use of *ʾāhēb* for Shechem's relationship to Dinah in Genesis 34 see Ackerman, "The Personal Is the Political," 457.

93. Westermann, *Genesis 1–11*, 236, 251; Arnold, *Genesis*, 63, 66.

94. On the dialogue of the man and woman in the garden in the Song of Songs as communicative intimacy see Davidson, *Flame of Yahweh*, 603.

95. Ibid., 630–31.

96. Westermann, *Genesis 1–11*, 290–91.

97. Gen 30:1-6; 35:16-20; 42:36; cf. Carine M. Mandarossian, "Laboring Women, Coaching Men: Masculinity and Childbirth Education in the Contemporary United States," *Hypatia* 18 (2003): 113–34, at 118–20, 125.

kind of knowing that the couple experiences in the moment of sexual union—although Gen 2:24; 4:1; 5:3 do not explicitly say this—would seem to reach a higher stage of disclosure when such union bears fruit in the birth of a new human being.[98]

This quest for knowledge is open-ended and infinite. Yet the desire for knowledge resides in a human couple that also have programmed into their physical constitution a strong desire to form a primordial unity: "Therefore, a man leaves behind his father and mother and joins to his woman, and they become one flesh" (Gen 2:24). If they had remained in the Garden such a unity might have been possible. But with their expulsion that unity will be elusive and frustrating. The intense longing of the lovers in the Song of Songs for one another anticipates their sexual union as an experience of the paradisiacal quality of a garden (Song 6:2), yet such an experience of union remains a matter of anticipation in the Song rather than one of fulfillment.[99]

The sexual transgressions with which Hosea charges Israel in Hosea 4 exemplify the frustrations and shortcomings humans experience in properly channeling sexual desire. Their intuition and foretaste of the unity possible with others, their environment, and God only intensifies their desire to reach this complete union without traversing the painful pathway of self-knowledge.[100] The sexual activities in the environs of the hilltop shrines testify to human efforts to use the gifts of nature for limited human ends. By contrast, the knowledge operative in the process of childbirth is participatory and obedient to the fundamental rule of the divine.[101] The challenge before humans who have eaten the fruit of the knowledge of good and evil is to keep searching for wholeness that can come about only with the presence of God.[102] Such divine presence is part of erotic experience, but erotic experience must wait upon this divine presence and deal with the ambiguity and finiteness of the human capacity to know. Infinite desire within a finite being demands another form of knowing than that of acquiring information and control (cf. Prov

98. Gen 24:60; Van der Toorn, *From Her Cradle to Her Grave*, 70; cf. John Paul II, *The Theology of the Body* (Boston: Pauline Books & Media, 1997), 79.

99. J. Cheryl Exum, *Song of Songs*, OTL (Louisville: Westminster John Knox, 2005), 246, 263; Davidson, *Flame of Yahweh*, 553.

100. On the culpability of the fathers and seniors of the Israelite families see A. A. Macintosh, *Hosea* (Edinburgh: T & T Clark, 1997), 159–60.

101. Robin H. Jarrell, "The Birth Narrative as Female Counterpart to Covenant," *JSOT* 97 (2002): 3–18, at 4.

102. Westermann, *Genesis 1–11*, 254–55.

30:18-19).[103] It is the patient and reverent kind of knowing that comes with getting to know another person. Getting to know God is a privilege of humans, but it challenges them beyond their capacities.

Erōs and the Maintenance of the Sacred Boundaries of the Israelite Household

Monogamy was the usual practice within Israelite households.[104] A recurrent reason for departing from this practice was the barrenness of the wife (Gen 16:1; 30:1; 1 Sam 1:2). The woman's status within the household depended on her capacity to give birth to offspring who would perpetuate the patriarchal life and the household (Gen 18:12; 30:1).[105] It is curious that the husband's sperm is designated as the carrier of life, yet when pregnancy does not occur, the woman bears the brunt of the frustration over the lack of an heir.[106] The Israelites understood well the essential role of the woman in the reproductive process, but when infertility occurred they gave the benefit of the doubt to the male.[107] The

103. David M. Carr, *The Erotic Word: Sexuality, Spirituality, and the Bible* (New York: Oxford University Press, 2003), 85; Davidson, *Flame of Yahweh*, 620–21. Leo Strauss, *On Plato's Symposium* (Chicago: University of Chicago Press, 2001), 138, notes that "the genuinely erotic human beings cannot say what they desire because the desire is in a way self-contradictory. But the self-contradiction points to a deeper truth which the soul divines without being able to state it clearly. There is a disproportion between the infinity of the love and the finiteness of the embrace. Men cannot say what they desire; a god must say it for them" (cf. *Symp*. 192b5-d2).

104. Roland deVaux, *Ancient Israel*, 2 vols. (New York: McGraw-Hill, 1965), 1:24–25; Davidson, *Flame of Yahweh*, 177–78.

105. Ibid., 453–57; Malul, *Knowledge, Control, and Sex*, 355. Keefe, *Woman's Body and the Social Body in Hosea*, 149, quotes Gerda Lerner, *The Creation of Patriarchy* (New York: Oxford University Press, 1986), who notes that "the presence of goddess worship in an ancient Near Eastern society does not offer evidence of social structures of female freedom and bodily autonomy. Rather patriarchal control of female sexuality, backed by the laws of the state, was a formative and foundational feature of ancient Near Eastern civilizations."

106. Malul, *Knowledge, Control, and Sex*, 359. Plato averred that the sperm originated in the brain and marrow of the male (*Timaeus* 73b-c, 86c, 91c-d); see Angela Hobbs, "Female Imagery in Plato," in *Plato's Symposium: Issues in Interpretation and Reception*, ed. James H. Lesher, Debra Nails, and Frisbee C. C. Sheffield, 252–71 (Cambridge, MA: Center for Hellenic Studies of Harvard University Press, 2006), at 263. On the power of male sperm in the writings of Galen, Aristotle, and Hippocrates see Thomas Laqueur, *Making Sex: Body and Gender from the Greeks to Freud* (Cambridge, MA: Harvard University Press, 1990), 38–42, 54–55; Sarah B. Pomeroy, *Families in Classical and Hellenistic Greece: Representations and Realities* (Oxford: Clarendon Press, 1997), 96.

107. Malul, *Knowledge, Control, and Sex*, 366–67. However, Baruch A. Levine, "'Seed' versus 'Womb': Expressions of Male Dominance in Biblical Israel," in *Sex and Gender in the*

solution to the lack of an heir was to secure a second wife or a concubine (Gen 16:2) or to adopt (Gen 15:3)—although adoption seems to have been rarely practiced.[108] The traditional practice of monogamy kept erotic sexual expression focused on the relationship of husband and wife with the primary goal of procreation (cf. Tob 8:7).[109] In this reproductive activity the couple participated in God's action of bringing life into the world and so acted analogously to God.

The status of a woman in the Israelite community changed with a shift in her sexual role. If she became barren or a widow she declined in status.[110] Her role in reproduction established her place in the household as the complement to her husband. On the basis of their biological or anatomical makeup, man and woman were not regarded as reversible parts. The woman was closely tied to nature through childbearing and nursing. Even though the woman was indispensable to the family, she was subordinate in decision-making power to the man who governed the household. Malul contends that whenever a social structure is articulated the differentiated parts will define themselves over against one another and thus will stand in tension.[111] This process of defining male and female over against one another has legitimacy insofar as it sees the interplay between similarities and differences as an ongoing dynamic anchored in particular contexts that admits of no definitive, timeless list of masculine and feminine characteristics.[112]

Those individuals who did not fit into the male-female project for procreation (e.g., celibates, barren women, and old women) were re-

---

Ancient Near East: Proceedings of the 47th Rencontre Assyriologique Internationale, Helsinki, July 2–6, 2001, 2 vols., ed. Simo Parpola and Robert M. Whiting, 337–43 (Helsinki: Neo-Assyrian Text Project, 2002), at 339, notes with regard to the Piel of *rḥm* in Hos 2:25, which links the notion of "womb" with that of "mercy, pity": "This may be taken to mean that the deepest love is realized sexually between male and female, and between mother and child, and that the child is first and foremost the fruit of the mother's womb, not of the father's seed."

108. Jacob Milgrom, *Leviticus 17–22*, 1787.

109. Othmar Keel, *Song of Songs* (Minneapolis: Fortress Press, 1994), 34; Larry Lyke, "The Song of Songs, Proverbs, and the Theology of Love," in *Theological Exegesis: Essays in Honor of Brevard S. Childs*, ed. Christopher Seitz and Kathryn Greene-McCreight, 208–23 (Grand Rapids: Eerdmans, 1999), at 211.

110. Malul, *Knowledge, Control, and Sex*, 372.

111. Ibid., 295.

112. Cf. Rodney Needham, "Introduction," in *Right & Left: Essays on Dual Symbolic Classification*, ed. idem (Chicago: University of Chicago Press, 1973), xi–xxxix, at xxv–xxx.

garded as outsiders to the social structure of ancient Israel.[113] One bearing such a liminal status might be described as an inhabitant of the wild. Malul notes that sex is a primary criterion for deciding who has a liminal status. For example, if certain individuals refrain from sex they would be regarded as liminal characters. So if the holy is defined as a liminal reality it is not part of the structure of the profane sphere but stands over against it. With such a picture of the liminal or antistructural sphere one would conclude that sex was to be kept separate from people and things that were designated as holy. But it seems that the Israelites believed that the holy could coexist with the profane and become an energizing power within the everyday world. If so, there is a need to identify the kinds of sexual expression they regarded as compatible with the holy. For example, the Priestly Writer categorizes any form of seminal emission as polluting and requires the man to stay away from the sanctuary for a day or perhaps longer in order not to defile it; however, the writer of the Holiness Code has nothing to say about such emissions but is more concerned about defiling mixtures of sexual substances—e.g., sexual relations with a menstruant (Lev 18:19), anal intercourse between males (Lev 18:22), or bestiality (Lev 18:23). These instances point to the distinctive strategies of the Priestly Writing and the Holiness Code for maintaining the boundary between the sacred and the profane.[114]

According to the book of Hosea, sexual relations outside the married relationship were condemned not only for women but also for men (Hos 4:14; cf. Amos 2:7). The promiscuity of the men at the hilltop shrines doubled back on the transgressors' household in such a way that their daughters became promiscuous. Even though the various pentateuchal law collections do not explicitly condemn extramarital sexual activity of men with women who are not bound to another household,[115] the ideal of monogamous fidelity as expressed by Gen 2:24 may well have been upheld in practice. Sexual boundary violations attacked the integrity of the household, the matrix of relationships that shaped the identity of its members and thus had a sacred character.

113. Malul, *Knowledge, Control, and Sex*, 401, 440.

114. Jacob Milgrom, *Leviticus 17–22*, 1567–71; Saul M. Olyan, "'And with a Male You Shall Not Lie the Lying Down of a Woman': On the Meaning and Significance of Leviticus 18:22 and 20:13," *Journal of the History of Sexuality* 5 (1994): 179–206, at 200–3; Brenner, *The Intercourse of Knowledge*, 144–46.

115. Carol Meyers, *Exodus* (Cambridge: Cambridge University Press, 2005), 176; Jon Berquist, *Controlling Corporeality: The Body and the Household in Ancient Israel* (New Brunswick, NJ: Rutgers University Press, 2002), 102.

Homosexual activity was either prohibited or severely curtailed in ancient Israel. Saul M. Olyan has argued that Lev 18:22 outlaws anal intercourse but leaves open the possibility for other forms of sexual exchange by same-sex couples.[116] He asserts that the main concern in the Holiness Code (Leviticus 17–26) concerning same-sex intercourse is the defilement of the land that would result from the mixing of semen and excrement.[117] In the historical narratives the stories about the close relationship between Jonathan and David suggest that there was a sexual dimension to their friendship. In David's elegy over Saul and Jonathan after their death at the battle of Gilboa, David says of Jonathan: "Distress has come upon me because of you, my brother Jonathan; you were very special to me; your love was more wonderful to me than the love of women" (2 Sam 1:26). Ackerman argues that Jonathan is portrayed as the feminine partner in this relationship in order to make David appear to be the dominant one who has a more legitimate claim on the kingship.[118] Thus the narrative assumes that the audience would regard a feminine-like claimant on political power as less fit to rule than a more masculine-like one. Ackerman contends that the positive presentation of homosexual innuendo in the David/Jonathan stories—in contrast to the pejorative view of homosexual relations in the rest of the Old Testament—is due to the liminal status of both Jonathan and David in this narrative in which both David and Jonathan are trapped in a state of in-betweenness vis-à-vis the power and authority of Saul.[119]

116. Saul M. Olyan, "'And with a Male You Shall Not Lie the Lying Down of a Woman,'" 187–88, 204–6; Susan Ackerman, *When Heroes Love: The Ambiguity of Eros in the Stories of Gilgamesh and David* (New York: Columbia University Press, 2005), 26; Jerome T. Walsh, "Leviticus 18:22 and 20:13: Who Is Doing What to Whom," *JBL* 120 (2001): 201–9, at 201, 208–9; Daniel Boyarin, "Are There Any Jews in 'The History of Sexuality'?" *Journal of the History of Sexuality* 5 (1995): 333–55, at 337.

117. Olyan, "'And with a Male You Shall Not Lie the Lying Down of a Woman,'" 203.

118. Ackerman, *When Heroes Love*, 221–23. Jean-Fabrice Nardelli, *Homosexuality and Liminality in the Gilgameš and Samuel*, Classical and Byzantine Monographs 64 (Amsterdam: Adolf M. Hakkert, 2007), 38–40, argues that Jonathan is nowhere portrayed as a submissive partner to David or the recipient of sexual favors, but rather their sexual relationship is covered up in the narrative. With regard to Lev 18:22, Olyan, "'And with a Male You Shall Not Lie the Lying Down of a Woman,'" 205, notes that anal intercourse is prohibited absolutely in the land of Israel; neither class status nor fear of feminization was a factor from the perspective of the Holiness Code.

119. Ackerman, *When Heroes Love*, 210–12. Nardelli, *Homosexuality and Liminality*, 46–47, 58–62, cites Walsh, "Leviticus 18:22 and 20:13," 207–8, on the limitation of the prohibition of these verses to anal intercourse between two men and then argues that this later law of

The threat of homosexual rape in Genesis 19 and Judges 19 is strongly censured. Interpreters emphasize that the crime in both of these stories is one of violence against a guest stranger.[120] Yet the most shocking aspect of these stories lies in the alternatives the host presents to the aggressive mob. In Genesis 19, Lot offers to give his unmarried daughters to the men of Sodom in place of the men who were visiting (v. 8). In Judges 19 the elderly Ephraimite hosting the Levite in Gibeah offers his virgin daughter and the Levite's concubine to the men of Gibeah instead of the Levite himself (v. 25). Ackerman contends that the hosts offer the women to the angry mobs because a greater dishonor to the community would arise from allowing a man to be treated as the passive partner in a sexual union than from letting them rape a young woman.[121] Whatever the precise reason for the dishonor attributed to these homosexual couplings, the stories use these threatened violent acts of male-to-male anal intercourse to accent the depravity of men in Sodom and Gibeah and to suggest that their behavior polluted these two cities. Both Sodom and the tribe of Judah were subsequently purged of their offenders so that life in the land could return to equilibrium.

The kind of connectivity to which *erōs* aspires suggests that the other-centered dimension of work, in which one carries out services that contribute to the common good, is an example of an erotic activity. Individuals can join with others in a common effort that will bind them more closely together.[122] Such erotic activity is nonsexual, but it has bonding potential that approximates many instances of sexual union. The purpose of placing humans in the Garden of Eden in Genesis 2 was that they might till the soil. Such work was not onerous labor but an activity that brought

---

the Holiness Code would not have applied to the late eleventh century BCE; he contends that the Samuel narratives suggest that David and Jonathan developed a reciprocal sexual relationship rather than a hierarchical one according to the active/passive model.

120. Claus Westermann, *Genesis 12–36*, trans. John J. Scullion (Minneapolis: Augsburg, 1985), 301, claims that the narrative deals with two crimes: "unnatural lust (Lev 18:22) and the violation of the right of guests to protection." Walter Brueggemann, *Genesis* (Atlanta: John Knox, 1982), 164, grants that Genesis 19 may be addressing a sexual disorder, but that is less the issue than the "general issue of a society organized against God." However, Terence Fretheim, *Abraham: Trials of Family and Faith* (Columbia, SC: University of South Carolina Press, 2007), argues that Genesis 19 does not condemn homosexual relations as unnatural acts. Susan Niditch, *Judges*, OTL (Louisville: Westminster John Knox, 2008), 193, states that this passage seems to be less about homosexuality and more "about a larger theme in sexual ethics in which one partner subdues, owns, and holds unequal power over the other."

121. Ackerman, *When Heroes Love*, 224.

122. Carr, *The Erotic Word*, 37; Meyers, *Discovering Eve*, 110.

them into harmony with the environment. Thus erotic activity in ancient Israel was wider than the sexual. Forms of nonsexual erotic activity would have been vital to the well-being of the Yahwistic cult in ancient Israel.

The patriarchal household was the basic building block of Israelite society according to the books of Hosea and Genesis. A central goal of erotic sexual expression in this agricultural society was procreation. When sexual expression was channeled toward the monogamous relation of husband and wife, the larger erotic dimension of other relationships and activities had to be properly directed so as not to compromise the vitality and integrity of the matrix of household relationships, the sacred core of the family.

Summary

To a reader of the book of Hosea in the Persian period (539–333), transcultural Israel was called to love YHWH, who is described as a husband and a parent in Hosea 2 and 11. But in the canonical memory Israel's capacity to relate properly to YHWH has already been called into question in the golden calf episode in Exodus 32. The rebelliousness of the child in Hosea 11 parallels that of the Israelites in their worship of the golden calf. The problem of syncretistic worship seems to be perennial. The Israelite priests are charged with depriving the people of "knowledge of YHWH," i.e., both objective and subjective knowledge that promotes the correct understanding of YHWH and right relationship to him. The corrupt priests with their mechanical sacrifices have silenced the symbolic dimension of these offerings and thus closed off an important avenue for coming into right relationship with YHWH.

The metaphor of Israel's marriage to YHWH highlights the covenantal relationship. As the wife, Israel was expected to be exclusively loyal to her husband YHWH. Her promiscuity (i.e., her worship of Baal) resulted in the birth of illegitimate children. The way Baal compromised the loyalty of the Israelites to YHWH did not seem to be so much by drawing them into his sanctuaries to acknowledge him and to dissociate themselves publicly from YHWH. Rather, the problem was one of syncretism: the Israelites thought that what YHWH expected of them overlapped with what Baal had typically requested. Which baalistic practices could be "baptized" into Yahwism, and which ones had to be kept strictly separate?

Sexual activity at the hilltop shrines was condemned (Hos 4:13). Was such activity a figure of speech for apostasy or syncretism? Or did such activity actually take place? The evidence for sexual activity in sacred marriage rituals and for cultic prostitution is fragmentary in extrabiblical sources. But within an agricultural economy the concern for fertility would seem to have made its way into the worship practices of the Canaanite and Israelite peoples. The symbolic potential of sexual union for communication with the divine is evident in the use of the marriage metaphor by Hosea and by extrabiblical texts. The erotic dimension of the marital metaphor could be communicated linguistically and need not have been carnally enacted in order to become a reality in the imaginations and behavior of the Israelites. Nevertheless, the translation of this metaphor into worship practices could potentially have taken the form of sexual copulation between cultic officials in sanctioned rituals or between cultic employees and individuals within the community in the form of prostitution. The allusions to "cultic prostitution" in Hos 4:14, 17 may literally refer to copulation in Baalistic shrines or may figuratively refer to Israelites' giving their loyalty to Baal. The consensus of critics seems to have shifted from literal to figurative copulation over the past decade due to the absence of clear data for sexual rites or cultic prostitution within the cults of the ancient Near East. However, to identify Baalism only with hierarchical, stratifying political power to the exclusion of concerns with agricultural success ignores the agricultural imagery of passages like Hos 2:23-24. Yahwistic worshipers would be concerned not only with an egalitarian social structure but also with fertility.

How could sexuality be expressed in Israel's relationship with YHWH? If copulation and genital emissions were prohibited in sacred space in the Yahwistic community, could the vital energies associated with the erotic have any place within Israel's relationship with YHWH, or were these erotic energies simply to be repressed? In Hos 2:16 YHWH "allures" Israel into the wilderness. The wooing that occurs here is expressed in figurative terms, but not in a disembodied way. The movement into the wilderness under the sway of YHWH's erotic speech is not to remain in the sphere of mere fancy but is to become enfleshed in Israel's behavior. This region between the literal and the figurative embodiment of an erotic relationship with YHWH is the place of decision for YHWH or for Baal. For YHWH to be respected and to become manifest, the sphere of the holy or the separate must be created. This creation of a sphere of differentiation is what is lost in syncretism.

In light of the marriage metaphor, the ambiguities involved in coming into right relationship with YHWH in worship are analogous to those of courtship and marriage. In light of Hosea's use of the marriage metaphor to communicate the dynamics of the covenant relations, Israel could not afford to screen the erotic and sexuality out of its relationship with

YHWH. In the world created by Hosea's message an exclusive married relationship with YHWH prohibited Israelites from marrying other gods, but they were free to marry humans.[123] This emphasis on an exclusive monogamous relationship with YHWH would have influenced the flow of erotic energies within the patriarchal household to keep the centripetal force of *erōs* from devolving into promiscuity.

Mesopotamia: Sexuality as a Life-force Spanning the Cosmos

In Mesopotamia divine reality is present in all three tiers of the cosmos: heaven, earth, and netherworld. The anthropomorphized gods express their sexuality not only in heaven and on earth but also in the netherworld. Sexuality and the erotic function within the family life of the gods and have an impact on the vitality of the earthly sphere. Meaningful interaction between the human and the divine transpire in sexual relations, whether literally or metaphorically conceived. The potential of sexuality and the erotic to enhance life in all three spheres of the cosmos will be examined primarily on the basis of texts from the love songs of Dumuzi and Inanna; the myths of "Enki and Ninhursaga," "Nergal and Ereshkigal," and *The Descent of Inanna*; and the *Epic of Gilgamesh*. The three main issues guiding the investigation of these texts will be addressed in successive subsections as follows: (1) how the erotic and sexual dimension of divine life in Mesopotamia was communicated in story and ritual to enhance understanding of the vital forces essential to cosmic order; (2) how erotic and sexual experience influenced the growth of Enkidu and Gilgamesh; and (3) how erotic experience reshaped sociopolitical arrangements.

The Role of the Erotic Within the Pantheon

Mesopotamian deities in the third millennium number more than three thousand. The god list AN has two thousand entries. By around 1200 BCE the number of recognized deities seems to have diminished, for Tablets VI-VII of the *Enūma Elish* list only six hundred, with three hundred in heaven and three hundred below the earth.[124] Given the wide

123. In the later Christian tradition a celibate was married to God but was not free to marry another human.

124. Jean Bottéro, "The Religious System," in idem, *Mesopotamia: Writing, Reasoning, and the Gods*, trans. Zainab Bahrani and Marc Van de Mieroop (Chicago: University of Chicago Press, 1992), 201–30, at 216.

geographical area and a history spanning more than three millennia, Mesopotamia can be said to have a pantheon in the sense that a syncretistic dynamic brought a measure of coherence and unity to this developing array of gods.[125] At the top of this pantheon in the third millennium were the following seven deities: An, Enlil, Enki, Ninhursag, Nanna-Sin, Utu, and Inanna.[126] These deities were anthropomorphic representations of spheres or powers of nature: An was the sky god; Enlil, "lord wind," ruled the space between the sky and the earth; Enki was the god of fresh water, which was located in a massive underground reservoir known as the Abzu/Apsu; Ninhursag was the mother goddess; Nanna-Sin was the moon god; Utu was the sun god; and Inanna, represented by the planet Venus, was the goddess of sex and war.[127] Each of these deities resided in a temple whose staff honored them by attending to the human-like physical and emotional needs attributed to each deity's cult statue. Most of these deities had a consort and offspring such that the temple was structured as if it were a family or a household.[128]

Within and between the households of these various gods, marital relations were vital for sustaining the households and spheres of influence of the deities. In the third millennium a cycle of stories about Dumuzi, the god of the date palm and the flocks, and Inanna, the goddess of sex, related episodes about their courtship, marriage, and dying/rising.[129] These two deities were responsible for the fertility not only of dates, flocks, and humans but also of fertility in general. When iconographical evidence of the Uruk Vase from the end of the fourth

125. Wilfred G. Lambert, "The Historical Development of the Mesopotamian Pantheon: A Study in Sophisticated Polytheism," in *Unity and Diversity: Essays in the History, Literature, and Religion of the Ancient Near East*, ed. Hans Goedicke and J. J. M. Roberts, 191–99 (Baltimore: Johns Hopkins University Press, 1975), at 195, 197–98; idem, "The Pantheon of Mari," *MARI* 4 (1985): 525–39, at 527–30. Jeremy Black and Anthony Green, *Gods, Demons and Symbols of Ancient Mesopotamia* (Austin, TX: University of Texas Press, 2000), 147; Bottéro, "The Religious System," 216–17.

126. Samuel Noah Kramer, *The Sumerians: Their History, Culture, and Character* (Chicago: University of Chicago Press, 1963), 122.

127. Jacobsen, *Treasures of Darkness*, 20. Wilfred G. Lambert, "Ancient Mesopotamian Gods: Superstitition, Philosophy, Theology," *Revue de l'Histoire des Religions* 207 (1990): 115–30, at 123–25, is skeptical of the claim that divine symbols point to a preanthropomorphic stage of Mesopotamian religion or to an earlier theriomorphic stage.

128. Frans A. M. Wiggermann, "Theologies, Priests, and Worship in Ancient Mesopotamia," *CANE* 2:1859–64; Bottéro, "The Religious System," 212, 215.

129. Jacobsen, *Treasures of Darkness*, 25–73; Tryggve N. D. Mettinger, *The Riddle of Resurrection: "Dying and Rising Gods" in the Ancient Near East*, ConBibOT 50 (Stockholm: Almqvist & Wiksell, 2001), 204, 212–13.

millennium[130] is combined with the literary accounts of the stories about Dumuzi and Inanna, a case can be made that a sacred marriage ritual was celebrated annually on New Year's Day with the goal of renewing the prosperity of the kingdom and securing a good fate for the king.[131] However, the date of New Year's Day for the celebration of the ritual, which would have symbolized cosmic renewal for the coming year, has been recovered only from the Inanna-Iddindagan hymn from Isin.[132] Alternative proposals associate this sacred marriage with the coronation[133] and legitimation of the king,[134] with the production of a royal heir,[135] with the installation of the EN-priestess,[136] or with the composition of courtly and secular poetry. Common to these proposals is that the aim of the ritualized sexual joining of Dumuzi-Inanna was to bring prosperity to the earthly realm, for which fertility was indispensable.[137] The most likely date for such a ritual would have been New Year's Day.[138]

130. Zainab Bahrani, *The Women of Babylon: Gender and Representation in Mesopotamia* (London: Routledge, 2001), 138.

131. Yitschak Sefati, *Love Songs in Sumerian Literature: Critical Edition of the Dumuzi-Inanna Songs* (Ramat Gan: Bar-Ilan University, 1998), 47–49.

132. Jacob Klein, "Sacred Marriage," *ABD* 5:868. Walther Sallaberger, "Ur-III Zeit," in Walther Sallaberger and Aage Westenholz, *Mesopotamien. Akkade-Zeit und Ur-III Zeit*, OBO 160/3 (Fribourg: Universitätsverlag, 1999),121–414, at 155–56, argues that the sacred marriage was celebrated at a high point in the year and was not linked with a particular calendar date. See also Barbara Böck, "Überlegungen zu einem Kultfest der altmesopotamischen Göttin Inanna," *Numen* 51 (2004): 20–46, at 37.

133. Johannes Renger, "Heilige Hochzeit. A. Philologisch," *RlA* 4 (1972–75), 251–59. Jerrold Cooper, "Sacred Marriage and Popular Cult in Early Mesopotamia," in *Official Cult and Popular Religion in the Ancient Near East*, ed. Eiko Matsushima, 81–96 (Heidelberg: C. Winter, 1993), at 87, rejects this proposal of coronation as the setting for the sacred marriage and promotes that of the New Year's festival.

134. Henri Frankfort, *Kingship and the Gods* (Chicago: University of Chicago Press, 1978), 295–99.

135. William Hallo, "The Birth of Kings," in *Love and Death in the Ancient Near East*, ed. John H. Marks and Robert M. Good, 42–52 (Guilford, CT: Four Quarters Publishing Co., 1987), at 49. Cooper, "Sacred Marriage and Popular Cult in Early Mesopotamia," 90, contends that the problem of incest in this model of producing a royal heir disqualifies it.

136. Douglas Frayne, "Notes on the Sacred Marriage Rite," *Bibliotheca Orientalis* 42 (1985): 5–22.

137. Klein, "Sacred Marriage," *ABD* 5:868. Lapinkivi, "The Sumerian Sacred Marriage and Its Aftermath," 10–11, acknowledges that the relationship of the king and the goddess brought prosperity to the land but cautions that the sacred marriage was not "*essentially* or *exclusively* a fertility ritual."

138. Klein, "Sacred Marriage," *ABD* 5:868; Lapinkivi, *Sumerian Sacred Marriage*, 245.

The erotic dimension of the relationship between Dumuzi and Inanna is illustrated in the following excerpt from the ceremony for the dressing of the bride from the song titled by Sefati "Meeting in the Storehouse (DI T)":[139]

> The maiden amid cries of joy has sent someone to her father! Inanna, moving as in a dance (for joy), has sent someone to her father, (saying): "O that they rush into my house, (into) my house for me! O that they rush into my house, (into) my house, for me who am the mistress; O that they rush into my house, the Giparu for me! And when they have set up my pure bed for him; O that they spread thereon my lustrous lapis lazuli (hued) straw for me. O that they have the man of my heart come in to me; O that they have my Amaushumgalanna come in to me; O that they put his hand in my hand for me; O that they put his heart next to my heart for me. Not only is it sweet to sleep hand in hand with him, sweetest of sweet is too the loveliness of joining heart to heart with him." (35-47)[140]

This passage highlights the excitement of Inanna at the anticipated approach of her bridegroom Dumuzi. As she is about to open the door to him, Inanna recounts how a bed has been set up for the couple in the *giparu*, an ancient storeroom within the temple.[141] She yearns for the closeness and the warmth of her lover as she invites him as the bridegroom into her chamber to consummate the marriage.

Jacobsen links this particular nuptial account in the "Meeting in the Storehouse (DI T)" with the renewal of the date palm so that it might produce an abundant harvest. The epithet describing Dumuzi here is Amaushumgalanna, which Jacobsen translates as "the one great source of the date clusters."[142] He represents the date clusters that will soon line the shelves of the storeroom, for which Inanna is the numen. Inanna expresses a warm, excited confidence at her approaching union with Dumuzi, a disposition that, according to Jacobsen, the community is invited to emulate as it looks to the coming year's harvest.[143]

Dumuzi is a complex figure. In origin he may have been a shepherd-king in Bad-Tibira or a fisherman-king in Erech. Upon his deification,

139. Sefati, *Love Songs*, 247–51.

140. Translation from Jacobsen, *Treasures of Darkness*, 34–35.

141. Klein, "Sacred Marriage," *ABD* 5:867.

142. Jacobsen, *Treasures of Darkness*, 36. Sefati, *Love Songs*, 74, n. 91, notes that the meaning of Amaushumgalanna is disputed and that Falkenstein translates it:"the mother is a heavenly dragon."

143. Jacobsen, *Treasures of Darkness*, 36.

temples were constructed for him in Girsu and Bad-tibira where he was worshiped as a minor deity until the OB period.[144] As a representative of the economy of a particular community (e.g., shepherding, fishing, date growing), Dumuzi was believed to unite sexually with the higher-ranking goddess Inanna in order to bring renewed life to the local community.[145] In these sexual liaisons Dumuzi was the passive partner in the sacred marriage rite, which seems to reflect his human origin.[146] After 1800 BCE the official cult for Dumuzi vanishes, but he lives on not only as a literary figure in the Dumuzi-Inanna stories and lyric poems but also as a dying and rising god within the canonical laments.[147]

According to royal inscriptions and hymns the sacred marriage rite was enacted in the Mesopotamian cult in the Ur III-Isin periods (ca. 2100 to 1800 BCE).[148] The reigning king represented Dumuzi. The representative of Inanna is assumed to be an EN-priestess,[149] although the female partner is also variously designated as a hierodule (NU.GIG), a concubine (LUKUR),[150] and a "divine lady" (NIN.DINGIR).[151] Klein notes that this variation in the identification of the female partner has led to questions of whether the female partner was actually the cult statue of Inanna, in which case the sexual joining of Dumuzi and Inanna would not have involved sexual relations between a human couple within the sanctuary.[152] This more abstract way of symbolizing the sacred marriage in

144. Klein, "Sacred Marriage," *ABD* 5:866, 868.

145. Jacobsen, *Treasures of Darkness*, 43.

146. Leick, *Sex and Eroticism in Mesopotamian Literature*, 56, claims that "in Mesopotamian literature, the woman's voice dominates the poetic discourse. She speaks of her desire and demands the gratification of her sexual needs, while the male voice is often an imagined response to her pleas."

147. Klein, "Sacred Marriage," *ABD* 5:867, 868; Cooper, "Sacred Marriage and Popular Cult in Early Mesopotamia," 94–95. Gwendolyn Leick, *Sex and Eroticism in Mesopotamian Literature*, 104, claims that erotic relationships of humans with the gods was limited to the Ur III period.

148. Cooper, "Sacred Marriage and Popular Cult in Early Mesopotamia," 83; Lapinkivi, *Sumerian Sacred Marriage*, 14.

149. Douglas Frayne, "Notes on the Sacred Marriage Rite," *BibOr* 42 (1985): 5–22, at 12–22. Cooper, "Sacred Marriage and Popular Cult in Early Mesopotamia," 87–88, criticizes Frayne's identification of the roles of the EN with NIN.DINGIR, identifying the problem of incest in the ritual as described by Frayne as the most serious drawback to the identification of the EN with the NIN.DINGIR.

150. Renger, "Heilige Hochzeit," *RlA* 4:256.

151. William Hallo, "The Birth of Kings," 49.

152. Klein, "Sacred Marriage," *ABD* 5:867. Leick, *Sex and Eroticism in Mesopotamian Literature*, 111, notes that there is no evidence that an Ur III king engaged in sexual intercourse within the ritual of sacred marriage. See also Martti Nissinen, "Song of Songs and

which the partners were the statues of the male and female deities was practiced at Lagash in the Ur III period and was the form of the sacred marriage that survived in the Mesopotamian tradition after 1800 BCE. Thus human sexual activity as a component in rituals, which is clearly described in Sumerian hymns honoring Shulgi of Ur (ca. 2050 BCE) and Iddindagan of Isin (ca. 1959 BCE), seems to have been eliminated from the Mesopotamian cult after 1800 BCE.[153] Cooper contends that the primary purpose of the sacred marriage ritual was the king's establishing ties with the gods; the sexual and fertility aspects of the sacred marriage built on the socioreligious one of strengthening the network of relationships between the gods, the king, and the people.[154]

The sacred marriage ritual illustrates the dominant Mesopotamian viewpoint that the fundamental purpose of sexuality is "the reproduction and creative organization of the universe."[155] The coupling of a male-female pair to produce offspring is the dynamic process by which not only species of animals and plants but also the world order itself is sustained. Among Mesopotamian artifacts, naked females, apparently intended to emphasize the female role in fertility and reproduction, are much more frequent than nude male figures or phallic symbols.[156] The only Mesopotamian god whose phallic characteristics are emphasized is the Sumerian god of fresh water, Enki. His life-giving characteristics are echoed in the Sumerian ideogram for "water," which also means "semen."[157]

In the second part of the story of "Enki and Ninhursaga," Enki is presented as a male sowing his seed and ready to subdue with violence those who would resist him. He encounters Nintud/Ninhursaga ("mistress of the foothills") alone in the marshland:

> Alone, the wise one, for Nintud—the mother of the land, Enki, the wise one, Nintud [the mother of the land], was digging his phallus

---

Sacred Marriage," 201. Hallo, "The Birth of Kings," 49, contends on the basis of the texts and numerous artistic representations that physical intercourse between the king and a priestess took place in the ritual of the sacred marriage in order to engender a royal heir.

153. Klein, "Sacred Marriage," *ABD* 5:867; Cooper, "Sacred Marriage and Popular Cult in Early Mesopotamia," 85; cf. Kelle, *Hosea 2*, 134–35.

154. Cooper, "Sacred Marriage and Popular Cult in Early Mesopotamia," 90–92.

155. Leick, *Sex and Eroticism in Mesopotamian Literature*, 20.

156. Ibid., 21.

157. *The Sumerian Dictionary*, ed. Åke W. Sjöberg, et al. (Philadelphia: Babylonian Section of the University Museum, 1984–[1998]), vol. A, part 1, p. 1; Marten Stol, *Birth in Babylonia and the Bible: Its Mediterranean Setting*, Cuneiform Monographs 14 (Groningen: Styx, 2000), 4.

> in the dyke, sliding his phallus into the reed. The great one (Nintud) pulled his phallus aside, saying: "No one will take me in the marsh." (So) Enki called: "By the life of heaven I adjure you. Lying down in the marsh, lying down in the marsh, that is joyous." Enki, his mouth uttered "Oh Damgulnuna."[158]

Enki's sexual aggression against Nintud/Ninhursaga, a ruling god in the Sumerian pantheon, can only be described as rape. Yet when he pronounces that Ninhursaga is Damgulnuna he identifies this great goddess with his consort in Eridu. This performative utterance by Enki changes their relationship in this narrative into a married one; therefore Ninhursaga allows him to have relations with her.[159] Ninhursaga becomes pregnant and gives birth to Ninisiga ("mistress of the verdure," 75-87). Enki repeats the same aggressive behavior toward his daughter as he did toward Ninhursaga. She gives birth to Ninkurra ("mistress of the mountains," 97-107). Enki likewise forces her, and she gives birth to Nin-imma ("lady female genitals," 126A). Enki then forces Nin-imma, who then gives birth to Uttu (126L-126CC).[160] At this point the account has Ninhursaga intervene and advise Uttu (the spider goddess of weaving) to protect herself against Enki.[161] When Enki approaches Uttu she demands marriage, with its accompanying gifts. When Enki disguises himself as a gardener delivering cucumbers, apples, grapes, and beer to Uttu, she opens the door to him.[162] He proceeds immediately to subdue her and have sex with her (180-85). When Uttu cries out, Ninhursaga removes Enki's semen from Uttu and casts the semen to the ground, where eight plants grow up: a wood plant, a honey plant, a vegetable plant, esparto grass, an *Atutu* plant, an *aštaltal* plant, an *amharu* plant, and one other (191-97).[163] When Enki sees these plants, he is determined to find out their nature. Enki's assistant Isimud cuts each of the plants and gives them to Enki, who then eats them, which enables him to know

158. Translation from Dina Katz, "Enki and Ninhursaga, Part Two: The Story of Enki and Ninhursaga," *Bibliotheca Orientalis* 65 (2008): 320–42, at 322; see also Thorkild Jacobsen, *The Harps That Once . . . Sumerian Poetry in Translation* (New Haven: Yale University Press, 1987), 191.

159. Katz, "Enki and Ninhursaga, Part Two," 322, 340.

160. Here I follow the reconstruction of the narrative and the translation of the names by Jacobsen, *The Harps That Once*, 195–97.

161. Jacobsen, *Treasures of Darkness*, 112–13.

162. Katz, "Enki and Ninhursaga, Part Two," 328.

163. Katz, Enki and Ninhursaga, Part Two," 330, 332, says that Ninhursaga's role in the creation of the plants indicates that a male and a female deity are involved in their creation, even though mother earth seems to assume the female role.

their hearts and determine their fates. Ninhursaga then curses Enki so that he lies dying (220-21). A fox convinces Ninhursaga to go to Nippur, where the Anunnakū are able to counteract her potent curse on Enki (231-51). Ninhursaga then places Enki in her womb and provides the environment in which the fertile plants within him can come to birth (252-71).

Enki's sexual exploits with five goddesses in the second part of "Enki and Ninhursaga" each result in pregnancy and birth. The emphasis is on the creative power of Enki's semen, which forms an analogue to the life-giving character of water—the lack of which in the primeval city of Dilmun in part one of "Enki and Ninhursaga" prompts Ninsikila (Enki's consort) to appeal to Enki.[164] His preoccupation with sowing his seed and not paying attention to the fact that it is his own daughters with whom he is having intercourse results in resentment from the more powerful Ninhursaga. The remedy she provides for releasing the painful plants from within him is to offer her womb in order to bring about the birth process of the four gods and four goddesses that reside within him and need to be brought to birth. The male Enki cannot usurp the female role in procreation.[165] Enki's phallocentric behavior nearly kills him.[166]

Since the netherworld has a steady stream of new recruits it has no need to try to regenerate itself through sexual activity and procreation. Thus it is understandable that Ereshkigal, queen of the netherworld and sister of Inanna, would never have had sexual relations. But the arrival of Nergal/Erra in the netherworld introduces her to the experience of sex. In the later version (first millennium BCE) of the story of "Nergal and Ereshkigal," Ereshkigal appeals to the celestial gods Anu, Enlil, and Ea to return Nergal to her, for he has become her lover:

164. Ibid., 340–42; Leick, *Sex and Eroticism in Mesopotamian Literature*, 39. Jerrold Cooper, "Enki's Member: Eros and Irrigation in Mesopotamian Literature," in *DUMU-E$_2$-DUB-BA-A: Studies in Honor of Åke W. Sjöberg*, Occasional Publications of the Samuel Noah Kramer Fund 11, ed. Hermann Behrens, Darlene Loding, and Martha T. Roth, 87–89 (Philadelphia: University Museum, 1989), argues that Enki's raw sexuality forms a counterpoint to the female sexuality foregrounded in Sumerian love poetry and has its rationale in Enki's fundamental role in irrigation agriculture.

165. Katz, "Enki and Ninhursaga, Part Two," 332, 338.

166. Jacobsen, *Treasures of Darkness*, 112–13. Katz, "Enki and Ninhursaga, Part Two," 332, notes that the death of Enki—analogous to that of Inanna—would be a drought. According to Leonore Tiefer, "The Medicalization of Impotence: The Normalizing of Phallocentrism," *Gender and Society* 8 (1994): 363–77, at 365, phallocentrism can be defined as a "preoccupying interest and focus on the penis/phallus in sexuality discourse."

> Ever since I was a young girl, I have not experienced the fun of young women or the playfulness of young girls. That god whom you sent me has had intercourse with me. Let him lie with me. Send that god to me that he might become my husband and stay overnight with me. Am I impure? Am I defiled? Can I not render verdicts for the great gods—the great gods who live in the netherworld? (V:2'-8')[167]

Ereshkigal has attempted to seduce Nergal by passing before him naked on her way to her bath. On the second attempt she overcomes his resistance. This resistance had been reinforced by Ea's counsel that he neither eat nor engage in sex while he was in the netherworld (iii 36'-48').[168] To do so would establish a claim of the netherworld on him. But, overcome by her attractiveness, Nergal has sex with her for seven days and then escapes to the upper world (iv 5'-25'). Ereshkigal sends Namtar to the great gods in heaven with the request (as quoted above in v 2'-5') that Nergal/Erra be returned to her. Namtar reports back to Ereshkigal that he could not find the god he was looking for in the heavenly assembly, but Ereshkigal recognizes the bald god as one disguised by Ea (v 39'). Namtar had not recognized him. Then Nergal descends to the netherworld and passes through the seven gates (vi 18'-28')—a feat he is probably able to accomplish because of his status as a messenger (iv 48').[169] He rushes to her throne, embraces her, and has sex with her for seven days (vi 29'-42'). Nergal's happy embrace of Ereshkigal suggests that he may have been ready to be confined in the netherworld and to forfeit his place among the celestial gods. In light of Ea's charge that Nergal only pretended not to comprehend Namtar's signals of kneeling before him as Ereshkigal's messenger (ii 10') and that he willingly makes the return journey and shows no fear (ii 10'-20'), it may have been Nergal's hidden intent on his return journey to Ereshkigal to share rule with her over the netherworld.[170] In the earlier MB version of this story, when

167. Edition: O. R. Gurney, "The Sultantepe Tablets (Continued): VII: The Myth of Nergal and Ereshkigal," *Anatolian Studies* 10 (1960): 105–31, at 122.

168. Neil Walls, *Desire, Discord, and Death: Approaches to Ancient Near Eastern Myth* (Boston: American Schools of Oriental Research, 2001), 141–45.

169. Erica Reiner, "Nergal and Ereshkigal: Epic into Romance," in *Your Thwarts in Pieces, Your Mooring Rope Cut: Poetry from Babylonia and Assyria* (Ann Arbor: Horace H. Rackham School of Graduate Studies at the University of Michigan, 1985), 50–60, at 57.

170. Walls, *Desire, Discord, and Death*, 135–37. Wilfred G. Lambert, "The Theology of Death," in *Death in Mesopotamia: XXVIe Rencontre Assyriologique Internationale*, Mesopotamia 8 (Copenhagen: Akademisk Forlag, 1980), 53–66, at 62, notes that Ereshkigal rose in influence in the Sumerian sphere in the late third millennium to be regarded as sole ruler of the netherworld; Nergal, as city god of Kutha in the Akkadian sphere, rose in influence in

Nergal makes his way to Ereshkigal's throne room he physically subdues her and threatens her with death until she promises that he can be her husband (ll. 80-83).[171] But in the later version of the story Ereshkigal is captivated by him and yearns to be his wife. The experience of nonstop sexual relations for seven days is one she apparently wants to repeat indefinitely.[172] This experience of sexual relations has been denied her previously and would not have been part of the experience of the dead.

As a goddess resident in the netherworld, Ereshkigal is nevertheless immortal. Her question to Anu, Enlil, and Ea was whether the experience of sexual relations was defiling for her (v 7'). In the Israelite and Greek worlds death was a potent impurity.[173] However, in Mesopotamia death does not seem to be depicted as a defiling force. Cooper notes that "a human's actual sphere was properly the netherworld; the same word in both Sumerian (KI) and Akkadian (*erṣetu*) signifies both the earth's surface and the netherworld beneath it."[174] However, there is a chasm between heaven and the netherworld, as shown by Anu's statement to Ereshkigal that she cannot come up to heaven to be part of the banquet of the gods but must send a messenger (C, i 31'-37').[175] But Walls questions whether Anu has the authority to confine Ereshkigal to the

---

the OB period; they are referred to as husband and wife in OB religious texts. On the statue inscription of Kurigalzu from the first half of the fourteenth century Nergal is identified as the foremost deity of the netherword (see Niek Veldhuis, "Kurigalzu's Statue Inscription," *JCS* 60 [2008]: 25–51, at 27).

171. Foster, *Before the Muses*, 512; Rivkah Harris, *Gender and Aging in Mesopotamia* (Norman: University of Oklahoma Press, 2000), 133–34.

172. Walls, *Desire, Discord, and Death*, 145, explains the intense sexual relationship of Nergal and Ereshkigal in the netherworld in light of George Bataille's link of desire and death or of prohibition and eroticism (*The Accursed Share* [New York: Zone Books, 1991], 2:95–101).

173. Jacob Milgrom, *Leviticus: A Book of Ritual and Ethics* (Minneapolis: Fortress, 2004), 38; Baruch Levine, *Numbers 1–20* (New York: Doubleday, 1993), 457; Parker, *Miasma: Pollution and Purification in Early Greek Religion* (Oxford: Clarendon Pewaa, 1983), 3–4, 32–33. On the insufficiency of Milgrom's explanation of sexual impurity in the Priestly system as a form of death see Jonathan Klawans, *Purity, Sacrifice, and the Temple: Symbolism and Supersessionism in the Study of Ancient Judaism* (Oxford and New York: Oxford University Press, 2006), 57.

174. Jerrold S. Cooper, "The Fate of Mankind: Death and Afterlife in Ancient Mesopotamia," in *Death and Afterlife: Perspective of World Religions*, ed. Hiroshi Obayashi, 19–33 (New York: Greenwood Press, 1992), at 28.

175. Reiner, "Nergal and Ereshkigal," 51.

netherworld, since other deities can enter and exit her realm (e.g., Namtar, Kakka, Nergal).[176]

Ereshkigal's question about being defiled by sexual intercourse is not answered by the great gods. Edzard regards her plea to Anu as a rhetorical question in light of Hutter's argument that Nergal was the one who sought her out and should carry the responsibility for their sexual encounter.[177] So the question of impurity arises from the illicit character of their sexual encounter.[178] Van der Toorn notes that Ereshkigal remains impure after bathing, probably because of the extramarital nature of her liaison with Nergal.[179] Ereshkigal may have been making the case that Nergal was obliged to return to her as her partner. According to MAL §55, a man who had sex with a virgin was obliged to marry her.[180] According to the view that Ereshkigal was no longer fit to rule the netherworld, Gurney translates Ereshkigal's question as a declarative statement: "I am sexually defiled, I am not pure, I cannot execute the judgments of the great gods" (v 7').[181] Her sexual experience with Nergal constituted a rite of passage that would have disqualified her from ruling. Also contending that Ereshkigal had to change and allow Nergal to share her rule, Harris claims that the aggressive, autonomous actions required of her as sole ruler would have been an unacceptable inversion of gender roles in Mesopotamian society.[182] Nevertheless, Ereshkigal does not surrender her royal rule, but rather exercises it in demanding the return of Nergal.[183]

In her lament that she had been denied the play and pleasure of girls by her assignment to the netherworld Ereshkigal presents herself as one whose life was like that of the demoness Ardat-lilî. This demoness was

176. Walls, *Desire, Discord, and Death*, 166.

177. Manfred Hutter, *Altorientalische Vorstellungen von der Unterwelt: Literar- und religionsgeschichtliche Überlegungen zu "Nergal und Ereškigal"* (Fribourg: Universitätsverlag; Göttingen: Vandenhoeck & Ruprecht, 1985), 98; D. O. Edzard, "Review of Manfred Hutter, *Altorientalische Vorstellungen von der Unterwelt*," *ZA* 79 (1989): 124–27, at 126–27; Walls, *Desire, Discord, and Death*, 154.

178. Tzvi Abusch, "Ishtar," *DDD* 452–56, at 454, notes that in the earlier tradition Ereshkigal was regarded as mother and virgin; she gave birth to "young who die before their time."

179. Karel van der Toorn, *Sin and Sanction in Israel and Mesopotamia* (Assen and Maastricht: Van Gorcum, 1985), 17.

180. Walls, *Desire, Discord, and Death*, 155.

181. Gurney, "The Sultantepe Tablets (Continued): VII: The Myth of Nergal and Ereshkigal," 123. Jacobsen, *Treasures of Darkness*, 230, accepts Gurney's translation of v 7'.

182. Harris, *Gender and Aging in Mesopotamia*, 140.

183. Walls, *Desire, Discord, and Death*, 158.

pictured as seeking sexual gratification from sleeping men; her sexual frustration seems to have arisen from her premature death so that she did not experience the joys of marriage or childbirth.[184] Ereshkigal presses her case with the celestial gods to have Nergal as her lover/husband; if not, she will unleash the dead to devour the living (iv 9'-12').

Ereshkigal's sister Inanna/Ishtar was the patron of eroticism and sensuality in Mesopotamia.[185] As noted earlier in the Dumuzi/Inanna stories, she played a preeminent role in sustaining fertility in the earthly realm. In the "Descent of Ishtar," after Ishtar has been imprisoned in the netherworld Papsukkal, the vizier of the great gods, intercedes with Sin and Ea, saying:

> Ishtar descended to the netherworld and has not come back up. Since that time when Ishtar descended to the netherworld, the bull does not mount the cow; the donkey does not impregnate the jenny; the young man does not have sex with the young woman publicly. The young man has slept in his room; the young woman has slept alone. (ll. 85-90)[186]

Therefore if sex and eroticism are put to death, life on earth will diminish and slowly die out. If Ishtar's behavior during her descent to the netherworld can be interpreted as her way of putting to death her sexuality, it is instructive that the warlike side of her character is dominant. She approaches the gate of the netherworld and insists that she be allowed to enter. She says to the gatekeeper: "If you do not open the gate so that I can come in, I will strike the door; I will break the bolt; I will strike the doorjamb; I will pass through the doors" (ll. 16-18).[187] Has Ishtar transmuted her sexual energies into warlike aggression? Ishtar succeeds in entering and making her way to the throne room of Ereshkigal, but there Ereshkigal visits sixty diseases upon Ishtar that result in her death.

Ishtar cannot remain in the realm of death. Through the wiles of Ea, an androgynous cultic figure[188] named Asushunamir is able to deceive

184. Ibid., 153–54; JoAnn Scurlock, "Death and Afterlife in Ancient Mesopotamian Thought," *CANE*, 1890.

185. Jeremy Black and Anthony Green, *Gods, Demons and Symbols of Ancient Mesopotamia* (Austin, TX: University of Texas Press, 2000), 108–9; Miroslav Marcovich, "From Ishtar to Aphrodite," *Journal of Aesthetic Education* 30 (1996): 43–59, at 45–46, 49; Leick, *Sex and Eroticism in Mesopotamia*, 53.

186. Borger, *BAL*, 1:100; see also Foster, *Before the Muses*, 502.

187. Borger, *BAL*, 1:96.

188. *Kulu'u* (*KAR* 1 rev. 6'); *assinnu* (*CT* 15 46 rev. 12; Borger, *BAL*, 1:101 Nin. 92 // Ass. Rs. 7).

Ereshkigal into releasing Ishtar.[189] But a substitute will be necessary. Thus Tammuz/Dumuzi takes her place; he becomes the dying/rising deity who resides in the netherworld for part of the year and in the earthly sphere for the other part.[190]

According to the lengthier, more complete account in the Sumerian *Descent of Inanna,* Inanna ascended from the netherworld on the condition that she supply a substitute. So she made her way upward accompanied by a group of rangers described as follows:

> The men who followed her to him, the men who followed Inanna to him, knew not food, knew not drink, ate not (offerings of) flour strewn, did not drink libated water. They took the wife from a man's lap, took the child from the wet-nurse's breast.[191]

These nonhuman, demonic creatures from the netherworld, who typically abduct women and children, eventually find Dumuzi/Tammuz and carry him off to the netherworld.[192] This episode about Inanna's aggressive, demonic bodyguards lends her profile an association with the netherworld and contributes to the development of a cautious, circumspect attitude toward her.[193]

Sex and eroticism play an essential role in the Mesopotamian pantheon, which spans the three-tiered cosmic community of the heavens, the earth, and the netherworld. The sacred marriage rite, as practiced

189. A. R. George, "Babylonian Texts from the Folios of Sidney Smith, Part Three: A Commentary on a Ritual of the Month Nisan," in *If a Man Builds a Joyful House: Assyriological Studies in Honor of Erle Verdun Leichty*, ed. Ann K. Guinan et al., 173–85 (Leiden: Brill, 2006), at 175; Erica Reiner, "The Descent of Ishtar: From Myth to Narrative," in *Your Thwarts in Pieces, Your Mooring Rope Cut*, 29–47, at 44. A. D. Kilmer, "How Was Queen Ereshkigal Tricked? A New Interpretation of the Descent of Ishtar," *UF* 3 (1971): 299–309, at 301, 304–5, on the basis of the Sumerian *Descent of Inanna* (ll. 255, 260), claims that Asushunamir tricked Ereshkigal by imitating her groans as a mother giving birth; such empathy moved Ereshkigal to complete an oath, of which Asushunamir had recited the first half; this oath bound Ereshkigal to release Ishtar.

190. "Inanna's Descent," ll. 222–351, in Jacobsen, *The Harps That Once*, 218–26.

191. Translation: "Inanna's Descent," ll. 284–90, in Jacobsen, *The Harps That Once*, 222–23; Jacobsen, *Treasures of Darkness*, 59–60; see also "Dumuzi's Dream," ll. 89–90, in Jacobsen, *The Harps That Once*, 34.

192. Inanna's Descent," ll. 342–55; Jacobsen, *Treasures of Darkness*, 60–61; Leick, *Sex and Eroticism in Mesopotamian Literature*, 226. See also Walter Farber, "Lamaštu," *RLA* 6 (1980–83): 439–46; JoAnn Scurlock, "Baby-Snatching Demons, Restless Souls and the Dangers of Childbirth: Medico-Magical Means of Dealing with Some of the Perils of Motherhood in Ancient Mesopotamia," *Incognita* 2 (1991): 135–83, at 135, 138.

193. Leick, *Sex and Eroticism in Mesopotamian Literature*, 226.

around 2100–1800 BCE, may have sanctioned sexual relations between human partners as an integral part of a ritual designed to renew the fertility of the cosmos. The heavenly protagonists in this ritual, Dumuzi/Inanna, were regarded as responsible for fertility in the various local economies and for fertility in general. There was an erotic dimension to their sexual relations; they were not driven to unite simply out of a duty to sustain reproduction.[194] Inanna was the patron of sex and eroticism; Dumuzi was her passive partner.

Active male sexuality is illustrated by Enki, the god of fresh water. As the only Mesopotamian deity whose phallic behavior is celebrated, Enki demonstrates his considerable phallic power through his various exploits. However, he cannot co-opt the female role in reproduction without endangering his own existence. He is ultimately healed by the mother goddess, who places him in her womb so that birth can happen. Enki could not be allowed to die; water is essential to life. So his endangered life, like that of Inanna, must be rescued.[195]

Erotic experience, as seen in the case of Nergal and Ereshkigal, is compatible with the realm of death. But their sexual activity, unlike that of Inanna and Enki, does not issue in new life. Fertility and reproduction is not a goal of their sexual joining. The erotic experience fostered by Inanna/Ishtar—even if it was that of prostitutes and other examples of "free love"—was part of the earthly or celestial realms and could potentially issue in new vitality.[196]

The Relationship between Sex and Knowledge in the Epic of Gilgamesh

The power a woman's sexuality wields over a man was not limited to subduing his will but also initiated him, according to the *Epic of Gilgamesh*, into a new way of seeing the world. Thus a man's first experience of sex with a woman was a rite of passage. Sexual experience as a form of transformative knowledge is memorably illustrated by the transition

194. Beate Pongratz-Leisten, "Sacred Marriage and the Transfer of Divine Knowledge," 50–51, argues that the metaphor of the sacred marriage aimed to bolster the king's authority by articulating the king's familial ties with the divine world; see also Nissinen, "Song of Songs and Sacred Marriage," 202–3.

195. Jacobsen, *Treasures of Darkness*, 63, 113, associates Enki's near death in this myth with the drying up of the rivers in the arid summer and Inanna's dying and rising with the emptying and replenishment of the storehouse with fresh meat in late spring/early summer.

196. Bottéro, "'Free Love' and Its Disadvantages," in *Mesopotamia: Writing, Reasoning and the Gods*, 185–98, at 196–98.

of Enkidu from the wild man running with the animals to the civilized rival of Gilgamesh. At the initiative of the father god Anu, the birth goddess Aruru created Enkidu to be a rival of heroic proportions to Gilgamesh. She clothed him with animal skins and set him in the wild where he lived as if he were one of the animals (*Gilg*. I:109-12). A hunter encounters Enkidu and is frightened by him (*Gilg*. I:113-21). He realizes that this humanlike creature has been dismantling his traps, so he decides to go to Gilgamesh in Uruk for advice on how to deal with this threat to his livelihood. Gilgamesh gives him the following advice:

> Go, my hunter. Take along with you Shamhat the prostitute (*ḫarimtu*). When the animals approach the watering place, let her remove her garment; let her reveal her attractiveness (*kuzubša*). When he sees her, he will approach her. His animals will become estranged from him (*inakkiršu*) who had grown up with them. (*Gilg*. I:162-66)

Gilgamesh believes in the power of a woman's charms to subdue a strong man. Later, when Ishtar proposes marriage to him, he resists, for he knows not only her exploitative character as a spouse but also the positional authority she will have over him as a goddess in this relationship (*Gilg*. VI:21-79).

The hunter enlists the services of Shamhat and takes her on a three-day journey to the steppe on which Enkidu roams with the animals. After they have waited at a watering hole for two days, Enkidu and his animal companions arrive (*Gilg*. I:167-77). The hunter identifies Enkidu and urges Shamhat to approach him:

> Shamhat removed her clothes. When she revealed her private parts, he took in her attractiveness. She was not afraid; she took in his breath; she made ready her garment and he lay down upon her. She carried out for the primeval man the woman's craft; his sexual desire caressed her. For six days and seven nights Enkidu, erect, had intercourse with Shamhat. After he was filled with her sexual delights, he set out toward his animals. When the gazelles saw Enkidu, they started roaming; the animals of the wild distanced themselves from him. Enkidu had corrupted his pristine body. His knees were at a standstill as his animals went forward. Enkidu was impeded; his running was not as it had been, but he had reason (*ṭēmu*) and broad understanding (*rapaš ḫasīsa*). (*Gilg*. I:188-202)

Shamhat is in charge of this experience. The visual impact of her vulva (*urša*, l. 189) is magical. Thereafter Shamhat confidently gives directions as she shows Enkidu "the work of a woman" (*šipir šinnište*, l. 192). Although the seven-day experience of lovemaking is highly pleasurable for Enkidu, its chief impact is the transformation it effects in him: (1) he loses his innocence and can no longer approach the animals; (2) his legs are weaker, so that he can no longer run with the animals; (3) he gains the capacity to plan or to reason.

Now that he has been alienated from the wild, Shamhat prepares Enkidu for his entry into the city of Uruk.[197] She tells him of the dreams Gilgamesh has dreamed about Enkidu and their prospective friendship (I:245-300). Shamhat continues Enkidu's process of initiation by taking him to the shepherd's camp, where the shepherds feed him bread and beer (II:44-51). At this point Enkidu is ready to enter the city and encounter Gilgamesh.

Gilgamesh is about to enter the wedding house to initiate a new bride into the world of sexual experience (II:109-11). Enkidu, apparently aware after his experience with Shamhat that this royal practice of *ius primae noctis* is exploitative and a violation of the marriage bond, blocks Gilgamesh's way to the wedding house.[198] They engage in a fierce wrestling match. The text is broken at this point; the struggle may have ended in a draw or perhaps Gilgamesh came out the winner (cf. *Gilg.* VII:96). The key point in this physical encounter between two strong rivals is that their equality in strength has prepared the way for a close friendship.

The question whether the friendship between Gilgamesh and Enkidu is simply an intimate relationship or also a sexual one has drawn a divided response from scholars.[199] Gilgamesh's mother Ninsun recounts and interprets Gilgamesh's first dream about Enkidu as follows:

197. Harris, *Gender and Aging in Mesopotamia*, 123, notes that Shamhat is a maternal figure who teaches Enkidu how to eat, drink, and dress, as if he were a child. Walls, *Desire, Discord, and Death*, 31, notes that Shamhat is a skilled teacher in the erotic arts analogous to Diotima as a teacher/initiator in Plato's *Symposium;* cf. Nardelli, *Homosexuality and Liminality*, 18.

198. A. R. George, *The Babylonian Gilgamesh Epic*, 2 vols. (Oxford and New York: Oxford University Press, 2003), 1:456; Walls, *Desire, Discord, and Death*, 30.

199. Harris, *Gender and Aging in Mesopotamia*, 127; Jacobsen, *Treasures of Darkness*, 218–19. Benjamin Foster, "Gilgamesh: Sex, Love and the Ascent of Knowledge," in *Love and Death in the Ancient Near East*, 21–42, at 22, contends that the relationship between Gilgamesh and Enkidu is not a sexual one. Ackerman, *When Heroes Love*, 77, 80, argues that the equality and collegiality of the relationship between Gilgamesh and Enkidu makes the label "homosexual" inappropriate for their relationship, since it implies that one partner is active and the other passive. The Mesopotamians expected that a man would not take the passive position in sexual relations.

> The stars of heaven were before you; like a clump from the sky (*kiṣir ša anim*) one fell near you. You tried to lift it, but it was too difficult for you. You tried repeatedly to move it, but you were not able to budge it. Then you lifted it and laid it at my feet, and I, I put it on the same level as you. You loved it (*tarâmšu*). You caressed it like a wife. A strong partner will come to you, a rescuer of a friend. He is the strong one among the powerful in the land. Like a clump from the sky, his power is strong. You will love him (*tarâmšu*). Like a wife, you will caress (*taḫabbubu*) him. As the strong one, he will repeatedly save you. (*Gilg*. I:261-72)

The basis for their attraction seems to be their remarkable similarity in physique and strength. This relative equality could support the claim that their relationship is a friendship without a sexual dimension.[200] On the other hand, A. D. Kilmer argues that the content of both of Gilgamesh's dreams reveals that the relationship of Gilgamesh with Enkidu was a sexual one. In the first dream the term for meteorite (*kiṣru*) sounds somewhat like *kezru* (a male cultic prostitute). In the second dream the term for axe (*ḫassinnu*) sounds like *assinnu* (a cultic eunuch who assumed the woman's role in sexual acts).[201] This dream may be saying, then, that Gilgamesh is the active partner and Enkidu the passive one.[202] George

200. Foster, "Gilgamesh: Sex, Love and the Ascent of Knowledge," 33; cf. Henri I. Marrou, *A History of Education in Antiquity*, trans. George Lamb (New York: Sheed and Ward, 1956), 27–28. With regard to the lovers in Plato's *Phaedrus*, Martha Nussbaum, *Fragility of Goodness*, 219, writes: "The best human life involves ongoing devotion to another individual. This involves shared intellectual activity; but it also involves continued madness and shared appetitive and emotional feeling. The best lovers are said to deny themselves sexual intercourse. But this, as we have said, is because they feel that in intercourse they risk forfeiting other valuable non-intellectual elements of their relationship: the feelings of tenderness, respect, and awe."

201. A. D. Kilmer, "A Note on an Overlooked Word-play in the Akkadian Gilgamesh," 128–29 in *Zikir Šumim: Assyriological Studies Presented to F. R. Kraus on the Occasion of His Seventieth Birthday*, ed. G. van Driel, et al., 128–29 (Leiden: Brill, 1982). On Enkidu's induction into the class of temple servants by Ninsun (*Gilg*. III.116-28) see George, *Gilgamesh Epic*, 461–62; for Enkidu's sexual role toward Gilgamesh as analogous to the Greek *paidagogos* see A. D. Kilmer, "The Investiture of Enkidu in the Epic of Gilgamesh," in *Sex and Gender in the Ancient Near East*, 283–88.

202. Ackerman, *When Heroes Love*, 120. Nardelli, *Homosexuality and Liminality*, 8, claims that Enkidu is portrayed as Gilgamesh's sexual partner. However, Harris, *Gender and Aging in Mesopotamia*, 127, interprets the portrayal of Gilgamesh and Enkidu as husband and wife as instances of the literary device of "category inversion" in terms of gender and family relationships rather than promoting this kind of "intense relationship between men."

contends that the language of the dreams clearly reveals the sexual nature of Enkidu's relationship with Gilgamesh.[203]

When Enkidu learns of his impending death he curses Shamhat for having introduced him to the city life of Uruk. After he has vented his frustration with a lengthy series of curses intended to reduce Shamhat to a life of poverty and abuse (VII:102-23), Shamash reprimands him by reminding him of the special treatment Shamhat has extended to him: she has given him food, drink, and clothing and has prepared him to have Gilgamesh as a friend (VII:134-38). What seems to alter Enkidu's disposition most decisively is Shamash's statement that Gilgamesh, the princes of the earth, and the people of Uruk will honor him and mourn for him at the time of his burial (VII:139-47). Enkidu then showers words of blessing on Shamhat to counteract the curses he has uttered (VII:151-61).

When Shamash reminds Enkidu of the blessings Shamhat showered on him he does not mention the sexual initiation that was emphasized in *Gilg*. I:188-95. Does this imply that at this late stage in Enkidu's life journey the learning gained from sexual experience was short-lived and without enduring significance?[204] Foster contends that sex belongs to the lowest level of human knowledge.[205] As Enkidu faces death he appears to be satisfied with the awareness that others have valued him and will miss him, particularly his close friend Gilgamesh. The measure of immortality conferred by an honorable burial is minimal, but within the Mesopotamian worldview it provides him a resting place in the netherworld.[206]

For Gilgamesh, the death of Enkidu overturns his own life. His unwillingness to let go of Enkidu at his death shows how strongly their lives have become intertwined through their friendship and their heroic ventures against the Bull of Heaven at the Cedar Mountain.[207] Gilgamesh is thrust back upon himself and undertakes an extreme journey to the ends of the cosmos through which he hopes to avoid death. Foster points

203. George, *The Babylonian Gilgamesh Epic*, 454.

204. Foster, "Gilgamesh: Sex, Love and the Ascent of Knowledge," 40, claims that for the author of the Nineveh tablets Enkidu's sexual episode with Shamhat was not necessary.

205. Foster, "Gilgamesh: Sex, Love and the Ascent of Knowledge," 22. Harris, *Gender and Aging in Mesopotamia*, 34, regards Foster's viewpoint on sexual experience as a low level of knowledge as a "hellenic" perspective that does not reflect the Mesopotamian sensibility.

206. George, *The Babylonian Gilgamesh Epic*, 488, 528–30.

207. Harris, *Gender and Aging in Mesopotamia*, 39, judges that the Mesopotamians would have seen the relationship of Gilgamesh and Enkidu as immature since it lay outside the domestic sphere.

out that in Gilgamesh's journey toward greater self-awareness he has come to the point, with the loss of Enkidu, at which he had to move beyond trying to preserve himself.[208] However, Ackerman contends that Gilgamesh's cosmic journey is not an individual one of self-discovery but rather a social drama in which he separates from the social group, goes into crisis, tries to reenter, and finally is able to do so. Something happens in the process such that he and the social group begin to relate to one another differently in the reintegration.

When Gilgamesh comes to the shores of the cosmic ocean prior to his voyage to the island where Utnapishtim resides, he enters a garden paradise populated with carnelian and lapis lazuli trees full of attractive fruit (*Gilg*. IX:173-94). Other jeweled objects likewise abound in the place.[209] It is here that he finds Utnapishtim's boatman Urshanabi, the one who will ferry him across the cosmic ocean and the waters of death. But as Gilgamesh moves about in the garden, Shiduri, the divine alewife who lives by the shore, is watching him (*Gilg*. IX:196–X:1). She is a liminal, wise figure who will challenge him with the futility of his efforts to overcome death.[210] In the OB version she counsels him to accept the limits of the human condition and enjoy the pleasures of family and the goods of the earth that are given to mortals, and not to squander these blessings in a vain quest to be immortal. In the later Nineveh version this sage advice is transferred to Utnapishtim (X:295-300, 319-22), who counsels Gilgamesh that the quest for the immortality of the individual is futile, whereas the immortality of the species is assured (X:308-11).[211] He compares transient humans to the mayfly on the flood waters in the spring: swarms of them hover over the waters but disappear instantly and hardly leave a trace. Nevertheless, mayflies return every spring.[212] After Gilgamesh has slept for six days and nights and has failed the test to show that he has been divinized, the wife of Utnapishtim urges that Gilgamesh be awakened and sent on his way back to the sphere of mortals in Uruk (*Gilg*. XI:212-30).[213]

208. Foster, "Gilgamesh: Sex, Love and the Ascent of Knowledge," 22.

209. Cf. Ezek 28:13; George, *The Babylonian Gilgamesh Epic*, 497.

210. Ibid., 498–99; Harris, *Gender and Aging in Mesopotamia*, 123–24.

211. Harris, *Gender and Aging in Mesopotamia*, 44, 47, notes that Sin-leqi-unninni is more interested in secret knowledge that will transform the initiand than in the wisdom to be gained in domestic life.

212. George, *The Babylonian Gilgamesh Epic*, 506.

213. George, *The Babylonian Gilgamesh Epic*, 521–22, notes that "not only is man at the mercy of sleep—he is also born a liar (219–20)."

The Nineveh version of the *Epic of Gilgamesh* opens and closes with references to the wall of Uruk (I:11-22; XI:322-28) and the inscription of the epic on lapis lazuli that is deposited in the foundation stone of the wall (I:24-28). These objects symbolize the wisdom Gilgamesh brought back to Uruk and to civilization as a result of his exploits.[214] The prologue celebrates Gilgamesh as the one "who saw the watery-depths, the foundation of the land. . . . He acquired universal wisdom. He saw what was secret and opened up the concealed; he retrieved an understanding from before the flood" (I:3, 6-8). Foster claims that this wisdom is the transcendent reality that makes Gilgamesh aware that what he is truly longing for is not the discovery of himself, but rather of enduring knowledge.[215]

Gilgamesh could not have reached this point of valuing wisdom more than his own self if he had not benefited from the strategic interventions and wise counsel of women: the prostitute Shamhat, his mother the goddess Ninsun, the goddess Ishtar, the divine alewife Shiduri, and the divinized wife of Utnapishtim.[216] Each of these figures is a voice from the margin; they are not characters of everyday domestic life. By reason of their status, gender, and experience they bring important perspectives and directives so that Gilgamesh can reflect and act in ways that will bring him more fully into contact with wisdom.

Erōs *and the Maintenance of the Sacred Boundaries of the Mesopotamian Household*

Initial sexual experience can alter one's self-understanding and one's relationship to a social group. Enkidu moved from the world of animals to the world of human civilization as a result of the sexual initiation afforded him by the prostitute Shamhat. In the myth "Nergal and Ereshkigal," Ereshkigal, queen of the netherworld, entered into a power-sharing arrangement with Nergal when she had sexual relations with him and proposed marriage to him. Enkidu, at a later moment of regret that his life was soon to end in a premature death, lamented the loss of innocence he had suffered through his sexual experience with Shamhat. Ereshkigal wondered before the celestial gods Anu, Enlil, and Ea if she had become impure through her sexual relations with Nergal and if this experience had impaired her capacity to rule over the gods in her realm.[217] The

214. Ibid., 445.

215. Foster, "Gilgamesh: Sex, Love and the Ascent of Knowledge," 22.

216. Harris, *Gender and Aging in Mesopotamia*, xi.

217. Foster, *Before the Muses*, 520.

regrets of these two individuals were only momentary. The sexual union, which proved energizing to the lives of both Enkidu and Ereshkigal, was compatible with their statuses and ways of life. Neither of these individuals was concerned about securing heirs or reproducing a household.

Monogamy and sexual relations within the context of marriage seem to have been the dominant practice in Mesopotamia. Enkidu tried to prevent Gilgamesh from entering the bridal chamber to initiate the bride into the world of sex. After his experience with Shamhat, Enkidu seems to have understood the profound personal significance of sexual initiation and did not want Gilgamesh to continue exercising this royal prerogative in Uruk. In the myth "Enki and Ninhursag," when Enki tried to have sex with Ninhursag, she permitted him to do so only after he had pronounced that she was his wife. This monogamous ideal in Mesopotamian literature seems to have reflected the ideal of monogamy in everyday life in ancient Mesopotamia, although it was not legislated as essential to the matrix of household relationships.[218]

Same-sex relations that were collegial and equal like that of Gilgamesh and Enkidu seem to have been regarded as constructive. Their relationship was erotically charged, but the sexual acting out of their relationship is not narrated. However, if a Mesopotamian man assumed the role of a woman in sexual relations, such relations were frowned upon or condemned. It may be that forbidden sexual relations constitute the "abomination" (*asakku*) alluded to in the following excerpt from the poem *Ishum and Erra*:

> [In Uruk, the Sutaeans] removed the performers (*kurgarrû*) and singers (*assinnū*) of Eanna—whose masculinity Ishtar had changed to femininity to create reverence among the people—the ones who carry swords, razors, sharp knives, and flint blades, who regularly take part in abominable acts (*asakkū*) in order to give joy to the heart of Ishtar. (*Erra* IV:55-58)[219]

Because Ishtar was the patron of sex and eroticism, the sexual activities of everyone came under her purview: e.g., those of married couples, prostitutes, and transgendered cultic actors.[220] The legitimacy of Ishtar's

218. With reference to the third and second millennia BCE see J. N. Postgate, *Early Mesopotamia: Society and Economy at the Dawn of History* (London: Routledge, 1992), 106; Robert McCormick Adams, *The Evolution of Urban Society: Early Mesopotamia and Prehispanic Mexico* (Chicago: Aldine, 1966), 82.

219. Edition: Luigi Cagni, *L'epopea di Erra*, Studi Semitici 34 (Rome: Istituto di Studi del Vicino Oriente, Universite di Roma, 1969), 110.

220. Tzvi Abusch, "Ishtar," *DDD* 452–55.

cult points to the Mesopotamians' attentiveness to sexual diversity. They assigned a place for marginal forms of sexual expression within their religious system.[221] This Mesopotamian strategy for dealing with the dynamic reality of *erōs* aimed to channel rather than repress the energy of this relational passion.

Ishtar is a sign of otherness. She is the epitome of sex appeal; therefore she attracts but at the same time repels. Those who are drawn to her are also afraid she will swallow them up.[222] Thus the emotional response Ishtar evokes is analogous to what a human experiences when confronted with the holy: it is simultaneously fascinating and frightening.[223] Ishtar raises fear of death not only in those who confront her in battle but also in those with whom she makes love. She has been described as a paradoxical deity, one within whom contradictory tendencies are at war. This characterization of Ishtar has much explanatory power because it captures the tensive dynamic of the erotic within the human and divine spheres.[224] However, Bahrani argues that Ishtar transcends these contradictions by being a sign of the Other. The warring contradictions within her person—e.g., sex versus violence; femaleness versus violence—place her beyond the pale. Such otherness has a pragmatic value: she becomes an ultimate sign of difference, one over against which Mesopotamian culture defines itself.[225] Perhaps there is room for both models—the paradoxical Ishtar, and Ishtar the Other—in trying to deal with such a potent, polymorphous reality as *Erōs*.[226] Ishtar provides a place for diverse forms of sexual expression that are incompatible with the matrix of relationships in the Mesopotamian household. In this indirect way she helps the household maintain its integrity.

Summary

The lush growth of plant life in the spring of the year captivates the senses and the imagination. The vital power springing from the earth to

221. Leick, *Sex and Eroticism in Mesopotamia*, 168–69.

222. Zainab Bahrani, *The Women of Babylon*, 153.

223. Tikva Frymer-Kensky, *In the Wake of the Goddesses: Women, Culture, and the Biblical Transformation of Pagan Myth* (New York: Free Press, 1992), 29; Bahrani, *The Women of Babylon*, 152–53.

224. Rivkah Harris, "Inanna-Ishtar as Paradox and a Coincidence of Opposites," *History of Religions* 30 (1991): 261–78, at 263.

225. Bahrani, *The Women of Babylon*, 151.

226. On the resemblance of *Erōs* to Proteus see Stanley Rosen, *Plato's Symposium*, 2d ed. (New Haven: Yale University Press, 1987), 236.

bring newness signals the resilience of life in the face of death. The renewal of the life-force in the household is essential to the family. This life-force is manifest in a concentrated way in both the household and the city in the conception and birth of children, in the planting and harvesting of crops, in recovery from serious illness, and in politico-military victories over dangerous forces. These examples of life triumphing over death show that the ritual of sacred marriage celebrated annually at the New Year's festival in various Mesopotamian cities aimed to promote the prosperity of the kingdom through communion of the king with Inanna/Ishtar. The erotic drive for wholeness was initially enacted in the carnal union of the king with the goddess as a sacramental way of channeling divine vitality to the king and his realm. But after 1800 BCE this carnal union was transmuted into a more abstract symbolic enactment of the union of the goddess's statue with that of the king. This essential goal of the sacred marriage was to promote the prosperity of the earthly kingdom; such prosperity encompassed the force of fertility but was wider in scope; it included various other ways in which life triumphed over death.

The Sumerian love songs celebrating Dumuzi and Inanna foster communication between the human community and the gods who are believed to oversee agricultural success and the security of the community. The sacred marriage ritual with which many of these songs are linked provided the opportunity to come into greater communion with Inanna/Ishtar, Dumuzi, and other deities. The erotic goal of communion was illustrated in sexual copulation, but it was more profoundly perceived as entwined in the wider web of relationships constituting the household and the kingdom. Scholars have recently argued that the goal of the sacred marriage was not fertility but rather prosperity; a more narrow understanding of sexual union as physiological act has given way to the wider, more enduring forms of communion symbolized by the joining of king and goddess.

The phallic power of Enki symbolized the irrigation works essential to the Mesopotamian economy. The ambiguity of Enki's sexual activities embedded in mythic narratives poses issues of gender conflict, boundary transgression, and fragile institutions that offer the audience an opportunity to reflect on the ways of disorder within nature and the human community. The rape and incest perpetrated by Enki in the myth "Enki and Ninhursaga" raises questions about the ethical order of the cosmos analogous to the unethical behavior of deities in the Greek tradition. Just as water can be destructive as well as beneficial, so also is Enki. Personifying sweet water essential to life as the god Enki provides an avenue to appeal to this natural reality through prayer and ritual. Enki's erotic, sexual power as it impacts nature and the human community is essential subject matter of prayer and ritual.

The life-giving potential of the erotic and sexual is manifest in the extreme case of Ereshkigal. As a goddess she lives in the realm of the dead. But the myth "Nergal and Ereshkigal" emphasizes how her love for Nergal has brought her a new sense of vitality, one that can flourish even in the midst of death. Within the context of the first millennium version of this myth Ereshkigal is not concerned about offspring. Her realm acquires a constant stream of new members from the earth. So the erotic and the sexual are imagined as having a potency that can operate among the gods who are surrounded by death. The descent of Inanna/Ishtar results in this deity becoming a dying and rising goddess. Her capacity to overcome death is dependent on the assistance of the larger divine world: viz., the wiles of Enki/Ea and his messenger Asushunamir.

Erotic sexuality plays a strategic role in the growth of Enkidu and Gilgamesh. Enkidu is transformed from the wild, natural state in which he keeps company with the gazelles to the civilized friendship of Gilgamesh through the assistance of the liminal figure Shamhat, a prostitute associated with the temple of Ishtar/Inanna in Uruk. Through intense sexual relations with Shamhat, the eating of bread and drinking of beer, and the wearing of clothing, Enkidu is initiated into the basic ways of life of Uruk. In accord with his destiny as a rival of Gilgamesh, Enkidu wrestles with Gilgamesh, accompanies him on heroic adventures, and faces premature death as a penalty for their trespasses on divine prerogatives. The close friendship between Enkidu and Gilgamesh creates bonds so strong that Gilgamesh cannot resume normal life in Uruk without protesting against death and trying to overcome its power in his life. His futile quest for immortality does not come up empty. He is still mortal, but he has the knowledge that this condition is inescapable and so learns how to function within such limits to create knowledge and relationships within his realm that will live on after him. Without the power of *erōs* channeled into meaningful friendship Gilgamesh would not have made constructive use of his semi-divine strength.

The ambiguity of erotic sexuality is evident in the sacred marriage ritual and in the exploits of Enki, Nergal, Gilgamesh, and Enkidu. But such ambiguity in which the shadow of sex plays off the light of *erōs* is embodied in the figure of Ishtar/Inanna. Her interactions with other gods and humans show how she is intertwined with sociopolitical processes but cannot be contained by them. She is a paradoxical other who makes humans aware of the polymorphous forces of sex and love operative in human communities and helps humans be attentive to these forces without presuming to domesticate them.

Greece: *Erōs* of the Body Versus *Erōs* of the Soul

In the *Symposium*, a drinking party of young aristocrats frames Plato's account of Socrates' views on the place of *erōs* in the life of the city and the individuals within it. Through the rhetorical form of a dialogue Plato can offer multiple views on a topic and have Socrates promote a particular idea or line of argument, then leave the reader wondering where Plato himself stands on the issue. The private character of this gathering and the festive atmosphere of a banquet suggest that the participants will be more disposed to express their feelings about the reality of love. In this setting Plato fosters an open and inclusive dialogue while at the same time promoting a picture of how erotic sexuality should be channeled and transmuted in the quest for the beautiful and the good. The ambiguity of erotic sexuality lends itself to Plato's dialogical approach because it is a reality manifest in the concrete particulars of individuals' experience rather than in abstract generalities reached by screening out the subjective and emotional aspects of life. In the following examination of Plato's *Symposium* three issues provide an outline for the discussion: (1) the speakers describe the character and activities of *Erōs* and make their case for the manifestation of this reality as a deity, or as a cosmic force, or as a being intermediate between gods and humans; (2) in their efforts to praise *Erōs* the speakers describe the landscape for the pursuit of wisdom; and (3) although the speakers' love of wisdom promotes reasoned discourse in a city, they do not adequately address the need to reproduce and protect the citizenry.

Erōs: *A God or a Demiurge Within the Ancient Greek World?*

The driving desire of love that impels individuals to lay down their lives for others (*agapē*) or to forsake rational calculations in the pursuit of the desired object (*Erōs*) is an intense manifestation of a pervasive force that is vital for the welfare of communities and the order of the cosmos. *Erōs* is an unsettling, ambiguous reality: it can lead either to the rapid growth or to the sudden loss of that for which one has labored and is destined. The attractive and frightening aspects of this wide-ranging power of love have given rise to numerous stories and theoretical reflections by the ancient Greeks that try to make sense out of love and to provide guidance in dealing with it. In the ancient Greek tradition two main categories emerged for classifying *Erōs*: it is either (1) a personal power within intimate relationships (i.e., a deity) or (2) a fundamental cosmic power (i.e., a demiurge).[227] *Erōs* is not merely an idea or a mental construct, for it is too dynamic or unstable to be classified as such.[228]

Within the Olympic pantheon, erotic experience is the specialty of Aphrodite.[229] Earlier we recounted the scene in *Iliad* 14.153-340 in which Hera seduced Zeus with the aid of a magical strap secured from Aphrodite.[230] This strap incited an insatiable desire in Zeus to have sex with Hera.[231] Aphrodite had also stirred this same power of passionate love in Paris, leading him to abduct Helen and thus caused the Trojan war (*Il.* 3.442-45). Later, in the tenth year of that war, when Paris is wounded in a duel with Menelaus and rescued by Aphrodite, he is once again smitten with desire for Helen as he recovers in Priam's palace. Even in his humiliated condition he notes how intense his desire is for Helen:

> Do not, o woman, reprove my heart with harsh blame. For now Menelaus has prevailed with Athena's help, but I will reverse it on another occasion. For gods are also on our side. But come now, let us go to bed and renew ourselves with love, for never yet has love (*erōs*) enfolded my perception (*phrēn*) in this way—not even when I seized you from pleasant Lacedaemon and sailed away in seagoing vessels and made love to you in bed on the island of Cranae—as now I long for you and sweet desire takes hold of me. (*Il.* 3.438-44)

Paris is here completely caught up in the passion of the moment. Helen accedes to his desire only because she has been intimidated by Aphrodite

227. Strauss, *On Plato's Symposium*, 97, 100, 140.

228. Rosen, *Plato's Symposium*, 210.

229. Stephanie Budin, *The Origin of Aphrodite* (Bethesda, MD: Capital Decisions Limited, 2003), 21.

230. See chap. 1 above.

231. Jacqueline and Vassos Karageorghis, "The Great Goddess of Cyprus or the Genesis of Aphrodite in Cyprus," in *Sex and Gender in the Ancient Near East*, 1:263–82, at 277; Christopher Faraone, *Ancient Greek Love Magic* (Cambridge, MA: Harvard University Press, 1999), 5–6; Richard Janko, *The Iliad: A Commentary*, vol. 4: *Books 13–16* (Cambridge: Cambridge University Press, 1992), 184–85. Sue Blundell, "Clutching at Clothes," in *Women's Dress in the Ancient Greek World*, ed. Lloyd Llewellyn-Jones, 143–69 (London: Duckworth and the Classical Press of Wales, 2002), at 156–57, notes that the magical strap Hera hides between her breasts is a *kestos himas*; Hera has already put on a *zōnē*, "belt," with a hundred tassels; the *zōnē* is the object typically signifying the containment or opening up of a woman's sexuality.

right before she enters Paris's room. Aphrodite has summoned Helen from the city wall and enchanted her (*Il.* 3.389-95), but when Helen recognizes Aphrodite she lashes out at her for manipulating her emotions and urging her to have sex with Paris while the rest of the inhabitants of the city are distraught at the events of the war (*Il.* 3:399-412). Aphrodite angrily warns her: "O hard-hearted one, do not irritate me lest I be angry and abandon you and detest you, just as I now love you abundantly" (*Il.* 3:414-15). Even though Helen is not inebriated with the madness of *Erōs*, she suffers a strong measure of coercion from the circumstances to submit to its demands. Homer holds the goddess Aphrodite responsible for designing these circumstances. Here Helen's erotic experience (i.e., her encounter with Aphrodite) triggers more intentional resistance than mindless passion (*Il.* 3.389-417).[232]

According to Hesiod's *Theogony*, Aphrodite was born from the white foam emitted from the severed genitals of Uranus ("sky") when he was castrated by his son Cronus as he made love to his wife Gaia, "earth" (*Theog*. 168-93). Hesiod then goes on to explain about Aphrodite:

> *Erōs* attended her and beautiful *Himeros* followed her when she was born and first went with the tribe of immortals. She held this honor from the beginning and obtained this portion among humans and the immortal gods: the chatter of young women, the smiles and deceptions, the sweet delight and gentleness of love. (*Theog*. 201-6)

The violence of Cronus toward Uranus was initiated by Gaia, who sought relief from Uranus's blocking the exit of the hundred-handers from her womb (ll. 150-61) and from his exorbitant need to have sex with her.[233]

With the birth of Aphrodite, *Erōs*—along with *Himeros* (desire)—becomes subordinate to her. But Hesiod has previously located the origin of *Erōs* in the first generation along with Chaos ("featureless void"), Tartarus ("the interior of the earth"), and Gaia ("earth") (*Theog*. 116-23).[234] Hesiod describes this primordial *Erōs* as the one "who is love, the most beautiful among the immortal gods, the one who relaxes the limbs, the one who overpowers reason and wise planning within the hearts of all gods and all humans" (ll. 120-22). *Erōs*, then, is the force that will draw all things together, and *Eris* ("strife") will be the force that drives them

232. Geoffrey S. Kirk, *The Iliad: A Commentary*, vol. 1 *Books 1–4* (Cambridge: Cambridge University Press, 1985), 321–24.

233. Jenny Strauss Clay, *Hesiod's Cosmos* (Cambridge: Cambridge University Press, 2003), 19.

234. Clay, *Hesiod's Cosmos*, 15–16.

apart (l. 226)—a reality that is born on the heels of the violence between Uranus and Gaia and her offspring. Although Hesiod describes *Erōs* in personal terms he also makes clear that it is a fundamental, ungenerated reality essential for procreation. Hesiod's genealogy of the cosmos pictures the gods as a divine family. Since this divine family does not lose members through death, the family tree increases in complexity and diversity as the generations of the gods unfold.[235]

Parmenides (ca. 490 BCE), who argued that change is illusory, located the gods in the illusory world of becoming.[236] He contends that even though humans talk about things being born and dying, they are deceived. If they look beyond appearances they will know that what is real is complete and unchanging. In this illusory world of becoming, there is a tension between light and darkness (DK 28B10; 28A35). For Parmenides *Erōs* is an early god but is not in the first generation as in Hesiod's *Theogony*. Parmenides claimed, according to the character Phaedrus in Plato's *Symposium*, that "the very first of all the gods that she devised was love" (*Symp*. 178b11). The "she" in this quotation seems to be the goddess cryptically described by Parmenides in the following passage:

> The narrower ones are filled with pure fire and those thereafter with night. Then a portion of flame comes to them. In the midst of these is a *daimōn* who directs all things. She began all things through abominable intercourse and childbirth. She sent a female to join with a male and in a reverse, complementary direction the male with the female. (DK 28B12; Simplicius's *Commentary on Aristotle's Physics*, CAG IX, 31.13-17; 39.14-16)

Parmenides's view that *Erōs* is subordinate to and subject to a goddess parallels the view of Hesiod that *Erōs*, though earlier in time, was made an attendant to Aphrodite. The radical difference between the views of Hesiod and Parmenides is that Hesiod sees *Erōs* as genesis or the process by which the gods who rule the cosmos come into existence; by contrast, Parmenides regards change as illusory and heterosexual relations and childbirth as "vile" (DK 28B12.4-6).[237]

235. Ibid., 14.

236. John Burnet, *Early Greek Philosophy*, 4th ed. (London: A & C Black, 1930), 192; Strauss, *On Plato's Symposium*, 47.

237. David Roochnik, *Retrieving the Ancients* (Malden, MA: Blackwell, 2004), 15–16, 42–45.

Among Plato's dialogues, the *Symposium* is the only one devoted to a god and the only one whose title designates an occasion.[238] During the course of this drinking party six of the eight attendees deliver speeches on the nature of *Erōs*. The first speaker, Phaedrus, claims that *Erōs* is the oldest of the gods (*Symp*. 178c). He appeals to Hesiod and Parmenides to support his claim. The fifth speaker, Agathon, the young, attractive host for the event, thinks that *Erōs* is the youngest and highest of the gods (*Symp*. 195b). Aristophanes contends that *Erōs* is the most philanthropic of the gods, i.e., a god who values humans for their own sake and not for the sacrifices they offer (*Symp*. 193c-d). The sixth and final speaker is Socrates. He bases his view that *Erōs* is a *daimōn* (i.e., an intermediary between gods and humans)[239] on a teaching he received many years earlier from the woman Diotima, an instructor in the mystery cults (*Symp*. 201d).[240]

The second speaker, Pausanias, emphasizes that the most important question in trying to come to terms with *Erōs* is how *Erōs* is integrated into a person's behavior. Pausanias argues that *Erōs* is not noble in himself; his nobility depends on the sentiments he produces in humans (*Symp*. 183e). He contends that there are two kinds of *Erōs*, which receive their definition in response to the profile of Aphrodite one encounters: (1) the elderly Aphrodite Ourania, "Heavenly Aphrodite," or (2) the younger Aphrodite Pandemos, "Common Aphrodite" (*Symp*. 180e). Pausanias claims that Common Aphrodite is associated with base *Erōs*: this is the *Erōs* that moves male and female to unite to produce offspring; this form of *Erōs* is vulgar because it is focused on the body. By contrast, noble *Erōs* is associated with Heavenly Aphrodite and is focused on the

238. Strauss, *On Plato's Symposium*, 16, 189. Oswyn Murray, "The Affair of the Mysteries: Democracy and the Drinking Group," in *Sympotica: A Symposium to the Symposion*, ed. idem, 149–61 (Oxford: Clarendon Press, 1990), at 150, notes that the *symposion* was primarily an aristocratic gathering whose heritage can be traced from Homer through Alcaeus and the aristocratic factions of sixth-century Athens to the fifth century with the emergence of mass democracy.

239. In *Apology* 26c Socrates defends himself against the charge of atheism by claiming that a *daimōn* is a god; see Strauss, *On Plato's Symposium*, 189.

240. Strauss, *On Plato's Symposium*, 24, 184, 230, notes that Diotima ("honored one of Zeus") is from a place in Arcadia called Mantinea, a name that suggests *mantis*, "soothsayer"; since Diotima is "the complete owner of wisdom," her speech is a revelation of mysteries (*Symp*. 209e5-210a4). See also Rosen, *Plato's Symposium*, 225–26; Luce Irigaray, "Sorcerer Love: A Reading of Plato's *Symposium*, 'Diotima's Speech,'" in *Feminism and the History of Philosophy*, ed. Genevieve Lloyd, 68–78 (New York: Oxford University Press, 2002), at 70.

soul.[241] Pausanias claims that this elderly Aphrodite is purely male; therefore noble *Erōs* takes the form of the attraction of male to male (*Symp.* 181b-c). He then goes on to explain how the customs of various cities regulate the practice of this noble *Erōs* in the form of pederasty: i.e., the befriending of young boys by older men in order to educate them and improve their souls.[242] But his final point is that a beloved becomes subject to a lover in order that he might grow in wisdom and virtue (*Symp.* 184c): the lover gains physical gratification through pederasty, while the beloved receives wisdom and virtue through philosophy.[243]

Eryximachus, the third speaker and a physician, argues that *Erōs* is a cosmic force. He bases his comments on the teaching of Empedocles, who sees the cosmos as composed of four basic elements: water, air, fire, and earth (*Symp.* 186e, 188a-b). Empedocles says that change happens by the recombination of these four elements. One might argue that Empedocles agrees with Parmenides that no real change happens—there is only a reshuffling of what has always existed. The forces that drive this process of recombination are *Erōs* (love) and *Eris* (strife). These forces operate not simply in human relations but throughout the entire cosmos (DK 31B17). Eryximachus builds on this theory to claim that a physician can intervene in this cosmic process in which love of "like for like" is a mark of strife in order to change this conflicted love into one of harmony. Moved by his physical passions and confident in human technical ability, Eryximachus demotes the traditional gods to servants of cosmic *Erōs*, which he understands to be the force that promotes harmony between human activity and the motions of the cosmos (*Symp.* 187e).[244]

The fourth of the six speakers in the *Symposium* is Aristophanes, the comic playwright. He, like Phaedrus, Pausanias, and Eryximachus, extols the practice of pederasty. Aristophanes makes his case for this form of same-sex love by arguing that in primordial times there were three kinds

241. Frisbee C. C. Sheffield, *Plato's Symposium: The Ethics of Desire* (Oxford: Oxford University Press, 2006), 28.

242. Strauss, *On Plato's Symposium*, 51, 66, 72, 120, 141; cf. Marrou, *A History of Education in Antiquity*, 29–31. Jan Bremmer, "Adolescents, *Symposion*, and Pederasty," in *Sympotica*, 135–48, at 136, 142, explains that the *symposion* evolved from the common meals of warrior groups in the Archaic age. He notes that the link between the *symposion* and pederasty becomes visible in vase painting in the late seventh century BCE, whose scenes show that pederasty was associated with initiatory rituals in Athens, Crete, and Sparta.

243. Rosen, *Plato's Symposium*, 87–88; Luc Brisson, "Agathon, Pausanias, and Diotima in Plato's *Symposium: Paiderastia* and *Philosophia*," in *Plato's Symposium: Issues in Interpretation and Reception*, 229–51, at 243.

244. Rosen, *Plato's Symposium*, 118–19.

of creatures: (1) the male as offspring from the sun, (2) the female as offspring from the earth, and (3) an androgynous creature as offspring of the moon. He contends that these primordial creatures were round, with four hands, four legs, two faces, one head with four ears, and two sets of sexual organs. These creatures were ambitious and aggressive. After they made an assault on the Olympian gods, Zeus and the council of the gods punished them by cutting them in two (*Symp*. 190b-c). The tendency of these severed creatures thereafter was to yearn for the other half so as to once again become whole. This yearning is *Erōs* (*Symp*. 191d); it is the "sexual desire of the body" rather than "the psyche's erotic striving toward the Ideas."[245] By this model of the severed round creatures Aristophanes offers a definition for what it feels like to "be in love": i.e., that the beloved makes the lover feel whole.[246] Aristophanes conceived of *Erōs* in terms of mutuality. He focused on the horizontal attraction of body to body and ignored the vertical attraction of the mind for ideas.[247] For Aristophanes spirituality is dependent on sexuality; humans are caught in the perpetual cycle of desire and satisfaction.[248] Aristophanes understands humanity to be "perpetually at war with self, gods, and cosmos."[249] The cosmos could fall apart at any moment.

Aristophanes claims that if humans understood *Erōs* they would build more temples to him (*Symp*. 189c-d). On the other hand, Aristophanes' description of *Erōs* as a yearning for a lost wholeness seems to confirm the instincts influencing religious practices in fifth-century Athens that this yearning as such does not have the profile of an independent deity. As Strauss explains, there seems to be little need to personify this yearning within Aristophanes' description because its origin is rationally explained and its movements seem quite predictable.[250]

245. Ibid., 138.

246. Richard Hunter, *Plato's Symposium* (New York: Oxford University Press, 2004), 67.

247. Strauss, *On Plato's Symposium*, 140. Rosen, *Plato's Symposium*, 147–48, notes that for Socrates and his followers wisdom began by gazing at the stars, but for Aristophanes humans come to awareness of their humanity by looking downward at their navel and genitals.

248. Rosen, *Plato's Symposium*, 143, notes the bondage of Ares with Aphrodite within the trap devised by Hephaestus in *Od*. 8.334-42. Rosen also claims (p. 158) that Aristophanes alludes to a solution to this perpetual cycle of desire and satisfaction: a suspension of all sexual intercourse for a time (*Symp*. 193b6-c3).

249. Ibid., 157.

250. Strauss, *On Plato's Symposium*, 131, notes that for Aristophanes *Erōs* is the never-ending desire of a finite creature for wholeness: i.e., "a movement of nature, of impaired

Aristophanes' description of erotic desire as one that drives a person to fill a gap resembles Diotima's claim that *Erōs* is a needy one. Yet Diotima views *Erōs* as having an intermediate status that transcends the perpetual cycle of opposites.[251] He is a *daimōn* who is linked with Aphrodite by having been conceived on the birthday of Aphrodite. Diotima tells the story of how *Poros* ("contrivance") became drunk and had relations with *Penia* ("hunger") who was begging at the gate. *Penia* became pregnant with *Erōs*.[252] Diotima then explains that *Erōs*

> is always poor and far from being tender and beautiful as most people imagine. Rather he is hard and rough, barefoot and homeless, always lying on the ground without blankets, sleeping in doorways or along roads in the open air. Since he has his mother's nature, he is always needy. But in line with his father, he is one who plots to get what is beautiful and good. He is courageous, eager, and earnest; an extraordinary hunter, always creating contrivances; and one who desires and enables attentiveness; a lifelong lover of wisdom; adroit in matters of magic, witchcraft, and sophistry. (*Symp*. 203d)

According to this account sexual intercourse was practiced before *Erōs* came into being. The subordinate rank of *Erōs* is revealed by the fact that he is a lover of the beautiful and not one who possesses beauty. The lover is the one who is lacking the beautiful and so strives for it with cleverness.[253] Therefore Diotima claims that the lover is inferior to the beloved, who is the beautiful one. She challenges Socrates to rethink the nature of love:

> It seems evident to me from what you have said that you think the loved one, and not the lover, to be love. Therefore, I think that for you love appears to be beautiful in every respect. So the loved one is the one who is beautiful, graceful, perfect, and blessed. But the lover has a much different profile, as I have described him. (*Symp*. 204c)

Diotima's definition of the lover as needy and distressed makes love appear as a mixed blessing. There is the lively sense of desire that accompanies the perception of a beautiful object, but there is also the realization

---

nature, against law. The direction of *Erōs* is inverse to the direction of the action of the Olympian gods."

251. Rosen, *Plato's Symposium*, 157.

252. Rosen, *Plato's Symposium*, 234, claims that because *Erōs* is the offspring of an intoxicated Olympian god he is presumably the agent of intoxication, even though he himself is not intoxicated.

253. Sheffield, *Plato's Symposium*, 42–43.

that this desire will never be satisfied.[254] Is it better never to feel this hunger in the first place? Or is there a constructive way in which to advance toward the beautiful through the urging of this hunger?

Aristophanes' view of *Erōs* as a persistent, driving hunger for a mutual relationship that will give a sense of wholeness is illustrated in the character Haemon in Sophocles' *Antigone*. Haemon is the son of the newly installed king of Thebes, Creon, the uncle of Antigone and her two brothers Polyneices and Eteocles. Antigone and Creon are locked in a life-and-death struggle over Creon's decree that because of Polyneices' traitorous actions toward Thebes his corpse is not to be buried but rather exposed to carrion-eating birds and animals (ll.27-38). While Antigone will not compromise her love and loyalty toward her brother Polyneices and her deceased family members, Creon will not compromise his commitment to defend the polis against traitors.[255] Haemon, who is engaged to Antigone, sides with her against his father. After Creon has Antigone entombed alive, Haemon discovers her, tries to murder Creon, but fails, and then commits suicide (ll. 1220-40). This disarray in Creon's family leads Creon's wife Eurydice to commit suicide (ll. 1301-5). This tragic turn of events testifies that the desire *erōs* stirred within Haemon controlled his world to such an extent that he no longer thought life worth living without his fiancée Antigone. But the love that moves Antigone and Creon to be single-minded in their devotion to principle is not *erōs* but rather *philia*.[256] Antigone's *philia* is united with death (ll. 891-92), whereas Creon's *philia* is united with abstract civic structures—that is, the viability of the polis demands that the citizens be patriotic and so those who defy this necessity must be punished regardless of their person or status. Neither Antigone nor Creon speaks of *erōs* where *erōs* means "mutuality."[257] Yet the fates of Haemon and Eurydice testify that the demands of *erōs* cannot be ignored without consequence.[258]

Antigone's sister Ismene quietly offers Antigone an alternative way of navigating the tensions between family and polis. She counsels against open defiance of Creon's decree:

254. Ibid., 43.

255. Martha Nussbaum, *Fragility of Goodness*, 55–60.

256. Ibid., 63; Rush Rehm, *Marriage to Death: The Conflation of Wedding and Funeral Rituals in Greek Tragedy* (Princeton: Princeton University Press, 1994), 59–60.

257. Arlene W. Saxonhouse, *Fear of Diversity: The Birth of Political Science in Ancient Greek Thought* (Chicago: University of Chicago Press, 1992), 71.

258. Ibid., 72.

> Now then, look at the two of us alone remaining. We will be destroyed in a most terrible way if with the force of custom we circumvent the vote and power of rulers. It is necessary to consider the fact that we two are women, who should not start a fight with men. Since we are ruled by stronger forces, it is necessary to obey these orders, and even those that are more painful. So I will ask those under the earth for pardon, since I am hard-pressed by these orders and so will obey those in office. To do something excessive makes no sense. (*Antig*. 58-68)

Ismene tries to balance conflicting demands. One might argue that she adopts a more challenging, nuanced course than Antigone by trying not only to love her sister but also to remain faithful to the city. Saxonhouse claims that Ismene's effort to balance opposites (i.e., love of family versus love of polis) is a "necessary *erōs* . . . [that] alerts us to the particularity or specificity of the individual rather than the uniform and exchangeable."[259] This kind of political *erōs* that pays attention both to individuals and to the limitations of the circumstances can be seen as a careful, painstaking desire for the beautiful. This kind of *erōs* is a slow burn that cannot afford to exhaust itself in moments of intense feeling as did Haemon's frustrated *erōs* that led to his suicide. The ache of Ismene's desire to be one with her family and yet mindful of the reality of a city's demand for loyalty leaves her in an extended time in which the longed-for communion will elude her.

Ismene's *erōs* finds a place within Diotima's view of *Erōs* as a *daimōn* who incites within humans the desire for the beautiful. Diotima's *Erōs* is an intermediary who effects a link between the human condition and the ideal. Diotima shook up the world of the young Socrates when she first instructed him around 440 BCE.[260] She made him see that *Erōs* is an aching desire issuing from a lack or a need and is not the sweet experience of being loved. The sexual dimension of erotic experience is radically reconfigured when it is imagined as an experience of a driving hunger rather than as the satisfaction of a strong desire; the need for this satisfaction must have weighed heavily on Haemon (*Antig*. 781-800).[261] But Ismene's political *Erōs* finds confirmation in Diotima's teaching that an important kind of "worship" to be offered to *Erōs* is to love one's own,

259. Ibid., 73.

260. For Diotima as a historical character in Socrates' past see Strauss, *On Plato's Symposium*, 184; A. E. Taylor, *Plato: The Man and His Work* (New York: Meridian Books, 1957), 224. For Diotima as a fictional character see Hunter, *Plato's Symposium*, 81.

261. Hunter, *Plato's Symposium*, 80; Rehm, *Marriage to Death*, 62–63.

one's kin, and one's fatherland. Two additional forms of worship of *Erōs* are to love the beautiful (i.e., glory, moral virtue) and to love the good from the most mundane to the most ethereal instances of the good.[262] These ways of serving *Erōs* honor this intermediary between gods and humans as the attractive force that holds the cosmos together. In these ways of serving *Erōs*, Diotima points beyond the mutuality of political *Erōs* to the higher goal of longing for the good (*Symp*. 211e-212a).[263]

Erōs *as the Desire to Possess the Beautiful and the Good*

The goal of the conversation and speechmaking at the home of the tragic poet Agathon, as recounted in the *Symposium*, was to praise the god *Erōs*. But, as Strauss notes, the first three speeches fail to praise *Erōs*, for they talk about *Erōs* in terms of something outside of *Erōs* rather than directing their attention to *Erōs* as such.[264] First, Phaedrus praises *Erōs* for the warm feeling and adulation *Erōs* can bring to the beloved; the amount of praise Phaedrus extends to *Erōs* is based on selfish gain. Second, Pausanias praises *Erōs* for the moral virtue he believes *Erōs* calls forth. For him, Noble *Erōs* is the mean between repression and complete license. Thus *Erōs* leads the beloved to bestow favors on the lover from whom he seeks virtue. However, Socrates criticizes this view as a weak attempt to justify the older lover's love of youth in bloom.[265] Third, Eryximachus praises *Erōs* in terms of its capacity to bring harmony to individuals and communities through technical skill, science, and art. This harmony or integration is equivalent to the pleasure *Erōs* generates.[266]

The final three speeches succeed in praising *Erōs* as such. Aristophanes, as a comic poet, is faced with the formidable task of praising *Erōs* in light of the ugly or the base. He praises *Erōs* as the rebellious trait within humans that challenges the particular restrictions of civilized life while at the same time recognizing that restrictions are necessary for civilized life. He lauds the role of *Erōs* in this restless striving for unity, even though the level of integration desired is unattainable.[267] Next Agathon praises *Erōs* as beauty incarnate. The beauty of *Erōs* is young, delicate, and pliant in shape. The beauty and goodness of *Erōs* moves poets

262. Strauss, *On Plato's Symposium*, 240–41.

263. Angela Hobbs, "Female Imagery in Plato," 271.

264. Strauss, *On Plato's Symposium*, 54.

265. Ibid., 83.

266. Ibid., 54, 106; Hunter, *Plato's Symposium*, 57–59.

267. Strauss, *On Plato's Symposium*, 54, 127, 134, 137; Hunter, *Plato's Symposium*, 68–69; Kahn, *Plato and the Socratic Dialogue*, 268.

to create, whether it be the gods, tragedies, or comedies.[268] Finally, Socrates claims that *Erōs* is neither beautiful nor ugly but intermediate between them.[269] *Erōs* is the power that binds all things together (*Symp.* 202e3-7).[270]

Diotima's first lesson for Socrates was that there is something between good and bad (*Symp.* 201e8-202a9). Between *phronēsis* ("understanding") and ignorance, there is right opinion. This right opinion can be checked in terms of universal agreement: for example, one may not be able to explain why there are lakes, trees, and birds, but we trust that they exist and will conform to their nature. This right opinion is important for making wise practical decisions; its main deficiency is that we do not know why this right opinion is true, and thus it participates in ignorance. This stage between ignorance and wisdom is philosophy: one loves what one desires but does not possess.[271] To the extent that this beloved object participates in the beautiful and the good it incites a love (*philia*) for wisdom (*sophia*) that can be described as erotic (209c, 210b-211b).[272]

The poets contend that there is a reality higher than reason. The tragic poets try to stir the emotions of fear and pity in their audience, thus providing the fictional space in which to work through tensions and contradictions they experience in the households and in the city. In the *Republic*, Plato regarded such emotional purging as dangerous for the people since it moved them into an imaginary world, which was simply weakening their perception of the truth that was already clouded by the shadowy world of everyday life (602c4).[273] Plato, like Parmenides, urged people to look beyond the appearances of things to the true reality.[274] In the *Symposium*, Socrates enters into a contest with a tragic poet (Agathon) and a comic poet (Aristophanes) in which the goal is a

268. Strauss, *On Plato's Symposium*, 54, 160, 162, 171.

269. On the paradoxical, demonical character of Socrates see Sarah Kofman, "Socrates and His Twins (The Socrates[es] of Plato's *Symposium*)," in *Feminism and the History of Philosophy*, 41–67, at 49.

270. Strauss, *On Plato's Symposium*, 54, 190.

271. Ibid., 187, 197.

272. Ibid., 196–97; Rosen, *Plato's Symposium*, 200; Gabriela Roxana Carone, "The Virtues of Platonic Love," in *Plato's Symposium: Issues in Interpretation and Reception*, 208–26, at 221–22; Sheffield, *Plato's Symposium*, 50–52, 56.

273. Thomas Gould, *The Ancient Quarrel Between Poetry and Philosophy* (Princeton: Princeton University Press, 1990), 81, 216–17, 221.

274. Rosen, *Plato's Symposium*, 251, states that Socrates "is a lover of nature and *logos* rather than of myth. He comes to philosophy from physics and cosmology rather than from religion and poetry."

poetic one: to adorn *Erōs* through praise.[275] He recognizes that poets aim to cultivate political prudence and virtue; they wish to educate statesmen and legislators.[276] However, the philosopher focuses on the capacity of *nous*, "reason," to see realities that cannot fully be put into words (*Symp.* 192b5-d2).[277] This pointing beyond to a larger, invisible reality is a poetic capacity philosophy shares.[278] The philosopher would contend, however, that the difference between the philosopher Socrates and the tragic poet Sophocles is that Socrates is occupied with discovering the truth and not with inventing it.[279] Gould describes this challenge that Socrates and Plato posed to the poets and tragedians as a redefinition of Dionysus in which Dionysus would never do anything dangerous or destructive. In this new Platonic form of Dionysian religion, Dionysus is an ally of *Erōs* in generating the energy that lifts the soul to the divine.[280]

What causes this desire known as *Erōs* (*Symp.* 207a5-7)? A person can only love what he or she perceives to be good. Parents make many sacrifices for their children; they will even forfeit their lives for the sake of their own children. So the "love of their own" takes precedence over their very selves. In the sexual union of man and woman the desire for this action extends beyond that of bringing a particular child to birth. This productive activity is a way humans act like gods.[281] An underlying, perhaps unconscious motive for a couple to have a child is the desire for immortality—an immortality of the species rather than of the individual.[282]

If this drive for immortality assumes the form of love of fame, one may strive to do virtuous things that will be remembered in the polis (*Symp*. 197a). But Diotima does not regard the polis as sempiternal (*Symp.* 209); it needs the avenging gods and the beautiful gods to sustain it.[283] The poets who seek fame do it for the sake of self-expression. Humans become who they are by repeatedly reproducing themselves. One who stands before what is good and beautiful and reproduces it realizes the self (*Symp*. 207c5-208b5).[284]

275. Strauss, *On Plato's Symposium*, 26, 201.

276. Ibid., 229.

277. Ibid., 138; Sheffield, *Plato's Symposium*, 67, 129–34.

278. Rosen, *Plato's Symposium*, 200–1.

279. Strauss, *On Plato's Symposium*, 229.

280. Gould, *The Ancient Quarrel Between Poetry and Philosophy*, 60, 228–29.

281. Sheffield, *Plato's Symposium*, 76, 86.

282. Strauss, *On Plato's Symposium*, 206–7; Rosen, *Plato's Symposium*, 248–49.

283. Strauss, *On Plato's Symposium*, 209.

284. Sheffield, *Plato's Symposium*, 76, 91, 100.

The ascent toward the beautiful and the good is driven by love. One begins the ascent by love of one beautiful body. Then one learns to love two beautiful bodies and then all beautiful bodies, perceiving that each of them participates in the reality of beauty (*Symp*. 211c-d).[285] But then one must recognize that the beauty of the soul manifested in the sharing of ideas and arguments about virtue is of greater worth than the beauty of bodies (*Symp*. 210c).[286] With the mind set on the beauty of knowledge, one comes to the great sea of beauty from which come to birth many beautiful ideas and theories (*Symp*. 210d).[287] If one truly perceives the beautiful in these objects and ideas, one will recognize that the beautiful is unchanging and complete (*Symp*. 211a-b, 212a).[288] Those things that participate in the beautiful come to be and pass away, but the beautiful is always one in form. Plato shares with Parmenides the conviction that being, or what is real, is unchanging. Parmenides holds this view in the context of a homogeneous cosmos (i.e., Being is one continuous whole, DK 28B8.22-25), whereas Plato does so in the context of a heterogenous ideal cosmos (i.e., Being pervades a multiplicity of ideal Forms, *Rep*. 508e).[289]

The transition from loving beautiful bodies to beholding ideas indicates that the intellectual life is higher on the ascent than the affective life. But there needs to be a higher stage yet in which the intellectual and affective are brought together.[290] In the highest stage of the ascent one beholds the beautiful itself and is together with it. Such beholding of the

285. Rosen, *Plato's Symposium*, 243, notes that erotic pursuit of happiness takes the following three forms: love of property, love of the body, and love of the psyche (*Symp*. 205d4-5); there is no acorporeal lover.

286. Rosen, *Plato's Symposium*, 216, notes: "Friendship may be defined as the form of love in which there is no erotic desire for the friend, but a shared possession of desire for some other thing." In criticism of this Socratic anthropology Judith Butler, *Gender Trouble: Feminism and the Subversion of Identity* (New York: Routledge, 1990), 12, states: "In the philosophical tradition that begins with Plato and continues through Descartes, Husserl, and Sartre, the ontological distinction between soul (consciousness, mind) and body invariably supports relations of political and psychic subordination and hierarchy. The mind not only subjugates the body, but occasionally entertains the fantasy of fleeing its embodiment altogether. The cultural associations of mind with masculinity and body with femininity are well documented within the field of philosophy and feminism."

287. Sheffield, *Plato's Symposium*, 115–23.

288. Ibid., 145.

289. Strauss, *On Plato's Symposium*, 55; Geoffrey S. Kirk, John E. Raven, and Malcolm Schofield, *The Presocratic Philosophers*, 2d ed. (Cambridge: Cambridge University Press, 1983), 251; Roochnik, *Retrieving the Ancients*, 47, 132–33.

290. Lloyd P. Gerson, "A Platonic Reading of Plato's Symposium," in *Plato's Symposium: Issues in Interpretation and Reception*, 47–67, at 63,

beautiful is identical to being together with the good; such an experience is one of complete happiness. This experience of happiness that comes in beholding the good is a form of *Erōs* that transcends the *Erōs* of bodies but can only be reached by way of the love of beautiful bodies.[291] The multiple beautiful bodies bring one to copy good things and thus to possess them (*Symp*. 206c-d); these good things give one a sense of happiness along the way (*Symp*. 204e5).[292] The experience of beholding is not one of complete union with the beautiful object, for there must be a separation between the perceiver and the object perceived.[293] There is communion but not a merger. For Plato this rational beholding of ideas replaces the personal relationship with the gods. But within the subsequent Platonic tradition Plotinus emphasizes that the striving of rational beings to know all that is knowable is fueled by a desire to be with the Good. The intellectual and the affective are integrated in this final stage of being with the Good.[294]

The speakers in the *Symposium* set out to praise *Erōs*. Socrates provides the most complete description of *Erōs* in his retelling of the teaching he claims was imparted to him about twenty-five years earlier by Diotima (cf. *Symp*. 201d). He celebrates *Erōs* for fueling the desire to seek the good and the beautiful. This desire is the love of wisdom that moves the philosopher; it is the desire that moves the poet to strive for virtue; it is the desire that moves one to have access to what is good from the most mundane to the most ethereal instances. Yet in this ascent toward the beautiful and the good the ways in which the affective and intellectual interrelate is not examined. Pausanias makes the distinction between noble *Erōs* and base *Erōs*, yet the ways in which this powerful passion of *Erōs* can overturn lives and be a destructive force have not been addressed by Socrates. Strauss claims that Socrates employs a form of Odyssean rhetoric in which he cleverly aims to succeed in the contest of praising *Erōs* by not mentioning the darker sides of this passion.[295]

In the *Republic* the soul is described as tripartite: reason, desire, and emotion (*Rep*. 441e–443e). Reason is expected to rule over desire and

291. Cf. Christopher Rowe, "The Symposium as a Socratic Dialogue," in *Plato's Symposium: Issues in Interpretation and Reception*, 11–22, at 10–11.

292. Rosen, *Plato's Symposium*, 240–41; Sheffield, *Plato's Symposium*, 81, 135.

293. Gerson, "A Platonic Reading of Plato's *Symposium*," 47–67, at 63. Rosen, *Plato's Symposium*, 230, notes that Diotima says with regard to the intermediary role of *Erōs* that "in human terms, there is no more direct intercourse, whether sexual or noetic, between gods and men" (*Symp*. 203a).

294. Gerson, "A Platonic Reading of Plato's *Symposium*," 58.

295. Strauss, *On Plato's Symposium*, 179.

emotion. The *Phaedrus* likewise has this tripartite view of the soul (*Phaedrus* 246b-c), but more room is given to desire and emotion to play a constructive role in personal development. In the *Phaedrus* the search for truth is fueled not simply by the intellect but by passion and personal love (*Phaedrus* 244a). Philosophy is not purely intellectual activity but is also a form of madness.[296] The principle of movement that lies at the origin of everything is within the immortal soul itself (*Phaedrus* 245). In this dialogue Phaedrus reads a speech composed by Lysias (231a-234c) exhorting the beloved to form a relationship only with a nonlover, since a lover will have desire for pleasure that will tend to overrule his desire to do what is right.[297] Socrates follows this speech with one in which he elevates the intellectual faculty (*logistikon*) as sufficient for the apprehension of truth; the nonintellectual elements are blind, tend to excess, and make no contribution to a person's cognitive function (237b-244a).[298] These two opening speeches reflect the ascetic views of the *Republic* and the *Phaedrus*; there is a compelling logic for someone at the outset of a career who wishes to advance by cultivating the most advantageous relationships with those who are established and can help one to move into the adult, professional world.[299]

The opening speeches of the *Phaedrus* are examples of how the power of incantation-like language can be used to defuse the mania of *Erōs*.[300] Just as the love charms of a lover aim to control the beloved,[301] so also these speeches aim to corral the unruly aspects of *Erōs* so that the intellectual portion of a person can be in control (*sōphrosunē*). In the *Phaedrus* these two speeches are delivered at the outset (231a-244a) so as to be countered in the main portion of the dialogue (244a-257b). In the *Republic* the person aims to grow by detaching the intellect from the other parts of the personality (*Rep.* 509d-511e). But here in the *Phaedrus* the nonintellectual elements are given an important role in personal development. First of all, emotions can energize a person and enable one to act in positive ways. Second, there are some insights that can be gained only through the guidance of the passions;

296. Nussbaum, *Fragility of Goodness*, 201; Rosen, *Plato's Symposium*, 206–7.

297. David A. White, *Rhetoric and Reality in Plato's Phaedrus* (Albany: SUNY Press, 1993), 40–41.

298. Nussbaum, *Fragility of Goodness*, 206; Josef Pieper, *Enthusiasm and Divine Madness* (South Bend, IN: St. Augustine's Press, 2000), 20–36.

299. Nussbaum, *Fragility of Goodness*, 207–8.

300. Ibid., 203.

301. Christopher Faraone, *Ancient Greek Love Magic* (Cambridge, MA: Harvard University Press, 1999), 5–6, 17–18; John Winkler, *Constraints of Desire: The Anthropology of Sex and Gender in Ancient Greece* (New York: Routledge, 1990), 94.

thus the emotions are believed to have a cognitive content. For example, an emotional response to beauty is not merely sensual but also involves fear and reverence (250d-e).[302] Therefore in the *Phaedrus* the soul's ascent towards the beautiful and the good needs the feverish, constant motion of the nonintellectual parts of the person. The search for truth is necessarily a passionate pursuit; falling in love is an essential moment in the ascent to truth (251a-252c). Therefore one can say that the intellect has a sexual element vital to personal wholeness.[303] Love of the abstract is not love; a person must love some particular being.[304]

Erōs *and the Maintenance of the Sacred Boundaries of the Greek Household*

Plato proposed a law that would fine any man over thirty-five years old who had not produced offspring (*Laws* 774a-e). The channeling of sexuality toward procreative purposes was a necessity, but it did not exhaust the creative potential of sexuality and *Erōs*. The Greek gods engaged in sex simply on the grounds of pleasure and relationships; by contrast, humans had to do so for the survival of the species.[305] Among animals there is no erotic dimension to sexuality; they are programmed to breed according to mating seasons. According to Diotima the gods did not have sexual relations with humans (*Symp*. 203a).[306]

Women receive little attention in the gathering of male intellectuals in Plato's *Symposium*. Even the young woman musician is dismissed by Eryximachus (*Symp*. 176e). However, Diotima holds an honored place as a wisdom teacher.[307] Within Greek society of Plato's time women held a distinctive position biologically and sociologically. Because of their intimate connection with nature in pregnancy and childbirth, women were that mysterious Other to the male perspective that typically shaped the ancient Greek texts.[308] Sociologically they belonged to two house-

302. Nussbaum, *Fragility of Goodness*, 214–15; Pieper, *Enthusiasm and Divine Madness*, 83–88.

303. Nussbaum, *Fragility of Goodness*, 217–18.

304. Strauss, *On Plato's Symposium*, 199; Nussbaum, *Fragility of Goodness*, 220–21.

305. Strauss, *On Plato's Symposium*, 132.

306. Ibid., 190.

307. Morag Buchan, *Women in Plato's Political Theory* (London and New York: Routledge, 1999), 53, claims that even though the woman Diotima teaches the erotic ladder of ascent to the Good, she describes a masculine soul.

308. Ibid., 82–88; Anne Carson, "Dirt and Desire: The Phenomenology of Female Pollution in Antiquity," in *Constructions of the Classical Body*, ed. James I. Porter, 77–100 (Ann Arbor: University of Michigan Press, 1999), at 84–85.

holds: first their father's and then that of their husband.[309] Since they married at a young age they became the longstanding members in their husbands' households by the time they were grandmothers. Usually their husbands were ten to fifteen years older than they and would have preceded them in death, so that the women became the key players in the re-creation of the culture of the household through the generations. As nurturers and as residents within the private sphere of the household they wielded considerable influence over it.[310] The *Erōs* that led female and male to join sexually was not aimed simply at pleasure but rather at immortality. The birth of offspring was a form of love of one's own, which also had the benefit for nature of continuing the species.[311]

In the *Symposium*, Socrates is presented as completely erotic but not as a lover of bodily things (215-16, cf. *Theages* 130d-e).[312] As an embodied being he is a beloved one, as Alcibiades' account of his attempts to seduce Socrates attest (*Symp.* 216c-219d).[313] But Socrates' nonresponse to Alcibiades points to Socrates' conviction that *Erōs* of the soul is higher than that of the body. When individuals share ideas and find themselves excited over the realities they have contacted through such thinking and speaking, this kind of intellectual friendship is the *Erōs* of the soul that is of higher nature than the *Erōs* of the body manifested in sexual relations. The beauty of Socrates' soul draws the love of his students or disciples.

The *Symposium* praises *Erōs* but criticizes pederasty. Pausanias, Eryximachus, and Aristophanes mount arguments in favor of pederasty. Pausanias tries to justify pederasty but finds himself demonstrating how it is immoral: i.e., it is exploitation of a boy by a man.[314] Eryximachus

309. Pomeroy, *Families in Classical and Hellenistic* Greece, 70–71.

310. Lynn Foxhall, "Pandora Unbound: A Feminist Critique of Foucault's History of Sexuality," in *Rethinking Sexuality: Foucault and Classical Antiquity*, ed. David Larmour, et al., 122–37 (Princeton: Princeton University Press, 1998), at 125–26, 130; Josiah Ober, *Political Dissent in Democratic Athens* (Princeton: Princeton University Press, 1998), 50–51.

311. Strauss, *On Plato's Symposium*, 203, 207, 222; Rosen, *Plato's Symposium*, 252–53.

312. Gould, *The Ancient Quarrel Between Poetry and Philosophy*, 226, 230. Rosen, *Plato's Symposium*, 71, notes that Plato regarded pederasty as unnatural (*Laws* 836b-e), for the natural end of sexual intercourse is procreation (*Laws* 838e). On the rhetoric and practice of pederasty see Paul W. Ludwig, *Eros and Polis: Desire and Community in Greek Political Theory* (Cambridge: Cambridge University Press, 2002), 28–31, 230–35.

313. On Socrates as a satyr-like trickster who is outwardly mischievous but inwardly resourceful and persuasive (*Symp.* 218c-219d), see Sheffield, *Plato's Symposium*, 188–91.

314. Strauss, *On Plato's Symposium*, 66; cf. John J. Winkler, "Laying Down the Law: The Oversight of Men's Sexual Behavior in Classical Athens," in *Before Sexuality: The Construction of Erotic Experience in the Ancient Greek World*, ed. David Halperin, John Winkler, and Froma Zeitlin, 171–209 (Princeton: Princeton University Press, 1990), at 173, 185–86.

celebrates the art of medicine as the harmonizing of opposites in nature but contradicts this principle in his pederasty, where he claims that similar things love similar things (cf. *Symp*. 187b).[315] Aristophanes defends pederasty through his claim that the male type of original human derived from the sun was superior to the others. These original humans were severed because of their rebellion; so the erotic effort at reunion aims to overcome *nomos* ("customary and positive law") to restore *physis* ("nature," *Symp*. 189d-e).[316] For Aristophanes erotic striving is a matter of overcoming artificial barriers.[317] The two halves that seek to be reunited could be base. Thus for Plato erotic striving was not limited to mutuality between bodies but aimed to spur on the intellect in its search for truth, beauty, and goodness.[318] This higher goal of *Erōs* moves the lover of beauty beyond the love of particular individuals to the love of the form of the beautiful in which beautiful things participate (*Symp*. 210b-211c).[319]

In Sophocles' *Antigone*, the sisters Antigone and Ismene give voice to two different strategies for negotiating the tension between love of family and love of homeland. Antigone is singleminded in her devotion to her family, whereas Ismene wrestles with the options before her as a woman in a male-dominated kingdom. Ismene is ready to engage the complexities of her situation and acknowledge the limitations of any approach to dealing with Creon's harsh decree exposing her brother's remains to carrion-eating animals. Ismene loves her family but is more open to recognizing the claims the city and its ruler Creon make on her. Her political *Erōs* moves her to take seriously the here-and-now demands of embodied existence within a family and a city, but at the same time she reveres her ancestors. By contrast, Antigone fights to the bitter end for the honor of her family, even if it means joining them prematurely in the afterlife. Ismene judges her situation to be one in which it is better to try to negotiate the conflicting claims of family and city than to force a crisis that might yield a worse condition; thus the ongoing tensions between the claims of the family and those of the city take the form of an antinomy (a conflict that does not submit to a rule). Antigone judges the position of Creon toward her traitorous brother to be totally unacceptable and provokes a confrontation with him in which there must be

315. Strauss, *On Plato's Symposium*, 100.

316. David Cohen, *Sexuality and Society: The Enforcement of Morals in Classical Athens* (Cambridge: Cambridge University Press, 1994), 187, 191.

317. Strauss, *On Plato's Symposium*, 134.

318. Sheffield, *Plato's Symposium*, 77–78.

319. Ibid., 155–62.

a winner and a loser; thus Antigone would categorize her conflict with Creon as a contradiction (a conflict that cannot continue in its current form).[320]

The desire for bodily immortality came to expression not only in having offspring but also in the creation of works of art and culture or by performing heroic deeds that would live on.[321] Living on in the memories of a people is a more dynamic form of enduring life than producing an artifact that then must be viewed by subsequent generations in order to bring it back to life. Yet the artifact would have greater durability than a live conversation. In the *Phaedrus*, Socrates extolled the virtue of the educator who passed on wisdom to others through direct speech. The give-and-take of dialogue and debate could supply context to one's statements. When statements are written down, the living context of the original author fades and interpreters may distort what has been said. But Plato seems to have had a different opinion about the value of written communication. Since he has written dialogues, he seems to honor written works as a form of bodily immortality.[322]

Plato's emphasis in the *Symposium* on the *Erōs* of the soul over that of the body would create a more detached, contemplative citizenry. But the *Erōs* of the body is indispensable because it promotes not only procreation but also acts of heroism and patriotism essential to the survival of the polis. Plato balances his emphasis on the *Erōs* of the soul with that of the body in the *Phaedrus*; in this dialogue the *Erōs* of the body is necessary to fuel the lover of wisdom to search for the Good with passion.[323] Thus, for the vitality of the body politic, citizens should aim to integrate *Erōs* of the body with that of the soul.

Summary

Erōs is a vital force that moves humans to act so as to connect with other humans or other tangible or intangible realities. This energy for connection pervades personal relationships and so can be imagined as

320. Cf. Fredric Jameson, *The Political Unconscious: Narrative as a Socially Symbolic Act* (Ithaca, NY: Cornell University Press, 1981), 114; idem, *The Seeds of Time* (New York: Columbia University Press, 1994), 4–5, 70; Jonathan Culler, *The Pursuit of Signs* (Ithaca, NY: Cornell University Press, 1987), 39.

321. Strauss, *On Plato's Symposium*, 225, 239; Rosen, *Plato's Symposium*, 260.

322. Strauss, *On Plato's Symposium*, 250, 252.

323. Buchan, *Women in Plato's Political Theory*, 89–90), contends, however, that the love extolled in the Phaedrus is male-to-male love and that the female role in reproduction is spiritualized as the birth of knowledge.

having a personality of its own (i.e., as a deity). But as an energy that suffuses creation, *Erōs* has the character of a demiurge or a cosmic force. Parmenides relegates *Erōs* to the world of becoming, the illusory world of change. In Hesiod's *Theogony*, *Erōs* appears more as a power rather than as a personality under the direction of Aphrodite. This Hesiodic emphasis on *Erōs* as a power evolves into an intermediary between gods and humans at the hands of Plato's Diotima. This two-faced reality of *Erōs* as a named, personal force and as an anonymous, impersonal force highlights the intimate yet uncontrollable character of *Erōs*, which can penetrate the inner sanctuary of a person to build up or tear down. If *Erōs* is a deity, its activity in this inner sanctuary would seem to be constructive (thus the views of Phaedrus and Agathon); however, if *Erōs* is a cosmic force it may simply react to the individual as part of a larger cosmic process and thus is ready to break down the individual identity (thus the views of Pausanias, Eryximachus, and Aristophanes). Pausanias treated *Erōs* as a cosmic force that influenced one's feelings to act in a certain way and so distinguished between the heavenly Aphrodite (*Erōs* of soul) and the common Aphrodite (*Erōs* of body). Erixymachus regarded *Erōs* as the integrating force in the body that continually countered the disintegrating forces of strife. Aristophanes identified *Erōs* as the yearning for completion by finite, fragmented humans. This yearning locates *Erōs* within the body as a sexual reality and subordinates the spiritual desire for wholeness to this embodied quest for mutuality. By contrast, Phaedrus and Agathon put more emphasis on the personal characteristics of *Erōs*. Phaedrus identifies *Erōs* as the oldest of the gods, while Agathon sees him as the youngest. They regard *Erōs* as a reality to be desired for itself; it is good to have *Erōs* present with oneself for the good he provides.

Socrates quotes his teacher Diotima in order to portray *Erōs* as an intermediary: a combination of the characteristics of a personal god and a cosmic force. Diotima had revolutionized Socrates' understanding of *Erōs* as a youth by instructing him that *Erōs* is not a sweet feeling within which to rejoice but rather a hungry yearning that causes distress and restlessness. But Socrates praises *Erōs* for such an unsettling influence because it energizes humans to search for wholeness. Socrates' picture of *Erōs* differs from that of Aristophanes in that he sees the yearning as an ascent to the beautiful and the good, whereas Aristophanes sees the yearning for mutuality as a perpetual, cyclical dimension of the human condition. Socrates' *Erōs* of the soul differs from Aristophanes' *Erōs* of the body.

The pictures the various speakers in the *Symposium* have of *Erōs* shape the way they deal with erotic sexuality in their lives. Phaedrus, Pausanias, Erixymachus, and Aristophanes favor the practice of pederasty in which the elder *erastes*, "lover," leads the younger *erōmenos*, "beloved," to higher stages of excellence (*aretē*) in exchange for sexual favors. But the dialogue exposes the shortcomings of each speaker's view of *Erōs*: Phaedrus sees *Erōs* as a warm feeling; Pausanias uses *Erōs* to promote a self-serving understanding of virtue; Erixymachus places *Erōs* in the service of pleasure; Aristophanes sees *Erōs* as an ingrained rebellious trait that would only grow stronger if the human were to recover its lost wholeness; in his view the conflicted human condition is irreparable. Agathon praises *Erōs* as beautiful and in every way a reality one should strive to embrace. Socrates' Diotima steers a middle course by picturing *Erōs* as midway between the beauty of Agathon's *Erōs* and the ugliness of Aristophanes's *Erōs*. Although no one of the other speakers has provided a sufficient description of *Erōs*, each proceeds on what they regard as the proper course in which to deal with *Erōs* in their lives and try to come to a better understanding and resolution of this reality of love. Diotima identifies this dynamic intermediate state between ignorance and wisdom as "love of wisdom": *Erōs* of the soul pushes one upward toward the beautiful and the good. In the *Phaedrus*, Plato instructs that the passion of the *Erōs* of the body should be brought together with the striving of the *Erōs* of the soul in order to move with all one's being toward the Good.

The implications of this ladder of ascent to the Good for social and political relations are profound. The interior spiritual world promoted by Plato provides a powerful avenue for dealing with human aggression and promoting personal and communal growth. Critics of Plato's vision point out that it tends to denigrate the body, foster a dualistic anthropology, and favor a masculine soul.

Synthesis: Transmuted Sex and the Erotic Desire for the Divine

Love is a fundamental force in the divine sphere. Its ambiguity manifests its power as a creator and destroyer of boundaries. Thus the cosmic polarities of order and chaos, life and death, light and darkness, and true and false are interrelated through the agency of love. This passionate, affective reality operates according to a logic that often appears mysterious to one whose world is shaped by rational logic. This otherness of *erōs* has surfaced repeatedly in this chapter concerned with mapping out the place of the erotic in the divine economies of ancient Israel, Mesopotamia, and Greece. In addressing the demands of *erōs* in one's life, an ongoing challenge is to avoid reducing this reality to sex, work, or one of its manifestations, thus short-circuiting the impetus of *erōs* toward communion with the good.[324]

The Presence and Function of the Erotic Within the Divine Realm

Erōs is a primary constituent in relationships among the gods and between gods and humans. From the late eighth through the fifth century BCE, as the Israelites and Judahites suffered invasions and deportations, the voice of the YHWH-alone movement gained strength.[325] A primary locus of the YHWH-alone perspective is the book of Hosea. Through the family metaphors of parent and husband Hosea provides a window into the heart of YHWH, who is in anguish over the punishment he must visit on Israel for its syncretism and apostasy. Through imagery from the household Hosea emphasizes that Israel owes exclusive devotion to YHWH as a wife does to her husband.

In the Mesopotamian tradition the family model for imagining the divine sphere orders the deities according to the temple households in the various cities. As the territorial states of Akkad and Babylonia developed in the third and second millennia, the political organization of the gods took the form of a monarchical state, and the number of gods was reduced from over three thousand to six hundred. The *Enūma Elish* narrates how Marduk gained the position of king of the gods by his heroic defense of his ancestral royal household. Although Marduk's rise to power in this household was not linked to marriage, the importance of courtship and marital imagery for picturing divine power is evident in the love songs of Dumuzi and Inanna. Even though divine erotic relationships at times went awry (e.g., "Enki and Ninhursaga"), they were vital to the web of relationships constituting the households of the Mesopotamian gods.

In the Greek pantheon of the first millennium BCE, erotic relationships are a force field within which strife arises and harmony is forged. The divine overseer of the erotic sphere spanning heaven and earth is the goddess Aphrodite. Her birth is described in Hesiod's *Theogony* as

324. On the issue of whether a person is to be loved for himself/herself or as an instantiantion of the good see the discussion in Sheffield, *Plato's Symposium*, 154–82, esp. 161–62, 172, 175, 181.

325. Bernhard Lang, *Monotheism and the Prophetic Minority: An Essay in Biblical History and Sociology* (Sheffield: Almond Press, 1983), 30.

the result of a battle between the primordial divine couple, Gaia and Uranus. Because of Uranus's hypersexuality and violence, Gaia had her son Cronus castrate her husband Uranus. Foam from Uranus's severed genitals was the substance from which Aphrodite was born. *Erōs* and *Himeros* were then imagined to be her auxiliaries (*Theog.* 168-206). Thus family relations among the gods, replete with intimacy and violence, provide an idealized picture of the dynamics of *erōs* in the traditions of ancient Israel, Mesopotamia, and Greece.

In these three cultural traditions *erōs* was revered as a divine emotional force pervading the cosmos that eludes easy characterization. According to Hosea, YHWH was not only the anguished parent forced to exercise tough love toward a rebellious child but also a cuckolded husband who forsook jealous vengeance and instead wooed an adulterous wife, confused and controlled by misdirected love. In Hos 2:16, YHWH speaks to the heart of Israel to draw her into the wilderness where she might gain perspective on the true workings of the powers of fertility and generativity in the land of Israel. YHWH is the husband of Israel and the land, and also a parent to the Israelites who live in it. He has bestowed his love on this land as a divine gift, but Israel has abandoned his love and attributed his divine gifts to other gods. These other gods are both fertility deities (Baal/Asherah) and political deities (Baal and his bureaucratic gods) who seek to centralize the resources in the land to the detriment of the traditional Israelite farming families. YHWH was likewise responsible for the fertility and security of the land and its inhabitants. Hosea's charge is that the Israelites do not distinguish YHWH from Baal; they are syncretists.

By contrast, the Mesopotamians felt obliged to be attentive to a number of deities who promoted fertility and security in their territory. Enki, the god of sweet water and overseer of the irrigation works, was intimately involved in agricultural success but was also depicted in the myth of "Enki and Ninhursaga" as bringing about fertility through rape and incest. Typically, the erotic force bringing fertility in Mesopotamia was symbolized by Inanna/Ishtar, particularly in her sexual relations with Dumuzi. But this marital relationship of Dumuzi and Inanna is not to be understood narrowly in terms of a sexual relationship but more widely as a vitality that brings well-being to the land. This vitality or generativity of *erōs* is shown in the myth of "Nergal and Ereshkigal" to extend even into the netherworld through the sexual union of these two deities. After 1800 BCE the annual rite of sacred marriage seems not to have been carnally enacted in the temple with a king and a priestess playing the roles of Dumuzi and Inanna. Rather, the symbolic dimension of the sacred marriage as a communing of Inanna/Ishtar with the king was enacted by placing statues of Dumuzi and Inanna in Inanna's bedchamber. The goddess's empowerment of the king shows a more wide-ranging conception of the erotic dimension of this divine-human relationship than a symbolic sexual union.

This understanding of *Erōs* as a personal and cosmic force that is much wider than sexuality is unfolded in Plato's *Symposium*. In this early-fourth-century composition Plato has four of his six speakers at a drinking party celebrate the cosmic significance of *Erōs*. The second speaker, Pausanias, claims that male homosexual love promotes a higher form of soul-based *Erōs* than heterosexual love—a bodily form of *Erōs* designed to produce offspring. The third speaker, the physician Eryximachus, draws on the theories of Empedocles, which picture *Erōs* ("love") countering *Eris* ("strife") in the integrating and disintegrating movements of the cosmic elements of water, air, fire, and earth. The fourth speaker, the comic playwright Aristophanes, regards *Erōs* as a rebellious force in which humans try to assert themselves against the gods and the limits of their condition. To curtail this rebellious tendency the gods split these primordial humans in two so that an immediate form of their *Erōs* is the insatiable desire to be reunited with one's lost half. However, Socrates' Diotima claims that *Erōs* is an intermediary linking the divine and the human and binding the various parts of the cosmos together.

Thus the human experience of *Erōs* provides a microcosm for understanding the cosmic operations of *Erōs*. Plato shows that *Erōs* is a natural force with cosmic range that should be addressed on a linguistic, rational basis. The need to identify *Erōs* properly and to avoid reducing it to a carnal form that can be manipulated mechanically is a concern shared by Plato and Hosea and seems to be operative in the transformation of the Mesopotamian sacred marriage rite into a more abstract symbolic form.

The Relationship Between Sex and Knowledge

Erōs is a divine force inherent in both carnal and spiritual knowledge. It offers an explanation for the insatiable human drive for knowledge. This drive to know as much as possible is a characteristic that overlaps with the drive for sexual union. The Israelite tradition explains that the alienation the drives for sex and knowledge try to overcome is exacerbated by efforts in which humans either try to save themselves or look to gods other than YHWH for assistance. Powerful *erōs* can give the impression that this force by itself can unite humans with the divine. Hosea condemns those Israelites who carry out illicit sexual unions in the environs of the Yahwistic sanctuaries (4:14). Such ecstatic forms of human interaction within a religious context can give the false impression that carnal activities can generate union with and knowledge of YHWH. But the transgression in the Garden of Eden robbed humans of their original innocence and left them in a state in which the couple's awareness of their sexuality complicated their relationship with one another. Discernment of how to engage and channel the force of *erōs* in one's life admitted of no easy solutions, although the temptation to reduce *erōs* to controllable forms or to repress it was ever ready to hand.

In the Mesopotamian *Epic of Gilgamesh,* the wild man Enkidu gained the capacity to plan and reason but lost the ability to run with the animals through his sexual union with the prostitute Shamhat. He irreversibly entered into the civilized sphere where he gave up eating grass and began to eat bread and drink beer. By wrestling with Gilgamesh to impede his sexual union with young women on the eve of their marriages, Enkidu came to know another who was equal to him in physical strength. Through their equality and collegiality Enkidu and Gilgamesh became the closest of friends, in a type of interpersonal knowing that advanced their understanding of the human and cosmic orders. Their friendship and love would push them toward a recognition of a reality bigger than their individual selves.

In Plato's *Symposium,* Diotima claims that *Erōs* is not a god and is neither beautiful nor good. Instead, *Erōs* is a demiurge that acts like a pauper. *Erōs* is homeless and insatiably hungry. This strong desire is triggered by looking upon a beautiful person or thing. Such beholding creates an awareness of what one lacks and so urges one to try to gain this beauty for oneself by reproducing it.

The recognition that many important practical decisions in life cannot be guided by more than probabilities leads one to search for truth and to accept one's limitations. Philosophy is this quest for truth in which one may have the right opinion but not be able to say why. The lover of wisdom tries to find an explanation. This state of knowledge between truth and ignorance triggers a desire to learn more and more. The desire to know can move the tragic poet to compose a tragic narrative; it can move the philosopher to define a virtue like justice. In his battle against the poets Socrates argues that the poet invents truth, whereas the philosopher is obliged to discover it. The philosopher relies on reason (*nous*) to behold the beautiful and the good, whereas the poet tries to create realities that will manifest the beautiful through emotion. The restless striving of reason, if prompted by the beautiful and the good, can lead to transcendence of self.

The desire for knowledge took the form of a quest for immortality in ancient Israel, Mesopotamia, and Greece. The penalty for eating the fruit of the knowledge of good and evil was the humans' conflicted state of awareness of their limits. Death became an issue for humans. With the death of Enkidu, Gilgamesh experienced a deep sense of loss that led him to try to find a way out of his mortal condition. He began searching for something within or around him that would allow him to transcend death. The enduring reality Gilgamesh eventually found turned out to be the knowledge of the human condition he bequeathed to civilization—an acceptance of human finitude that he gained through his heroic pressing of human limits. In Plato's *Symposium* the soul that beholds a beautiful body will move on to recognize that this reality of beauty is manifest in many bodies, since they participate in the beautiful. It is this beautiful and good that will draw one to try to gain it by imitating it and by being in its presence. *Erōs* is the unending desire for the true and the beautiful. This immortality of the soul is superior to the forms of immortality that come with (1) having offspring and living on in some attenuated form in them or (2) creating a name for oneself through one's virtuous life, heroic exploits, or exemplary productions. For the immortal soul, the beholder never merges with the beautiful and the good but enjoys a form of communion in which the erotic longing is fed so that it is a form of vitality rather than an enervating force.

Erōs *and the Sacred Boundaries of Person and Household*

Erōs was an important force shaping the sociopolitical structures of ancient Israel, Mesopotamia, and Greece. The primary purpose of sexual relations was reproduction. Extramarital sex that undercut the marriage bond and the integrity of household relationships was condemned in all three cultures. Same-sex activities were marginalized in Israel to liminal situations or were linked with transgressions that violated the sacred character of persons, households, and the land. In Mesopotamia same-sex activities were placed under the care of Ishtar and thus were allowed a place on the margins. However, the homosocial relationship between Enkidu and Gilgamesh receives an honored place in the tradition; this erotically charged relationship does not explicitly refer to sexual relations between them. Sexual relations that involved gender inversion were condemned in the Middle Assyrian Laws. In classical Athens pederasty was practiced in aristocratic circles and so comes to expression in Plato's *Symposium*. However, the critical stance of the dialogue toward pederasty tries to move the guide for the young beyond his own self-serving interests toward an examination of how his interest in improving the young is a participation in the good. The *Erōs* of the body is dominated by the *Erōs* of the soul in this Platonic-Socratic educational model.

The recognition that sexual activities apart from procreation could be generative of life finds support in the Song of Songs in Israel, in Ereshkigal's desire for her lover Nergal in Mesopotamia, and in those sexual relations that lead to a reality outside the self. The powerful passion of *erōs* is indispensable to life, yet its potential to be destructive requires that it be approached with circumspection.

Chapter Four

Virginity and Chastity: Feminine Ideals Integral to the Patriarchal Household

When creaking bones and the diminishing capacity to read fine print become realities for a person, one is reminded of how much the human body belongs to a sphere beyond an individual's control. This knowledge of being part of nature is presupposed throughout a day's routines but becomes an issue when the body does not function in the way to which one has become accustomed. One quickly recognizes, however, that this problematic character of the body has manifested itself in various guises throughout one's life. One also realizes that one's body has been a matter of concern not only for oneself but also for one's family and the communities of which one is a part. From the moment of birth when one is separated from one's mother, one is also dependent on mother and father and the network of relationships that shape the family's life. And so the adage that "I can never say who I am unless I can also say who we are" is grounded in the sociobiology of birth and nurture. The capacity of an individual to negotiate this interplay between the "I" and the "we" is vital to the common good. The intertwined character of the individual and the social identity of embodied beings means that within the matrix of social and natural relations one will need to maintain a measure of equilibrium and vitality if a meaningful life is to be lived.

The quest for a meaningful life in a body that is sliding towards death has led humans from the earliest times to come to terms with the invisible forces that traverse one's body and shape human existence. This quest for meaning unfolds within a cosmic context, which the peoples of ancient Israel, Mesopotamia, and Greece believed to consist of three levels: heaven, earth, and the underworld. For humans on earth, forces from all three levels impact their bodies daily and call upon them as agents to both accept and configure their place within the larger whole. Finding one's place can be seen as maintaining one's integrity within a dynamic whole in which constructive and destructive forces impinge upon one. A potent form of disequilibrium is defilement, where the matter that is out of place threatens one's sense of self or identity.[1] If this displaced matter and its residue are not properly identified and removed, a person could lose his or her sense of self either through neglect or misguided zeal. Sexual forces both within and outside persons can threaten the integrity of individuals and communities. A window for viewing the power of sexuality in the maintenance of personal and physical integrity is provided by the ideal and practice of virginity.

This chapter will begin by establishing a working definition of female virginity for ancient Israel, Mesopotamia, and Greece and posing the question of the extent to which sexual constraint for males assumed the form of virginity. Then texts from each culture will be examined to see how the household promoted the ideal of virginity and what social institutions outside the household, if any, were created to facilitate a life of abstinence from sexual relations. The following four questions will be addressed to the texts of each of the cultural traditions: (1) how did the household's protection of women maintain the integrity of the community? (2) how did the household try to keep matter in place and control its boundaries? (3) how did the society foster social equilibrium by urging male sexual constraint as a counterbalance to female virginity? and (4) to what extent did the patriarchal household respond to the constraints of the human condition without exploiting the marginalized?

Definition of Virginity

One of the more complete definitions of female virginity in the Old Testament is the account of the defeat the tribes of Israel visited upon the tribe of Benjamin in Judges 20–21. This narrative begins with an account of how a contingent of Israelite forces went out against the inhabitants of Jabesh-gilead because they had failed to send representatives to a tribal coalition assembled at Mizpah. The Israelite forces were given the following charge:

1. Mary Douglas, *Purity and Danger: An Analysis of the Concepts of Pollution and Taboo* (London: Routledge & Kegan Paul, 1966), 3–4.

> "Go, strike the residents of Jabesh-gilead with the edge of the sword, including the women and the children. This is the thing you shall do; every male and every woman that has had sexual intercourse with a male you shall place under the ban." They found among the residents of Jabesh-gilead four hundred young virgins (*naʿărâ bĕtûlôt*) who had never had sexual relations with a male (*ʾăšer lôʾ yādĕʿâ ʾîš lĕmiškab zākār*) and brought them to the camp at Shiloh in the land of Canaan. (Judg 21:10-12)

The dispute over the meaning of *bĕtûlâ* centers on whether the term itself means "young woman of marriageable age" or "virgin." If the former, then the clause "who had never slept with a man" is necessary in order to describe the woman as a virgin. But if *bĕtûlâ* itself means "virgin," then the clause is redundant and is perhaps used for emphasis.[2] Carolyn Pressler contends that *bĕtûlâ* must mean "virgin" in Lev 21:13-14, where the high priest is limited to taking a *bĕtûlâ* for a wife, and in Ezek 44:22, where a priest is limited to taking a *bĕtûlâ* of Israelite descent or a widow of an Israelite priest. If *bĕtûlâ* simply meant "girl of marriageable age," then these requirements for the high priest and priests would scarcely distinguish them from the average Israelite male.[3]

From an androcentric perspective a virgin is a young woman who has never had the sperm of a man within her. The improper spilling of semen defiles the young woman.[4] Mieke Bal claims that a person with this androcentric view believes that a daughter's coupling with a male severs her relationship with her father. Through this action she loses her "integrity, bodily wholeness, purity, cleanliness."[5] This male perspective on female virginity is not in accord with that of many feminist interpreters, who see the nubile stage as a transition point between *naʿărâ*, "a phase of near-ripeness," and *ʿalmâ*, "a married woman before her first pregnancy."[6] In this developmental schema the woman "who has not

2. Tikva Frymer-Kensky, "Virginity in the Bible," in *Gender and Law in the Hebrew Bible and the Ancient Near East*, *JSOTSup* 262, ed. Victor H. Matthews, Bernard M. Levinson, and Tikva Frymer-Kensky, 79–96 (Sheffield: Sheffield Academic Press, 1998), at 79; Gordon Wenham, "*Bĕtûlāh* 'A Girl of Marriageable Age,'" *VT* 22 (1972): 326–48; Carol Meyers, *Exodus* (Cambridge: Cambridge University Press, 2005), 194.

3. Carolyn Pressler, *The View of Women Found in the Deuteronomic Family Laws*, BZAW 216 (Berlin and New York: de Gruyter, 1993), 27.

4. Mieke Bal, *Death & Dissymmetry: The Politics of Coherence in the Book of Judges* (Chicago: University of Chicago Press, 1988), 72.

5. Ibid.

6. Ibid., 48; Peggy L. Day, "From the Child Is Born the Woman: The Story of Jephthah's Daughter," in *Gender and Difference in Ancient Israel*, ed. eadem, 58–74 (Minneapolis: Fortress

known a man" is one who has not yet borne a child rather than one who is sexually innocent.[7] Frymer-Kensky refers to this Israelite emphasis on premarital virginity as a form of "cultural supervaluation of virginity."[8] Bal argues that premarital virginity prevents young women from gaining the knowledge that comes with sexual experience: a knowledge that would trigger in them a sense of their autonomy and thus constitutes a threat to the patriarchal household.[9] Exum notes that "patriarchal literature, and thus the Bible in general, reflects the underlying attitude that a woman's sexuality is to be feared and thus carefully regulated. Patriarchy severs the relationship between eroticism and procreation."[10]

In Mesopotamia, the Sumerian term e-nu-gi$_4$-a, "virgin," is formed by adding the syllable –nu (the sign of the negative) to the word for "bride" (e-gi$_4$-a) so that a virgin is simply one who is not married. Such a one may have had sexual experience and still be described as an e-nu-gi$_4$-a.[11] The Akkadian term *batultu* (KI.SIKIL.TUR) is rendered by Jerrold Cooper as "a girl barely nubile to adolescent," which is a stage prior to *ardatu* (KI.SIKIL), "an older adolescent girl."Cooper writes that *ardatu* and *batultu* came to mean "virgin" since a young woman was expected to be sexually innocent at the time of marriage.[12] Marten Stol notes how there has been a scholarly debate over whether *batultu* means "girl of marriageable age" or "virgin," but he is emphatic that it means "virgin."[13] Martha Roth notes that in NB marriage contracts, in thirteen of forty-two contracts investigated the woman to be married is identified as a *batultu* and is almost certainly a virgin because she is often only about fourteen years old.[14] In the *Code of Hammurapi*, instead of an abstract term for

Press, 1989), at 59; cf. J. Cheryl Exum, *Tragedy and Biblical Narrative: Arrows of the Almighty* (Cambridge: Cambridge University Press, 1992), 67.

7. Bal, *Death & Dissymmetry*, 51.

8. Frymer-Kensky, "Virginity in the Bible," 82.

9. Bal, *Death & Dissymmetry*, 53.

10. Exum, *Tragedy and Biblical Narrative*, 68; see also Athalya Brenner, *The Intercourse of Knowledge: On Gendering Desire and 'Sexuality' in the Hebrew Bible*, Biblical Interpretation Series 26 (Leiden: Brill, 1997), 18, 29–30, 178.

11. Jerrold S. Cooper, "Virginity in Ancient Mesopotamia," in *Sex and Gender in the Ancient Near East: Proceedings of the 47th Rencontre Assyriologique Internationale, Helsinki, July 2–6, 2001, CRRAI* 47, ed. Simo Parpola and Robert M. Whiting, 91–112 (Helsinki: Neo-Assyrian Text Corpus Project, 2002), at 93.

12. Ibid., 91, 93.

13. Marten Stol, "Private Life in Ancient Mesopotamia," *CANE*, 485–501, at 489; idem, "Women in Mesopotamia," *JESHO* 38 (1995): 123–44, at 128.

14. Martha Roth, "Age at Marriage and the Household: A Study of Neo-Babylonian and Neo-Assyrian Forms," *Comparative Studies in Society and History* 29 (1987): 715-47, at 743.

"virginity," a negative formulation is used: "who has not known a man" (*ša zikaram lā idû*, *CH* 130).

In Greece a *parthenos* was a young woman who was not married and had not borne a child (i.e., a *gynē*).[15] At Olympia for certain athletic events the young women were divided into three groups: *parthenoi* ("unmarried women"), *nymphai* ("brides"), and *gynai* ("wives") (Pausanias 5.16.3).[16]

Giulia Sissa emphasizes that a young woman who had had premarital sexual encounters was expected to keep these secret. So while the term *parthenos* could refer to a girl who had had sexual relations and perhaps children, this crossing of the boundary from sexual innocence was not to be public knowledge and thus should be excluded from the definition of *parthenos*.[17] In light of her study of the virgin goddess Hestia, Eleanor Irwin concludes that for the Greeks "virginity by definition excluded sexual submission to a male."[18]

The concept of "virgin" for one who has not yet experienced sexual joining with another person is usually applied to females.[19] But the question may be posed whether this concept could be predicated of a male in the cultures of ancient Israel, Mesopotamia, and Greece. In such a case the male would be acting counterculturally by adopting a behavioral trait typically attributed to women. This ideal of male virginity arises centuries later in Christian circles, so that Stephen Benko offers the following transgendered definition of the Christian virgin: "someone who has not engaged in sexual activity, whether male or female."[20] Because such examples of male virginity in the record of ancient Israel, Mesopotamia, and Greece are almost nonexistent, it will be necessary, for the most part, to examine forms of temporary sexual restraint by males if

15. Giulia Sissa, *Greek Virginity*, trans. Arthur Goldhammer (Cambridge, MA: Harvard University Press, 1990), 76, 87–93.

16. Susan Guettel Cole, "Domesticating Artemis," in *The Sacred and the Feminine in Ancient Greece*, ed. Sue Blundell and Margaret Williamson, 27–43 (London and New York: Routledge, 1998), at 33.

17. Sissa, *Greek Virginity*, 98; David Cohen, *Law, Sexuality, and Society: The Enforcement of Morals in Classical Athens* (Cambridge: Cambridge University Press, 1994), 164.

18. Eleanor Irwin, "The Invention of Virginity on Olympus," in *Virginity Revisited: Configurations of the Unpossessed Body*, ed. Bonnie MacLachlan and Judith Fletcher, 13–23 (Toronto: University of Toronto Press, 2007), at 17, claims that a *parthenos* did not become identified as masculine or feminine prior to marriage but exhibited both masculine and feminine characteristics like the Amazons.

19. Anthony Giddens, *The Transformation of Intimacy: Sexuality, Love and Eroticism in Modern Societies* (Stanford, CA: Stanford University Press, 1992), 51.

20. Stephen Benko, *The Virgin Goddess: Studies in the Pagan and Christian Roots of Mariology*, Studies in the History of Religions 59 (Leiden and New York: Brill, 1993), 11.

we are to recognize that males refrained from sexual relationships as if they were virgins.

Israel. Virginity: Commitment to the Common Good or to the Patriarchal Good?

The household is a living web of relationships in which the joys and sorrows of the various parts impact the quality of life of the whole. The virgin body signified wholeness not only of the individual but also of the household. Thus the virginity of the daughters of a household became a symbol that marked the boundaries of a household and facilitated life-giving exchanges between households. Without marriage a household is not born or sustained. The practice of virginity was enjoined upon the young women of a household and so raises questions about the importance of sexual constraint by males in upholding the integrity of the household. A recurring question in the following section is whether the women gain a sense of belonging in the household through their contributions or are exploited by a male-dominated household structure. This section will examine these issues in the following four parts: (1) Female virginity was central to the honor of the patriarchal household, as shown in Deut 22:13-22, 27-28 and Genesis 34. (2) The bodily wholeness inherent in the practice of virginity finds an analogue in the practice of sexual purity enjoined by the regulations of Leviticus 15, 18–19. (3) The discipline of avoiding adultery as addressed in Genesis 39 and Proverbs 7 exemplifies a form of male sexual constraint continuous with what would be required of a male virgin. (4) The sacrifice of virginity falls heavily upon the young women of the household, as shown in Judg 11:29-40.

Virginity as a Sign of Individual and Communal Integrity

The patriarchal culture of ancient Israel expected that the daughters within a household would be virgins at the time of their marriage. Three laws in Deuteronomy 22 highlight the importance given to premarital virginity: vv. 13-19 prescribe a legal procedure for countering the slander spread by a husband who is dissatisfied with his new wife on the grounds that she was not a virgin at the time he married her; vv. 20-22 prescribe the punishment of stoning for a woman who was discovered to have forfeited her virginity prior to marriage; and vv. 28-29 legislate that a man who is caught having sexual relations with an unbetrothed woman must pay her father fifty shekels of silver and marry her without the option of divorce. The procedure outlined in vv. 13-19 would probably have been initiated by the father of the accused woman.[21] In this scenario it seems that the husband has spread rumors in the community that he had been hoodwinked by the father and daughter into believing that the woman was untainted by the semen of another man. He has claimed that on their wedding night he did not find "evidence of her virginity" (*bĕtûlîm*, v. 14): i.e., bloody sheets. Richard Nelson notes that

> it is well known (to moderns at least) that the absence of blood on the occasion of first intercourse proves nothing about virginity. Perhaps the intended effect of this law was to encourage parents to obtain and preserve the "evidence of virginity" and to discourage husbands from raising such a socially destructive charge.[22]

Since the husband's allegation proved to be unfounded, he was obliged to pay the father one hundred silver shekels (i.e., twice the bridewealth) and to remain married to the woman without the option of divorce. The monetary compensation suggests that the husband may have been trying to swindle the father into returning the bridewealth to the husband on the grounds that the bride was not a virgin as expected. With his deceitful charge exposed, the husband was obliged to take steps in restoring the honor of the father, the daughter, and their household.[23] But if the charge had proved to be true, then the woman would have been guilty of a crime (*nĕbālâ*, v. 21) that undermined the social order. Because she had experienced sexual intercourse while still under her father's authority, she had defiled her father's house and the community. Stoning by the men of the city was intended to purge this evil from the community.

Finally, the third law in this section (vv. 28-29) makes the claim that a man who has forced an unbetrothed Israelite woman to have sex has objectively changed her by taking away her virginity. The law prescribes that he bring her into his household as his wife and sustain her in perpetuity. The law does not state that the father of the woman would have the option to prevent this "rapist" from marrying his daughter; as stated, the law requires the father to accept the settlement of fifty shekels (cf. Exod 22:15-16).[24] From these three family laws dealing with a "young woman" (*naʿărâ*) we can conclude that her virginity was important not

21. Jon Berquist, *Controlling Corporeality* (New Brunswick, NJ: Rutgers University Press, 2002), 67; Frymer-Kensky, "Virginity in the Bible," 95.

22. Richard D. Nelson, *Deuteronomy*, OTL (Louisville: Westminster John Knox, 2002), 270.

23. Pressler, *The View of Women Found in the Deuteronomic Family Laws*, 29.

24. Nelson, *Deuteronomy*, 273.

only to her moral reputation as an individual but also to the integrity and viability of the father's household. From an economic standpoint her virginity assured a future husband that children borne by her within his household would have him as progenitor and thus be legitimate heirs to his property.[25]

If the foregoing Deuteronomic law concerning an unbetrothed woman accosted in a field (22:28-29) is applied to the case of Shechem's having sexual relations (*ʿinnâ*) with Dinah,[26] then it would seem that Shechem's desire to marry Dinah (Gen 34:3, 8) and the readiness of Hamor, Shechem's father, to pay a bridewealth (*mōhar*, Gen 34:12) in an amount as high as Jacob and his sons might set it, should have paved the way for the marriage of Dinah and Shechem.[27] Fleischman contends that Shechem departed from the usual Canaanite pattern of negotiating with the bride's family prior to taking her by following the less common Canaanite practice of "marriage-by-abduction, in which the groom, without the permission of the bride's parents, took her and had sexual intercourse with her to consummate the marriage." Then negotiations with the bride's family would take place.[28] As Fleishman explains, the people of Shechem did not regard Shechem's sexual actions as felonious; a just monetary compensation in terms of a dowry could redress the dishonor suffered by the bride's family.[29] But Jacob's sons objected that their sister Dinah could not marry an uncircumcised man; the value system of the Shechemites did not coincide with that of Jacob and his sons.[30] Jacob's sons deceitfully demanded that every man in Hamor's city undergo circumcision. Although circumcision was practiced at

25. Frymer-Kensky, "Virginity in the Bible," 81.

26. Nicholas Wyatt, "The Story of Dinah and Shechem," *UF* 22 (1990): 433–58, at 435–36, argues that the three verbs in Gen 34:2 (*lāqaḥ, šākab, ʿinnâ*) should be translated as referring not to rape, but to intercourse. Joseph Fleishman, "Why Did Simeon and Levi Rebuke Their Father in Genesis 34:31?" *JNSL* 26 (2000): 101–16, at 101–3, discusses the options for translating the verbs and concludes that Shechem's having intercourse with Dinah was an "outrage" (Gen 34:7) in the eyes of Jacob and his sons whether the action was rape or not.

27. With reference to Gen 34:12, *HALAT* 525, 618 defines *mōhar* as "Brautgeld" and *mattān* as "Gabe, Geschenck." However, Wyatt, "The Story of Dinah and Shechem," 438, n. 14, proposes on the basis of parallel terms in *KTU* 1.24 ([*trḫt*] and *mhr*) that Gen 34:12, 14 refer to Shechem's paying not only the brideprice/bridewealth (*mattān*) but also the dowry (*mōhar*).

28. Fleishman, "Why Did Simeon and Levi Rebuke Their Father?" 102–3.

29. Ibid., 105.

30. Ibid. David Cohen, *Law, Sexuality, and Society*, 185, refers to Isocrates (*Cyprians* 36), where revenge leading to civil strife is exacted to regain family honor lost through aggressive sexual relations against a family member in classical Greece.

various times by Egyptians, Edomites, and Sidonians, it became a mark of distinction for the Israelite male in the postexilic period.[31] In the Israelite tradition circumcision is clearly differentiated from castration, for no castrated male was to be allowed into the worshiping assembly (Lev 21:24; Deut 23:2).[32]

The wholeness of the circumcised male was to be complemented by the wholeness of the virginal female.[33] Thus the defilement (*ṭāmēʾ*, Gen 34:13, 27) Dinah had suffered at the hands of Shechem was regarded by her brothers as an outrage (*nĕbālâ*, Gen 34:7). However, instead of trying to become reconciled to the people of the land, the brothers secretly plan to purge the area of uncircumcised men so that they might occupy the land free from this foreign influence (cf. Deut 7:1-5).[34] After Simeon and Levi kill all the males who were immobilized by the pain of circumcision, the other brothers take the wives, children, and wealth of the citizens of Hamor's city (vv. 25-29). The brothers' goal of purging the area of non-Israelites was, from their viewpoint, a justification for lying in their negotiations with Hamor and Shechem. However, Jacob has serious misgivings about his sons' deceitful actions and fears reprisals by the other Canaanites and Perizzites in the area (v. 30).[35] The brothers, contrary

31. Daniel Block, *The Book of Ezekiel: Chapters 25–48* (Grand Rapids: Eerdmans, 1998), 218; Lawrence Boadt, *Ezekiel's Oracles against Egypt: A Literary and Philological Study of Ezekiel 29–32*, BibOr 37 (Rome: Biblical Institute Press, 1980), 123, 162–63. Wyatt, "The Story of Dinah and Shechem," 438, argues that circumcision in the earlier version of the story would have been an expected premarital ritual that the father-in-law would have required of a future son-in-law. Daniel Boyarin, *Carnal Israel: Reading Sex in Talmudic Culture* (Berkeley: University of California Press, 1993), 7, notes that in the subsequent centuries, reaching into Graeco-Roman times, circumcision localized "sexuality, genealogy, and ethnic specificity in bodily practice."

32. Berquist, *Controlling Corporeality*, 37, sees a contradiction between the practice of circumcision as an entrance rite to the worshiping assembly and the exclusion of sexually mutilated individuals from that assembly.

33. John Goldingay, "The Significance of Circumcision," *JSOT* 88 (2000): 3–18, at 7, argues that circumcision became a sign aimed at "the disciplining of procreation, of sexual activity itself, and of masculinity." Alternatively, Meir Malul, *Knowledge, Control, and Sex: Studies in Biblical Thought, Culture, and Worldview* (Tel-Aviv–Jaffa: Archaeological Center Publication, 2002), 339, 408, claims that this premarital ritual of exposing the male element was aimed at giving it greater visibility as a symbol of patriarchal authority.

34. Frymer-Kensky, "Virginity in the Bible," 91; Fleishman, "Why Did Simeon and Levi Rebuke Their Father?" 107. Berquist, *Controlling Corporeality*, 100, notes that this purging shares features of the *ḥerem* that aims to prepare a territory for Israelite occupation (Josh 2:1-14).

35. Frymer-Kensky, "Virginity in the Bible," 91; Fleishman, "Why Did Simeon and Levi Rebuke Their Father?" 107; Deborah L. Ellens, *Women in the Sex Texts of Leviticus and*

to the wishes of Jacob (cf. Gen 49:5-7), choose to restore the honor of Jacob's household by demonstrating that they can maintain the boundaries of the community.[36] However, instead of this violent reprisal raid, the honor of their household could have been restored, as Deut 22:28-29 stipulates, through the payment of the bridewealth, the option Jacob appears to have chosen.[37]

Virginity and Bodily Wholeness

The violation of a woman's virginity is an act that cannot be reversed. Restoration of the woman, the household, and the community can only come about through adaptation to her objectively changed condition. This ideal of the bodily wholeness of the virgin parallels the regulations for bodily wholeness mapped out in Leviticus 15. The concern of Leviticus 15 is to monitor genital emissions and make provision for how the body can once again be made whole and presentable before YHWH. A woman who is menstruating is expected to stay at home for seven days and be careful to identify the chairs or bed she uses, because whatever she sits or lies upon will contract her uncleanness and have the potential to communicate it to another person (Lev 15:19-23). For a man who has an emission of semen, he must bathe and remain away from the sanctuary until sunset; any cloth or object made from animal skins upon which the semen falls shall likewise be washed and kept away from the sanctuary until evening (15:16-17). For those cases involving abnormal discharges, the man (15:2-12) or the woman (15:25-27) is highly contagious and must take special care to contain and remove the impurity (15:13-15, 27-30). Jonathan Klawans, following the lead of Howard Eilberg-Schwartz, argues that the "intensity" of the impurity is proportional to the controllability of the emission.[38] That is, the emission of semen by

---

Deuteronomy: A Comparative Conceptual Analysis, Library of Hebrew Bible/Old Testament Studies 458 (New York and London: T & T Clark, 2008), 197.

36. Fleishman, "Why Did Simeon and Levi Rebuke Their Father?" 109–10, claims that Simeon and Levi, whose mother Leah was also the mother of Dinah, rebelled against Jacob's authority in taking vengeance on behalf of their sister and regarded a compromise as treating their sister "like a whore" (Gen 34:31). On the contagion of dishonor see Mary Douglas, *Leviticus as Literature* (New York: Oxford University Press, 1999), 146–47.

37. Frymer-Kensky, "Virginity in the Bible," 90–91; Fleishman, "Why Did Simeon and Levi Rebuke Their Father?" 108.

38. Jonathan Klawans, "Pure Violence: Sacrifice and Defilement in Ancient Israel," *HTR* 94 (2001): 133–55, at 144; Howard Eilberg-Schwartz, *Savage Judaism: An Anthropology of Israelite Religion and Ancient Judaism* (Bloomington: Indiana University Press, 1990), 195.

the man is more controllable than the menstrual flow by the woman, with the result that the man needs only to wash and remain away from sancta until evening. But the woman must be cautious about communicating her impurity for seven days, and then on the eighth day she must bring to the priest a bird for a purification offering and a bird for a burnt offering. The discipline of remaining faithful to these purificatory expectations and procedures tends to make one's daily life into an offering to God analogous to the offering of an animal in sacrifice.[39] In both cases one's own life or the life of the animal must be characterized by physical wholeness in order to be presentable to God (Lev 1:3, 10; 15:15, 30).

Control over the portals of the body is a physical, ritual discipline that has an ethical analogue in the laws mapped out in Leviticus 18–20. At the midpoint of this central section of the Holiness Code (Leviticus 17–26) is God's command: "You must be holy as I the Lord your God am holy" (Lev 19:2).[40] This command is illustrated in a series of laws among which are those that aim at eliminating syncretistic worship (18:3, 21; 20:2-6) and at maintaining proper boundaries among members of a household (18:6-20; 20:10-21). The concentric circles of relatedness in the Israelite community (Fig. 4.1) link the individual to the household and to the larger community and show the interdependent character of individual and communal responsibility. If the Israelites maintain physical and moral integrity they will be taking essential steps toward imitating YHWH that will permit them to live on his land in his presence (Lev 18:24-30; 20:22-26).

To enter into the cultic sphere and draw closer to the symbolic space in which YHWH's presence was concentrated demanded a higher measure of imitation of YHWH than daily life could normally sustain.[41] The distinctive character of this encounter with YHWH is captured in the narrative of the Hebrews' arrival at the base of Mount Sinai after their flight from Egypt (Exodus 19). YHWH commanded Moses to "instruct and consecrate (*qiddaštām*) the people" (v. 10) so that they might be ready for his appearance on the mountain on the third day. They were to wash their clothes, avoid touching the mountain, and refrain from sexual rela-

39. Douglas, *Leviticus as Literature*, 188, claims that the rules on contamination and uncleanness in Leviticus treat the body and the tabernacle as "analogues of one another." See also Dale Launderville, *Spirit and Reason: The Embodied Character of Ezekiel's Symbolic Thinking* (Waco, TX: Baylor University Press, 2007), 105–6.

40. Jacob Milgrom, *Leviticus: A Book of Ritual and Ethics* (Minneapolis: Fortress Press, 2004), 7; Douglas, *Leviticus as Literature*, 52, 54, 234–35.

41. Klawans, "Pure Violence," 142–43.

Embodied Relatedness of the Israelite Community

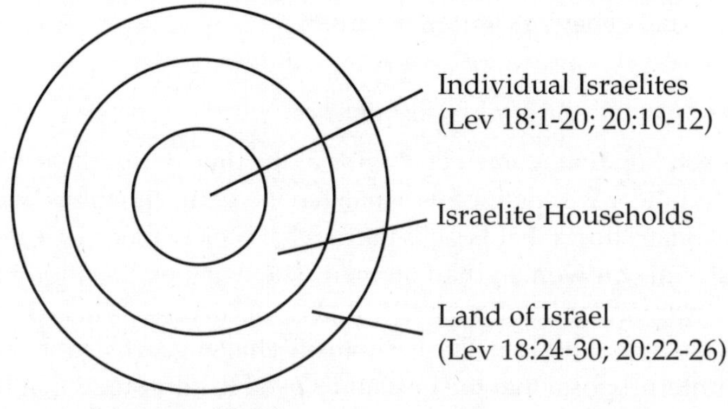

Leviticus 18–20

Fig. 4.1.

tions with a woman (vv. 11-15). The stipulation that sex was to be kept out of the sanctuary can be seen as a form of imitating YHWH, who transcends sex and gender.[42]

The suspension of sexual activity for limited times in order to participate in the cult of YHWH is a workable practice. The extension of the time of this sexual abstinence for women until the time of marriage would have been more demanding; however, girls typically married at about the age of fourteen. The channeling of male and female sexuality required more than a set of norms articulated in legal codes; institutional practices in the household and community needed to be maintained in order for the vision of the legal code to be enacted.[43] Jon Berquist describes Israel's way of approaching sexuality as one in which sexuality was treated as an integrative force within a network of power relations that was configured according to the needs of particular groups. He contrasts this approach with one that sees sexuality primarily as an unruly force requiring regulation by norms, which would at times be violated.[44] Berquist's view can be seen as defending the constructive potential of the Israelite system for channeling sexuality against charges

42. Ibid., 142. Eilberg-Schwartz's claim (*Savage Judaism*, 145) that YHWH had a phallus that the editors of the Hebrew Bible were reluctant to allow in print is, according to Mark S. Smith, *The Origins of Biblical Monotheism: Israel's Polytheistic Background and the Ugaritic Texts* (New York: Oxford University Press, 2001), 92–93, without foundation in the text and runs counter to the way YHWH is described from the earliest to the latest levels of the biblical texts.

43. Berquist, *Controlling Corporeality*, 162–65.

44. Ibid., 78, 106.

like that of Foucault, who argues that cultural efforts to map out the terrain of sexuality are defensive measures that inevitably reduce the varieties of sexual behaviors within nature.[45]

Male Sexual Constraint: An Understated Practice

The expectation that women be virgins at the time of marriage and the fact that adultery was defined as a man having sexual relations with a married woman shows that Israel's patriarchal society placed greater sexual constraints on women than on men. The usual explanation for more restrictive standards for women is that it was necessary to be sure of the paternity of the children. Frymer-Kensky challenges this rationale with the counterproposal that the husband's need to be assured that he is the progenitor of the offspring who will inherit his estate could be met by designating any children born in the first nine months of marriage to the wife's natal household.[46] However, the rationale concerning inheritance is insufficient to account for Israel's requirement of premarital chastity. Frymer-Kensky refers to Freud's ruminations about incestuous feelings between father and daughter and sees the possessiveness of the father as a significant factor in his desire that his daughter be joined to no other male prior to her marriage.[47] If males were not similarly constrained in their premarital and extramarital sexual relations, the charge that Israel's laws on virginity and adultery reflect the male's urge to dominate gains more force. If the only legitimate place for sexual relations for women is within marriage, one might argue that in terms of fairness and partnership between the sexes the same restriction should apply to males. If the move to level the playing field were to designate the requirements for female chastity as applicable to both genders, then males would be required to be virgins prior to marriage and exclusively faithful to one wife during marriage. The identification of constraints on male sexuality that are in continuity with the practice of virginity is the subject of the following examination.

At the beginning of the story of Joseph's rise to power in Egypt (Genesis 39–41) the wife of his Egyptian master Potiphar, "a court official

45. Michel Foucault, *The History of Sexuality*, vol. 1: *An Introduction*, trans. Robert Hurley (New York: Pantheon, 1978), 11–12; Berquist, *Controlling Corporeality*, 96; Boyarin, *Carnal Israel*, 11.

46. Frymer-Kensky, "Virginity in the Bible," 81.

47. Ibid., 85.

of Pharaoh" (*sārîs*, Gen 39:1),[48] repeatedly tries to seduce him. She begins her seduction by gazing at him, a visual form of sexual connection (Gen 39:7). Then she addresses him with the succinct, direct imperative "lie with me," a phrase she will repeat three more times in the course of the story in her efforts to have him accede to her desire (vv. 7, 10, 12, 14). Joseph resists her initial entreaty with a rather lengthy protest in self-defense:

> Look, my master does not oversee along with me what goes on in the household. Everything he possesses he has put under my control. He does not act as one greater in this household than me. He has not held back anything from me except you, because you are his wife. So how could I do this great evil and sin against God? (Gen 39:8-9)

Erotic desire is not constituted simply by feeling; it also has cognitive content.[49] Thus the reasons Joseph provides for refraining from having sex with Potiphar's wife are (1) ingratitude and disloyalty to his master and her husband and (2) sin (*ḥaṭṭāʾt*, v. 9) against God. This is the only mention of God by a character in the story, although Yhwh is referred to by the narrator seven times in the frame of the story (vv. 2, 3, 5, 21, 23).[50] Joseph identifies the potential adulterous act as "this great evil" (*hārāʿâ haggĕdōlâ hazzōʾt*, v. 9); it seems he regards this transgression as a taboo similar to the prohibition against eating the fruit of the tree of the knowledge of good and evil (Gen 2:17; 3:3-7, 11). If he succumbs to her temptation he will have crossed a threshold in his relationship with his master over which he will not be able to return.

Joseph resists her, but she is persistent day after day (v. 10). Finally she increases her aggressiveness one day, seizes his garment as he flees, and tries to stir up xenophobia in the servants in order to gain their support against Joseph by saying: "my husband brought us a Hebrew to toy with us" (v. 14). She then charges that Joseph had tried to have sexual relations with her (v. 15). When the master returns that evening she repeats her story to him, but alters her phrasing in her appeal to the master:

48. Theodore Jennings, *Jacob's Wound: Homoerotic Narrative in the Literature of Ancient Israel* (New York: Continuum, 2006), 187–88, argues that Potiphar is a married eunuch who can have sexual relations but not offspring.

49. Martha Nussbaum, *The Fragility of Goodness: Luck and Ethics in Greek Tragedy and Philosophy*, rev. ed. (Cambridge: Cambridge University Press, 2001), xviii.

50. W. Lee Humphreys, *Joseph and His Family: A Literary Study* (Columbia: University of South Carolina Press, 1988), 120.

"The Hebrew slave, whom you brought us, came to me to toy with me" (v. 17). The wife is shrewd, while Potiphar is impulsive.[51] She effectively places Joseph in a dilemma from which there is no exit.[52] His master has been detached from the affairs of the household (v. 8). Even though Potiphar is furious at Joseph for this alleged adultery, he does not have Joseph put to death but rather places him in one of Pharaoh's prisons (v. 20), for which he has oversight.[53]

Joseph's sexual restraint stands in marked contrast to the loose behavior of Judah toward Tamar (Gen 38:16-18). Judah had married a Canaanite wife (v. 2) who bore him three sons (vv. 3-5) and then passed away (v. 12). He is portrayed in this story as an unmarried man who would have sex with prostitutes at festival times (vv. 13-16). Unbeknownst to him, however, he has sex with his daughter-in-law Tamar (v. 18). Since she is a member of Judah's household and obliged to produce an heir for her deceased husband—Judah's son Er—Judah is expected to keep her from illicit sexual relations (v. 24). When Tamar brings forward Judah's signet, cord, and staff she demonstrates that he is the father of the child she is carrying (vv. 25-26). Bill T. Arnold points out that in some cultures a father-in-law was obliged to perform the levirate if the deceased husband's brother did not do so.[54] From Judah's perspective this way of fulfilling the levirate was not a route he would have chosen. In light of Judah's embarrassment at Tamar's success in becoming pregnant by him he appears in a less favorable light than Joseph, whose sexual restraint makes him appear wiser and more circumspect.

This profile of a young man who has the potential to rise through the administrative ranks if he avoids missteps along the way is the subject of Proverbs 1–9.[55] Carol Newsom claims that the father figure in these chapters gives voice to the values of the landed aristocrat or the senior bureaucrat.[56] Within Proverbs 1–9, chapter 7 constitutes the tenth and final lecture delivered by the father/teacher to his sons/pupils and is

51. Ibid., 72.

52. Susan Tower Hollis, "The Woman in Ancient Examples of the Potiphar's Wife Motif, K2111," in *Gender and Difference in Ancient Israel*, 28–42, at 29, 38.

53. Bill T. Arnold, *Genesis* (Cambridge: Cambridge University Press, 2008), 333, n. 598, notes that because Potiphar is "captain of the guard" (Gen 39:1) he is responsible for overseeing Pharaoh's prison (Gen 40:7; 41:12).

54. Ibid., 327; cf. Harry Hoffner, "Hittite Laws," *COS* 2, 19:118 §193.

55. Richard Clifford, *Proverbs*, OTL (Louisville: Westminster John Knox, 1999), 2.

56. Carol A. Newsom, "Woman and the Discourse of Patriarchal Wisdom: A Study of Proverbs 1–9," in *Gender and Difference in Ancient Israel*, 142–60, at 144; Raymond C. Van Leeuwen, "Liminality and Worldview in Proverbs 1–9," *Semeia* 50 (1990): 111–44, at 113.

the fourth of five explicit warnings about the forbidden woman (Prov 2:16-19; 5:1-23; 6:20-35; 9:13-18).[57] The forbidden woman is "the primary image of otherness"; she is "a figure of ambivalence, both frightening and attractive."[58] The teacher relates an incident that he observed from his window as he looked down on the street below. Youths were congregated there in the twilight of the evening. Then a woman, dressed like a prostitute, came toward one of them. With her frantic movements and loud manner she tried to lure him to have sex with her. She noted that she had just completed a vow and so was celebrating it with a banquet. Her husband was gone on a long journey.[59] The youth succumbed. The teacher described this simple youth as one who "goes like an ox brought to the slaughter or edges[60] like a stag toward the net[61]" (7:22). He thinks he is going to enjoy a banquet, but little does he know that he will be the victim.[62] So the teacher concludes his lecture with the exhortation

> And now, children, listen to me, and pay attention to the words of my mouth. Do not let your hearts turn to her ways; do not stray into her paths. For many are those she has brought down and vast in number are all her victims. Her house is comprised of the ways to Sheol, realities that descend to the chambers of death. (vv. 24-27)

This example story is about two different kinds of love: love of sexual pleasure versus love of wisdom. Clifford notes that, according to this story, if one loves wisdom one will be protected against the deceptions of the forbidden woman (7:4-5).[63] Wisdom, personified as a woman, gives two long speeches (1:20-33; 8:1-36) in which she "invites people into a long-term, marriage-like relationship with her. The relationship is founded on her truthfulness, bounty, and closeness to God."[64]

57. Clifford, *Proverbs*, 84.

58. Newsom, "Woman and the Discourse of Patriarchal Wisdom," 148. Neil Walls, *Desire, Discord, and Death: Approaches to Ancient Near Eastern Myth* (Boston: American Schools of Oriental Research, 2001), 137–38, compares the foreign woman of Proverbs 7 to Ereshkigal in "Nergal and Ereshkigal" as a dangerous woman who threatens to seduce and lead one to death.

59. For an alternative reading of the *ʾiššâ zārâ* in Prov 7:5 as an unmarried woman see Herbert Marbury, "The Strange Woman in Persian Yehud: A Reading of Proverbs 7," in *Approaching Yehud: New Approaches to the Study of the Persian Period*, ed. Jon L. Berquist, 167–82 (Atlanta: Society of Biblical Literature, 2007), at 169–71.

60. Read *kĕʿakkēs*.

61. Read *môsēr ʾayyāl*.

62. Clifford, *Proverbs*, 86; Van Leeuwen, "Liminality and Worldview," 128.

63. Clifford, *Proverbs*, 85–86; Van Leeuwen, "Liminality and Worldview," 129–30.

64. Clifford, *Proverbs*, 28; cf. Van Leeuwen, "Liminality and Worldview," 131.

In contrast to the foolish young man in Prov 7:7-23, Joseph resists the persistent advances of Potiphar's wife and eventually wins an honored position within the kingdom of Pharaoh. The folk motif informing the story of "Joseph and Potiphar's Wife" portrays the hero as one who survives the dilemma created by a seductress within a household and then is able to rise to a national level of leadership.[65] Joseph's capacity to exercise sexual restraint is due in no small part to his fear of the Lord (Gen 39:9). The narrator emphasizes the way in which YHWH was present with Joseph and made him prosper (Gen 39:5-6, 21-23). The pursuit of wisdom heralded in Proverbs 1–9 likewise aims to have the divine presence guide one on the path of life (Prov 8:35).

The marriage-like relationship one enters with Woman Wisdom has an erotic dimension: "love" (8:17), "delighting in" (8:30-31), a man watching and waiting at her gate (8:34).[66] The person who pursues wisdom is not repressing the erotic component of life but is directing it toward a divine, transcendent source that comes to abide in the human sphere in the form of Woman Wisdom. Sexual renunciation, like that practiced by the Hebrews at the base of Mount Sinai in Exodus 19, is a way to prepare oneself to receive the divine presence. Given the trouble Judah experienced through searching out a prostitute in the story of Tamar, it seems that Genesis 38 and 39 combine to promote the message that sexual relations outside of marriage, whether with an adulteress or a prostitute, endanger a man's reputation and life. These chapters promote the ideal of a chaste wisdom figure in Joseph, whose response in a time of temptation provides a model of the character and discipline necessary for one aspiring to live as a male virgin.

The Purpose of the Sacrifice of Virginity

The sacrifice required of virgins by the patriarchal households and the Yahwistic faith must have elicited resistance and protest from women. Because the hierarchy of the patriarchal household was firmly entrenched in Israelite culture, protests by women would have had to be indirect to have an impact. The story of the sacrifice of Jephthah's daughter in Judges 11 has moved generations of readers to question Jephthah's resoluteness in fulfilling his vow. Why would Jephthah sacrifice the first living being that crossed the threshold of his house to greet him on his return from a victory over the Ammonites (vv. 30-36)? Jephthah mourns

65. Hollis, "The Woman in Ancient Examples of the Potiphar's Wife Motif," 37.

66. Newsom, "Woman and the Discourse of Patriarchal Wisdom," 156.

when he sees that his daughter is the first one to meet him, but he states nevertheless: "I am not able to retract my vow" (v. 35). Susan Niditch wonders why this particular vow (*nēder*, Judg 11:30) must be completed, whereas the oath (*ḥay-*Yhwh, 1 Sam 14:39) Saul took concerning his son Jonathan—that whoever broke the fast imposed on the Israelite troops would die—was not carried out (1 Sam 14:43-45).[67] But a *nēder* ("vow") is a solemn promise made directly to the Lord: "If you indeed will place the Ammonites under my power, then . . ." (Judg 11:30),[68] whereas the *ḥay* ("oath") expressed by Saul in 1 Sam 14:24 has the form of an imprecation without direct address to God: "Cursed (*ʾārûr*) be the one who . . . ."[69] The higher degree of solemnity of a vow (*nēder*) over an oath (*ḥay*) calls for a higher level of commitment in fulfilling it (cf. Deut 23:22-24; Prov 7:14).[70]

The narrative in Judges 11, in contrast to every other passage mentioning human sacrifice in Israel, does not condemn the sacrifice of Jephthah's daughter but rather presents it as one that seems to have been accepted by Yhwh.[71] This acquiescence to human sacrifice as an unfortunate but necessary step under the circumstances makes the narrative all the more troubling to the reader.[72] It poses an enduring protest to the sacrifice of Jephthah's daughter, but it can also be seen to raise questions about the ways in which patriarchal authority exploits women.[73]

67. Susan Niditch, *Judges*, OTL (Louisville: Westminster John Knox, 2008), 134.

68. Jacques Berlinerblau, *The Vow and the 'Popular Religious Groups' of Ancient Israel: A Philological and Sociological Inquiry*, *JSOTSup* 210 (Sheffield: Sheffield Academic Press, 1996), 86–87.

69. Heintz-Dieter Neef, "Jephta und seine Tochter (JDC. XI 29-40)," *VT* 49 (1999): 206–17, at 217. David Marcus, *Jephthah and His Vow* (Lubbock, TX: Texas Tech University Press, 1985), 18–19, 55, notes the similarity in the structure of Jephthah's vow with the other four descriptions of a vow (Gen 28:20-22; Num 21:2; 1 Sam 1:11; 2 Sam 15:7-8).

70. Cf. Karel van der Toorn, "Prostitution (OT)," *ABD* 5:511–12.

71. Niditch, *Judges*, 133; Mikael Sjöberg, *Wrestling with Textual Violence: The Jephthah Narrative in Antiquity and Modernity* (Sheffield: Phoenix Press, 2006), 61, 63. Exum, *Tragedy and Biblical Narrative*, 60, notes: "In Judges 11, God neither requires nor rejects human sacrifice."

72. Thomas Römer, "Why Would the Deuteronomists Tell About the Sacrifice of Jephthah's Daughter?" *JSOT* 77 (1998): 27–38, at 37, argues that a post-Deuteronomic redactor added this story of the sacrifice of Jephthah's daughter in light of the sacrifice of Iphigeneia in the Greek tradition in order to counterpoint the Deuteronomic theology of retribution and highlight the ambiguity operative in divine justice.

73. Bal, *Death & Dissymmetry*, 50–51.

The narrative does not say that Jephthah actually sacrificed his daughter.[74] As with Iphigeneia in Euripides' *Iphigeneia at Tauris*, she may have been spared and a substitute provided. Medieval Jewish exegetes interpreted this "sacrifice" as one in which Jephthah commits his daughter to a life of perpetual virginity.[75] As she is Jephthah's only offspring, this would deprive him of a biological heir.[76]

The annual four-day ritual (Judg 11:40) that the narrative says was carried out to mourn the virginity of Jephthah's daughter (11:37-39) suggests that this remembering of Jephthah's daughter was not merely a matter of the literary record but also lived on in the practices of the communities of Gilead—even though it is not attested elsewhere in the OT or in extant extrabiblical texts.[77] Mikael Sjöberg argues that this ritual did not simply serve to keep the memory of Jephthah's daughter alive; more important, it protested the way in which the daughter lost her virginity (*bĕtûlâ*, vv. 37, 39). Sjöberg claims that Jephthah "sacrificed" his daughter by arranging her marriage; therefore this ritual marked the rite of passage of a young woman from her status as a virgin in her father's house to that of a wife in the house of her husband.[78] This transition seems to have been framed in terms of a lament because a young woman was compelled to marry the man her father approved. According to the narrative this memorial rite or "protest ritual" was initially celebrated by the daughter of Jephthah and her female companions on a mountain free from male observation (vv. 37-38); this was a place apart where these young women could give expression to a view of reality alternative to that of the patriarchal household.[79] This interpretation, however, would be more compelling if there was a reference in the narrative to the actual transfer of the daughter through marriage; there is no mention of a hus-

74. The daughter inherits the patrimony if a father has no sons (Num 27:1-11). See Neef, "Jephta und seine Tochter," 206–7; David Marcus, *Jephthah and His Vow*, 9–11.

75. Ibid., 8–9.

76. Naomi Steinberg, "The Problem of Human Sacrifice in War: An Analysis of Judges 11," in *On the Way to Nineveh: Studies in Honor of George M. Landes*, ed. Stephen L. Cook and Sarah C. Winter, 114–35 (Atlanta: Scholars Press, 1999), at 128, argues that Jephthah's sacrifice of his daughter "creates and maintains the descent line between Yahweh and Israel."

77. Exum, *Tragedy and Biblical Narrative*, 67.

78. Sjöberg, *Wrestling with Textual Violence*, 65; cf. Day, "From the Child Is Born the Woman, 58–74, at 58, 60.

79. Niditch, *Judges*, 135; Sjöberg, *Wrestling with Textual Violence*, 66–68.

band for the daughter.[80] Thus the daughter's mourning of her virginity could just as well refer to the fact that her father's vow confined her for the rest of her life to a status of perpetual virginity in which his beloved daughter remains within his own household.[81]

Another notable counterpoint to the legitimacy of the authority of the patriarchal household over marriage and childbirth is the place of Jephthah in this account. He was initially cast out of his father's household by his brothers on the grounds that he was the son of a prostitute (vv. 1-3).[82] But immediately the story shows the Gileadites imploring the strong warrior Jephthah to return to defend them against the Ammonites (vv. 5-6). Thus the control the patriarchal household exercises over the legitimacy of offspring and the virginity of wives and daughters is limited and operates within a larger sphere of reality that can overrule patriarchal priorities.

The narrative of Judges 11 keeps open the question whether the curtailment of women's sexual autonomy by the patriarchal household is in accord with the constraints of the human condition or is merely a power play by men.[83] Exum calls attention to the ambiguous character of YHWH's silence in the narrative.[84] She notes that the "spirit of YHWH" comes upon Jephthah just before he makes his regrettable vow (v. 29). This raises questions about who gave expression to this vow.[85] Was it Jephthah? Or was it YHWH speaking through Jephthah?

Jephthah was a negotiator.[86] He made the Gileadites pledge that he would be both commander (*qāṣin*, v. 11) and head (*rōʾš*, vv. 8, 9, 11) over them (1) if they brought him back from exile and (2) if YHWH granted him victory over the Ammonites. Here Jephthah is grounding his future

80. I am indebted to my student Joan Spring for her insightful critique of Sjöberg's interpretation.

81. Marcus, *Jephthah and His Vow*, 50–51, summarizes ten points in support of the view that Jephthah consecrated his daughter to a life of perpetual celibacy and juxtaposes these to eight points in favor of seeing Jephthah's sacrifice of his daughter as an act he literally carried out.

82. Sjöberg, *Wrestling with Textual Violence*, 53–55.

83. Carole R. Fontaine, "Hosea," in *A Feminist Companion to the Latter Prophets*, ed. Athalya Brenner, 40–59 (Sheffield: Sheffield Academic Press, 1993), at 54.

84. Exum, *Tragedy and Biblical Narrative*, 59.

85. Ibid., 46–47, 49–50; Sjöberg, *Wrestling with Textual Violence*, 51, 63. Steinberg, "The Problem of Human Sacrifice in War," 118–19, notes that the spirit of YHWH explains Jephthah's feeling of communion with YHWH—perhaps a linking of the human and divine levels in terms of kinship.

86. Exum, *Tragedy and Biblical Narrative*, 54; Sjöberg, *Wrestling with Textual Violence*, 58–60.

authority over the Gileadites on (1) human election by the elders and (2) divine election through military victory. When Jephthah sends messengers to the Ammonite king he tries to negotiate peace with them through a lengthy discourse on how YHWH has chosen Israel to inherit the land of Gilead (vv. 12-27). Because of Jephthah's strong investment in his skills as a warrior and rhetorician, perhaps YHWH moved Jephthah to make his vow in order to punish him for encroaching on divine sovereignty through his efforts to become a kinglike ruler in Gilead.[87] The necessity imposed on Jephthah for carrying out this vow would make him aware of how dependent he was on YHWH. Niditch notes that "implicit in the war vows in Num 21:2-3 and Judg 11:30 are threads in this deep mythological understanding of the way life works."[88] Costly sacrifices seemed to have to be made to a higher power in order for life to go forward. In light of Deut 23:22-24 (cf. Qoh 5:3-4; Prov 20:25), once Jephthah uttered the vow he had no choice but to carry it out.[89] Jephthah "sacrificed" —literally or figuratively— his daughter to YHWH in the hope that this would strengthen his bond with YHWH.[90]

Jephthah's daughter has no name. She is a virgin, that is, one who "had not experienced sexual intercourse with a man" (v. 39). Now she accedes readily to the costly reality of the vow her father has made and protests only by asking for a delay of implementation of the vow in order to lament with her female companions on the mountains. Her demeanor openly supports the patriarchal ideology. Yet when she and her companions withdraw to the mountains they have the potential to work together to redefine patriarchy.[91]

Another nameless woman who is sacrificed in response to patriarchal values is the concubine (*pîlegeš*, 19:1) of the Levite from the hill country of Ephraim in Judges 19. She herself is not a virgin but is paired with the virgin daughter (*bittî habbĕtûlâ*, v. 24) of the elderly Ephraimite who gives them emergency lodging in Gibeah.[92] When a Benjaminite mob converges on the Ephraimite's house and demands that he hand the Levite traveler

87. Exum, *Tragedy and Biblical Narrative*, 48; Sjöberg, *Wrestling with Textual Violence*, 60–63. Phyllis Trible, *Texts of Terror: Literary-Feminist Readings of Biblical Narratives* (Philadelphia: Fortress Press, 1984), 97, claims that Jephthah made this vow on his own, which is an act of unfaithfulness because it tries to manipulate YHWH.

88. Niditch, *Judges*, 133; cf. Neef, "Jephta und seine Tochter," 209–10.

89. Ibid., 215–16; Berlinerblau, *The Vow and the 'Popular Religious Groups' of Ancient Israel*, 87.

90. Niditch, *Judges*, 134.

91. Exum, *Tragedy and Biblical Narrative*, 66, 69; Bal, *Death & Dissymetry*, 67.

92. Ibid., 92.

over to them so that they might rape him, the elderly Ephraimite offers them his virgin daughter and the Levite's concubine (19:24). This costly proposal on the part of the Ephraimite shows that he believes the degradation his Levite guest would suffer would outweigh that which threatens his daughter and the Levite's concubine.[93] However, respect for the laws of hospitality is not sufficient to explain the elderly Ephraimite's choice. He wants to prevent homosexual rape, which he labels "this sacrilege" (*hanněbālâ hazzōʾt*, v. 23). Eventually he gives them the Levite's concubine, whom they abuse so severely that she dies the next morning (vv. 25-26). This crime of rape and murder leads to civil war between a coalition of the Israelite tribes and the Benjaminites as the Israelites try to "root out this evil[94] from Israel" (20:13). According to the logic of the narrative, the offering of the concubine substituted a less potent form of defilement for a more potent one—namely, the severe defilement that would have come upon Israel through the rape of the Levite. In the patriarchal society of Israel the defilement brought about by homosexual rape was more severe than that incurred by heterosexual rape. One explanation for the severity of this crime is that the perpetrator treated a man as if he were a woman.[95] Such gender reversal—a collapsing of the fundamental distinction between man and woman according to the Priestly perspective (Lev 18:22)—would unleash a sense of cosmic chaos.[96] Another explanation is that homosexual rape humiliates the victim by treating him as if he were a woman prisoner of war who was raped; in other words, the rape is a power play.[97] However, the sense of chaos is unleashed in an even more virulent form with the Levite's dismemberment of his concubine's body, by which he responds to the dishonor shown him by the treatment of his concubine and summons the other Israelite tribes to purge this evil in Gibeah from their midst (Judg 19:29-30).[98]

93. Ibid., 92–93; Niditch, *Judges*, 193. Trible, *Texts of Terror*, 74, emphasizes the callous disregard of the old man and the master toward these two women who are offered up to satisfy the desires of males.

94. Read *hārāʿâ*.

95. Ken Stone, "Gender and Homosexuality in Judges 19: Subject-Honor, Object-Shame?" *JSOT* 67 (1995): 87–107, at 96–98.

96. Brenner, *The Intercourse of Knowledge*, 133; S. Tamar Kamionkowski, *Gender Reversal and Cosmic Chaos: A Study of the Book of Ezekiel*, *JSOTSup* 368 (Sheffield: Sheffield Acadmic Press, 2003), 8–9; David Carr, "Gender and the Shaping of Desire in the Song of Songs and Its Interpretation," *JBL* 119 (2000): 233–48, at 240.

97. Niditch, *Judges*, 193.

98. Niditch, *Judges*, 193–94; Stone, "Gender and Homosexuality in Judges 19," 101. Trible, *Texts of Terror*, 83, notes that the violence against the concubine justifies violence

Summary

The sense of integrity or wholeness associated with virginity provides a context for channeling sexual activity that stretches from the individual through the family and community to the divine sphere. Sexual relations are a powerful factor in whether an individual is in harmony with his or her social context. The requirement for young women that they be virgins at the time of marriage emphasizes that initial sexual intercourse is a transformative event: once one has experienced it, one cannot go back to one's previous state. To hold up this ideal of premarital virginity as a norm would be a positive but probably insufficient step to support chastity in practice. Thus Israelite priests developed a model of bodily integrity in which genital emissions had to be monitored in order to keep impurities from accumulating in the communal atmosphere. Such intrusive regulations kept Israelite men and women mindful of their living on YHWH's land, close to his symbolic dwelling place, the temple. This practical awareness of the connection between the physical body, the social body, and the cosmic body (i.e., the sphere spanning heaven and earth) fostered a sense of communal identity and reverence for creation. Thus sexual restraint and abstinence make sense only in light of the common good, whose ultimate form is right relationship with YHWH.

When the male-dominated hierarchy in Israel ignores the cosmic context of sociopolitical authority its actions toward those under its charge tend to become exploitative. Thus Judah is ready to purge his daughter-in-law Tamar from his household, only to be shown that he himself unknowingly has made her pregnant when he thought he was having sex with a prostitute (Gen 38:24-25). Joseph's more circumspect approach to sexual relations indicates that he is protected by God's presence, which in Proverbs would be expressed as Woman Wisdom. Joseph's channeling of erotic desire according to wisdom helps him to see and respect the larger relational context within which sexual relations take their rightful place and can serve as an integrative force. From Joseph's example one can argue that the ideal of sexual abstinence—continuous with that of male virginity— can make a rightful claim on Israelite men alongside the ideal of female virginity in Israel. Otherwise the ideal of premarital chastity for women may seem to be merely a form of exploitation by a patriarchal society.

---

against four hundred virgins of Jabesh-gilead and two hundred daughters of Shiloh; "the Israelite males have dismembered the corporate body of Israelite females."

The place of sexual restraint as a constructive contribution to equilibrium in a society demands wise discernment in particular contexts. The story of Jephthah's sacrifice of his daughter to fulfill a war vow raises questions about the significance of virginity for women. If the sacrifice is interpreted figuratively, then two main alternatives for understanding Jephthah's vow present themselves: (1) he pledged his daughter to a life of perpetual virginity; thus she and her companions mourned the fact that she would not be a wife and a mother; (2) he arranged the marriage of his daughter; thus she and her companions were mourning the loss of her virginity as she was about to enter into the household of her future husband. Both alternatives seem possible. The sacrifice in each alternative is intensified by the fact that her father makes a vow for her that shapes her future in a fundamental way. The picture of Jephthah presented in Judges 11 leaves open the question of how much his judgment was influenced by the spirit of YHWH. His impulsive, rash vow to sacrifice his daughter may well not have been entirely of his own making. If YHWH influenced him, then pledging his daughter to a life of perpetual virginity or sending her forth from his household to be married at a young age may well have been part of YHWH's plan. Jephthah mourns over the impending sacrifice his daughter faced but then seems to distance himself from her (11:35).[99] Such handing over of a woman for "a higher goal" is shockingly described in the case of the rape and murder of the Levite's concubine in Judges 19. These two stories in the book of Judges raise the question of whether and to what degree these sexual regulations reflect the authority of YHWH or the authority of a male elite.

Mesopotamia. Virginity: An Alternative Lifestyle Compatible with the Patriarchal Household

In Mesopotamia, virginity was practiced by young women prior to marriage and by cloistered women with a special calling for a lifetime. The honor of the father's household compelled members of the household to protect its nubile young women. Whenever dark spots showed up on the honor of the household this was not simply a signal for behavioral changes but also a time for restoring the integrity of the matrix of household relationships. This symbolic character of the patriarchal household called for a plurality of approaches to navigate the contradictions of embodied existence, particularly the erotic and sexual dimensions of social experience. This section on virginity and sexual restraint

99. Bal, *Death & Dissymetry*, 63; Sjöberg, *Wrestling with Textual Violence*, 60–61.

will address the following four topics: (1) Premarital virginity seems to have been the dominant practice, but its formulation as an ideal of physical wholeness is not explicit. (2) The ideal of bodily wholeness comes to expression when the integrity of the matrix of household relationships is violated by transgressors from without and within. (3) The sacrifice of virginity takes on a lifelong character in the cloistered life of the OB *nadītu*-women. (4) The sexual restraint required for a virgin is a feminine virtue that receives only one male instantiation in the character of Enkidu in the *Epic of Gilgamesh*; otherwise, virginity for males appears to be an extreme to be avoided.

The Expectation of Premarital Virginity for Women

The various Mesopotamian law collections do not explicitly state that a young woman must be a virgin at the time of marriage. However, there are many texts that suggest this was commonly expected. For example, the *Laws of Lipit-Ishtar* from Isin around 1930 BCE contain the following regulation about premarital virginity: "If a man claims that another man's virgin daughter has had sexual relations but it is proven that she has not had sexual relations, he shall weigh and deliver 10 shekels of silver" (¶33).[100] This law resembles the law of Deut 22:13-19 in that it tries to limit slander against a virgin daughter but is different in that no bloody linens (i.e., "evidence of virginity") are required—a type of evidence which Cooper notes is nowhere mentioned in Mesopotamian texts.[101] If three percent of a shekel equaled a day's wage,[102] then this fine of ten shekels amounted to the wages for more than 330 days.[103] Probably of more significance than the financial compensation would have been the symbolic significance of the fine: the slanderer would have

100. Martha T. Roth, *Law Collections from Mesopotamia and Asia Minor*, 2d ed., SBL Writings from the Ancient World Series 6 (Atlanta: Scholars Press, 1995), 33.

101. Cooper, "Virginity in Ancient Mesopotamia," 94. However, the notion of bridal sheets is celebrated in the Sumerian hymn "Bridal Sheets" in which Utu, Inanna's brother, has arranged for her marriage with Amaušumgalanna; see Thorkild Jacobsen, *The Harps That Once . . . Sumerian Poetry in Translation* (New Haven: Yale University Press, 1987), 13–15.

102. Marvin Powell, "Wir müssen alle unsere Nische nutzen: Monies, Motives, and Methods in Babylonian Economics," in *Trade and Finance in Ancient Mesopotamia*, MOS Studies 1, ed. Jan G. Dercksen, 5–23 (Leiden: Nederlands Historisch-Archaeologisch Instituut, 1999), at 14.

103. Daniel Snell, "Methods of Exchange and Coinage in Ancient Western Asia," *CANE*, 1487–97, at 1492, notes that a shekel of silver in Larsa-Girsu in the Ur III period was equivalent to 8.5 bushels of barley.

had to publicly acknowledge that he was at fault. Thus the reputation of the young woman and her family would be restored.[104]

A text that has been interpreted as defining a virgin as one who has not been penetrated by a male is the following Mari letter from Buqāqum, a governor in a strategic region of the kingdom of Mari, to king Zimrilim, from the eighteenth century BCE:

> The wife of Sin-iddinam disclosed the following: "Before Sin-iddinam married me, I came to an agreement with the father and the son. When Sin-iddinam went away from his household, the son of Asqudum wrote this statement: 'I want to marry you.' He kissed my lips. He touched my vulva, but his penis did not enter me. I said: 'I will not commit an unpardonable sin against Sin-iddinam.' In my household, I have not done what should not be done against my fiancé /husband (*bēlīja*)." (ll. 29-40)[105]

If the woman is understood to be a betrothed girl, then the issue is that she has not lost her virginity. Even though she engages in intimate contact with another man in her fiancé's (Sin-iddinam's) absence, she has not been penetrated by a male.[106] But Cooper interprets her agreeing with father and son as an indication that she herself was negotiating the marriage rather than her father; therefore she must have been older than an adolescent. Thus Cooper interprets her protest to be that she has not engaged in sexual relations with another man in her husband's absence.[107] Alternatively, the young woman's statement, "I came to an agreement with the father and the son" (*amgur abam u māram*, l. 31), may reflect a practice of her giving her assent in part of the betrothal process, as suggested in Rebekah's agreement to depart with Isaac's servant when asked in Gen 24:57. The context does not make it clear that the young woman negotiated her marriage independently of her father. If so, the text can

104. Elisabeth Meier Tetlow, *Women, Crime, and Punishment in Ancient Law and Society*, vol. 1: *The Ancient Near East* (New York: Continuum, 2004), 17, claims that this law is concerned primarily about the injury to the girl's father and not to the girl; cf. Cooper, "Virginity in Ancient Mesopotamia," 101–2.

105. *Edition: ARM* XXVI, §488, ll. 29–40, published by S. Lackenbacher in *Archives epistolaires de Mari* II/2, ed. Dominique Charpin, 423–24 (Paris: Editions Recherche sur les Civilisations, 1988); cf. Marten Stol, "Private Life in Ancient Mesopotamia," *CANE*, 485–501, at 489–90.

106. Stol, "Private Life in Ancient Mesopotamia," 489–90; idem, "Women in Mesopotamia," *JESHO* 38 (1995): 128.

107. Cooper, "Virginity in Ancient Mesopotamia," 96.

be seen as a statement by the young woman that she was a virgin at the time of her betrothal and marriage.

A frequent way to verify that a woman was a virgin in the Ur III and OB periods was for the woman or her female companions to take an oath.[108] In the following OB legal text this oath-based testimony is provided by female witnesses that a woman, Ama-sukkal, was a virgin. Her story begins with the fact that she had paid a man named Enlil-issu nineteen shekels of silver to marry her.[109] Four years later she increased the amount by five shekels.[110] He still did not complete the marriage contract. After waiting another six years, Ama-sukkal went to court accompanied by female witnesses who testified (1) that she had not insulted Enlil-issu, (2) that she was a "virgin" (*nunzû*), and (3) that Enlil-issu was holding out for more money. But Enlil-issu refused to marry her, saying that he would rather die. The court decided in favor of Ama-sukkal, and so Enlil-issu returned her money.[111] Cooper notes that *nunzû* is based on the Sumerian nu-nu-zu, "she did not know (a man)" and interprets this to mean that this woman, because she negotiates the marriage on her own behalf, is probably a widow or divorcée who has not yet slept with Enlil-issu.[112] Alternatively, Ama-sukkal may simply be making the case that she was a virgin at the time of her marriage proposal.

The foregoing three texts from the early second millennium BCE have been interpreted by a number of scholars as indicating that a young woman was expected to be a virgin at the time of marriage. However, Cooper questions the extent to which premarital virginity was an ideal; clearly virginity was not a prerequisite to marriage since prostitutes contracted marriages.[113] An economic point at issue, though, was the size of the brideprice/bridewealth. Virginity may have been attested through the oath-based testimony of others. But most likely, as Cooper states, the absence of virginity could only be known by pregnancy or by a woman's being caught having intercourse with a man.[114]

108. Ibid., 94–96.

109. BE 6/2 40; Raymond Westbrook, *Old Babylonian Marriage Law*, AfO Beiheft 23 (Horn, Austria: F. Berger, 1988), 43, 114–15.

110. BE 6/2 47; Westbrook, *Old Babylonian Marriage Law*, 43–44, 115.

111. BE 6/2 58; Westbrook, *Old Babylonian Marriage Law*, 44, 116; Cooper, "Virginity in Ancient Mesopotamia," 95.

112. Ibid., 95–96.

113. Ibid., 100–2; Stol, "Private Life in Ancient Mesopotamia," 493; Richard Henshaw, *Male and Female: The Cultic Personnel, The Bible and the Ancient Near East*, Princeton Theological Monograph Series 31 (Allison Park, PA: Pickwick, 1994), 212.

114. Cooper, "Virginity in Ancient Mesopotamia," 99.

Protection of a Wife or Daughter: The Ideal of Bodily Wholeness for Women

Since the virginity of a woman and the exclusive fidelity of a wife were valuable to the head of a household, one might think that measures would have been taken to shield women from the gaze and advances of men. In Babylon it appears that women took the veil at the time of marriage and probably wore it in public.[115] A law from the *Middle Assyrian Laws* (*MAL* 40) stipulates that a veil is to be worn by wives, widows, Assyrian women, daughters of an *awīlu* (a citizen), an *esirtu* ("concubine") who walks with her mistress, and a *qadiltu* ("a consecrated woman") who is married. But if prostitutes and slave women go about veiled, they are to be severely punished.[116] Anyone who discovers a prostitute or a slave woman doing so and fails to report her will be subject to a similarly severe punishment. The fact that Assyrian women were not confined within the walls of a house is evident in the protasis of the following law:[117]

> If a man's wife should walk along a street and a man seizes her and says, "I want to have sex with you"—she must not yield but rather guard herself. If he should take her by force and have sex with her—whether they find him on top of the man's wife or witnesses testify that he had sex with the woman—they shall put the man to death. But there is no penalty for the woman. (*MAL* 12)[118]

Presuming that the wife was veiled, the rapist would have known she was off limits. Capital punishment would seem to have deterred rape and other crimes against women. Thus even though the head of the Mesopotamian household had considerable anxiety over his wife's sexuality, the women were not secluded and watched, except in the Assyrian harem.[119]

115. A. R. George, *The Babylonian Gilgamesh Epic* (New York: Oxford University Press, 2003), 188, 498; Karen Rhea Nemet-Nejat, *Daily Life in Ancient Mesopotamia* (Peabody, MA: Hendrickson, 1998), 136–37.

116. Godfrey R. Driver and John C. Miles, *The Assyrian Laws* (Oxford: Clarendon Press, 1935), 129–30.

117. Sophie Lafont, *Femmes, Droit et Justice dans l'Antiquité orientale: Contribution à l'étude du droit pénal au Proche-Orient ancien*, OBO 165 (Fribourg: Editions Universitaires; Göttingen: Vandenhoeck & Ruprecht, 1999), 109.

118. Edition: Driver and Miles, *Assyrian Laws*, 386; see also Martha T. Roth, *Law Collections from Mesopotamia and Asia Minor*, 157–58.

119. Cooper, "Virginity in Ancient Mesopotamia," 102, contends that such heavy surveillance was absent even though the husband worried about his wife's fidelity as seen in the phrase "the man's wife will fornicate over and over again" (*aššat amēli ittanajjak*),

Rape of a virgin was a serious offense. On a literary level the tyrannical Gilgamesh, the young king of Uruk, may have engaged in the rite of *ius primae noctis*:[120] "[Gilgamesh] does not release [a daughter to her] mother . . . . [Very strong, resplendent, experienced] . . . Gilgamesh does not release a young woman to [her] bride-[groom]. The warrior's daughter is the wife of [the young man]" (*Gilg*. 1: 72, 75-77; cf. 1: 90-92).[121] If he was deflowering brides, the subsequent narrative calls such behavior into question and has the mother goddess Aruru create Enkidu who will be able to subdue Gilgamesh (*Gilg*. 1: 101-12; 2: 111-12). *MAL* 55 legislates the following:

> If a man seizes with force a young woman—who resides in her father's household, has not been betrothed, whose "narrows" (i.e., womb?) have not been opened, who is not married, and there are no claims against her father's house—and rapes her—whether in the heart of the city or in the countryside or in the street at night or in a granary or during the city festival—the father of the young woman shall take the wife of the one who had sex with the young woman and have her raped. He shall not return her to her husband, but shall take her. The father shall hand over his daughter who was violated to the one who had sex with her for marriage. (*MAL* A, viii, 6-41)[122]

The androcentric perspective of these laws is painfully evident in the talionic fate that befalls the wife of the rapist: she too will be raped and then banished from her husband's household. Then the maiden who was raped will take her place in the fornicator's household. The logic appears to be (1) that the maiden has been indelibly marked by the rap-

---

Alamdimmû X:56; see Barbara Böck, *Die babylonisch-assyrische Morphoskopie*, AfO Beiheft 27 (Vienna: Institut für Orientalistik der Universität Wien, 2000), 35, 120–21.

120. The OB Pennsylvania tablet reads: "He [Gilgamesh] will have sexual intercourse with the one destined to be a wife: he is first, afterwards the bridegroom. This is decreed by divine resolution: at the cutting of the umbilical cord, she was allotted to him" (*Gilg*. OB II:159-64, edition in George, *The Babylonian Gilgamesh Epic*, 1: 178). George, in ibid., 1:188, 449, n. 20, notes that in Uruk—contrary to custom elsewhere—Gilgamesh, instead of the bridegroom, parts the veil of the bride; regarding *ius primae noctis*, George notes that Jacobsen once argued this point but then later abandoned it.

121. Restored text edition from George, *The Babylonian Gilgamesh Epic*, 1:542.

122. Text: VAT 10000, in Otto Schroeder, *Keilschrifttexte aus Assur verschiedenen Inhalts*, Wissenschaftliche Veröffentlichungen der Deutschen Orient-Gesellschaft 35 (Leipzig: J. C. Hinrichs, 1920), 13; edition: Driver and Miles, *Assyrian Laws*, 422; see also Roth, *Law Collections from Mesopotamia and Asia Minor*, 174–75.

ist's sperm such that she should be allowed to be his wife,[123] and (2) that the maiden should be regarded as the fornicator's primary wife and not be placed in a situation in which she must compete with the former wife. If the restoration of the phrase "whose [womb (?)] is not opened" is correct,[124] then the law clearly states that her virginity has been violated. This loss of sexual innocence and the implanting of the fornicator's seed in her is a driving force in the formulation of this law. This point is reinforced by the fact that if the fornicator has no wife he simply must marry the maiden without the option of divorce and pay triple the bridewealth.

Was the concept of the "intact virgin" known in Mesopotamia? Cooper argues that it was not. He cites the following passage from the Sumerian myth "Enlil and Ninlil" in which the young Ninlil protests Enlil's advances:

> My vulva is small and has not learned to stretch! My lips are small and have not learned to kiss! My mother will learn of it and slap my hand! My father will learn of it and lay hold of me! And then, when I tell my girl friend . . . ![125]

Enlil then takes her away and has intercourse with her. Cooper notes that the text does not mention blood or pain in this initial experience of sex. He then assembles examples from the Sumerian myths "Enlil and Sud" and "Enki and Ninhursag," and the Akkadian myth "Nergal and Ereshkigal" to argue the point that the first experience of sex does not seem to have been traumatic for the young woman and that the presence or absence of virginity was not manifest in physical signs.[126] In a similar vein, Gwendolyn Leick contends that Sumer did not accent the girl's loss of sexual innocence but rather her passage "from sexual immaturity to sexual maturity."[127] Cooper notes that the belief in the existence of the hymen as a physical structure in the vagina emerged only in the modern era.[128] Therefore both Cooper and Leick contend that the Mesopotamians did not interpret the status of virginity in terms of physical wholeness but rather as a stage in

123. Driver and Miles, *Assyrian Laws*, 56–57; cf. Lafont, *Femmes, Droit et Justice*, 98.

124. Driver and Miles, *Assyrian Laws*, 422; Roth, *Law Collections from Mesopotamia and Asia Minor*, 174.

125. Translation in Cooper, "Virginity in Ancient Mesopotamia," 97.

126. Ibid., 97–99.

127. Gwendolyn Leick, *Sex and Eroticism in Mesopotamian Literature* (London and New York: Routledge, 1994), 47.

128. Cooper, "Virginity in Ancient Mesopotamia," 100; cf. Sissa, *Greek Virginity*, 110–11.

the maturational process. However, Lafont's claim that the deflowering of a free virgin has consequences of a physical nature cannot be dismissed, particularly in light of the Mesopotamians' awareness of impurity—a metaphysical reality with physical manifestations.[129]

Consciousness of purity or wholeness was part of the Mesopotamian experience.[130] Although there is no series of regulations on genital emissions comparable to those found in Leviticus 15, consciousness of defilement from these emissions is attested in the Mesopotamian record. With regard to the contagious character of menstruation, Stol notes that

> women were thought to menstruate for six days—"hit by the weapon," as the Babylonian expression ran. During this period they were considered unclean and did not have to work. A man touching a woman in this situation shared her condition and was regarded as being unclean for six days.[131]

The following incantation recited in order to secure pure water for a ritual illustrates this attitude toward menstrual blood: "Water of the ocean, the wide sea, into which a mother-to-be has not gone down, and in which an impure woman had not washed her hands."[132] With regard to seminal emissions, the following chronic condition occasions an incantation ritual imploring Ištar and Dumuzi to heal an afflicted one:

> If the limbs of a man are limp like a sick person, and his feet and stomach-lining are loose/slack, and he talks much without saying anything and his sexual potency is frustrated and either in his urine or continually he has a flow of semen as if he were having sex with a woman, that man is unclean; his god and goddess have abandoned him; his words are not acceptable.[133]

129. Lafont, *Femmes, Droit et Justice*, 97–98; cf. E. Jan Wilson, *"Holiness" and "Purity" in Mesopotamia*, AOAT 237 (Kevelaer: Butzon & Bercker; Neukirchen-Vluyn: Neukirchener Verlag, 1994), 67, 87.

130. Karel van der Toorn, *Sin and Sanction in Israel and Mesopotamia* (Assen and Maastricht: Van Gorcum, 1985), 17–18, 29–33.

131. Stol, "Private Life in Ancient Mesopotamia," 490; van der Toorn, *Sin and Sanction in Israel and Mesopotamia*, 31.

132. *AMT* 10 1 iii 1–2; quoted in Wilfred G. Lambert, "Prostitution," in *Aussenseiter und Randgruppen: Beiträge zu einer Sozialgeschichte des Alten Orients*, ed. Volkert Haas, 127–57 (Konstanz: Universitätsverlag, 1992), at 145.

133. Edition: Walter Farber, *Beschwörungsrituale an Ištar und Dumuzi*, Akademie der Wissenschaften und der Literatur 30 (Wiesbaden: Franz Steiner, 1977), 236; see also van der Toorn, *Sin and Sanction in Israel and Mesopotamia*, 32.

Karel van der Toorn claims that the Mesopotamian and Israelite regulations on genital emissions arose out of widespread folk beliefs linked to an instinctive aversion to the loss of reproductive bodily fluids and were not simply the creation of priestly legislators of the sixth-fifth centuries BCE.[134]

Care was taken to keep a sanctuary free from defilement. For example, in the prologue to the *CH*, Hammurapi is hailed as "the one who purifies the rituals of the Eabzu temple" (*mubbib šuluḫ* E.ZU.AB; *CH* I: 66). As a matter of etiquette in the presence of a god, since the god was of a higher status, a person would take care to keep his or her body pure.[135] For example, in the *Maqlû* ritual that aimed to burn away the negative influences of witchcraft the leader of the ritual says: "I washed my hands, I purified my body in the clean spring water issuing from Eridu" (VII:119).[136] Thus there was an awareness on a bodily level that one's life needed to signify reverence for the gods who ruled the cosmos.

An Old Babylonian Community of Celibate Women: The Nadiātum *of Sippar and Nippur*

A unique institution that existed only during the First Dynasty of Babylon (1894–1595 BCE) was a community of celibate women associated with a particular temple, of which the best documented is the community dedicated to Shamash at Sippar. Here two hundred *nadiātum* (= *nadītum*-women) lived in a "cloister" (*gagû*) consisting of a walled-off section of the city where the *nadiātum* owned their own homes.[137] The largest number of extant documents mentioning these *nadiātum* are contracts and letters, which speak primarily about the economic and social dimensions of their lives but only secondarily about the religious dimension.[138] Fortunately, the abundant sources provide sufficient information for a fairly nuanced portrait of their way of life.

134. Karel van der Toorn, *From Her Cradle to Her Grave: The Role of Religion in the Life of the Israelite and the Babylonian Woman*, trans. Sara J. Denning-Bolle (Sheffield: JSOT Press, 1994), 53–54; see also Benjamin Kedar-Kopfstein, "Blood," *TDOT* 3 (1978), 237.

135. Van der Toorn, *From Her Cradle to Her Grave*, 49.

136. Edition: Gerhard Meier, *Die assyrische Beschwörungssammlung Maqlû*, AfO Beiheft 2 (Osnabrück: Biblio-Verlag, 1967), 51.

137. Rivkah Harris, *Ancient Sippar: A Demographic Study of an Old-Babylonian City (1894–1595 B.C.)* (Istanbul: Nederlands Historisch-Archaeologisch Instituut te Istanbul, 1975), 188.

138. Ibid., 307.

A *nadītum* of Shamash at Sippar or of Ninurta at Nippur was not allowed to marry or to have children.[139] The term *nadītum* means "(1) abandoned, uninhabited; (2) uncultivated, fallow; (3) laid (foundation), placed; (4) spit-out, strewn, scattered; (5) fallen, lax."[140] In light of her suspension of her capacity to bear children, the *nadītum* is like a field that lies fallow (meaning 2). Since she transferred from her father's household to the *gagû*, the *nadītum* reflects meanings 3 and 4. With regard to meaning 5, there is a debate over whether the *nadītum* was expected to be chaste. On the basis of the extant data Benno Landsberger assumed that the *nadītum* promised to live a chaste life.[141] But Finkelstein counters that there is no text that speaks of a vow of chastity.[142] Also there is an entry in the OB lexical list *Proto Lu* that equates *nadītum* with *qadištum* by identifying both terms as possible renderings of the Sumerian LUKUR. Harris dismisses such equivalences as unreliable because of the lateness of the list, reflecting a period in which the term LUKUR was no longer understood technically.[143] But Lambert accepts this data, which "suggests that the *nadītum* was a prostitute."[144] He claims that the business activities of the *nadītum* were compatible with her work as a prostitute and concludes that "at least in some periods and areas the *nadītum* was a prostitute."[145] In order to assess Lambert's conclusion, we need to describe the role of the *qadištum*.

The *qadištum*, "the consecrated woman," is mentioned in Babylonian and Assyrian texts spanning the first two millennia BCE. Joan Westenholz notes that she is only infrequently mentioned as dedicated to a god with a particular ritual function, although these references increase in MA and NA texts.[146] However, Harris points out that the sources mentioning

139. Ibid., 303, 306; Elizabeth Stone, "The Social Role of the *Nadītu* Women in Old Babylonian Nippur," *JESHO* 25 (1982): 50–70; Ulla Jeyes, "The *Nadītu* Women of Sippar," in *Images of Women in Antiquity*, ed. Averil Cameron and Amélie Kuhrt, 260–71 (Detroit: Wayne State University Press, 1983), at 267.

140. *CAD* N, part 1, 66–67.

141. Benno Landsberger, "Jungfräulichkeit: Ein Beitrag zum Thema 'Beilage und Eheschliessung,'" in *Symbolae Iuridicae et Historicae Martino David Dedicatae*, 2 vols., ed. J. A. Ankum, Robert Feenstra, and William F. Leemans, 2:41–105 (Leiden: Brill, 1968), at 58.

142. Jacob J. Finkelstein, "On Some Recent Studies in Cuneiform Law" *JAOS* 90 (1970): 243–56, at 246.

143. Rivkah Harris, "The *Nadītu* Woman," in *Studies Presented to A. Leo Oppenheim* (Chicago: The Oriental Institute of the University of Chicago, 1964), 106–35, at 107.

144. Lambert, "Prostitution," 154, n. 14.

145. Ibid., 138.

146. Joan Goodnick Westenholz, "Tamar, *Qĕdēšā*, *Qadištu*, and Sacred Prostitution in Mesopotamia," *HTR* 82 (1989): 245–65, at 251–54, refers to the MA text *KAR* 154, in which

the *qadištum* at Sippar are letters and legal or economic texts and not religious or literary ones.[147] Lambert counters that on the basis of the OB text *Ana iṭtišu* VII iii 7-10 the *qadištum*'s social location is "on the street" and not as part of a household.[148] But according to the *Laws of Lipit-Ishtar* 22 from Isin in the twentieth century BCE a daughter who became a *qadištum*, an *ugbabtum*, or a *nadītum* was still considered to be a member of her father's household because she was an heir equal to her brothers.[149] Thus Westenholz notes that within the categories of the OB legal system the *qadištum* is grouped with women (*nadītum, kulmašītum, ugbabtum*) whose sexual expression is guided by the law codes in contrast to those women whose sexual expression lay outside the bounds of the law codes (*harimtum, šamhatum, kezertum*).[150] The *qadištum* could marry, own property, have children, and serve as a wet nurse.[151] According to the OB poem *Atra-hasīs*, the *qadištum* operated a maternity hut in which she attended to the spiritual needs of the mother giving birth while the midwife tended to her physical needs.[152] Thus the *qadištum* in OB times lived on the margins of the normative social structure centered on the patriarchal household and offered a diversity of services. Apart from *Ana ittišu* VII iii 7-10, there is no indication that the *qadištum* served as a prostitute.

---

the *qadištu* has a ritual role along with a sanga-priest; in a procession in the temple of Adad she intones and sustains the *inhu*-chant and lifts up the statue of Shamash. Lambert, "Prostitution," 144, refers to *KAR* 321 obv. 5–7, where a *qadištu* is carrying out a purification ritual at childbirth.

147. Harris, *Ancient Sippar*, 303, notes that the *qadištu* at Sippar were devoted to the god Adad.

148. Lambert, "Prostitution," 141, notes that *Ana ittišu* was edited by Landsberger and identified by him as composed in OB Nippur. See also Westenholz, "Tamar, *Qĕdēšā, Qadištu*," 250–51.

149. Henshaw, *Male and Female: The Cultic Personnel*, 208. This inclusion of the *qadištu, ugbabtu,* and *nadītu* in their natal household seems to be reflected in the MB lexical list *Malku*, where these women take their place in the systematic arrangement of the members of the household (see Anne Draffkorn Killmer, "The First Tablet of *Malku* = *Šarru* Together With Its Explict Version," *JAOS* 83 [1963]: 421–46, at 427, entries 126–35; Lambert, "Prostitution," 144).

150. Westenholz, "Tamar, *Qĕdēšā, Qadištu*," 251.

151. Ibid., 252.

152. Wilfred G. Lambert and Alan R. Millard, *Atra-hasīs, the Babylonian Story of the Flood* (Winona Lake, IN: Eisenbrauns, 1999), 1: 290; Lambert, "Prostitution," 143; Westenholz, "Tamar, *Qĕdēšā, Qadištu*," 252.

With reference to the *Proto Lu* list and *Ana ittišu* VII iii 7-10, Lambert argues that the *nadītum* could have served at times as a prostitute.[153] If she did, she must have used some form of contraception to avoid pregnancy because the *nadītum*, unlike the *qadištum*, was not permitted to bear children.[154] But why this discrepancy in the application of the prohibition on marrying and bearing children if the *nadītum* and the *qadištum* are regarded as equivalent? On the basis of *Atra-hasīs* one could argue that the *nadiātum* were denied the normal human company of husband and children as a way of countering overpopulation.[155] But such an argument seems to ignore the religious role of the *nadītum*.

The *nadītum* of Shamash is a *kallatum*, which identifies her either as a "daughter-in-law" of the deities Shamash and his bride Aja[156] or as the "betrothed" of Shamash.[157] The *kallatum* was the young girl from her betrothal to the consummation of her marriage, during which time she lived in her father-in-law's household and was expected to remain chaste as a virgin.[158] Harris contends that no marriage took place as she entered the cloister of Shamash.[159] Rather, she was initiated into the household of Shamash on the festival of *šebût šattim* (in December/January) in which she was given the betrothal gift (*biblum*) by her father-in-law Shamash;[160] at this time she had the "rope of Shamash" placed on her arm as a sign of her adoption as daughter-in-law, and she also might change her name to express her devotion to Shamash or Aja.[161] But Westbrook counters that Shamash brings the *biblum* as the groom and not as the father-in-law, because in standard OB practice the groom brings both the *biblum* and

153. Lambert, "Prostitution," 138.

154. Finkelstein, "On Some Recent Studies in Cuneiform Law," 246, n. 15; cf. Robert D. Biggs, "Conception, Contraception, and Abortion in Ancient Mesopotamia," 1–13, in *Wisdom, Gods, and Literature: Studies in Assyriology in Honour of W. G. Lambert*, ed. A. R. George and Irving L. Finkel, 106–35 (Winona Lake, IN: Eisenbrauns, 2000), at 107; Julia Assante, "From Whores to Hierodules: The Historiographic Invention of Mesopotamian Female Sex Professionals," in *Ancient Art and Its Historiography*, ed. A. A. Donohue and Mark D. Fullerton, 13–47 (Cambridge: Cambridge University Press, 2003), at 26.

155. Lambert, "Prostitution," 139.

156. Harris, *Ancient Sippar*, 307; eadem, "The *Nadītu* Woman," 116.

157. Westbrook, *Old Babylonian Marriage Law*, 66.

158. *CAD* K 82B; Jeyes, "The *Nadītu* Women of Sippar," 265–66; cf. Westbrook, *Old Babylonian Marriage Law*, 17–18.

159. Harris, *Ancient Sippar*, 308.

160. Harris, "The *Nadītu* Woman," 112–13. Jeyes, "The *Nadītu* Women of Sippar," 265, notes that a "bridal gift" (*terḫatum*) was also given at initiation, but it seems to have remained in the cloister rather than being given to the father as the *biblum* was.

161. Harris, *Ancient Sippar*, 308; eadem, "The *Nadītu* Woman," 113, 128.

terḫatum.[162] Furthermore, he states that Aya is "the mistress" to the *nadītum*, a relationship analogous to that of the *nadītum* of Marduk and a *šugītum* ("secondary wife"). Therefore Westbrook argues that the *nadītum* of Shamash was a secondary wife to Shamash.[163] Whether as a daughter-in-law or secondary wife of Shamash, the *nadiātum* was expected to remain chaste.[164]

On the second day of the festival of *šebût šattim* the *nadītum* of Shamash was obliged to honor the memory of her sister *nadiātum* and make intercession for them.[165] One of the ongoing duties of the *nadītum* apparently was to be present in the sanctuary for extended periods to make intercession for the city, relatives, and other interested parties.[166] As a votary of Shamash she was believed to have a special line of communication to the deity.[167] Erišti-Aya, daughter of Zimri-Lim of Mari and a *nadītum* at Sippar, refers to herself as a *šurinnum* ("emblem, standard") of a deity who makes intercession for the king before Shamash and Aya.[168] The *nadītum*'s special relationship with Shamash and Aya is accented by her standard use of a salutation like the following: "May Šamaš and Aja, the Bride, keep you well."[169] Harris notes, however, that there is no evidence that the *nadiātum* were priestesses with a specialized cultic role to perform.[170]

If the religious role of the *nadītum* is to be reconciled with the function of a prostitute, then prostitution would need to bear more significance than as an erotic release for the client. Lambert argues that "in ancient Mesopotamia all prostitution was by definition sacral, because the sexual act was a natural force working for the well being of the human race and was a power personified in the goddess Inanna/Ištar."[171]

162. Westbrook, *Old Babylonian Marriage Law*, 66.

163. Ibid., 108–9.

164. Jeyes, "The *Nadītu* Women of Sippar," 265, writes that Aya also was designated a *kallatum*.

165. Harris, *Ancient Sippar*, 308; eadem, "The *Nadītu* Woman," 113–14, 121–22; Jeyes, "The *Nadītu* Women of Sippar," 264.

166. *ARM* X 38; 36:14-15; 37:7-8; 39:20; van der Toorn, *Family Religion in Babylonia, Syria and Israel*, 114. On *nadītum* as *karibtum* see *ARM* X 42:4; *AbB* 1, 61:7; *AbB* 7, 139:3.

167. Harris, *Ancient Sippar*, 308; eadem, "The *Nadītu* Woman," 120; Henshaw, *Male and Female: The Cultic Personnel*, 194; Bernard Batto, *Studies on Women at Mari* (Baltimore: Johns Hopkins University Press, 1974), 96.

168. Ibid., 97.

169. *CT* 29 11a:4; *CT* 29 11b:3; *CT* 6 27a:4; *YOS* 2 64:4, as cited by Harris, "The *Nadītu* Woman," 117, 119. *ARM* X 40:1′-10′; 36:13-18.

170. Harris, *Ancient Sippar*, 303.

171. Lambert, "Prostitution," 143.

However, the absence of explicit data on the cultic roles of the *nadītum* and *qadištum* has rendered suspect the existence of sacred prostitution in Mesopotamia.[172] So the debate between Lambert and Landsberger/ Harris/Renger over whether the *nadītum* functioned at times as a prostitute or lived a chaste life turns on how to interpret the entry in *Proto Lu* implying that there is an equivalency between the *nadītum* and the *qadištum* because both words are possible renderings of the Sumerian LUKUR. More data on the economic and social functions of the *nadītum* should bring further light to the issue.

The cloistered *nadiātum* of Shamash at Sippar and of Ninurta at Nippur acted primarily as private individuals.[173] In Sippar the wall that enclosed the cloister was repeatedly repaired by the kings of Babylon, and its four gates were supervised by civil officials.[174] The marks of the cloister at Nippur are not as clear as they are at Sippar, yet this communal space seems to have been in place for them as well.[175] Stone speculates that the cloistered status of the *nadiātum* may have had more to do with their unmarried status than with a role in religious ritual.[176] The cloister at Sippar contained a granary, an administrative building, and perhaps a dormitory for workers. The administrative staff was comprised of an overseer, a director of personnel, a female scribe, a scribe of the *nadiātum*, a judge of the cloister, an overseer of the *ugbabtum*-women, a steward farmer, and an official over the workers. The workers consisted of female weavers, servant girls, female cooks, an overseer of the sailors, a Sutean guard for the sesame field, and several others.[177] These administrators and workers at Sippar freed the *nadiātum* from many daily tasks so that they could devote themselves to their religious, financial, and scribal activities.[178]

The *nadiātum* at both Sippar and Nippur belonged to the upper class and were significant landowners. At Sippar successive generations of women from the same families joined the cloister.[179] They typically brought

172. Westenholz, "Tamar, *Qĕdēšā*, *Qadištu*," 260–63; Stephanie Budin, *The Myth of Sacred Prostitution in Antiquity* (Cambridge: Cambridge University Press, 2008), 17–32.

173. Harris, *Ancient Sippar*, 306; Stone, "The Social Role of the *Nadītu* Women," 55, 67.

174. Harris, *Ancient Sippar*, 188.

175. Stone, "The Social Role of the *Nadītu* Women," 56.

176. Ibid., 62.

177. Harris, *Ancient Sippar*, 189, 199.

178. Ibid., 306, 310–12; Stone, "The Social Role of the *Nadītu* Women," 66–67.

179. Batto, *Women at Mari*, 98, refers to *ARM* X 43.15-17, in which Erišti-Aya indicates that it was not entirely her choice to enter the cloister; there was considerable parental pressure.

large dowries with them, which may point to a reason for the rise of the *nadītum* institution: it served as a way to keep the family's wealth from dispersing to other households by way of dowries.[180] For if the father who dedicated his daughter as a *nadītum* to Shamash did not state in writing that she could freely dispose of her property, then when the father died the brothers of the *nadītum* were expected to take her property and in return to supply her with "rations, ointment, and clothing as required by her share of the estate" (*CH* §178; xxxvii: 82-84). But if they were delinquent in supplying her with her just portion she could find another tenant farmer who would take care of the land and supply her with her portion. She could not sell the property, for title to it belonged to the brothers (*CH* 178).[181] This law was presumably also in effect at Nippur, but the dowries of the *nadiātum* there typically consisted more of moveable property than of agricultural land.[182] However, at Nippur there was a close relationship between the *nadītum* and her brothers. If property were part of her dowry, the brothers could not sell it while she was alive; they were to provide her with a living allowance and protect her rights.[183] On the other hand, if the *nadītum*'s father put in writing that she had clear title to the property and could sell it to whomever she wished, her power and autonomy were significantly enhanced (*CH* §179).

The *nadiātum* at Sippar and Nippur were heavily involved in real estate transactions. Harris notes that at Sippar from around 1830 to 1712 BCE *nadiātum* were the lessors in fifty-three of fifty-nine leases, but from circa 1711 to 1595 BCE they were lessors in only twenty-nine of sixty-six leases. She speculates that the decrease in the seventeenth century over the previous century may have been a consequence of greater centralization of land management by the Babylonian kings. The *nadiātum* in Sippar were also creditors in silver and staples, and they entered into partnerships in order to increase their financial power.[184] In Nippur from about 1895 to 1719 BCE *nadiātum* were the buyers of property from a man in five of twenty-three transactions, whereas in seven of twenty-three transactions a man bought property from the *nadiātum*. In seven of fifteen transactions a man borrowed money from a *nadītum*; in two of fifteen transactions a *nadītum* borrowed money from a man; and in four of fifteen

180. Harris, "The *Nadītu* Woman," 109; Jeyes, "The *Nadītu* Women of Sippar," 264–65.

181. Harris, *Ancient Sippar*, 310.

182. Stone, "The Social Role of the *Nadītu* Women," 58.

183. Ibid., 59–60; Batto, *Women at Mari*, 99–100; see *ARM* X 36.22-26.

184. Harris, *Ancient Sippar*, 311–12.

transactions a *nadītum* rented property from a man.[185] Stone claims that the documentation from Nippur is more representative of actual economic activity than that at Sippar, for the Sippar data includes a *nadītum* in almost every case, which seems to overstate the influence of the *nadiātum* in the economy of Sippar.[186]

Stone proceeds to make a case that the *nadiātum* of Nippur in the nineteenth and eighteenth centuries BCE played a pivotal role in property transactions when individual ownership of property developed at the expense of ownership by patrilineal lineages. She notes that because the *nadiātum* belonged to their natal household and to the "household" of the cloister, they could play a mediating role between men in different lineages who wished to buy and sell property. The customs of patrilineage allowed the members of the lineage to sell their property only to one another. So if a *nadītum* of one lineage could buy property from a relative, she in turn could sell this property to a man from another lineage since she belonged to a non-traditional household. Stone's argument to explain the important role of the *nadiātum* in property transactions is that their liminal position with regard to the patrilineal descent allowed them to assist members of that lineage to adjust to the economic reality of exchanging property across lineages. Such an exchange needed to occur because of the increasing power of the state, a form of political organization that favored private rather than lineage ownership of property.[187]

The involvement of *nadiātum* in commercial and property transactions inevitably landed them in conflicts that resulted in lawsuits. The following case illustrates how the troubles of commercial life made their way into the life of the cloister:

> To my lord say: Thus says Eli-eresa, daughter of Nur-Adad, your servant: Concerning Sin-iddinam, the son of Ilšu-bani, because he is a native of my city of Sippar . . . to him . . . I left my garment with him. After he had my garment in his possession for three months, he paid an insufficient amount. He held back a half shekel and twenty corn of silver from the purchase price. For the remainder of the silver, I went to him. As if I were not a servant of Šamaš, he struck me terribly. What ought not to happen in the land, he did to me. Two days later, I went to him and said: "Why did you treat me that way?" He replied: Stop! It is not for you (to speak). Have I not

185. Stone, "The Social Role of the *Nadītu* Women," 63.

186. Ibid., 50–52; Jeyes, "The *Nadītu* Women of Sippar," 262.

187. Stone, "The Social Role of the *Nadītu* Women," 64–67.

> struck the throats of five *nadiātum* of Šamaš from Ebabbar? Who has ever taken something from me?" My lord, my judge, decide my case with Sin-iddinam. (*AbB* 1 §34, ll. 1-25)[188]

The *nadiātum* in Sippar employed female weavers and owned slaves who could also do this work. Here it seems a product from the cloister has been handed over to a hometown merchant who has swindled the *nadītum*. Through his macho rhetoric, as reported by the offended *nadītum*, the merchant pays no respect to her religious status as a servant of Shamash.

A *nadītum* in Sippar was given at least one slave—and probably many more—by her father upon her entry into the cloister.[189] A *nadītum* not only hired out her slaves at harvest time, she also engaged in slave trade. Contracts from Sippar indicate that *nadiātum* were the lessors in thirty-five of forty-three transactions for the seasonal labor of slaves and that they were the buyers in twenty out of thirty-seven contracts for the sale of slaves.[190]

A *nadītum* was the head of her own household. This kind of autonomy and agential power may have been a significant attraction for young women, moving them to forego marriage in order to become *nadiātum*. Others may have wanted to escape the burdens of childbearing.[191] Many women died in childbirth at that time. On the assumption that Babylonian women had at least a voice in whether or not to marry a particular man, it may be that some women did not find suitable husbands and so preferred to become *nadiātum*.[192] It may be that the father chose one of his daughters to become a *nadītum* so that she might make intercession for the family and also keep her dowry, particularly its landed portion, within the family. A tradition of entering the cloister developed in some families.[193] Older *nadiātum* could adopt younger *nadiātum*, who were often relatives, to care for them in their old age; since the *nadiātum* were financially independent, the cloister was not respon-

188. Edition: Fritz R. Kraus, *Altbabylonische Briefe in Umschrift und Übersetzung* [*AbB*], vol. 1 (Leiden: Brill, 1964), 30.

189. Harris, *Ancient Sippar*, 312. Batto, *Women at Mari*, 100–2, notes that Erišti-Aya at Sippar may have had at least three to seven slaves (*ARM* X 38.12-21; 39.15-19; 42.1′-6′).

190. Harris, *Ancient Sippar*, 312.

191. Ibid., 309.

192. Stone, "The Social Role of the *Nadītu* Women," 65.

193. Harris, "The *Nadītu* Woman," 124–26; Jeyes, "The *Nadītu* Women of Sippar," 263, 270, 272.

sible for them in their declining years.[194] Through a combination of social, economic, and religious factors the *nadiātum* held high social status and wielded significant financial power during the OB period.[195]

It is difficult to imagine that the cloistered *nadiātum* of Sippar and Nippur in the OB period would have functioned as prostitutes. Lambert notes on the basis of an unpublished LB text that the label *nadītum* for a class of women persisted into the first millennium, when they had a part to play in a ritual during the month of Kislimu (November/December) in the Esagil temple in Babylon.[196] The functions the *nadiātum* acquired after the OB period could have expanded to include prostitution. However, such an activity seems incompatible with their profile in the OB period, as Landsberger, Renger, and Harris have argued.[197]

Male Sexual Constraint: A Concern for Boundaries

Male virginity as a way of life analogous to that of the *nadiātum* is not attested in Mesopotamia. It is difficult to find examples of males who held up the ideal of virginity as a discipline even for a limited time. If males did not marry until they were well into their twenties they either had to practice sexual abstinence or visit prostitutes.[198] Sexual abstinence is not presented as an ideal in the extant Mesopotamian record. According to Cooper the only male character in Mesopotamian literature who is identified as a virgin is Enkidu.[199] When he is initiated into civilized life by the prostitute Shamhat he loses his animal-like innocence to become part of the human sphere in which "copulation, kissing, and prostitution" were regarded as ME's or "essences."[200] Enkidu's impending death makes him think that his initiation into human life was a mistake. He curses Shamhat. But Shamash counsels him about the gift of friendship he received in this civilized life and so Enkidu balances out his curses of Shamhat with blessings. This ambiguity of good and bad is constitutive of the human condition. Even though Enkidu becomes rec-

194. Ibid., 270; Harris, *Gender and Aging in Mesopotamia*, 110.

195. Jeyes, "The Nadītu Women of Sippar," 262.

196. Lambert, "Prostitution," 138.

197. Jeyes, "The Nadītu Women of Sippar," 266–67, 272.

198. Roth, "Age at Marriage and the Household, 747.

199. Cooper, "Virginity in Ancient Mesopotamia," 102.

200. Wim van Binsbergen and Frans Wiggermann, "Magic in History: A Theoretical Perspective, and Its Application to Ancient Mesopotamia," in *Mesopotamian Magic: Textual, Historical, and Interpretative Perspectives*, Ancient Magic and Divination 1, ed. Tzvi Abusch and Karel van der Toorn, 3–34 (Groningen: Styx, 1999), at 23.

onciled to his fate and affirms the human life he experienced, it is instructive that the reality of death made Enkidu have strong reservations about having lost his virginity and having moved toward a way of life that typically would have marriage on the horizon.

Males were obliged to respect the marital and household relationships of others in the community, so adultery and rape were forbidden. The sexual omens of Tablet 104 of the series *Šumma ālu* address the contradictory character of sexuality with behavioral recommendations that typically offer advice in particular circumstances but resist being generalized into laws or principles.[201] Nevertheless, a principle operative in the omen series *Šumma ālu* is that extremes should be avoided. One teaching, which Ann Kessler Guinan singles out as threading its way through the sex omens of *Šumma ālu,* is that males should exercise sexual constraint for the sake of their social advancement and well-being.[202] In the Mesopotamian composition from the end of the second millennium, known as "Counsels of Wisdom," a male audience is urged to avoid marrying slave girls, because they will be disruptive of the household, and prostitutes, because they will not be respectful or obedient (66-80).[203] Thus sexual constraint was no doubt exercised by Mesopotamian males. However, an ideal of lifelong chastity is nowhere enjoined on men as it would have been on women who were to remain unmarried and not to bear children, as was the case for the *nadiātum* of Shamash at Sippar.

Summary

Young Mesopotamian women were expected to be virgins at the time of marriage. One definition of virginity was the woman's not having been penetrated by a male. The Mesopotamians did not identify a physical structure like an intact hymen as a criterion for virginity. But even if there were no verifiable bodily benchmarks for identifying a virgin, this does not mean that the experience of losing one's sexual innocence did

201. Ann Kessler Guinan, "Erotomancy: Scripting the Erotic," in *Sex and Gender in the Ancient Near East*, 185–201, at 191.

202. Ann Kessler Guinan, "Auguries of Hegemony: The Sex Omens of Mesopotamia," in *Gender and Body in the Ancient Mediterranean*, ed. Maria Wyke, 38–55 (Malden, MA: Blackwell, 1998), at 40; Rivkah Harris, *Gender and Aging in Mesopotamia* (Norman: University of Oklahoma Press, 2000), 93–95.

203. Wilfred G. Lambert, *Babylonian Wisdom Literature* [*BWL*] (Oxford: Clarendon Press, 1960), 102–3. On instances of Mesopotamian public authorities intervening to restrain extramarital sexual relationships that were otherwise legal see Raymond Westbrook, "The Enforcement of Morals in Mesopotamian Law," *JAOS* 104 (1984): 753–56.

not imprint its effects on the embodied character of the person involved. If one highlights the first sexual experience as a rite of passage, the emotional change effected by this experience has physical ramifications. How to measure such effects is a different question from the fact that this first sexual experience has a bodily impact. The symbolic character of the body, whereby one's experiences imprint themselves on one's physical appearance, is too commonplace to need proof. Yet measuring such changes and identifying specific causes is a different kind of concern from attentiveness to the fact that the mind or spirit has an impact on the body. The latter concern wishes to see how the body functions as a symbol of which physicality is an essential component.

Virginity in Mesopotamia can be seen as a symbol of physical wholeness. Such wholeness did not have to be verified by producing bloody bridal linens, as may have been the case in Deut 22:9-13. But when a virgin was raped, her rapist was obliged to marry her. If he already had a wife, the violated virgin was to replace her in the rapist's household. It seems there was a physical bond forged between the rapist and the violated virgin that needed to be maintained. The cultural practice seems to have said that because her virginal state no longer existed, she should be married. This sense of the physical integrity of a virgin is part of Mesopotamian consciousness of the distinction between the pure and the impure. Even though the containment of genital emissions is not mapped out in a series of regulations as in Leviticus 15, similar sentiments are expressed about the "wrongness" of frequent emission of semen by the male and the contagious character of menstruation.

This sense of the wholeness of the virgin may be a driving factor in cloistering the *nadiātum*-women. The extant letters, contracts, and legal texts provide much information on the socioeconomic dimension of *nadītum*-life, but only fragments about its religious purpose. The fact that the *nadiātum*-women of Sippar could not marry or bear children distinguishes them from *qadištum*-women. To explain this restriction simply in terms of avoiding the dispersal of the family inheritance overlooks the stipulation in *CH* 179 that a father could empower a *nadītum* to dispose of her property to those outside the family. This practice seems to have been operative in Nippur, where the *nadiātum* functioned as financial managers who could buy and sell property across lineages. Even if a family were moved by an economic or social motive to place a daughter in the liminal situation of a *nadītum*, this motive would be insufficient to support a common effort by multiple families over the span of more than three hundred years. The upper-class status of many *nadiātum* indicates that this cloistered way of life with its entrepreneurial activities was an honorable vocation.[204] The religious explanation that the *nadītum*'s task was to make intercession for the family extending through the generations and for the city seems to be vital to understanding this institution unique to the sociopolitical circumstances of the OB period. Just as a temple exercised important economic functions in the community alongside its religious focus, so also could the cloister of *nadiātum* in Sippar and Nippur have carried out economic activities alongside its primary vocation as a community of votaries linked with Shamash and Ninurta respectively.

An ideal of male virginity was nonexistent in Mesopotamia. However, it surfaces ever so momentarily in the experience of Enkidu when he was faced with death. He then wanted to return to his sexually innocent way of life with the animals prior to meeting the prostitute Shamhat. He was ready to jettison his sexual experience with Shamhat and his relationship with Gilgamesh and the people of Uruk until Shamash counseled him that their concern for him transcended death. They would honor him after he had died. This promise of enduring affection was enough for him to counteract his curses of Shamhat with blessings. Otherwise, the sexual restraint involved in keeping one's life on track was a matter of concern in the laws and omens.

Greece. Virginity: Negotiating an Ideal Within the Limits of the Human Condition

The ideal of virginity cultivates habits aimed at sustaining the boundaries of the patriarchal household. The dynamic character of *erōs* reveals that it is an integral part of human life and cannot be co-opted by human strategies and social structures. The approach to *erōs* that is attentive to its demands but cautious about its tendencies to excess requires that the reality of *erōs* be woven into the practices of the household. The conformity of the personal dimension of *erōs* to the limits prescribed by the household depends on the decisions of its individual members. The survival of the household depends on shaping the imagination and values of the members so that they constructively bring the energy of *erōs* into the household but keep at bay its destructive excesses. The practice of virginity was a disciplinary measure that aimed to allow *erōs* its rightful place in the life of the household. This section will examine

204. Harris, "The *Nadītu* Woman," 108–9.

the practice of virginity in ancient Greece according to the following four topics: (1) the societal expectation of premarital virginity was fostered but not directly enforceable; (2) the household's need for its members to practice virginity and sexual constraint was communicated by the example of the virgin goddesses Hestia, Athena, and Artemis; (3) the maintenance of purity demanded attentiveness to the inbreaking of the biological processes of birth, sex, and death into the life of the household; and (4) the quest for lifelong male virginity may become hubristic rather than heroic if the one practicing this virginity is not attentive to the demands of Aphrodite.

The Reception of the Prohibition of Premarital Sex for Women

A young Greek woman was expected to be a virgin at the time of her marriage. This ideal of sexual innocence was not always achieved in real life because the woman might have borne a child and yet have been categorized as a *parthenos*.[205] Nevertheless, the ideal of virginity was to be respected by keeping illicit sexual encounters secret.[206] If an unmarried woman had sexual relations with a man and became pregnant, the father of the household was authorized to disown her and declare her to be an outsider. Her sexual behavior was tied to the honor of the household because her bodily wholeness was representative of the integrity of the household.[207] In the sixth century BCE Solon enacted a law demanding that an Athenian father dismiss a pregnant unmarried daughter from his household.[208] The severity of this punishment for illicit sexual relations is evident when viewed in light of Solon's legislation forbidding a man to sell a daughter or a sister into slavery.[209] In fifth-century Athens the severity of the punishment for adultery was lessened: the wife was expelled from the household and prohibited from partici-

205. Sissa, *Greek Virginity*, 342–43; Cole, "Domesticating Artemis," 33.

206. Sissa, *Greek Virginity*, 89; Cohen, *Law, Sexuality, and Society*, 164; cf. Ken Dowden, *Death and the Maiden: Girls' Initiation Rites in Greek Mythology* (London: Routledge, 1989), 2.

207. Cheryl Ann Cox, *Household Interests: Property, Marriage Strategies, and Family Dynamics in Ancient Athens* (Princeton: Princeton University Press, 1998), 69; cf. Carol Delaney, "Seeds of Honor, Fields of Shame," in *Honor and Shame and the Unity of the Mediterranean*, ed. David D. Gilmore, 35–48 (Washington, DC: American Anthropological Association, 1987), at 42–43.

208. Walter K. Lacey, *The Family in Classical Greece* (London: Thames and Hudson, 1968), 115; cf. Plutarch, *Solon*, 23:2.

209. Ibid.; Sissa, *Greek Virginity*, 87.

pating in religious functions but was not subjected to corporal punishment or sold into slavery.[210]

In the marriage ceremony the bride's virginity was symbolized by the veil.[211] Sissa explains that the wedding ritual was to prefigure discreetly the sexual initiation of the wedding night and to be both a beginning and a mirror of all married life.[212] As significant as the gift-giving and the change of the bride's name were to this rite of passage, probably the most dramatic moment of the ceremony was the "unveiling" (*anakalyptēria*) of the bride. The wedding night began with a procession with torches and singing from the household of the bride's father to that of the father of the groom, who hosted the banquet. Sissa explains that "the meal offered by the father of the groom stands for the solemn reception of a faceless female stranger into the male *oikos*."[213] Therefore when the groom lifts the veil of the bride and expresses to the assembled guests his approval of her, he is ritually saying that this is the first time he has seen her. Most likely he has already become acquainted with her, but this unveiling prefigures the undressing of the bride in the bridal chamber.[214] The ritual states the ideal that the couple will not have had sexual relations prior to their wedding night. Thereafter the veil was to be part of her attire as a wife. If she was bereaved of her husband as was Andromache of Hector (*Il.* 22.468-72), she would tear off her veil in anguish, indicating the end of her marriage.[215]

The wedding procession and the unveiling emphasize two "gazes" at the bride: (1) that of friends and neighbors in the public acknowledgment of the transfer of the bride to the groom's household and (2) that of the groom at the moment of unveiling.[216] The visual contact of the

210. Demosthenes, "Against Neaera," 87; Cynthia Patterson, *The Family in Greek History* (Cambridge, MA: Harvard University Press, 1998), 131.

211. See above, chap. 2.

212. Sissa, *Greek Virginity*, 93–94.

213. Ibid., 98; see also William D. Furley, *Studies in the Use of Fire in Ancient Greek Religion* (New York: Arno Press, 1981), 185, 195.

214. Sissa, *Greek Virginity*, 98. Aphrodite A. Avagianou, "*Hieros Gamos* in Ancient Greek Religion: The Human Aspect of a Sacralized Ritual," in *Sacred Marriages: The Divine-Human Sexual Metaphor from Sumer to Early Christianity*, ed. Martti Nissinen and Risto Uro, 145–71 (Winona Lake, IN: Eisenbrauns, 2008), at 156, n. 54, notes the debate on the point in the marriage ceremonies when the *anakalyptēria* occurred and contends that it was a ceremony in the morning after the bride and groom had spent the night together; the same view is held by Rush Rehm, *Marriage to Death: The Conflation of Wedding and Funeral Rituals in Greek Tragedy* (Princeton: Princeton University Press, 1994) 142.

215. Sissa, *Greek Virginity*, 95.

216. Ibid., 98.

groom with the bride marks the point at which "the intact boundary of her person is violated."[217] The erotic dimension of this gaze is consistent with that of the voyeuristic gaze—which the virgin goddess Athena repelled by placing the Gorgon on her aegis, with the result that men who looked upon her lustfully would suffer serious, if not fatal, consequences.[218] The prophet Teresias was blinded for looking upon Athena at her bath.[219]

During the wedding procession the guests and onlookers shouted *hymēn, hymenaios*. Sissa explains that the ancients speculated at length on the etymology of the word *hymēn*, linking it with "living together" (*hymenaiein*) "in harmony" (*homonoein*) or with some figure by the name of Hymenaeus.[220] But Aristotle and the Hippocratic doctors say nothing about a membrane veiling the female genitals known as the *hymēn*.[221] Sissa concludes: "The Greek hymen lacked none of the qualities needed to become the impossible-to-mend protective veil over the virgin's *aidoion*—the hymen as we know it. Yet plausible as it may have been, such a role was never assigned to it."[222]

Since the Greeks did not rely on anatomical investigations to verify virginity of a young woman, they had to resort either to divination or to ordeals. Sissa describes the following two tests at Ephesus. (1) A woman swears that she has been chaste, and her words are recorded on a tablet that is hung about her neck; she is then required to step into a "revelatory liquid" that reaches up to the lower part of her calves. If nothing happens, she has been truthful; but if she has lied, then the waters of the Styx are riled and rise up to cover the tablet about her neck. (2) At a cave of Pan, if a young woman enters who is a virgin, the pipes of Pan put forth a sweet sound; but if she has had a secret sexual experi-

217. Anne Carson, "Dirt and Desire: The Phenomenology of Female Pollution in Antiquity," in *Constructions of the Classical Body*, ed. James I. Porter, 77–100 (Ann Arbor: University of Michigan Press, 1999), at 91.

218. Callimachus, *Hymn to Athena*, 51–136; Irwin, "The Invention of Virginity on Olympus," 17.

219. Timothy Gantz, *Early Greek Myth* (Baltimore: Johns Hopkins University Press, 1993), 530.

220. Sissa, *Greek Virginity*, 106, who quotes Photius in his *Chrestomathia* of Proclos in Albert Severyns, *Recherches sur la Chrestomathie de Proclos, première partie: Le codex 239 de Photius*, vol. 2 (Liège: Faculté de philosophie et lettres, 1938), 49–50; commentary on pp. 194–204.

221. Sissa, *Greek Virginity*, 110–11.

222. Ibid., 111.

ence the pipes give a mournful howl.[223] These local tests seem to be more anecdotal in character than established practices.

The Ideal Virginity of the Goddesses Hestia, Athena, and Artemis

The Greek ideal of virginity is embodied in the divine world by the goddesses Hestia, Artemis, and Athena.[224] These three deities are singled out in the *Homeric Hymn to Aphrodite* as the only beings among the gods, humans, and beasts who have been able to resist the erotic power of Aphrodite.

Hestia was the firstborn of Cronus, but she was also the first of Cronus's children to be swallowed by Zeus and the last to be released from inside him as a second birth.[225] She was courted by Poseidon and Apollo but rejected them and swore an oath of perpetual virginity. Since she had turned away from marriage, Zeus gave her an honored place at the center of every household as the one who tends the hearthfire (*Homeric Hymn to Aphrodite*, ll. 21-32).[226] Jean-Pierre Vernant identifies this honored place not only as the center of the domestic space but also as the *omphalos* ("navel") that has contact with heaven and the netherworld.[227] Hestia's location at the hearth is also a place of purity as seen in the following exhortation by Hesiod: "Do not, when physically defiled, show yourself near the hearth in your house, but avoid it" (*Op.* 733-34). Because of her virgin status within her natal household she symbolizes "the fixity, permanence, and seclusion" of the household.[228]

She also represents political power as she becomes manifest in the city council, its treasury, and the very exercise of political authority.[229] Hestia's role of promoting unity among the diverse citizens is illustrated in the communal sacrifices in fourth-century Cos. The citizens gather at Hestia's altar, from which the sacrificial victim is divided and distributed among them; Hestia presides over this movement to and from the center.[230] As Marcel Detienne notes, there is an abstractness about Hestia:

223. Ibid., 85.

224. Ibid., 83.

225. Marcel Detienne, *The Writing of Orpheus: Greek Myth in Cultural Contact*, trans. Janet Lloyd (Baltimore: Johns Hopkins University Press, 2002), 62.

226. Furley, *Use of Fire in Ancient Greek Religion*, 187–89.

227. Jean-Pierre Vernant, *Myth and Thought among the Greeks* (London: Routledge & Kegan Paul, 1983), 128.

228. Ibid., 132.

229. Detienne, *The Writing of Orpheus*, 63.

230. Ibid., 66.

"she is an idea, a pure form of something that incorporates both the end and the beginning, ubiquitous yet with a fixed center, an idea that imposes order on all the space that surrounds her."[231] The paired opposite of Hestia is the messenger god Hermes, who represents movement, contact with the outside world, and exchange with others.[232]

Athena is the virgin goddess who won the role of protector of Athens against Poseidon. According to an account in Herodotus 8.55 and Apollodorus 3.14.1, the Olympian gods chose Athena, who had planted an olive tree on the Acropolis, instead of Poseidon, who had produced a "sea" near the Acropolis.[233] In another version of this account by Varro (first century BCE) the people of Athens selected Athena over Poseidon. Her profile, then, is of one who accepted the traditional passive role of the female in politics, but in matters of war she was arrayed in full armor and symbolized the values of self-control and order in the military.[234] Walter Burkert describes her as a graceful aide who is there when solutions need to be found but whose intervention does not detract from the accomplishments of the one she aids.[235]

In Athena's honor the Parthenon was built in 447–432 BCE as a replacement for the temple destroyed by the Persians in 487; it celebrates the Athenian triumph over the Persians. The sculpture engraved on the exterior of the building was linked with the words engraved on her forty-foot statue in its interior.[236] Her role as a civilizing force weaves its way through the artistic narratives of the metopes and the frieze. The metopes depict battles between the Greeks and the Amazons, the Greeks and the Trojans, the Lapiths and the Centaurs, and the Olympian gods and the giants. This visual narrative announces that Athena will overcome those who are rebels in terms of gender (female warriors), adultery (the Trojan Paris's abduction of Helen), bestial lust (drunken Centaurs' rape of Lapith women), and cosmic war (the Titans' battle against Zeus

231. Ibid., 63.

232. Vernant, *Myth and Thought among the Greeks*, 130; Detienne, *The Writing of Orpheus*, 64.

233. Sue Blundell, "Marriage and the Maiden: Narratives on the Parthenon," in *The Sacred and the Feminine in Ancient Greece*, 47–70, at 53.

234. Ibid., 55.

235. Walter Burkert, *Greek Religion* (Cambridge, MA: Harvard University Press, 1985), 141.

236. Kenneth Lapatin, "The Statue of Athena and Other Treasures in the Parthenon," in *The Parthenon: From Antiquity to the Present*, ed. Jenifer Neils, 261–91 (Cambridge: Cambridge University Press, 2005), at 266–67.

and the Olympians).[237] The frieze pictures the procession closing the Panathenaea festival, which occurs every fourth year. The cavalry in the procession symbolizes the transfer of aristocratic values from the family to the polis.[238] In these depictions Athena supports marriage as the primary paradigm of an ordered civilization.[239] She herself resists marriage in the world of the gods and pushes marriage into the human sphere.[240] Clad in mannish dress, the ideal virgin warrior Athena emphasizes the difference of her femininity from that of mortals by heightening it.[241]

Artemis is the virgin goddess of the hunt who watches over young women as virgins and then later as childbearers (*Homeric Hymn to Aphrodite*, ll. 14-20). Her sanctuaries were typically located at the borders of a territory in order to link that vulnerable region with the city at the center; however, she also had sanctuaries on hills overlooking thoroughfares and in the agora section of cities, to which she brought a sense of the wilderness.[242] Artemis was the lookout, "a god of turning points," who watched over vulnerable areas or dangerous passageways.[243] When her rituals in border sanctuaries excluded males, the women participants were particularly vulnerable. Their only protection was Artemis. At Brauron, the well-known shrine of Artemis that guarded an important harbor on the east coast of Attica,[244] it was said that the ancient Pelasgians from Lemnos had kidnapped Attic women and kept them as concubines

237. Katherine A. Schwab, "Celebrations of Victory: The Metopes of the Parthenon," in *The Parthenon*, 159–97, at 167. On role reversal in Heracles' battle with the Amazons in Euripides' *Ion*, in which the feminine is the civilized, saving force, see Froma Zeitlin, "Mysteries of Identity and Designs of the Self in Euripides' *Ion*," in her *Playing the Other: Gender and Society in Classical Greek Literature*, 285–338 (Chicago: University of Chicago Press, 1996), at 326–27.

238. Blundell, "Marriage and the Maiden," 57–60; Jenifer Neils, "'With Noblest Images on All Sides': The Ionic Frieze of the Parthenon," in *The Parthenon*, 199–223, at 120, 211–15, 220, notes that the horsemen seem to represent a "heroization or aggrandizement of Athenian warriors" in relation to victories at land and at sea, including the battle of Marathon.

239. Schwab, "Celebrations of Victory," 168.

240. Froma Zeitlin, "Mysteries of Identity," 323, notes that "Athena retains her virginity [and] yet participates in motherhood" by resisting sexual union with Hephaestus and casting his semen into the soil from which Erichthonius is born.

241. Blundell, "Marriage and the Maiden," 47–48.

242. Susan Guettel Cole, *Landscapes, Gender, and Ritual: The Ancient Greek Experience* (Berkeley: University of California Press, 2004), 180–83, 195–96.

243. Ibid., 184, 187.

244. Cole (ibid., 193) notes that water held an important place both in the landscape of Artemis's sanctuaries and in her rituals.

(*pallakai*). In order to hide their crime the kidnappers killed the women and their children, which prompted Artemis to send a disease that attacked their crops, herds, and humans (Herodotus 6.138-39).[245] Susan Guettel Cole explains that initiation rituals in outlying sanctuaries that put women at risk were intended to test the strength of the community's security and to honor Artemis as a protector. Such rituals were an important component of the religious system.[246] Also at Brauron was the annual ritual known as the *arkteia*, in which young girls played the part of she-bears as preparation for pregnancy and childbirth. At Athens this ritual was regarded as a prerequisite to sexual intercourse.[247] Artemis required a young woman to participate in rituals at strategic points in her maturation process: before puberty, at marriage, at first pregnancy, at childbirth, and at key stages in the growth of the child. If a young woman skipped one of these rites she ran the risk of angering Artemis.[248] The women's rituals honoring Artemis were not so much individual as communal rites of passage: they were key moments in the community's process of reproducing itself.[249]

In her rites of initiation the virgin hunter goddess Artemis required young women to retreat to the wilds like the maenads of Dionysus or like the women in the Athenian Thesmophoria (*Hom. Hymn to Aphrodite* 118; *Il.* 16.180-83; *Od.* 6.155-57; cf. Eur. *Bacchae*, l. 33).[250] Here the women were freed from the constraints of the patriarchal household. Their virginity had to be intact as they came before Artemis in their collective dancing at the festival of Brauron. In this liminal state their erotic appeal was strong. Artemis was perpetually in this potent state of virginity, ripe for marriage. She was also protective of the virginity of young women and would punish those who would compromise it. So the majority of the young women who transitioned toward marriage had to be careful to offer sacrifice to Artemis in order to appease the potential anger of Artemis at the relinquishment of their virginity.[251] In the ritual at Brauron

245. Cole (ibid., 179–80) refers to the Messenians' kidnapping of Lakedaimonian young women (*parthenoi*) from the sanctuary of Artemis Karyatai on the border where the territories of Argos, Arkadia, and Lakonia converged (Pausanias 4.16.9-10). A similar Messenian kidnapping of Lakedaimonian *parthenoi* from the sanctuary of Artemis Limnatus on the western border of Lakonia is reported in Pausanias 4.4.3 and Strabo 6.3.3.

246. Cole, "Domesticating Artemis," 29.

247. Ibid., 31, 33.

248. Ibid., 33–34.

249. Ibid., 29.

250. Dowden, *Death and the Maiden*, 100, 104.

251. Burkert, *Greek Religion*, 151.

the young women identified themselves as she-bears; they were replacements for the bear killed by the brothers of the young women.[252] Thus they were human sacrifices offered to Artemis to calm her anger, just as Iphigenia was to be sacrificed at Aulis in order to replace the stag Agamemnon had killed in her sacred grove. In Euripides' *Iphigenia at Aulis*, Artemis replaces Iphigenia at the last moment with a doe (ll. 1581-89). So also the young women at Brauron are replaced by animal sacrifices. Richard Seaford argues that women's resistance to marriage is implied within this Brauronian ritual: they retreat to the wild; they become like animals; they perform sacrifice.[253] In this ritual time in the wild in service of Artemis they reject the men of their households and polis. This role of counterpointing the order of the male-dominated domestic and civic order is one that Artemis shares with Dionysus (cf. *Od.* 11.326; Eur. *Bacchae* 1056; cf. Eur. *Helen* 543).[254]

These three idealized divine virgins play essential roles in the maintenance of the household and marriage. Hestia with her intact virgin body symbolizes the integrity of the patriarchal household and the collective responsibility all of its members have in upholding its honor. Athena has a unique bond with her father Zeus in that she was born from her father's head after he had swallowed her mother Metis. He did so because an oracle warned him that the offspring of the pregnant Metis would usurp his sovereignty as he had done to his father, Cronus (Hesiod, *Theog*. 886-900, 924-26).[255] In line with the fact that Athena was not born from a mother, she identifies with all things male, except for marriage (cf. Aesch. *Eum*. 735-38).[256] Artemis likewise is a daughter of Zeus, but as the goddess of the hunt or of the wild she serves the essential function of counterpointing the status quo so that it might be renewed with intact boundaries. Artemis's role in the cycle of women's maturation is essential to the household and the polis.[257]

252. Ibid.

253. Richard Seaford, "Dionysus as Destroyer of the Household: Homer, Tragedy, and the Polis," in *Masks of Dionysus*, ed. Thomas H. Carpenter and Christopher A. Faraone, 115–46 (Ithaca, NY: Cornell University Press, 1993), at 122.

254. Ibid.

255. Martin L. West, in his edition of Hesiod's *Theogony*, 397, notes that Zeus's marriage with Metis, the first of his seven marriages, comes to an unusual end with the birth of Athena but was effective for ending the palace coups in the divine household.

256. Blundell, "Marriage and the Maiden," 49.

257. Cole, *Landscapes, Gender, and Ritual*, 195–97; eadem, "Domesticating Artemis," 33–34.

The virginal status of Hestia, Athena, and Artemis frees them from defiling processes in marriage and childbirth so that they might promote the integrity of the relationships of the household. This defense of the sphere of the household became increasingly important in the sixth century as the state intruded into the affairs of the household with laws regulating dowries, making adultery a public offense, and establishing an only daughter as an *epiklēros* whose son would then be regarded as the rightful heir to his grandfather's estate.[258] As a human example, Antigone's conflict with Creon illustrates how a virgin and *epiklēros* (Soph., *Antig.* 917-18) could so fully identify herself with her household that she would confront the power of the state in a life-or-death struggle. Her single-minded intensity in her effort to honor her brother with burial (*Antig.* 904-28) has a maenad-like quality that refuses to compromise with the polis.[259] Her protest is essential to justice in the polis and shows how her Dionysian-inspired self-sacrifice (*Antig.* 891-904, 1118-51) can be constructive for the polis in the long run.[260]

Sexual Defilement: The Violation of Communal and Personal Boundaries

According to legend, a priestess of Artemis Triklaria had sexual relations with her lover in the sanctuary because her parents opposed her relationship with him. The polis of Patrai, in which this sanctuary of Artemis was located, then suffered plague (*loimos*) and famine (*limos*) for the priestess's threefold sin: (1) she had violated the purity of the sanctuary; (2) she had not observed the requirement of sexual purity for a priestess; (3) she had turned away from the expectation that every unmarried woman refrain from sex. The famine sent by Artemis was so severe that the Delphic oracle instructed the people to sacrifice the priestess and her lover to Artemis and to repeat this sacrifice each year with another couple. The point of the story is clear: if female virginity is not preserved, the whole community will suffer defilement and then be punished by Artemis.[261] Sacrilegious actions did not harm Greek deities but rather bounced back on the perpetrator of these actions disrespectful of one or more deities.[262]

258. Blundell, "Marriage and the Maiden," 47.

259. Seaford, "Dionysus as Destroyer of the Household," 130, identifies similarities in Antigone's desolation and that of Agave in Euripides' *Bacchae* (1383–87).

260. Ibid., 120–21, 139.

261. Cole, "Domesticating Artemis," 30.

262. Robert Parker, *Miasma: Pollution and Purification in Early Greek Religion* (Oxford: Clarendon Press, 1983), 145–46.

In the shame culture of Athens the foregoing legend would put pressure on a young woman to be quite reserved in her dealings with men. An exacting standard of modesty would dictate her dress, behavior, and movements within the community.[263] Not only did her behavior have an impact on the honor of her father's household, it could also trigger calamities for the entire city. As noted earlier, Solonian laws called for a father to dismiss from his household a daughter who had lost her virginity and for a husband to do likewise to a wife who had committed adultery. This harsh law was predicated on the belief that the kinship structure could not tolerate the presence of a corrupted woman within the household. This corruption (*diaptheirein*) was believed to have an objective character such that subjective factors like the seduction of the wife or daughter would not change the need to expel.[264] If a daughter was pregnant, her illegitimate fetus was also to be sent away.[265]

Dirt is matter out of place.[266] It defiles when it disrupts the social context in which it is found.[267] Parker identifies *katharmos*, "cleansing," as the opposite of *miasma*, "defilement," and lists the following four characteristics of a person who is *miaros*: (1) the person is ritually impure; (2) the impurity is contagious; (3) the impurity is dangerous; and (4) this danger is not of a secular origin.[268] He notes that pollution arises from involuntary acts and so is not to be understood according to ethical categories like sin.[269] He also claims that the category of "disgusting," which refers to actions that are devoid of a proper sense of shame, is too broad to define *miasma*.[270] The term *agos*, "disgusting, outrageous, shameless," overlaps with *miasma* but carries the sense that this revolting action offends what is sacred. Therefore when Oedipus describes himself as *enagēs* he is in "the grip of an avenging power," which will contaminate those with whom it comes into contact.[271] What is *agos* is midway between an impersonal pollution and the angry visage of a deity. To counteract the former one would carry out a purification, but for the latter one would offer a sacrifice to appease the deity.[272]

263. See Phaedra's speech in Euripides, *Hippolytus* 385–89; Cox, *Household Interests*, 69; Carson, "Dirt and Desire," 86.

264. Sissa, *Greek Virginity*, 87.

265. Ibid., 88.

266. Douglas, *Purity and Danger*, 35–36; Carson, "Dirt and Desire," 87.

267. Parker, *Miasma*, 121.

268. Ibid., 3–4.

269. Ibid., 2.

270. Ibid., 4–5.

271. Ibid., 8; Burkert, *Greek Religion*, 81, 270.

272. Parker, *Miasma*, 9.

Sacred space was demarcated in order to facilitate the manifestation of a deity. The demarcation came not only by way of physical structures but also by actions, of which an important kind were purifications. So those measures aimed at keeping birth, death, and sexuality out of the sanctuary accented the gulf that separates deities from humans.[273] These actions pollute because they are an uncontrolled entry of the biological into the social sphere;[274] the impure humans would need to undergo purification in order to stop the spread of the contagion and keep it from contacting the holy. Birth and death within a sanctuary were regarded as sacrilegeous, that is, showing a lack of due respect for the god who dwelt there. For example, no one was permitted to die on the island of Delos or to bring the remains of someone there since the entire island was regarded as sacred (Herodotus 1.64.2).[275] A woman who had just given birth was secluded for the first forty days of her pregnancy but was then encouraged to visit temples.[276] However, the Greeks did not regard menstruation as an impurity, but rather as facilitating a woman's role as a potential mother.[277] The Hippocratic writer saw the menstrual flow of blood as a healthy purging that should not be impeded.[278] To do so would be to expose a girl to madness.[279] Parker concludes that "in the classical period, to judge from the surviving evidence, the threat which woman poses to ordered society proceeds not from the dark recesses of her body but of her mind."[280]

The integrity of the Greek household called for a working harmony between its diverse parts. In addition to the parents, children, and relatives, it could include concubines (*pallakes*), slaves, prostitutes (*hetairai*), and friends.[281] The danger posed to the husband's relationship to his

273. Ibid., 66. Burkert, *Greek Religion*, 271, defines *hagneia* as "the inviolate state required when dealing with the gods, the absence of sexuality, blood, and death." He points to Persephone and Demeter as *hagnai theai* who repeatedly come into contact with sexuality and death but are untouched by these forces since they are cloaked by the force field of *hagnos* that creates reverential distance and by *hieros* that establishes boundaries.

274. Parker, *Miasma*, 63.

275. Ibid., 33.

276. Ibid., 48–49.

277. Ibid., 100. Sissa, *Greek Virginity*, 116, notes that the physician Soranus of Ephesus (first-second century CE) advised against permanent virginity.

278. Hippocrates, "Prorrhetic II," 218–93, at 270–71, in *Hippocrates* VIII, LCL 482 (Cambridge, MA: Harvard University Press, 1995).

279. Sissa, *Greek Virginity*, 121; Ann Ellis Hanson, "The Hippocratic *Parthenos* in Sickness and Health," in *Virginity Revisited*, 40–65, at 43.

280. Parker, *Miasma*, 103; cf. Euripides, *Hippolytus* 636–42.

281. Cox, *Household Interests*, 168.

wife by the presence of concubines and *hetairai* is emphasized by the trouble brought upon Deianira by Heracles' promiscuous ways in Sophocles' *Trachiniae* (357-79, 460, 545-51).[282] The concubine who was designated to give birth to free children was distinguished from the one who was to give birth to slave children. Illegitimate offspring of the father (*nothoi*) were not allowed to inherit his property.[283] There was a special section of the household designated for free and slave women; this was a functional arrangement for completing household tasks rather than a strategy for guarding against female promiscuity.[284] Also foreign friends (*xenoi*) were often present within the house; they might use their wealth or capacity to create alliances to leverage power relationships in the household.[285] If *hetairai* were present they were usually either foreigners or lower-class women. While some were entertainers and a few could be the intellectual equals of men, the majority were *pornai* from the brothels located in the Peraeus or the Cerameicus.[286]

In Plato's vision of how life should be lived in the Greek household in the *Laws*, he proposed a number of strategies to sustain the procreative potential of the household. He argued that every male citizen was obliged to marry (773e-774a) in order to beget children (772e). In his plan adultery was defined in the same terms for husband and wife rather than the one-sided expectation that the wife be exclusively faithful to her husband. Plato emphasized sexual fidelity during the childbearing years but tolerated a moderate amount of adultery thereafter. To persuade his audience to observe these standards he proposed that adultery, homosexual relations, and union with prostitutes be regarded as equivalent to incest, which was abominable to the gods and dishonorable in society. Plato argued that if a man committed any one of these transgressions and failed to keep it secret he should be stripped of his citizenship (841).[287]

282. See chap. 2 above, and Charles Segal, "Trachiniae," in *Tragedy and Civilization: An Interpretation of Sophocles* (Cambridge, MA: Published for Oberlin College by Harvard University Press, 1981), 60–108, at 75–76.

283. Cox, *Household Interests*, 172. On Pericles' alteration of the law in order to include his concubine Aspasia and her son within his household, see chap. 2 above, p. 138.

284. Patterson, *The Family in Greek History*, 126, 128; Cohen, *Law, Sexuality, and Society*, 149.

285. Cox, *Household Interests*, 202–3.

286. Ibid., 174.

287. Patterson, *The Family in Greek History*, 133–37, 171, notes that prostitution was institutionalized early in the sixth century BCE to serve the needs of male citizens, who typically did not marry until they were thirty years of age.

Chastity and the Ideal of Male Virginity

Complete chastity was regarded as extreme by the Greeks. A more honorable way of life was the exercise of *sōphrosynē*, "self-control." [288] Cohen notes that according to folk belief in Italy, Spain, and Greece men were to be careful not to allow women to drain their sexual energy from them.[289] The expectation of complete chastity was imposed on girls and young women in premarital situations. Since the majority married by age fourteen or shortly thereafter, this ideal may well have been realizable. But since young men often did not marry until closer to thirty years of age they were not expected to remain chaste prior to marriage. Since women were regarded as off-limits first by the household of their father and then by that of their husband, the only options for sexual relations open to unmarried men were liaisons with foreign women, slaves, prostitutes, or males.[290] After marriage the wife was to be exclusively faithful to her husband, but the husband was not legally bound to refrain from sexual relations with other unmarried women or with men who were slaves.[291] Thus chastity was regarded primarily as a feminine virtue.[292]

In Euripides' *Hippolytus* the two main characters are Hippolytus, a bastard son of Theseus, king of Troezen near Athens, and Phaedra, the wife of Theseus and the stepmother of Hippolytus. Hippolytus is a young, unmarried man who boasts of his chastity. When he defends himself before his father, he says: "You perceive the light and the earth here. In these places, there is no man more chaste than I, even though you would not say so" (993-95). Hippolytus is proud of his strong devotion to Artemis. After a hunt with his companions he goes to the altar of Artemis and prays:

> Greetings, Artemis, most beautiful among the young women on Olympus, I have prepared this garland for you from an untouched meadow. No shepherd considers feeding his flock there, nor has an iron implement ever entered it. Only the bees in springtime pass

288. David Grene, "Introduction, Euripides, *Hippolytus*," in *Three Greek Tragedies in Translation* (Chicago: University of Chicago, 1942), 155–68, at 156.

289. Cohen, *Law, Sexuality, and Society*, 142.

290. Cox, *Household Interests*, 172; John J. Winkler, "Laying Down the Law: The Oversight of Men's Sexual Behavior in Classical Athens," in *Before Sexuality: The Construction of Erotic Experience in the Ancient Greek World*, ed. David Halperin, John Winkler, and Froma Zeitlin, 171–209 (Princeton: Princeton University Press, 1990), at 178–83.

291. Cox, *Household Interests*, 187–90, 195, 207.

292. Froma Zeitlin, "The Power of Aphrodite: Eros and the Boundaries of the Self in Euripides' *Hippolytus*," in *Playing the Other*, 219–84, at 222.

> through this untouched meadow. Reverence tends it with pure water from the river. Those who receive chastity toward all things by nature rather than by instruction may pick flowers there; the wicked are not permitted to do so. (70-81)

The wild is the sphere of Artemis. The meadow in which Hippolytus gathers flowers is a sacred space. Zeitlin notes that this bounded meadow is a spatial analogue to the bounded character of Hippolytus's chaste body.[293] Both places keep what is alien outside their boundaries. Hippolytus's strong devotion to Artemis seems to have given him the daring to withdraw from the duty of honoring Aphrodite.[294] When his elderly servant questions his neglect of Aphrodite, he replies: "I, who am chaste, greet her at a distance . . . . Concerning gods and humans, one cares about one and another another" (102, 104). In ancient Greece young men would be chaste when they wanted Artemis to assist them on a hunt, but this was for a limited duration. Hippolytus, however, is taking on the discipline of chastity over the long term—a challenge neither women nor men in ancient Greece would have accepted because it was one only the virgin goddesses could meet.[295] Therefore Aphrodite feels offended and plans to make him recognize her reality in his life (21-23). She will do so indirectly by having Phaedra, his stepmother, fall madly in love with him (24-28).

Phaedra battles valiantly against this lovesickness (176-300). She recognizes that some deity has afflicted her with this madness and that it puts her in a compromised position in which both her honor and that of her household are endangered, and so she longs for death (239-49). Phaedra describes to the women of Troezen (i.e., the chorus) the battle she has been waging against this illicit desire:

> When *erōs* wounded me, I was considering how I might deal with it as well as possible. So I began by keeping the illness quiet and

293. Ibid., 232. Hanna M. Roisman, *Nothing Is As It Seems: The Tragedy of the Implicit in Euripides' Hippolytus* (Lanham, MD: Rowman & Littlefield, 1999), 29, claims that Hippolytus says he is not interested in sex, but it is on his mind as he visits the meadow.

294. Robin Mitchel-Boyask, "Euripides' *Hippolytus* and the Trials of Manhood (The *Ephebia*?)," in *Rites of Passage in Ancient Greece: Literature, Religion, Society*, ed. Mark W. Padilla, 42–66 (Lewisburg, PA: Bucknell University Press, 1999), at 45, notes that Hippolytus's identity at the fluid margins violates Artemis's normal functions as one who promotes transitions from one stage of life to the next.

295. Zeitlin, "The Power of Aphrodite," 238, 255. Roisman, *Nothing Is As It Seems*, 7–8, contends that Hippolytus does not rule out marriage in the future (cf. *Hipp*. 1140–41; 1425–26).

> hidden. For no one should trust the tongue, which knows how to criticize the alien thoughts of men but by this it brings very many evils. Then I imagined that I might prevail and deal well with my foolishness through self-control (*sōphronein*). Finally, when I still was not successful in dealing with Aphrodite, I decided that the best solution was to die, which no one disputes. I would rather that my good deeds be noticed and my shameful ones not have many witnesses. (393-404)

She also is committed to *sōphrosynē*, "self-control," but sees that the irrational has irrupted into her life and endangers her social standing.[296] The nurse who forces Phaedra to reveal what is troubling her is shocked when she hears of Phaedra's love for her stepson Hippolytus and notes: "The chaste ones do not willingly love evil but nevertheless love it. Aphrodite is surely not a deity. But, if possible, something greater than a deity, which has utterly destroyed her, me, and the household" (359-61).

The nurse, who is intent on helping Phaedra recover, decides against Phaedra's wish to conceal her secret passion from Hippolytus and reveals it to him (520-24).[297] Upon hearing of Phaedra's love for him, Hippolytus is filled with righteous indignation; Phaedra overhears the commotion he makes in the house and feels there is no exit except death (575-76, 596-97, 599-600). In her disclosure to Hippolytus the nurse makes him swear an oath that he will speak of Phaedra's love for him to no one (611). He expresses his ambivalence about this oath by saying: "The tongue swore, but the mind was non-committal" (612). But he remains faithful to his word even though it means that his father Theseus believes he has raped Phaedra (882-86, 1057-58, 1164-65).[298] Zeitlin points out that his fidelity to this oath is of a piece with his commitment to chastity. To lie would be to taint his conscience and defile himself, which Hippolytus, virtuous as he is, would avoid at all costs, even death.[299]

Phaedra is well aware that the revelation of her illicit passion would fit the stereotype of the adulterous wife. She states to the women of Troezen:

296. Roisman, *Nothing Is As It Seems*, 39, 47, 50, 56, 77, 90, describes Phaedra as a seductress who is in full control as she tries to trap Hippolytus (*Hipp.* 239-49).

297. Roisman, *Nothing Is As It Seems*, 47, 65, describes the nurse as obtuse and excessively loyal (with *philia*) to Phaedra (*Hipp.* 253-66).

298. Charles Segal, *Oedipus Tyrannus: Tragic Heroism and the Limits of Knowledge* (New York: Twayne Publishers, 1993), 8, notes that the plot of Euripides' *Hippolytus* seems to be the reverse of Sophocles' *Oedipus Tyrannus*: i.e., the protagonist is falsely accused of incest with his stepmother and is killed by his enraged father.

299. Zeitlin, "The Power of Aphrodite," 251.

> I recognized well what it is to be a woman in these things—an object of hate to all. As one who might utterly perish, this one began to defile the marriage-bed initially with foreign men. This evil for women began in upper-class households. Whenever the shameful seems honorable for the nobles, then it will very much seem to be so for the lowly. I hate women who are chaste in words but secretly acquire a reckless boldness. (407-414)

To avoid this lecherous reputation, Phaedra determines to leave behind a letter at the time of her suicide that accuses Hippolytus of having raped her. It is this letter that bursts the bubble of Hippolytus's chaste reputation. Even though the claim is false, Theseus believes it. Hippolytus cannot refute it without breaking his oath. This dilemma leads Hippolytus to accept exile and settle merely for a strong protest that the allegation is false (983-1035, 1055-56). Zeitlin explains that this false accusation puts Hippolytus in the same compromised situation Phaedra had been placed in by Aphrodite. Now Hippolytus is her double, that is, he will struggle for his life and honor in the face of this false accusation. He must deal with the "other" in his experience: he cannot live in splendid isolation away from the human contact that demands that one take risks in relating to the "other." Hippolytus has been forced to leave his Eden-like enclosure of adolescence and pass over into the adult world where the touch of the "other" brings one to a new level of self-awareness.[300]

Hippolytus has to make a significant adjustment in order to die to his reputation as a chaste person. This does not mean that he forfeits the practice of chastity, but he does have to deal with the reality that he has no means of refuting the allegation of rape. In the interim between first hearing of Phaedra's passion for him and his resolve to accept exile from his irate father Hippolytus vents his feelings about women in a strongly misogynistic speech that reflects Greek attitudes found in the story of Pandora in Hesiod's *Theogony* (570-601) and *Works and Days* (54-95).[301] He advocates imploring the gods to create men directly, and not through women. He accuses women of being a drain on the resources of their father's household and then those of their husbands (616-39). Hippolytus

300. Ibid., 234.

301. Roisman, *Nothing Is As It Seems*, 37–38, 110–11, interprets Pandora as threatening because she is first of all a seductress, a courtesan. Furley, *Use of Fire in Ancient Greek Religion*, 192, refers to Edmund Leach's *Culture and Communication* (Cambridge: Cambridge University Press, 1976), 74–75, where this misogyny is explained as arising from the foreignness of the new wife; such a view changes as time progresses and she becomes the mother of legitimate children.

feels defiled by the very suggestion that he would have sexual relations with Phaedra and violate, as he says, "the untouchable character of my father's marriage bed" (650-52). The threatening character of the report of her passion leads Hippolytus to say: "I am going to a flowing stream to cleanse myself by washing out my ears. How could I be a sinner since I cannot even hear such things without regarding myself as defiled?" (653-55).[302]

When Phaedra's letter is opened after her suicide, Hippolytus can keep the "other" out of his inner space no longer. Zeitlin argues that this is when Hippolytus's claim to be *parthenos* is gone. No longer can he refuse "to allow an 'other' to intrude upon his visual and tactile space."[303] Hippolytus's relationship with Artemis embodies the ideals of maidenhood, where sexual purity means that "what is objectively untouched is what is subjectively contained."[304] The womb of the virgin remains sealed. But Zeitlin notes that the *parthenos* figure is liminal and poised to enter the complex and compromised arena of human relations. Thus Hippolytus "may well be the potential bride as well as the bridegroom and it is this status that will socially lead him into the wider sphere of feminine experience exemplified by his secret double, Phaedra."[305] In this intersubjective relation with an "other," the adult self emerges.[306] Hippolytus had waylaid the emergence of this adult self by his suppression of *erōs*, a reality that is both outside as an "other" and within as a beast.[307]

Hippolytus is an illegitimate son who is trying to demonstrate that he possesses the qualities necessary to be an heir to the household.[308] From his perspective, virtue can be learned; it is not simply given by birth. This question of foreigners gaining control of households and, as property owners, exercising their right to speak in the polis assembly became an important issue in fifth-century BCE Athens.[309] When Pericles designated his son from his concubine Aspasia as a legitimate heir to his household he introduced controversy into the polis that was probably

302. Roisman, *Nothing Is As It Seems*, 18, contends that Hippolytus is not fearful of sex but of sex outside of wedlock.

303. Zeitlin, "The Power of Aphrodite," 234.

304. Ibid., 235.

305. Ibid.

306. Ibid., 234, 236.

307. Ibid., 223, 229.

308. Mitchel-Boyask, "Euripides' *Hippolytus* and the Trials of Manhood," 53–54. Roisman, *Nothing Is As It Seems*, 8, 38, notes how Theseus himself had come to Troezen as a self-imposed exile for having slain the Pallantids.

309. Ibid., 178–79.

strong around the time of his death in 429 BCE.[310] Euripides' *Hippolytus* was performed one year later in 428 and probably entered into this debate over the criteria for a legitimate heir by portraying the tragic fate of Hippolytus, a bastard son who displayed exemplary virtue but was undermined by a deceitful letter. The reception by the audience may well have been divided: Athenians who were worried about the erosion of their voting power by an increasing immigrant population would probably have said that the demise of Hippolytus was an unfortunate necessity, whereas those who had immigrated probably sympathized with him as a tragic figure.[311] As a virtuous, tragic figure Hippolytus may be regarded as one who sacralized virginity: its "untouchability bears a metaphysical charge transcending the laws of nature and even of gender."[312]

As Hippolytus lies dying after his chariot crashes on the rocks of the sea cliff near Skiron, Artemis appears and informs Theseus of Hippolytus's innocence (1284-1312).[313] She indicates that Hippolytus will be remembered by maidens in their ritual on the eve of their marriages:

> To you, unfortunate one, because of your troubles, I will give you the greatest honors in the city of Troezen. Unmarried young women, prior to their marriage, will cut their hair for you. Through a lengthy period, you will harvest the great sorrow of their tears. Forever the poetry of young women will be concerned about you. And Phaedra's love for you will not be silenced by falling into anonymity. (1423-30)

This occasion on which young women would bid farewell to their virginity would be the time when Hippolytus's virginity would be remembered.[314] He would be a mirror image of them, that is, "a reversed image" that both reflects the truth and creates an illusion.[315] On the other hand,

310. Martin Ostwald, "Athens as a Cultural Centre," CAH, rev. ed., vol. 5: *The Fifth Century B.C.*, 306–69, at 309–10, 368.

311. Roisman, *Nothing Is As It Seems*, 178.

312. Zeitlin, "The Power of Aphrodite," 235.

313. Mitchel-Boyask, "Euripides' *Hippolytus* and the Trials of Manhood," 46–52, notes how Hippolytus's death in the area of Skiron recalls an event in Theseus's own relationship to his father. Roisman, *Nothing Is As It Seems*, 152–53, explains how Theseus never accepts Hippolytus as a legitimate son; reconciliation between father and son is not reached.

314. Rehm, *Marriage to Death*, 29, 52, notes that brides offer a lock of hair prior to marriage and mourners do likewise when visiting a grave.

315. Zeitlin, "The Power of Aphrodite," 270; Charles Segal, "Theatre, Ritual and Commemoration in Euripides' *Hippolytus*," *Ramus* 17 (1988): 52–74, at 62–64.

Hippolytus's embodiment of both feminine and masculine characteristics could be saying that virginity is a state that transcends gender.[316]

Summary

Greek society in archaic and classical times respected the competing claims of the goddesses Aphrodite and Artemis. They legislated strict laws against premarital sex for women and then tried to sustain the impression that these laws were observed always and everywhere. Tests for virginity, where they occurred, took the form of ordeals or divinations; there was no physically verifiable standard such as an intact hymen.

The virgin goddesses Hestia, Athena, and Artemis created in the important sphere of the imagination a picture of the benefits conferred by a chaste life. Hestia symbolized the wholesome integrity of the household where purity was respected. Athena was identified with the civilizing force threading its way through the activities that created the polis. Artemis was the goddess who enforced chastity for unmarried women and assisted young mothers in childbirth and the early years of nurturing their children. Rituals in Artemis's sanctuary provided an opportunity for women to express their feelings of resistance to marriage as structured within a patriarchal household.

The sense that there is something foreign in one's personal space is a feeling of defilement. This feeling also has an analogue within the body of the community and the cult. Removal of such involuntary irruptions of the biological into the social are effected by purifications and sacrifices. The ancient Greeks were attentive to the defiling character of birth, death, and sex but did not regard genital emissions as contaminating. The patriarchal Greek household protected itself against the possibility of female promiscuity but also, from Plato's perspective, had in place the potential structures for sexual continence among males.

The ideal of male virginity as a way of life existed only in the imaginary world of Greek tragedy. In practice males would remain chaste for activities such as the hunt and preparation for battle, but as a behavior to be observed over the long term it was regarded as violating the structures of life. This violation is articulated in Euripides' *Hippolytus* as a dishonoring of Aphrodite. The proud young virgin Hippolytus is faithful to Artemis, but Aphrodite will make him pay his dues for embracing chastity and completely ignoring the demands of *erōs*. Hippolytus's

316. Zeitlin, "The Power of Aphrodite," 235.

stepmother Phaedra wrestles with the strong erotic passion Aphrodite has inflicted on her. Phaedra's nurse tries to overcome this tension between *erōs* and chastity that is driving Phaedra toward the grave, but her efforts to resolve the tension only hurry the movement. The tension between sexual restraint and *erōs* cannot be readily resolved and at some level of intensity takes the form of an antinomy within human existence that needs to be respected and monitored. The nurse's intervention to lower the painful intensity of the *erōs* besetting Phaedra only results in death for both Phaedra and Hippolytus. Phaedra tries to avoid the label of the adulterous wife but does so in a way that results in her fulfilling the stereotype of the adulterous wife who frames the young lover by falsely accusing him of raping her. The accused Hippolytus, sworn to secrecy about Phaedra's passion for him by the nurse, can only protest that his virginity is as pure as can be found anywhere. In his initial anger at Phaedra he voices the misogynistic attitudes found in the Greek society of his time.

Synthesis: The Role of Virginity in Maintaining Bodily Integrity

The context within which one views a person or an object will have a decisive impact on how that object is understood. If virginity is pictured as a female practice that is imposed on young women before marriage in ancient Israel, Mesopotamia, and Greece, it may appear that the patriarchal household is manipulating women to its own advantage. If, however, virginity is viewed as a form of sexual restraint outside of marriage that is vital to the equilibrium of individual and social bodies in these three ancient societies, it can be seen as a practice that tries to honor the place of diverse agents—divine and human—in the cosmic community. The discipline of virginity aims to see the divine, the human, and the animal dimensions of life within a cosmic context in order to negotiate the limits that shape one's destiny and to encourage sufficient openness to the presence of "the other." Virginity is an exercise in communal living that helps one honor the agential status of women, men, and deities. The neglect of deities and the treatment of women and men as property are two ways to dishonor these agents and distort the equilibrium in a community. An individual who exercises the discipline of virginity avoids the illusion of being completely autonomous and embraces the reality that the "other" is part of one's own existence.[317] Having

317. Yvonne Sherwood, "Boxing Gomer: Controlling the Deviant Woman in Hosea 1–3," in *A Feminist Companion to the Latter Prophets*, 101–125, at 120, contends that biblical

a "big view" of one's status as an agent is fundamental to one's assessment of the value of virginity as an ascetical practice.

The Protection of Women and the Integrity of the Community

The ideal of the virginal status of unmarried women in Israel was transgressed by Shechem's forcing Dinah to have sex with him (Gen 34:2). This violation of Dinah's boundaries was also a violation of the communal boundaries of Israel. The brothers of Dinah demanded that Hamor (Shechem's father) compensate Jacob (Dinah's father) and that all the males of Hamor's city be circumcised. In light of the brothers' strategy, Dinah would continue as a part of a household within the Israelite community by incorporating the households of Hamor's community. However, the brothers' slaying of the sons of Hamor was a hidden tactic of purging the sons of Hamor from their households so as to incorporate the women, children, and territory of Hamor's households into the Israelite community. Such an aggressive redrawing of communal boundaries left Jacob perplexed.

In Mesopotamia the laws against adultery and rape prescribed severe penalties to prevent these boundary violations. The laws were designed to protect the interests of the heads of households. According to the Middle Assyrian Laws from the latter part of the second millennium BCE, if a daughter was raped by a man who was married, his wife had to be raped and then the daughter put in her place as his new wife. In this harsh law communicated to the society in the northern part of Mesopotamia the talionic principle did not recognize the individual agency of the wife; she was identified with the man as belonging to him. The daughter was then to serve as a link between these two households and thus as an extension of the influence of the father's household into that of the man who had raped his daughter. Even though the daughter transferred from one household to the other, she must have maintained emotional and relational ties with her natal household.

In Greece the women's rituals honoring Artemis in sanctuaries at the boundary of a territory exposed these women to raids from neighboring men. Religiously the practice called on the protection of Artemis. Politically and militarily it tested the territory's assessment of its capacity to repel invaders. These rituals in the boundary sanctuaries were important transition points in the women's maturation. To avoid the risk of

---

interpreters try to tame the harlot Gomer because they find "autonomous female sexuality" to be "a fearful specter."

the invasion of the alien other was to curtail the growth of women who were vital to the reproduction and vitality of the community.

Pollution as "Matter Out of Place" and as Diminishment of Control

Efforts to maintain one's personal boundaries can veer to the extremes of either rigidity or laxness. The middle way of integration is more challenging. But by endorsing this middle way one is better able to identify when an effort to control a situation is counterproductive. If a family or community is shamed by boundary violations of one of its members there may be a tendency to tighten controls so that this shameful situation does not recur. But such tightening of control may go so far as to produce more such violations by refusing to recognize the irrational dimension of the erotic force that needs to be acknowledged.

An individual in the ancient societies of the eastern Mediterranean basin had no identity apart from a family or a community. There was a collective character to human existence in ancient Israel, Mesopotamia, and Greece that extended beyond the family to membership in a communal body (royal body) and from there to a place in a cosmic body (a royal body whose true sovereign is the king of the gods). When this larger view of the cosmic body was lost, the lower levels pretended to be the sovereigns and so tended to exploit those under their power in order to sustain their illusion of power and autonomy. This monarchical model for explaining the interdependence of the cosmos contextualizes the question of individual autonomy and freedom as one that can only be addressed in a collective context.

On a practical day-to-day level a discipline that monitors the reproductive portals of the body can help individuals be aware that they are part of a larger human and cosmic community. The regulations for genital emissions in Leviticus 15 tended to be intrusive into everyday life, but they produced a constructive mindfulness—in contrast to a destructive obsessiveness. These priestly regulations operated on the principle that the irruption of biological forces into the social cannot not go unregulated if communal life is to be maintained. But they were also aware that efforts to eradicate these larger biological forces would stifle the vitality of an individual and community. The wisdom of the regulations in Leviticus 15 is that they prescribe manageable means of purification that can be repeated as necessary. They do not aim to offer a once-and-for-all magical solution for containing these biological forces. In extant Mesopotamian texts there are various statements on the impurity of genital emissions, but there is no systematic attempt to regulate them as in

Leviticus 15. In Greece, the term *miasma* referred to "pollution." Although menstruation and genital emissions were not regarded as contagious, there was a concern to respect sacred space by keeping it free from sexual activities and materials. Sacred marriage texts do appear in parts of the Mesopotamian and Greek traditions, but such actions were not a form of sacred prostitution but rather a sanctioned erotic component of the ritual.

The Holiness Code in Leviticus 18–20 calls upon Israel to be holy: i.e., to imitate God through upright ethical and proper cultic behavior. In Mesopotamia a form of proper religious behavior was the intercessory worship offered by the *nadiātum*; their life behind the walls of the cloister had a votive character with the potential to elevate them in the estimation of the larger community as individuals with a special link to the gods who governed their lives. In Greece the young women were expected to imitate the virginity of Artemis; therefore those about to be married were to offer sacrifices to Artemis to appease her anger at their relinquishing their virginity. Artemis promised Hippolytus at the end of Euripides' *Hippolytus* that he would receive honorable mention when the bride-to-be ritually cut her hair prior to her wedding day (1425-26).

Gender Equity: Female Virginity Versus Male Constraint

The burden of maintaining the purity of the patriarchal line seems to have rested primarily on the women of the households in ancient Israel, Mesopotamia, and Greece. The wife was allowed to have sexual relations only with her husband, whereas the husband could theoretically have had sexual relations with any unmarried woman. In Mesopotamia and Greece the husband could have had homosexual relations as long as he did not act the part of a woman in them. Saul Olyan has argued that the same rule was in effect in ancient Israel according to Lev 18:22. This double standard, which gave greater freedom of sexual expression to men, could be rectified either by relaxing the sexual restraints on the wife or increasing them on the husband. The latter alternative would be an expectation of the discipline of male virginity for limited or extended periods.

Male virginity could take the form of abstinence from sexual relations (1) from youth until marriage or (2) during an extended time of cultic service. The purpose of the first form would be to allow sexual relations only in the context of heterosexual marriage. In the second form it would respect the principle that most sanctuaries were to be kept free from sexual matters. This form of cultic service by a male virgin would be an analogy to the service of the Greek women who were Pythian priestesses for Apollo. After young priestesses had been raped at the sanctuary in Delphi it was decided to appoint older women beyond their childbearing years as priestesses and dress them like young women.

The skills of sexual restraint required of a male virgin would be in continuity with those required to resist the temptation to adultery. In Genesis 39, Joseph resists the repeated propositions by Potiphar's wife. Euripides' character Hippolytus finds his stepmother's passion for him inconceivable. The Mesopotamian laws against adultery make it clear that similar forms of restraint by males were required there. These scenarios counsel a man to be circumspect and attentive to the bigger picture. Joseph's gratitude and respect for his master and his fear of God shield him from the temptation of Potiphar's wife. Hippolytus's strong commitment to virginity leaves him no room to even contemplate the possibility of sexual relations with any woman, much less incestuous relations with his stepmother. Euripides portrays Hippolytus in such a way that one can read him as overly judgmental and not attuned to the ways of Aphrodite, for Phaedra does not choose to love him; this passion is visited on her by Aphrodite. Around the figure of Hippolytus lurks the question whether he is too well defended to accept this power of Aphrodite in his world. As a Mesopotamian example of a male exercising sexual constraint toward the erotic advances of a woman, Gilgamesh rejects the proposal of Ishtar to marry him since he knows her history of marital infidelity and harsh treatment of her former husbands (*Gilg*. VI: 22-79).

The wherewithal to practice sexual restraint is offered through the pursuit of wisdom. Proverbs 7 assures the young man that if he is attentive to Woman Wisdom he will be protected from the Forbidden Woman. The pursuit of wisdom promoted by the Mesopotamian "Counsels of Wisdom" urges its male audience to avoid marrying slave girls, because they will be disruptive of the household and prostitutes because they will not be respectful or obedient (66-80). Euripides' Hippolytus claims that he lives chastely by honoring the gods above all and by keeping noble company (*Hippolytus* 996-1002).

The Patriarchal Household: An Institution Constrained by the Human Condition or a Source of Exploitation?

Marriages were arranged in ancient Israel, Mesopotamia, and Greece by the father (or perhaps the brother) of the bride. The brides were very young. The father's decision may have been received by some of the daughters as a call to sacrifice their virginity. Some scholars claim that mourning the loss of virginity is the import of the ritual young women are said to perform annually in remembrance of Jephthah's daughter. Thus the human sacrifice of Jephthah in the story would find an analogue in the ritual in the form of the girl's transition from virgin to wife. Alternatively, a case can be made that Jephthah vowed his daughter to a life of perpetual virginity—a lifelong sacrificial process in which her ties to her father's household remained intact. The reaction of mourning to a father's announcement of an arranged marriage may well have occurred among Mesopotamian and Greek daughters. In OB Mesopotamia fathers were known to designate one of their daughters as a *nadītum* to Shamash or Ninurta or Marduk—a cloistered life of perpetual virginity in which her ties to her father's household remained intact.

The ritual lament in Judg 11:37-40 occurs on the mountains, a place apart in which the young women keep one another company. In this place that is their own for a while they can construct an alternative reality to that of the patriarchal household. It would seem that for many of the cloistered *nadiātum* an appealing part of their celibate way of life was the opportunity to live in a sphere in which they were able to act as agents: viz., scribes (politics), entrepreneurs (business), and votaries (religious matters). In the Greek maidens' ritual in Artemis's sanctuary on the eve of their marriage they were appeasing Artemis, which means they were attending to their impending loss of virginity. Their depiction of Artemis as angry over this change probably reflects the ambivalence of the young women about the prospect of married life.

The exploitation of women of which the patriarchal household was capable is emphasized in the story of the rape of the concubine in Judges 19. The virgin daughter of the host is also offered as a possible victim to the abusive mob in Gibeah. The lower status of women in ancient Israel is accented by the fact that the host would offer his daughter and the guest's concubine to the mob in order to prevent the homosexual rape of the guest. The humiliation of the guest by accenting his subservience in subjecting him to gender reversal is regarded by the host as more heinous than the rape of the two young women. In Assyria, if a man is raped, the perpetrator is raped and then castrated (*MAL* A20), and if a husband rapes the daughter of another man, that man can have the wife of the husband raped (*MAL* A55). The voice of the wife is of no account in this talionic punishment. The lower status of women in ancient Greek society comes to expression in Hippolytus's angry speech after he is falsely accused by Phaedra's letter of having raped her (Eur. *Hipp.* 616-50). He repeats many of the misogynistic attitudes found in Hesiod (*Theog.*

570-601; *Op.* 54-95). It may be that these attitudes would have seeped into the subconscious of Greek males and perhaps were ready for use once a man felt deeply betrayed by a woman.

The decision of Jephthah to follow through on his sacrifice of his only daughter is preceded by mention of the "spirit of YHWH" coming upon him. Whether this human sacrifice was interpreted literally or figuratively, one wonders about the extent to which the father of a household was called upon to have members of his household make sacrifices for the common good arising from his perception of the will of God or the gods. Even in the setting of the ancient world in which a sense of collective responsibility was stronger than in the modern Western world, Jephthah's vow is extreme.

Chapter Five

Composite Guardian Figures: Tension at the Cosmic Junctures

Sex is a topic that typically generates almost immediate attention. Whether this interest is oriented toward pleasure or resistance, the topic of sex is one that is rarely received in complete neutrality. Each interlocutor has something at stake in how the structure and function of this relational reality are mapped out. Some will cling tightly to traditional sexual rules of a religious tradition while others will insist that the sexual desires of individuals should be free to manifest themselves in all their diversity.

Sexuality is a tangible yet invisible reality embedded in the dynamics of the cosmos. As a relational reality sex is not simply the terrain of an individual but, rather, is necessarily a social or communal concern. As an emotional and physical reality that joins the bodies of individuals, sex exercises its world-shaping function at those junctures that join individuals to one another and into communities. The procreative union of male and female brings together the divine, human, and bestial spheres of the cosmos to reproduce the human species from one generation to the next. Yet this primary form of human coupling does not exhaust the ways sexuality joins together or separates individuals and communities. Sexual desire varies among individuals in terms of intensity and object choice (i.e., heterosexual/homosexual, bestial, or sublimated objects such as wisdom, work, prayer). As an elemental cosmic force, sex is a reality that demands the attention of individuals and communities. To ignore sex or repress it is to be excessively vulnerable to the inevitable surprises this force will visit on the rigid or unsuspecting. Such visitations can transform or undermine one's world. The discourse one has at hand shapes one's response to these visitations.

Discourse about sex is a primary factor in whether the sex drive is carefully monitored or given free rein. Michel Foucault argued that the monastic discipline of suppressing the sex drive through talking about it and confessing its manifestations was extended to the population at large by the Council of Trent in its emphasis on the confession of sexual sins.[1] He contended that this channeling of the sexual drive battled against the diverse forms sexual desire could take and thus reduced the impact of sex as a life force.[2] In the nineteenth century Nietzsche had argued that such moral directives had curtailed the life-giving force of the bodily drives.[3] Both Nietzsche and Foucault argued for greater freedom of sexual expression. Foucault understands the body as a force field in which social power, knowledge, and pleasure battle to shape the discourse that defines the structure and function of sexual desire.[4]

The body of an individual is tied to larger natural, social, political, and economic bodies. Each of these bodies promotes its views of how the body of the individual is to be understood. For example, an economist may champion the view of the individual as a consumerist body rather than as a laboring body.[5] But a politician may disagree and promote a plan for increasing worker productivity instead of supporting measures to increase the flow of cheaper imported goods. The religious leader may preach the benefits of sexual abstinence over the use of contraceptives in order to regulate family size. The psychologist may argue for greater tolerance of diverse sexual expression on the basis of his empirical research. These diverse, interacting discourses compete in defining how the sexual energies of an individual are to be channeled.[6]

If the categories and directives for sexual expression are too restrictive for an individual, the person may despair over his or her incapacity to conform or may become nihilistic—that is, take the attitude that the

1. Michel Foucault, *The History of Sexuality*, vol. 1: *An Introduction*, trans. Robert Hurley (New York: Pantheon, 1978), 19–20.

2. Ibid., 23.

3. Friedrich Nietzsche, *Twilight of the Idols*, trans. Duncan Large (Oxford: Oxford University Press, 1998), 4:23; Terence Turner, "Bodies and Anti-bodies: Flesh and Fetish in Contemporary Social Theory," in *Embodiment and Experience: The Existential Ground of Culture and Self*, ed. Thomas J. Csordas, 27–47 (Cambridge: Cambridge University Press, 1994), at 37; Bernard Reginster, *The Affirmation of Life: Nietzsche on Overcoming Nihilism* (Cambridge, MA: Harvard University Press, 2006), 32–33.

4. Foucault, *History of Sexuality*, 1:11; Turner, "Bodies and Anti-bodies," 35.

5. M. L. Lyon and J. M. Barbalet, "Society's Body: Emotion and the 'Somatization' of Social Theory," in *Embodiment and Experience*, 48–66, at 52.

6. Ibid., 56.

world imposing such restrictions is not organized as it ought to be.[7] Alternatively, the individual may regard these restrictions as essential to the vitality of the sexual drive itself. Geoffrey Harpham argues that sexual desire and the repression of that desire are countervailing forces that arise simultaneously in the depths of human consciousness.[8] If there were no restrictions on the sex drive it would spread itself thin and diminish. Harpham contends that sexual discipline stabilizes the body as it undergoes persistent change.[9] This principle of an internal check and balance on the sex drive is transcultural, although its configuration and application are specific to its time and place. By contrast, Foucault had a negative view of sexual asceticism, believing that it stifled sexual expression out of fear of the sex drive's potential to go to excess and upset personal and social equilibrium.[10]

Because the sex drive is a powerful, elemental force it has the potential to upset the cosmic order. The sex drive has a tendency not only to go to excess but also to be polymorphous in its expression. Both of these tendencies transgress against the categories that aim to impose order on untidy experience. When such transgressions occur, something comes to be out of place, which then is labeled "dirt." Mary Douglas notes that something can be defined as "dirt" only within the context of a system.[11] It is such a cultural system that provides the fundamental categories of the discourse by means of which a child is socialized. The language a child learns from her or his parents contains categories that exert a profound influence on the child's subsequent channeling of the sexual drive.

Sexual material or activity that is out of place is particularly defiling if it comes into contact with sacred space or objects. Evidence for this incompatibility of the sexual and the sacred can be found not only in biblical Israel but also in the ancient cultures of Mesopotamia and Greece.[12]

7. Reginster, *The Affirmation of Life*, 28.

8. Geoffrey Galt Harpham, *The Ascetic Imperative in Culture and Criticism* (Chicago and London: University of Chicago Press, 1987), 54; see also Leo Strauss, *Natural Right and History* (Chicago: University of Chicago Press, 1953), 130.

9. Harpham, *The Ascetic Imperative*, xv.

10. Foucault, *The History of Sexuality*, 1:50, 56.

11. Mary Douglas, *Purity and Danger: An Analysis of the Concepts of Pollution and Taboo* (London: Routledge & Kegan Paul, 1966), 35–36.

12. For example, Mesopotamian mouth-washing rituals were used to initiate or rejuvenate cultic statues for cultic use; see Christopher Walker and Michael Dick, *The Induction of the Cult Image in Ancient Mesopotamia: The Mesopotamian Mīs Pî Ritual*, SAALT 1 (Helsinki: Neo-Assyrian Text Corpus Project, 2001), 233. Greek purification rituals used spring water

Unless sexual expression was specifically designated as part of a religious ritual (e.g., sacred marriage), it was to be kept out of the sanctuary. Even within the cult of Ishtar, the goddess of sex, the ways in which sex could be expressed in her cult were ritualized and defined.[13] Transgressors were punished, and the results of their actions were purged from sacred space. The sacred present in the world stood in danger of losing its distinctiveness and so needed to be hedged in by prohibitions.[14]

Dual sexuality—i.e., the simultaneous possession of both male and female identity—challenged the authority of the polarities fundamental to the traditional cosmic order in ancient Mesopotamia, Israel, and Greece.[15] Luc Brisson distinguishes this simultaneous possession of both sexes and genders from bisexuality, in which the actions manifesting each sex and gender would be sequential rather than simultaneous.[16] Thus dual sexuality is functionally equivalent to asexuality;[17] this androgynous state is equivalent to a third gender.[18] Such an androgyne stood outside the normal human categories and thus elicited a mixed reaction: on the one hand the androgyne was revered as a divine prodigy,[19] but on the other hand was feared as an evil omen or a corrupting

---

and sea water to cleanse cultic statues and their accessories; see Robert Parker, *Miasma: Pollution and Purification in Early Greek Religion* (Oxford: Clarendon Press, 1983), 212.

13. John Maier, "Gender Differences in the First Millennium: Additions to a Canonical Lamentation," in *Sex and Gender in the Ancient Near East: Proceedings of the 47th Rencontre Assyriologique Internationale, Helsinki, July 2–6, 2001*, CRRAI 47, ed. Simo Parpola and Robert M. Whiting, 345–54 (Helsinki: Neo-Assyrian Text Corpus Project, 2002), at 347.

14. Douglas, *Purity and Danger*, 21.

15. Luc Brisson, *Sexual Ambivalence: Androgyny and Hermaphroditism in Graeco-Roman Antiquity*, trans. Janet Lloyd (Berkeley: University of California Press, 2002), 5; Will Roscoe, "Priests of the Goddess: Gender Transgression in Ancient Religion," *History of Religions* 35 (1996): 195–230, at 222; Deut 22:5.

16. Brisson, *Sexual Ambivalence*, 1.

17. Ibid., 72; Brigitte Groneberg, "Der sumerisch-akkadische Inanna/Ištar: Hermaphroditos?" *WO* 17 (1986): 25–46, at 37. Instead of referring to a being with dual sexuality as a hermaphrodite and a being with dual gender as an androgyne, I will use the term androgyne to indicate a creature with characteristics of male and female sex and masculine and feminine gender.

18. Julia Asher-Greve, "Decisive Sex, Essential Gender," in *Sex and Gender in the Ancient Near East*, 11–26, at 19–21; Roscoe, "Priests of the Goddess," 203; Saana Teppo, "Sacred Marriage and the Devotees of Ištar," in *Sacred Marriages: The Divine-Human Sexual Metaphor from Sumer to Early Christianity*, ed. Martti Nissinen and Risto Uro, 75–92 (Winona Lake, IN: Eisenbrauns, 2008), at 89–91.

19. Mircea Eliade, *Mephistopheles and the Androgyne* (New York: Sheed & Ward, 1965), 110–11.

influence.[20] The favorable assessment of the androgyne was typically reserved for gods or primordial humans in mythical narratives, while human androgynes born into families or communities were usually exposed or eliminated.[21] With regard to gender, for a god to be an androgyne was a mark of excellence since it signaled "totality, completeness."[22] But a human androgyne was treated as a threatening misfit: the cowardly soldier was labeled a woman (Nah 3:13; cf. Jer 31:32) and the aggressive, active woman was categorized as a warrior or Amazon (*Il.* 3.189; 6.186).[23]

In classical Greece the totalizing aspect of the human androgyne was valued only as a temporary state within rites of initiation for adolescent youth as they transitioned to adulthood. So in the Oschophoria (October grape festival in honor of Athena) and Anthesteria (three-day festival in February–March in honor of Dionysus) as the *ephebe* moved into the role of the hoplite he would dress in women's clothing at the beginning of the rite prior to being clothed in his armor.[24] This ritual gesture marked the young man's movement from the private realm of the household to the public realm of politics.[25] To be stalled out in the liminal state of androgyny was to suffer the fate of a tragic character like Pentheus in Euripides' *Bacchae*; the capacity to live within the tension of dual genders seems to have been beyond that of a human and could be borne only by a god like Dionysus.[26] Androgyny was a distinguishing characteristic of gods at the beginning of the divine genealogy or of the primal human as the mythical ancestor of humans.[27]

20. Brisson, *Sexual Ambivalence*, 14–15.

21. Ibid.

22. Eliade, *Mephistopheles and the Androgyne*, 110; Groneberg, "Der sumerisch-akkadische Inanna/Ištar: Hermaphroditos?" 41–42. Gwendolyn Leick, *Sex and Eroticism in Mesopotamian Literature* (London and New York: Routledge, 1994), 157, claims that Inanna/Ishtar was not bisexual or androgynous.

23. Brisson, *Sexual Ambivalence*, 61. According to Plato's *Laws* III (695a-b, 697e), those who are raised in a protected, courtly setting by women and eunuchs lack the courage and discipline necessary for the battlefield.

24. Louise Bruit Zaidman and Pauline Schmitt Pantel, *Religion in the Ancient Greek City* (Cambridge: Cambridge University Press, 1989), 77, 199; Charles Segal, *Dionysiac Poetics and Euripides' Bacchae* (Princeton: Princeton University Press, 1982), 170; Pierre Vidal-Naquet, *The Black Hunter: The Forms of Thought and the Forms of Society in the Greek World*, trans. Andrew Szegedy-Maszak (Baltimore: Johns Hopkins University Press, 1986), 114–17.

25. Segal, *Dionysiac Poetics and Euripides' Bacchae*, 164–65, 168.

26. Ibid., 176.

27. Eliade, *Mephistopheles and the Androgyne*, 111.

The presence of male and female characteristics in each human is a combination of genetic endowment and socialization.[28] Genetic endowment locates one within either the male or female sex, but since the nineteenth century CE this category is further differentiated by sexual orientation.[29] In the area of gender, feminine and masculine roles are constructed and sustained by socialization.[30] The sexual polarity of male and female is paralleled by the gender polarity of masculine and feminine. How these four categories combine within each individual tells the story of that person's identity as a sexual being. A stable male or female identity requires continuity in the midst of the exchange of characteristics from each of the four categories.[31] Such changes happen in

28. Judith Butler, *Gender Trouble: Feminism and the Subversion of Identity* (New York: Routledge, 1990), 17, provides a definition of gender she finds in the polarized, heterosexual forms of representation of the person: "'Intelligible' genders are those which in some sense institute and maintain relations of coherence and continuity among sex, gender, sexual practice, and desire." Such models fear discontinuity and incoherence in sexual and gender identity and thus move to suppress such divergences.

29. Thomas Laqueur, *Making Sex: Body and Gender from the Greeks to Freud* (Cambridge, MA: Harvard University Press, 1990), 51–52, states that, even though same-sex desire was acknowledged by the ancient Greeks, they categorized the male partner who acted as a passive, receptive female as "deeply flawed, medically and morally."

30. Judith Butler, *Gender Trouble*, 6, states: "The presumption of a binary gender system implicitly retains the belief in a mimetic relation of gender to sex whereby gender mirrors sex or is otherwise restricted by it. When the constructed status of gender is theorized as radically independent of sex, gender itself becomes a free-floating artifice, with the consequence that *man* and *masculine* might just as easily signify a female body as a male one, and *woman* and *feminine* a male body as easily as a female one." Laqueur, *Making Sex*, 61–62, claims that in the one-sex model dominant in the early Greek and Christian traditions in which the woman was the inverse of the man and not ontologically distinct, there paradoxically were a series of polarities in this one sex: fatherhood / motherhood, male / female, man / woman, culture / nature, masculine / feminine, honorable / dishonorable, legitimate / illegitimate, hot / cold, and right / left. Tikva Frymer-Kensky, *In the Wake of the Goddesses* (New York: Free Press, 1992), 142, notes: "In contrast to such gender-specific thinking, the biblical story of Adam and Eve presents women and men as the true suitable companions to each other. . . . Male and female are created at the same time, and they are both created in the image, the likeness of god. The differences between male and female are only a question of genitalia rather than of character. This view of the essential sameness of men and women is most appropriate to monotheism."

31. Criticizing the ruling heterosexual model of sex and gender that marginalizes women, Butler, *Gender Trouble*, 7–8, states: "For Beauvoir, women are the negative of men, the lack against which masculine identity differentiates itself; for Irigaray, that particular dialectic constitutes a system that excludes an entirely different economy of signification. Women are not only represented falsely within the Sartrian frame of signifying-subject and signified-Other, but the falsity of the signification points out the entire structure of

terms of physical growth, social interaction, and social change. The goal of adult maturity dictates that a solid male or female identity incorporates both feminine and masculine characteristics into a way of living that is either male or female. Pure androgyny and dual sexuality constitute a liminal state of being that humans cannot sustain.[32]

When a person asks "what is good for a human?" this question is posed from a particular standpoint and perspective. A person will respond to it by reflecting on the order that emerges from one's own experience and how he or she has found her place within that order. It is the narrative of one's own experience that supplies the essential data for the discovery of an ethical world order. Yet this narrative is not merely subjective; it is a communally generated narrative in which socially cooperative and morally meaningful activities have occurred.[33] Therefore when sexual desire and activity transgress against this ethical world order the resulting personal distress can take on the character of cosmic chaos, that is, a situation in which one has lost a fixed point and the world seems to be awash in formlessness.[34] How to negotiate this chaos calls for reflection on the four categories of male, female, masculine, and feminine. At one extreme Foucault would advocate the free, uninhibited expression of sexual desire;[35] at the other a monastic discipline would call for the sublimation of corporeal sexual desire into a spiritual yearn-

representation is inadequate." Later she states: "The binary regulation of sexuality suppresses the subversive multiplicity of a sexuality that disrupts heterosexual, reproductive, and medicojuridical hegemonies."

32. The god Dionysus is androgynous, but Pentheus struggles with it; see Segal, *Dionysiac Poetics and Euripides' Bacchae*, 29. The primitive human in the Garden of Eden has been identified by some scholars as androgynous, but outside this primeval setting this composite of male/female and masculine/feminine is a challenge: see Nick Wyatt, "Androgyny in the Levantine World," in idem, *The Mythic Mind: Essays on Cosmology and Religion in Ugaritic and Old Testament Literature*, 238–55 (London and Oakville, CT: Equinox, 2005), at 238; Johannes C. de Moor, "The Duality in God and Man: Gen 1:26-27 as P's Interpretation of the Yahwistic Creation Account," in *Intertextuality in Ugarit and Israel*, OTS 40 (Leiden: Brill, 1998), 112–25, at 120–21.

33. Christopher Gill, "The Human Being as an Ethical Norm," in *The Person and the Human Mind: Issues in Ancient and Modern Philosophy*, ed. idem, 139–61 (Oxford: Clarendon Press, 1990), at 154; Strauss, *Natural Right and History*, 135–37; Alasdair MacIntyre, *After Virtue* (Notre Dame, IN: University of Notre Dame Press, 1981), 240.

34. S. Tamar Kamionkowski, *Gender Reversal and Cosmic Chaos: A Study of the Book of Ezekiel*, *JSOTSup* 368 (Sheffield: Sheffield Academic Press, 2003), 7–8, 132; Julie Galambush, *Jerusalem in the Book of Ezekiel*, SBLDS 130 (Atlanta: Scholars Press, 1992), 101–2; Athalya Brenner, *The Intercourse of Knowledge: On Gendering Desire and 'Sexuality' in the Hebrew Bible*, Biblical Interpretation Series 26 (Leiden: Brill, 1997), 133.

35. Foucault, *History of Sexuality*, 1:57.

ing for God.[36] In both extremes there is a yearning for life, but each alternative envisions a radically different strategy for finding life.

An "in-between" figure is the androgyne, who is imagined as holding all four categories of male, female, masculine, and feminine simultaneously. The imaginary examples of the androgyne in myth and the real-life examples among cultic personnel and palace administrators from the traditions of ancient Israel, Mesopotamia, and Greece illustrate how composite beings negotiated the exchanges among individual and corporate bodies. Composite mythical beings, asexual or androgynous primal humans, eunuchs, and androgynous cultic officials mediated between the visible and invisible spheres at points of vulnerability in the cosmic structure. This chapter will examine the profile and function of these composite, androgynous figures in the traditions of ancient Israel, Mesopotamia, and Greece to describe more closely the unique contribution of these liminal figures to cosmic order. The following three questions will be addressed to the texts of each tradition: (1) How does the attitude toward life as a gift rather than as a dynamic force to be shaped according to human goals shift the context within which one assesses one's quality of life? (2) How does the ongoing tension and complementarity between male and female (sex) and masculine and feminine (gender) allow for both change and continuity? (3) How do androgynes or composite figures exercise a distinctive role in promoting harmony between the divine, human, and bestial dimensions of human existence?

Israel: Balancing of the Human, Bestial, and Divine Aspects of Life Through the Integration of Heart and Mind

Humans strive to find their place within a dynamic, shifting environment. To get one's bearings, both introspection and environmental scanning are required to map how one has gotten to the place one currently occupies. A vital dimension of this search is a reconstruction of one's origins. This creative picturing of the past in the tradition handed on to us foregrounds certain aspects of human existence and marginalizes others. This picture of human origins takes narrative and poetic form and demands engagement from those who read it or hear it recited. This act of completing the picture demands faithful listening, but it also calls

36. John Kitchen, "Cassian, Nocturnal Emissions, and the Sexuality of Jesus," in *The Seven Deadly Sins: From Communities to Individuals*, Studies in Medieval and Reformation Traditions 123, ed. Richard Newhauser, 73–94 (Leiden and Boston: Brill, 2007), at 87.

for connecting the dots or filling the gaps. In the following reconstruction of human life in the Garden of Eden, a guiding principle will be to allow the texts to say as much as possible about these primordial human figures, even if the data lead to contradictions or aporia. The insights these texts offer on how to put together the bestial and divine aspects within human existence will be valuable for how we go about using our time and energy in interaction with God and with other humans. The following three topics will be examined in light of texts from Ezekiel 28, Genesis 1–3, Deuteronomy 22, and Isaiah 56: (1) How can humans accept life as a gift and rejoice in its beauty without becoming self-absorbed and intent on seizing life as if it were one's own possession? (2) How can humans bring together the masculine/feminine and male/female dimensions of human existence so as to symbolize the reality of God who transcends and yet encompasses gender and sexuality? (3) How can asexual androgynes find a place within a God-centered community?

The Primal Human in Ezekiel 28: The Composite Guardian Figure in Eden

The royal figure in the garden of God in Ezekiel 28:11-18 is described as "perfect in beauty" (*kĕlîl yōpî*) and "full of wisdom" (*mālēʾ ḥōkmâ*, vv. 12-14). He is a primal human who walked about among "the stones of fire" (*ʾabnê ʾēš*, v. 14).[37] As such, he appears to be a godlike figure who encompassed the totality of characteristics that could be bestowed on a human.[38] This figure is identified as male in gender, but because the narrative in Ezekiel 28 is not concerned about issues of procreation, his sexual functions are not described. The jewels that adorn him (v. 13) may be a mark of his status but also may point to a numinous power, which in Mesopotamian culture would link him with the astral powers.[39] The narrative praises his reception of this beauty and wisdom but criticizes his use of that wisdom to generate wealth and shape a commercial empire. The ideal primal human in Ezek 28:11-18 would be mindful that wealth and wisdom are given to him in order to use these gifts constructively. The narrative calls for discerning the limits of the human agent by being mindful of the sovereignty of Yhwh.

37. Dexter Callender Jr., "The Primal Human in Ezekiel and the Image of God," in *The Book of Ezekiel: Theological and Anthropological Perspectives*, SBL Symposium Series 9, ed. Margaret Odell and John Strong, 175–93 (Atlanta: Scholars Press, 2000), at 177, 191.

38. Daniel Block, *The Book of Ezekiel:Chapters 25–48* (Grand Rapids: Eerdmans, 1998), 105.

39. Erica Reiner, *Astral Magic in Babylonia*, *TAPA* 85, Part 4 (Philadelphia: American Philosophical Association, 1995), 127–28.

In the MT of Ezek 28:14 this primal human is identified as a cherub: *ʾat-kĕrûb*, "you are a cherub."[40] The cherub figure was a composite creature that, according to the description in Ezek 1:5-11, was humanoid in outline, with the feet of a calf, four wings equipped with human hands, and four faces (those of a human, a lion, an ox, and an eagle). Here the humanoid component seems to resemble the *kusarikku* ("bull-man") figure in Mesopotamian iconography.[41] Since a single cherub figure served as a mount for the deity in Ps 18:11, the cherub in Ezekiel 28 may have had this function, but its primary responsibility in Ezek 28:14 was to serve as a guardian (*hassōkēk*), the appointment to which position seems to have been ritualized by an anointing (*mimšaḥ*).[42] As a composite figure, consisting of human and animal characteristics, such a creature was positioned to be a powerful protector of the deity's interests.

The combination of bestial and human parts symbolized not only the cherub's supernatural character but also its potential for rebellion. If the cherub is identified with the primal human, then in Ezek 28:15b the primal human has rebelled; he is one in whom "iniquity was found." This tainting of the God-given perfection of the primal human was apparently caused by commercial activities that led to violence (Ezek 28:16; cf. 27:12-25).[43] The Lord God (*ʾădōnāy* YHWH, 28:2, 12) will not only cast him out as

40. But the LXX and Syriac translate two words as if the Hebrew were *ʾet-kĕrûb*, "with a cherub." Therefore the MT identifies the primal human as a cherub, and the LXX and Syriac claim that the primal human was assisted by a cherub. See James Barr, "'Thou Art the Cherub': Ezekiel 28.14 and the Post-Ezekiel Understanding of Genesis 2–3," in *Priests, Prophets and Scribes: Essays on the Formation and Heritage of Second Temple Judaism in Honour of Joseph Blenkinsopp*, *JSOTSup* 149, ed. Eugene Ulrich, 213–23 (Sheffield: JSOT Press, 1992), at 217.

41. Baruch Halpern, "The Assyrian Astronomy of Genesis 1 and the Birth of Milesian Philosophy," *Eretz-Israel* 27 (*Hayim and Miriam Tadmor Memorial Volume*), ed. Israel Eph'al, Amnon Ben-Tor, and Peter Machinist, 74–83 (Jerusalem: Israel Exploration Society, 2003), at 75–76, 78; Christoph Uehlinger and Susan Müller Trufaut, "Ezekiel 1, Babylonian Cosmological Scholarship and Iconography: Attempts at Further Refinement" *TZ* 57 (2001): 140–71, at 153; Maria DeJong Ellis, "An Old Babylonian *kusarikku*," in *DUMU-E$_2$-DUB-BA-A: Studies in Honor of Åke W. Sjöberg*, Occasional Publications of the Samuel Noah Kramer Fund 11, ed. Hermann Behrens, Darlene Loding, and Martha T. Roth, 121–35 (Philadelphia: University Museum, 1989), at 124–28; Frans A. M. Wiggermann, *Mesopotamian Protective Spirits: The Ritual Texts*, Cuneiform Monographs 1 (Groningen: Styx & PP Publications, 1992), 174–79.

42. Alternatively, *HALAT* 608 lists *māšaḥ* II, "to measure," in which case *kĕrûb mimšaḥ*, "the cherub who measures out," would be a distributor or boundary-keeper; cf. Dexter E. Callender Jr., *Adam in Myth and History: Ancient Israelite Perspectives on the Primal Human*, HSM 48 (Atlanta: Scholars Press, 2000), 110.

43. Block, *The Book of Ezekiel: Chapters 25–48*, 53.

a profane thing but will also drive him out from among the "stones of fire" (v. 16), that is, from his position with the other deities.[44]

The primal human, who was filled with wisdom and endowed with perfect beauty, was not content to serve as a signet (*ḥōtēm*, 28:12) or representative for YHWH.[45] Instead he decided to act as if he were the sovereign and to extend his power through cleverness in trade and violence (Ezek 28:16). In the lament in 28:1-10 the thoughts of the prince of Tyre are described; he is portrayed in Ezek 28:11-18 as the earthly counterpart of the primal human. The prince of Tyre experienced great success in his trading ventures, which he attributed to his wisdom or cleverness (vv. 4-5). He became narcissistic and elevated himself to the rank of El and claimed to occupy a "divine throne in the heart of the seas" (vv. 2, 17).[46] The wisdom of the prince of Tyre led to his downfall (vv. 3-6, 17).

The breastplate worn by the primal human indicates that he is a sacral as well as a royal figure (Ezek 28:13). His breastplate has nine of the twelve stones contained on the breastplate of the high priest in Exodus 28. The function of the stones of the high priest's breastplate is to make intercession for each of the twelve tribes of Israel within the holy of holies.[47] It seems, then, that this garden on the mountain of God, in which the primal human serves, functions like a sanctuary.[48] When the primal human transgresses he must be purged from the garden as if he were an idol; he is reduced to dust on the earth (Ezek 28:18; cf. Deut 9:21; Job 28:6). As a royal-priestly figure, the primal human abandoned the perfection bestowed on him to establish his own power independently of YHWH. In casting him down, YHWH cast him before the kings of the earth so that the humiliation of the prince of Tyre (i.e., the primal human)

44. Hugh R. Page, Jr., *The Myth of Cosmic Rebellion: A Study of Its Reflexes in Ugaritic and Biblical Literature*, *VTSup* 65 (Leiden: Brill, 1996), 151–54.

45. Callender, "The Primal Human in Ezekiel," 189.

46. Moshe Greenberg, *Ezekiel 21–37*, AB 22A (New York: Doubleday, 1997), 592–93; Callender, *Adam in Myth and History*, 123–24.

47. Robert Wilson, "The Death of the King of Tyre: The Editorial History of Ezekiel 28," in *Love and Death in the Ancient Near East: Essays in Honor of Marvin H. Pope*, ed. John H. Marks and Robert M. Good, 211–18 (Guilford, CT: Four Quarters Publishing, 1987), at 215–16; Cornelis Houtman, *Exodus*, vol. 3, *Chapters 20–40* (Leuven: Peeters, 2000), 503. By contrast, Block, *The Book of Ezekiel: Chapters 25–48*, 112, contends that the gemstones were probably inlaid in the figure of the king of Tyre and were not intended to link this king with the Israelite high priest.

48. Lawrence Stager, "Jerusalem and the Garden of Eden," *Eretz-Israel* 26 (1999): 183–94, at 188–89; Jon Levenson, *Resurrection and the Restoration of Israel: The Ultimate Victory of the God of Life* (New Haven: Yale University Press, 2006) 85.

might become a spectacle. The primal human must acknowledge his hubris.[49]

The garden scene of Eden on the mountain of God seems like an ideal setting in which one would want to remain. Royal gardens in the ancient Near East had this function of providing a place apart that symbolized the potential of the king to bring peace and civility to the land.[50] The fundamental expectation of the king in Ezekiel 28 is that he acknowledge what he has been given and be an obedient servant of the Gift-giver (see also the wife Jerusalem in Ezek 16:11-19).[51] However, he claims the gifts as his own and acts as if he were sovereign. He is somehow incapable of living with the "perfection of wisdom" and the "fullness of wisdom" (28:12). When pictured as a guardian cherub, the primal human fails as a boundary-keeper by his interior weakness: that is, his heart, the locus of thinking and feeling, is in the wrong place.[52] The competing human, bestial, and divine forces within this composite primal human/cherub highlight both the human potential to promote cosmic harmony and the danger of cosmic and personal disintegration resulting from failure to acknowledge YHWH as sovereign.

The Asexual Primal Human in Genesis 2 as an Inadequate Image of the Divine

In the other, better-known Eden story in Gen 2:4b–3:24 the primal human is also placed in an idyllic garden by the Lord God (*YHWH ʾĕlōhîm*, 2:7, 15). It has been planted with trees, which are fed by a subterranean water source (Gen 2:6, 8-9; cf. Ezek 31:7-9; Jer 17:12-13; Ps 1:3).[53] These trees, which are pleasant to look at (v. 9), will supply the primal human with an ongoing food supply. Its task will be to cultivate the garden (v. 5). This work will resonate with it and not be onerous, for God fashioned

49. Daniel Bodi, *The Book of Ezekiel and the Poem of Erra*, OBO 104 (Fribourg: Universitätsverlag, 1991), 158–59.

50. Mirko Novák, "The Artificial Paradise: Programme and Ideology of Royal Gardens," in *Sex and Gender in the Ancient Near East*, 443–60, at 446–49; William P. Brown, *Seeing the Psalms* (Grand Rapids: Eerdmans, 2002), 67–68.

51. Greenberg, *Ezekiel 21–37*, 592–93; Callender, *Adam in Myth and History*, 123–24. On the culpability of the king of Tyre on the basis of "general, collective principles" rather than Israelite covenantal law see Stephen L. Cook, "Cosmos, Kabod, and Cherub: Ontological and Epistemological Hierarchy in Ezekiel," in *Ezekiel's Hierarchical World*, ed. Stephen Cook and Corrine Patton, 179–97 (Atlanta: Society of Biblical Literature, 2004), at 196.

52. Dale Launderville, *Spirit and Reason: The Embodied Character of Ezekiel's Symbolic Thinking* (Waco, TX: Baylor University Press, 2007), 180.

53. Callender, *Adam in Myth and History*, 43, 46–47.

the earth creature (*hāʾādām*) from the soil (*hāʾădāmâ*, v. 7).[54] After God had molded this creature from the soil he breathed into it "the breath of life" (*nišmat ḥayyîm*) so that it became a "living being" (*nepeš ḥayyâ*, v. 7).

The kind of food one eats defines one's place on the cosmic hierarchy.[55] God ordered the earth creature not to eat from one tree that stood in the center of the garden: the tree of the knowledge of good and evil. The penalty for transgressing this taboo was to be death (v. 17). The reason the tree is named as possessing "the knowledge of good and evil" is debated; however, the identification of "good and evil" as a merism indicating that the fruit carried within it the ability to know everything is a likely explanation.[56] When the earth creature ate from this fruit it would no longer be content to cultivate trees in the garden and eat from their fruit. It would want to be in charge of the garden. The fruit from this tree belonged only to God. This motif of being metamorphosed into another kind of being by eating food belonging to another sphere of being is found in other ancient myths: for example, the Mesopotamian sage Adapa would have become immortal had he eaten of the food offered him by Anu, the king of the gods; the Greek goddess Persephone was required to spend one-third of every year in Hades because she ate from the pomegranate when she was detained in Hades. Once the fruit from the tree of the knowledge of good and evil was eaten, enlightenment occurred; there was no turning back to a simpler life.[57]

The earth creature God had formed was alone. In the creation story in Genesis 2:4b-25 the earth creature is grammatically treated as masculine in gender (through masculine singular pronouns and suffixes), but

54. Phyllis Trible, *God and The Rhetoric of Sexuality* (Philadelphia: Fortress Press, 1978), 80, notes with reference to the wordplay *ʾādām* / *ʾădāmâ* that God chooses to make distinctions that promote harmony rather than opposition.

55. William Hallo, "Adapa Reconsidered: Life and Death in Contextual Perspective," *Scriptura* 87 (2004): 267–77, at 272–74. This notion is illustrated in the Mesopotamian *Myth of Adapa* (see Shlomo Izre'el, *Adapa and the South Wind: Language Has the Power of Life and Death* [Winona Lake, IN: Eisenbrauns, 2001], 115, 121) and in the Greek myth of Hades' abduction of Persephone in the *Homeric Hymn to Demeter* (373).

56. Nahum Sarna, *Genesis* (Philadelphia: Jewish Publication Society, 1989), 19; Claus Westermann, *Genesis 1–11: A Commentary*, trans. John J. Scullion (Minneapolis: Augsburg, 1984), 243; Meir Malul, *Knowledge, Control, and Sex: Studies in Biblical Thought, Culture, and Worldview* (Tel-Aviv and Jaffa: Archaeological Center Publication, 2002), 441.

57. The notion of "taboo" entails this phenomenon of a barrier crossed that cannot be undone: i.e., an irrevocable change in circumstances as in a rite of passage; see Victor Turner, *The Ritual Process: Structure and Anti-Structure* (New York: Aldine de Gruyter, 1969), 168, 171; Mary Douglas, *Purity and Danger* (London: Routledge & Kegan Paul, 1966), 10, 21–22, 165.

this seems to be primarily a consequence of the structure of the Hebrew language, which necessarily categorizes persons and objects as masculine or feminine. According to Phyllis Trible the gender and sex of the earth creature do not yet exist.[58] After God had paraded all the animals of the garden before the earth creature, God judged that none of them would be "a suitable partner for the earth creature" (v. 20). In line with his procedure for creating the earth creature from the soil and thus fashioning a bond between them, God created the woman by taking a rib from the earth creature and fashioning her. The existence of sex and gender first becomes explicit with the creation of woman (*ʾiššâ*, v. 23); it is at this point that the earth creature (*hāʾādām*) is identified as a "man" (*ʾîš*, v. 23). Trible interprets v. 23 to mean that there is continuity and discontinuity between the *hāʾādām* and the *ʾîš*, but the *ʾiššâ* is entirely new. She understands the earth creature to have been asexual but not explicitly androgynous—"the ambiguity of one flesh becoming two creatures."[59]

One might argue that the earth creature in Gen 2:7 is an androgyne by reading it in sequence with Gen 1:27, which says that "God created the earth creature (*hāʾādām*) in his image (*bĕṣalmô*), in the divine image (*ṣelem ʾĕlōhîm*) he created him (*ʾōtô*); male (*zākār*) and female (*nĕqēbâ*) he created them (*ʾōtām*)." Here the text is explicit about *hāʾādām* ("the earth creature" or "humanity") containing both the male and the female.[60] The dual-sexed, androgynous character of the earth creature would have been more strongly emphasized if a dual pronominal suffix had been in use at the time of the writing of this text. But as Johannes de Moor points out, dual forms of personal pronouns and verbal forms were phased out in an early stage of Biblical Hebrew, which then required the use of either the plural or the singular in designating a dual object.[61] Likewise in

58. Trible, *God and the Rhetoric of Sexuality*, 80–81, 98.

59. Ibid., 98. Herbert Huffmon, "Gender Subversion in the Book of Jeremiah," in *Sex and Gender in the Ancient Near East*, 245–53, at 245, states that in the Hebrew Bible "there is no acknowledgment of androgyny or any 'third gender.'" Peter Jones, "Androgyny: The Pagan Sexual Ideal," *JETS* 43 (2000): 443–69, at 460, argues that the androgyne is "the physical symbol of the pagan spiritual goal, which is the merging of two seemingly distinct entities, the self and God, and a mystical return to the state of godhead prior to creation."

60. Wayne A. Meeks, "The Image of the Androgyne: Some Uses of a Symbol in Earliest Christianity," *History of Religions* 13 (1974): 165–208, at 185, notes with reference to Gal 3:28 that the primal human in Gen 1:26-27 was androgynous and that Christian initiation was believed by some early Christians to reverse the division of Gen 2:21-22.

61. Daniel Sivan, *A Grammar of the Ugaritic Language* (Leiden: Brill, 1997), 54; Bruce Waltke and Michael O'Connor, *Introduction to Biblical Hebrew Syntax* (Winona Lake, IN: Eisenbrauns, 1990), 14.26; 15.2.5b.

Ugaritic, the dual was often indicated by using plural forms and sometimes by singular ones.[62] From these hints that an archaic dual form underlies the text of Gen 1:27, de Moor offers the following interpretation: "In my opinion it is worthwhile to consider the possibility that the alternation between plural and singular as a designation of the first human being goes back to an original use of the dual as a designation of a dual personality, an androgynous creature, both man and woman."[63] To follow de Moor's line of argument one step further, the original human creature would not only have been an androgynous (masculine/feminine) being but also a hermaphrodite (possessing both male and female sex organs). But human reproduction as we know it would not have been possible for the hermaphrodite.

By contrast, Ed Noort argues that the male and the female in Gen 1:27 were created simultaneously and separately rather than being united in a composite first earth creature. He appeals to the purpose of the narrative in Genesis 1 as one that aims to explain how fertility happens and how the earth regenerates itself. Therefore both male and female must be designated in order to explain how the human species will be able "to be fruitful and multiply" (Gen 1:28).[64]

Since according to Gen 1:26-27 the earth creature is theomorphic, the theological implication would seem to be that if the earth creature is an androgyne, then God must be also. De Moor sees the argument as turning on how one interprets the term *ṣelem*, "statue, image, drawing." He claims that the more literal, physical meaning of *ṣelem* is intended in Gen 1:26-27. So if a statue were to be made of God, it would have to incorporate the features of both the male and the female.[65] Perhaps this statue would portray God as a Siamese twin, or perhaps in some more exotic form such as Aristophanes' round androgynes in Plato's *Sympo-*

62. Johannes de Moor, "The Duality in God and Man," 120.

63. Ibid., 120–21.

64. Ed Noort, "The Creation of Man and Woman in Biblical and Ancient Near Eastern Traditions," in *The Creation of Man and Woman: Interpretations of the Biblical Narratives in Jewish and Christian Traditions*, Themes in Biblical Narrative 3, ed. Gerald P. Luttikhuizen, 1–18 (Leiden and Boston: Brill, 2000), at 7–8. Athalya Brenner, *The Intercourse of Knowledge*, 12, regards *hāʾādām* as male and doubts that it is bisexual or androgynous.

65. Mark S. Smith, *The Origins of Biblical Monotheism: Israel's Polytheistic Background and the Ugaritic Texts* (New York: Oxford University Press, 2001), 89, notes: "Unfortunately, the examples claimed for divine androgyny in Ugaritic and other ancient Middle Eastern texts are unconvincing; it would be more persuasive to view this language at most as vestigial from an older form of Yahwistic cult that acknowledged Asherah as Yahweh's consort, hence male and female."

sium 189d-190a. However, such a literalistic interpretation of a statue is not in accord with the way statues functioned in the cultures of the ancient Near East.

In Mesopotamia, after the statue of Marduk had been fashioned by a craftsman its mouth was opened, a ritual signaling that the deity lived within the statue.[66] The *Enūma Eliš* regarded Marduk's statue as a symbolic, sacramental representation of his ineffable divinity (*EE* I.86-100).[67] The statue manifested the presence of the deity but did not claim to literally describe it. So when Marduk is described as a god with four eyes and four ears, this symbolizes the extraordinary capacity of Marduk to see and hear and thus supports the picture of Marduk as a god who is "beyond understanding, too difficult to perceive" (*EE* I:94). When the statue of Marduk was taken in procession, some observers in Babylon probably regarded this statue as a literal description of Marduk, but this interpretation reduced the symbolic dimension of Mesopotamian myths and rituals of the official cult.[68] Therefore, *ṣelem* in Gen 1:27 should be interpreted as referring to a dynamic, figurative sense of a sacramental image rather than to a static, literal sense of a physical copy.[69]

In Israel an iconic rendering of YHWH would clearly not have been possible in the wake of the Deuteronomic reform of the seventh century BCE (Deut 4:15-20). Likewise, the Israelite tradition prior to the seventh century refrains from describing the enthroned YHWH.[70] In Isa 6:1, YHWH

66. Christopher Walker and Michael Dick, *The Induction of the Cult Image in Ancient Mesopotamia: The Mesopotamian Mīs Pî Ritual*, SAALT 1 (Helsinki: Neo-Assyrian Text Corpus Project, 2001), 14.

67. Thorkild Jacobsen, "The Graven Image," in *Ancient Israelite Religion: Essays in Honor of Frank Moore Cross*, ed. Patrick D. Miller Jr., Paul D. Hanson, and S. Dean McBride, 15–32 (Philadelphia: Fortress Press, 1987), at 16–20.

68. Riekele Borger, *Die Inschriften Asarhaddons, Königs von Assyrien*, AfO Beiheft 9 (Graz: by the author, 1956), 89, #57 AsBbE, 21–24; Angelika Berlejung, "Washing the Mouth: The Consecration of Divine Images in Mesopotamia," in Karel van der Toorn, *The Image and the Book: Iconic Cults, Aniconism, and the Rise of Book Religion in Israel and the Ancient Near East* (Leuven: Peeters, 1997), 45–72, at 45; Launderville, *Spirit and Reason*, 133–34.

69. John Kutsko, *Between Heaven and Earth: Divine Presence and Absence in the Book of Ezekiel*, Biblical and Judaic Studies 7 (Winona Lake, IN: Eisenbrauns, 2000), 67, 102; Westermann, *Genesis 1–11*, 146.

70. For speculation that the Jerusalem temple had an anthropomorphic statue of YHWH see, in *The Image and the Book* (n. 68 above), Christoph Uehlinger, "Anthropomorphic Cult Statuary in Iron Age Palestine and the Search for Yahweh's Cult Images," 152–53; Karel van der Toorn, "The Iconic Book Analogies Between the Babylonian Cult of Images and the Veneration of the Torah," 242; and Herbert Niehr, "In Search of YHWH's Cult Statue in the First Temple," 73–95.

is imagined as an enthroned deity but is not physically described; the same reticence is evident in Exod 24:9-11, which says that God shared a meal with Israelite leaders, but where the description of God refers only to One whose feet were on a sapphire pavement. Ezekiel is more daring in describing YHWH as One who has a humanlike form with the appearance of electrum from the waist up but of fire from the waist down (Ezek 1:26-28). However, Ezekiel frames this description of YHWH within an elaborate vision that emphasizes its metaphorical character. Trygvve Mettinger characterizes Ezekiel's description as one that is both aniconic and anthropomorphic.[71] Such a contradiction indicates that Ezekiel is saying that YHWH exceeds the human capacity to picture him.

If one speculates on the meaning of Gen 1:26-27 prior to its reception by the priestly author one has shifted the ground for interpreting this pericope. De Moor hypothesizes that an early stage of the tradition of Gen 1:26-28 made the claim that the God of Israel was an androgynous deity. He refers to portrayals of creator gods in the ancient Near East (e.g., Aten, Amun-Re, Enlil, Marduk, Kumarbi, Ilu, and Ahura-Mazda) as androgynous.[72] It is conceivable that some early interpreter could have read *ṣelem* in a physical sense and portrayed YHWH in the form of a statue. But even if such a statue were recovered, it is questionable—particularly in light of the *Enūma Eliš's* interpretation of the Marduk statue—that the Israelite community would have understood a statue of YHWH to be a literal rather than a figurative description of YHWH.

A physicalist depiction of God is not in accord with Genesis 1, where God primarily interacts with the earthly sphere by means of his word.[73] When vegetation (vv. 11-12), sea creatures (vv. 20-21), and earth creatures are created, God commands the earth and the waters to produce them. He is described as making (*ʿāśâ*) the sun and the moon (v. 16) and the earth creatures (v. 25); however, the sun and moon belong in the dome over the earth and thus transcend the earthly sphere, while the earth creatures are brought forth by the earth rather than being directly fabricated by God (v. 24).[74] Thus the priestly writer consistently portrays God as transcendent to the earthly sphere. In this context, then, it would seem

71. Tryggve N. D. Mettinger, *The Dethronement of Sabaoth: Studies in the Shem and Kabod Theologies*, ConBOT 18 (Lund: Gleerup, 1982), 25.

72. De Moor, "The Duality in God and Man," 123.

73. Westermann, *Genesis 1–11*, 81.

74. Westermann, *Genesis 1–11*, 87–88. David M. Carr, *The Erotic Word: Sexuality, Spirituality, and the Bible* (New York: Oxford University Press, 2003), 24, emphasizes that Genesis 1 contains other ways of creating besides divine royal decree.

more likely that the reference to God as a being that encompasses both male and female is intended to communicate the point that the reproductive potential of the male and the female is contained within God in some transcendent, inchoate form.[75] God is not defined by the human categories of male, female, masculine, and feminine. While the coupling of male and female symbolizes the creative power of God, it does not define this divine power.[76] The God of Genesis 1 may have a spiritual form of androgyny but clearly not a physical one—which in effect means that God is asexual and without gender.[77]

In the Sethite genealogy of Genesis 5 the fruitfulness of the divine blessing of fertility is realized in the enormous lifespans of the antediluvians.[78] Adam lived for 930 years, Seth for 912, Enosh for 905, but Methuselah outperformed them all with 969 years. This genealogy begins with a restatement of Gen 1:27-28: "When God created an earth creature (*ʾādām*), he made it (*ʾōtô*) in the likeness (*dĕmût*) of God: male (*zākār*) and female (*nĕqēbâ*) he created them. He blessed them (*ʾōtām*) and called their name *ʾādām* on the day he created them" (Gen 5:1-2). Noort argues that this genealogy affirms that the reason for the differentiation of sexes in Gen 1:27 and 5:2 is to prepare the way for the sexual coupling that will lead to an abundance of offspring. He claims that this sexual differentiation is oriented toward the future abundance of offspring rather than to a statement about the origin of sexual and gender identity.[79] Furthermore, it is important to note that the way in which God creates Adam is stated differently from the way Adam produces offspring: the latter "begets" (*wayyôled*) a son "in his likeness" (*bidmûtô*, 5:3).[80] This sexual form of reproduction is not predicated of God; rather, God "creates" (*bārāʾ*)—an important indication that the God of Israel transcends sexuality.[81] Thus if one argues that the procreative potential of male and female is present in God, this presence takes the form of an archetype in which there is no

75. Wyatt, "Androgyny in the Levantine World," 238, defines androgyny as an archetype within gods or primordial humans that contains both genders, and later this archetype is reified as separate genders.

76. Noort, "The Creation of Man and Woman," 9. Carr, *The Erotic Word*, 24, argues that God is "faintly erotic" in Genesis 1 but yet "is not sexually erotic like the gods of Egypt, Mesopotamia, and other cultures."

77. Frymer-Kensky, *In the Wake of the Goddesses*, 144; Smith, *The Origins of Monotheism*, 144.

78. Westermann, *Genesis 1–11*, 348.

79. Noort, "The Creation of Man and Woman," 8.

80. Callender, *Adam in Myth and History*, 38.

81. Westermann, *Genesis 1–11*, 99.

sexual coupling; the reason for mentioning this sexual differentiation in God would be to affirm the necessity and value of this sexual differentiation for the subsequent process of human procreation.[82] According to this line of argument the simultaneous existence of male and female within the Godhead takes the form of an archetype rather than of physical shape and activity.

As we have seen in Gen 2:4b–3:24, the earth creature is incomplete. This creature needs a companion. This asexual creature must be refashioned into two separate beings whose gender and sex are opposite but complementary. As a single, isolated being, the earth creature is insufficient. The emotional and sexual coupling of male and female is celebrated in Gen 2:24 as a realization of what God intends for humans. In a sequential reading of the creation stories this coupling can be seen as an instantiation or partial realization of the archetype of the male and the female of primordial humanity, which was created in the image of God (Gen 1:26-27).[83]

According to Genesis 3 the creation of woman led to further complications for human life in the Garden. Paired with the serpent as a dialogue partner, the woman is a wisdom figure.[84] She is the first one to interpret a statement by God when she expansively restates the prohibition regarding the tree of the knowledge of good and evil: "You shall not eat from it, and you shall not touch it, lest you die" (3:3).[85] Once the fruit is eaten, the human couple become aware of their limitations at the same time that they acquire the divine desire to know everything. Sexual relations, which had been spontaneous, now become self-conscious and vulnerable to shame (vv. 7-11).[86] This new, more complicated form of existence impinges on their work within the Garden. No longer is there a harmonious relationship to the soil. Rather, the man must toil with the assistance of the woman to extract a livelihood from labor-intensive grain production.[87] The woman will not only share in this agricultural toil but will also need to face repeated pregnancies with their life-threatening agonies (3:16a). The man is commissioned "to rule over her," that is, to

82. Wyatt, "Androgyny in the Levantine World," 254; Noort, "The Creation of Man and Woman," 8.

83. Wyatt, "Androgyny in the Levantine World," 238; cf. Noort, "The Creation of Man and Woman," 11.

84. Carol Meyers, *Discovering Eve: Ancient Israelite Women in Context* (New York: Oxford University Press, 1988), 91.

85. Westermann, *Genesis 1–11*, 239–40.

86. Ibid., 250–51; Carr, *The Erotic Word*, 40.

87. Meyers, *Discovering Eve*, 105.

make sure that the indispensable activity of reproduction not be avoided (3:16b).[88] The toil she will face in having children will not be limited to labor pains, but will also include the ongoing task of parenting.[89] Thus the creation of woman expanded the potential of the earth creature from that of a solitary individual to that of a social, communal being. This social existence held out promise for a fulfilling companionship and also provided the means by which humans could reproduce themselves. But now both of these plusses have become complicated by their decision to disobey God's prohibition and to gain a divine form of wisdom that would repeatedly tempt them to be their own masters. The new pains from their compromised relationship to the soil and to one another would only fuel repeated efforts to remake the human condition. The various forms of sexual expression that would arise in their new, more complicated circumstances (cf. Leviticus 18–19) would only render the monogamous, heterosexual ideal of Gen 2:24 more challenging.[90]

The desire to return to the uncomplicated existence of the Garden is symbolized by the cherubim stationed at the boundary of Eden. Equipped with their divine form of wisdom, the human couple now are perceived as a threat to take the divine prerogative of immortality, which would in effect metamorphose them from humans into gods (3:22).[91] To prevent such forcible taking of divine status, God stations the cherubim at the east edge of Eden with a "flaming, rotating sword" (3:24). This expulsion from the Garden can be seen as a form of purification. The dirt or defilement of the human rebellion is to be rectified by placing the humans outside the Garden and so restoring the integrity of the Garden and the clarity of its boundaries.[92] As creatures combining within themselves the attributes of humans and beasts, the cherubim transcend the bestial and human spheres and take on a supernatural character. As servants of God, these cherubs, like guardian deities, fend off threats to God's prerogatives and distinctiveness. In light of Ezek 28:11-18, humans were created with the potential to be cherubs or guardians of Yhwh's

88. Ibid., 114–16.

89. Ibid., 106, 116.

90. Richard M. Davidson, *Flame of Yahweh: Sexuality in the Old Testament* (Peabody, MA: Hendrickson, 2007), 3–4, constructs a biblical theology of sexuality in which the Edenic pattern of Genesis 1–3 with its heterosexual, monogamous ideal is determinative. By contrast, Carr, *The Erotic Word*, 24, 36–37, speaks of Genesis 1–3 as affirming human sexualities where diversity of sexual expression is acknowledged.

91. Westermann, *Genesis 1–11*, 272.

92. David P. Wright, "Holiness, Sex, and Death in the Garden of Eden," *Bib* 77 (1996): 305–29, at 307–8, 323, 327.

sovereignty. But in the current post-Eden situation humans must strive to integrate the human and bestial components of their being by means of God's help (cf. Ezek 36:26-27).

Eunuchs and Prohibited Mixtures in Ancient Israel

Composite creatures like the cherubim inspired awe since they wielded a power that transcended the normal categories of earthly existence.[93] For a man to confront them would show his blindness to his limits and his refusal to accept his place in the cosmic hierarchy. The transgression of categories by supernatural beings manifests their transcendence. However, if human beings mix or transgress categories, it is usually a sign of chaos. Eunuchs and "androgynous" cultic personnel were marginal figures shunned by many. But eunuchs played important roles in palace administration, while the "androgynous" cultic personnel in Mesopotamia were responsible for lamentations and performed significant roles in the cult of Ishtar, a goddess with androgynous traits.[94] Legislation excluding these anomalous types from the Israelite assembly and from entry into the sanctuary indicates that eunuchs (2 Kgs 9:32; Isa 56:4-5) and perhaps androgynous cultic personnel (cf. 1 Kgs 18:28; Ezek 8:14) were present in the land of Israel.

Deuteronomy 23:2 legislates that no Israelite male who has been castrated or whose testicles have been crushed may be admitted into the Israelite assembly (*biqhal* YHWH), which presumably would have dealt with both cultic and communal matters. The ideal of completeness required of priests seems here to be extended to the people as a whole (Lev 21:18-20; 22:24).[95] Thus they seem to have regarded a form of mutilation that deprived a male of his procreative capacity as incompatible with the presence of YHWH. Just as a blemished animal was unfit for sacrifice,

93. Wiggermann, *Mesopotamian Protective Spirits*, 163; Othmar Keel and Christoph Uelinger, *Gods, Goddesses, and Images of God in Ancient Israel*, trans. Thomas Trapp (Minneapolis: Fortress Press, 1992), 168–69; Dale Launderville, "Ezekiel's Cherub: A Promising Symbol or a Dangerous Idol?" *CBQ* 65 (2003): 165–83, at 165–69; Samuel Terrien, "The Omphalos Myth and Hebrew Religion," *VT* 20 (1970): 315–38, at 329.

94. Stefan M. Maul, "*kurgarrû* and *assinnu* und ihr Stand in der babylonischen Gesellschaft," in *Aussenseiter und Randgruppen: Beiträge zu einer Sozialgeschichte des Alten Orients*, ed. Volkert Haas, 159–71 (Konstanz: Universitätsverlag, 1992), at 163; Rivkah Harris, "Inanna-Ishtar as Paradox and a Coincidence of Opposites," *History of Religions* 30 (1991): 261–78, at 266; cf. Leick, *Sex and Eroticism*, 157.

95. Richard D. Nelson, *Deuteronomy: A Commentary*, OTL (Louisville: Westminster John Knox, 2002), 278; Joseph Blenkinsopp, *Isaiah 56–66*, AB 19B (New York: Doubleday, 2003), 138.

so also an Israelite who was maimed in terms of his generative capacity was disallowed. In line with this reasoning may have been an abhorrence of the practice of castration in cults in western Asia.[96] One reason for the exclusion of a castrated male from the assembly may have been his incapacity to father an heir; thus he would have been an outsider to the property and inheritance practices that defined the Israelite male's membership in the Israelite community (cf. Mic 2:5).[97] Kurt Galling argues that this law, along with those in Deut 23:2-8, was administered from a border sanctuary like that of Gilgal.[98] Here the cultic personnel would have been occupied with admitting immigrants or resident aliens into the land. This law would have articulated a clear boundary.

Foreigners whose reproductive capacities had been compromised were still admitted to the land of Israel. In the late seventh–early sixth century BCE it appears that eunuchs served within the royal government of Judah, for the Ethiopian Ebed-Melech is described as an *ʾîš sārîs*, "eunuch" (Jer 38:7).[99] His loyalty to king Zedekiah positioned him to assist Zedekiah in protecting Jeremiah from the Jerusalemites who regarded Jeremiah as a traitor (Jer 38:7-13). It is possible that Ebed-melech was the overseer of Zedekiah's harem (Jer 38:22).[100] The role of overseer of the royal harem was probably the most distinctive task of the eunuch. Here he was able to demonstrate his loyalty to the king and would not be able to beget offspring with the royal women who could then make a claim on the property and power of the royal household. Eunuchs were typically found performing this task plus other administrative roles for the

96. Lynn E. Roller, "The Ideology of the Eunuch Priest," in *Gender and Body in the Ancient Mediterranean*, ed. Maria Wyke, 118–35 (Malden, MA: Blackwell, 1998), at 119; Roscoe, "Priests of the Goddess," 198–99; Terrien, "The Omphalos Myth," 327–28. Leick, *Sex and Eroticism*, 225, notes: "[Castration] is alien to the Mesopotamian religious system and was probably an import from western Syria and the Levant, where, at least in Hellenistic times, the cult of the Dea Syria involved the self-inflicted removal of genitals in ecstatic rituals."

97. Nelson, *Deuteronomy*, 278; A. H. D. Mayes, *Deuteronomy* (Grand Rapids: Eerdmans, 1981), 315.

98. Kurt Galling, "Das Gemeindegesetz in Deuteronomium 23," in *Festschrift Alfred Bertholet zum 80. Geburtstag*, ed. Walter Baumgartner, 176–91 (Tübingen: Mohr, 1950), at 187–90; Nelson, *Deuteronomy*, 278; Mayes, *Deuteronomy*, 315.

99. Hayim Tadmor, "The Role of the Chief Eunuch and the Place of Eunuchs in the Assyrian Empire," in *Sex and Gender in the Ancient Near East*, 603–11, at 605; Roland de Vaux, *Ancient Israel*, vol. 1: *Social Institutions* (New York: McGraw-Hill, 1965), 121; William Holladay, *Jeremiah 2: A Commentary on the Book of the Prophet Jeremiah, Chapters 26–52* (Minneapolis: Fortress Press, 1989), 140, 289.

100. Jack R. Lundbom, *Jeremiah 37–52*, AB 21C (New York: Doubleday, 2004), 70.

palace. Like Ebed-melech, a eunuch would often be a protector of the king as well as his loyal servant.[101]

In early postexilic Judah (late sixth century BCE), a debate arose within the community over the admissibility of foreigners and eunuchs to the Yahwistic community. In Isa 56:3-5 the prophet proclaims a message of radical openness to foreigners and eunuchs that was sure to meet with resistance from the majority of those who adhered to the priestly tradition:

> Let not the foreigner say, when he would ally himself with the Lord, "The Lord will surely set me apart from his people." And do not let the eunuch say, "Look, I am a dried up tree." For thus says the Lord: "To the eunuchs who observe my sabbaths and choose what I desire and firmly grasp my covenant, I will set up for them within my house and walls a monument and a name better than sons and daughters. I will set up for them an everlasting name, which will not be cut off."

This prophetic pronouncement presented a direct challenge to the exclusion of eunuchs in Deut 23:2. The prophet contends that one who observes the Sabbath and carries out the divine will is acceptable to YHWH and can be admitted into his sanctuary. Physical requirements concerning intact male reproductive organs can be overridden by a faithful, internalized relationship to YHWH.[102] The inner community debate on this issue resurfaces around the expectation of choosing what is pleasing to YHWH, for in Isa 65:12 and 66:4 the prophet's opponents are condemned for displeasing YHWH. The inclusive attitude of the prophet reaches a crescendo in Isa 66:21, where he says concerning the foreigners who come on pilgrimage to Jerusalem to worship YHWH: "Some of them I will take as priests and Levites, says the Lord." For those schooled in the priestly tradition (cf. Ezek 44:1-14) this laxity in enforcing the rule of Deut 23:2 would have seemed like a defilement that was sure to double back on the community.[103]

Other purity prescriptions in the Deuteronomic corpus related to transgression of cultural categories are briefly listed in Deuteronomy 22.

101. Tadmor, "The Role of the Chief Eunuch," 603, 607.

102. Blenkinsopp, *Isaiah 56–66*, 139.

103. Steven Tuell, "The Priesthood of the 'Foreigner': Evidence of Competing Polities in Ezekiel 44:1-14 and Isaiah 56:1-8," in *Constituting the Community: Studies on the Polity of Ancient Israel in Honor of S. Dean McBride*, ed. John T. Strong and Steven S. Tuell, 183–204 (Winona Lake, IN: Eisenbrauns, 2005), at 198, 201–2.

The prohibition of cross-dressing in Deut 22:5 forbids men and women to put on articles of clothing exclusively designated for the opposite gender. Such an action is an "abomination to YHWH" (*tôʿăbat* YHWH). It was thought to cause ritual impurity (cf. Lev 19:19).[104] Deuteronomy 22:9-11 has been dubbed "a farmer's code of conduct."[105] Here various mixtures are prohibited: (1) two different kinds of seed are not to be sown in a vineyard; if one does so, they must be withdrawn from ordinary use until the time designated for their interdiction has passed (Lev 19:23-25; Deut 20:6).[106] (2) A farmer is not to harness an ox together with a donkey to his plow; most likely these two animals were incompatible and forcing them to work together would be detrimental to the animals, the farmer, and the public. Alternatively, Carmichael suggests that this law prohibits crossbreeding of an ox and a donkey (cf. Lev 19:19).[107] And (3) a person is not to wear cloth that consists of wool and linen woven together. This may refer to a belief that the mixture of animal and vegetable products produces holiness and thus was appropriate only for vestments (Exod 29:29; cf. 26:1).[108] Jacob Milgrom notes that this mixture of two types of cloth (*šaʿaṭnēz*) is appropriate only for sacred vestments: the lower cover of the tabernacle and curtain at the entry to the holy of holies (Exod 26:1, 31), the high priest's ephod, breastplate, and belt (Exod 28:6, 15), and the priest's belt (Exod 39:29). He claims in light of Num 15:37-41 that a redactor adhering to the Holiness Code (Leviticus 17–26) legislated that ordinary Israelites include a blue woolen thread on the fringe of their linen garments as a reminder that they were to keep the cultic and ethical ordinances of the Holiness Code so that they might be holy through such imitation of the Lord (Lev 19:2).[109]

Summary

The primal human in Eden in Ezekiel 28 is a divinized royal figure who has the potential to bring together the divine, human, and animal dimensions of existence. As a cosmic boundary-keeper, his crucial step

104. Nelson, *Deuteronomy*, 267; Daniel Boyarin, "Are There Any Jews in 'The History of Sexuality'?" *Journal of the History of Sexuality* 5 (1995): 333–55, at 342–43.

105. Nelson, *Deuteronomy*, 268.

106. Ibid., 269.

107. Calum M. Carmichael, *Laws of Deuteronomy* (Ithaca, NY, and London: Cornell University Press, 1974), 159–60; Mayes, *Deuteronomy*, 308.

108. Nelson, *Deuteronomy*, 269.

109. Jacob Milgrom, "Law and Narrative and the Exegesis of Leviticus XIX 19," *VT* 46 (1996): 544–48, at 546–47.

must be to keep his heart in the right place, that is, the locus of his thinking and feeling must locate him at the proper level in the cosmic hierarchy. His failure is that his heart becomes arrogant and his gifts of wisdom and beauty lead him to become narcissistic. His wisdom devolves into a form of cleverness that is directed toward his commercial activities, which give him a sense of his own autonomous power. The idolatry of the primal human/prince of Tyre disqualifies him from continuing in his position as boundary-keeper. His arrogance is a rebellious move to take over God's place in the hierarchy, and thus he defiles himself. God purges him from his mountain sanctuary and from his political position as a divine king. Somehow the primal human's wisdom undermines rather than sustains his relationship with God.

In the Garden of Eden in Gen 2:4b–3:25, God creates the primal human from the soil so that it might cultivate the soil of the Garden and enjoy the blessings of this idyllic environment. God notices that a solitary existence is not good for this earth creature; apparently divine accompaniment and the presence of animals have not been sufficient. The earth creature needs someone more akin to itself. God creates woman from the rib of the earth creature, who then becomes a man complemented by a woman. The earth creature had neither sex (male/female) nor gender (masculine/feminine), that is, the earth creature is an asexual being who also appears to be ungendered.[110] In the previous creation story (Gen 1:26-28) humankind is differentiated into male and female components that complement one another. Their differentiation has its place within their unity; this unity-in-difference is the way humankind images God. Genesis 2:24 addresses this goal of man and woman coming into right relationship. Their embodied corporeal harmonization of the male/female and masculine/feminine has the potential to sacramentally symbolize the way God creates and interacts with humans. According to Gen 1:26-27 the separate identities of male and female and their subsequent sexual union is vital to the fertility of humans and the future of the created world.[111] Their right relationship to one another as sexual beings symbolizes the transcendent image of an asexual God.

The eating of the fruit of the tree of the knowledge of good and evil shows humans' curiosity and their desire for autonomy. The attractiveness of wisdom distorts their judgment; they transgress the taboo and lose their innocence. Thereafter they must deal with a more complicated

110. On early Christian efforts to transcend gender through sexual renunciation see Roscoe, "Priests of the Goddess," 204–5.

111. Cf. Wyatt, "Androgyny in the Levantine World," 254.

relationship with their environment, with their own sexuality, and with God. Their inability to turn back is highlighted by the cherubim as boundary-keepers that now enforce the mortal condition of humans.

The transgression of cosmic categories leads to personal, communal, and environmental chaos. The various prescriptions against the mixing of sex/gender, agricultural seeds, animals, and types of fabric point to the Israelites' concern with purity and order within their community. Their sense of order is tied to their sense of the wholeness or integrity of their individual and communal bodies.

Mesopotamia: Composite Mythic and Human Figures as Mediators of Integrative Divine Power

A flourishing garden provides its inhabitants with nourishment, aesthetic delight, and a sense of security. As a product of both nature and culture, a garden provides a model of how human efforts can be integrated with the forces of nature to produce a communally inviting atmosphere. In southern Mesopotamia irrigation was necessary for the growth of plants and trees. To sustain these irrigation works the technical resources of the community needed to be coordinated by the king. This royal figure, as a manager of vital aspects of agricultural production, can be mythicized (1) into a primordial androgynous figure who strives to bring together the resources of the land and the community or (2) into a divinized king who is married to the life-force symbolized by Inanna/Ishtar. On the earthly plane the differentiation of masculine and feminine tasks is an ongoing effort that works itself out against the backdrop of primordial commonality. Along with historical reconstructions of specific topics (e.g., eunuchs in Assyria), this section will examine excerpts of mythical (*Atrahasis, Erra and Ishum, Enūma Elish,* "Descent of Ishtar"), ritual (NA state ritual), hymnic ("Sacred Marriage of Iddin-Dagan"), lament ("Uru-amirabi"), omen (*Šumma ālu*), and legal (*MA Palace Decrees,* land-grant) texts. The following three main questions will be addressed: (1) How does the idealized king symbolize the embodied life-force of the land in his maintenance of the royal garden? (2) How are the distinctive roles of male/female and masculine/feminine promoted and yet complemented by androgynous mythical and human figures essential to communal harmony? (3) How do androgynous or asexual human agents mediate between the forces of life and death that suffuse the bestial, human, and divine spheres of human existence?

Mesopotamian Primordial Androgynous Figures as Symbols of the Unity of Humanity

Royal gardens showcased the king's prowess as a gardener and a hunter.[112] As a gardener the king held a key role in maintaining the fertility of the land. On a technological level he was responsible for maintaining the irrigation and flood works necessary for agriculture in the southern part of Mesopotamia.[113] On a symbolic level he needed to honor the gods and maintain justice in the land so that agricultural success would be granted.[114] Included in such honoring was the practice of sacred marriage, which until about 1800 BCE was believed to be enacted annually in many Mesopotamian cities by the ritual coupling of the king and a priestess of Inanna.[115]

The garden had a practical function of supplying fruit and vegetables to the palace, but this purpose was outstripped by the symbolic significance of the garden as an inviting, civilized space in the midst of an environmentally challenging geographical region.[116] In the first millen-

112. Mirko Novák, "The Artificial Paradise: Programme and Ideology of Royal Gardens," in *Sex and Gender in the Ancient Near East*, 443–60, at 452.

113. Johannes M. Renger, "Institutional, Communal, and Individual Ownership or Possession of Arable Land in Ancient Mesopotamia From the End of the Fourth to the End of the First Millennium B.C.," *Chicago-Kent Law Review* 71 (1995): 271; Christopher J. Eyre, "The Agricultural Cycle, Farming, and Water Management in the Ancient Near East," *CANE*, 185; Daniel T. Potts, Mesopotamian Civilization: The Material Foundations (Ithaca, NY: Cornell University Press, 1997), 19–21.

114. Hammurapi celebrated the construction of a canal with the words: "When Anum and Enlil gave me the land of Sumer and Akkad to rule (and) placed their halter in my hand, I dug the canal (named), 'Hammurapi is the prosperity of the people,' which brings abundant water to the land of Sumer and Akkad. I returned its two banks to cultivation. I repeatedly heaped up piles of grain. I established everlasting waters for the land of Sumer and Akkad. I gathered together the scattered peoples of the land of Sumer and Akkad. I procured grazing land and a watering place for them. I shepherded them with plenty and abundance. I settled them in peaceful dwellings" (edition: Douglas Frayne, *The Royal Inscriptions of Mesopotamia. Early Periods*, vol. 4: *Old Babylonian Period (2003–1595 BC)*, RIME 4 [Toronto: University of Toronto Press, 1990] E4.3.6.7, 10–37).

115. Pirjo Lapinkivi, "The Sumerian Sacred Marriage and Its Aftermath," in *Sacred Marriages*, 7–41, at 22–23; Jerrold Cooper, "Sacred Marriage and Popular Cult in Early Mesopotamia," in *Official Cult and Popular Religion in the Ancient Near East*, ed. Eiko Matsushima, 81–96 (Heidelberg: Universitätsverlag, 1993), at 90–92; Jacob Klein, "Sacred Marriage," *ABD* 5: 868.

116. Stephanie Dalley, "The Hanging Gardens of Babylon at Nineveh," in *Assyrien im Wandel der Zeit: XXXIXe Rencontre Assyriologique Internationale, Heidelberg 6.–10. Juli 1992*, CRRA 39, Heidelberger Studien zum Alten Orient 6, ed. Hartmut Waetzoldt and Harald Hauptmann, 19–24 (Heidelberg: Heidelberger Orientverlag, 1997).

nium BCE the Assyrian kings expanded these gardens to form "universal parks." The palaces at the center of these parks were constructed to provide a panoramic view of the garden.[117] Among the spectacles to take place in this garden was the royal lion hunt, a contest designed to celebrate the king's capacity to maintain the borders of the kingdom against chaotic forces.[118] Beginning with Tiglath-Pileser I (1114–1076), who transplanted to his garden trees and plants from all parts of the known world, down to the time of Ashurbanipal (668–627), Assyrian kings constructed gardens and palace complexes that communicated by their design, iconography, and ritual activities that the king was godlike in his rule over the kingdom and empire.[119]

The "perfect king" in the Ur III period (2112–2004) was depicted in iconography as a masculine vessel incorporating female characteristics.[120] Kings such as Gudea were celebrated as builders by being depicted with a mixture of male and female features: shaven head and nude upper body, wearing a skirt, and carrying a basket on their heads (masculine features); somewhat pronounced breasts and soft facial features (feminine traits); beardless (gender neutral).[121] Irene Winter has identified as visual representations in the Gudea statues of the able and just ruler his height, his broad chest, and his bulging biceps, along with his wide ears and attentive eyes.[122] If the warrior attributes are identified as more masculine and the pious attentiveness as more feminine on the spectrum of gendered attributes in ancient Mesopotamian society, the image of Gudea presented by his statues combined masculine and feminine features. Julia Asher-Greve notes that the dominant masculine features with somewhat weaker feminine features constituted the understanding of royal androgyny in southern Mesopotamia at that time. This androgynous king was revered as a primordial human who symbolized humankind. Later the model of "the heroic king" would depict the king in

117. Novák, "The Artificial Paradise," 446.

118. Chikako E. Watanabe, *Animal Symbolism in Mesopotamia: A Contextual Approach*, WOO 1 (Vienna: Institut für Orientalistik, 2002), 76–88; Elnathan Weissert, "Royal Hunt and Royal Triumph in a Prism Fragment of Ashurbanipal (82-5-22,2)," in *Assyrian 1995: Proceedings of the 10th Anniversary Symposium of the Neo-Assyrian Text Corpus Project, Helsinki September 7–11, 1995*, ed. Simo Parpola and Robert M. Whiting, 339–58 (Helsinki: Neo-Assyrian Text Corpus Project, 1997).

119. Novák, "The Artificial Paradise," 443–60, esp. 444–49.

120. Asher-Greve, "Decisive Sex, Essential Gender," 11.

121. Ibid., 12.

122. Irene J. Winter, "The Body of the Able Ruler: Toward an Understanding of the Statues of Gudea," in *DUMU-E$_2$-DUB-BA-A*, 573–83, at 578–83.

exclusively masculine terms, emphasizing his beard and lionlike features.[123] Although the models of both the "perfect king" and the "heroic king" celebrate the king as a builder of civilization, only that of the "perfect king" takes into account the indispensable feminine component in this effort.[124]

The primordial human (*lullû*), according to the *Atrahasis* story, was created to be a builder of irrigation and flood works, temples, and other public works projects (I:195-97). The Igigū-gods, who had been laboring on these projects, revolted against the Anunnakkū gods (I:5-6, 37-49).[125] Enki, the god of wisdom, proposed to Enlil, the king of the gods, that the mother-goddess (Mami or Nintu) create a human being (I:190). Enki directed that the leader of the rebel gods (Aw-ila) be slain so that his blood might be mixed with clay to make the first human (I:203-15). Nintu did so. The heartbeat of the human was to be a sign of the rebel god's blood within him (I:225-31).[126] As Asher-Greve explains, this primordial human was either androgynous or without sex because the subsequent humans were created by taking bits of clay from the body of this primordial human and fashioning seven males and seven females.[127] Reproduction by heterosexual coupling could then proceed to build the needed workforce.

The Mesopotamian king, whose body symbolized the body politic, was portrayed primarily as masculine but did have androgynous form in the "perfect king" of the Ur III period. In the mythical narrative *Atrahasis* the primordial human can be seen as androgynous. These semidivine or mythical figures stand at the margins of the human condition

123. Asher-Greve, "Decisive Sex, Essential Gender," 12.

124. Ibid., 13. Stephanie Dalley, "Evolution of Gender in Mesopotamian Mythology and Iconography with a Possible Explanation of *ša rēšēn*, 'the man with two heads,'" in *Sex and Gender in the Ancient Near East*, 117–22, at 120–21, claims that the classification of nouns into animate/inanimate in Sumerian rather than into masculine/feminine as in Akkadian must have predisposed Sumerian speakers to accept a common gender.

125. The Anunnakkū prior to the MB period referred to the gods in general but thereafter to the gods of the underworld; the Igigū in the OB period referred to the ten great gods but from the MB period onward to the gods of heaven. See Jeremy Black and Anthony Green, *Gods, Demons, and Symbols of Ancient Mesopotamia* (Austin, TX: University of Texas Press, 1992), 34, 106.

126. William Moran, "The Creation of Man in Atrahasis I 192–248," in *The Most Magic Word*, CBQMS 35, ed. Ronald S. Hendel, 75–86 (Washington, DC: Catholic Biblical Association, 2002), at 85–86.

127. Asher-Greve, "Decisive Sex, Essential Gender," 11; Benjamin Foster, *Before the Muses: An Anthology of Akkadian Literature*, 3d ed. (Bethesda, MD: Capital Decisions Limited, 2005), 270; *Atrahasiṣ* (Late Assyrian version) I iii 15′-31′.

and so can incorporate characteristics of both genders and sexes in order to act constructively for the ordering of the world.[128] This constructive, civilizing role of the king is symbolized by his task as keeper of the royal garden.

Socialization into the Categories of Sex and Gender

While the creation of male and female humans made possible the physical reproduction of humans it left open the question of the masculinity and femininity of each of these human creatures. In Mesopotamia sexual identity was determined by a person's sexual organs, but gender identity was subject to the processes of socialization.[129] "Heroism" was a ME in Sumerian culture: i.e., it was an "essence" or a traditional value or fact that carried the weight of what would later be known as natural law.[130] If a man was to be "a man" he should act heroically when the circumstances called for this. Another ME was prostitution, which obviously did not mean that women were required to be prostitutes, but it did warn against efforts to eradicate this profession as abnormal.[131] Marriage was not a ME, but intercourse and kisses were.[132] So intercourse was not valued solely as a procreative act. However, in the *Atrahasis* story, having children is ranked higher than marriage (I: 246-305).[133] Socializing the young into the masculine or feminine model is accented

128. Groneberg, "Der sumerisch-akkadische Inanna/Ištar: Hermaphroditos?" 36–37.

129. Asher-Greve, "Decisive Sex, Essential Gender," 19.

130. Wim van Binsbergen and Frans Wiggermann, "Magic in History," in *Mesopotamian Magic: Textual, Historical, and Interpretative Perspectives*, Ancient Magic and Divination 1, ed. Tzvi Abusch and Karel van der Toorn, 3–34 (Groningen: Styx, 1999), at 23; Jack Lawson, *The Concept of Fate in Ancient Mesopotamia of the First Millennium: Toward an Understanding of Šimtu* (Wiesbaden: Harrassowitz, 1994), 64, 131. Gertrud Farber Flügge, *Der Mythos "Inanna und Enki" unter besonderer Berücksichtigung der Liste der me*, Studia Pohl 10 (Rome: Biblical Institute Press, 1973), 117–19, notes that the ME's are essences that are evidenced in particular groups of individual existents; the ME's are divine powers or attributes that make a thing or reality what it is and thus are constitutive of civilization.

131. Ibid., tablet II, v. 39, 53; see also *COS* 1.523; Jerrold Cooper, "Prostitution," *RlA* 11 (2006), 12–21, at 13–14; Neil Walls, *Desire, Discord, and Death: Approaches to Ancient Near Eastern Myth* (Boston: American Schools of Oriental Research, 2001), 21.

132. Farber Flügge, *Der Mythos "Inanna und Enki,"* tablet II, v.37-38; see also *COS* 1.523.

133. Asher-Greve, "Decisive Sex, Essential Gender," 17. Bernard Batto, "The Institution of Marriage in Genesis 2 and Atrahasis," *CBQ* 62 (2000): 621–31, at 628, argues that *Atrahasis*, 271–76, 291–305, emphasizes the origin of the institution of marriage as a greater concern than that of sexual attraction and as closely linked with procreation.

in the following birth incantation from the Ur III period: "If it is male, he holds in his hand a weapon and an ax, which is his strength of heroship. If it is a female, she holds in her hand a spindle and a decorated comb."[134] Boys were taught a trade or sent to the Edubba to learn the scribal craft; girls were kept at home to learn homemaking skills from their mothers.[135]

The socialization process linked male or female gender identity to heterosexual desire. Homosexual behavior was allowed under certain circumstances: e.g., active homosexual relations with certain cult personnel in Ishtar's cult were regarded as having relations with the goddess and therefore propitious.[136] Passive homosexual relations lowered the status of a male and were presumably avoided. According to *MAL* 19 and 20, to accuse another male of passive homosexual relations or to rape another male lowered the status of that male and thus were actions punished by the law of talion.[137] Departures from the dominant heterosexual model marginalized a person.[138]

The sex omens on tablets 103-104 of the omen series *Šumma ālu* address a range of sexual activities including heterosexual intercourse, masturbation, and anal intercourse. These omens are designed to speak to male erotic experience and the vulnerabilities of a man's body.[139] The omens primarily address sexual interactions at the boundaries of male and female bodies and the ominous character of bodily emissions.[140] Ann Kessler Guinan identifies four main types of binary classification at work within these omens: "hierarchy (domination/subordination), sex (male/female), gender (masculinity/femininity), sexuality (penetration/receptivity)."[141] The omens help a man reflect on how his sexual desires fit within his social circumstances. A general principle in the omens is

134. Translation from Willem H. P. Römer, "Geburtsbeschwörungen," *TUAT* 2 (1986–1991), 204–7, as quoted in Asher-Greve, "Decisive Sex, Essential Gender," 13.

135. Ibid., 15.

136. *Šumma ālu*, tablet 104, omens 13, 14 (*CT* 39, 45, 32); Ann Kessler Guinan, "Auguries of Hegemony: The Sex Omens of Mesopotamia," in *Gender and Body in the Ancient Mediterranean*, 38–55, at 45; Groneberg, "Der sumerisch-akkadische Inanna/Ištar: Hermaphroditos?" 36.

137. Guinan, "Auguries of Hegemony: The Sex Omens of Mesopotamia," 45–46.

138. Roscoe, "Priests of the Goddess," 222; Asher-Greve, "Decisive Sex, Essential Gender," 19.

139. Guinan, "Auguries of Hegemony," 38.

140. Ibid., 41.

141. Ibid., 40.

that it is more constructive for a man to switch his sexual energies away from a woman toward projects that will enhance his public *persona*.[142]

Transgressions of the categories of sex and gender mapped out in the dominant heterosexual model raised anxieties and were regarded as ominous. Castration, impotency, asceticism, and congenital sexual anomalies placed a male outside the typical categories.[143] The presence of these abnormal realities in the community was regarded as threatening to its integrity. The anxiety associated with the blending of gender categories arose not simply from lack of clarity over gender roles but also from the fear that such anomalous behavior was tied to magical powers.[144] An aggressive woman who would take over a man's role was feared as a danger to the world order. For example, according to the *Sumerian King List*, Ku-baba briefly ruled over Kish after the flood (*SKL* 40-94) and thereby was regarded as having set the stage for the downfall of Kish.[145] Thus those who inverted male and female behavior or mixed gender roles within the human community were feared and marginalized.

On the mythical plane, however, androgynous humans and composite beings played strategic roles in the maintenance of cosmic order. The divinized "perfect king" of the Ur III period was depicted as androgynous, but he was regarded as partially divine. In the *Gilgamesh Epic* the wild man Enkidu runs with the animals and shares many of their traits (*Gilg*. I.109-33). But when he is initiated into the society of Uruk by the temple prostitute Shamhat he is in the anomalous situation of being an adult who needs to be socialized.[146] Shamhat takes the active role of instructing Enkidu (*Gilg*. II.29-51). Asher-Greve notes that in his listening and speechlessness Enkidu exhibits feminine characteristics.[147] In his companionship with Gilgamesh, Enkidu will also be a follower. So in the intimacy of their "buddy" relationship one can see Enkidu assuming

142. Ibid., 40.

143. Roscoe, "Priests of the Goddess," 222.

144. Asher-Greve, "Decisive Sex, Essential Gender," 19–20. Sarah Kofman, "Socrates and His Twins (The Socrates[es] of Plato's *Symposium*)," in *Feminism and the History of Philosophy*, ed. Genevieve Lloyd, 41–67 (New York: Oxford, 2002), at 49, 61, refers to the paradoxical, androgynous character of Socrates who exercises a "magico-magnetic power" on others (e.g., Alcibiades in *Symposium* 215e).

145. Asher-Greve, "Decisive Sex, Essential Gender," 19.

146. Ibid., 14–15. Richard A. Henshaw, *Female and Male: The Cultic Personnel, The Bible and the Rest of the Ancient Near East*, Princeton Theological Monograph Series 3 (Allison Park, PA: Pickwick, 1994), 215, claims that the Shamhatu type of prostitute seems to be different from the *ḫarimtu* type (*CT* 18, 19). Cf. Gilg. I:140; VI:158.

147. Asher-Greve, "Decisive Sex, Essential Gender," 14–15.

the feminine role. But physically—except for his hair—Enkidu is strongly masculine.[148] His androgyny assists the hearer of this mythic narrative in thinking about the boundary between the animal and the human and about the place of heterosexual relations (through his transformative sexual relations with Shamhat) and of a "buddy" relation (through his close friendship with Gilgamesh).[149] This mythic narrative affords the opportunity to reflect upon the contradictions that arise between male/female, masculine/feminine, and superior/subordinate in human experience and to bring them into a modus vivendi.[150]

From Sumerian times onward it appears that sex and gender roles were clearly distinguished in Mesopotamian society. However, Guinan notes that overt descriptions of expected sexual behavior tend to produce strong countercurrents. Thus omen literature offered advice on particular boundary issues that provoked reflection but could not be generalized into laws or principles.[151] Mythical narratives shaped the Mesopotamian imaginary by charting out the contours of the masculine and feminine roles and male and female behavior. The deities or heroes could combine or reverse these distinctive roles of sex and gender because they belonged to another sphere of cosmic reality. But if a human being experienced a reversal of gender or sex roles it would have created anxiety in the person and in the social group. Anxiety over fluidity in these basic categories of human life raised questions about magical powers that might influence one's life and environment. Mythical narratives and omen literature were two means Mesopotamians could use to negotiate the personal and social boundaries of sex and gender.

Composite Figures as Guardians of Cosmic Junctures

A primary function of composite creatures was to stand guard at the cosmic borders separating heaven, earth, and the netherworld.[152] The

148. Jean-Fabrice Nardelli, *Homosexuality and Liminality in the Gilgameš and Samuel*, Classical and Byzantine Monographs 64 (Amsterdam: Adolf M. Hakkert, 2007), 18–19, dismisses scholarly claims that Enkidu and Gilgamesh exhibit androgynous traits.

149. Jerrold S. Cooper, "Buddies in Babylonia: Gilgamesh, Enkidu, and Mesopotamian Homosexuality," in *Riches Hidden in Secret Places: Ancient Near Eastern Studies in Memory of Thorkild Jacobsen*, ed. Tzvi Abusch, 73–85 (Winona Lake, IN: Eisenbrauns, 2002).

150. Cf. Fredric Jameson, *The Political Unconscious: Narrative as a Socially Symbolic Act* (Ithaca, NY: Cornell University Press, 1981), 80, 183.

151. Ann Kessler Guinan, "Erotomancy: Scripting the Erotic," in *Sex and Gender in the Ancient Near East*, 185–201, at 191.

152. Dalley, "Evolution of Gender in Mesopotamian Mythology," 118.

scorpion-men, half-human and half-scorpion, were sentinels who resided as male-female pairs at the twin cosmic mountains: one in the east where the sun rises and the other in the west where the sun sets (*Gilg*. IX.37-45).[153] The *mušhuššu*, the snake-dragon that provided the mount for Marduk, had the body of a snake, the front legs of a lion, the back legs of a bird, a serpentine neck, and a head with horns.[154] This terror-inspiring animal was engraved on the Ishtar Gate in Babylon and on the gates and walls of temples to alert all who approached that the space beyond it belonged to Marduk and had to be respected. In neo-Hittite/Aramean sites of the NA period, there are stone sculptures with a human head and an animal head. NA texts refer to these composite creatures as *kūribu* (cognate to Hebrew *kĕrûb*).[155] Stephanie Dalley claims that the composite creatures at the entryways to ancient Near Eastern palaces and temples were often of dual sex and gender.[156]

The fish-man, an androgynous, composite creature consisting of a man and a *purādu*-fish, was revered as a founder of Mesopotamian cities.[157] Fish were hermaphrodites and so could reproduce without copulation. They obviously were not troubled by the great flood and thus could be a point of continuity between pre- and post-flood civilization. These fish-men, belonging to the domain of Enki, were regarded as sages who brought civilization from the gods to humans.[158] Of the Seven Sages honored in the Mesopotamian tradition, Adapa, who founded Eridu, was the first. His Sumerian name Ù.TU.A.AB.BA means "born in the sea."[159] The main story about him relates that his fishing boat capsized one day, and in his distress he cursed the South Wind, which broke the wind's wing. This wind brought moist, humid air to Mesopotamia. The god

153. A. R. George, *The Babylonian Gilgamesh Epic*, 2 vols. (Oxford and New York: Oxford University Press, 2003), 1: 492–93; cf. Groneberg, "Der sumerisch-akkadische Inanna/Ištar: Hermaphroditos?" 36–37.

154. Theodore Lewis, "CT 13.33-34 and Ezekiel 32: Lion-Dragon Myths," *JAOS* 116 (1996): 28–47, at 35; Wiggermann, *Mesopotamian Protective Spirits*, 154, 157.

155. Dalley, "Evolution of Gender in Mesopotamian Mythology and Iconography," 118. Talmud Yoma 54a identifies the cherub figure as being both male and female.

156. Dalley, "Evolution of Gender in Mesopotamian Mythology and Iconography," 119.

157. Wiggermann, *Mesopotamian Protective Spirits*, 183, describes the *kulullû*, "fish-centaur," as a composite creature whose upper body (except the head) is human and lower body is a *purādu*, "carp." He notes that this monster is sometimes confused with the fish-*apkallu*. See also J. C. Greenfield, "Apkallu," *DDD* 72–74.

158. Dalley, "Evolution of Gender in Mesopotamian Mythology and Iconography," 120.

159. Izre'el, *Adapa and the South Wind*, 1.

Anu, when he was informed that the human Adapa was the one who had disabled the wind, became angry. Izre'el points out that Anu was upset that a human was invested with power to interfere with the regularities of nature: the issue was a transgression of divine authority rather than the possession of excessive wisdom.[160] This fish-man Adapa was able by the power of his language to control a natural force.[161] When Anu summoned him to heaven, Ea counseled Adapa not to eat or drink; however, Ea said that he could accept clothing and be anointed. Ea deceived Adapa, for if he had eaten this divine food he would have become immortal—a transformation Ea did not want to happen to Adapa. From Ea's perspective, Adapa was more important as a composite being and boundary-keeper than he would be if he were to be divinized.[162]

Composite figures in art and mythical narrative provided a response to the human desire to know how to communicate with the invisible powers that shape human life. Their task of facilitating communication between humans and the gods required that they not only maintain and guard the boundary between humans and the gods but also that they serve as mediators and messengers who travel between the spheres of heaven, earth, and the netherworld to promote harmony and appropriate interaction among these three spheres.

Cultic Officials as Androgynous Boundary-Keepers

The task of traversing heaven, earth, and the netherworld in order to keep intact the boundary between them is carried out by mythical composite figures. But the story of boundary-keeping intersects with human history when cultic personnel associated with Ishtar have a part to play in the story. The *kurgarrû* and *assinnu* were real-life actors in ritual who could at the same time symbolize mythical beings.[163] In a state ritual acted out in Esagil in Babylon in the NA period in which Marduk and Nabû defeat Anu and Enlil, the *kurgarrû* represent gods allied with the victorious Marduk and Nabû.[164] Their celebration of this victory is described as follows:

160. Ibid., 129, 132–33.

161. Ibid., 134–35. On this curse as a type of magical language see Piotr Michalowski, "Adapa and the Ritual Process," *Rocznik Orientalistyczny* 51 (1980): 77–82, at 79.

162. Izre'el, *Adapa and the South Wind*, 120.

163. Stefan M. Maul, "*kurgarrû* and *assinnu*," 163.

164. Alasdair Livingstone, *Mystical and Mythological Explanatory Works of Assyrian and Babylonian Scholars* (Oxford: Clarendon Press, 1986), 131.

> The cult dancers (*kurgarrû*) of the battle-field cavort, play about, beat clappers, halloo, lift up [. . .] together, and twitter. They are the brothers, who concerning Enlil and Anu, gave their cries, poured out their sheen on them, broke their [. . .] and [sent down] to the Apsû. (K3476 [obverse] line 15)[165]

Their noisy ecstasy points to their participation in the invisible realm of Ishtar. Maul claims that the *kurgarrû* are like shamans in their capacity to mediate between the two cosmological levels of heaven and earth.[166] The reference to their earlier "pouring out their sheen" on Enlil and Anu indicates that the cultic actors on the mythic level were gods who attacked Anu and Enlil with their divine radiance (*melammû*).[167] This kind of ecstatic behavior by the *kurgarrû* also occurs in the procession preceding the annual sacred marriage rite in Isin as described in the Sumerian hymn titled "The Sacred Marriage of Iddin-Dagan and Inanna":

> Daggers and clubs rage before her—before holy Inanna, before her eyes they are parading—the *kurgarrû*s mounted (on chariots), swing the clubs—before holy Inanna, before her eyes, they are parading—gore is covering the daggers, blood sprinkles,—before holy Inanna, before her eyes they are parading—in the courtyard, the (place of) assembly of the temple administrators, they are shedding blood, (as) loudly resounds there (gay music of) tigi-harps, tambourines, and lyres.[168]

In this ritual in which the *kurgarrû* are playing war they carry weapons as well as musical instruments.[169] The blood that is sprinkled may be

165. Translation in ibid., 123.

166. Maul, "*kurgarrû* and *assinnu*," 163. Cooper, "Buddies in Babylonia," 82, n. 60, notes his unease with the application of a term like "shamanism" to Babylonian figures.

167. Jean Bottéro, *Religion in Ancient Mesopotamia*, trans. Teresa L. Fagan (Chicago: University of Chicago Press, 2001), 38, defines *melammû* (Sumerian ME, "power,"and LÁM, "incandescent") as "an extraordinary density of being" or "prodigious luminosity residing in the gods," which attracts and intimidates. A. Leo Oppenheim, "Akkadian *pul(u)ḫ(t)u* and *melammu*," *JAOS* 63 (1943): 31–34, at 33–34, notes that cult personnel would wear a "terror-inspiring *melammu* mask," which functioned as a divine nimbus in their battles with demons.

168. Translation by Jacobsen in *COS* 1.173, p. 556. Basic edition: Willem H. P. Römer, "Hymne an Inanna-Dilibad. Heilige Hochzeit Iddindagāns mit der Göttin," in *Sumerische 'Königshymnen' der Isin-Zeit* (Leiden: Brill, 1965), 128–208, at lines 72–79, pp. 130–31.

169. Barbara Böck, "Überlegungen zu einem Kultfest der altmesopotamischen Göttin Inanna," *Numen* 51 (2004): 20–46, at 29–33.

their own, for Maul claims that they engaged in self-mutilation in this dance.[170]

Closely associated with the *kurgarrû* is the *assinnu*. The *assinnu* first appears in Mari in the eighteenth century BCE as a prophet of Annunītum (a form of Ishtar).[171] In the NA period he functions within the cult of Ishtar.[172] The androgynous character of the *kurgarrû* and *assinnu* is evident in the following passage from *Erra and Ishum* concerning the inhabitants driven from Uruk by Sutaean invaders:

> [The Sutaeans] removed the performers (*kurgarrû*) and singers (*assinnū*) of Eanna—whose masculinity Ishtar had changed to femininity to create reverence (*ana šupluḫ*) among the people—the ones who carry swords, razors, sharp knives, and flint blades, who regularly take part in abominable acts in order to give joy to the heart of Ishtar. (*Erra* IV:55-58)[173]

This sex change to produce an androgynous cultic official is referenced also in the following curse in an inscription of Esarhaddon: "May Ishtar, the lady of war and battle, turn his masculinity into femininity" (Mnm. A, lines 55-56).[174] In the lamentation "Uru-amirabi," Ishtar is said to describe herself as one who is ". . . wise. I make right into left. I make left into right. I turn a man into a woman. I turn a woman into a man. I am the one who causes the man to adorn himself as a woman. I am the one who causes the woman to adorn herself as a man."[175] The gender inversion signaled by cross-dressing manifests Ishtar's presence as a paradoxical deity. Because Ishtar was believed to metamorphose basic biological and cultural categories she evoked both fear and reverence (cf. *Erra*

170. Maul, "*kurgarrû* and *assinnu*," 164; Römer, "Hymne an Inanna-Dilibad,"166–67. Saana Teppo, "Sacred Marriage and the Devotees of Ištar," 79, suggests that self-mutilation is an action through which the devotees identify with Ištar in the netherworld.

171. *ARM* X 6:5; William L. Moran, "New Evidence from Mari on the History of Prophecy," *Bib* 51 (1969): 15–56, at 33.

172. Henshaw, *Female and Male*, 284.

173. Edition: Luigi Cagni, *L'epopea di Erra*, Studi Semitici 34 (Rome: Istituto di Studi del Vicino Oriente, Universite di Roma, 1969), 110; see also Foster, *Before the Muses*, 904.

174. Edition: Riekele Borger, *Die Inschriften Asarhaddons*, 99; cf. Henshaw, *Female and Male*, 292. See also Donald J. Wiseman, "The Vassal Treaties of Esarhaddon," *Iraq* 20 (1958): 75, 616-17; Groneberg, "Der sumerisch-akkadische Inanna/Ištar: Hermaphroditos?" 40.

175. Translation by Mark E. Cohen, *Canonical Lamentations of Ancient Mesopotamia* (Potomac, MD: Capital Decisions Limited, 1988), 2:596. See also Konrad Volk, *Die Balag-Komposition Uru-Àm-ma-ir-ra-bi: Rekonstruktion und Bearbeitung der Tafeln 18 (19'ff), 19, 20 und 21 der späten, kanonischen Version*, Freiburger Altorientalische Studien 18 (Stuttgart: Franz Steiner, 1989), tablet 20:64-69, pp. 143–44, 150.

IV:52).[176] In the hymn "The Sacred Marriage of Iddin-Dagan and Inanna" another cultic performer known as a sag-ur-sag, "guardian," honors Ishtar by reversing a normal practice by which men dress for battle:

> Their right arms are clothed with cloth in male fashion, before holy Inanna, before her eyes, they are parading—the queen of heaven, Inanna, I will hail! On their left arms they have pulled the cloth down and off—before holy Inanna, before her very eyes they are parading—the great queen of heaven, Inanna, I will hail! Playfully, with painted buttocks, they engage in single combat—before holy Inanna, before her eyes they are parading.[177]

Jacobsen notes that the usual practice was for men to keep the right arm uncovered for freedom of movement.[178] The remaining description of their display indicates that they were scantily clad to the point of obscenity, a tactic designed to catch Ishtar's attention and entertain her.[179]

The capacity of the *assinnu* to enter into the netherworld unharmed made him a valuable mediator when one was troubled by its denizens. In the "Descent of Ishtar to the Netherworld" the earthly sphere languishes because Ishtar has been captured and held in the netherworld as a corpse (76-80). Therefore Ea is petitioned to find a solution. He creates an *assinnu* named Asushunamir ("he is resplendent as he comes forth," 92)[180] and sends him to win the favor of Ereshkigal so that she will swear to reward him. Perhaps the device by which he wins her favor is by voicing a lament on her behalf.[181] Alternatively, Ereshkigal may be attracted to the charming but impotent Asushunamir.[182] When Asushunamir requests the return of Ishtar to the upper world, Ereshkigal becomes angry; nevertheless, she

176. Maul, "*kurgarrû* and *assinnu*," 159.

177. Translation by Jacobsen in *COS* 1.173, 60–65, p. 555; see Willem H. P. Römer, "Hymne an Inanna-Dilibad," 60–65, p. 130.

178. Jacobsen, *COS* 1.173, p. 555, n. 10. Böck, "Überlegungen zu einem Kultfest der altmesopotamischen Göttin Inanna," 33, argues that this inversion ritual, as is typical of carnival, aimed to strengthen the rules and boundaries of the moral and political order through this momentary ritual inversion. For a reference to cross-dressing in the cult of Inanna on the fourteenth-century Kurigalzu statue see Niek Veldhuis, "Kurigalzu's Statue Inscription," *JCS* 60 (2008): 25–51, at 26, 43.

179. Cf. Julia Assante, "Sex, Magic and the Liminal Body in the Erotic Art and Texts of the Old Babylonian Period," in *Sex and Gender in the Ancient Near East*, 27–52, at 27–28.

180. Foster, *Before the Muses*, 502, n. 3.

181. A. D. Kilmer,"How Was Queen Ereshkigal Tricked? A New Interpretation of the Descent of Ishtar," *UF* 3 (1971): 299–309, at 301, 304–5.

182. Walls, *Desire, Discord, and Death*, 152.

honors her oath (100-25). As a devotee of Ishtar, the *assinnu* would strongly participate in the life of the goddess.[183] Perhaps it is the androgynous character of Asushunamir that allows him to pass unharmed into the netherworld.[184] Foster notes that it is not clear how he was shielded on his descent but speculates that "perhaps a male in female costume 'partook of both worlds' or could pass anywhere as an itinerant entertainer."[185]

The numinous power believed to be wielded by the *kurgarrû* and *assinnu* may well account for the mixed reaction they aroused. On the one hand they were sought out for their capacity to banish abnormalities of mind or nature by siphoning off evil.[186] On the other hand they were feared for their capacity to curse and so were grouped with sorcerers and witches (*Maqlû* IV:83; VII:92).[187] Martti Nissinen accents the professional character of the *kurgarrû* and *assinnu*. Even though these individuals may not have been literally castrated, they lived as if they had been.[188] Nissinen describes their role as basically asexual: a sign of their total dedication to Ishtar.[189] One may note, however, that according to a sex omen in *Šumma ālu*, sexual contact with the *kurgarrû* and *assinnu* was propitious.[190] Sex omens were intended to provoke reflection rather than to prescribe particular actions. Guinan notes that sex omens were sometimes contradictory in order to deal with ambiguous character of sexuality; in other words, an omen may prescribe a particular way of addressing a sexual concern with the expectation that the recipient would oppose

183. Martti Nissinen, *Homoeroticism in the Biblical World*, trans. Kirsi Stjerna (Minneapolis: Fortress Press, 1998), 33.

184. Maul, "*kurgarrû* and *assinnu*," 163; Lambert, "Prostitution," 151; A. R. George, "Babylonian Texts from the Folios of Sidney Smith, Part Three: A Commentary on a Ritual of the Month Nisan," in *If a Man Builds a Joyful House: Assyriological Studies in Honor of Erle Verdun Leichty*, ed. Ann Kessler Guinan, et al., 173–85 (Leiden: Brill, 2006), at 175; Henshaw, *Female and Male*, 288.

185. Foster, *Before the Muses*, 502, n. 3; cf. Rivkah Harris, *Gender and Aging in Mesopotamia* (Norman: University of Oklahoma Press, 2000), 129.

186. Roscoe, "Priests of the Goddess," 216.

187. Maul, "*kurgarrû* and *assinnu*," 164.

188. Nissinen, *Homoeroticism in the Biblical World*, 33–34; Teppo, "Sacred Marriage and the Devotees of Ištar," 86. In the *Descent of Ishtar* the *assinnu* is cursed by Ereshkigal by being castrated (*KAR* 1 rev. 19′, ed. Borger, *BAL* I, 101 Ass. Rs. 20); see A. R. George, "Babylonian Texts," 175.

189. Nissinen, *Homoeroticism in the Biblical World*, 33–34.

190. *Šumma ālu*, tablet 104, #13, 14; Guinan, "Auguries of Hegemony," 45; cf. Teppo, "Sacred Marriage and the Devotees of Ištar," 81.

it.[191] The dialectic between the opposing views was apparently regarded as a constructive way for an individual to address a sexual issue.

Androgynous male dancers and singers who served Ishtar were respected and feared as mediators of her elemental erotic power. Love and strife are forces that characterize Ishtar. The *kurgarrû* and *assinnu* were cultic actors who symbolized her presence in her cultic rituals. The gender inversion ascribed to these cultic officials was believed to be effected by the paradoxical Ishtar, who moved these officials into a primordial state of androgyny to promote communication between earth, heaven, and the netherworld. Their lamentations and carnivalesque ritual performances aimed to assist the dynamic of dying and rising in the community essential to its revitalization. Their holiness linked with Ishtar provoked awe and fear.

Eunuchs at the "Sacred" Boundaries of Palatial Culture in Assyria and Persia

The term *ša rēšēn*, "one of the two heads," has been identified more generally as an Assyrian or Babylonian palace official or more specifically as a eunuch. Dalley, who has identified a number of androgynous creatures in Mesopotamian mythology and iconography, contends that *ša rēšēn* did not become a designation for a eunuch until after NA times.[192] She speculates that the practice of bringing foreigners into the Assyrian court and indoctrinating them in Assyrian culture and ideology to prepare them to be provincial officials may have triggered the association of eunuchs with the primeval androgynes with two heads. Therefore the castration such foreigners would have undergone would have been figurative rather than literal. In the most extreme case of such figurative castration they would have been emptied of their native culture and indoctrinated into Assyrian ways. In a more moderate scenario these officials-in-training would have been able to balance the claims of both cultures, with priority given to the Assyrian.[193]

In recent years, scholars who focus on the Assyrian evidence have tended to identify the *ša rēši* as a eunuch in NA times. A. Kirk Grayson

191. Guinan, "Erotomancy: Scripting the Erotic," 191.

192. Stephanie Dalley, "Review of R. Mattila, *The King's Magnates*," SAAS 11 (Helsinki: State Archives of Assyria Project, 2000), *Bibliotheca Orientalis* 58 (2001): 197–206, at 198; von Soden (*AHw* 974A) claims that *šūt rēši* were not eunuchs.

193. Dalley, "Evolution of Gender in Mesopotamian Mythology and Iconography," 121.

noted that there is no evidence to affirm or deny that the *ša rēši* was a eunuch, yet he is convinced that this identification is correct.[194] Hayim Tadmor likewise claims that *ša rēši* means "eunuch" and is the term from which the biblical *sārîs* was borrowed.[195] Karlheinz Deller also identifies the *ša rēši* as a eunuch; he proposes that *rēšu* ("round object") refers to testicles in *ša rēšēn*, a title which he translates as "the one of crushed testicles."[196] The title or label *ša rēši* is applied to a wide range of positions from high palace officials to lowly servants in households, but almost never to temple administrators.[197]

From the ninth to the seventh centuries BCE in Assyria a corps of palace and provincial eunuchs played key roles in the administration of the empire. Records on the Assyrian bureaucracy in the ninth-eighth centuries indicate that 10 percent (19 of 147) of the officials were eunuchs, but Grayson believes the actual number of eunuchs was much higher.[198] By the time of Sargon II (721–705) that number had increased significantly.[199] The eunuchs were not simply scribes or office workers but were also ranking officers in the military—which suggests that eunuchs in these positions were not effeminate.[200] The *rab ša rēši*—the biblical *rab-sārîs* (2 Kgs 18:17)—was the military leader in charge of the royal guardsmen.[201] A eunuch was especially suited for this position since he was more likely than a typical general to maintain absolute loyalty to the king. The eunuchs were drawn primarily from prisoners of war, but some of the high-ranking ones originated from the Assyrian nobility.[202]

194. A. Kirk Grayson, "Eunuchs in Power: Their Role in the Assyrian Bureaucracy," in *Vom Alten Orient zum Alten Testament*, AOAT 240 (Neukirchen-Vluyn: Neukirchener Verlag, 1995), 85–97, at 90.

195. Tadmor, "The Role of the Chief Eunuch," 606.

196. Karlheinz Deller, "The Assyrian Eunuchs and Their Predecessors," in *Priests and Officials in the Ancient Near East*, ed. Kazuko Watanabe, 303–11 (Heidelberg: Universitätsverlag, 1996), at 304–5.

197. Grayson, "Eunuchs in Power," 90, 94–95; Deller, "The Assyrian Eunuchs and their Predecessors," 303, 308; Tadmor, "The Role of the Chief Eunuch," 603–4.

198. Grayson, "Eunuchs in Power," 93. On the basis of administrative lists from Ur III, Kazuya Makaewa, "Animal and Human Castration in Sumer, Part II: Human Castration in the Ur III Period," *Zinbun* 16 (1980): 1–55, at 51–52, argues that the Sumerian AMAR-KUD applies to lower-class boys and young men, of whom many were war captives, who were assigned to a wide range of tasks for which castration would have diminished their temptation to flee.

199. Grayson, "Eunuchs in Power," 93.

200. Ibid., 96–97.

201. Tadmor, "The Role of the Chief Eunuch," 607.

202. Grayson, "Eunuchs in Power," 95.

The legendary Semiramis (Sammu-ramat, the mother of Shamshi-Adad V [823–811]) was reported by the Roman historian Ammianus Marcellinus (writing in the fourth century CE; 16.6.17) to have appointed the first eunuchs to the Assyrian harem.[203] The eunuchs began to play an increasingly important role in the government because they provided a buffer for the king against usurpers. In 826–820 BCE an internal crisis arose in the Assyrian royal government when two sons of Shalmaneser III (858–824) were vying for the kingship: Ashur-daʾin-apli, the eldest, and Shamshi-Adad V, the winner. In this context the office of the chief eunuch, a confidant with military clout, rose in significance. In 798 the eunuch Mutakkil-Marduk was chosen to have his name be the eponym for that year—an administrative practice in which one of the king's top officials was selected to oversee events for the New Year's festival and to have his name attached to bureaucratic documents for the year. It was the first time this honor was bestowed on a eunuch.[204]

In the middle of the eighth century two rebellions arose that were led by government officials rather than by royal sons: (1) a series of conflicts in 763–758, and (2) a rebellion in Calah in 746 that brought Tiglath-Pileser III (744–727) to power. Two key factors causing these rebellions were the weakness of the reigning king and the longevity of the officials who started the uprisings.[205] In the time of Tiglath-Pileser III the chief eunuch became a troubleshooter in the provinces. The king would often send him to replace a rebellious provincial governor with one more compliant with his centralization policy. Another boost in the power of the chief eunuch came during the reign of Sargon II (721–705), when the king divided the power of the *turtānu* (palace herald and chief cupbearer) by taking the land of Kummuh in east Anatolia and assigning it to a new official known as the left *turtānu* and leaving the rest for the current *turtānu*, who then became known as the right *turtānu*. This move enhanced the power of the lower-ranking chief eunuch.[206]

The eunuchs' loyalty to the king was strengthened by the status, wealth, and sense of solidarity granted by the position. The induction

203. Vern L. Bullough, "Eunuchs in History and Society," in *Eunuchs in Antiquity and Beyond*, ed. Shaun Tougher (London: Classical Press of Wales and Duckworth, 2002), 1–17, at 5; Tadmor, "The Role of the Chief Eunuch," 607.

204. Ibid., 608.

205. A. Kirk Grayson, "The Struggle for Power: Challenge to Absolute Monarchy in the Ninth and Eighth Centuries," in *Priests and Officials in the Ancient Near East*, 253–70, at 268.

206. Tadmor, "The Role of the Chief Eunuch," 608.

of a young man into the ranks of the eunuchs probably had to occur at an early age—if he were literally castrated—for castration was usually fatal for an adult male.[207] His induction was ritualized by a name-giving and clothing ceremony.[208] Therefore the young man was leaving behind his family and former identity in order to become part of the king's government. Nevertheless, those eunuchs who came from noble Assyrian families would seem to have maintained some ties with their families. Many eunuchs received significant landholdings from the king. Even though such lands reverted to the crown at the death of the eunuch, he enjoyed their usufruct and wielded much power from these holdings during his lifetime.[209] An example of the privileges the king would bestow on the eunuch as a landholder was the exemption from taxes, as the following excerpt from a seventh-century BCE document attests:

> NN, eunuch of Ashurbanipal, king of Assyria, an official worthy of good favor, who, from the "succession" to the exercise of kingship, has been committed to the king, his master, and whose heart is fully loyal to his lord, who serves me in fidelity and walks about in safety, who has advanced with a good reputation within my palace, and has kept guard over my kingship—according to my own inclination and counsel, I planned to do him a favor by establishing a grant for him. The fields, orchards and people that he gained under my patronage and built into his own household, I made tax-exempt. I put it in writing and sealed it with my royal seal. I gave them to NN, the eunuch, who reveres my kingship. (SAA XII, 29, 11-29)[210]

This passage highlights the royal favor that accrued to a eunuch because he was a longstanding confidant to the king. A eunuch had much to gain from his association with the king in terms of power and prestige.

Even though most eunuchs were valuable allies in court intrigues, there were exceptions.[211] In 671–670, during the reign of Esarhaddon, the chief ministers of the king conspired to put the chief eunuch—a high-ranking military officer—on the throne. A letter tells how these ministers coerced a Babylonian diviner named Kudurru to provide an extispicy (reading of entrails) predicting the chief eunuch's accession to the king-

207. Dalley, "Review of R. Mattila, *The King's Magnates*," 199.

208. Deller, "The Assyrian Eunuchs and their Predecessors," 306.

209. Ibid., 305–8.

210. Edition: Laura Kataja and Robert M. Whiting, *Grants, Decrees and Gifts of the Neo-Assyrian Period*, SAA XII (Helsinki: Helsinki University Press, 1995), 32.

211. Grayson, "The Struggle for Power," 260.

ship (SAA X 179).[212] This conspiracy was discovered and the chief eunuch—either Ša-Nabû-šû or Aššur-nasir—was executed.[213] Other eunuchs seem to have been part of the conspiracy, for a letter dating to 670 describing the efforts of an agent of Esarhaddon to apprehend eunuchs probably is to be linked to the suppression of this conspiracy.[214] This collective action by eunuchs points to another dimension of their identity: they formed a subgroup within the royal bureaucracy whose members identified with and supported one another.[215] Extant Assyrian records indicate that only one chief eunuch (Sin-Šum-lišir) ever held the throne, and he did so only for three months at the end of the reign of Assur-etil-ilani (623) when the Babylonian prince Nabopolassar was about to take over the land.[216]

An important function for eunuchs in Mesopotamia in the second and first millennia BCE and then in Persia from the sixth to the fourth centuries BCE was to serve the king's wives.[217] The term "harem" refers to what is "separate, forbidden, taboo."[218] The quarters of the wives and concubines of the king were private, just as were the women's quarters in the typical Mesopotamian household. Yet the royal household participated in the king's symbolization of the kingdom by his body. The activities of the royal women within the palace and the image they created by their involvement in the governance of the kingdom were important to the public relations of the monarchy. It may be that the cloistered view of the life of royal women in Mesopotamia is heavily influenced by the picture of the royal harem of the Ottoman empire in the seventeenth to nineteenth centuries CE. But even in this relatively well-documented lifestyle of the harem too little has been said about the important contributions of the royal women in the areas of philanthropy

212. Martti Nissinen, *References to Prophecy in Neo-Assyrian Sources*, SAAS VII (Helsinki: Neo-Assyrian Text Corpus Project, 1998), 133–34.

213. Ibid., 147–48. Tadmor, "The Role of the Chief Eunuch," 609, notes that according to the Assyrian Chronicles 86:29; 127:27 Esarhaddon executed a number of magnates in 670, including the chief eunuch Aššur-Nasir.

214. Nissinen, *References to Prophecy*, 131–32.

215. Grayson, "Eunuchs in Power," 96.

216. Tadmor, "The Role of the Chief Eunuch," 610.

217. Lloyd Llewellyn-Jones, "Eunuchs and the Royal Harem in Achaemenid Persia (559–331)," in *Eunuchs in Antiquity and Beyond*, 19–49, at 21, 31.

218. *Ḫarāmû* "to separate," *CAD* H 89–90; *ḫarāmu* II, "absondern," *AHw* 323A; Heb. *ḥāram*, "ban, devote, exterminate" *BDB* 355B; Arab. *ḥaruma*, "be prohibited, forbidden, unlawful, become sacred" *BDB* 355B.

and public relations.[219] If the starting point for understanding the harem is that these women were important authority figures rather than passive sex objects, the available evidence on Mesopotamian royal women emerges in a new light. The records of women at Mari in the eighteenth century BCE and of NA royal women indicate individuals who were educated and entrusted with important roles in the royal government.[220] For example, Esarhaddon promoted the image of his mother Naqia as a voice of authority within the royal government.[221] Reliefs at Assurbanipal's North Palace in Nineveh portray the queen dining outdoors with the king. Elna Solvang argues that the royal women in Assyria were involved in governing activities and significantly shaped the image of the royal administration in the public's eye.[222]

Keeping the quarters of the royal women safe and free from intruders appears to have been a key responsibility of the eunuchs. They themselves were expected to relate to the royal women with integrity. The code of conduct for the eunuchs in Assyria may well have been carefully crafted along the lines of the following palace regulations from the reign of Tiglath-Pileser I (1114–1076):[223]

> If a woman of the palace has exposed her hips and is not covered by a loincloth and calls out to a palace attendant, saying, "Come that I might send you," and he delays to speak with her, he shall be struck one hundred times. The eyewitness against him shall take his clothing, but as for him they shall bind a skirt around his hips. If a palace attendant speaks with a woman of the palace, he shall come no nearer to her than seven steps. (*MADP* 21)[224]

Surveillance was effected by having the eunuchs report on one another; there were severe penalties for not doing so and substantial rewards for

219. Elna K. Solvang, "Another Look 'Inside': Harems and the Interpretation of Women," in *Orientalism, Assyriology and the Bible*, ed. Steven W. Holloway, 374–98 (Sheffield: Phoenix Press, 2007), at 395–97.

220. Bernard F. Batto, *Studies on Women at Mari* (Baltimore: Johns Hopkins University Press, 1974), 29, 73, 87, 135–38.

221. Sarah C. Melville, *The Role of Naqia/Zakutu in Sargonid Politics*, SAAS 9 (Helsinki: Neo-Assyrian Text Corpus Project, 1999), 92.

222. Solvang, "Another Look 'Inside,'" 395–96.

223. Llewellyn-Jones, "Eunuchs and the Royal Harem," 36; Solvang, "Another Look 'Inside,'" 394.

224. Edition: Ernst Weidner, "Hof- und Harems-Erlasse assyrischer Könige aus dem 2. Jahrtausend v. Chr.," *Archiv für Orientforschung* 17 (154–56:) 257–93, at 287–88; see also Martha T. Roth, *Law Collections from Mesopotamia and Asia Minor*, 2d ed., SBL Writings from the Ancient World 6 (Atlanta: Scholars Press, 1997), 206.

complying. Nevertheless, the eunuchs spent considerable time with the royal women. They were the escorts for the women on outings such as the royal lion hunt.[225] Evidence that the bonds between the eunuchs and these women could become quite strong is given by Xenophon, the late fifth to early fourth century BCE Greek soldier-historian, who reports that three eunuchs committed suicide over the corpse of their beloved mistress (*Cyropaedia* 7.3.15).

As the royal household in Persia grew in size, so also did the demand for eunuchs as servants. Artaxerxes I (465–424) had eighteen sons, but Artaxerxes II (404–358) had 118.[226] Most of the eunuchs in the Persian court after the time of Darius I (522–486) were foreigners who were imported and trained at a young age.[227] They would have grown up with royal sons and would probably have become their confidants, which largely accounted for the power of the eunuchs.[228] Their close relationship with the royal women enabled them to be a communication link between these cloistered women and the public realm of the Persian court—a role that increased the eunuchs' influence but also made them vulnerable to charges of duplicity.[229]

Eunuchs transferred from their natal households to become servants and guardians of the royal family: the king, the royal women, and their children. If they were from foreign lands they could mediate Assyrian or Persian culture to their native culture. Foregoing paternity and family property, they chose to gain the status, power, and property the royal government offered them. Eunuchs functioned throughout the range of palace functions from head of the royal body guard to menial servant duties. They were prized for their loyalty to the royal household and respected for their sense of solidarity with one another. The protection of the royal family emphasizes their distinctive role as ones who maintain the boundaries of the royal household. There is a sacred character to the function of maintaining boundaries, even if they are not the boundaries of a sanctuary per se. They were specially charged with negotiating the link between the royal women and the public. Because they have foregone procreative sex, their erotic world would either take on an asexual character or move toward a more androgynous form.

225. Llewellyn-Jones, "Eunuchs and the Royal Harem," 38.

226. Herodotus 7.187; Llewellyn-Jones, "Eunuchs and the Royal Harem," 33–34.

227. Herodotus 3.92; Llewellyn-Jones, "Eunuchs and the Royal Harem," 33.

228. Ibid., 41.

229. Ibid.

Guardian Figures and Magic

Androgynous beings who were able to traverse the divide between earth and the netherworld or between earth and heaven were both revered and marginalized. The numinous power they were able to bring to bear on a situation made these figures into a source of either blessings or curses. Their protective function at particularly vulnerable locations on the individual and communal bodies shows their potential to address ordinary human anxiety. The androgynous cultic officials of Ishtar with their ecstatic rituals could be offputting (cf. *Erra* IV:58), yet these officials were respected for their capacity to draw evil away from individuals and out of the community so as to restore well-being.[230]

Magical power was also exercised by Adapa when his curse broke the wing of the south wind. Language in its normal operations brings order into human experience and shapes the human environment. But this capacity to alter what appears to be the "essence" of things (MEs) in nature penetrates to the heart of reality. The power to alter the ME was labeled a *šīmtu*, "fate, destiny."[231] When Marduk assumed the kingship in the *Enūma Elish* he demonstrated that he had the power to change destinies and alter the ME (*EE* IV:25-27). From that point on he shared with his father Ea the role of patron of magic.[232] He would be appealed to in incantations and exorcisms to change a bad destiny or bring protection. Since Marduk was king of the gods, the kind of magic he sponsored was white rather than black magic. This white magic was incorporated into the established political order as a force that would be used to keep the status quo or the interests of the powerful intact.[233] Magic was not simply to be a weapon wielded by the marginalized.

The apotropaic function of figurines and plaques at doorways of homes and of statuary at the entrances to palaces and temples drew on this form of "white magic" to promote well-being. The majority of plaques depicted guardian figures that were called upon to ward off evil spirits. They were placed at gates, doorways, windows, crossroads, beds, and entrances to shrines—places that were vulnerable to both visible and invisible forces. Some of these plaques contained sexual scenes designed to arouse the onlooker and were often placed in high-traffic

230. Groneberg, "Der sumerisch-akkadische Inanna/Ištar: Hermaphroditos?" 39–41; Maul, "*kurgarrû* and *assinnu*,"163–64.

231. Van Binsbergen and Wiggermann, "Magic in History," 23; Lawson, *The Concept of Fate in Ancient Mesopotamia of the First Millennium*, 64, 131.

232. Binsbergen and Wiggermann, "Magic in History," 29.

233. Ibid., 17–19.

areas in houses for young and old alike to see. The purpose of these erotic plaques, dating from around 2000 to 1700 BCE, was to protect the house and bring well-being by attracting the attention of Ishtar.[234] It was believed that if she were favorable to a household she would bring fertility and vitality. In the OB period Ishtar's vulva, which symbolized this goddess of sex, was regarded as a propitious sight.[235] However, later such a sight seems to have been more ambiguous. In the Standard Babylonian version of the *Gilgamesh Epic* of the first millennium Gilgamesh refuses Ishtar's marriage proposal because her presence seems to portend only death or castration (*Gilg*. VI:22-79).[236]

A location in which Ishtar's presence was strongly petitioned was the tavern. The tavern was the special preserve of the *ḫarimtu*, "prostitute." As the patron of prostitutes, Ishtar was called upon to bring about an enchanting atmosphere in the tavern. The purpose of accenting erotic attraction in this setting was not so much for sex but rather for seizing individuals and moving them from an everyday disposition to one that was highly charged.[237] This change in bodily/psychic energy was the unique contribution the combination of beer and *erōs* could provide to the clientele. As the divine *ḫarimtu*, Ishtar is both male and female inside the tavern; she is the embodiment of pure desire. As such, Ishtar was sought as a kind of elemental power of existence.[238] Her presence provided the kind of magic the clientele found renewing.

Mythical guardian figures manage their surplus of power minimally at one remove from the way human guardian figures carry out their roles. Mythical figures are supernatural and should be able to perform greater deeds. Yet human figures who perform exorcisms and recite incantations draw on divine power through solemn formulas so as to banish evil and bring well-being. Magical uses of rituals and words were activities employed by the establishment under the patronage of Ea and Marduk. Magical objects such as erotic plaques were used to protect and vitalize a household by appealing to Ishtar to bring blessings. One important area of revitalization was the psychic renewal effected by beer and *erōs* mediated by the barmaid/prostitute. Ishtar was the elemental life-force operative in the activities of the tavern who lifted the spirits of its patrons caught by the force-field of the netherworld.

234. Assante, "Sex, Magic and the Liminal Body," 27–28.

235. Leick, *Sex and Eroticism in Mesopotamia*, 94.

236. Assante, "Sex, Magic and the Liminal Body," 30.

237. Ibid., 33.

238. Ibid., 32.

Summary

According to the *Atrahasis* story, the primordial human was molded from clay as an androgynous being (I: 210-30). This stage quickly gave way to the fabrication of seven males and seven females who then would copulate in order to reproduce (I: 255-60 + K 3399+3934, obv. iii:1-21). Procreation was a higher priority than the companionship of male and female in *Atrahasis*. In line with this priority, heterosexual desire was the dominant model for explaining and guiding erotic interactions. According to the Middle Assyrian Laws (19-20), gender inversion, particularly a male's submission to homosexual penetration, would marginalize a person (*Erra* IV: 55-58). The sex omens of the omen-series *Šumma ālu* deal with male anxieties over male/female relations and bodily emissions. One overriding piece of advice in these omens is to choose to enhance one's public *persona* rather than to pursue a sexual relation with a woman. Transgressive sexual behavior induced anxiety not only by bringing instability or fluidity through the mixing of categories but also by risking association with the powers of black magic.

Mythical portrayals and narratives are particularly valuable for the way they help us think about the basic issues of human existence. The static model of the "perfect king" in Ur III iconography mythologized the reigning king. The androgynous character of this king painted a picture of a complete, primal human who incorporated basic polarities of existence in his person: e.g., divine/human, human/bestial, male/female. In the portrayal of Enkidu's initiation into human culture by the prostitute Shamhat (*Gilg*. I:188-202) we are provided with a more dynamic exploration of the interplay between the polarities of human/animal, nature/culture, and masculine/feminine. In the initiation rite itself the powerful Enkidu is speechless and has feminine-like hair; in other words, he appears to be an androgyne who is fundamentally a male but with pronounced female characteristics. His androgynous character, then, will be a key factor in understanding his buddy relationship with Gilgamesh: was this relationship sexual or asexual in character? An appreciation for primitive androgyny in mythic prototypes perhaps favors the asexual character of the erotically charged relationship of Gilgamesh with Enkidu.

Composite creatures like the scorpion-man, the *mušhuššu*, and the fish-man can move into two different levels of cosmic reality (earth and heaven, or earth and the netherworld) and so can mediate between these two realms. This capacity is fundamental to a cosmic boundary-keeper. The androgynous, two-headed *kurību* from the Hittite/Aramean regions in NA times, which parallels the biblical cherub, indicates how the reality of sex and gender is encompassed and transcended: a being that is simultaneously both male and female can be seen as asexual and genderless. The erotic energy of the cherub would be focused on the deity it serves.

On the earthly level, cultic figures are granted a role that allows them to participate in the mythic realm in ritual time. The androgynous *kurgarrû* and *assinnu* were believed to have been metamorphosed in gender and sex by Ishtar. Cross-dressing, self-laceration, and ecstatic dancing and singing put them in a different world. In their liminal status within the cult they were regarded as shamanlike mediators. But outside the cult of Ishtar they were apparently regarded as abnormal or ominous.

Substantial yet less than definitive evidence exists that eunuchs staffed the Assyrian bureaucracy and military in significant numbers from the ninth century BCE onward. They were drawn primarily from prisoners of war, but some were from the Assyrian nobility. Inducted at a young age into the ranks of the eunuchs, a young man working within the palace could expect to enhance his social status, political power, wealth, and solidarity with the royal family and other eunuchs. The king valued eunuchs for their loyalty, the nonhereditary character of their bureaucratic position, and their care for the royal harem. In times of court intrigue the eunuchs, who tended to identify both with the king and with other eunuchs, could form a buffer between the king and the usurpers. A number of the eunuchs rose in the ranks of the military, which probably originated from the eunuchs gaining leadership over the king's bodyguard. As with all institutional arrangements, there are exceptions to the rule. There were some ambitious eunuchs who tended to appear when the king was weak. Because they themselves had served for some time, these eunuchs were able to forge strategic alliances with the powerful in the kingdom. The only eunuch to sit on the Assyrian throne was Sin-Šum-lišir, who did so for three months in 623 BCE. Eunuchs continued to have an important function in the region in subsequent centuries; especially noteworthy was their substantial presence in the Persian court.

Androgynous beings can be strong protectors of cosmic boundaries, or they may be usurpers who undermine these boundaries. The numinous power at their disposal is a dynamic, elemental force within a culture that demands attention. Strategies to negotiate between the free expression of erotic power and the transmutation of sexual energies into other culturally constructive tasks constitute a vital issue for a community of embodied humans.

Greece: The Interplay of Mythic and Human Androgyny in Euripides' *Bacchae*

In late-fifth-century Athens many would have liked to see the return of a strong ruler like Pericles. Beginning with the plague in 430 and extending through the debacle of the Athenian defeat on the expedition to Sicily in 413, these years were marked by the long-drawn-out war with Sparta that drained the vitality of the polis. In the midst of this general malaise, Euripides' *Bacchae* (ca. 408–406) explores the ways in which the irrational breaks into the life of Athens' shadow city Thebes. Pentheus, the young king of Thebes, does not know how to relate to the women of the city stirred up by Dionysus but only tries to control them. This immaturity reveals the deficiencies in his view of the complementarity of the masculine and feminine dimensions of experience. In the person of Dionysus, the divine sphere of reality provokes a crisis in which the bestial dimension of life overwhelms the civilized order in order to reconstitute it with a new equilibrium. In the following investigation of the *Bacchae* these four questions will be addressed: (1) Is the life-force that sustains the citizens and natural environment of the city of Thebes a malleable, exploitable entity, or is it a personal, divine reality that expects to be attended to and reverenced? (2) Is Pentheus's effort to control the women of Thebes a reflection of his personal struggle to allow the feminine dimension of his own person to have its rightful place? (3) Is Pentheus's cross-dressing a sign that he is no longer fit to rule as king of Thebes, or is it potentially a carnivalesque interlude that will move him to pass beyond the adolescent, voyeuristic stage in his relations with women? (4) Is the sacrificial death of Pentheus at the hands of the maenads a revelation of the deep alienation of the women of Thebes from the patriarchal household and *polis*, or is it an aberration induced by Dionysus to shock the inhabitants of Thebes into recognizing his reality?

Dionysian Polarities: The Unfolding of the Amoral Life-force

In Euripides' *Bacchae*, Pentheus, the king of Thebes, dismisses the god Dionysus as irrelevant and must pay for this grave error with his life. Dionysus, who disguises himself as a human stranger from Asia Minor, enters Thebes and incites the women to retreat to the mountains.[239] Pentheus orders that this stranger be imprisoned but discovers that when

239. On the Macedonian context as the place in which Euripides composed this play and on the dancing madness induced by divine possession see E. R. Dodds, "Introduction," ix–lv, at xi–xiv, xx, in his edition of Euripides' *Bacchae* (Oxford: Clarendon Press, 1944).

he tries to put the shackles on him it is as if he is trying to subdue a bull (619-20). When Pentheus hears a report of the women of Thebes on the mountain he plans to order the military to bring them back (781-83). But Dionysus offers to return them peacefully (803). At the same time he offers Pentheus the opportunity to observe the revels of the women on the mountain, if he will disguise himself as a maenad in women's clothing (821-36; 912-17). Pentheus agrees. When Pentheus complains of not being able to see the maenads, Dionysus elevates him—in phallic fashion—by bending low the top of a fir tree, having Pentheus take his place there, and then returning the tree to its upright position (1059-74). The maenads spot him immediately in his new location and topple the tree in their warlike mania (1075-1113). Pentheus's mother Agave, driven by extreme Dionysian mania, dismembers him, impales his head on a stake, and parades him back to Thebes under the impression that she is carrying the head of a young lion (1113-45). When her father Cadmus coaxes her back to her senses she recognizes the horrible murder she has carried out and plans to go into exile (1144-1371). Cadmus and Agave commiserate with one another (1372-74).

The horror of a mother dismembering her son manifests the amoral, elemental power of Dionysus.[240] Pentheus had intruded on the secret Dionysiac rites of the women (1105-9), but his guilt is mitigated by the fact that Dionysus had lured him into visiting the mountain (811-24). When Agave realizes that it is her son's head she has paraded on a stake she is crushed by this unthinkable, violent crime carried out by her own hands under the impulse of Dionysus—a daemonic, natural force (1282, 1288, 1375-76).

As Agave and her father Cadmus console one another at this irreversible tragedy, the audience is led to reflect on the irrational dimension of life that can erupt and destroy the lives of individuals.[241] Cadmus confronts Dionysus with the charge that his punishment was too harsh and claims that "gods should be exempt from human passions" (1347). But Dionysus replies that "long ago my father Zeus ordained these things" (1348). The members of the audience will most likely agree with Cadmus and judge that the world order shaped by Zeus can be unjust.[242] This view that humans are victims of an unjust world order ruled by the gods led

240. Martha Nussbaum, "Introduction," in Charles K. Williams, *The Bacchae of Euripides*, vii–xliv (New York: Farrar, Strauss & Giroux, 1990), at xix–xx.

241. Ibid., vii.

242. Thomas Gould, *The Ancient Quarrel between Poetry and Philosophy* (Princeton: Princeton University Press, 1990), 39–41.

Plato to decree that tragic poets who promoted such views should not be allowed to remain in the ideal Greek city. He argued that the pity for a victim evoked by the tragic play appeals to the lowest part of the human psyche and gives the citizens a distorted view of themselves and the human condition. Plato claimed that the poetic illusion created by a play like *The Bacchae* moves the audience further from the true reality, which even now they perceive only in shadows (*Rep*. 602c).[243]

As king of Thebes, Pentheus responds to the threat he perceives Dionysus to pose to the boundaries of Thebes by the use of physical force. He tries to enclose Dionysus in prison. Dionysus appears to metamorphose into a bull, but this is only in Pentheus's imagination, for as Pentheus sweats and labors to subdue this bull, Dionysus in his human form sits calmly watching him (617-22).[244] When Pentheus hears of the revels of the maenads on the mountains he fears they are engaged in orgies and threatens to bring out the army in order to bring them back to their safe enclosure in the households in the city. Dionysus warns him that such a measure will be futile; he will be fighting against a god (787-91). Pentheus's strategy for sustaining the boundaries of Thebes is narrow and simplistic. The bull Pentheus tries to shackle is within Pentheus himself. As a symbol of fertility and sexual power the bull points to an elemental force of nature that eludes rational control; this fundamental life-force must be respected and negotiated with rather than coerced.[245] Dionysus, who sits calmly watching Pentheus labor against this force, is an anthropomorphized expression of this elemental life-force—the dimension of life that underlies and goes beyond the conscious, rational existence of humans. The grin Dionysus has when he is being attacked by Pentheus indicates how futile a direct confrontation with Dionysus can be. Dionysus, known for his indirection and trickery, must be met on his own terms.[246]

The blasphemy with which Pentheus and Agave are charged is a denial of the divinity of this irrational force and a lowering of inhibitions toward manipulating or coercing this force (43-46, 537-55, 793-94, 1297).

243. See chaps. 3 and 6 above. Renate Schlesier, "Mixtures of Masks: Maenads as Tragic Models," in *Masks of Dionysus*, ed. Thomas H. Carpenter and Christopher A. Faraone, 89–114 (Ithaca, NY: Cornell University Press, 1993), at 95.

244. Gould, *The Ancient Quarrel between Poetry and Philosophy*, 226.

245. Nussbaum, "Introduction," xix–xx, explains how human morality is not self-sufficient but depends on sudden and strange exits into the divine and the bestial; Pentheus's obsession with preventing such exits constitutes a bestial act.

246. Ibid., vii.

But Pentheus's strategy of going to war against this force is a recipe for rigidity and self-defeat.[247] As Dionysus points out to him, he ends up fighting against himself in trying to remove Dionysus from Thebes (506). In Pentheus one sees the inevitability of a clash with Dionysus if one's instincts and real emotional needs are not addressed.[248] The alternative offered by Dionysus is to welcome him (802, 804). He is also the god of wine, who can bring life-giving energy to an individual and a community (770-75). The recognition of Dionysus is the acceptance of the principle that fluidity is essential to the healthy life.[249] To deny the reality of Dionysus portends that sudden, unexpected irruptions will plague one's emotions and social interactions.[250] Pentheus's attempt to prevent the appearance of Dionysus only serves to reveal him and to turn Pentheus into a beast.[251]

The respect Dionysus expects from Pentheus and the people of Thebes is an ongoing attentiveness to the life-force within and around them. This attentiveness would take the form of negotiating the following set of Dionysian polarities: the Olympian versus the chthonic god; the bestial versus the divine; civic versus rural religion; masculine versus feminine; barbarian versus Theban; wine for the rich versus wine for the poor; native birth versus foreign upbringing; honoring Thebes versus threatening its destruction.[252] The successful balancing of these polarities promises to bring the vitality that comes through harmony with the basic life-force of the cosmos. However, this balance was often won in the midst of paradox or by sitting on the horns of a dilemma. The challenge of respecting Dionysus often takes the form of staying with a set of circumstances in life even when they no longer make sense.[253]

As king of Thebes, Pentheus symbolizes the community. His struggles are not simply his own but aim to bring together the divine, human, and animal spheres within a dynamic hierarchical ordering that makes

247. Nussbaum, "Introduction," xxii, notes that "the *Hippolytus*, produced in 428, is very close to *The Bacchae* in its portrayal both of the violence of erotic desire and of the impoverished character of a life that attempts to close it off completely."

248. Segal, *Dionysiac Poetics and Euripides' Bacchae*, 162; Nussbaum, "Introduction," xxviii; Dodds, "Introduction."

249. Nussbaum, "Introduction," xli; Marcel Detienne, "Forgetting Delphi between Apollo and Dionysus," *Classical Philology* 96 (2001): 147–58, at 154–55.

250. Schlesier, "Mixtures of Masks," 98, 102.

251. Segal, *Dionysiac Poetics and Euripides' Bacchae*, 29; Nussbaum, "Introduction," xx.

252. Segal, *Dionysiac Poetics and Euripides' Bacchae*, 10; see also Schlesier, "Mixtures of Masks," 89–90.

253. Nussbaum, "Introduction," vii.

the world inhabitable for the community.[254] The tensive ordering of polarities, or the coincidence of opposites, communicates a sense of coherence within a geometric model of society and cosmos. However, within a concrete life situation such contradictory, paradoxical relations can be enervating. In many crisis situations it seems that only Dionysus—and not his human followers—can sustain the coexistence of opposites.[255]

The way in which polarities of mythic narratives are negotiated in ritual differs from the way this occurs in a tragic play. In ritual, myth aims to reconcile opposites,[256] whereas in tragedy myth aims to explode these polarities.[257] The benevolent view of the natural order within which a reconciling ritual operates assumes that harmony can be achieved through narrative and logical strategies.[258] However, in tragedy the mythical narrative takes the tension between opposites to such an extreme that (1) divine intervention (*deus ex machina*) is required to resolve a conflict or (2) the protagonists are devoured by the circumstances. The latter alternative is illustrated in the tragic dismemberment of Pentheus by his raving maenad mother. When Agave comes to her senses she knows that she did not will this horrible murder, but she also knows that the violent energy emerged from within her and worked through her hands. Agave identifies this inexplicable irruption of violence from within her as Dionysus (1296, 1326-27). She and Pentheus are accused by the chorus for being blasphemous (1327-28, cf. 43-46, 537-55, 793-94, 1297). The play

254. Ibid., xvi–xx. The cosmic significance of the right ordering of the divine, human, and bestial is emphasized in Hesiod's category of the monsters born from the incestuous unions of members of the family of Pontus: e.g,, Phorkys' union with Keto produces the Graiai and Gorgons (*Theog*. 270–77). Jenny Strauss Clay, "The Generation of Monsters in Hesiod," *CP* 88 (1993): 105–16, at 108, 114, notes that "the breaking of categories makes the monsters appear as if anti-cosmos."

255. Albert Henrichs, "'He Has a God in Him': Human and Divine in the Modern Perception of Dionysus," in *Masks of Dionysus*, 13–43, at 31.

256. Gould, *The Ancient Quarrel between Poetry and Philosophy*, 84.

257. Segal, *Dionysiac Poetics and Euripides' Bacchae*, 14, 212.

258. Charles Segal, "Greek Tragedy and Society: a Structuralist Perspective," in *Greek Tragedy and Political Theory*, ed. J. Peter Euben, 43–75 (Berkeley: University of California Press, 1986), at 45, 48. With regard to Levi-Strauss's view of myth as a tool for resolving contradictions, Marcel Henaff, in *Claude Levi-Strauss and the Making of Structural Anthropology* (Minneapolis: University of Minnesota Press, 1998), 137, notes: "Symbolism is an operating system, an instrument of organization. We do not ask what an instrument means, but what purpose it serves, what it allows to be produced. Symbolism produces order in a set of tangible elements, order that is intelligible from the perspective of the homologies, oppositions, and inversions that it brings into play. In sum, this is what Levi-Strauss calls the 'savage mind.'"

suggests, but does not guarantee, that she and Pentheus could have avoided their tragic fates if they had allowed Dionysus a respected place in their day-to-day lives.[259] Denying the reality of Dionysus is an example of failing to integrate the supernatural into the social order so that a tensive balance can be maintained between the rational and the irrational, the public and the private, the social order and one's personal order.[260] But such openness to the ambiguous Dionysus carries with it the threat that one's social code might need to be rearranged.[261]

As the plot of the *Bacchae* unfolds, Dionysus's control over events becomes more evident. The tragic performance honors Dionysus—this amoral necessity in the cosmos experienced as the life-force.[262] The audience observes the masked actors of *The Bacchae* on the stage and realizes that these actors function as symbols: by their presence and their actions they both reveal and conceal Dionysus.[263] Therefore a tragic play is a sacral performance. The dilemmas of human existence are approached differently than in the rational discussions of thinkers like Socrates, Democritus, or Protagoras.[264] The ambiguity associated with masked actors is antagonistic to the either/or approach to truth in a rational discussion.[265] However, even when Plato tries to talk about the irrational forces in the lowest level of the psyche he must resort to mythic imagery and narrative. For example, in the *Phaedrus* (229de) he draws on the mythic figures of Chimera, Pegasus, Gorgon, and Typhon to explain psychic tensions.[266] These figures function like symbols that both reveal and conceal as an interpreter engages them.

The performance of a tragic play honors Dionysus by recognizing the life-force suffusing human life and its environment. The audience of

259. Nussbaum, "Introduction," xxxv–xxxvii, xl–xli.

260. Segal, *Dionysiac Poetics and Euripides' Bacchae*, 206.

261. Ibid., 25. Nussbaum, "Introduction," xvi–xvii, emphasizes that this play produced anxiety not so much because boundaries are transgressed as because boundaries are depicted as fluid and shifting.

262. William Arrowsmith, "Introduction to the Bacchae," *The Complete Greek Tragedies*, vol. 3: *Euripides*, ed. David Grene and Richmond Lattimore, 530–41 (Chicago: University of Chicago Press, 1955), at 537; Segal, *Dionysiac Poetics and Euripides' Bacchae*, 267.

263. Ibid., 275, 281, 283; Catherine M. Bell, *Ritual: Perspectives and Dimensions* (New York: Oxford University Press, 1997), 159.

264. Segal, *Dionysiac Poetics and Euripides' Bacchae*, 270; Helene P. Foley, *Ritual Irony: Poetry and Sacrifice in Euripides* (Ithaca, NY, and London: Cornell University Press, 1985), 59.

265. Schlesier, "Mixtures of Masks," 95; Segal, *Dionysiac Poetics and Euripides' Bacchae*, 13.

266. Gould, *The Ancient Quarrel between Poetry and Philosophy*, 213–14; Luc Brisson, *Plato the Myth Maker* (Chicago: University of Chicago Press, 1998), 11.

the play is emotionally engaged and must commiserate with the tragic characters crushed by irrational forces and piece their lives back together. The tragic poet claims that Dionysus will not be co-opted; the desire of the life-force to be recognized cannot be denied by morality and rationality. Thus Euripides' Dionysus grins at Socrates.

Pentheus's Efforts to Control the Feminine

In the *parodus* (i.e., the first song of the chorus as it comes on stage), Dionysus accuses the women of Thebes of denying that Zeus was his father (26-31). They were saying that Semele, the daughter of Cadmus, the founder and first king of Thebes, had become pregnant by a human. In retribution for this denial, Dionysus says:

> So I stung them with madness out of their homes. With frenzied minds they dwell on the mountains where they must wear the attire of my revels. Every woman—the women who were offspring of Cadmus—I drove out of their homes in madness. Mingled together with the daughters of Cadmus, they sit under the green fir trees without a shelter on the rocks. (32-38)

This withdrawal of the women from their patriarchal households to form a group at a location outside the city reflects an old myth in which all the women are possessed by a god; this differs from the Demeter rituals of the annual feast of Thesmophoria (October) by not being associated with a particular sanctuary overseen by a priesthood.[267] In this festival the *thiasos*, "group," Dionysus forms among the maenads is designed to renew their close links with nature, most evident in the reproductive process.[268]

Males are aware of their biological dependence on females.[269] After Pentheus has been dismembered by his mother Agave, her father Cadmus says to her: "And me, who does not have a male child, I see that this shoot from your womb, O suffering one, has been most shamefully and basely killed" (1305-8). Men resist the close tie to nature that women

267. Burkert, *Greek Religion*, 291, cf. 242–45. Richard Seaford, "Dionysus as Destroyer of the Household: Homer, Tragedy, and the Polis," in *Masks of Dionysus*, 115–46, at 122–23, 134, 137, argues that Dionysus presents a latent threat to both the household and the polis by undermining the gender division on which the polis is based.

268. Dodds, "Introduction," xviii, argues that Dionysus's cult aimed to recover the potency of nature that had been lost through the repression generated by reason and social custom.

269. Segal, *Dionysiac Poetics and Euripides' Bacchae*, 173.

represent, for it compromises the masculine desire for autonomy, immortality, and transcendence.[270] The Athenians even went so far as to claim that their ancestor Erichthonius was a snakelike composite born from the soil of Athens, which had earlier received the semen of Hephaestus cast off by Athena.[271] The male desire to suppress the female role in reproduction is answered by the women in their desire for the ritual solidarity of maenadic gatherings.[272] These ritualized opportunities to let off steam resulted in a strengthening rather than an undermining of the patriarchal order of the household and city.[273]

The mountain revels gave a woman an exhilarating sense of freedom, as expressed by the chorus in its third stasimon:

> Then I will set my bare feet in the dances that last throughout the night. Roused to Bacchic frenzy, I will cast my neck into the watery air just as a fawn cavorting in the grassy meadow delights when it escapes the dreaded hunt by going outside the guards and over the finely-woven nets. With the shouting hunters urging on the racing dogs, she, with intense sprints and storm-like speed, bounds over the expanse of the river plain and then delights in solitary regions without humans in the shaded undergrowth of the forest. (862-78)

Like a fawn far from the hunt, the maenad can commune with nature in an uninhibited way. She has left behind the oppression and cultural baggage of the patriarchal order and is free to express herself as the natural environment invites.[274] As part of a chorus whose civilized flute music and dancing have given way to the frenzied excesses of the tympanum, the maenad is moved by a divine madness to revel in a sphere free of male oppression. Previously the chorus of the women of Thebes had condemned the heavy-handed rule of Pentheus (539-550) and cried out: "Dionysus, son of Zeus, do you see how your prophets are under

270. Ibid., 163. Cf. Catherine Clement and Julia Kristeva, *The Feminine and the Sacred* (New York: Columbia University Press, 2001), 15–16.

271. Euripides, *Ion* 267; see chap. 1 above. Nussbaum, "Introduction," xiv, notes that the snakes that entwine themselves around the maenads and lick the blood on their faces (698, 767–68) are "emblems of fertility and murderousness." Segal, *Dionysiac Poetics and Euripides' Bacchae*, 129, notes that there is an echo of Pentheus's father's name Echion (*echis*, "snake") in the ancestral name Erichthonius (540–42); see also Gould, *The Ancient Quarrel between Poetry and Philosophy*, 215.

272. Foley, *Ritual Irony*, 237.

273. Seaford, "Dionysus as Destroyer of the Household," 122–23, 134. On the destructive, death-dealing madness of the maenads see Schlesier, "Mixtures of Masks," 100–2.

274. Segal, *Dionysiac Poetics and Euripides' Bacchae*, 91–92; Nussbaum, "Introduction," xi.

constraint in their conflicts? Come down from Olympus, brandishing your golden wand, and restrain the violence of the murderer" (551-56). Dionysus responds with earthquake and lightning, which causes the maenads to bow down in fear and awe (586-603). But then Dionysus comes among them in human guise (604-7). His presence will make known that Pentheus and the patriarchal order have tried to control what cannot be controlled.[275]

Charles Segal contends that the male desire to control the feminine is manifested in the uneasiness of Western male consciousness with the dark, material, passionate part of itself.[276] Martha Nussbaum notes that because Pentheus secretly desires the condition of womanly passivity at the same time that he scorns it, he is vulnerable to being tricked by Dionysus into going to the mountain to observe the secret rites of the maenads.[277] His curiosity manifests not only a need for control but also a secret desire for pleasure. Here Pentheus is longing for a knowledge that is forbidden to him: a knowledge of the women's Bacchic mysteries (473-90).[278] His efforts to close off erotic desire manifest the paradox of pleasure: at the same time one resists it, one longs for it (487-88).[279]

Pentheus's desire to return the women of Thebes from the mountain and to enclose them manifests the delusion of phallic control.[280] Such a delusion will be exposed when the tree on top of which Pentheus is perched to view the women's secret rites comes tumbling down under their attack (1110-13). The tree, which, like the bull, is under the control of Dionysus, reveals the desires of Pentheus that he cannot admit.[281] When Pentheus makes known to Dionysus his suspicion that the women engage in lustful actions in their rituals on the mountain (486), Dionysus gives him an ambiguous response, a characteristic Dionysian slipperiness to which the seer Teiresias had earlier responded: "Dionysus does not force women to be chaste. It is necessary to see that chastity is in place in a woman's character always and in all things. Even in the Bacchic rituals, the chaste woman will not be corrupted" (314-18).

275. Foley, *Ritual Irony*, 228; Segal, *Dionysiac Poetics and Euripides' Bacchae*, 21–22.

276. Ibid., 158.

277. Nussbaum, "Introduction," xxxviii; see also Segal, *Dionysiac Poetics and Euripides' Bacchae*, 28–29, 197.

278. Ibid., 52.

279. Ibid., 9–10; Nussbaum, "Introduction," xxxix.

280. Segal, *Dionysiac Poetics and Euripides' Bacchae*, 204–5. On a spy infiltrating the Thesmophoria see Aristophanes, *Thesmophoriazusae* 585–634.

281. Segal, *Dionysiac Poetics and Euripides' Bacchae*, 206; Foley, *Ritual Irony*, 209.

The secret character of these rites (470) tends to trigger such suspicions on the part of male outsiders.[282] But Teiresias, who has been termed "a theological sophist,"[283] departs from the traditional role of the seer (*mantis*) to persuade through argumentation (i.e., eristic). Here he argues that a woman's nature rather than her circumstances determines her conduct.[284]

Pentheus's desire to be in control masks his desire for pleasure—the joy of being carried along by a life-giving experience. He seeks the forbidden knowledge of maenadic rituals so that he might participate in them at a distance and feel as if he has more control over the erotic dimension of polis life. Pentheus's desire to control the women of the polis reveals his inability to relate to them and allow them a place in the life of the polis outside the household. However, the life-force suffusing the members of the polis and its natural environment has a personal identity that will not be dismissed as mere raw material for polis construction. Dionysus has more authority over the women than Pentheus has.

Pentheus's Androgyny Revealed

Because the maenads are warriorlike in defending their mountain retreat, Dionysus advises Pentheus to go disguised as a maenad (828-42). Pentheus expresses disbelief at the suggestion that he should be found in a woman's dress (836), but this scene of the cross-dressing of Pentheus becomes a "metatragic symbol" of the identity of opposites.[285] The coexistence of masculine and feminine characteristics in Pentheus's behavior reveals the reality of Dionysus in Pentheus's life. Dionysus is one who becomes manifest in contradictions; his presence reveals the sameness within polarities.[286] In this scene Dionysus influences Pentheus's consciousness so as to remove his resistance to cross-dressing (850-53). Ritually this clothing scene—analogous in symbolic function to the arming

282. For the view that there were sexual activities in Dionysian rituals see Euripides, *Ion*, 544–55. Michael Jameson, "The Asexuality of Dionysus," in *Masks of Dionysus*, 44–64, at 60–61, notes that ancients and moderns alike insist that Dionysian revels were chaste; see also William Arrowsmith, "Introduction to the *Bacchae*," in *The Complete Greek Tragedies*, vol. 3: *Euripides*, ed. David Grene and Richmond Lattimore, 530–41 (Chicago: University of Chicago Press, 1955).

283. G. M. A. Grube, *The Drama of Euripides* (London: Methuen, 1941), 404, as cited in Paul Roth, "Tiresias as *Mantis* and Intellectual in Euripides' *Bacchae*," *TAPA* 114 (1984): 59–69, at 59–60.

284. Ibid., 60.

285. Segal, *Dionysiac Poetics and Euripides' Bacchae*, 223.

286. Ibid., 30.

scene in epic (*Il.* 16.130-54)[287]—is a form of dedication of Pentheus to Dionysus.[288] Ironically, Pentheus becomes the androgynous symbol of the maenadic women of Thebes.[289]

When Pentheus first comes face to face with the stranger Dionysus after he has been apprehended in Thebes, Pentheus says to him:

> So you, stranger, have a body attractive to women, for which very thing you are present here in Thebes. Your long hair is not for wrestling; it flows down the cheeks, full of desire. You have a white complexion by taking care to avoid the sun's rays and be under shade. You seek love through beauty. (453-59)

With a mocking tone Pentheus describes the adolescent Dionysus with his pronounced feminine characteristics. It was only in Athenian art toward the end of the fifth century BCE that Dionysus was given this appearance of a beardless youth. In earlier Archaic art down to the late fifth century he was depicted as a full-bearded, full-grown, youthful male.[290] He is typically shown in the company of females (nymphs and maenads) and males (satyrs and sileni).[291] Whenever he is shown alone with maenads his sexuality is latent.[292] The symbol of his presence is the phallus, yet there are frequent references to his feminine features. He presents the paradoxical figure of "the effeminate god of the phallus" who is detached and unconcerned with sex.[293] Michael Jameson notes that the coexistence of the elements of both genders in Dionysus may cancel one another out and result in his transcendence of sexuality.[294]

Whenever Dionysus takes possession of a person, his merger with that one effaces his or her identity and upon separation leaves that person in a different condition. Prior to the scene of Dionysus's clothing, the visible Dionysus is quoted as addressing the following prayer to himself, or to the invisible Dionysus:

287. Ibid., 169.

288. Foley, *Ritual Irony*, 209. Sue Blundell, "Clutching at Clothes," in *Women's Dress in the Ancient Greek World*, ed. Lloyd Llewellyn-Jones, 143–69 (London: Duckworth and the Classical Press of Wales, 2002), at 153, notes how the long skirt in which Pentheus is clad signifies his feminization (Eur. *Bacchae* 935–38).

289. Segal, *Dionysiac Poetics and Euripides' Bacchae*, 29.

290. Jameson, "The Asexuality of Dionysus," 48, 50.

291. Ibid., 45.

292. Ibid., 45–46.

293. Ibid., 44–45.

294. Ibid., 44.

> Dionysus, now is the time for your action. You are not far off. Let us repay him. First, put him out of his mind by infusing him with a buoyant frenzy. With his wits about him, he will never agree to put on feminine apparel. But if driven out of his mind, he will put it on. After his earlier boasts in which he was so threatening, I want him to bring on himself the derision of the Thebans when he is led through the streets appearing as a woman. (849-56)

Cross-dressing was part of two initiation rituals in which male adolescents passed from the private realm of the household to the more public and less personal collective realm governed by the warrior code of the city, where one's status was based on performance rather than family ties.[295] In the Oschophoria, two young males dressed in feminine attire led a procession from the sanctuary of Dionysus in Athens to a shrine of Athena in Phaleron. In the initiatory rite for ephebes (males between the ages of sixteen and twenty) in the festival of Anthesteria, Dionysus is portrayed as changing from male to female clothes; the male initiand is required to act out feminine values of effeminacy, emotionality, illusion, magic, and trickery.[296] The purpose of these rites within a two-year structured transitional period was to facilitate the maturation of young men from adolescents to citizens and warriors. Dionysus was typically an agent promoting this transition. But when Dionysus takes possession of Pentheus he does so in order to punish him and so he stalls him in adolescence.[297] His relations with women are voyeuristic rather than relational (813). He regresses to an ephebe spying on women in the mountain rather than progressing to be a hoplite bearing arms on behalf of the city (838).[298]

A general goal of Dionysiac rituals in the festivals of Oschophoria and Anthesteria was to provide individuals with the opportunity to participate in the madness of Dionysus so that they might use this divine energy to be renewed or to grow. In the extreme cases portrayed in the *Bacchae* this dissolving of cultural and psychological boundaries when possessed by Dionysus metamorphoses Pentheus and Agave into animals and destroys their grasp on reality and human identity.[299] A boundary-keeper is one who is able to move unharmed between different levels of cosmic reality: the divine, human, and animal. But for Pentheus and

295. Segal, *Dionysiac Poetics and Euripides' Bacchae*, 168; Foley, *Ritual Irony*, 214.

296. Segal, *Dionysiac Poetics and Euripides' Bacchae*, 170.

297. Ibid., 160, 169; Nussbaum, "Introduction," xxxiv.

298. Segal, *Dionysiac Poetics and Euripides' Bacchae*, 199; Foley, *Ritual Irony*, 214.

299. Segal, *Dionysiac Poetics and Euripides' Bacchae*, 31.

Agave their movement toward the bestial level of existence is one that overwhelms and destroys them.[300]

The initiation rites of the ephebes mark a point of transition from the predominantly feminine nurturing of the household to the predominantly masculine sphere of the military and politics. Masculine and feminine characteristics are present in the adolescent boys, but at the time of initiation the balance shifts to the masculine. In the reality of polis life, androgyny gives way to a stronger gender differentiation. Only the god Dionysus can sustain a pure androgynous existence. But because of Pentheus's hubris, Dionysus keeps him in a liminal state in which he cannot make an appropriate transition to his masculine identity.

Maenadic Madness and the Sacrifice of Pentheus

In his maenadic dress Pentheus is transformed into a passive sacrificial animal who is paraded through the streets of Thebes on his way to the mountain (915-70). He is like a scapegoat representing the maenads who have fled from the city.[301] In their raving on the mountain he will become an outsider who enters into their group and is dressed as they are. He is the "odd one" among their group whom they can all unite against to destroy so as to relieve group tensions and restore equilibrium and increase solidarity. This form of human sacrifice in which there is a confusion between the human and the animal is a perversion of normal sacrificial ritual in which the violence is carried out on the animal and is disguised.[302]

The hostility toward Pentheus is direct, vivid, and shocking. The dismemberment (*sparagmos*) of Pentheus, initiated and overseen by his mother Agave, is horrifying:

> First his mother, like a priestess, began the slaughter by coming against him. He ripped off his hair-band that the wretched Agave might recognize him and not kill him. Touching her cheek, he said: "I, mother, am your son Pentheus to whom you gave birth in the house of Echion. Have pity on me, mother! Do not kill your son for my sins." But she was foaming at the mouth and her distorted eyes were rolling. She was not aware that it was necessary to think; she was possessed by Bacchus. Pentheus did not persuade her. She took his left arm in her hands and stood upon the miserable one's ribs;

300. Nussbaum, "Introduction," xxxv–xxvii.

301. Segal, *Dionysiac Poetics and Euripides' Bacchae*, 29; Foley, *Ritual Irony*, 31.

302. Ibid., 206.

> then she tore off his shoulder. This was not by her own strength, for the god had made this easy in her hands. Meanwhile, Ino was working on the other side to tear off his flesh. Then Antinoë and the whole Bacchic throng came upon him. Together, they were all raising a loud noise: the moaning king as long as there was breath in him and those raising shouts of triumph. One carried an arm; another a foot with its boot. His ribs were stripped clean in the rending. Everyone's hands were smeared with blood as they played catch with Pentheus's flesh. (1114-36)

Under the influence of Dionysus, the mother Agave and the two aunts Ino and Antinoë are transformed into wild beasts. So while Pentheus is the passive sacrificial animal, they are the aggressive, bloodthirsty animals. Here Dionysus becomes manifest in the massive irruption of violence, which shows that this god has become a beast—a movement not depicted elsewhere in Greek tragedy with such starkness.[303] Just as the body of Pentheus—the sacral king who has the potential to bring together the spheres of the divine, the human, and the animal[304]—is dismembered and scattered, so also has the royal household of Thebes been dismembered in this process.[305] Dionysus's grin in response to this scene of horror accents the extent to which this god has become a beast.

The sequence of actions by which Pentheus is brought to the mountain and killed parallels in a number of respects, as Helene Foley explains, the ritual sequence in a Greek festival of *pompē*, *agōn*, and *kōmos*.[306] The *pompē* ("procession") occurs when Dionysus has Pentheus dressed as a maenad and paraded through the streets. A typical Dionysian *pompē* would invite the crowd to speak ribald jests and heap abuse on the persons on parade.[307] The *agōn* is a contest or struggle that could take various forms: e.g., a debate, trial, or athletic contest.[308] Pentheus will resemble a returning failed champion; Dionysus predicts that he will be

303. Segal, *Dionysiac Poetics and Euripides' Bacchae*, 31–32, 304. On the character of Dionysus in rituals according to sources other than myths and tragedies see Dirk Obbink, "Dionysus Poured Out: Ancient and Modern Theories of Sacrifice and Cultural Formation," in *Masks of Dionysus*, 65–86, at 80, 86; Noel Robertson, "Orphic Mysteries and Dionysiac Ritual," in *Greek Mysteries: The Archaeology and Ritual of Ancient Greek Secret Cults*, ed. Michael B. Cosmopoulos, 218–40 (London and New York: Routledge, 2003), at 223–24.

304. Segal, *Dionysiac Poetics and Euripides' Bacchae*, 31

305. Foley, *Ritual Irony*, 207; Seaford, "Dionysus as Destroyer of the Household," 124.

306. Foley, *Ritual Irony*, 208.

307. Ibid., 211–12.

308. Burkert, *Greek Religion*, 105–6.

carried home like an infant in his mother's arms (967-68).[309] The *kōmos*, which is a celebration or revelry in honor of gods or heroes, takes the form of "a victory song for the god and a revel/potential feast for Agave and the chorus."[310]

The sacrificial character of Pentheus's death is also reflected, as Foley explains, in the following five parallels between the steps by which Pentheus was led to his death and the process by which an animal was prepared for slaughter: (1) Just as the sacrificial animal was decorated with gilded horns, so is Pentheus dressed in maenadic attire. (2) Just as the animal was pelted with grain, so is Pentheus showered with branches. (3) Just as there was a silent moment before the animal was slaughtered, so there is a hush in the forest after Dionysus summons the maenads to bring vengeance on Pentheus for his earlier blasphemy (1079-85). (4) Just as there was an inducement for the animal to make a religious error and nod in "consent" to its own punishment, so also is Pentheus lured to the mountain to spy out the secret maenadic rites, for which he acknowledges his misdeed (1120). (5) Just as there was the *ologē* ("shrill cry") by the women at the moment of the animal's slaughter, so also do the maenads shriek as they dismember Pentheus (1132).[311] Foley notes, however, the following two ways in which the sacrifice of Pentheus departs from the usual procedure in order to accent the horror of this human sacrifice: (1) the unwilling victim is torn apart by the maenads instead of being methodically divided by a knife; (2) the parts of Pentheus's body are scattered and are of no benefit to the community, whereas an animal's carcass is a source of food for the community. Even though the parts of his body are later gathered and buried by members of his family, there is no positive energy for the royal family or the city through his sacrificial death.[312] This human sacrifice is a perverted one that leaves the family and city disintegrated.[313]

When Pentheus repents before his raving mother that he has done wrong he is acknowledging a more fundamental transgression than his spying on the secret maenadic rites: he is referring to his blasphemy of Dionysus. His efforts to control the women of Thebes and to banish Dionysus from Thebes indicate his unwillingness to come to terms with the fundamental tie of humans to nature and the uncontrollable dimension

309. See Pindar's description of the returning defeated athletes in *Pythian* 8.83–87; Foley, *Ritual Irony*, 212.

310. Ibid.

311. Ibid., 210.

312. Ibid., 211.

313. Seaford, "Dionysus as Destroyer of the Household," 115–46, at 123.

of the life-force. As the play progresses, Dionysus emerges from the shadows and assumes greater control of events. He becomes a larger reality within which individual preoccupations are subsumed and diminished in urgency. From the perspective of Dionysus the death and dismemberment of Pentheus is like a "divine joke" found at the end of Old Comedy.[314] This detachment of Dionysus from the tragedy of Pentheus tells us that this god who has been revealed is real, but he is an amoral, elemental force—the necessity of nature.

The audience that watches this play must put the pieces back together. Agave and Cadmus commiserate with one another and so invite the audience to do likewise.[315] Plato feared that this propagation of a view of a god as amoral or immoral would let the audience off the hook from finding the real causes of the demise of the royal family of Thebes.[316] Rather than constructing spectacles that placed the blame for humanity's troubles on the gods, Plato thought that humans should take responsibility and try to live more insightful and disciplined lives. Plato's intellectual religion recognizes that *miasmata*, "defilements," can take control of individuals or communities.[317] But humans can see the part these *miasmata* have played and recognize that they can take steps to improve the situation. Plato was quite concerned about *miasmata* because of his dedication to the view of the purity of the transcendent realm.[318] He encouraged an effort to ascend out of the cave of this world of shadows and into the bright light where the true reality is revealed. The manifestations of the essences or forms of this upper world were captured through intuitive flashes—there was an enthusiastic or divinely induced component to this intellectual ascent.[319] Plato defined Dionysus as the god who assisted in this ascent: a god thoroughly consistent with the ethical order of the cosmos (*Phaedrus* 247a7).[320]

314. Foley, *Ritual Irony*, 219.

315. Nussbaum, "Introduction," xl, claims that the mutual compassion of Agave and Pentheus is what distinguishes them from the divine and the bestial.

316. Nussbaum, ibid., xvii–xviii, notes that the deepest belief of the citizens was that the gods were without weaknesses and had no need of moral virtues since they had no limitations.

317. Michel Despland, *The Education of Desire: Plato and the Philosophy of Religion* (Toronto: University of Toronto Press, 1985), 111–18; Paul Ricoeur, *The Symbolism of Evil* (Boston: Beacon, 1969), 33–46.

318. *Republic* IX.589 e4; Gould, *The Ancient Quarrel between Poetry and Philosophy*, 262.

319. Ibid., 237–38.

320. Gould, ibid., 229, notes the contradiction between Euripides' *Bacchae* 302–5 and Plato's contention that the gods always act ethically.

The sacrifice of Pentheus creates communal solidarity only in an audience that commiserates with Agave and Cadmus and tries to make sense of human life in the aftermath of tragedy. This kind of human sympathy is vital to navigating the tragedies of real life. However, Plato opposes this avenue for overcoming conflicts and releasing tension within the polis since this kind of solidarity is based on uniting the people against the gods and the unjust order of the world. Since Plato defines the real as the rational, he may well be one whom Euripides would see as a candidate to be blindsided by the irruption of the irrational in his experience. Euripides' plays alert us to human vulnerability and summon us to see life as a larger reality in which we are allowed to participate.

Summary

Pentheus, the royal boundary-keeper of the city of Thebes, feels threatened by the arrival of the Stranger from Asia Minor. When Pentheus meets this visitor whom he has tried to imprison he recognizes the pronounced feminine features of this young man. The god Dionysus has assumed the human form of an androgynous adolescent in order to confront Pentheus and the people of Thebes with his reality as the life-force that suffuses them and is beyond their control. Dionysus also makes his presence known in the forms of a thunderbolt and an earthquake, but his primary manifestation is in human form. The grin of Dionysus in the midst of human suffering indicates a detachment from the human condition in which he is the amoral necessity of the life-force and not a symbol of an ethical world order.

The key question for Pentheus, the symbol of the community of Thebes, is how he understands the threat of this Stranger and how he will respond to it. Pentheus's automatic response to this threat, which he does not fully understand, is to contain it. He tries to imprison Dionysus but discovers that he is fighting against himself. The more intensely he fights, the more exhausted he gets. The life-force he is trying to bring under control sits at the side and grins at the blindness of Pentheus's futile efforts to control him. Pentheus's strategy of control is not able to give the necessary space for the life-force to rule in Thebes and its people. He has made the fatal error of denying the reality of Dionysus, who is unforgiving and intends to prove the mistaken attitude of Pentheus by having him pay with his life.

Dionysus is a deity who becomes manifest in the dynamics of the symbol. The symbol reveals and conceals a reality. This reality cannot be controlled, but must be engaged. The polarities of life from a Dionysian perspective—the Olympian versus the chthonic god, the bestial versus the divine, civic versus rural religion, masculine versus feminine, barbarian versus Theban—reveal that Dionysus is most vividly present as the tensive reality that is suspended between two poles. From a human perspective this tension can be exhilarating, but also exhausting. To dwell perpetually at the center of paradox or on the horns of a dilemma is an existence manageable only by the god Dionysus; humans can live with contradiction only for limited times. The notion of the coincidence of opposites can bring coherence intellectually to the nonlinear character of life, but it is a much different exercise to deal with contradiction in the concrete rather than in the abstract. When the contradictions of a mythic narrative are brought into ritual, the goal is reconciliation of the competing polarities. When such contradictions are brought into tragedy, the tension between these polarities is exaggerated to the breaking point.[321] The dynamics of tragedy demand that the audience pick up the pieces and try to put the community back together again. When performed, the tragic play itself is a ritual within the sanctuary (i.e., the theater) of Dionysus. The sacral context of the tragic play addresses the dilemmas of life in a context different from that of the rational examinations of a philosopher or a rhetorician. Context is decisive for seeing and understanding the real dilemmas of life. The rigid Pentheus, focused on controlling life, does not recognize the character of the life-force within him until his life-force is about to be snuffed out at the hands of his mother, whose mind has been taken over by this life-force (Dionysus). In this extreme context of losing his life he recognizes Dionysus.

Pentheus's strategy of control is exposed in its distorting limitedness in his way of dealing with the feminine aspect of experience. When the maenads, possessed by Dionysus, flee to the mountains, he is ready to bring them back by military force. The women experience this time apart from household and city as exhilarating and rejuvenating. Their close ties with nature through the reproductive process threaten the male boundary-keeper intent on autonomy, immortality, and transcendence. Their way of life is more attuned to the life-force that suffuses and encompasses the individual and the community.

Pentheus's own desire to commune with nature breaks through when Dionysus offers him the option of going to the mountain to view the rites of the maenads. This temptation to spy out the secret maenadic rites may point to his continuing desire to gain information so that he

321. Seaford, "Dionysus as Destroyer of the Household," 137.

might control the feminine aspect of experience, but it also reveals—although Pentheus would probably not admit this—his desire to participate in this feminine reality. The feminine dimension of Pentheus's person points to the essential sameness of human existence as lived by males and females. The sameness within the difference of the polarities indicates that the male will have feminine characteristics and the female will have masculine characteristics. This androgynous character of Pentheus mirrors the androgynous character of Dionysus. When Dionysus takes control of Pentheus's mind and leads him to agree to cross-dress and so to commit to Dionysus, he in effect makes Pentheus publicly renounce his previous blasphemy that the androgynous character of the life-force was an illusion.

When Dionysus seizes an individual, the resulting madness can lead to maturation or disintegration. In more typical transition points in life this madness is positive energy. For example, it allows an adolescent male to cut ties with the private realm of the household and take up his place among the competing members of the public realm. In Pentheus's case Dionysus decrees punishment for him and thereby freezes him in his adolescent phase so that he is unable to move beyond a voyeuristic relation to women and thus to commit to a responsible, productive relationship with women and others. When Pentheus is exposed for his spying on the secret rites of the maenads he becomes the "other" among them who is also dressed like them. He is sufficiently marginal to serve as the scapegoat who, when sacrificed, will call forth jubilation and solidarity among the maenads. Human sacrifice is a perverted sacrificial ritual in which the boundaries between the human and the bestial have collapsed. The jubilation of the maenads is madness. Agave, when she comes to her senses, will painfully realize the insanity of her Dionysian-induced crime.

The rigid, controlling Pentheus is put on the rack by the intervention of Dionysus. His fate is to be one ripped apart by his mother and members of his own family. The feminine force he regards as foreign is intimately intertwined with his own existence. To deny or repress this androgynous life-force is self-defeating and leads to disintegration—so graphically communicated by the dismemberment of Pentheus's body.

Plato has a different picture of Dionysus as the life-force that fuels the transitions toward the contemplation of the pure forms. The inspiration that moves the lover of truth to catch glimpses of the pure forms is a manifestation of Dionysus. Plato categorically denies that Dionysus is a bestial deity. An amoral or immoral god is a contradiction in terms that appeals to the lower part of the human psyche, a part of humans that desires to see themselves as victims of the human condition. So the philosophic wisdom of Plato has a quarrel with the tragic wisdom of Euripides. Plato indicates that this quarrel is an ancient one arising from the depths of the psyche. Plato wants to banish the tragic poets from his ideal city. Does Plato's way lead to happiness? Or is Plato, like Pentheus, caught up in a self-defeating quest?

Synthesis: The Role of Composite Guardian Figures in the Integration of the Divine, the Human, and the Animal

The boundary-keeping function incumbent on every human being is exemplified in a paradigmatic way by the sacral king. Such a king shows how vital it is to be attentive to the context in which one lives. The prince of Tyre in Ezekiel 28 is imagined as a primal human figure who has been blessed with beauty and wisdom on God's mountain so that he might mediate these gifts to the people of Tyre. The "perfect" Mesopotamian king in the Ur III period was urged by his court poets to see himself as a divine being who channeled the vitality of the heavenly sphere into the human realm. Pentheus in Euripides' *Bacchae* holds the symbolic position of king in Thebes where he is to strive to mediate between the divine, human, and animal spheres in the collective life of the city. The self-understanding of each king is vital to the strategy he will use in trying to keep these three cosmic spheres in right relationship to each other. These spheres are distinct but must interact appropriately if the cosmos is to avoid falling into chaos. The self-understanding and strategy of a king is either duplicated or complemented by other members of the kingdom. Thus his approach to maintaining cosmic boundaries can inform the boundary-keeping efforts of people throughout the kingdom.

The attitude of the king toward the divine is crucial to the way he exercises power. The king of Tyre becomes arrogant and regards himself as an autonomous sovereign ruler who can rule absolutely. The first human couple wonders about increasing their status to that of gods, even though they have been warned not to do so. The king of Assyria builds lavish universal gardens to symbolize his power and worldwide rule. Pentheus denies the reality of the god Dionysus and goes about trying to suppress any inroads this deity might make into the kingdom of Thebes. In each of these cases the human places more trust in what can be seen and touched than in the invisible and partially known. The transgression arises from paying insufficient attention to this other reality and entertaining doubts about its seriousness.

The way the divine is imagined is critical to the way one approaches it. In a monotheistic model the human's focus is to be on loyalty and obedience to the one sovereign. In a polytheistic model the human's attention is to be as inclusive of the divine powers as possible. The monocentric monotheistic model promises that wholeness and well-being will arise from bringing the heart into right relationship with the sovereign. The polycentric polytheistic model promises equilibrium and well-being in balancing the competing demands of opposites. Because a polytheistic system is often monarchically organized, it shares many features of a monotheistic model. Likewise, a monotheistic model sees the polarities and competing interests of human experience operating at lower levels of the cosmic hierarchy and so incorporates some features of the polytheistic model. But the impact on one's life of a monotheistic model over against a polytheistic one is significant; each employs different strategies for maintaining boundaries between the animal, human, and divine parts of existence. The context within which one goes about drawing boundaries is fundamental to the task of understanding the symbolic character of humans' relationships with the divine and the animal.

The primal human in Eden is asexual and pre-gendered. Both sex and gender appear in the story with the creation of the woman. However, in a sequential reading of Genesis 1–2 one might argue that the two sexes and genders presented in Gen 1:26-28 exist in archetypal form in the original earth creature in Gen 2:7 from whom the LORD God takes the rib in order to create the woman. Insofar as the primal human in Ezek 28:11-19 was a cherub, this composite creature was imagined to be perfect as long as it remained in right relationship with YHWH. Perhaps the perfection of this cherub entailed that it possess the full range of human characteristics—feminine as well as masculine. In Mesopotamia the divinized Ur III king was androgynous and was regarded as a primal human representing humanity. In Euripides' *Bacchae*, Pentheus mirrors Dionysus as an androgyne. But even though he is a sacral king, Pentheus is not a primal human. His characterization as an androgyne is one that he resists and tries to suppress throughout the play. Pentheus's repression of the feminine in his own psyche is one of the explanations offered for his efforts to control the women of Thebes and to keep the influence of Dionysus outside the bounds of his kingdom. To the extent that the Ur III king embraces the model of the androgynous perfect king he forms a counterexample to Pentheus in his strategy for dealing with the question of androgyny. In the Israelite tradition the original earth creature appears to have been both asexual and ungendered; however, one might argue that in an inchoate, potential form both feminine and masculine characteristics were present in the original earth creature and became explicit with the creation of the first couple in Gen 2:7, 21-24. Thereafter the relation between male and female, feminine and masculine is shaped according to the heterosexual model of Genesis 1–2 where the goal of male and female relationship is to reestablish a unity (Gen 1:26-28; 2:24) by way of heterosexual union and procreation. In Genesis 2, if the original earth creature is imagined as an androgyne, this duality of sex and gender within one creature gives way to heterosexual companionship. At first glance it would seem that Pentheus would be more at home in the heterosexual model offered by Genesis 2. However, the first couple is urged to form a complementary union in which male and female characteristics come together as a unity. In this restored unity neither the male nor the female can be regarded as a foreign "other" by the opposite sex; such a difference-in-unity may be seen as having an androgynous character.

A composite being is also concerned about how the bestial level of existence relates to the human and the divine. As identified with the king of Tyre, the cherub figure in Ezekiel 28 has allowed its raw natural power as a "primitive bison" to unite with its human cleverness to try to usurp divine authority. Likewise, in Mesopotamia the *kusarriku* and the *mušhuššu* have a rebellious potential through the combination of human and animal characteristics. As Pentheus fights against Dionysus, who appears as a bull, the bestial dimensions of his own being come to the fore. Dionysus's way of punishing Pentheus and ultimately having him dismembered emphasizes how much this god has become like a beast. When the distinctions between animal, human, and divine disappear, the cosmic order gives way to chaos.

The Mesopotamian Ishtar and the Greek Dionysus are androgynous deities. The female Ishtar and the male Dionysus exhibit strong characteristics of the opposite sex, indicating their propensity to incorporate opposites within themselves. Each deity manifests the characteristics of the opposite sex and gender within itself rather than silencing them. Rather than co-opting the other sex and gender, this holding together of opposites in oneself allows the other to maintain its voice. The resulting unity has a tensive, dynamic character. A deity can do this as an individual, but it is more typical for humans to need the support of other humans within a community to maintain this coincidence of opposites of gender and sex.

The monotheistic model of the Israelite tradition recognizes the reciprocal relationship between male and female as necessary for wholeness in human relationships and for the fertility of humanity. This productive unity symbolizes the dynamic character of the God of Israel, but it does not provide a picture of the God of Israel. The notion of humans as the "image of God" means a sacramental, symbolic figuring of the Godhead rather than a literal rendering. The God of Israel transcends sexuality and gender. However, if androgyny is defined as an asexual, genderless state it could be used in this non-bodily sense to describe the God of Israel.

Cultic or sacral officials dedicated to a god aim to symbolize the deity to whom they are dedicated. In Ezekiel 28 the perfect king was to symbolize God, who had bestowed wisdom and beauty on him. In Mesopotamia the male *kurgarrû* and *assinnu* were metamorphosed by Ishtar into females. Whether or not they were literally castrated is not known, but they functioned as if they were. This transgression of the basic cosmic categories of male/female and feminine/masculine symbolizes the character of Ishtar as a deity who holds opposites in tension within her. One way in which these cultic officials symbolized their coincidence of opposites was by cross-dressing. This same gesture of gender inversion is foisted upon Pentheus by Dionysus. Although Pentheus's mind has been taken over by Dionysus, this act of cross-dressing becomes a symbol of his alignment with Dionysus. Within the Israelite tradition such cross-dressing—that is, a confusion of the fundamental categories of male and female—was forbidden. The *kurgarrû* and *assinnu* were paradoxically both respected and marginalized in Mesopotamia. They were regarded as having the capacity to drive out evil but were also feared for their capacity to inflict it through curses. Pentheus, in his own mind, was completely dumbfounded by Dionysus's suggestion that he dress like a maenad. Such a symbolic act went contrary to his understanding of how reality was organized.

The paradox of the simultaneous presence of characteristics of masculine/feminine and male/female in one being—whether divine, human, or animal—constitutes a counterpoint to the human propensity to try to control the boundaries between heaven, earth, and the netherworld. The effective boundary-keeper is able to move in the spheres on each side of the boundary; composite beings symbolize this capacity to participate in two spheres of reality without being identified with either sphere—that is, they are intermediaries. The success of human efforts to hold opposites in tension and to know when to move beyond a particular tension and when to remain faithful to the legitimate yet irreconcilable differences of each side depends on keeping this process in a cosmic context in which the divine is a constant guide. Human intermediaries are to be respected and feared.

Chapter Six

Celibacy as a Proleptic Death and a Quest for Transcendence

Ascetical practices have as their initial goal the shaping of an individual's behavior into a form that is compatible with a larger social body. Beyond conformity, however, such practices usually aim to effect a deeper, more enduring transformation of a person's character that will contribute to the harmony required for a healthy social body. Because of its emphasis on procreation and the family, the ancient Israelite tradition speaks of the practice of refraining from marriage only by way of exception. Jeremiah is commanded by YHWH not to marry or have a family because judgment is coming against the land and death will be widespread (Jer 16:1-4). End-time thinking or the imminence of death leads to a reevaluation of the practice of marriage and family life in this particular instance. Celibacy, as a proleptic form of death, deprives an individual of typical human relationships of spouse and parenthood; however, this celibate way of living must find its significance within the larger social body and its traditions if this form of self-sacrifice is to make a positive contribution to the society and culture. The potential of celibacy to lead to a higher level of integration in the social body and in the individuals comprising it is illustrated by the way celibates use language to form bonds with God or the gods, with other humans—both living and dead—and with a culture. This linguistic capacity—a trait distinguishing humans from other animals—can shape the individual and the community into new forms that can be either a blessing or a curse for those involved.

Lifelong celibacy is an extreme measure that was enjoined only as an exception in ancient Israel, but less stringent variants of this discipline can be seen in the injunctions to refrain from sexual activity (Lev 18:6-23;

Prov 5:1-14; 7:24-27) and to pursue wisdom (Prov 3:13-18; 7:1-5; 8:1-36). The enlightenment and nourishment received from wisdom (Prov 8:10-21; Ps 19:8-12), a reality integral to the bonds of community, open the way for the kinds of sacrifices necessary to sustain the community in its cosmic context. The pursuit of wisdom in the cultures of Israel, Mesopotamia, and Greece will be examined in this chapter as a rationale for sexual restraint, even to the point of celibacy, for it opened the way to a new form of immortality: a transcendence of death through the word. The following three topics will be addressed in the examination of the texts from each tradition: (1) A crisis that brings one face to face with death impels an individual to find inner resources to move through death. (2) The engagement with the wisdom of the community's tradition generates a breadth of vision that will enable humans to find their place within the hierarchy of the cosmic community. (3) The technology of writing provides a new standing place for faithfully staying with the call to come into harmonious relationship with the divine, the human, and the animal.

Israel: The Promise of Enduring Life Through God's Word

The word of God that Jeremiah proclaimed to the Judahites in the late seventh century communicated a message of judgment and hope. He proclaimed this word as an embodied messenger, so that his actions and way of life were part of his message. The tradition recorded in the book of Jeremiah presents an account of Jeremiah's wrestling with God over the credibility of his mission. This prophetic *persona* goes into the depths as he is called to relinquish his reliance on human support and focus his life on trust in YHWH's presence with him. This rising to new life through YHWH's writing his torah on Jeremiah's heart brings coherence to the trauma Jeremiah was asked to undergo. From the perspective of the later tradition YHWH's command that Jeremiah refrain from marrying and having children was a call not to end his life but to transform it—not only for his own sake but also for the Judahite community. This invitation to transformation through attention to God's word—particularly through the means afforded by the celibate way of life—will be addressed according to the following three topics: (1) Jeremiah's experience of dying and rising in his wrestling with YHWH's commission foreshadows the exile and restoration of the Judahite community and so fosters an internalization of their relationship with YHWH (see Jeremiah 15–17). (2) The process of internalizing God's word from a written text demands that the immediacy of person-to-person communication be re-created through prayer, meditation, and communal worship and instruction (see Jeremiah 8; Psalms 19, 119). (3) Through the composition of the fixed text of YHWH's torah, Levitical scribes fostered the people's relationship to YHWH by teaching and persuading.

The Symbolic Character of Jeremiah's Celibacy

In the narrative of the book of Jeremiah the embattled Jeremiah is commanded to live a celibate way of life just after he has prayed his second "confession"—that is, his individual complaint—over the people's aggressive rejection of him (Jer 15:10-21).[1] YHWH says to him:

> You shall not marry a woman, and you shall not have sons or daughters in this place. Indeed, thus says the Lord concerning the sons and daughters to be born in this place and the mothers who give them birth and the fathers who beget them in this land: Of deadly disease they shall die; they shall not be mourned nor buried; they shall be like dung on the ground; by sword and famine they shall come to an end; their corpses shall be food for the birds of the sky and the animals of the land. (Jer 16:1-4)

Jeremiah has already complained that YHWH has caused him to be shunned by others in the community: "I did not sit with those who were entertaining one another; on account of your intervention, I sat alone, for you had filled me with a curse" (15:17). Now he was not to try to overcome this isolation through the companionship of a wife and children. This charge that YHWH has brought trouble upon a sufferer is expressed in a similar way in Ps 39:10—"I was speechless and did not open my mouth because you had done this"—and in Ps 88:19—"Companion and neighbor you have taken away from me; my only friend is darkness." Jeremiah's isolation intensifies in his next two "confessions" (Jer 17:14-18; 18:18-23) as he lashes out at those who persecute him. In his fifth and final "confession" (20:7-18) he even accuses YHWH of having deceived him and given him a word that has only been a source of derision and

1. William L. Holladay, *Jeremiah 1: A Commentary on the Book of the Prophet Jeremiah Chapters 1–25*, Hermeneia, ed. Paul D. Hanson (Philadelphia: Fortress Press, 1986), 467. Holladay (p. 358) provides the following commonly accepted list of Jeremiah's confessions: (1) 11:18–12:6; (2) 15:10-12, 15-21; (3) 17:9-10, 14-18; (4) 18:18-23; (5) 20:7-12, 14-18. In the second volume of his commentary, *Jeremiah 2: A Commentary on the Book of the Prophet Jeremiah Chapters 26–52*, Hermeneia, ed. Paul D. Hanson (Philadelphia: Fortress Press, 1989), 24, Holladay contends that the later additions to the book of Jeremiah were made in the fifth century BCE.

reproach. The confusion and anger Jeremiah expresses in his "confessions" matches that of others in the Israelite tradition who pray individual laments or complaints in response to misfortune.[2] The sharp edge of these complaints is the charge that YHWH himself, and not an anonymous form of bad luck, has brought about the misfortune.[3] In the context of this increasing tension YHWH commands Jeremiah to live as a celibate. This isolated way of life will serve as a message of judgment that the life of the Judahite community is about to come to an end.[4]

Critics debate whether Jeremiah's celibacy constitutes a symbolic action—that Jeremiah's isolation and celibacy are not simply part of his particular experience but are shared by the Judahite community.[5] William McKane denies that Jeremiah undertook celibacy as a symbolic action and claims that his refraining from family life simply indicates a "communal concern." He does not question the narrative's claim that Jeremiah was without a wife and children, but he doubts that Jeremiah adopted this unusual way of life in order to drive home his message of doom to the people of Judah.[6] In Jer 16:1-4 the prophet makes no protest against this command, whose effect would be to heighten his sense of

2. Holladay, *Jeremiah 1*, 358. On the prophet as a poet see Christoph Bultmann, "A Prophet in Desperation? The Confessions of Jeremiah," in *The Elusive Prophet*, OTSt 45, ed. J. C. de Moor, 83–93 (Leiden: Brill, 2001), at 90–93.

3. A. R. Diamond, *Confessions of Jeremiah in Context: Scenes of Prophetic Drama, JSOTSup* 45 (Sheffield: JSOT Press, 1987), 183, emphasizes that the theodicy theme should be the final arbiter in interpreting the "confessions" since the context emphasizes the justice of YHWH's judgment of faithless Judah more than the paradigmatic character of Jeremiah's suffering.

4. Holladay, *Jeremiah 1*, 469.

5. Kathleen M. O'Connor, "The Book of Jeremiah: Reconstructing Community after Disaster," in *Character Ethics and the Old Testament: Moral Dimensions of Scripture*, ed. M. Daniel Carroll R. and Jacqueline E. Lapsley, 81–92 (Louisville: Westminster John Knox, 2007), at 86; Corrine Patton, "Layers of Meaning: Priesthood in Jeremiah MT," in *The Priests in the Prophets, JSOTSup* 408, ed. Lester Grabbe and Alice Ogden Bellis, 149–76 (London and New York: T & T Clark, 2004), at 156. Robert P. Carroll, *Jeremiah: A Commentary*, OTL (Philadelphia: Westminster, 1986), 109, 117–18, 120, 123, 130, contends that the "confessions" are multivalent compositions of the exilic community reacting to the exile, which depict the prophet as a representative figure who is a victim and object of persecution.

6. William McKane, *Jeremiah: Introduction and Commentary on Jeremiah I–XXV*, ICC (Edinburgh: T & T Clark, 1986), 367, dates Jer 16:1-9 to the exilic age, which Jack Lundbom, *Jeremiah 1–20*, AB 21A (New York: Doubleday, 1999), 761, regards as too late and contends that it should be dated to the early years of Jehoiakim or earlier. Holladay, *Jeremiah 1*, 468, dates it to 601 BCE. Robert P. Carroll, *Jeremiah*, 340–41, also denies that Jeremiah's celibacy has a symbolic character on the grounds that the people do not react to his celibate example in the way that a symbolic action typically evokes (cf. Ezek 24:15-24). However, the hostility

isolation. McKane suggests that Jeremiah found celibacy to be a sensible way of life for him to follow, given the overwhelming demands of his prophetic vocation and the unsettled sociopolitical circumstances of his time.[7] Jack Lundbom counters that Jer 16:1-9 is not to be reduced to an exilic text that merely reflects back on a reconstructed prophetic experience that has no basis in history.[8] With a similar belief that contact with Jeremiah's authentic prophetic experience can be reached, R. E. Clements claims that the book of Jeremiah communicates real life experiences of the prophet essential to his message, even if it is not possible to reconstruct a biography of Jeremiah from the sources.[9] The editorial arrangement of Jeremiah's poetry and life story presents the experience of a flesh and blood figure with whom the reader is encouraged to identify.[10] The narrative as it currently stands, a product of theological reflection on Jeremiah and his message, incorporates this command to celibacy within the sequence of his five confessions, in which Jeremiah's anguished experience serves as a paradigm for the trauma the Judahites would undergo with the destruction of Jerusalem.[11] In the final form of the book of Jeremiah, YHWH reveals to the Judahites that not only will their land and possessions be taken from them but also their families, so that they will stand like Jeremiah before YHWH, stripped of all the normal supports of daily life. Jeremiah's celibate way of life symbolizes the challenges that would face the Judahites after the destruction of Jerusalem in 586 BCE.[12]

of the people toward Jeremiah as a prophet of doom would be a response to his celibate commitment, one that he lived out rather than preached as a covenantal practice.

7. McKane, *Jeremiah I–XXV*, 33–64, 367.

8. See n. 6 above for Lundbom's dating of Jeremiah.

9. Ronald E. Clements, "Jeremiah's Message of Hope: Public Faith and Private Anguish," in *Reading the Book of Jeremiah: A Search for Coherence* (Winona Lake, IN: Eisenbrauns, 2004), 135–47, at 139.

10. Louis Stulman, *Jeremiah* (Nashville: Abingdon, 2005), 16–17; Clements, "Jeremiah's Message of Hope," 142–43; cf. Kathleen M. O'Connor, *The Confessions of Jeremiah: Their Interpretation and Their Role in Chapters 1–25*, SBLDS 94 (Atlanta: Scholars Press, 1987), 148, 154.

11. Holladay, *Jeremiah 1*, 467–68, argues that this call to celibacy must have been integrated into his "confessions" at an early point, just after the rewriting of the second scroll (Jer 36:27-32), which declared the destruction of Jerusalem to be inevitable, ca. 601 BCE. Carroll, *Jeremiah*, 341–42, sees the editorial picture of Jeremiah as that of a celibate prophet, which he contends, in turn, prevents the recovery of the historical Jeremiah as celibate.

12. Clements, "Jeremiah's Message of Hope," 141; J. G. McConville, *Judgment and Promise: An Interpretation of the Book of Jeremiah* (Winona Lake, IN: Eisenbrauns, 1993), 72, 75–76; Leslie C. Allen, *Jeremiah*, OTL (Louisville: Westminster John Knox, 2008), 189–90.

The celibate way of life for Jeremiah was to last for the duration of his life but nevertheless was to be short-term, for the end of the Judahite way of life as they knew it was believed to be near. He was not advised to take up the celibate way of life as a survival strategy—the counsel to travel lightly so as to shield oneself from deprivation. Rather, he was commanded to withdraw from normal social interaction because those forms of interaction were about to come to an end for the Judahites.[13] The agents of this coming wholesale destruction were to be pestilence, sword, and famine. The extent of the predicted destruction would be so severe that the Judahites would not even be able to bury their dead (Jer 16:4). The normal state of affairs for the members of a family would have been burial with one's ancestors: one's remains would have been placed with those of the preceding generations (Gen 25:7-11; 1 Kgs 13:22; 2 Kgs 14:16, 22). However, the coming massive destruction Jeremiah announced would have made it impossible for the family members to provide an honorable burial for one another. In the societies of the ancient Near East, and presumably within the Israelite family, an unburied corpse meant that the spirit of the person was roaming the wasteland between earth and the netherworld in search of rest. This restless spirit was believed to be deprived even of the occasional consolation that would have come by way of memorial offerings from the living members of the family.[14]

The prohibition in Jer 16:5-9 calling for avoidance of mourning rituals emphasizes in the here and now for Jeremiah how the Judahite family would be deprived of the consolation of family relationships. Cross-culturally, mourning rituals provide the means by which grieving family members come to terms with the transition of a loved one into the afterlife.[15] The family members fast, weep, wear torn or soiled clothing, and put dust on their heads to symbolize their participation in the loved one's death.[16] The practices of shaving one's head and gashing oneself, prohibited by Deut 14:1, are listed in Jer 16:6 as if they had been typical

13. Carroll, *Jeremiah*, 339. Herbert Huffmon, "Gender Subversion in the Book of Jeremiah," in *Sex and Gender in the Ancient Near East: Proceedings of the 47th Rencontre Assyriologique Internationale, Helsinki July 2–6, 2001*, CRRAI 47, ed. Simo Parpola and Robert M. Whiting, 245–53 (Helsinki: Neo-Assyrian Text Project, 2002), at 247–48, notes how the prediction of a short-term future contrasts with that in Jer 29:4-7 and 42:10.

14. Dale Launderville, *Spirit and Reason: The Embodied Character of Ezekiel's Symbolic Thinking* (Waco, TX: Baylor University Press, 2007), 309–20.

15. Ibid., 289–345.

16. Saul M. Olyan, *Biblical Mourning: Ritual and Social Dimensions* (New York: Oxford University Press, 2004), 40–41.

mourning practices among the Judahites.[17] At the conclusion of the seven-day period of mourning the family members would share in a funeral meal as a sign of their solidarity and their readiness to return to normal life.[18] YHWH orders Jeremiah to stay away from these rituals because, he says, "I have taken away my peace (*šālôm*) from this people . . . my covenantal love (*ḥesed*) and compassion (*rĕḥāmîm*)" (Jer 16:5). This *šālôm* is the sense of wholeness or integration that pervades the life of the community and the individuals within it when the people are in right relationship with YHWH (cf. Jer 9:24).[19] It is not a peace humans can claim for themselves, but rather a gift that accompanies their attentiveness to YHWH.[20] Therefore when the false prophets oppose Jeremiah's message of doom and alternatively proclaim peace (14:13), YHWH declares that they are liars and have not been sent by him (14:14). As a punishment they will be consumed by sword and famine with no one to bury them (14:15-16).

In Jer 14:1–15:4 the Judahites recognize that something is amiss in their relationship with YHWH when a drought (perhaps in 601 BCE) devastates their land.[21] They engage in fasting (14:12; 36:9) and a public ritual in which they confess their wrongdoing (14:7). Their prayer retains, however, complaints typical of communal laments: "O hope of Israel, its savior in time of distress, why should you be like a resident alien in the land, like a wanderer who pitches a tent for the night? Why should you be like a bewildered man, like a warrior who is unable to save?" (14:8-9). Their identification of YHWH's absence as arising from his

17. Ibid., 114–23. Necromancy (Deut 18:11) and tithes offered to the dead were forbidden (Deut 26:14).

18. Ibid., 47–48. Marvin Pope, *Song of Songs*, AB 7C (New York: Doubleday, 1977), 216–21, describes the *marzēaḥ*-house as a place of bacchanalian celebration and funeral feasts—a stance that resonates with the similarity in imagery for weddings and funerals; see Rush Rehm, *Marriage to Death: The Conflation of Wedding and Funeral Rituals in Greek Tragedy* (Princeton: Princeton University Press, 1994), 7–9, 32; Tzvi Abusch, "Ishtar's Proposal and Gilgamesh's Refusal: An Interpretation of *The Gilgamesh Epic*, Tablet 6, Lines 1-79," *History of Religions* 26 (1986): 143–87, at 157. By contrast, Jon Levenson, *Resurrection and the Restoration of Israel: The Ultimate Victory of the God of Life* (New Haven: Yale University Press, 2006), 49–51, separates the *marzēaḥ*-house in Jer 16:5 as a place of mourning from the wedding celebration in Jer 16:8 as part of his argument that there is very little evidence of the *marzēaḥ* in the Hebrew Bible.

19. Holladay, *Jeremiah 1*, 471.

20. Carroll, *Jeremiah*, 339.

21. Holladay, *Jeremiah 1*, 427–28. Mark J. Boda, "From Complaint to Contrition: Peering through the Liturgical Window of Jer 14,1–15,4," *ZAW* 113 (2001): 186–97, at 195, dates the drought to the time of Zedekiah around 587.

disorientation is a projection of their own confusion about the way he is treating them. Their repentance has not yet reached far enough; they still regard themselves as victims of the drought. Therefore YHWH rejects their petition for assistance and orders Jeremiah not to intercede for them (14:11-12; 15:1-4).[22]

Jeremiah, like Moses before him (Exod 32:11-14), seems to have wanted to intercede for the people (14:17-18).[23] But YHWH has consistently given him a word of judgment to speak to the people. As the hostility against him mounts, Jeremiah pleads with YHWH to defend him against those who mock him (17:14-16, 18; 18:21-23). But he also expresses uneasiness toward YHWH: "You have certainly become for me like a deceitful stream whose waters are unreliable" (15:18); "Do not become destruction for me" (17:17a). The delay in the predicted doom for Jerusalem has given his opponents evidence for claiming that he is a false prophet (17:15-16; cf. 28:10-16).[24] The beginning of Jeremiah's final "confession" (20:7-13) suggests that he himself has begun to have serious doubts about the veracity of the message the Lord has given him to speak: "O Lord, you have seduced me, and I was seduced; you were too strong for me, and you have prevailed. I have become one who is toyed with all the day; everyone ridicules me" (20:7).[25] Thus even though Jeremiah has been set apart from the people as YHWH's messenger there is considerable overlap between the response he gives to YHWH's message of doom and that which the people give. He resists, questions, and denies. But YHWH keeps the pressure on Jeremiah (20:9), and Jeremiah responds by complaining vehemently.

The "confessions" of Jeremiah are shaped according to the genre of the individual lament. They probably reflect the literary *persona* of Jeremiah more than the historical Jeremiah.[26] But this literary *persona* is the product of traditionists who have reflected on Jeremiah's ministry and have the benefit of knowing how history unfolded in the decades following Jeremiah's preaching. So their portrayal of Jeremiah in the "confessions" is not a mere imaginative construct but draws forth from the story of his ministry truthful dimensions of his mission of which he

22. Holladay, *Jeremiah 1*, 427–29.

23. Boda, "From Complaint to Contrition," 191.

24. Holladay, *Jeremiah 1*, 461, 504–7.

25. Ibid., 548, 552–53.

26. David Jobling, "The Quest of the Historical Jeremiah: Hermeneutical Implications of Recent Literature," *USQR* 34 (1978): 3–12, at 3–6; Corrine Patton, "Layers of Meaning: Priesthood in Jeremiah MT," in *The Priests in the Prophets*, 149–76, at 157.

himself was probably unaware.[27] Furthermore, the genre of the individual lament is a dynamic rhetorical form that engages its audience. Therefore readers of the confessions of Jeremiah in the context of the narrative of his ministry and the collection of his oracles in Jeremiah 11–20 are challenged to wrestle in their own experience with the question of whether YHWH is a God who draws them into painful dilemmas that test them to the breaking point.[28] When we read Jeremiah's story, we wonder if YHWH was asking too much of Jeremiah.

If we do ask the question about the fairness of YHWH's dealings with Jeremiah, we have moved into the paradigm of the lament and away from that of the penitential prayer.[29] In the latter we would acknowledge our own sinfulness when confused by the misfortunes in human experience. In the former we would protest more strongly to God to remedy the situation or to bring understanding.[30] The use of penitential prayer is no guarantee that we are being obedient to YHWH. In fact, YHWH's rejection of the people's confession of sin in Jer 14:7, 20 illustrates that if such a confession is superficial it will only distance us from YHWH. The vigorous complaints of Jeremiah in his "confessions" can help us to examine the depth of our commitment to YHWH.

The resistance of the people to Jeremiah's message of doom and repentance leads Jeremiah to describe their condition as follows: "The sin of Judah is inscribed with an iron stylus; with an emery point it is chiseled on the tablet of their hearts" (17:1). The fundamental question is how their hearts stand in relation to YHWH.[31] Jeremiah goes on to deliver an oracle in which he contrasts the one who trusts in mortals with the one who trusts in YHWH. The former is "like a juniper in the desert that does not see good when it comes" (17:6).[32] But the latter shall be "like a tree planted near water that sends forth its roots along the watercourse, sending out its roots by the stream. It has no fear when

27. Clements, "Jeremiah's Message of Hope," 139, 142; McConville, *Judgment and Promise*, 69–72.

28. Clements, "Jeremiah's Message of Hope," 142; Stulman, *Jeremiah*, 24–25.

29. Boda, "From Complaint to Contrition," esp. 187, 196–97.

30. Richard J. Bautch, *Developments in Genre between Post-Exilic Penitential Prayers and the Psalms of Communal Lament*, SBL Academia Biblica 7 (Atlanta: Society of Biblical Literature, 2003), 2–6.

31. Holladay, *Jeremiah 1*, 487–88, detects sexual innuendo in the terms "iron pen" (*bĕ ʿēṭ barzel*) and "engraved, plowed" (*ḥărûšâ*); thus Judah's rebelliousness "involves a preoccupation with male sexuality: the concerns of Baal have taken over Judah's heart."

32. McKane, *Jeremiah I–XXV*, 390, argues that *ʿarʿār* does not refer to a tree in v. 6; the imagery here is that of a destitute, isolated person who trusts in human power.

heat arrives; its leaves stay green; in the year of drought it is not worried, and it does not stop bearing fruit" (17:8). In the deep distress of his second "confession" Jeremiah accused YHWH of being "like a deceitful stream whose waters are unreliable" (15:18). But now in the more reflective mode at the beginning of Jeremiah 17 the prophet takes a longer view of a person's relationship with YHWH and testifies, echoing the language of Psalm 1, that YHWH is an everflowing stream of water (cf. Jer 2:13).[33] Jeremiah 17:5-8 teaches that trust in YHWH is more fundamental than morality; trust in God is a prerequisite for the capacity to act uprightly.[34]

YHWH's command that Jeremiah live as a celibate is given in light of the doom predicted to descend upon Judah. But the detachment required in responding to this command strips away the relationships to wife and children that are constitutive of a father's role in a household. He is required to stand before YHWH in need of a relationship that will sustain him. The image of the sturdy, resilient tree that can resist a drought describes the one whose heart trusts in YHWH.[35] He is the one who has survived the test YHWH brings against mind and heart to find out what truly lies within a person (17:10). Such testing, which seems so extreme in the life of Jeremiah, is necessary, for "the heart is too serpentine to comprehend; it is incurable—who can know it?" (Jer 17:9).[36] This disorientation at the center of the human person is problematic not only epistemologically but also ontologically: we not only cannot crack the mystery of human perversity, we also must deal with this characteristic weakness within ourselves and others.

33. Holladay, *Jeremiah 1*, 489–90, contends that Jer 17:5-8 is modeled on Psalm 1 and serves as an affirmation of faith in response to 15:18-19 and as an introduction to the confessional material in Jeremiah 17, 18, and 20.

34. Rodney Sadler, Jr., "Jeremiah 17:5-11," *Interpretation* 58 (2004): 59–61, at 60. McKane, *Jeremiah I–XXV*, 392–94, sees 17:5-8 directed to the individual and not to a king or statesman; the universal reach of its teaching is not confined to Israel's corporate experience. Trust in YHWH is more interior and fundamental than the issue of public idolatry.

35. James Crenshaw, "Deceitful Minds and Theological Dogma: Jer 17:5-11," in *Utopia and Dystopia in Prophetic Literature*, Publications of the Finnish Exegetical Society 92, ed. Ehud Ben Zvi, 105–21 (Helsinki: Finnish Exegetical Society; Göttingen: Vandenhoeck & Ruprecht, 2006), at 120, describes this advice as utopian or as an instance of "whistling in the dark."

36. Tzvi Novick, "*ʿqb hlb mkl wʾnš hûʾ mî ydʿnû* (JEREMIAH 17:9)," *JBL* 123 (2004): 531–535, interprets this phrase as referring to the "unfathomability" rather than the "sinfulness" of the human heart and so argues for the translation "too serpentine to comprehend."

The solution offered in Jer 31:31-34 to the complexity of the human heart is its divine reprogramming. The Sinai covenant the Israelites had failed to keep will be replaced in the coming days (31:31).[37] At some indeterminate date in the future, but in a time perceived to be near enough to have an impact on one's current understanding of life, YHWH will intervene and act, as he says:

> I will put my torah within them and write it on their hearts. I will be their God, and they will be my people. No longer will they instruct their friends and relatives saying, "Know the Lord." Indeed, they will all know me, from the least to the greatest, says the Lord, because I will forgive their iniquity and will no longer remember their sin. (31:33-34)

By YHWH's gracious acting, he will place his torah on their hearts.[38] They will know him without effort. This utopian view differs from that of the book of Deuteronomy, which repeatedly exhorts the Israelites to learn and teach the words of YHWH:

> Let these words that I command you today be upon your hearts. Repeat them to your children and say them when you are sitting at home and walking on the road, when you are lying down and standing. You shall bind them as a sign on your hands and as pendants on your forehead. You shall write them on the doorposts of your houses and on your gates. (Deut 6:6-9)

The unconditional divine promise of Jer 31:31-34 is closer to the promise in Deut 30:6, in which Moses says that YHWH will circumcise the hearts of the Israelites so that their devotion may be undivided, and to the statement in Deut 30:14 concerning the nearness of God's command and

37. William Holladay, *Jeremiah 2*, 165, argues that Jer 31:31-34 is authentic to Jeremiah and was probably preached shortly after the fall of Jerusalem (Jer 39:2) on the temple site to pilgrims as a "counter-proclamation to the recitation of Deuteronomy in Jerusalem at the festival of booths." By contrast, Karel van der Toorn, *Scribal Culture and the Making of the Hebrew Bible* (Cambridge, MA: Harvard University Press, 2007), 200, argues—on the ground that Jer 31:31-34 is a secondary insertion in Jeremiah 26–45 added after the *Vorlage* of LXXJer was written—that this passage is a product of theological reflection after the Deuteronomic editors made their contribution to the book of Jeremiah. Holladay, *Jeremiah 2*, 8, dates LXXJer to ca. 200 BCE and its *Vorlage* to a time prior to the end of the fifth century.

38. Holladay, *Jeremiah 2*, 198, contends that this interior space is not only the bodies of the Judahites but also the city and temple as interior locations in the land and the city.

its presence in their hearts.[39] The gracious yet dominant action of YHWH to reshape the hearts of the Israelites so that they will remain faithful to the covenant seems to minimize the significance of human choice. The similarity of this radical divine action to the heart transplant and placing of the divine Spirit in the exiles in Ezek 36:26-27 suggests that the editors responsible for Jer 31:31-34 were influenced by that passage.[40] The intent of these promises of eschatological salvation, instead of minimizing free will, is to accent the power of torah to bring about unity between YHWH and Israel, among the Israelites, and within each Israelite. This integrative power of torah can overcome the deficits in the thinking and perceiving apparatus at the center of the human person—the heart. The extravagant promise of Jer 31:31-34 aims to get the Israelites back on their feet.[41] For an Israelite to be hopeful demands that he or she love YHWH with the whole heart, soul, and strength (Deut 6:4).

The Word of God: Educator of the Human Person Within the Cosmic Community

Language is a divine gift that is indispensable for human consciousness. When someone has suffered a serious accident and is alive but in a coma we typically refer to this one as in a vegetable-like state. If one happens to be able to express himself or herself but is reduced to inarticulate groans, we may refer to such a one as animal-like. Thus the distinguishing feature of a human is the capacity to speak. Within this use of language there are forms of expression that create reality; such expressions have been labeled as "performative" in character. For example, when a bride and groom say successively to one another "I do" in the public ceremony before a socially commissioned officiant they have created a new reality in which they will shape their lives for the foreseeable future. These powerful linguistic actions penetrate to the roots of personal existence. For a devoted Roman Catholic the priest's words of absolution for con-

39. William McKane, *A Critical and Exegetical Commentary on Jeremiah XXVI–LII*, ICC (Edinburgh: T & T Clark, 1986), 825.

40. Corrine Patton, "Pan-Deuteronomism and the Book of Ezekiel," in *Those Elusive Deuteronomists: The Phenomenon of Pan-Deuteronomism*, *JSOTSup* 268, ed. Linda Schearing and Steven McKenzie, 200–15 (Sheffield: Sheffield Academic Press, 1999), at 204–5, 212, 214. With regard to Jer 31:31-34, Holladay, *Jeremiah* 2, 164, notes: "it is important to stress that theologically the striking message of the passage is not typical of anything else in the exilic or postexilic period"—a point Holladay regards as favoring this passage as an authentic expression from Jeremiah.

41. McKane, *Jeremiah XXVI–LII*, 827.

fessed sins have a healing power that can be transformative. The performative use of language has what might appear to be a "magical" power in its capacity to create or reshape important boundaries of human existence. But the performative utterance depends upon who is speaking and under what circumstances and thus does not have the mechanical predictability inherent in a properly constructed magical act.[42]

Rituals run the risk of becoming mechanical and magical if the participants do not open their hearts to the reality that is to be engaged. In Jer 14:10 YHWH rejects the Judahites' petition for forgiveness of their sins because they are not committed to following him but are guilty of "loving to wander." The kind of turning that qualifies as true repentance requires a fixed point, a turning of the heart (cf. Jer 8:4-5).[43] Without such a fixed point the person's turning merely contributes to further disorder and chaos.

Writing is more stable than spoken words, but this visual form of speech carries the additional potential for distortion since the words are detached from their author. Even if the author's intention is held up as the criterion for interpreting the written words, this intention may be difficult to recover.[44] Jeremiah has trouble with certain scribes of his time. He reports a judgment YHWH renders on the scribes for distorting the torah (Jer 8:8) and then claiming to be wise on the basis of their knowledge of written texts. But Jeremiah declares that these wise ones will be "put to shame, shattered, and captured" (8:9).[45] The torah that has been

42. John R. Searle, *Mind, Language and Society. Philosophy in the Real World* (New York: Basic Books, 1998), 150; John B. Thompson, "Introduction" to Pierre Bourdieu, *Language and Symbolic Power* (Cambridge, MA: Harvard University Press, 1991), 8–10; Jürgen Habermas, "Comments on John Searle's 'Meaning, Communication, and Representation' (1998)," in *On the Pragmatics of Communication* (Cambridge, MA: MIT Press, 1998), 269; Armin Burkhardt, "Speech act theory—the decline of a paradigm," in *Speech Acts, Meaning and Intentions: Critical Approaches to the Philosophy of John R. Searle*, ed. idem (New York: de Gruyter, 1990), 117–18.

43. Holladay, *Jeremiah 1*, 278–79.

44. William M. Schniedewind, "The Textualization of Torah in Jeremiah 8:8," in *Was ist ein Text? Alttestamentliche, ägyptologische und altorientalische Perspektiven*, BZAW 362, ed. Ludwig Morenz and Stefan Schorch, 93–107 (Berlin: de Gruyter, 2007), at 97, argues that the battle in Jer 8:8 is not over which text the term "torah" refers to but rather over the "authority of any written text as opposed to oral tradition." By contrast, Holladay, *Jeremiah 1*, 281, frames the issue as: "the contrast here is between the 'law of Yahweh' and the 'lie of the scribes.'"

45. Holladay, *Jeremiah 1*, 276–77, 281–83, proposes that YHWH is the speaker of Jer 8:4-13, in which he brings an accusation against a people who refuse to change; the lie of the scribes (i.e., royal bureaucrats) exacerbates this "deadly complacency."

distorted may be the scroll that was recovered from the temple at the time of Josiah, which initiated a purge of all non-Yahwistic cult objects and personnel from the Jerusalem temple and from the land (2 Kgs 22:1–23:27). Josiah had this text validated by the prophetess Huldah (2 Kgs 22:14-17).[46] The king then gave the support of the monarchy to the vision and directives of this document and began his purge of the land. Jeremiah's criticism of false reliance on the written torah seems to be that those using this authoritative document claim to have a wisdom that Jeremiah believes keeps them from listening to YHWH. This battle between oral prophecy and written law testifies to a tension that is necessary for an honest, ongoing interpretation of the word of God.[47] Without this debate between prophets and scribes the memory of God's instruction and attentiveness to God's continuing guidance would be lost.[48]

The composition and editing of the torah did not end at the time of the deposition in the temple of the torah that Josiah recovered. Rather, the Torah that was promulgated by Ezra in the fifth century, which presumably was the Pentateuch in penultimate form, was a combination of priestly and nonpriestly torah.[49] The juxtaposition of this diverse source material, which has been labeled JEPD in the longstanding pentateuchal documentary hypothesis, reveals that the Mosaic Torah promulgated by Ezra was a compromise document. Complementary and competing voices within the postexilic Judahite community were incorporated into this foundational, charter document so that the members of this community in the fifth century (Yehud) might share a common vision of life. The resources required for this scribal, scholarly effort may well have

46. Marvin Sweeney, *I & II Kings*, OTL (Louisville: Westminster John Knox, 2007), 444; idem, *King Josiah of Judah: The Lost Messiah of Israel* (New York: Oxford University Press, 2001), 19–20, 41, 45.

47. Schniedewind, "The Textualization of Torah," 95, claims that the heart of the debate between oral and written traditions is "whether a text-artifact was understood as autonomous or embedded in the community." He notes further (pp. 100–2) that the term *dĕbar YHWH* is infrequent in legal texts—except for the Chronicler (1 Chr 10:13; 2 Chr 34:21; 35:6)—and virtually absent in wisdom texts; it is a term more at home in the prophetic tradition (Deut 5:4-5).

48. William Schniedewind, *How the Bible Became a Book: The Textualization of Ancient Israel* (Cambridge: Cambridge University Press, 2004), 116–17.

49. David M. Carr, *Writing on the Tablet of the Heart: Origins of Scripture and Literature* (New York: Oxford University Press, 2005), 170; Meindert Dijkstra, "The Law of Moses: The Memory of Mosaic Religion In and After the Exile," in *Yahwism After the Exile*, ed. Rainer Albertz and Bob Becking, 70–98 (Assen: Van Gorcum, 2003), at 92.

exceeded those available to the small community of Yehud.[50] This deficit may have been supplied by funds from the imperial Persian treasury, for, according to Ezra 7:14-16, Ezra was commissioned by the emperor to implement the Torah and to take along silver and gold contributed by the king and his counselors.[51]

The Torah promulgated by Ezra seems to have formed the basis for the Pentateuch, which then became the most authoritative teaching in Yehud and in the Jewish communities in other lands.[52] These first five books of the Bible narrate events from premonarchical times and are designated as the bearers of a timeless truth that is not to be changed (Deut 4:2). Deuteronomy 17:14-17 exhorted Israelite kings to meditate daily on the Torah, which in 622 BCE was probably Deuteronomy 12–26 but in the time of Ezra was most likely a form of the Pentateuch.[53] According to Josh 1:8 the warrior Joshua, who was about to clear the land of Canaan of inhabitants inimical to the Yahwistic way of life, was commanded to take on the mindset of this Torah as follows: "This scroll of the Torah must not leave your mouth. You must vocalize it day and night so that you are careful to act according to all that is written in it" (Josh 1:8; cf. Deut 1:3-5; 5:32-33; 6:6-9, 24-25; 31:9-13, 24-26). This same exhortation to attend

50. Ehud Ben Zvi, "What Is New in Yehud? Some Considerations," 32–48 in *Yahwism After the Exile*, at 46.

51. Konrad Schmid, "The Persian Authorization as a Historical Problem and as a Biblical Construct: A Plea for Distinctions in the Current Debate," in *The Pentateuch as Torah: New Models for Understanding Its Promulgation and Acceptance* (Winona Lake, IN: Eisenbrauns, 2007), 23–38, at 27, 31, 37–38. Lester Grabbe, *Ezra–Nehemiah* (London: Routledge, 1998), 150, questions whether there was a historical Ezra who brought a law from Mesopotamia and contends that the Torah was taking shape during the Persian period and only completed prior to 200 BCE; see also Daniel Smith-Christopher, "The Mixed Marriage Crisis in Ezra 9–10 and Nehemiah 13: A Study of the Sociology of the Post-Exilic Judaean Community," in *Second Temple Studies. 2. Temple and Community in the Persian Period*, *JSOTSup* 175, ed. Tamara C. Eskenazi and Kent H. Richards, 243–65 (Sheffield: Sheffield Academic Press, 1994), at 265.

52. Schniedewind, *How the Bible Became a Book*, 115–16. Joseph Blenkinsopp, *Ezra–Nehemiah*, OTL (Philadelphia: Westminster, 1988), 66, 153–55, says that this law "cannot simply be equated with the Pentateuch." He identifies it primarily as the laws of Deuteronomy along with some ritual legislation from the Priestly source and the Holiness Code. The traditional view in Judaism is that this law was the Pentateuch.

53. Carr, *Writing on the Tablet of the Heart*, 153; cf. Richard Nelson, *Deuteronomy*, OTL (Louisville: Westminster John Knox, 2002), 222–25. On the Deuteronomistic historian's reversal of the restrictions on royal authority in Deut 17:14-20 in Josiah's reform as recounted in 2 Kings 22–23 see Bernard M. Levinson, "The Reconceptualization of Kingship in Deuteronomy and the Deuteronomistic Historian's Reconceptualization of Torah," *VT* 51 (2001): 511–34, esp. 525–27.

carefully to the words of YHWH's torah is emphasized, as we have seen, in Ps 1:2, but here the content of that torah is the collection of psalms in the Psalter.[54] By chanting and meditating on the written text of the Psalter a person could nurture a living, dialogical relation with YHWH, which illustrates what it means to be in covenant with YHWH.

By the end of the fifth century BCE the various psalms that had been repeatedly prayed within the Israelite community and had assumed a revered position in its tradition were organized into a sequence of five books, mirroring the Mosaic Torah.[55] The strategic emphasis of Psalm 1 on torah piety was complemented not only by the editorial organization of the Psalter into five books but also by Psalms 19 and 119, which extol the virtues of the torah. Psalm 19 consists of three parts: vv. 2-7, the nighttime firmament and the rising sun sing praise to YHWH; vv. 8-11, the torah mediates between heaven and earth by enlightening and nourishing the faithful ones; vv. 12-15, the beauty of creation and the torah stir holy fear within the faithful who dare to stand before YHWH. The middle section of this psalm extols the capacity of the torah to shape the life and behavior of the one who meditates on it. The wisdom offered by the torah opens a way for the faithful to share in the divine life of YHWH.[56] The unity with YHWH, with creation, and within the faithful ones generated through meditation on the statutes of the torah mirrors that which existed in Eden prior to the transgression of the taboo regarding the tree of the knowledge of good and evil.[57] Thus the wisdom of the torah is an antidote to the mortality that accompanied the consumption of the fruit of the tree of knowledge of good and evil. The numinous power of the torah is evident in the trepidation the psalmist feels after having meditated on the law of YHWH. The psalmist's fear is associated with the strong desire not to lose this relationship with YHWH by way of a hidden fault or an arrogant attitude (Ps 19:13-14). According to Psalm 19, those who are struck by the beauty of creation and the words of the torah are given a wisdom that unites them with YHWH and brings them redemption (Ps 19:15). This is not a secret wisdom but is written throughout creation and is accessible to all.[58]

54. Gerald Henry Wilson, *The Editing of the Hebrew Psalter*, SBLDS 76 (Chico, CA: Scholars Press, 1985), 206–7.

55. Ibid., 207–8; van der Toorn, *Scribal Culture and the Making of the Hebrew Bible*, 125–26, notes that 1 Chr 16:36 quotes the doxology at the end of Book IV of the Psalter (Ps 106:48).

56. Richard J. Clifford, *Psalms 1–72* (Nashville: Abingdon, 2002), 40–41.

57. Peter Craigie, *Psalms 1–50*, WBC 19 (Waco, TX: Word Publishing, 1983), 182.

58. Van der Toorn, *Scribal Culture and the Making of the Hebrew Bible*, 166.

Psalm 119, a torah psalm, is the longest in the Psalter and seems to have been composed in the fifth century at the time of Ezra. This acrostic psalm, consisting of twenty-two eight-line stanzas for a total of 176 lines, communicates a sense of the totality and completeness of YHWH's torah.[59] The artistry of the psalm is not limited to the device of beginning each stanza with a sequential letter of the Hebrew alphabet. There are eight key words for "torah" in Psalm 119 (*tōrâ, ʿēdôt, dābār, ʾimrâ, piqqûdîm, ḥuqqîm, miṣwôt, mišpaṭîm*). Eighty-eight instances of these eight key words occur in the first part of the psalm (vv. 1-88), and eighty-nine in the second part (vv. 89-176).[60] Each of these torah words is repeated approximately twenty-two times, or an average of once per line. However, only five of the stanzas use each of the eight words only one time; within these five stanzas the order and arrangement of the eight torah words vary.[61] David Noel Freedman notes that the number eight "does not carry as much content, portent, and symbolism as the number 7 . . . . It connotes completeness and totality and perfection and carries connotations of the important number 4."[62] In sum, then, this psalm, which has often been dismissed as repetitive and wooden, manifests an underlying pattern with subtle variations on a technical level. The repetition of the torah words may have induced meditation on the mystery of the torah, where the torah is not be identified specifically with the Pentateuch but rather includes the oral teaching of the elders along with the written tradition.[63] The psalm's repeated mulling over of the virtues of the torah, in which there are sophisticated word plays and subtle technical variations, may well have communicated to the hearer or pray-er that there is an ethical order to the world that often goes unnoticed. Yet within this order the individual experiences dissonance as shown by the fact that ninety verses contain either a petition or a lament or both.[64]

The genre of this psalm may best be described as that of an individual complaint because the psalmist repeatedly struggles with YHWH's word.[65] Clifford notes that the psalmist goes through a complex, nonlinear

59. David Noel Freedman, *Psalm 119: The Exaltation of the Torah* (Winona Lake, IN: Eisenbrauns, 1999), 88–89.

60. Ibid., 26; Richard J. Clifford, *Psalms 73–150* (Nashville: Abingdon, 2003), 209.

61. Freedman, *Psalm 119*, 78.

62. Ibid., 28–29.

63. Erhard S. Gerstenberger, *Psalms, Part 2, and Lamentations*, FOTL 15 (Grand Rapids: Eerdmans, 2001), 315.

64. Clifford, *Psalms 73–150*, 211.

65. Will Soll, *Psalm 119: Matrix, Form, and Setting*, CBQMS 23 (Washington, DC: Catholic Biblical Association, 1991), 90.

process in which he complains of peril, rejoices in hope, and begs for enlightenment and fidelity to commandments.[66] His complaints begin in vv. 17-24 and intensify in the following stanzas until the psalmist reaches a low point in his fortunes in the *kaph*-stanza (vv. 81-88). Here he petitions YHWH to act against his persecutors, who have nearly destroyed him (v. 87). Yet even in these verses the psalmist notes that he has not forgotten YHWH's precepts (v. 87), and when he is restored, his primary goal is to keep YHWH's decrees (v. 88). The sudden shift to a confident mood—typical of individual laments—in the following stanza (*lamedh*, vv. 89-96) is communicated by the psalmist's celebrating the stability of the torah: "Your word, O Lord, is everlasting; it stands as firm as the heavens. From generation to generation your faithfulness endures; you have given permanence to the earth and it stands. According to your rulings they still stand firm; indeed, all things are your servants" (vv. 89-90). This conviction that life is to be lived within the sphere of the torah is striking; the world of nature and history is not held up as revelatory in this psalm. So while Psalm 19 celebrates nature as a medium of revelation and the Pentateuch narrates YHWH's saving actions in history, Psalm 119 regards revelation as occurring in the medium of the word.[67] The ups-and-downs of experience pivot on how the psalmist responds to YHWH's word. This psalm focuses on the individual's relationship with YHWH, with the communal dimension of that relationship as a backdrop. The conclusion to be drawn from this psalm is that one ought to be attentive to YHWH's torah through prayer and study. To have this torah as one's constant companion is the way to happiness (v. 1) and blamelessness (v. 9).

A striking feature of this psalm is the way YHWH's word shapes the heart (vv. 2, 58, 80, 111, 145, 161). The psalmist's freedom is respected in this dialogue with the word, for the psalmist cannot access the power of the word unless he does so with his whole heart. This dedication to the torah is emphasized by the psalmist's claim to take delight in YHWH's torah: "In your statutes I take delight; I will not forget your words" (v. 16; see also vv. 24, 47, 70, 77, 92, 143, 174). But the psalmist is realistic about his weakness and his tendency to lose focus in relating to YHWH, and so he cries out: "Give me discernment that I may observe your law and keep it with all my heart" (v. 34; see also vv. 32, 36, 69, 80). Like Jeremiah, the psalmist recalls that fidelity to YHWH's word can bring

66. Clifford, *Psalms 73–150*, 211.

67. Soll, *Psalm 119*, 91–92; Clifford, *Psalms 73–150*, 216; Gerstenberger, *Psalms, Part 2, and Lamentations*, 313.

opposition from the proud and powerful (vv. 23, 150) but proclaims that YHWH's promise sustains him (vv. 24, 50-53). The psalmist proclaims that the torah helps him not only to cope with suffering but also to learn from it (vv. 73-76, 143). So by meditating wholeheartedly on YHWH's torah (vv. 15, 23, 27, 48, 78, 97, 99, 148) the psalmist hopes to be transformed by YHWH's word (vv. 99-100, 130). The promise held out by Psalm 119 is that wholehearted searching for YHWH will result in YHWH's strengthening whoever does so and filling him or her with understanding through his presence.[68]

The Power of the Written Word Within the Politics of Piety

The individual "I" of Psalm 119 is representative of the members of the Yahwistic community.[69] The struggles this "I" has with YHWH's torah provide a written medium for others in the community to engage in the process of being transformed by YHWH's word. An aspect of the psalmist's commitment to YHWH's torah is his disdain for those who scoff at YHWH's word; therefore this psalm, as Gerstenberger notes, has a confessional character: that is, the psalmist's identity as a worshiper of YHWH comes to expression through the praying of this psalm.[70] So even though the psalm nourishes an interior piety through prayer that can be engaged in a variety of social contexts, the psalmist still connects with the Yahwistic community. This torah-centered piety is never simply a vertical relationship of an individual with YHWH but always includes a horizontal dimension in which the individual's relationship with YHWH has an impact on communal relationships. The community then has a vital interest in the nature of the prayers and sacred texts used by its members.

A sacred text in the Israelite tradition is a writing authorized by the community for fostering a person's relationship with YHWH. The written text symbolizes the presence of YHWH.[71] As noted with regard to Psalm 119, engagement with a sacred text opens the possibility for this word to shape and strengthen a person's heart. The writing and interpretation of this text, as illustrated by the Levites' explanation of the Mosaic Torah

68. Clifford, *Psalms 73–150*, 216; Gerstenberger, *Psalms, Part 2, and Lamentations*, 314; cf. Ben-Zvi, "What Is New in Yehud?" 45.

69. Gerstenberger, *Psalms, Part 2, and Lamentations*, 314–15.

70. Ibid., 315.

71. Schniedewind, *How the Bible Became a Book*, 24; Karel van der Toorn, "The Iconic Book: Analogies Between the Babylonian Cult of Images and the Veneration of the Torah," in *The Image and the Book: Iconic Cults, Aniconism, and the Rise of Book Religion in Israel and the Ancient Near East*, ed. idem (Leuven: Peeters, 1997), 229–48, at 229, 248.

in Nehemiah 8, cannot be simply a subjective, private activity. Just as Jeremiah confronted the scribes for their use of the written torah in the late seventh century (Jer 8:8-9), so also the Levites, priests, and prophets wrestled with the proper way to incorporate written texts into the life of the exilic and postexilic communities.[72]

The Levites hold a unique position in the Israelite tradition as custodians of the written word of YHWH (Deut 31:9-13).[73] The initial composition of the book of Deuteronomy, which is believed to have been the scroll recovered in the renovation of the temple at the time of Josiah, seems to have been an early version of Deuteronomy 12–26, which consisted of diverse legal materials from the sanctuaries and cities of the Northern Kingdom.[74] The Levites are a likely group of Northern refugees to have brought these materials to Jerusalem at the time of the Assyrian conquest of the Northern Kingdom in 732–722 BCE. As priests in the northern sanctuaries the Levites would probably have been responsible not only for offering sacrifice but also for composing necessary written materials.[75] The spheres of the palace and temple overlapped in most Western Asiatic kingdoms, and the priests were the group in which scribal skills were concentrated.[76] Karel van der Toorn notes that on the basis of epigraphic evidence the Hebrew script was standardized in the North and the South by 850 BCE.[77] So the northern Levites, as refugees in Judah bereft of their own sanctuaries, may well have sought employment in Judah not only as cultic assistants but also as scribes.

Josiah's reform in 622 as guided by the scroll recovered from the temple reveals the growing power of the scribal circles. The scribal version of the Mosaic Torah embodied in the scroll gained the support of the monarchy in its program of purging Jerusalem and Judah of non-Yahwistic cults (2 Kgs 23:4-20). The written Torah not only provided leverage for Josiah in his reforming efforts but also opened the way for increasing the status and power of the scribes within the kingdom. The significance of the scribes for sustaining the traditions of the Yahwistic community rose as the political community suffered destruction and

72. Blenkinsopp, *Ezra–Nehemiah*, 189, 291; van der Toorn, *Scribal Culture and the Making of the Hebrew Bible*, 107.

73. Ibid., 96; Carr, *Writing on the Tablet of the Heart*, 139; Dijkstra, "The Law of Moses," 85–86.

74. Richard Nelson, *First and Second Kings* (Louisville: John Knox, 1987), 255; Sweeney, *King Josiah of Judah*, 24.

75. Van der Toorn, *Scribal Culture and the Making of the Hebrew Bible*, 84.

76. Ibid., 96; Carr, *Writing on the Tablet of the Heart*, 152.

77. Van der Toorn, *Scribal Culture and the Making of the Hebrew Bible*, 89.

deportation.[78] Just as the Levitical refugees from the North showed their resilience in being able to preserve their traditions and have them acknowledged by the Judean monarchy, so also the scribes were able to navigate the destruction of Jerusalem in 586.

The rising significance of the scribes can be seen in the four successive editions of the book of Deuteronomy as reconstructed by van der Toorn: (1) The Covenant edition (Deut 6:4-9; 12:1–16:17; 26; 28) would have been composed shortly after 622 BCE by legal scholars, for whom an important agenda was to update the "Covenant Code" of Exodus 21–23. (2) The Torah edition, probably composed in 590–570 by a Levitical priest, incorporated Deut 16:19–18:22 into the earlier edition, which gave the text a utopian character. (3) The History edition, which includes passages (e.g., Deut 1:1; 34:10-12) added by the editors of the Deuteronomistic history in the exilic period, emphasizes the role of Moses as the ideal prophet and gives a negative assessment to Israel's history. (4) The Wisdom edition, probably written by a Babylonian Jew in the early Persian period, promotes the intellectual superiority of the Jewish way of life envisioned in the Torah.[79] In the book of Deuteronomy the Levites emphasize their role as legal interpreters of the Torah and allow their part in sacrificial matters to fade into the background.[80]

In the trajectory of Levitical fortunes stretching from 730 to 400 BCE the scribal role becomes increasingly important to members of this priestly group. However, the Levites were not a monolithic group.[81] In the initial years of their flight from the North and their recovery from the closing of rural sanctuaries at the time of Josiah's reform there must have been considerable conflict between the Zadokite priests in charge in Jerusalem and the Levites (cf. Ezek 44:9-31), but the subsequent history shows the adjustments that were made. Many Levites assumed the duties of cultic assistants at the Jerusalem sanctuary and had to accept their status as subordinate to the Aaronide priests (Num 18:21-24). In Chronicles the Levites likewise acknowledge the higher rank of the Aaronide/Zadokite priests but are not answerable to them.[82] However, the Levites in the Deuteronomic tradition regarded all priests as Levites, saw themselves

78. Dijkstra, "The Law of Moses," 91; van der Toorn, *Scribal Culture and the Making of the Hebrew Bible*, 167; Schniedewind, *How the Bible Became a Book*, 149, 164, 165–66.

79. Van der Toorn, *Scribal Culture and the Making of the Hebrew Bible*, 151–66.

80. Ibid., 168; Schniedewind, *How the Bible Became a Book*, 110–11, 113.

81. Antje Labahn, "Antitheocratic Tendencies in Chronicles," in *Yahwism After the Exile*, 115–35, at 132.

82. Ibid., 130.

as heirs to the prophets, and emphasized their status as guardians of the Torah (Deut 17:14) and of the Ark (Deut 31:24-29).[83] The Levites with scribal skills were able to use these to gain employment in the Persian government. In the description of the reforming efforts of Davidic kings in Chronicles, the Levites play important roles: e.g., judges in Jehoshaphat's reform (2 Chr 19:4b-11) and administrators for Josiah (2 Chr 35:1-19). Antje Labahn argues that the Levites in Chronicles did not abandon their sacred duties as cultic servants, prayer leaders, musicians, and preachers but expanded their duties as civil servants.[84] This civil function grew under the Persian rulers, who needed local officials to collect taxes, control trade routes, and assist provincial administrators with correspondence and financial matters.[85] The Levitical authors of Chronicles seem to have acknowledged the higher rank of the priests in cultic matters, for they were more invested in the status system that was developing outside the cultic sphere from opportunities opened up by the Persian government.[86] The scribal craft provided Levites with the opportunity to advance to upper-middle-class status.[87] In the context of the Second Temple the Levites became the scholars (2 Chr 34:13; Neh 8:7-8).

Writing can be an avenue for promoting compromise and reconciliation between competing traditions. Ezra the scribe promulgated the Mosaic Torah that brought together both the priestly and nonpriestly traditions, the texts of the Aaronites and the Levites. But writing can also become a powerful tool for co-opting the traditions of a particular group. The Pentateuchal texts depict Moses as an ideal leader who functions without a temple and emphasizes wholehearted devotion to the Torah.[88] The Deuteronomists promote the view that Moses is the ideal prophet and thus establish him as the standard against which the written collections of other prophets are to be measured. Moses is rarely mentioned in the preexilic prophetic writings.[89] When the oracles of Isaiah are put in written form, handed on, and expanded by supplementation (e.g, the

83. Van der Toorn, *Scribal Culture and the Making of the Hebrew Bible*, 92, 96, 100, 107; Carr, *Writing on the Tablet of the Heart*, 139; Labahn, "Antitheocratic Tendencies in Chronicles," 124–25.

84. Ibid., 122; Steven McKenzie, *1–2 Chronicles* (Nashville: Abingdon, 2004), 363–64.

85. Labahn, "Antitheocratic Tendencies in Chronicles," 122.

86. Ibid., 130.

87. Van der Toorn, *Scribal Culture and the Making of the Hebrew Bible*, 105.

88. Ben-Zvi, "What Is New in Yehud?" 45.

89. Dijkstra, "The Law of Moses," 96.

addition of Isaiah 40–55 and Isaiah 56–66),[90] there are viewpoints on the accessibility of the Yahwistic sanctuary (Isa 56:3-8) that stand in tension with those of the Mosaic Torah (Deut 23:1-8).[91] With Ezra's promulgation of the Mosaic Torah the Isaianic traditions would be under increased pressure to adapt.

Through its appeal to Moses and the Law the community of Yehud was shaped according to the model of a normative, enclave religion.[92] Meindert Dijkstra claims that writing gives rise to an elite, which then employs reflexive, systematic thinking to direct proper teaching and learning (Exod 24:7, 12; Deut 4:14; 17:19).[93] Dijkstra also points to Ezra's efforts at reforming the community as resembling those of Joshua insofar as he is guided by the Mosaic Torah and wants to remove non-Yahwistic influences from the land. However, Ezra's primary focus was on teaching the Torah. Although Ezra resembles Joshua in trying to purge the land of non-Yahwistic groups that endanger the integrity of the Yahwistic community, such steps were less significant to his agenda than the public reading and Levitical teaching of the Torah.[94] In the confessions in Ezra 9 and Nehemiah 9, Ezra is portrayed as a reformer and scribe of the Torah who promoted repentance and change of heart through obedience to the Torah (Ezra 9; Nehemiah 8–9). For an individual to obey the Torah wholeheartedly would provide a sense of belonging to a particular group that would counter the experience of "getting lost" within the empire.[95]

Summary

Jeremiah's celibacy is a discipline that forces him to depend more fully on YHWH. This trusting relationship between a Judahite and YHWH

90. H. G. M. Williamson, *The Book Called Isaiah: Deutero-Isaiah's Role in Composition and Redaction* (Oxford: Clarendon Press, 1994), 240–41.

91. Joseph Blenkinsopp, *Isaiah 56–66*, AB 19B (New York: Doubleday, 2003), 138–39; Rainer Albertz, *A History of the Religion of Israel*, vol. 2: *From the Exile to the Maccabees* (Louisville: Westminster John Knox, 1994), 370; Steven Tuell, "The Priesthood of the 'Foreigner': Evidence of Competing Polities in Ezekiel 44:1-14 and Isaiah 56:1-8," in *Constituting the Community: Studies on the Polity of Ancient Israel in Honor of S. Dean McBride*, ed. John T. Strong and Steven S. Tuell, 183–204 (Winona Lake, IN: Eisenbrauns, 2005), at 198, 201–2.

92. Dijkstra, "The Law of Moses," 95; Sara Japhet, "People and Land in the Restoration Period," in her *From the Rivers of Babylon to the Highlands of Judah: Collected Studies on the Restoration Period* (Winona Lake, IN: Eisenbrauns, 2006), 96–116, at 108.

93. Dijkstra, "The Law of Moses," 85, 95.

94. Ibid., 91.

95. Bob Becking, "Law as Expression of Religion (Ezra 7–10)," in *Yahwism After the Exile*, 18–31, at 31; Albertz, *A History of the Religion of Israel*, 2:375.

is promoted by the contrast between the shrub in the desert (the one who trusts in humans) and the tree near ever-flowing waters (the one who trusts in YHWH). Jeremiah follows YHWH's command and becomes a living symbol for the Judahite community of the traumatic times in store for them because their sin is indelibly inscribed on their hearts and so they are unable to keep YHWH's *šālōm* in their midst. Without YHWH's *šālōm*, disease, famine, and sword descend on the community. Jeremiah symbolizes the Judahite community not only by his deprivations that foreshadow those to come more fully upon the community but also by his resistance to the chastisement YHWH brings against him. His call to a celibate way of life—not long-term, but as an exceptional way to live because the end of the kingdom is near—is situated in the midst of the five "confessions" of Jeremiah that occur in Jeremiah 11–20. In these "confessions" Jeremiah complains bitterly about the opposition from the community to the word of judgment YHWH has given him to speak to them. He also expresses his anxiety that YHWH may have set him up as a false prophet since his words of disaster have not yet been realized in Judah. This inner anguish of Jeremiah illustrates YHWH's proverbial statement about the human heart: "The heart is too serpentine to comprehend; it is incurable—who can know it?" (Jer 17:9). YHWH is putting intense pressure on Jeremiah; his heart is placed in a crucible where YHWH tests it as a metallurgist would test silver or gold for its purity (Jer 17:10). One can survive this test only through YHWH's intervention. In the oracle of salvation in Jer 31:31-34 YHWH promises to inscribe his law on the hearts of the Judahites. This oracle emphasizes the gracious, redemptive action of YHWH, but its drastic character of reprogramming the human heart seems to suspend human freedom. Nevertheless, the emphasis in this oracle is on the power of YHWH's word in the torah to bring reconciliation with YHWH. Once YHWH's *šālōm* is present, all other relationships fall into place.

The symbolic significance of Jeremiah's celibacy lies in its emphasis on removing all forms of human reliance that might compromise the wholehearted trust in YHWH that the covenant requires (cf. Deut 6:4-9). The desire for YHWH's word to come and work in one's heart is the first step that seems to be suggested by the utopian oracle of salvation in Jer 31:31-34. This kind of dramatic intervention of YHWH would mark the end of human history as we know it. But it emphasizes the importance of focusing on YHWH's word in his torah as the means for gaining life and wholeness. The cultivation of such wholehearted devotion to YHWH is the goal of Psalm 119—and of the entire Psalter. This lengthy psalm aims to foster meditation on the torah. The torah is a world unto itself:

one who studies and meditates on the torah will come to know YHWH through the joys of YHWH's enlightenment and nourishment but also through the struggles that the torah will trigger within the person praying the psalm and with other members of the community. This wrestling with YHWH fosters a living, embodied revelation of torah. If the written word of YHWH becomes a static entity that does not challenge the hearts of those who hear it, the torah of YHWH will have been made into a lie (Jer 8:8-9). Sacred writing was a powerful medium for Yehud's interiorizing its relationship with YHWH, but this blessing can be distorted if the written word becomes an end in itself and loses its symbolic character of embodying, yet pointing beyond itself to YHWH. The tension between scribes, prophets, and priests is a creative force in the divine-human relationship in the Israelite tradition.

Mesopotamia: Linguistic Protection Against the Power of Death

The capacity for self-reflection and symbolic thinking arising from the human capacity to speak drives humans to find meaning in life. It is not enough to simply be able to live one's years in which the pleasures balance out the pains; humans yearn for their lives to be part of a larger narrative. This story of humans as the servants of the gods pervades the myths of the third millennium BCE and is rearticulated when disaster strikes the human community. When humans meet death in one of its many faces and survive, they not only try to make sense out of the experience but also seek for ways to shield themselves from it. Contemplative and technical knowledge combine to construct a meaningful world that will shield us from the terror of death. How Mesopotamians constructed a shield of meaning against death will be examined not only through excerpts from *Ludlul bēl nēmeqi*, the myth of Adapa, an incantation, and royal correspondence, but also through a reconstruction of the theological disciplines that arose in the early first millennium. The following three topics will be addressed: (1) The experience of being rescued from death through divine intervention provides a new standpoint from which to understand the structure and functions of the divine world. (2) A breadth of vision is necessary in pursuing knowledge about human and cosmic origins so as to distinguish between knowledge oriented toward acceptance of human limits and that oriented toward changing them. (3) The technology of writing created a new framework for paying attention to the revelation the gods were believed to have inscribed in the cosmos and so created a new means for enlisting divine help against the force of death.

The Plight of Those Who Suffer Divine Abandonment

YHWH's command that Jeremiah live as a celibate would have increased his sense of isolation. To lose one's family connections was equivalent to descending into Sheol with no one to remember one through either honorable burial or memorial offerings. To the observer, Jeremiah's growing isolation signaled divine abandonment. Jeremiah was conflicted: he knew YHWH was with him, but he was deeply distressed over what YHWH was asking him to endure. This same dilemma of undergoing intense suffering, particularly in terms of social ostracism, which leaves the sufferer wondering about how the divine realm is treating him, is the main concern of the Babylonian poem *Ludlul bēl nēmeqi* from the Kassite period (fourteenth-twelfth century BCE).[96] In this four-tablet composition, which has been hailed as one of the finest Babylonian literary productions,[97] the author Shubshi-meshre-shakkan, a literate noble who had held influential political positions, wrestles with the issue of how to react to the divine realm when one is afflicted with misfortune.[98]

After an opening hymn celebrating the supremacy of Marduk as a god who intervenes in human life in contrasting, contradictory ways (I:1-40), Shubshi-meshre-shakkan notes how Marduk became angry with him, which resulted in his protector god and goddess abandoning him.[99]

96. Wilfred G. Lambert, "*Ludlul bēl nēmeqi*," *BWL*, 21–62, at 26.

97. Paul-Alain Beaulieu, "The Setting of Babylonian Wisdom Literature," in *Wisdom Literature in Mesopotamia and Israel*, SBLSymposium 36 (Atlanta: Society of Biblical Literature, 2007), 3–19, at 9.

98. Lambert, *BWL* 21; the same author, in "Some New Babylonian Wisdom Literature," in *Wisdom in Ancient Israel*, ed. John Day, Robert P. Gordon, and H. G. M. Williamson, 30–42 (Cambridge: Cambridge University Press, 1995), at 33–34, argues that Shubshi-meshre-shakkan may well have been a governor of that name under king Nazimuruttaš (ca. 1324–1298 BCE).

99. Daniel E. Fleming, "Job: The Tale of Patient Faith and the Book of God's Dilemma," *VT* 44 (1994): 469–82, at 478, argues that this opening hymn defines *Ludlul bēl nēmeqi* as a didactic hymn in praise of Marduk for his anticipated saving actions such that all the sufferer's subsequent protests cannot be read as part of an individual lament. In the edition published by Lambert (*BWL*, 21–62) in 1960 the first tablet had not yet been recovered (Donald J. Wiseman, "A New Text of the Babylonian Poem of the Righteous Sufferer," *Anatolian Studies* 30 [1980]: 101–7); thus *Ludlul bēl nēmeqi* was read as the Babylonian Job. William Moran, "The Babylonian Job," in *The Most Magic Word*, CBQMS 35, ed. Ronald S. Hendel, 182–200 (Washington, DC: Catholic Biblical Association, 2002), at 191, identifies the genre of *Ludlul bēl nēmeqi* as akin to a hymn of thanksgiving: the fulfillment of a promise to a penitent who has asked for healing. On the lyrical character of *Ludlul bēl nēmeqi* see Brigitte Groneberg, "Toward a Definition of Literariness as Applied to Akkadian Litera-

This initiates the long litany of ills that ravaged the sufferer: physical weakness, psychological distress, and social hostility (I: 47-69). The sufferer, once strong and proud, begins to buckle under this pressure (I: 70-78). He then describes at length his growing alienation from his family, friends, and fellow citizens:

> Within my extended family, I became isolated. Whenever I would go down the streets, fingers were pointed at me. Whenever I entered the palace, eyes would peer at me. My city glared at me like an enemy. My land was strange and savage. My brother turned into a stranger. My friend turned into a bad person, a demon. My companion would intensely denounce me. My colleague "dirtied" his weapon for bloodshed. My good friend tormented me. Publicly, in the assembly, my male slave cursed me. My female slave slandered me in front of a crowd. My confidant saw me and became terribly afraid. My family categorized me as not one of their own. For whoever might speak well of me, a pit was opened. Whoever slandered me was promoted. For whoever spoke ill of me, a god became his helper. For whoever said, "it is enough," death came quickly to him. To the one who never assists, his life became lucky. I had no one to accompany me; I saw no mercy. Among the commoners and riffraff, my property was divided. In the mouth of my canals, they deposited silt. In my fields, the work-song was eliminated. Like a hostile city, my city became very silent. They allowed another to take over my position. For my duties, they appointed a stranger. (I:79-104)[100]

This list of woes describes one whose life is slipping away. What was once a vibrant and meaningful existence is now one in which the whole fabric of life is unraveling. Not only did his brother and best friend oppose him, but also anyone who presumed to show him compassion or defend him was put to death. They took his property as if he were an enemy and gave it to another. This besieged individual was demonized and excluded.

At the beginning of Tablet II the sufferer notes that his misfortune steadily increased over the course of a year. He found no way to reverse this course. He prayed to his protector gods (II: 4-5); he called on the diviner (*bārû*), the dream interpreter (*šā'ilu*), the exorcist (*mašmaššu / āšipu*; II: 6-9). But these three experts could not find a solution. The sufferer

---

ture," in *Mesopotamian Poetic Language: Sumerian and Akkadian*, Cuneiform Monographs 6 (Groningen: Styx, 1996), 59–84, at 71–73.

100. Edition: A. R. George and F. N. H. Al-Rawi, "Tablets from the Sippar Library. VII. Three Wisdom Texts," *Iraq* 60 (1998): 187–206, at 193–94.

compares his situation to that of an impious person who has spurned the gods (II: 13-22), but he emphasizes how conscientious he has been in bringing prayer and food offerings to the deities and participating in religious rituals of the city (II: 23-32). He was not simply in attendance at these services for the gods, he also invested himself in them and took an active role in instructing others about the deities honored in these rituals. But his extreme suffering called into question whether his way of serving the deities was on the right track: "If only I knew that these things are acceptable to a god! What seems good to oneself could be a sin to a god. What in one's own estimation is impure, could be good to one's god" (II: 33-35).[101] The sufferer's world has been turned on its head. The ways of the gods completely escape him (II: 36-38). Moran notes that what is unique in this passage is that the gods expect humans to obey unknown and inaccessible standards of behavior, which may even go so far as to invert good and evil.[102] In the second half of Tablet II (lines 50-107) the sufferer describes at length the physical symptoms of the disease the demons have inflicted on him.[103] His family make funeral preparations for him (II: 114-15).

Tablet III begins with an indirect reference to Marduk: "His hand was burdensome, I was unable to bear it" (line 1).[104] Lambert, who notes that *Ludlul bēl nēmeqi* spends the bulk of its time speaking about Marduk's restoration of the sufferer and that only Tablet II justifies labeling this poem "the Babylonian Job," regarded this phrase as centrally important to the poem; it blames Marduk—albeit cautiously—for the sufferer's troubles.[105] However, Moran argues on the basis of the Nimrud text of Tablet I that the sufferer ascribed his troubles to the abandonment of his personal gods and does not blame Marduk, whom he regards as a god whose "judiciousness checks anger."[106] This identification of Marduk as a god of mercy as well as of wrath is clearly stated in Tablet I: "Just as his hand is burdensome, so his heart is merciful. Just as his weapons are

101. Lambert, *BWL* 40.

102. Moran, "The Babylonian Job," 190.

103. Erica Reiner, "'This Year and into the Next . . . .' The Second Tablet of *Ludlul bēl nēmeqi*: Intricate Texture of a Learned Poem," in *Your Thwarts in Pieces, Your Mooring Rope Cut: Poetry from Babylonia and Assyria* (Ann Arbor, MI: Horace H. Rackham School of Graduate Studies at the University of Michigan, 1985) 101–18, at 109.

104. Edition: Lambert, *BWL* 48.

105. Lambert, *BWL* 23; idem, "Studies in Marduk," *Bulletin of the School of Oriental and African Studies* 47 (1984): 1–9, at 6; idem, "Some New Babylonian Wisdom Literature," 32.

106. Moran, "The Babylonian Job," 192.

murderous, so his temperament is life-giving" (I: 33-34).[107] With this cosmic god rescue will come quickly and unpredictably.[108] Thus Lambert interprets Tablet I as consistent with the subsequent three tablets of the poem in portraying Marduk as "first savage, but then later relenting" (*eziz u muštal*, cf. *Enūma Elish* VI:137; An=Anum II:181).[109]

Tablet III then describes three dreams that come to the dying sufferer. The main character in the first dream is a strong, well-dressed young man—whom Foster suggests is the sufferer himself in his prime[110]—who claims to have been sent by the Lady (probably Ṣarpanitum; III: 8-15). When he tries to relate this dream to his family they dismiss it as delirium. But a second dream follows immediately in which he sees a man, who is holding a tamarisk purifying rod, come and pour water over him and pronounce an incantation (III: 21-28). In the third and final dream a godlike young woman with a radiant face intervenes to declare his deliverance; then a bearded young man, who is an exorcist (*mašmaššu*), appears in the dream carrying a tablet with the words declaring his release (III: 29-41). Then the healing of the sufferer is described in III: 2′-36′ as a reversal of the afflictions described in II: 50-107. Finally, in Tablet IV the healed sufferer gives thanks and praise to Marduk for saving him from death. Is Marduk the sovereign deity who brought this suffering on Shubshi-meshre-shakkan and then healed him after he had undergone this test? Or is Marduk the saving god who healed the sufferer after he was abandoned by his protector gods? Moran has proposed the latter alternative and argues that the point of *Ludlul bēl nēmeqi*, which foregrounds the hymn in praise of Marduk in Tablet 1 and refrains from mentioning Marduk until the third dream promising the sufferer's deliverance, is to celebrate the advent of the new Marduk religion toward the end of the second millennium.[111] The earlier interpretations of *Ludlul bēl nēmeqi* defended the first option: that the point of this wisdom composition is to declare Marduk's sovereign power to initiate and to end individual misfortune.

Shubshi-meshre-shakkan is brought to the end of his strength and is moved to acknowledge the sovereignty of Marduk because of the

107. Edition: George and Al-Rawi, "Tablets from the Sippar Library. VII. Three Wisdom Texts," 193. See also Moran, "The Babylonian Job," 193.

108. Ibid., 194.

109. Lambert, "Some New Babylonian Wisdom Literature," 32–33.

110. Benjamin Foster, *Before the Muses: An Anthology of Akkadian Literature*, 3d ed. (Bethesda, MD: Capital Decisions Limited, 2005), 392.

111. Moran, "The Babylonian Job," 187, 198.

miraculous healing given to him. Yet he proclaims that the paradoxical ways of the gods and the expectations they impose on humans are beyond human understanding. He does not adopt the confrontational style of Job in the face of undeserved suffering. He draws on the knowledge and exorcistic rituals of the *āšipu*, but they are ineffective. In the end the point of this composition is to praise the power and the mercy of Marduk, even though one may find paradoxical the kind of treatment one receives from this cosmic deity.[112]

The Pursuit of Wisdom and the Confrontation with Death

Humans tend to want to know more than it is possible for them to know. This desire to extend their knowledge beyond what is appropriate to humans' status in the cosmic community is the topic of the *Myth of Adapa and the South Wind*. Adapa is the first of the seven sages (*apkallū*): the primordial humans who are credited with bringing the arts and institutions of civilized life into the earthly sphere.[113] This narrative begins with Adapa, servant of Ea, carrying out his daily duties for the temple of Ea in Eridu, of which one is to supply fish from the sea. A strong south wind comes up and capsizes his sailboat, at which point he cries out: "O south wind, (and) the winds, your brothers. As much as [necessary to . . .] I will break your wing" (fragment B, 4'-6').[114] As soon as he has said this, the south wind quits blowing for seven days. This wind, associated with Ishtar and regarded as having a sexual, violent nature, brought humid air to southern Mesopotamia essential for agriculture.[115] When Anu learns of the lengthy cessation of the south wind he sends his vizier Ilabrat to find out the cause. When Anu discovers that it was the words of Adapa that broke the wing of the South Wind he becomes angry. Izre'el contends that Anu became angry not so much because the wind had not blown but rather because a human brought this about.[116]

Differing interpretations of the character of Adapa's speech have been offered. Piotr Michalowski categorizes Adapa's words as an incan-

112. Foster, *Before the Muses*, 394.

113. Shlomo Izre'el, *Adapa and the South Wind: Language Has the Power of Life and Death*, Mesopotamian Civilizations 10 (Winona Lake, IN: Eisenbrauns, 2001), 1, 116. Berossus describes Oannes-Adapa as a fish-man from the sea who brings civilizing arts (see Stanley Burnstein, *The Babyloniaca of Berossus* [Malibu: Undena Publications, 1978], 13–14).

114. Edition: Izre'el, *Adapa and the South Wind*, 16.

115. Ibid., 144.

116. Ibid., 129.

tation: their effectiveness here in controlling a natural force like the wind requires a special divine force.[117] In this case the transgression would be an excessive human wisdom that had devised an incantation with sufficient power to disable the South Wind.[118] But the words Adapa uses against the South Wind seem like ordinary speech; they have no repetitions or other stylistic features characteristic of an incantation.[119] Thus Shlomo Izre'el argues that Anu is incensed over Adapa's use of language to control the wind.[120] This human capacity that differentiates humans from animals and gives them divinelike power leads to confrontations between humans and the gods. Izre'el contends that the use of language is equivalent to intelligence or wisdom; therefore, when humans use language, the only remaining differentiator between gods and humans is the mortality of humans.[121] If Izre'el's interpretation is followed, the drama of Adapa's ascent to heaven to appear before Anu is whether the remaining barrier to divine status—mortality—will be removed. Ea advises Adapa not to eat any food given to him while in heaven, but such advice tricks Adapa into missing the opportunity to gain immortality. In this narrative Adapa seems to go about his business, oblivious to the threat Ea sees him posing to the distinction between gods and humans (ll. 57-61). According to Izre'el's view of Adapa's cursing of the wind as carried out by ordinary human language, the conclusion to be drawn from this narrative is that humans make themselves rivals to the gods by using the language and intelligence given them when they were created.[122] They did not transgress a taboo like that of Genesis 2–3, which resulted in rivalry between the divine and the human. However, Michalowski explains that the Adapa narrative may be an etiology for the art of the *āšipu*, that is, to keep the power of language from upsetting the

117. Piotr Michalowski, "Adapa and the Ritual Process," *Rocznik Orientalistyczny* 51 (1980): 77–82, at 79.

118. Michalowski, "Adapa and the Ritual Process," 80–81, states that Adapa stumbled upon this magical power in his use of it against the South Wind but was later equipped with the capacity to recite effective incantations. As a representative of humanity, Adapa shows how the practice of using incantations (*āšipūtu*) became institutionalized with divine approval.

119. Cf. Mariana E. Vogelzang, "Repetition as a Poetic Device in Akkadian," in *Mesopotamian Poetic Language: Sumerian and Akkadian*, 167–82, at 168.

120. Izre'el, *Adapa and the South Wind*, 131, 134.

121. Ibid., 120.

122. Ibid., 126.

order of the world its performative power is to be reserved for incantations in the hands of the *āšipu* and immobilized in ordinary speech.[123]

Adapa spoke against the South Wind because he was drowning (ll. 48'-54'). The confrontation with death stirs humans to use whatever means they have at their disposal to escape it.[124] Adapa may have drowned, but he was taken up to heaven to stand before Anu, where the stakes were higher than he imagined (ll. 35-41, 75-78). Since he did not see through the trickery of Ea and refrained from eating heavenly food that would have incorporated him into the divine sphere, Adapa was returned to earth to live out his human lifespan (ll. 81-85). According to this Adapa myth, human efforts to transcend death will require that they have sufficient wisdom to outmaneuver the stratagems of Ea.

The pursuit of wisdom repeatedly faces the issue of the proper limits for human understanding. Will pressing a question further lead to new understanding, or will it open up a flood of problems that might even threaten human existence? This search for the origins of order in the cosmos is necessarily a preoccupation with the reality of death. The effort to find the secret that will overcome death is associated in the Mesopotamian tradition with the flood-hero Ziusudra in the *Eridu Genesis*. Ziusudra was the last king before the flood and will be called upon to reestablish culture after the flood.[125] In the Standard Babylonian version of the *Gilgamesh Epic*, Ziusudra is known as Utnapishtim; he instructs Gilgamesh on the importance of respecting the limits appropriate to humans and urges him to transform his individual quest for immortality into that of a responsible king who strives to maintain the walls of his city Uruk and its sanctuaries and to establish justice (*Gilg*. X:266-322; I:11-23). Nevertheless, the desire to find the key to immortality is addressed by the motif of the plant of immortality, which Gilgamesh obtains but then loses on his return trip to Uruk when a snake devours it (XI:278-309). Gilgamesh must then face the fact that the wisdom that will benefit humans is not that which will remove the limits to human life (X:297-322) but rather a breadth of vision that will respect the place of human life within the hierarchy of the cosmic community (I:1-10).

123. Michalowski, "Adapa and the Ritual Process," 81.

124. Izreʾel, *Adapa and the South Wind*, 134–35, claims that Adapa uses the power of language only when he confronts death (cf. Prov 18:21, where language is seen to possess the power of life and death).

125. Beaulieu, "The Setting of Babylonian Wisdom Literature," in *Wisdom Literature in Mesopotamia and Israel*, 3–19, at 6.

The quest for secret knowledge did not end with Gilgamesh's failure to gain immortality. The diviners and scholars devoted a major portion of their lives to discovering what the gods were planning to do in the near future. The diviners (*bārû*) interpreted omens inscribed on the entrails of animals about to be sacrificed. If employed as a royal adviser, the diviner wielded considerable authority as the expert who could provide an immediate, direct response from the gods to particular questions within the community. As Alan Lenzi has explained, this vertical model of gaining information from the heavenly council contrasted with the horizontal model of the scribes, where knowledge was acquired through the ages, written down, and handed on.[126] The corpus of divination texts began to take shape in the OB period and guided the interpretation of omens inscribed by the gods on the inner organs of animals (i.e., extispicy and hepatoscopy). This corpus of texts gained authority as secret knowledge (*nisirti bārûti*) when the scribes claimed it was revealed by the gods Shamash, Adad, or Ea in antediluvian times.[127] Such privileged knowledge was handed on by the scholarly diviners through the ages.

Four other text corpora took on the character of secret divine knowledge: (1) Texts for teaching the art of exorcism (*āšipūtu*) designated this knowledge as secret wisdom disclosed by Ea.[128] The *āšipūtu* covered a range of functions including magic, medicine, and purification rituals as well as philological and esoteric knowledge associated with these matters. Thus, as Cynthia Jean notes, the translation of *āšipūtu* as "exorcism" can be misleading, particularly if exorcism is narrowly understood as the act of driving out a demon.[129] (2) The texts designated *kalûtu* contained secret knowledge from Ea concerning the art of lamentation or "soothing the heart of a god."[130] (3) The texts for the art of medicine were known as *asûtu*. This secret knowledge in the form of a written corpus was given by Ea to Gula, the goddess of healing.[131] (4) Finally, the corpus of astrological texts, known as *tupšarrūtu*, consisted of the collections of celestial omens titled *Enūma Anu Enlil*, of terrestrial omens titled *Šumma ālu*, and

126. Alan Lenzi, *Secrecy and the Gods: Secret Knowledge in Ancient Mesopotamia and Biblical Israel*, SAAS 19 (Helsinki: Neo-Assyrian Corpus Project, 2008), 121.

127. Ibid., 83.

128. *KAR* 44, rev. 5-13a; Lenzi, *Secrecy and the Gods*, 94.

129. Cynthia Jean, *La magie néo-assyrienne en contexte: recherches sur le métier d'exorciste et le concept d'āšipūtu*, SAAS 17 (Helsinki: Neo-Assyrian Text Corpus Project, 2006), 52.

130. Lenzi, *Secrecy and the Gods*, 96–97.

131. Wilfred G. Lambert, "The Gula Hymn of Bullutsa-rabi," *Or* n.s. 36 (1967): 105–32, at lines 144–46; Lenzi, *Secrecy and the Gods*, 98–99.

of calendrical omens known as menologies and hemerologies.[132] These four corpora plus that of the diviners contained the technical knowledge and wisdom for these five areas of expertise: divination of provoked omens (*bārûtu*), body-mind therapy (*āšipūtu*), medicine (*asûtu)*, lamentation (*kalûtu)*, and divination of unprovoked omens (*tupšarrūtu*). Lenzi argues that the scribes overseeing these corpora claimed that this secret knowledge was given by Ea in antediluvian times to the sages (*apkallū*) and handed on by the scribes through the generations.[133]

The master scribe who was knowledgeable in all five areas of ritual expertise was known as the *ummânu*.[134] In Assyria of the first millennium these *ummânū* came to play an increasingly important role in the royal government, for they "acted as mediators between the gods and the king in order to maintain proper cosmological balance."[135] The numerous ways in which misfortune could beset the kingdom led the king to try to construct a shield against these invisible threats. Assuming that the gods ruled the cosmos, the king employed these scholarly ritual experts in order to learn about bad fates and then to take measures to persuade the gods to change them. The corpus of celestial omens was arranged according to an acrographic principle (i.e., each line begins with the same cuneiform sign or group of signs), which allowed for repeating the protasis to cover as many permutations as possible.[136] For example, in the solar omen "If the eyes of the normal solar disk are closed and it rides the south wind: locusts will devour the land" (*EAE* 24 I:2) the protasis is varied by substituting the north wind as follows: "If the eyes of the normal solar disk are closed, and it rides the north wind: diminution of the herds, locusts will diminish the land" (*EAE* 24 I:3).[137] Then successively the east and west winds are substituted with a different apodosis for each. This effort to cover all the options in this expanding list moved scholars both to think more specifically of options and to be more com-

132. Ibid., 101–2.

133. Ibid., 104–9.

134. Ibid., 68–70.

135. Ibid., 76. See also van der Toorn, *Scribal Culture and the Making of the Hebrew Bible*, 60–61.

136. Erica Reiner, *Astral Magic in Babylonia*, *TAPA* 85, part 4 (Philadelphia: American Philosophical Society, 1995), 62. Stephanie Dalley, "The Influence of Mesopotamia on Israel," in *The Legacy of Mesopotamia*, ed. eadem (Oxford: Oxford University Press, 1998), 57–83, at 74, notes that the great lexical lists were also arranged by category.

137. Translated and edited by Wilfred H. Van Soldt, *Solar Omens of Enuma Anu Enlil: Tablets 23 (24)—29 (30)* (Leiden: Nederlands Historisch-Archaeologisch Instituut, 1995), 18.

prehensive in filling out the list. When an ill omen for the king was recognized, the *āšipu* could use a *namburbû* ("loosening") ritual to try to divert this misfortune. This way of dealing with the gods has been described by Dalley as a form of democratic counsel in which the ritual expert proposes to the gods an alternative fate to the bad one already decreed to try to persuade them to reconsider.[138] By drawing on the wide range of data supplied by the written corpora the scholar was able to bring reflection about past ways of dealing with particular issues to bear on contemporary problems and thus used knowledge to allay anxiety.[139]

The primary responsibility of these ritual experts in the royal court was to protect the king, but they jealously defended their roles against competitors, as illustrated by the following letter of Bel-ušezib, a well-known Babylonian astronomer, to Esarhaddon:

> I am Bel-ušezib, your servant and your dog who fears you [. . .]. Why [did the king, my lord sum]mon prophets and prophetesses w[hen I disclosed] the many [th]ings I had heard in Nineveh, (while) [I, who] blocked the exorcist with my mouth and [we]nt to pay homage to the crown prince my lord, who evaded execution [by fleeing] to the Tower, whose murder along with your servants [was plotted] every day, and who told the omen of the kingship of my lord the crown prince Esarhaddon to the exorcist Dadâ and the queen mother, saying: "Esarhaddon will rebuild Babylon and restore Esaggil, and [honor] me"—why has the king up until now not summoned me? (SAA X 109, lines 7'-16')[140]

Bel-ušezib is not only highly knowledgeable of the omen series *Enāma Anu Enlil* but also has much experience in applying this kind of data to political circumstances. Martti Nissinen notes that Esarhaddon has a high regard for the scholarly tradition of the astrologer and understands its place within Assyrian theology; nevertheless, Bel-ušezib is anxious about his status as an adviser to the king. The potential for falling out of favor was ever present, so it was important for Bel-ušezib to be summoned regularly by Esarhaddon so that he would know where he stood

138. Stephanie Dalley, "Occasions and Opportunities: 1. To the Persian Conquest," in *The Legacy of Mesopotamia*, 9–33, at 20.

139. Van der Toorn, *Scribal Culture and the Making of the Hebrew Bible*, 206–8; Beaulieu, "The Setting of Babylonian Wisdom Literature," 12, 15.

140. Translation: Simo Parpola, ed., *Letters from Assyrian and Babylonian Scholars*, SAA X (Helsinki: Helsinki University Press, 1993), 86, as quoted in Martti Nissinen, *References to Prophecy in Neo-Assyrian Sources*, SAAS 7 (Helsinki: Neo-Assyrian Text Corpus Project, 1998), 89.

with the king. In the complaint he airs in the letter above he reminds Esarhaddon of how he risked his own life for him when Esarhaddon's brothers turned against him as crown prince in 683–681 BCE. Now Bel-ušezib wonders why prophets and prophetesses are called upon as counselors rather than himself.[141] He also refers to the omen predicting that Esarhaddon would rebuild Esagil, Marduk's temple in Babylon, a primary objective in his pacification plan for Babylon.[142] Bel-ušezib notes that he forwarded this omen to the *āšipu* Dadâ, who apparently was expected to clear away any obstacles through intercessions, incantations, and rituals.[143]

While the written works of the extispicist and the celestial diviner have a decided technical character —a foreshadowing of an empirical method—the wide range of functions of the *āšipu* earn him the descriptor "doctor of body and mind."[144] Paul-Alain Beaulieu notes that the *āšipu* uses all forms of knowledge in order to establish a connection with the heavenly realm.[145] The description of these activities is furnished by an NA tablet (*KAR* 44) that has been dubbed the "Vademecum of the Exorcist."[146] This manual of the exorcist consists of three parts, corresponding to the stages of apprenticeship: (1) the *āšipūtu* of Esagil-kin-apli, an *apkallu* of Hammurapi,[147] (2) the *kakugallūtu*, "the exorcism corpus," and (3) the *išippūtu*, "esoteric knowledge."[148] The *āšipūtu* of Esagil-kin-apli are wide ranging, including exorcistic rituals, royal rituals, medical knowledge, incantations, and omen series; also some knowledge of medicine and magic—such as the production of amulets—is required. The *kakugallūtu* deal with *namburbû* rituals that respond to bad omens and with matters of a more cultural nature whose meaning is not yet clear.[149] The *išippūtu* deal with the secrets of the Apsû, noncanonical

141. Nissinen, *References to Prophecy in Neo-Assyrian Sources*, 91–92.

142. A. K. Grayson, "Assyria: Sennacherib and Esarhaddon (704–669 BC)," CAH vol. 3, part 2, *The Assyrian and Babylonian Empires and Other States of the Near East, from the Eighth to the Sixth Centuries B.C.*, ed. John Boardman et al., 103–41 (Cambridge: Cambridge University Press, 1982), at 132.

143. Jean, *La magie néo-assyrienne en contexte*, 132–35.

144. Beaulieu, "The Setting of Babylonian Wisdom Literature," 19.

145. Ibid.

146. Lenzi, *Secrecy and the Gods*, 85.

147. Jean, *La magie néo-assyrienne en contexte*, 62, claims that this reference to an *apkallu* from the OB period is intended to confer the authority of an ancient sage on this NA tablet.

148. Ibid., 72.

149. Ibid., 73–74; Lenzi, *Secrecy and the Gods*, 92–94.

incantations, and other hidden matters; divinely induced medical issues (e.g., paralysis, catatonic states, and muscular maladies caused by "the hand of god x" [*qāt* DN]); and treatments against demons and all illnesses.[150] As an illustration of the ritual activity of the *āšipu*, the following prayer addressed to Ea during the *bīt rimki* (a royal lustration) ritual for the protection of the king highlights the intercessory component of the *āšipu*'s work:

> O wise king, discerning creator, exalted leader, "goosehead" of the Eabsu . . . . The peoples of the land praise your important utterance. You give advice to the great gods. Ea, because of your life-giving incantation, those marked for death do not die. Lift up my head; say the name. In your instructions, may my utterances become known. At your command, may I become prosperous . . . . Ea, through your life-giving incantation, may everything evil, everything unfavorable be put to flight. May the incantation of Eridu loosen the bonds of the sorcerer and sorceress. (Ea 1a, vs. 29-30, rs. 3-8, 15-17)[151]

Enki is the god to whom one turns when one wants a solution to be engineered. His expertise surfaces most clearly in magic, for he knows the secrets of the spirit world and the ways to manipulate these hidden forces.[152]

Knowledge is an important antidote to death. The perception of a reality more enduring than the fleeting forms that populate daily life offers a standing place from which to contribute to the family and community. The pursuit of wisdom by Gilgamesh was a highly individualistic quest, but once the secret wisdom of Utnapishtim was conveyed to him he was ready to return to Uruk to act as a responsible king. But Mesopotamian kings regularly gathered diviners, prophets, and advisers about them so that they might navigate through the dangers that typically confront a king. The art of the diviner was refined into a highly technical skill with areas of specialization. These ritual and scholarly experts aimed to build a sacred canopy around the king in which divine counsel and assistance were regularly sought in order for the king and his land to prosper.

150. Jean, *La magie néo-assyrienne en contexte*, 75.

151. Edition: Werner Mayer, *Untersuchungen zur Formensprache der babylonischen "Gebetschwörungen,"* Studia Pohl, Series Maior 5 (Rome: Pontifical Biblical Institute, 1976), 443–46; see also Foster, *Before the Muses*, 643–44.

152. Samuel N. Kramer and John Maier, *Myths of Enki, the Crafty God* (New York: Oxford University Press, 1989), 100.

The Development of the Role of the Scribe from Recorder to Scholar

Since the invention of writing in the late fourth millennium as an aide to memory, the indispensable role of writing for record keeping has perdured. But apart from administrative purposes, writing, as Laurie E. Pearce notes, served three other main purposes as it developed in Mesopotamia: (1) to assist a performer such as a singer of a balag ("lament"); (2) to aid a teacher who has the students learn to write and become knowledgeable in the cultural tradition by reading texts, taking dictation, and studying texts; and (3) to make intercession through letters to gods, balag's on behalf of the scribe, prayers for success, or other texts as votive offerings.[153] So within the dominant oral culture of Mesopotamia writing began to increase in significance as a mode of communication complementary to speech.

The apprenticeship model for learning to write that arose in the third millennium expanded into the scribal school (E.DUB.BA, "tablet house") in the OB period. The master scribe (*ummânu*) was the entrepreneur responsible for a group of students from the beginning to the end of their education. He was not subject to the palace or the temple. There were no royal regulations regarding subjects or methods of instruction. In the OB E.DUB.BA, students learned four major subjects: language, literature, mathematics, and music.[154] The main activity of the students on a typical day was to prepare, write, and read tablets. The first step was for students to memorize materials and then to commit them to writing. David M. Carr emphasizes that the initial inscription of a text on the tablet of the student's heart through memorization was a significant step in the Mesopotamian educational process; it was a form of enculturation that kept the emphasis on the oral character of the cultural memory and used writing as an aid to memory.[155] Students began with lists (e.g., synonyms, kings, plants, animals) and then moved on to longer texts.[156] The scribal schools that spread throughout the ancient Near East in the second millennium immersed their students in a "stream of tradition" whose content included the belles lettres such as the *Gilgamesh Epic*, the *Myth of*

153. Laurie E. Pearce, "Statements of Purpose: Why the Scribes Wrote," in *The Tablet and The Scroll: Near Eastern Studies in Honor of William W. Hallo*, ed. Mark E. Cohen, Daniel C. Snell, and David B. Weisberg, 185–93 (Bethesda, MD: Capital Decisions Limited, 1993).

154. Laurie Pearce, "The Scribes and Scholars of Ancient Mesopotamia," *CANE* 2265–78, at 2272.

155. Carr, *Writing on the Tablet of the Heart*, 9–13.

156. Wolfram von Soden, *The Ancient Orient: An Introduction to the Study of the Ancient Near East* (Grand Rapids: Eerdmans, 1994), 145–53.

Adapa and the South Wind, and *Atrahasis*.[157] The spread of this scribal culture into the Canaanite sphere is attested by a fragment of the *Gilgamesh Epic* recovered at Megiddo.[158] The students were held accountable not only through a ranking system—"big brother" was highest, and "son of the tablet house" was lowest—but also through the master's key role in placing the scribe in a position on completion of the course of study. The master could also use corporal punishment to keep the students on track.[159] At the end of the OB period the E.DUB.BA ceased to exist and instruction reverted to the apprenticeship model.[160]

Toward the end of the second millennium the scribal school reappeared, but it was attached to the palace and in some cases to the temple. The focus of the curriculum shifted from the humanistic education of the OB period to theological education. This theological dimension became most evident in the second stage of their education in which they took the writing skills acquired in the initial stage and applied them to an area of specialization: divination through provoked omens (*bārûtu*), body-mind therapy (*āšipūtu*), medicine (*asûtu)*, lamentation (*kalûtu)*, and divination through unprovoked omens (*tupšarrūtu*). The scribes who became ritual experts in one of these areas of specialization were primarily practitioners. These skills were not learned simply for theoretical reasons but primarily for sustaining the king and the kingdom.

Competition for high-ranking scribal positions must have been substantial, even though certain scribal families seem to have kept some positions in their grasp for a number of generations.[161] Laurie Pearce estimates that approximately seventy percent of the scribes were employed in administrative work, about twenty percent as private entrepreneurs, and about ten percent in scientific or quasi-scientific activities.[162] As palace administrators the scribes would have kept records, collected taxes, supervised workers, and managed granaries. A privileged few would have assisted the king in his correspondence.

The most powerful among the palace scribes would have been those who specialized in one of the five "theological" disciplines. These ritual

157. A. Leo Oppenheim, *Ancient Mesopotamia* (Chicago: University of Chicago Press, 1964), 13.

158. Aaron Dempsky, "The Education of Canaanite Scribes in the Mesopotamian Cuneiform Tradition," in *Bar-Ilan Studies in Assyriology Dedicated to Pinhas Artzi*, ed. Jacob Klein and Aaron Skaist, 157–70 (Ramat Gan: Bar-Ilan University Press, 1990), at 164.

159. Pearce, "The Scribes and Scholars of Ancient Mesopotamia," 2272.

160. Ibid.

161. Van der Toorn, *Scribal Culture and the Making of the Hebrew Bible*, 60, 62.

162. Pearce, "The Scribes and Scholars of Ancient Mesopotamia," 2273.

specialists were the intellectuals in the royal court and advisers to the king. The model of royal rule that elevated these practical theologians to positions of power emphasized that the gods of the divine council ruled earthly affairs. If the king were to succeed he needed to be attentive to the deliberations that occurred in the divine council. Such deliberations could be learned directly through extispicy and hepatoscopy and through prophecy, but also through celestial and terrestrial omens. Once the will of the gods was discerned, it was important to try to persuade the gods to alter any fates that were unfavorable to the king. Some critics argue that this model of royal rule did not call for political thinking or planning but was merely reactive to threats to the status quo.[163] However, the success of Assyrian kings in expanding their rule throughout the ancient Near East attests that these kings were not blind to the political realities of the people they were ruling in Assyria or to the peoples they conquered. These theological disciplines created a framework in which debate and reflection on political alternatives could occur, but the element of public opinion seems to have surfaced rarely—perhaps only in times of revolt. The authority of the celestial diviners would have been increased by their ability to predict eclipses, planetary phases, and periodicity of various astronomical realities by the end of the eighth century BCE.[164]

The temple workshops (*bīt mummi*) in the first millennium became a locus for scholarly debate as well as for the production of texts.[165] The fact that these workshops were the places in which the cultic statues of the gods were produced and had their mouths opened—i.e., they were sacramentally brought to life so that they could receive food offerings—indicates that the scribes employed here had to have been inducted into a special group that was entrusted with privileged information.[166] The temple scribes were also responsible for developing significant libraries. The temple of Shamash at Sippar had over eight hundred tablets. The scribes were encouraged to donate tablets they had written to the collection. The only borrowers allowed to read the tablets were scholars.[167]

163. Wolfgang Röllig, "Aktion oder Reaktion? Politisches Handeln assyrischer Könige," in *Anfänge politischen Denkens in der Antike: Die nahöstlichen Kulturen und die Griechen*, ed. Kurt Raaflaub and Elisabeth Müller-Luckner, 105–13 (Munich: Oldenbourg, 1993), at 109.

164. Pearce, "The Scribes and Scholars of Ancient Mesopotamia," 2275.

165. Van der Toorn, *Scribal Culture and the Making of the Hebrew Bible*, 63–64.

166. Lenzi, *Secrecy and the Gods*, 132.

167. Van der Toorn, *Scribal Culture and the Making of the Hebrew Bible*, 64.

The rise in significance of the theological disciplines in the first millennium is of a piece with the phenomenon van der Toorn labels "the scribalization of prophecy."[168] On the basis of the shift in the way lexical lists were copied around 1300 BCE, van der Toorn argues that scribes began to copy texts with a reference text in front of them rather than writing the texts from memory and having them checked by a master scribe where the memory of the master was the standard. With this shift toward greater reliance on the written text the variability in traditional texts was minimized. Prior to 1300 BCE there would be no possibility of recovering an *ur*-text to a work such as the *Gilgamesh Epic* because the written text of this literary work had not yet been standardized. But with this new standard of a written text as the reference text, the origin of the written text became important as a way of bolstering the authority of a given text. Thus the scribes contended in most cases that the text was revealed in antediluvian times by the god Enki/Ea to the primordial sages (*apkallū*), who in turn handed it on to the master scribes (*ummânū*).[169] The scribes championed the image of the *ummânū* as an imitator of the *apkallū*. The scribal model of revelation can be described as horizontal: the communication from the gods occurred in primordial times and has traveled through history under the guardianship of the scribes. This model did not eliminate the vertical model of communication with the divine; prophecy and divination still involved direct communication, but even in these areas a corpus of texts overseen by the scribes constituted a check on the kinds of oracles and omens to be given a hearing. Van der Toorn argues that this shift to a scribal model of revelation did not come about in response to a social crisis but rather was a consequence of the rising influence of literacy and the written text.[170]

Adapa was revered as an *apkallu* of Eridu. As an antediluvian wisdom figure created and instructed by Ea, Adapa became in the tradition the patron of the *āšipū*. He was regarded as one who could bring about healing of body and mind. Adapa was never divinized, perhaps because he was not a king. But his divinelike knowledge elevated him above the typical human. As a patron of one of the four theological disciplines, his profile shows how the spoken word bolsters its authority in a tradition that takes on written form. The practical advice of the *āšipu* is regarded as having substance because it is informed by the tradition of the *āšipū* anchored in revelatory knowledge imparted by Enki/Ea. Writing and

168. Ibid., 203.
169. Ibid., 211.
170. Ibid., 217.

the interpretation of writing become increasingly important for communication with the gods and harmony in the kingdom.

Summary

Ludlul bēl nēmeqi describes the crisis into which Shubshi-meshre-shakkan is thrust by the withdrawal of his protector deities as the diminishment of his physical and psychological health, his property, and his place within the community. This catastrophic fall in his fortunes he attributes to Marduk's anger, but then he quickly goes on to speak of being abandoned by his protector deities. The reference to Marduk's devastating anger in the night balanced by his mercy in the morning in the opening hymn of *Ludlul bēl nēmeqi* (I: 4-6) appears to be a second order reflection in which Shubshi-meshre-shakkan comes to recognize Marduk as exercising extensive royal power among the gods. Since Marduk has rescued him from an almost impossible situation he must hold authority over the gods of pestilence, social chaos, and death. Marduk has answered the sufferer's prayer, and so he is to be praised for his mercy. In this poem Shubshi-meshre-shakkan's reflection on the ways of the gods arises out of the context of thanksgiving.

Confrontation with death is also the crisis in the *Myth of Adapa and the South Wind*. Adapa, a primordial *apkallu* from Eridu and the patron of the *āšipū*, uses language to immobilize the wind and so not only upsets the harmony in nature in southern Mesopotamia but also blurs the distinction between humans and gods. Ea, the god of wisdom, wishes for the *apkallu* to have wisdom but not immortality. Anu is ready to confer immortality on Adapa since he regards him as already godlike because of the wisdom Ea bestowed on him. This competition between Ea and Anu over how to deal with humans who have divinelike characteristics shows that there are hindrances to the human pursuit of wisdom that humans are not going to be able to understand readily. In *Ludlul bēl nēmeqi*, Shubshi-meshre-shakkan claimed that the gods hold humans to a standard of conduct they have not revealed to humans and so visit punishments on humans that seem to be undeserved. Adapa is tricked by Ea from gaining immortality; this measure may seem unfair, but Ea was intent on not allowing a human to become a god by simply having divinity bestowed by Anu. Furthermore, Ea would have lost the services of Adapa and, according to Michalowski, would not have channeled the dangerous magical power of language into the institutionalized form of the incantation, with the result that repeated human assaults on the natural order through the magical word would have upset the cosmic order.[171]

The effort to find a solution to death and the key to life is dramatized in Gilgamesh's journey to Utnapishtim. He is instructed by Utnapishtim to return to his station in life as king and to be concerned for others. Rather than trying to escape the human condition, he should try to work within it to improve it and thereby to win an everlasting place in the memory of the culture.

The effort to cope with death is also a preoccupation of the pursuit of wisdom by the scholars associated with the royal court. They have the capacity to write and are competent in one or more ritual specializations that aim not only to understand the plans of the gods but also to communicate and negotiate with them. They assume the fundamental unity of the cosmic community and wrestle with the contradictions and paradoxes that plague human experience. They approach the fact that something is out of place for humans not only by searching for understanding but also by taking action to shield themselves from evils. The divine world in Mesopotamia is monarchically organized but still bears the characteristics of a divine society with a plurality of gods. Some of the problems humans experience may be due to their lack of attention to a particular god. But if that god is Erra, the god of pestilence and famine, then human offerings to appease him are simply efforts to keep this deity from powerfully revealing his presence. The epilogue of *Erra and Ishum* honors Erra and thereby takes steps to keep him from acting (V: 39-61). In the tradition, Marduk joins with Ea as the patron of magic and makes incantations effective against those debilitating forces that plague human life. Thus Marduk achieves henotheistic status by the beginning of the first millennium BCE and is honored even by Assyrian kings such as Esarhaddon and Ashurbanipal, whose primary allegiance is to the god Ashur.[172] The scholarly ritual experts were expected to be concrete in addressing the dangers facing the king, but they also were expected to be comprehensive in constructing what might be termed a "culture of safety": they needed to try to consider every eventuality and to propose a way of dealing with each. The measures taken in dealing

171. Michalowski, "Adapa and the Ritual Process," 81.

172. Wilfred G. Lambert, "Ancient Mesopotamian Gods: Superstition, Philosophy, Theology," *Revue de l'Histoire des Religions* 207 (1990): 115–30, at 121; John A. Brinkman, *Prelude to Empire: Babylonian Society and Politics, 747–726 B.C.* (Philadelphia: University Museum, 1984), 69–73, 86–90.

with bad omens can perhaps be described more as negotiations than as manipulations, although exorcistic rituals have a pronounced magical, manipulative component.

Writing carried an aura for the general population. A corpus of texts that came to be regarded as arising from Ea's realm—the equivalent of descending from heaven in the Israelite context —bore an authority that would lead to its standardization and careful transmission through the centuries. The scribalization of heavenly communications seems to have begun around 1300 BCE. The bearers of this privileged, secret knowledge were scribes. To become a part of the inner circle of scribes or a scholar admitted into the *bīt mummi* ("temple workshop"), one had to be initiated and committed to maintaining a discreet silence about the wisdom entrusted to the scribes. Within this scribal guild, which had regional and international scope, one could advance to a higher social status if all worked well.[173] The art of writing and the pursuit of wisdom complemented one another for the most part, although each could be co-opted by royal power.

Greece: The Embodied Soul in the Search for Truth that Promotes Justice and Happiness

Conflict and disappointment make one painfully aware that one is not alone on this planet and that efforts must be made to find one's place within the larger whole in which life moves. The extent of this larger whole was not limited for the ancient Greeks to what one could see, touch, taste, or feel. Parmenides and Plato spoke of the intelligible, invisible, rational world as true and dismissed the world of change as illusory. In the Platonic model the immortal soul was journeying back to its original home. The context in which one seeks for everlasting life widens through internalization in Plato, but at the cost of devaluing the physical world. Aristotle sees the world as the home for humans but maintains that the road to the happiest life is one that involves a contemplative element. For the ancient Greeks there was a world beyond appearances that contextualized the world of change in which we experience death. So the discipline involved in sexual renunciation might not just be a means for finding happiness in this life but might also be an avenue toward an enduring life beyond death. Texts from Plato's *Republic*, *Phaedrus*, and *Philebus* and from Aristotle's *Nicomachean Ethics* offer information on this Greek pursuit of enduring wisdom. The following three propositions

173. Lenzi, *Secrecy and the Gods*, 160, 214.

will be examined in the Greek materials: (1) In situations of social injustice one searches to understand what constitutes the relational reality of justice and how it might be cultivated. (2) Critical engagement with others over the best way to live creates an environment within which justice can be forged. (3) The breadth of vision required for making practical decisions attentive to the particularities of the individuals and communities at hand requires the cultivation of moral and intellectual virtues by the members of a community.

Plato's Vision for the Rule of Reason in Classical Athens

The trial and execution of Socrates in 399 BCE revealed once again the shortcomings of human efforts to maintain justice in a community. Transferring authority from an aristocratic few to a larger assembly of representatives in the reforms of Ephialtes in 462 may have opened up the possibility of a more rational form of justice to many Athenians, but the process would only be as good as the people who were implementing it (cf. *Rep.* 443d-e). Socrates was committed to the rationality of the rule of law within a community. On principle, he refused to flee from Athens after receiving the death sentence. He contended that the laws of the city had shaped him and become part of him; thus he could not defy them by fleeing (*Crito* 51e-52a; *Apol.* 28e).[174] Even though the implementation of those laws was unjust in his case, Socrates chose to face death. On many occasions Socrates had been a critic of the way the popular assembly operated. He charged that rhetoric had more influence in the public forum than knowledge; thus leaders were more concerned about public opinion than about doing what was right (Plato, *Alcibiades* 119b).[175] Socrates' repeated challenges to the way democratic processes were enacted in Athens stirred his opponents to charge him with befriending tyrants. However, they could not bring this charge against him at his trial because an amnesty had been granted by the assembly to all who

174. Josiah Ober, *Political Dissent in Democratic Athens: Intellectual Critics of Popular Rule* (Princeton: Princeton University Press, 1998), 181; Leo Strauss, *Natural Right and History* (Chicago: University of Chicago Press, 1953), 133–37.

175. Monique Canto-Sperber, "Socrates," in *Greek Thought: A Guide to Classical Knowledge*, ed. Jacques Brunschwig and Geoffrey E. R. Lloyd; trans. Catherine Porter, 745–62 (Cambridge, MA: Belknap Press, 2000), at 751. See Plato's *Seventh Letter* 325c-d. Ober, *Political Dissent in Democratic Athens*, 164, argues that Plato withdrew from active political involvement to consider justice in the abstract because of the corrupt *morēs* of the democratic rulers of his time.

had sided with the Thirty Tyrants—a group who had seized power in Athens from 404–403.

A key factor in the transition from aristocratic to democratic rule in Athens was payment to jurors. In the 460s Ephialtes had arranged for jury pay, with the result that juries of hundreds or even thousands were assembled. The members of the Council (*boulē*) of Five Hundred that prepared materials for the assembly were also compensated. In the fifth century the funds for these payments were drawn from imperial revenues, gained by way of taxes from allies and tribute from subject peoples.[176] In the following decades this practice of paying jurors became so engrained in the Athenian way of government that it not only survived the demise of the Athenian empire but also was extended in 404 to provide pay for those who attended the assembly (*ekklēsia*).[177] In classical Athens only adult males were enfranchised. Of the forty thousand male citizens eligible to vote in the fifth century BCE it seems that only six thousand would have been able to participate, since this was the seating capacity of the Pnyx (the place of assembly).[178] The assembly was limited in its exercise of sovereign power by the practice of the *demes* (villages), of which many were quite influential, and by the tendency of the *boulē* (council), composed mainly of upper-class politicians, to take action without consulting the assembly.[179] Other shortcomings of the Athenian assembly were that it did not meet with enough frequency to develop an effective forum for debate and that it was vulnerable to the ambitions of demagogues like Cleon and Hyperbolus.[180]

Socrates may not have taken a personal interest in participating in Athenian political deliberations. During an elected term of service in the committee of fifty (*prutanis*) he was laughed at for not knowing the procedure for putting a question to a vote in the *boulē* (*Gorgias* 474a); however, Josiah Ober cautions that this "clumsiness" of Socrates in putting a question to vote as *prutanis* should not lead one to the conclusion

176. Simon Hornblower, "Greece: History of the Classical Period," in *The Oxford History of the Classical World*, ed. John Boardman et al., 124–55 (Oxford and New York: Oxford University Press, 1986), at 136.

177. Ibid.; T. H. Irwin, "Plato: The Intellectual Background," in *The Cambridge Companion to Plato*, ed. Richard Kraut, 51–89 (Cambridge and New York: Cambridge University Press, 1992), at 59, 62.

178. Hornblower, "Greece: History of the Classical Period," 136.

179. Ibid., 138–9.

180. Ibid., 139. Ober, *Political Dissent in Democratic Athens*, 200, notes that "the Athenian democracy was predicated specifically upon constructing reality through the social practice of performative speech."

that Socrates had avoided attending the Assembly.[181] Socrates did not hesitate to speak out against actions of the Assembly of which he disapproved. In 407 he opposed the Assembly's punishment of the Athenian generals who had not recovered the corpses of sailors who had fallen in the battle of Arginusae (*Apology* 32b). In 404, when the Thirty Tyrants commanded Socrates and four other citizens to bring Leon back from Salamis in order to execute him, Socrates refused to participate (*Apology* 32d). His sense of justice prohibited him from carrying out such actions; his focus was on what was just and true.[182]

Socrates' passion for truth directed his pedagogical efforts, in which he conversed with young men and challenged them to examine their presuppositions and so come to know themselves. Socrates located the authority of law in the individual decision to behave ethically rather than in the public assembly's collective endorsement of the law.[183] His efforts at urging the youth to become critical thinkers brought them into tension with conventional ways in need of reform. Such tensions stand behind the charges of promoting impiety and corrupting the youth that were brought against Socrates at his trial (*Apology* 40). Socrates' work of teaching the youth in the marketplace outwardly resembled that of the Sophists in the fifth century; their occupation was imparting the skills of rhetoric and logic to youth aspiring to be politicians and entrepreneurs.[184] Socrates' teaching at the edge of the marketplace illustrates that the intellectual in Greek society during the Archaic and Classical Ages had an interstitial character: this social role was in the process of moving from the aristocratic *oikos* to the public sphere of the polis.[185] The intellectual's role as teacher and researcher would take on a more institutionalized form in the fourth century BCE with the founding of Plato's Academy and Aristotle's Lyceum.[186]

Socrates' vision of how a city should be structured in order to promote the best life is presented in Plato's *Republic*, generally considered

181. Canto-Sperber, "Socrates," 747; Ober, *Political Dissent in Democratic Athens*, 194.

182. Ibid., 175; Canto-Sperber, "Socrates," 748.

183. Ober, *Political Dissent in Democratic Athens*, 181.

184. Irwin, "Plato: The Intellectual Background," 65; Ober, *Political Dissent in Democratic Athens*, 167–74.

185. Callicles (Plato, *Gorgias*, 484c) regards the philosopher as an unmanly escapist who flees from the responsibilities of public life and its concern over reputation, contracts, laws, etc.; see Ober, *Political Dissent in Democratic Athens*, 201.

186. Sarah C. Humphreys, *Anthropology and the Greeks* (London and Boston: Routledge & Kegan Paul, 1978), 212, 228, 235, notes that the intellectual countervoice in the politics of Athens also took poetic form in the performance of tragedies and comedies.

one of the middle dialogues (386–367 BCE). Plato (429–347) was born into an aristocratic family: his mother could trace her ancestry to Solon; his stepfather was a friend of Pericles; but his uncles Critias and Charmides were members of the Thirty Tyrants.[187] Plato sets the dialogue of the *Republic* at the home of Polemarchus (a wealthy immigrant executed by the Thirty Tyrants in 404 BCE) in the Athenian port of Piraeus.[188] The participants have just returned from celebrating a festival in honor of the Thracian goddess Bendix.[189] Polemarchus's father, Cephalus, is present in the house, and so Socrates asks him about what it is like to be elderly.[190] Cephalus emphasizes the serenity of old age, which he says is due in no small part to liberation from the sex drive. He claims that

> With regard to these desires and those within the household, there is only one cause, Socrates—not old age, but the people's character. If they are well-ordered and content, old age is moderately painful. But if not, Socrates, both old age and youth are difficult for such matters. (*Rep*. 329d)

In Cephalus's opinion liberation from the sex drive is even more important for one's serenity in old age than a sufficiency of money.[191] But Socrates probes further and has Cephalus admit that he had inherited his wealth and so was more detached from it than one who had worked hard to gain it (*Rep*. 330c). Cephalus claims that a distinct advantage of having wealth is that one can avoid cheating humans or shortchanging the gods in terms of offerings and so can have a clear conscience as one approaches death and the judgment of one's life (*Rep*. 330e-331b). Cephalus's piety is calculating. He is motivated by fear rather than by love (*erōs*) of the true and the good and thus blameworthy in the Socratic

187. Julia Annas, "Plato," in *Greek Thought: A Guide to Classical Knowledge*, 672–92, at 672; Irwin, "Plato: The Intellectual Background," 59.

188. Martha Nussbaum, *The Fragility of Goodness: Luck and Ethics in Greek Tragedy and Philosophy*, rev. ed. (Cambridge: Cambridge University Press, 2001), 136; Ober, *Political Dissent in Democratic Athens*, 215, notes that the port city of Piraeus was well known for its diverse population of metics and traders and its strong democratic ethos.

189. Robert Parker, *Athenian Religion: A History* (Oxford: Clarendon Press, 1996), 170–75.

190. Martin Ostwald, "Athens as a Cultural Centre," in CAH, 2d ed., vol. 5: *The Fifth Century B.C.*, 306–69, at 308, notes that Cephalus was a wealthy industrialist from Syracuse whom Pericles convinced to move to Athens, where he lived for thirty years.

191. David Roochnik, *Beautiful City: The Dialectical Character of Plato's Republic* (Ithaca, NY: Cornell University Press, 2003), 4, argues that a key question of the *Republic* is how a city is to deal with *erōs*.

world, even though Socrates does not directly challenge Cephalus on this point.[192]

The primary issue Socrates pursues with his interlocutors in the *Republic* is a definition of justice.[193] Cephalus offers an initial definition formulated by the lyric poet Simonides (ca. 556–468 BCE): one is just when one tells the truth and gives back what one has received. Socrates questions the second part of the definition by way of a counterexample: Should a person return a weapon to someone who has become deranged in the meantime? Cephalus acknowledges this weakness of his working definition (*Rep*. 331c-d). A second proposal is offered by Polemarchus: a just man is one who helps his friends and harms his foes (*Rep*. 332a). Socrates counters that this definition seems to come from a rich man and points out that harming an enemy diminishes a person's excellence. In this respect vengeance does not promote justice (*Rep*. 335e).

At this point (*Rep*. 336b) Thrasymachus, a sophist from Chalcedon near the Bosphorus, enters the conversation with a bluster and tries to subvert the elenchus by wanting Socrates to provide an answer to Socrates' own question rather than to point out repeatedly how the definitions offered by others are inadequate. Socrates listens to Thrasymachus and skillfully keeps him engaged in the dialogue.[194] Thrasymachus offers the controversial definition that justice is nothing but the advantage of the stronger. He claims that a shepherd-ruler makes decisions for his own advantage rather than for those he rules. Thrasymachus wants to leave at this point, but Socrates persuades him to stay and explain why he thinks the unjust man is better than the just man (*Rep*. 345b). In the course of their exchanges Socrates finds that Thrasymachus is arguing that injustice is "strong and beautiful" and has "all the qualities that we used to attribute to the just" (*Rep*. 349a). Thus Thrasymachus contends that "the unjust man is intelligent and good, the just man is not" (*Rep*. 349d). But Socrates then leads him by a series of questions to come to the opposite conclusion: "that the just man turns out to be wise and good; the unjust man bad and ignorant" (*Rep*. 350c). Socrates goes on to make

192. Darrell Dobbs, "The Piety of Thought in Plato's *Republic*, Book 1," *American Political Science Review* 88 (1994): 668–83, at 672. Julia Annas, *An Introduction to Plato's Republic* (Oxford: Clarendon Press, 1981), 20, notes that Cephalus's ethics are merely external: do the right actions with no attention to the spirit in which they are done; he dismisses Socrates' questions that would force him to think about his ethics.

193. Richard Kraut, "The Defense of Justice in Plato's *Republic*," in *The Cambridge Companion to Plato*, 311–37.

194. On Socrates' skill in keeping Polemarchus engaged in the inquiry see Dobbs, "Piety of Thought in Plato's *Republic*," 673.

the point that injustice causes discord with others and inner conflict for the unjust man (*Rep*. 352a). With Thrasymachus cornered, Socrates then ironically makes the gracious move of commending Thrasymachus for his generous participation in the discussion and accuses himself of having strayed off track from the question of "what is justice?" such that they are now no closer to a definition. In moving Thrasymachus to acknowledge the merit of an opposing position in the dialogue Socrates illustrates the importance of dialectic for shedding light on complex realities like justice that elude definition.[195]

Glaucon then poses the question whether there is "something good that we receive in order to embrace for its own sake rather than to possess for its consequences—for example, joy and pleasures that are harmless and from which nothing arises other than their enjoyment" (*Rep*. 357b).[196] He then varied this combination of an object's attributes of being good-in-itself or of having good consequences by asking about things that are not only good in themselves but also bring good consequences—for example, thinking, seeing, health. A third variation would be that the things are not good in themselves but bring good consequences—examples include exercise and earning a living. Then Socrates claims that he thinks justice belongs to the second combination: both good in itself and in its consequences. But Glaucon counters that the selfless behavior of the just person is rare and contends that greed will move the just as well as the unjust to try to acquire more if the opportunity presents itself (*Rep*. 360c-d). Glaucon contends that the unjust man will recognize that it pays to cultivate the appearance of being just; therefore the unjust man will offer sacrifices and give gifts so that he is regarded as just, even though he remains an unjust man. Adeimantus, a brother of Glaucon, then builds on this argument and claims that wandering priests and soothsayers offer sacrifices with promises that such actions will bring the offerers happiness in the next life (*Rep*. 364c).[197] They use quotations from Homer and Hesiod to claim that the gods can be manipulated by sacrifices (*Rep*. 364de-365a).

At this point the line of argument shifts because Adeimantus and Glaucon want to see what impact justice and injustice actually have on the soul of the individual (*Rep*. 367a-e). Socrates is pleased with the way

195. Roochnik, *Beautiful City*, 5–6.

196. Roochnik, *Beautiful City*, 56, notes that Glaucon's sustained questioning of Socrates is an illustration of the *erōs* driving the philosopher.

197. Parker, *Athenian Religion*, 55; Robert McGahey, *The Orphic Moment: From Shaman to Poet-Thinker in Plato, Nietzsche, and Mallarmé* (Albany, NY: SUNY Press, 1994), 20–21.

they present their counterargument. Socrates then proceeds to make his case by drawing an analogy between the three parts of the soul and the three parts of the citizen-body of the polis. The average citizen will try to maximize the goods he or she can acquire; the surplus will then call for auxiliaries (i.e., a military group) to defend it; then, to protect the soldiers from preying on one another and the other citizens there will need to be guardians entrusted with responsibility for the well-being of the whole. Socrates claims that all three citizen-types (citizen-at-large, auxiliary, and guardian) will be exhorted to be temperate and courageous. With regard to temperance he makes the case that proper love will be directed toward order and beauty and will have nothing to do with sex (*Rep*. 403a-b). Those who raise and educate children by means of poetry and gymnastics in this ideal city will be on the lookout for those individuals who seem to be unmoved by either fear or pleasure, for these have the potential to be auxiliaries or guardians (*Rep*. 413d-e). These potential auxiliaries or guardians are to be told a noble lie: that they were not born from humans but rather from the earth (*Rep*. 414c-e). This has the advantage of tying them to the soil of Athens so that they will defend it with all their being. But it also keeps them from looking to their parents as the ones to whom they belong. These youth are to be raised in common (*Rep*. 457d). Likewise, there is to be no private property for the auxiliaries and guardians so that they keep their attention focused on the good of the whole city and are not tempted toward individual gain (*Rep*. 416d-e). By testing the youth to see if they have the proper detachment from fear and pleasure and by prohibiting them from owning property and being part of a family structure the guardians of the city will be taking steps to minimize the potential of its auxiliaries and guardians to turn from being sheepdogs into wolves (*Rep*. 416a).[198] These guardians and auxiliaries will gain their happiness from a sense of being important contributors to the well-being of the whole of which they are a part. This concern for the well-being of the whole—that is, justice—has as its corollary the happiness of those who promote the well-being of the whole (*Rep*. 420b-c). Socrates notes with regard to these three classes (citizens-at-large, auxiliaries, guardians) that care must be taken to place the rightly endowed individuals in each category (*Rep*. 434a-435b).[199]

198. Ober, *Political Dissent in Democratic Athens*, 223, 228.
199. Roochnik, *Beautiful City*, 44.

Socrates constructs the analogy that just as there are three classes in the city, so also there are three parts to the soul.[200] He says that we can know that these parts exist by reflecting on the experience of feeling thirsty but refusing to allow oneself to take a drink. Here the rational part of the soul (*to logistikon*) exercises control over the desiring or lower part (*to epithumētikon*). The middle part of the soul—the spirited (*thumeides*)—exists to defend the soul against outside enemies; it is the part of the soul from which ambition issues.[201] Harmony reigns in the soul when the desiring and spirited parts agree to submit to the rule of the rational part (*Rep.* 442d). The emphasis in Books 5–7 of the *Republic* is the control of *erōs*.[202] Just as there is justice in the city when each of the three classes tends to what is proper to it, so also there is justice or harmony in the soul when its three parts do likewise. In the ideal city the citizens should have as their first order of business the maintenance of harmony in their own souls, and then they will be able to contribute this harmony to the well-being of the city as they carry out their proper functions (*Rep.* 443d-e).[203]

Socrates is convinced of the justice of the underlying world order in which the realities that truly exist are governed by the good (*Rep.* 508e-509a).[204] As narrated in Plato's *Apology*, Socrates claimed that no one can harm the just person (30c-d). The goodness the just person imitates and in which he or she participates establishes the just one in such a way that no one can take away this goodness. Socrates was convinced that the soul of Socrates—the real Socrates—would remain untouched by the

200. Ellen Wagner, "Introduction," in *Essays on Plato's Psychology*, ed. eadem, 1–32 (Lanham, MD: Lexington Books, 2001), at 6–13. John M. Cooper, "Plato's Theory of Human Motivation," in *Essays on Plato's Psychology*, 91–114, at 93, promotes the view that the rationale for the three parts of the soul is more solidly grounded in fact than the three classes in the city. However, Roochnik, *Beautiful City*, 26, 39, 62–64, argues that the soul acts as a whole and not as three parts; therefore the tripartite view of the soul must be set in tension with a unitary view of the soul as a passionate desire for truth.

201. Cooper, "Plato's Theory of Human Motivation," 107.

202. Roochnik, *Beautiful City*, 44. Nussbaum, *The Fragility of Goodness*, 206, 216, understands Socrates to be saying in the *Republic* that the freer the *logistikon* is from the other elements, the better will be the condition of the soul. She notes that such a sharp distinction between calculation and desire does not describe how the pursuit of wisdom, a quest fired by love, will occur.

203. Jonathan Lear, "Inside and Outside the *Republic*," in *Essays on Plato's Psychology*, 169–201, at 187.

204. Plato contends that the gods are always good (*Euthyphro* 6b). See Thomas Gould, *The Ancient Quarrel between Poetry and Philosophy* (Princeton: Princeton University Press, 1990), xv, xx; Nussbaum, *The Fragility of Goodness*, xv.

hemlock. His soul was already participating in the pure, stable realm of truth that existed beyond the appearances of things.[205] Socrates' mission was to engage others in this pursuit of truth and love of wisdom with the result that justice would emerge in this dynamic process of souls trying to find their proper place within the cosmic order. In his probing of the presuppositions of his dialogue partners Socrates brought the group into a quandary (*aporia*) about defining matters such as virtue, piety, and justice—realities about which they had assumed they had an adequate understanding (*Meno* 84a-c; *Euthyphro* 11b; Rep. 350c).[206]

Keeping the dialogue partners engaged was fundamental to Socrates' teaching method. Plato, who wrote the dialogues about Socrates, tried to capture the dynamic of engaging the audience by his invention of the genre of the dialogue. Socrates claims in the *Phaedrus* that writing distorts the search for truth because it keeps readers from using their memories (275a). Plato records this position in the context of a dialogue so that his own more positive assessment of the potential of writing can be examined.[207] Thus the written dialogue can engage a reader to use reason to examine his or her presuppositions in the search for truth just as a written tragic play can move a reader who becomes caught up in the action of the plot to experience fear and pity through empathy with the tragic characters. But such poetic engagement differs from that of critical reason. Plato banishes the tragic poet from his ideal city because he wants his citizens to use the highest parts of their soul, basing their actions on the truth and justice of the world order rather than engaging the lowest part of the soul by feeling pity for one another as victims of an unethical world order; in such a case their emotions cloud their perception of what is real (*Rep*. 398a, 598e-599b).[208] But as David Roochnik explains, Plato counters his condemnation of poetry in Books 8–9 of the *Republic* by using narrative and imagery to describe tyrants and other rulers from the types of regimes (548a, 553c, 559d-e); therefore he argues

205. Kraut, "The Defense of Justice in Plato's *Republic*," 327.

206. Charles H. Kahn, *Plato and the Socratic Dialogue: The Philosophical Use of a Literary Form* (Cambridge: Cambridge University Press, 1996), 180.

207. Ibid., 293, 372, 380, 388; Charles L. Griswold, Jr., *Self-Knowledge in Plato's Phaedrus* (New Haven: Yale University Press, 1986), 7, 13, 223–24.

208. Gould, *The Ancient Quarrel between Poetry and Philosophy*, xvi–xix, 11, 29–32; Nussbaum, *The Fragility of Goodness*, 30, 130. Dorothea Frede, "Disintegration and Restoration: Pleasure and Pain in Plato's *Philebus*," in *The Cambridge Companion to Plato*, 425–63, at 450–52, notes that Plato in the *Philebus* understands emotions to be mixtures of pleasure and pain that are disturbances of the soul; tragedies and comedies further exacerbate this disharmony in the soul.

that a dialectic between the logical mode of philosophy and the mythical mode of poetry operates within the dialogue of the *Republic*.[209]

In the Socratic-Platonic world disorder enters one's life through lack of knowledge. The remedy is the pursuit of truth and the love of wisdom. Socrates criticized the shortcomings of the democratic process but engaged passionately in educating the young to be critical thinkers.[210] This capacity to follow the line of argument and yet keep in view a larger context in which this discussion is unfolding is a positive consequence of valuing truth over rhetoric. For Socrates, winning a debate is not as important as recognizing the limits of what one knows. This effort of individuals to speak honestly to one another stabilizes competing elements within the polis. Even though the effort to define justice did not result in an acceptable definition, the dialogue contributed to the enlightenment of the participants about the dynamic within the city that promotes justice. The main lesson to be drawn from Socrates' way of teaching is that the process of pursuing justice is as important as achieving it, which means that justice itself diminishes in a static environment. An important consolation for the person who follows Socrates and values truth for its own sake is that one cannot be deprived of the good in which one participates. The "fixed point" in the Socratic world is the belief in a rational, ethical world order.

The Socratic-Platonic Educational Process

Socrates claims that knowledge of an object is clear, unchanging, and certain. He notes that many people see beautiful things, but the one who loves wisdom wants to perceive the beautiful itself. Socrates and his conversation partners agree that the lover of wisdom is the one who sees "the beautiful itself and the things that participate in it" and in doing so is wide awake and not dreaming (*Rep*. 476d). As humans we live in this world of shadows and are summoned to gain knowledge of the true, the good, and the beautiful. This process of gaining knowledge is described by Socrates through three metaphors; this figurative way of speaking reveals that he is tentative in speaking about the true, the good, and the beautiful out of reverence for their transcendent character (*Rep*. 506b-e; 509b). Even if logical discourse could unfold the mysteries of

209. Roochnik, *Beautiful City*, 94–104.

210. Ober, *Political Dissent in Democratic Athens*, 162–64, claims, on the basis of Plato's Seventh Letter, that Plato became disillusioned with the democratic regime at the execution of Socrates.

such fundamental realities, such an approach would be rhetorically ineffective (cf. *Phaedrus* 246a, 247c-e).

The first metaphor is that of the sun. If we stand before an object we cannot see it unless we have light. So also if we try to know an object, our minds need to be enlightened by the good. Socrates states the matter as follows: "The good begot the sun as an analogue to itself: i.e., as the good in the sphere of intelligible things is to reason (*nous*) and to the objects of reason, so is the sun in the sphere of visible things to sight and the objects of sight" (*Rep*. 508c).[211]

Socrates' second metaphor is that of the divided line (*Rep*. 509d-511e). The lower, proportionally shorter part of the line represents the world of sense experience; the upper part represents the world of the mind. Socrates then divides the lower part into two segments corresponding to the way objects are perceived by the senses: the lowest part is the image of something, such as an artist's drawing of a horse; the next

Divided Line

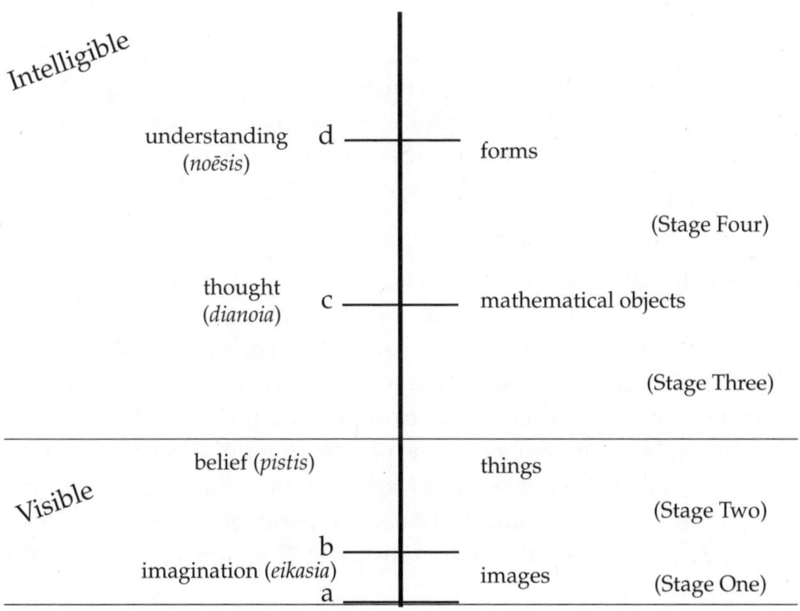

211. Edition: Paul Shorey, *Plato, The Republic* (Cambridge, MA: Harvard University Press, 1935), 102.

higher part is the object (i.e., the horse) as perceived by the senses. Because the perception of the horse directly by the eye or indirectly by the image created by an artist can change, the perceiver has not really grasped the essence of the horse. His sense perception of the horse is a combination of "what is" and "what is not" horse (*Rep*. 514b-c). To move to knowledge of the horse that is everywhere and always the same, the perceiver must "see" with the mind (*Rep*. 516b). So the person desiring to know moves to the upper part of the line, which is also divided into two segments. According to the lower part of this upper segment the mind thinks with the aid of images. This is illustrated by the way a geometer works when he uses figures such as triangles, rectangles, and diagonals in trying to grasp the form of an object (cf. the curriculum in *Rep*. 521c-535a).[212] The higher part of this upper segment of the line uses no images but is occupied with examining assumptions by means of the dialectic. For example, Socrates' effort to understand justice began with the working definitions of his interlocutors. Together they examined these definitions and tried to reach the essence of justice.[213] Socrates summarizes the process of knowing communicated by the four segments of the divided line as follows:

> Now corresponding to these four segments take four conditions that occur in the soul: align reason with the highest, understanding with the second, trust with the third, and imaging to the last. Arrange them proportionately, because to the extent that the object partakes of truth, each of these conditions partakes of clarity. (*Rep*. 513e)[214]

A key factor in the perception of truth is whether the object perceived is unchanging. If the object changes, it participates in "what is" and "what is not" and does not belong to the world of forms or eternal essences. Socrates reveals his concern to transcend the reality of death when he focuses his search on finding that which is unchanging and certain—characteristics of knowledge and truth that are free from death.[215]

Socrates' third metaphor for the process of coming to know the good is typically labeled the allegory of the cave. In an underground cave a group of individual humans have been imprisoned since birth in a stationary position facing the wall of the cave. These prisoners are unable

212. Roochnik, *Beautiful City*, 27, 35.

213. Kahn, *Plato and the Socratic Dialogue*, 157–64; Irwin, "Plato: The Intellectual Background," 68–70.

214. Edition: Shorey, *Plato, The Republic*, 116.

215. Roochnik, *Beautiful City*, 40, 120; Kahn, *Plato and the Socratic Dialogue*, 384–85.

Cave

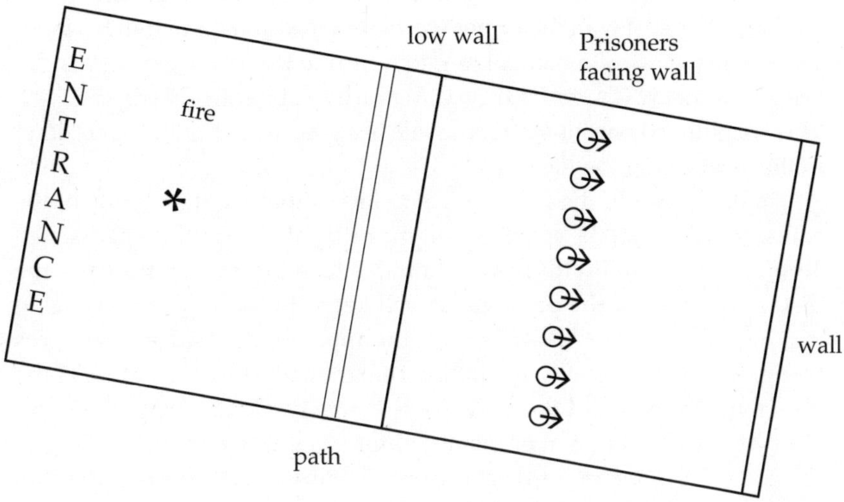

to turn their heads, but they can hear what is happening elsewhere in the cave. There is a low wall behind the prisoners with a walkway on the other side of it, and there is a fire beyond the walkway. Workers in the cave carry objects above their heads as they move along the walkway. Images of these objects are reflected on the wall in front of the prisoners by means of light from the fire. The prisoners confirm with one another the reality and differences of the images that are repeatedly paraded before them. For them these images are the actual objects. Then Socrates speculates on what would be the response of one of the prisoners if he were released and shown the objects. Socrates contends that the prisoner would resist this new knowledge; and if he were taken up the walkway leading out of the cave into daylight, his eyes would adjust to the bright light only with difficulty. Out of the cave, he would in time come to see the earthly things themselves and the heavenly bodies (i.e., the unchanging Forms). Eventually, he would also be able to catch glimpses of the sun and come to realize that it is "the one which provides the seasons and years and is the governor of all things in the visible sphere and somehow the cause of all those things that he used to see" (*Rep*. 516c).[216] Once he had seen this true realm he would pity the prisoners still in the cave, and on returning there he would

216. Edition: Shorey, *Plato, The Republic*, 126.

not participate in their games of identifying the images they see projected on the wall. The prisoners would be hostile toward this enlightened one who has returned from the upper world (*Rep*. 517a). The enlightened one would prefer to stay in the upper world, but it would seem that his inner sense of justice would compel him to return to the lower world to try to bring the other prisoners up the pathway to the upper world (*Rep*. 520b-c). This enlightened one illustrates the role of a guardian or philosopher-king in the ideal city of the *Republic*.[217]

In Books 5–7 of the *Republic*, Plato insists that the three parts of the soul—the desiring, the spirited, and the rational—are to be kept distinct. To mix the rational with the irrational is to subject the rational to the distorting effect of the passions, which keeps the soul from advancing to the realm of truth.[218] Plato regards the appetites as blind animal forces that grasp for an object with no discernment regarding the nature of the object. In Books 5–7 of the *Republic* he contends that the appetites tend to go to excess and have no potential for a cognitive understanding of the good. The way forward is to suppress the irrational parts of the soul so that the rational part (*logistikon*) can move toward the apprehension of truth.[219] The educational project of the city will be to turn "the eye of the soul" upward toward the good by disciplining from earliest childhood the appetites that would otherwise turn the soul downward (*Rep*. 518c-519b).

In the *Phaedrus*, however, Plato emphasizes that passion has a positive role to play in the pursuit of truth and the love of wisdom. In contrast to *Rep*. 398a-b; 598a-604a, where poets were regarded as creating images that were three degrees removed from reality (602c)—that is, at stage one rather than stage four of the divided line—poetry in the *Phaedrus* is regarded as a gift of the gods and valuable for education.[220] The *Phaedrus* opens with two speeches that denounce mania and praise self-control (*sōphrosynē*).[221] These anti-erotic speeches have the character of apotropaic speech-acts that wish to silence a potential source of inner chaos: they function like magical incantations that have a psychological impact. This drive toward a more stable, reliable inner harmony is of a piece with the confrontation with death; it is based on the soul's success in controlling

217. Roochnik, *Beautiful City*, 31, 56, 74–75; Nussbaum, *The Fragility of Goodness*, 138–41.

218. Roochnik, *Beautiful City*, 13–20, 90.

219. Nussbaum, *The Fragility of Goodness*, 206.

220. Ibid., 201.

221. Ibid., 203–4.

its desire for the material world so that it might rise upward to its true home.[222]

The picture in the first two speeches of the *Phaedrus* advocates the silencing of the bestial elements of the person so that the intellectual element can freely seek the truth.[223] But Plato places these two speeches first in order to counterpoint them. In the *Phaedrus*, Plato reimagines the human soul as a fevered entity in constant motion in which its impure elements have the potential to aid the soul's rise toward beauty.[224] The human soul, like the divine soul, is a self-moving entity.[225] The configuration of this self-moving entity is similar for gods and humans: a winged charioteer guides two winged horses. The difference between the human soul and the divine soul is that one of the horses in the human soul is evil (*Phaedrus* 246b; 253d-e).[226] This evil horse impedes the ascent of the human soul to heaven. By contrast, the souls of the gods rise effortlessly into the world of forms—such as temperance, justice, and courage—which they gaze upon and from which they derive nourishment. As the cosmic sphere revolves, the gods return to their place in the cosmos at the appropriate time and put their horses in the stable to rest (247b-c). By contrast, the human soul wrestles with a team of horses who work against one another. The charioteer is unable to keep the good and the evil horse working together with the result that the motion downward to the material sphere wins.[227] The inner turmoil in one soul clashes with

222. David A. White, *Rhetoric and Reality in Plato's Phaedrus* (Albany: SUNY Press, 1993), 40.

223. Nussbaum, *The Fragility of Goodness*, 206, 216.

224. Ibid., 216; Josef Pieper, *Enthusiasm and Divine Madness: On the Platonic Dialogue Phaedrus*, trans. Richard and Clara Winston (South Bend, IN: St. Augustine's Press, 2000), 75–76.

225. Douglas Blyth, "The Ever-Moving Soul in Plato's 'Phaedrus,'" *American Journal of Philology* 118 (1997): 185–217, at 210, notes that the reality of soul includes not only gods and humans but also plants and animals.

226. White, *Rhetoric and Reality in Plato's Phaedrus*, 88–90, 104–5, explains how the analogy of the soul with the charioteer and two horses does not map in a one-to-one fashion onto the tripartite soul of *Rep.* 443e; desire in the charioteer model is integral to the self-moving soul but has within the human soul an ineradicable rebellious element in the evil horse.

227. Ibid., 104, 112–13. The charioteer's breaking the wing of a horse immobilizes it and so seems to be analogous to the Mesopotamian sage Adapa's breaking the wing of the wind (*Adapa*, Frag. B 1-7); breaking a wing symbolizes a participation in death. In the *Epic of Anzu* (III: 6-15), Ninurta defeated the thunderbird Anzu, immobilizing it by cutting his pinions and robbing its faculty of speech of its power; see Erica Reiner, "The News of Victory," in *Your Thwarts in Pieces, Your Mooring Rope Cut*, 61–67, at 64.

other souls and the consequence is that the wings of the majority of the souls are broken before they can even glimpse the realities in the heavenly sphere (248a-c).[228] This struggle within the soul is part of its nature; the evil horse is present prior to the embodiment of the human and is ineradicable. The key task for the charioteer is to discipline the evil horse so that it goes along with the soul's desire to mount upward rather than sink downward (249c-e).[229]

Some human souls rise higher than others. Plato gives the following list, beginning with those who have seen more of the world of Forms and then moving toward those who have hardly seen anything: the philosopher, the lawful king or warlike warrior, the politician or businessman, the gymnast or doctor, the prophet or mystagogue, the poet, the craftsman or husbandman, the sophist or demagogue, and finally the tyrant (*Phaedrus* 248d-e). A primary reason that the soul of the philosopher rises higher than the others is that he is possessed of a madness that comes from seeing beauty on earth that then triggers his memory of the true beauty of the world of forms he had seen in a previous existence. "Whenever he sees something beautiful and remembers the true beauty, he feels his wings grow and longs to fly upward, but he is unable to do so; and looking upward like a bird, he neglects the things below" (*Phaedrus* 249d). The one who is possessed by this madness is called a lover. Only a few are able to move into this state because it requires a strong memory of the Forms from the previous world. But even those lovers of wisdom privileged to experience this madness do not understand their condition. The experience of sprouting new wings triggered by the perception of beauty is agonizing. This new vision of the ascent of the soul toward knowledge in the *Phaedrus* describes a creative interplay between poetry and philosophy in which the soul is not merely an active agent as in the *Republic* but also is receptive.[230]

As embodied souls, humans perceive beautiful objects that trigger a memory of its Form that it looked upon in its previous existence.[231] Often such a beautiful object is another human to whom one is attracted (253d-254e). Socrates says there is a warm glow that flows through the

228. White, *Rhetoric and Reality in Plato's Phaedrus*, 113, notes that the rivalry between disembodied human souls is due to a fundamental desire to get a closer view of reality.

229. Ibid., 97, 104.

230. Nussbaum, *The Fragility of Goodness*, 227.

231. Blyth, "The Ever-Moving Soul in Plato's 'Phaedrus,'" 193, 207, 211, notes that the soul's primary relation to the Forms generates *erōs* such that there is an ongoing erotic striving in the generation of the cosmos (cf. *Symp.* 201d-212c).

charioteer. The good horse reacts with modesty to this attraction, but the evil horse stirs carnal desire and tries to wear down the resistance of the charioteer and the good horse. But the charioteer remembers the true beauty of the Form and its relationship with the other Forms and the good, and fears following the urges of the evil horse. A fierce struggle ensues in which the charioteer must repeatedly subdue the evil horse through the bit in its jaws. The evil horse reproaches the charioteer for breaking a previous agreement in which there would be a place for carnal pleasure within the life of the soul. But the charioteer becomes more enlightened by his memory of the Forms and alters his attitude toward that agreement with the evil horse. Eventually, after severe discipline, the evil horse submits to the charioteer and fears to react carnally with the sight of the beloved (254e). If the lover and beloved are guided by love of wisdom in their friendship, they will avoid physical consummation of their love.[232] They are guided and strengthened by memory of the Forms—however fragmentary and episodic their knowledge of these Forms might be. Without this contact with the Forms, the lover and the beloved may live chastely out of a sense of duty but will occasionally lapse in times of weakness (256b-d). Socrates argues that those guided by wisdom will be happier and will return to their heavenly home after three one thousand-year cycles rather than ten (249a). The lover of wisdom experiences erotic attraction, struggles with it, but avoids acting on it by attentiveness to the true realities ordered by the Good that enable him to persuade the unruly horse within and so bring a working equilibrium to his soul.[233]

The way in which perception of the Good influences one's understanding of pleasure and knowledge is addressed in Plato's *Philebus* 23b-27c.[234] Here Plato explains that the Good manifests itself when an unbounded entity (*apeiron*) is subjected to a boundary (*peras*): for example, music is created when indeterminate sound—which can be high,

232. Helene P. Foley, "'The Mother of the Argument': *Eros* and the Body in Sappho and Plato's *Phaedrus*," in *Parchments of Gender: Deciphering the Bodies of Antiquity*, ed. Maria Wyke, 39–70 (Oxford: Clarendon Press, 1998), at 49, 68–69, notes that in the *Phaedrus* (255a-256a) the lover and beloved take mutual responsibility for the development of the relationship in contrast to the hierarchical model dominant in the tradition.

233. White, *Rhetoric and Reality in Plato's Phaedrus*, 165, 172.

234. John M. Cooper, "Plato's Theory of Human Good in the *Philebus*," in *Reason and Emotion: Essays on Ancient Moral Psychology and Ethical Theory* (Princeton: Princeton University Press, 1999), 150–64, at 150; Nussbaum, *The Fragility of Goodness*, 150.

low, slow, or fast—is subjected to numerical ratios.[235] Pleasure and knowledge are each comprised of both the bounded (*peras*) and the unbounded (*apeiron*). Thus the experience of pleasure and of knowledge can be explained as the imposition of ratios on entities that would otherwise be indeterminate.[236] The ratios in dialectics and higher mathematics produce pure knowledge in contrast to the mixed knowledge of the applied sciences (*Philebus* 55c).[237] Pure pleasure is something that is enjoyed for its own sake and not because it is a release from pain;[238] thus the experience of clear musical tones, pure colors, and learning would be forms of pure pleasure in contrast to the energizing experience of having completed a five-mile run. Plato contends that to properly appreciate pleasure one must situate it within the larger system of pleasures.[239] So if one has never experienced the pure pleasures of sense and intellect, that person will be prone to overtax the lower forms of pleasure in order to find life satisfying.[240] In light of the tripartite character of the soul, Plato recognizes that the fully satisfying life cannot be achieved only by pure pleasures and pure knowledge; the mixed forms of these realities have their place within the well-ordered life (*Philebus* 61e 7-9).[241]

There is a slight, but significant shift in the Socratic-Platonic educational model in the later dialogues of the *Phaedrus* and *Philebus.* Here pleasure receives a more positive assessment and is not simply grouped with the appetites.[242] Thus the experience of beauty is acknowledged as

235. Cooper, "Plato's Theory of Human Good," 151. Frede, "Disintegration and Restoration," 435, 456, notes that pleasures are judged almost from a scientific or medical point of view.

236. Cooper, "Plato's Theory of Human Good in the *Philebus*," 151; Seth Bernadette, *The Tragedy and Comedy of Life: Plato's Philebus* (Chicago: University of Chicago Press, 1993), 143.

237. Cooper, "Plato's Theory of Human Good in the *Philebus*," 155–56.

238. Ibid., 156.

239. Bernadette, *The Tragedy and Comedy of Life*, 152, notes that Socrates shapes his argument on the principle of symmetry: "there has been a match between the measurer and the measured . . . as when we fill a cup to the brim. Man the measure coincides with the pleasure of man."

240. Cooper, "Plato's Theory of Human Good in the *Philebus*," 158; Bernadette, *The Tragedy and Comedy of Life*, 153.

241. Cooper, "Plato's Theory of Human Good in the *Philebus*," 159; Frede, "Disintegration and Restoration," 427, 441.

242. Nussbaum, *The Fragility of Goodness*, 154, criticizes Plato's ascetical stance in the *Phaedo* and *Republic* as follows: "Most of us, again, do not pursue sexual activity merely as a source of release from a painful tension; it is connected with other complex ends such as friendship, self-expression, and communication; there are reasons why most of us do

pleasurable and is identified as a key element in the philosopher's quest for truth. The experience of earthly beauty—for example, the form of the human body—can trigger a memory of beauty itself as perceived by the soul in a previous existence unencumbered by the body. This memory can then be experienced as madness—a strong form of energy that can move the philosopher along the pathway toward the truth. The view of knowledge and pleasure as sharing a common structure as ratios of the bounded and unbounded opens the way toward appreciating the significance of pleasure in the harmonious soul.

The contemplation of beauty is vital to the restless striving toward harmony. The quest for wholeness cannot be achieved by ignoring the desiring part of the soul or putting it to death. This desiring part of the soul manifests erotic energy that moves a person to try to participate in the beautiful it has perceived. Because harmony can be achieved only in communion with the good, this quest for wholeness will always be incomplete during earthly life. A fundamental step in the quest is to keep expanding one's attention to the sea of beauty rather than seizing prematurely on one beautiful object and expecting that possessing or being with this instance of beauty will sustain life. Also, embodied objects subject to diminishment will move one to search for a more stable, enduring level of reality. However, glimpses of the beautiful will bring pleasure that will inspire one to keep searching. This pleasure in the soul can be seen as the imposition of bounds on the unbounded; by contrast, fluidity produces pain. Pure pleasures such as enjoying a beautiful choral performance or viewing the nighttime firmament are not sufficient to bring harmony to humans in their embodied existence. Lower pleasures are also required, such as eating a good meal or completing an exercise routine—pleasures that in part consist of release from hunger or exhaustion.

To become educated and formed by the beautiful requires that one search for and be receptive to the beautiful as manifested in its various embodiments. This wideness of vision can be created and sustained only by attending to all three parts of the soul: desiring, spirited, and rational. A passionless existence is premature death; a life guided by pleasure is mired in objects and activities that weigh down the soul and keep it from the communion with the good for which it is destined. The experience of beauty, truth, and goodness on the pathway inspires and nourishes

not take the option of becoming eunuchs. The *Republic* seriously underestimates the complexity of our appetitive nature when it ignores the aesthetic side of appetitive activity and the complex connections between such activity and other valuable ends."

the soul. The activity of searching for the Good is one that promotes harmony in the soul and justice in the community.

Aristotle: The Wise Ordering of Desire in the Rational Animal

On the issue of how to deal with the realities of misfortune or luck, Aristotle takes an approach compatible with that of the tragic poets. He accords a positive value to passion in the well-ordered life and so sees a creative interplay between poetry and philosophy akin to that in Plato's *Phaedrus* and at odds with the battle between poetry and philosophy staged by Plato in the *Republic*.[243] A key question for Aristotle in describing the well-ordered life is the extent to which the good human being is a passive recipient (i.e., a receiver of what one desires) as well as an active agent.[244] Aristotle found the tradition inadequate in dealing with the fact that a human is a self-moving animal: that is, humans are so constituted that they move toward entities outside themselves because they stand in need of an external thing or person.[245]

Although Aristotle was a student of Plato, his approach toward the world is shaped by his interest in biology and not by mathematics as was Plato's.[246] This attention to particular organisms in their immediate environment made Aristotle critical of theories that reduce the richness of particular entities in order to emphasize an overarching category: for example, the Socratic definition under which many particulars are subsumed, mechanistic explanations of living beings, or materialist explanations of the mind.[247] Aristotle can be characterized as an empiricist. However, his empiricism is not preoccupied with quantifiable data as is the empiricism of modern science but with attentiveness to the way things appear to the careful observer. The reality beyond appearances that is secured through instrumentation and computational models in

243. Ibid., 237. Gould, *The Ancient Quarrel between Poetry and Philosophy*, 83, notes: "In Jung, as in Aristotle, nature, dreams, and the 'lowest' part of the psyche are no longer considered the enemies of morality and rationality; they are expressions of nature at its most unerringly rational."

244. Nussbaum, *The Fragility of Goodness*, 238.

245. Plato, *Phaedrus* 245c5-9: "All soul is immortal. For that which is always moving is immortal." Blyth, "The Ever-Moving Soul in Plato's 'Phaedrus,'" 197, notes that Socrates contends here that "soul is responsible for whatever existence the whole cosmos has."

246. John Hermann Randall, *Aristotle* (New York: Columbia University Press, 1960), 61–63; David Roochnik, *Retrieving the Ancients* (Malden, MA: Blackwell, 2004), 160; Nussbaum, *The Fragility of Goodness*, 238–40.

247. Ibid., 259.

modern science is not part of Aristotle's functional world.[248] He sees organisms interacting with one another within a larger environment, a dynamic that can be observed as it reaches to the cosmic level.

In reflecting with his friends as to why he was sitting in prison prior to his execution, Socrates made clear that he was in prison because he had accepted the fact that the Athenians with the assistance of their laws had decided to condemn him. His sitting there was due to deliberation and choice and not to the mere movement of his bones and muscles, as if he were simply a chance configuration of air, earth, water, and fire as Empedocles had theorized (*Phaedo* 98c-99c). Nussbaum claims that by focusing in this passage from the *Phaedo* on rational decision making and overlooking forms of intentionality that a physiologist would attribute to perception and desire, Plato draws a clear distinction between humans and other animals. He groups animals with nonsentient, nondesiring entities that are simply acted upon by their environments. He draws a sharp distinction between actions initiated by the intellect and all other actions. Because he ignores actions initiated by perception and desire he sees little difference between the motions carried out by animals and the motions of processes like those of the digestive tract.[249] By contrast, Aristotle regards both physiological and psychological forces as constitutive of the human (*De Anima* 433a10-433b31).[250]

When Aristotle describes the human as a rational animal he respects the capacity of the senses to perceive reality. Reason works with the data supplied by the senses. In terms of the embodied character of the human, Aristotle sees that bodily appetites (*epithumia*) have a vital role to play in the life of the human along with the spirited component (*thumos*) and the rational judgment (*boulēsis*). Aristotle identifies a common motion in all three components: a "reaching out" (*orexis*, *De Anima* 433b12-25).[251] He posits that there is an element in humans and other animals that can be described as the "desiring part" (*orektikon*, *EN* 1102b31). It is this element that is at work when a human or an animal perceives an object and

248. E.g., for Aristotle, the form of an eye is the capacity to see; this function is the form of the eye rather than its oval shape (*De Anima* 412b11-22). This emphasis on function pervades Aristotle's teleological view of nature; see Steven Everson, "Psychology," in *The Cambridge Companion to Aristotle*, ed. Jonathan Barnes, 168–94 (Cambridge: Cambridge University Press, 1995), at 185; see also Randall, *Aristotle*, 65–67.

249. Plato, *Theatetus* 154a, 184c-186c; *Rep.* 436a-438d; Nussbaum, *The Fragility of Goodness*, 272.

250. John M. Cooper, "Some Remarks on Aristotle's Moral Psychology," in *Reason and Emotion*, 237–52, at 241, 247; Everson, "Psychology," 168, 179, 192–93.

251. Cooper, "Aristotle's Moral Psychology," 239.

then desires it (*EN* 1102b29-1103a3).[252] The remaining factor in whether the human or animal acts to secure the object is the judgment of whether it is possible to do so or not. Adults, whose characters have been formed, are able to choose (*proairesis*) whether or not to pursue a desirable object. So Aristotle understands human desire to be influenced by external objects but not determined by them (*EN* 1139a31-1139b5). In our lack of self-sufficiency we are oriented toward external objects, but we are not simply pushed and pulled by them.[253]

To live a good human life demands that a person be attentive to the particularities of the persons and things around one. *Phronēsis*, "practical wisdom," is a form of deliberation attentive to the human good rather than to the good in itself (*EN* 1141a31-32). Aristotle says: "So it appears then that a prudent person (*phronimos*) is able to deliberate well concerning matters that are good and useful to himself, not according to a part—e.g., what is for health or for strength—but what is for the good life as a whole" (*EN* 1140a25-28). This capacity to make good judgments depends on one's character—shaped through one's upbringing and virtuous action—and attentiveness to the specific good required for a particular time and place. For Aristotle there are knowable absolutes, such as the prohibition of adultery in order to safeguard the integrity of the family (*EN* 1107a9-19). He is not a relativist who doubts the human capacity for objective truth. In the realm of politics and ethics Aristotle claims that the laws of a city in accord with its "way of life" (*politeia*) serve as guides that allow one to tap the wisdom of the community and to counter one's biases (*EN* 1181b7-24).[254] So attentiveness to the particular entity is a priority that cannot ignore the patterns and categories that structure human experience in a particular community. Nussbaum contends that for Aristotle the way to develop better laws is not to search for harder, transcendent standards but rather to work within the concrete human context.[255] The person who cultivates the virtues will be trying to strike a balance between competing inner tendencies. The more one lives virtuously, the better one will be able to make good judgments (*boulēsis*) and decisions (*proairesis*), which are key components of *phronēsis* (*EN* 1141b6-16).

Aristotle advises that one cultivate virtues that reduce or eliminate troublesome passions. The means reason has for controlling nonrational desires is not only to point out bad consequences but also to try to per-

252. Nussbaum, *The Fragility of Goodness*, 273–75.

253. Ibid., 289.

254. Strauss, *Natural Right and History*, 136–37.

255. Nussbaum, *The Fragility of Goodness*, 304–5.

suade the desires to recede.[256] Desires that become well-trained can in turn help reason in making proper choices. In other words, according to Aristotle the passions are "intelligent and educable."[257] Furthermore, virtuous action requires an element of passion. So, for example, to contribute grudgingly does not qualify as a virtuous action. Yet on the other hand there is a risk in listening to the passions, for it may lead to an excessive, misdirected effect that will undermine one's life. So it is a matter of trying to balance competing tendencies and doing so in light of the circumstances before one. The person who is practically wise would not want to do away with the appetites or dissociate from them entirely (*EN* 1119a6-10). It is essential for a human to recognize that he or she has needs. Then one's attention can be focused on the most appropriate way to meet those needs. To try to be a human without hunger, thirst, or sexual needs would be to place oneself outside human society.[258]

Aristotle's attention to practical wisdom and to the particularities of human situations as the way to live the good human life is crowned in the tenth chapter of the *Nicomachean Ethics* with his acknowledgment of the important role contemplation plays in the happy life (*EN* 1177a6-19; 1177b17-26; 1178b7-8, 28-32).[259] Commentators have puzzled over how Aristotle's high valuation of theoretical activity fits together with his previous emphasis on the practical development of virtue. Cooper argues that Aristotle sees the cultivation of the range of virtues described in chapters three through six as fostering stability and peace so that a person can carry on theoretical activity.[260] This theoretical activity is valuable in itself apart from any further good it might produce. The one who engages in this form of contemplation is engaging the rational faculty, which is the best or most godlike element within humans. This contemplative activity is pleasant and fulfilling; thus the one who does so is happy. Aristotle contends that this contemplative activity is the most virtuous action humans can undertake because it brings to perfection the rational element within.[261]

256. Cooper, "Aristotle's Moral Psychology," 245.

257. Nussbaum, *The Fragility of Goodness*, 309.

258. Ibid., 309.

259. John M. Cooper, "Contemplation and Happiness: A Reconsideration," in *Reason and Emotion*, 212–36, at 216; Nussbaum, *The Fragility of Goodness*, 374–75.

260. Cooper, "Contemplation and Happiness," 217.

261. Ibid., 226.

Aristotle accords emotion a more positive role in the search for truth than Plato allowed. Plato's recognition of the importance of passion in the search for truth in the *Phaedrus* steps in the direction of a reconciliation between the poetic work of the tragedians and that of the philosopher (*Phaedrus* 251a-e, 256b-e),[262] but Aristotle takes this even further by embracing the capacity of the tragic play to disclose important truths about the human condition (*Poetics* 1450b3-7, 1452a1-20). Aristotle adopts the tripartite components of the Platonic soul—the desiring, spirited, and rational components—but he sees the soul as the form or activity of the living body. The survival of the capacity for rational thought (i.e., the active intellect, *De Anima* 430a10-25) after death is the only remnant of the immortal soul from Plato, but the individuality of the person does not continue in the disembodied active intellect. This Aristotelian attention to the mind-body unity accords with his biological functionalism, in which he aims to see the human person in the living environment of which it is a part. Aristotle emphasizes the practical reason of a person that is attentive to the particularities of the context in which one is operating (*EN* 1140b20-30). This attention to particularities is nevertheless operating out of the conviction that the world is purposefully organized (*EN* 1140b5-8). Theoretical or contemplative activity reveals this larger whole in operation and can help a person to make more informed judgments. Nevertheless, such contemplative activity bears its own reward in the happiness it bestows on the person who contemplates.

Summary

Plato is the rationalist who regards the real as rational.[263] He experienced the chaotic conditions in late-fifth-century Athens in which the Peloponnesian war was lost; the shift from democracy to tyranny and back to democracy indicates the disruption of normal life at that time. It is not surprising, then, that Plato imagines an ideal city ruled by philosopher-kings, that is, those best able to lead. His definition of knowledge as unchanging and certain manifests his belief that it transcends death. This search for knowledge moves one from a dream world to wakefulness. In this search unruly desires, such as sex, are to be controlled

262. Nussbaum, *The Fragility of Goodness*, 122-24, 214-18.

263. Frederick Copleston, *History of Philosophy*, vol. 1: *Greece and Rome* (Westminster, MD: Newman Press, 1960), 196, notes: "That the real is rational is a presupposition of all dogmatic philosophy, but it does not follow that the whole of reality can be rationalized by us." See also White, *Rhetoric and Reality in Plato's Phaedrus*, 69.

or suppressed so as not to impede rational activity.[264] Plato's educational model lends itself to the ascetical practice of celibacy. However, in his ideal city he does away with marriage and the family in the guardian class and proposes a discreetly administered program of social engineering in order to procreate and nurture children (*Rep*. 451c-461e).[265]

Aristotle is the moderate realist who regards the world of appearances perceived by the senses as real.[266] As an immigrant from Macedonia, Aristotle views Athens as a political unit with diverse parts. He does not think the city should be structured as if it were one large family that was replacing the natural families. His respect for diversity in the sociopolitical realm is probably also influenced by his work as a biologist, one who attends to organisms in their particularity and in their diverse living contexts. So also with humans; individuality is to be respected when proposing the cultivation of virtue, that is, the gifts and potential of individuals are to be engaged but not prescribed from a preexisting pattern. Aristotle defines humans as rational animals. The principle of movement of humans and other animals comes from within: they are self-moving organisms. The initiator of this movement is identified by Aristotle as desire (*orektikon*). Desire is a reality that threads its way through the appetites, to the spirited or courageous aspects of the person, and finally to the rational. This desiring element can be educated. By contrast, Plato regards appetites as nonintellectual forces that are no more educable than the movements of the digestive tract; therefore Plato believes the appetites must be channeled by the rational part of the soul. However, Aristotle believes that the energizing dimension of passion—an emotion arising from the lower, appetitive part of the soul—must be engaged if a person is to develop authentic virtue. At the center of virtuous activity is a balancing act between competing tendencies: for example, to be either cowardly or brash misses the intermediate, balanced response of courage. Virtuous activity promotes justice and affords happiness.

Aristotle is a thinker who has his feet firmly planted on the earth. Death is a natural reality for humans to accept rather than to try to transcend. Aristotle's attention to the animal dimension of human existence and to the particularities of individual humans is in accord with his view of death as natural. He can accept change as an integral part of human existence and not as evidence for decay or illusion. Although Aristotle

264. Nussbaum, *The Fragility of Goodness*, 158, 164.

265. Ibid., 159; Copleston, *Greece and Rome*, 235–37.

266. Diogenes Allen and Eric O. Springstead, *Philosophy for Understanding Theology*, 2d ed. (Louisville: Westminster John Knox, 2007), 115.

calls for a disciplined life in which the passions are to be kept in check, he would have no place for celibacy or the suppression of the sexual drive. He champions marital fidelity and family life (*Politics* 1261b17-1262b26).

Plato's tripartite view of the soul in the *Republic* provides a model for the discipline of celibacy. The skeptical view of the unruly appetites and the goal of subjecting the appetites and the spirited parts of the soul to the rational would be in accord with the discipline of celibacy. But what is even more helpful for the discipline of celibacy is the creative, transformative role of reason. The control of the appetites is not an end in itself; it is a discipline that allows the rational element—the true element of the soul and person—to develop. This reasoning activity lifts the person toward the true, the beautiful, and the good. Harmony in the individual soul is an essential element in the harmony of the sociopolitical body, a Platonic view Aristotle espouses. Aristotle values contemplative activity as the crown of all the virtuous activities and one that brings the rational animal to perfection. He regards the educational process as one that brings balance to potentially unruly appetites through virtuous activity, whereas Plato in the *Republic* advocates the elimination of such unruly appetites—a view he modifies in the *Phaedrus*. The models of Plato and Aristotle both call for discipline and rigor, but Plato's has an intensity that arises from battling against death. Aristotle regards the world as eternal, whereas Plato sees the virtuous soul as one that is about to take flight into the higher realm of truth.

Synthesis. Celibacy: Death to Oneself and the Rise of the Common Good

A crisis typically triggers survival instincts. When the cause of the crisis is not easily known, a response must be developed that will allow the individual or the group to regain a sense of agency. Jeremiah is a bellwether for the Judahite community that is about to suffer massive destruction and exile. His announcement of the imminence of this catastrophe will provide a basis from which the survivors can begin to make sense of what has happened to them. Jeremiah's symbolic action of celibacy as ordered by YHWH is part of this prophetic announcement of YHWH's judgment against Judah. The prohibition against having a family who will carry on one's name and physical line puts a death sentence on Jeremiah that would typically mean the complete extinction of a person. Jeremiah will not have the consolation of the type of immortality that comes from living on in his descendants. Celibacy is a form of dying to oneself that runs contrary to the basic family values of the Israelite tradition. The placement of this command in Jeremiah 16 in the context of his five confessions accents Jeremiah's sense of confusion and anger at what YHWH is causing him to endure.

In Mesopotamia in the late second millennium the royal official Shubshi-meshre-shakkan writes in *Ludlul bēl nēmeqi* of his experience of losing his wealth and health and suffering ostracism by his friends, family, and community. His confrontation with death, which he attributes to abandonment by his protector deities, leads him to cry out to the gods in deep confusion. Marduk rescues him and heals him at a point in his illness when no one gave him a chance.

Plato confronted death in the sociopolitical unrest of the late fifth century, which was a factor in the development of his picture of the ideal polis. His experience of the absence of justice in the city led him to advocate a three-class system for his ideal city in which the philosopher-kings ruled over the citizens and the soldiers. By analogy, in the soul of each citizen reason would rule over the desiring and spirited parts. This capacity of reason to rule depended on education in which the soul came to look upon the essences of things and persons and to advance toward the good.

Language distinguishes humans from animals. It is a power that makes humans like the gods. Adapa's pronouncing that the wing of the South Wind be broken points to the power inherent in the word. This word of Adapa may have been empowered by the magic of an incantation; alternatively, this powerful word may reveal the potent structure of language itself that humans often take for granted. In the questions Socrates posed to his interlocutors that assisted them in revising their presuppositions and looking at their worlds differently, he showed them the power of the word to connect the human thinker with the invisible world of truth.

This perception of a world of truth in which the essence of everything is organized under and participates in the good is fundamental to a worldview that believes the order of the cosmos is ethical. The belief in such an ethical world order is called into question by Jeremiah, Shubshi-meshre-shakkan in the *Ludlul*, and by tragic poets like Aeschylus, Sophocles, and Euripides.

The crucible in which Jeremiah was tested by YHWH forced him to cry out and to cling to YHWH's words of response to him. His dialogue with YHWH resulted in increasing pressure throughout his confessions, but it was precisely the words from YHWH that gave him hope—he was like a tree planted by a flowing stream (Jer 17:8). Gilgamesh sought for a way out of the human condition and pressed this challenging quest to the ends of the cosmos, where he crossed the waters of death. But there he received wise counsel directing him to forfeit his individualistic quest and go back to Uruk to serve as a responsible king who promotes justice.

The attentiveness to words of wisdom and life from a transcendent source guiding Jeremiah, Shubshi-meshre-shakkan, and Gilgamesh also sustains Socrates as one who believes that no one can harm him as long as he has been good, that is, that he has united his soul to the good through virtuous actions. The Socratic-Platonic quest to discover truth and be transformed by it finds an analogue in the citizen of Yehud who meditates on the torah of Psalm 119. This lifegiving teaching forms a sphere within which one's life can be joined to the life of YHWH by means of the divine word. This *šālôm* of YHWH that encompasses the pious psalmist is analogous to the reality the scholars in the Assyrian royal court sought for the king when they aimed to create a shield around him from all evil forces and to bring the benevolent ones to his assistance. Access to this divine word in the Israelite and Mesopotamian traditions was altered with the writing down of the tradition. The objectification of the divine word had the potential to communicate this word as a symbol but also ran the risk of co-opting the word and turning it into an idol. So the "scribalization of revelation" in Mesopotamia around 1300 BCE and thereafter has an analogue in the writing of the Torah in seventh-century Judah and thereafter. In fourth-century Athens, Plato wrote Socrates' oral encounters with his interlocutors in the form of dialogues and so engaged readers in assessing their presuppositions rather than in simply looking for secret knowledge that would deliver them from the human condition.

YHWH's command to Jeremiah to be celibate was not an isolated pronouncement. It was a directive that was of a piece with the plan of placing Jeremiah in a crucible so that his heart might be freed from secondary attachments and trust wholeheartedly in YHWH. This goal of union with YHWH through his word and the cutting away of all other forms of support is distinctive to the Israelite tradition. There is an emphasis on Marduk's word for the healing of Shubshi-meshre-shakkan, but it does not carry the intensity of the dialogue between Jeremiah and YHWH. Marduk is a god in a polytheistic system, whereas Jeremiah is directed toward worship of YHWH alone. This sustaining relationship with YHWH recontextualizes the life of celibacy. It is not simply a negation; instead it is a choice for an intense devotion to God rather than for an intimate relationship to a spouse and family—which also is a way toward union with God. In Plato and Aristotle the contemplative life points to this sustaining power of the word from the transcendent realm.

Chapter Seven

Communion with the Real: The Goal of Celibacy

Alienation is a salient feature of the human condition. Things are out of joint. So the question becomes how to deal with the alien forces in the environment and within our very selves. We can make a disciplined effort to try to control those forces inimical to human life such as viruses, noxious insects, and predatory animals and to shield ourselves from others that elude our mastery such as droughts, violent weather, and aging or the march of time. Many of the remarkable technological achievements of the modern era have been fueled by oil, coal, and fossilized remains that are limited in supply and threaten to destabilize the global climate. So the reality of limits to what human ingenuity can achieve without destroying itself reappears with vengeance. The wisdom of the story of the Garden of Eden reasserts itself. There is something fundamental that is out of alignment in the human community. We humans are not able to fix this on our own because such autonomous action over against the life and environment that have been given for our use is at the heart of the problem of alienation. Genesis 2–3 states that human failure to acknowledge the sovereign authority of YHWH resulted in a separation from his presence. This expulsion from his Garden meant that humans' relationship to the soil, to animals, to one another, and even to their own bodies would be problematic. The only remedy would be the restoration of God's presence.

The goal of celibacy is to come into communion with the divine and human inhabitants of the cosmic household. The matrix of relationships within the household is the place in which alienation is most keenly felt and is also the place in which harmony will be realized. Divine assistance and presence are essential to this harmony. The discipline of celibacy exists to call upon such divine presence and to symbolize that the matrix of household relationships that will overcome human alienation is the matrix of the cosmic household rather than that of the various human ones. The celibate serves as an intermediary between the cosmic and human households and symbolizes that the human family finds the source and fulfillment of its love—whether *erōs*, *agapē*, or *philia*—in the love of the divine cosmic family. Celibate love stands together with and serves married love in their mutual goal of upholding the matrix of family relationships—most immediately in their particular human families but at the same time in the enduring matrix of relationships of the cosmic family. This chapter will address these complementary ways of love within a household according to the following two topics: (1) the heterosexual love uniting a man and a woman with the ultimate aim of producing offspring is a sacramental action in which the divine presence creates and sustains the matrix of relationships in the household. (2) The forms of sexual renunciation continuous with and giving rise to celibacy in the cultures of ancient Israel, Mesopotamia, and Greece prior to the Hellenistic period testify—as shown in this study—that such renunciation arises from and is grounded in the enduring matrix of relationships that forms the cosmic household.

Erotic Poetry and the Encounter with the Divine

Erōs can be defined as a lack or need within a human being that carries within it the impetus to satisfy this need. So *erōs* is a human drive that projects outward. This erotic drive can manifest itself in work—an activity that Genesis 2 asserts is constitutive of human nature. One of the strongest manifestations of *erōs* is in sexual relations. Genesis 2:24 claims that this drive within man and woman to form one flesh is constitutive of human nature. This heterosexual attraction of humans was an established part of life in the Garden prior to the transgression of eating the fruit of the tree of the knowledge of good and evil. This primordial community of man and woman was an action taken by God to respond to the need of the earth creature for companionship. God judged that the Garden he visited from time to time in a humanlike way and that was populated with animals was insufficient for human well-being. This primal human appears to be a genderless, sexless being who may have had the potential to live forever. But Gen 2:18 says that God judged otherwise and made plans for a human community that was to be reproduced through sexual relations. Sexual relations between a man and a woman were regarded as integral to a Garden that was to be home for a human community. Was God's first action in creating a sexless, genderless human a mistake? Or was God's second step of creating the woman from the original earth creature to be seen as a constructive alternative, but nevertheless one that had not been God's first choice?

The primal human would seem to have been engaged in gardening as work and enjoying the garden by eating its fruit and residing among its flora and fauna. Such would have been the erotic experience (i.e., the reaching outward to commune with the environment) of this primal human. The addition of sexual relations to this creature's erotic repertoire would seem to have been an enhancement of its existence. Genesis 2:21-22 makes it clear that God took the initiative in creating woman and introducing sexual relations into the Garden. But in Genesis 3 the story shifts to the complications that arise from having a human community rather than simply a human being. The interlude between the creation of the woman and the complications arising from a human community must have been a time of harmony in which communication between the man and the woman on all levels of their persons—linguistically, somatically, psychologically—worked. It is in this interlude in the Garden that the erotic love celebrated in the Song of Songs may be said to belong.[1]

The erotic love celebrated in the Song of Songs does not speak directly about God's presence in the midst of that love. However, generations of readers in the Jewish and Christian traditions have interpreted this erotic encounter of the lovers as revealing powerful dimensions of the divine-human relationship. In the following two sections the sacramental character of this love and its capacity to reach beyond the bounds of death will be examined in light of texts from the Mesopotamian and Greek traditions that address these same concerns of uniting with the divine and overcoming the limitations of mortal existence.

The Evocative, Sacramental Character of Erotic Love in the Song of Songs vis-à-vis Mesopotamian and Greek Parallels

The confident, joyous affirmation of the goodness of erotic, romantic love between man and woman in the Song of Songs is unique in the Old

1. Othmar Keel, *The Song of Songs*, trans. Frederick Gaiser (Minneapolis: Fortress Press, 1994), 31–32; David M. Carr and Colleen M. Conway, "The Divine-Human Marriage Matrix and Constructions of Gender and 'Bodies' in the Christian Bible," in *Sacred Marriages: The Divine-Human Sexual Metaphor from Sumer to Early Christianity*, ed. Martti Nissinen and Risto Uro, 275–303 (Winona Lake, IN: Eisenbrauns, 2008), at 281; Gary A. Anderson, *The Genesis of Perfection: Adam and Eve in Jewish and Christian Imagination* (Louisville: Westminster John Knox, 2001), 44, 53.

Testament.[2] The majority of biblical writings express a cautious concern about the potential of *erōs* to go to excess and transgress sacred boundaries. For example, the preoccupation with preserving the premarital virginity of young women and with monitoring genital emissions (Leviticus 15) to keep intact the bodily wholeness of the members of the community emphasizes how this sexual code deliberately intruded into the daily lives of the people to keep them mindful of the boundary between the sacred and the profane. In the Song of Songs, however, such cultic and social anxieties are almost completely absent.[3] There are a few places where the lovers express an awareness of social strictures on the expression of their love (Song 1:6; 5:7; 8:8-9), but then quickly their fascination with one another drowns out these anxieties and allows them to be caught up in the joy of the present.[4] In the peak moments of this romantically charged world of the lovers the world in all its sensuous diversity achieves a harmony and communion that approximates paradise—a return to the primeval Garden.[5] This erotically charged, sensuous union of the lovers that brings them into harmony with creation would also seem to bring them into communion with God. Such a sacramental participation in the divine life through the sexual union of man and woman may be hinted at in Song 8:6 where love is described as *šalhebetyâ*, "the flame of YHWH."[6]

2. Keel, *Song of Songs*, 5, 17, identifies the Song of Songs as a collection of love poems, not by a single author, dating to a time between the eighth and sixth centuries BCE with an origin in the Northern Kingdom of Israel. J. Cheryl Exum, *Song of Songs*, OTL (Louisville: Westminster John Knox, 2005), 66, notes that proposals for dating the Song range from the eighth century to the second century BCE and no study has yet given a specific date for any individual part or parts of the collection.

3. Ibid., 68.

4. Ibid., 9–10, 25–26.

5. Patrick Hunt, *Poetry in the Song of Songs: A Literary Analysis*, Studies in Biblical Literature 96 (New York: Peter Lang, 2008), 103–6; cf. Martti Nissinen, "Love Lyrics of Nabû and Tašmetu: An Assyrian Song of Songs?" in *"Und Mose schrieb dieses Lied auf." Studien zum Alten Testament und zum Alten Orient: Festschrift für Oswald Loretz zur Vollendung seines 70. Lebensjahres mit Beiträgen von Freunden, Schülern und Kollegen*, AOAT 250, ed. Manfried Dietrich and Ingo Kottsieper, 585–634 (Münster: Ugarit-Verlag, 1998), at 618.

6. This word is a *hapax legomenon*, otherwise rendered as "a raging flame" (NRSV) or "a blazing fire" (NAB). Roland Murphy, "Dance and Death in the Song of Songs," in *Love and Death in the Ancient Near East: Essays in Honor of Marvin H. Pope*, ed. John H. Marks and Robert M. Good, 117–19 (Guilford, CT: Four Quarters Publishing, 1987), at 118, notes that if *šalhebetyâ* means "flame of YHWH" it is the only reference to God in the Song of Songs and would indicate a connection between divine and human love.

If this form of erotic, sexual love between man and woman holds this potential for communion with God, then for a celibate to deliberately refrain from such erotic activity for a lifetime would seem to be a rejection of a privileged means of access to God. The Jewish tradition, as Daniel Boyarin points out, takes the position that sexuality is a gift to be fully enjoyed in the upbuilding of the community.[7] However, the early Christian writer Ephrem advocated a celibate way of life by his appeal to the priestly figure in Eden who was charged with upholding the purity of the sanctuary.[8] This priestly figure in Eden in Ezek 28:12-13 can be identified with the earth creature in the better-known Eden story in Gen 2:7; this figure forms the common ground from which male/female and masculine/feminine emerge and from which they can never divorce themselves. Sex and gender are distinctions within the unity of humanity.[9] If so, this earth creature provided a model of the human wholeness God had first created and so could be appealed to as a model that had priority in time. But if a celibate is to forego the heterosexual erotic love modeled in Genesis 2, he or she should be aware of the positive potential of this expression of *erōs* to bring humans into communion with the divine.

The Song of Songs is love poetry that invites its readers to observe the intimate exchange of lovers. Although, as Cheryl Exum points out, there is a voyeuristic element in this observing, the experience escapes the pejorative aspect of such a label by engaging its readers in the full realization of this intimate love.[10] The lovers are always clothed in metaphors and never exposed as naked bodies to the dispassionate gaze of an onlooker as in cruder forms of erotica.

7. Daniel Boyarin, *Carnal Israel: Reading Sex in Talmudic Culture* (Berkeley: University of California Press, 1993), 6, n. 11, states: "the near-universal privileging of virginity, even for Christian thinkers who valorize marriage, produces an irreducible difference between that formation and rabbinic Judaism, for which sexuality and procreation are understood as acts of ultimate religious significance and for which virginity is highly problematic."

8. Ephrem *Hymns* 3.16-17; Gary A. Anderson, "Celibacy or Consummation in the Garden? Reflections on Early Jewish and Christian Interpretations of the Garden of Eden," *HTR* 82 (1989): 121–48, at 143–45; idem, "The Cosmic Mountain: Eden and Its Early Interpreters in Syriac Christianity," in *Genesis 1–3 in the History of Exegesis: Intrigue in the Garden*, ed. Gregory A. Robbins, 187–224 (Lewiston, NY: Edwin Mellen, 1998), at 207–8; Thomas Buchan, "Paradise as the Landscape of Salvation," in *Partakers of the Divine Nature: The History and Development of Deification in the Christian Traditions*, ed. Michael J. Christensen and Jeffrey A. Wittung, 146–59 (Madison, NJ: Fairleigh Dickinson University Press, 2007), at 149.

9. See chap. 5 above.

10. Exum, *Song of Songs*, 22–24.

The dialogue between the lovers begins with the woman's statement: "Let him kiss me with the kisses of his mouth" (Song 1:2). The woman's experience is given the unique opportunity of a public hearing in this patriarchal Israelite culture. In 1:2-7 she expresses her desire for intimacy with her lover. The Song begins *in medias res* of this erotic relationship; it will also end without a consummation in 8:14, where she says: "Run away, my beloved; become like a gazelle or a young stag on the balsamic mountains." The Song is about erotic desire rather than sexual consummation.[11] To keep such desire alive beyond death is a goal of the Song; the text confronts new generations of readers and brings back to life this experience of these two particular and, as yet, anonymous lovers with whom the readers can identify.[12] The evocative character of the opening statement is due not only to the fact that here a woman is speaking in an intimate tone; it also catches the attention of the ancient Israelite audience by speaking about a man and a woman kissing.[13] Of the thirty-one times that kissing (*nšq*) is mentioned in the OT, only one other time does it refer to a man kissing a woman (Gen 29:11). Twice *nšq* refers to women kissing other women (Ruth 1:9, 14). Usually *nšq* is used of men kissing other men, where it is a warm greeting expressing mutual well-being.[14] The intimate kissing that the woman desires at the beginning of the Song is alluded to again in 8:1 where she wishes that her lover would be perceived as her brother so that she could kiss him in public and not be censured.[15]

The intense desire that consumes lovers and transforms their world is introduced not only by the mention of intimate kissing but also by references to wine, perfume, and lovemaking. The woman says: "Your lovemaking (*dōdekā*) is more delightful than wine" (1:2). Later he will bring her to the "house of wine" for lovemaking (2:4). This kind of love (*dōd*) is sexual: kisses, caressing, sexual intercourse (7:12; Prov 7:18; Ezek 16:8; 23:17). There is nothing abstract about it at all; it brings a euphoria more delightful than that of wine.[16] She then states: "Your name is a spreading perfume" (1:3). The very mention of the name of her lover

11. Richard S. Hess, *Song of Songs* (Grand Rapids: Baker, 2005), 32.

12. Exum, *Song of Songs*, 95.

13. However, Keel, *Song of Songs*, 41, notes that male and female lovers kissing on the lips is attested in Sumerian literature ("Enlil and Ninlil" ll. 51-52); see Thorkild Jacobsen, *The Harps That Once . . . Sumerian Poetry in Translation* (New Haven: Yale University Press, 1987), 174, and in Egyptian literature of the second half of the second millennium BCE.

14. Exum, *Song of Songs*, 93.

15. Ibid.

16. Ibid.

catches the attention of women and stirs them as if he were near them. In these opening two lines of the Song the woman engages four of the five senses: touch (kissing), taste (wine), hearing (spoken name), and smell (perfume). Notably, she does not mention the sight of him, which seems to reflect a gender difference in erotic attraction in which for men sight is the usual means for triggering an erotic arousal.[17]

In the Mesopotamian tradition the Sumerian love songs of the deities Dumuzi and Inanna have the courtship of the couple as one of their themes.[18] These songs express the erotic desire of lovers who strive to develop a closer relationship, but the language they use tends to be more stereotypical and sexually explicit than that of the Song.[19] In the following excerpt from a text titled "The Women's Oath,"[20] Inanna exhorts Dumuzi to make an oath that he has not had sexual relations with other women:

> My brother, I will make you take an oath, oh my brother of beautiful eyes! Your right hand on my nakedness should be placed; your left hand on my head should be laid; when you have brought your mouth close to my mouth; by so (doing) you will take an oath to me. Thus is the oath of women, oh my brother of beautiful eyes. (ll. 20-26)[21]

The physical actions of the oath taking concretely anticipate the act of sexual intercourse. These words of Inanna are part of a short dialogue in which the two lovers extol one another's beauty.[22] This excerpt on oath taking, which itself is an erotically charged description, takes place within the context of lovemaking. Inanna's demand that Dumuzi pledge

17. Ibid., 14–15, 94.

18. Yitschak Sefati, *Love Songs in Sumerian Literature* (Ramat Gan: Bar-Ilan University Press, 1998), 94–97; Roland Murphy, *The Song of Songs*, Hermeneia (Minneapolis: Fortress Press, 1990), 48–49, 52.

19. Keel, *Song of Songs*, 28–29.

20. Yitschak Sefati, "An Oath of Chastity in a Sumerian Love Song (SRT 31)?" in *Bar-Ilan Studies Dedicated to Pinḥas Artzi*, ed. Jacob Klein and Aaron Skaist, 45–63 (Ramat Gan: Bar-Ilan University Press, 1990), at 50–51 notes that this bal-bal-e is a hymn with a dialogical character that seems to have been recited in the cult, probably at some point in the sacred marriage rite.

21. Translation by Yitschak Sefati, "The Women's Oath," in *Love Songs in Sumerian Literature*, 128–31; idem, *COS* 1.169A; idem, "An Oath of Chastity?" 52–53.

22. This dialogical structure is exemplified in the Akkadian love poem, *The Love Lyrics of Nabû and Tašmetu*; see Martti Nissinen, "Love Lyrics of Nabû and Tašmetu"; idem, "Song of Songs and Sacred Marriage," in *Sacred Marriages*, 173–218, at 209. Murphy, *Song of Songs*, 55, notes how this literary device of dialogue is present in a number of the Sumerian love poems but absent from Egyptian love songs.

that he has been a virgin parallels the expectation of the lovers in the Song that their love be committed rather than promiscuous (Song 2:16; 3:4; 4:12; 5:9; 6:3; 7:10; 8:2, 6).[23]

In Homer's *Iliad*, when Hera approaches Zeus wearing a talisman from Aphrodite that enhanced her charms to an irresistible degree, Zeus exclaims: "Now let us go to bed and find joy in lovemaking. For never before in this way has love (*erōs*) of goddess or mortal woman come upon me and taken control of the heart within me" (*Il.* 14:314-17). On the island of Lesbos in the early sixth century BCE, Sappho (ca. 630–575) describes in a lyric poem her strong erotic feeling for a woman whom she desires but whom she sees sitting next to a man:[24]

> For when I look at you for a moment, then it is no longer possible for me to speak; my tongue has snapped, at once a subtle fire has stolen beneath my flesh, I see nothing with my eyes, my ears hum, sweat pours from me, a trembling seizes me all over, I am greener than grass, and it seems to me that I am little short of dying. (Sappho 31:7-16)[25]

Next, in a context in which the conventions surrounding heterosexual marriage are invoked to channel the erotic attraction of a man and a woman, the following papyrus fragment contains a selection of blame poetry—presumably from the lyric poet Archilochus (ca. 680–645)—in which a seducer tries to persuade a young woman to have sex with him, but—according to David Campbell's restoration of a missing part of the papyrus—she probably replies: "My mother said not before marriage."[26] Later—after a missing section of the papyrus—she continues her resistance by urging him to pursue another woman (Neobule) in whom he was previously interested, but he dismisses this recommendation:

> I will listen to what you are urging. I am greatly stirred by desire.
> Do not, my friend, regard my hurrying ahead below the wall and

23. Hess, *Song of Songs*, 32; Sefati, "An Oath of Chastity?" 49; Murphy, *Song of Songs*, 53.

24. Henri I. Marrou, *A History of Education in Antiquity*, trans. George Lamb (New York: Sheed and Ward, 1956), 34–35; John Winkler, *Constraints of Desire: The Anthropology of Sex and Gender in Ancient Greece* (New York: Routledge, 1990), 178–80; Martin L. West, *East Face of Helicon: West Asiatic Elements in Greek Poetry and Myth* (Oxford: Clarendon Press, 1997), 527.

25. Translation David Campbell, *Greek Lyric*, 4 vols. (Cambridge, MA: Harvard University Press, 1982), 1:78–81.

26. David A. Campbell, *The Golden Lyre: The Themes of the Greek Lyric Poets* (London: Duckworth, 1983), 7.

> gate as excessive, for I will be in the orchard. Now know this. Let another man be the one who has Neobule. Ah! She is surely ripe. The blossom of youth has left her and the grace that was formerly upon her. She has never refrained from a surfeit. This raving woman has revealed the limits of her youth. Take her away to the ravens! May the king of the gods not repeatedly hold that I have such a woman. I will be a laughingstock for the neighbors. Rather I very much prefer you. For you are neither faithless nor treacherous. However, she is much too clever and makes many friends. (ll. 13-25)[27]

In this fragment from Archilochus and in the excerpt from the Mesopotamian "Women's Oath" the dialogue between the man and the woman concerns itself with social or personal expectations and does not foreground the mutual expression of erotic feeling in the present moment as in the Song of Songs. The level of mutuality in the dialogue between the lovers in the Song of Songs is remarkable—as striking as any other example of mutual expression of erotic feeling to be found in currently known love poems from the ancient Near East and Greece.[28]

In the Song of Songs the woman is the speaker in fifty-three percent of the text and the man in thirty-four percent.[29] So in the dialogue in 1:5–2:7 in which the lovers express strong admiration for one another the woman begins and ends these encomia and provides descriptions that are more solidly textured and evocative than those of the man:

> [Woman] While the king was with his banqueters, my nard gave off its fragrance. To me my lover is a pouch of myrrh, which lies at night between my breasts. To me my lover is a cluster of henna from the vineyards of En-gedi.
> [Man] Ah, my beloved, you are beautiful. Ah, you are beautiful. Your eyes are doves. (1:12-15)

This exchange takes place in a quiet garden-like setting amid the scents of cedar, cypress, unguents, and perfumes.[30] Here the courtly imagery (king's couch) merges with that of the countryside (vineyards of En-gedi) to provide a unique setting for the lovers to see themselves through the eyes of the other.[31]

27. Edition: Campbell, *The Golden Lyre*, 7.

28. Hess, *Song of Songs*, 32, 37; cf. Exum, *Song of Songs*, 51.

29. Hess, *Song of Songs*, 19.

30. On the garden as setting for feminine sexuality see Gwendolyn Leick, *Sex and Eroticism in Mesopotamian Literature* (London and New York: Routledge, 1994), 74.

31. Exum, *Song of Songs*,110–11.

In the Sumerian love song, "The Women's Oath," the lovers praise one another as they move toward intimate union.[32] The man begins the dialogue with praise of the woman, and she concludes it with praise of him:

> [Man] Your eyes—their gaze delights me, come my beloved sister! Your mouth—its utterance delights me, my mellifluous mouth of her mother. Your lips—their kiss delights me, come my beloved sister! My sister, your barley—its beer is delicious, my mellifluous mouth of her mother. Your wort—its liquor is delicious, come my beloved sister! (ll. 4-8)
> . . . [Woman] My blossoming one, my blossoming one, sweet is your allure! My blossoming garden of apple trees, sweet is your allure! My fruitful garden of celtis-trees, sweet is your allure! My (?) "Dumuzi-abzu by his own virtue," sweet is your allure! My pure figurine, my pure figurine, sweet is your allure! Alabaster figurine, adorned with the lapis lazuli diadem, sweet is your allure! (ll. 27-32)[33]

This exchange of praise by the fertility deities Dumuzi and Inanna seems to offer itself as a model for others in the land to imitate, for the intervening section of the poem (as described above) refers to an oath Dumuzi is to take that he has not had relations with other women. Thus in these Mesopotamian texts erotic attraction and sexual intercourse were avenues by which humans imitated the gods and came into harmony with the forces of nature.[34]

In Homer's *Odyssey*, Nausicaa, the daughter of king Alkinous and queen Arete of Phaeacia, becomes enamored of the visitor Odysseus. She is of marriageable age and expresses her admiration for him:

> Listen to me, white-armed serving women, to what I am going to say. Not all of the gods on Olympus are opposed to this man's mingling here with the godlike Phaeacians. Earlier he appeared to me to be worn, but now he is like the gods in the wide heavens. If only

32. On mutual love between male and female partners in a patriarchal gender matrix see Nissinen, "Song of Songs and Sacred Marriage," 210–11; David Carr, "Gender and the Shaping of Desire in the Song of Songs and its Interpretation," *JBL* 119 (2000): 233–48, at 241–42.

33. Translation in Sefati, *Love Songs in Sumerian Literature*, 129–30.

34. Tikva Frymer-Kensky, *In the Wake of the Goddesses* (New York: Free Press, 1997), 56; cf. Jerrold Cooper, "Sacred Marriage and Popular Cult in Early Mesopotamia," in *Official Cult and Popular Religion in the Ancient Near East*, ed. Eiko Matsushima, 81–96 (Heidelberg: Universitätsverlag, 1993), at 94–95.

> such a one would be named as a husband for me and would live here and agree to remain here. (*Od.* 6.239-45)

Homer tends to understate the intensity of erotic feeling or to communicate it indirectly.[35] If Odysseus were to reiterate his praise of Nausicaa, which he had earlier uttered in desperation as a shipwrecked stranger, she would be sure to invite a more intense relationship, if her father Alkinous would allow it. His previous words of praise are those befitting a suitor:

> I entreat you, my queen. Are you a goddess or a mortal? If you are a goddess, one of those who are in the wide heavens, I think you are like Artemis, the daughter of great Zeus, in looks, stature, and form. If you are one of the mortals, who reside on the earth, then your father and your queenly mother are triply-blessed and triply-blessed are your brothers. Very much must their hearts always be warmed with happiness because of you, when they see you, such a young shoot, approach to take part in the dance. But most blessed in heart beyond others is that man who offers a weighty bridewealth and leads you to his home. With these eyes, I have never yet seen a mortal like you, whether man or woman. Wonder holds me as I look at you. (*Od.* 6:149-61)

The wily Odysseus delivers this encomium of Nausicaa with the intent to win her favor but not to court her as a wife. The language preserved here seems to reflect that of erotic poems a suitor and a betrothed would use in their courtship.[36]

The love expressed by the man and woman in Eden has a sacramental character since it brings them into communion not only with each other but also with God and with their natural environment. In the other Eden story the royal priestly cherub-figure is the only human creature in the garden, but he is blessed with wisdom and the divine presence such that all is harmonious as he appears to serve as an intermediary for the earthly community of Tyre or Jerusalem. He is a solitary and so may symbolize the potential of the celibate to promote harmony in the divine-human relationship. The longing of erotic love between humans, between gods, or between God/gods and humans can generate the passionate intensity that is vital to cosmic harmony. The partial satisfaction of this longing fuels more intense longing. This longing between the human

35. Campbell, *The Golden Lyre*, 3.

36. Rebecca Hague, "Ancient Greek Wedding Songs: The Tradition of Praise," *Journal of Folklore Research* 20 (1983): 131–43.

lovers in the Song of Songs is communicated in dialogue. This dialogue form is also present in the Mesopotamian love song known as "The Women's Oath," yet the level of mutuality is not as intense since it presents the lovers as paying more heed to social expectations than is the case in the Song. In Homer's *Odyssey* the love expressed by Odysseus and Nausicaa has the potential to become a strong exchange of erotic feelings, but Homer does not develop Odysseus's relationship with Nausicaa. Sappho gives a vivid description of her erotic desire for a young woman, but this is a personal reflection rather than a dialogue between lovers.

Love as Strong as Death (Song 8:6) in Light of the Cosmic Journeys of Gilgamesh and Odysseus

The dialogue between the two lovers in Song 1:5–2:7 finds an analogue at the conclusion of the Song in 8:1-14. In this concluding dialogue the power of erotic love is juxtaposed with death and comes to expression in a way that transcends death. The woman says:

> Set me as a seal on your heart, as a seal on your arm. For love is as strong as death, devotion is as fierce as Sheol. Its flames are flames of fire, the flame of YHWH. Many waters are not able to quench love; rivers cannot wash it away. If a man were to give all the wealth of his household, he would be utterly despised. (8:6-7)

Here the intimacy of the love relationship is expressed by the woman's desire to either be imprinted on her beloved's heart and arm or to become his seal that is worn across his chest or on his arm.[37] In either case she longs to have her identity intertwined with his. Such a wish is in accord with the divine command in Gen 2:24, where the man and woman are to be drawn to one another and so become one flesh.[38] The power in love is declared to be as relentless as that of death. Just as death will eventually have its way, so also will love.[39] Its fiery passion is of such an intensity that the "many waters," which elsewhere are described as cosmic forces (Pss 29:3; 77:20; 93:4), cannot extinguish it.[40] Thus this statement

37. Exum, *Song of Songs*, 245, 250.

38. Richard M. Davidson, *Flame of Yahweh: Sexuality in the Old Testament* (Peabody, MA: Hendrickson, 2007), 21, 26–38.

39. Roland Murphy, "Dance and Death in the Song of Songs," 118; idem, *Song of Songs*, 197.

40. Murphy, "Dance and Death in the Song of Songs," 119.

in v. 7 indicates that love is locked in a struggle with death throughout life;[41] perhaps it indicates that love will eventually win over the forces of death. This love is treasure that cannot be given a price tag and cannot be exchanged. It is gained only through the engagement of one's being with that of another. This reaching out to the other without counting the cost is the pathway by which such love can become part of one's life. This section, along with the sayings in 2:7 and 3:5 that speak of not rushing love but allowing it to run its course, are the only places in which the Song reflects on the reality of love as such. Otherwise it speaks of love only through the concrete, particular exchanges of the lovers, the locus in which this unquenchable reality comes to be known.[42]

The struggle between love and death is a prominent theme in the *Epic of Gilgamesh*. Perhaps because Gilgamesh is two-thirds divine, he seems to avoid settling into a domestic way of life with a wife and children. His initial heterosexual encounters seem to involve his deflowering young women on the night prior to their marriages as a royal prerogative. His intimate relationship with Enkidu involves shared heroic adventures in which they team together to carry out divinelike feats of warriors. When Enkidu dies, Gilgamesh feels the absence of his friend so intensely that he sets out to try to find a way to avoid death, the inevitable one. He describes his anguish to the alewife Shiduri at the edge of the earth:

> Enkidu, whom I love very much (*ša arammušu danniš*), who traveled with me through every hardship, has departed according to the fate of humans. I wept over him day and night and did not hand him over for burial for seven days and seven nights until a worm fell from his nose, [thinking] "Perhaps my friend will get up at the sound of my voice." After he departed, I lost vitality. I wandered like a trapper in the wilderness. Now, alewife, I have seen your face, but death, which I continually fear, may I never see. (OB VA + BM, ii 2'-13')[43]

Shiduri then gives him advice on how to overcome his lovesickness. He is to seize the pleasures of the day and to make the most of the good things that mortal life has to offer, ranging from clean clothes to dancing and playing to children and a wife. Tzvi Abusch draws attention to the fact that Shiduri mentions clean clothes prior to bathing and the child

41. Exum, *Song of Songs*, 251; Keel, *Song of Songs*, 31–32,

42. Murphy, "Dance and Death in the Song of Songs," 119.

43. Edition: A. R. George, *The Babylonian Gilgamesh Epic*, 2 vols. (Oxford and New York: Oxford University Press, 2003), 1:275.

prior to the wife. These inversions of the expected order seem to draw attention to the wife, who is mentioned last: she is to be the answer to Gilgamesh's lovesickness over the departed Enkidu. Abusch notes, however, that Gilgamesh's statement about looking on the face of Shiduri contains within it his desire to know her in an intimate way,[44] and speculates that in the OB version of the *Epic* the goal of Gilgamesh's journey to the end of the earth was to find the goddess, who was a wisdom figure monitoring the boundary between earth and the netherworld.[45] Gilgamesh's desire for an intimate relationship with an immortal rather than with a mortal woman is frustrated by Shiduri, who advises him to marry and have offspring. Such going to seed would be a sign of his mortality. Gilgamesh's rejection of this proposal then leads to the idea of his journeying on to Utnapishtim. Nowhere in the *Epic* is Gilgamesh said to have had the intense kind of heterosexual erotic experience Enkidu had with Shamhat (*Gilg*. I:188-94). If Abusch is correct, it seems that Gilgamesh was trying to have such an experience with the wisdom goddess Shiduri. Gilgamesh's drive to be bigger than life makes him want to fight against death rather than accept the satisfaction that comes through domestic life.

With regard to the desire for a wife and family, Homer's Odysseus is the opposite of Gilgamesh. Odysseus fights through life-threatening obstacles to return home to Penelope and his family in Ithaca. One of his last stopping places on his return voyage is the island of Ogygia, located at the western end of the cosmic circle in the vicinity of the sun's daily entryway into the netherworld (*Od*. 7.239, 254; 12.448).[46] The island is inhabited by the goddess Calypso. She wants him to remain with her on the island. She exercises strong erotic influence over him, a kind of power that approximates that of a magical love charm.[47] So when the opportunity arises for Odysseus to leave the island, she exhorts him:

44. Tzvi Abusch, "Gilgamesh's Request and Siduri's Denial: Part I, The Meaning of the Dialogue and Its Implications for the History of the Epic," in *The Tablet and the Scroll: Near Eastern Studies in Honor of William W. Hallo*, ed. Mark E. Cohen, Daniel C. Snell, and David B. Weisberg, 1–14 (Bethesda, MD: Capital Decisions Limited, 1993), at 5.

45. Ibid., 5–7.

46. Nanno Marinatos, "The Cosmic Journey of Odysseus," *Numen* 43 (2001): 381–416, at 395, 399.

47. Daniel Ogden, "Binding Spells: Curse Tablets and Voodoo Dolls in the Greek and Roman Worlds," in *Witchcraft and Magic in Europe: Greece and Rome*, ed. Bengt Ankarloo and Stuart Clark, 1–90 (Philadelphia: University of Pennsylvania Press, 1999), at 35; Christopher Faraone, *Ancient Greek Love Magic* (Cambridge, MA: Harvard University Press, 1999), 5–6, 17–18.

> Are you still wanting to go home at once to your native land? In any case, may it go well for you. But if you knew within how much trouble lies in store for you before you reach your native land, you would stay right here with me to keep this house and become immortal, even though you want to see your wife for whom you continually long all days. Still I claim that I am not inferior to her in build or stature, since it is never fitting for mortals to vie with immortals in build or looks. (*Od.* 5.204-13)

Upon his successful return to Ithaca, his reunion with Penelope is described as follows:

> So when the two of them were renewed in the joy of lovemaking, they took delight in telling stories to one another. She, resplendent among women, had endured so much in her household halls as she looked upon the destructive suitors who, on account of her, were slaughtering many cattle and fattened sheep, and much wine was being drawn from the large jars. But Odysseus, born of Zeus, told all the hardships he had brought upon people and all the troubles he himself had suffered. She delighted in hearing them. Sleep did not descend upon her eyelids until he had recounted everything. (*Od.* 23.300-9)

Odysseus's love for Penelope was stronger than his desire for immortality. Thus it seems that the love he shared with her was stronger than death, for he desired it even if they would live together only for a limited number of years. Their depth of communion must have communicated a sense of harmony with nature, society, and the cosmos that transcended all other considerations.

Erotic love is a relentless force essential for the unity of the cosmos. From the perspective of the individual it can be an ambiguous power: it may generate a desire for communion with another that is lifegiving, but it may also narrow one's focus to one person and enslave one to a particular relationship. The relationship between the lovers in the Song, between the man and woman in Eden in Gen 2:24, and between Odysseus and Penelope are portrayed positively. However, the ambiguity emerges for Gilgamesh who, according to the storyline of the Nineveh version, journeys on to Utnapishtim rather than returning immediately to Uruk to embrace the joys of married and domestic life. For Gilgamesh the way to communion with others and the cosmos was not by way of marriage but through friendship and wisdom. The avenue of wisdom seems to have been the primary avenue open to the primal human in Eden for erotic fulfillment.

Summary

The superior quality of the love poetry of the Song of Songs emerges in its capacity to communicate passionate erotic love without devolving into pornography or other crude forms of expression. While the Mesopotamian poems on Dumuzi and Inanna have dialogues between lovers with erotically charged expressions, they do not sustain the same level of longing and erotic desire as that evoked by the Song. The Homeric love scenes aim to describe the experience of the lovers rather than to draw the reader into the experience of the lovemaking. Thus, from the perspective of love poetry, the Homeric love scenes tend to be reserved. The Song is distinctive in the attention it gives to the woman's experience of lovemaking; also there is a level of mutuality in the lovers' dialogue that is rarely matched in the love poetry of Mesopotamia and virtually absent in that of Greece. Sustaining the intensity of the lovers' desire is the primary goal of the Song; it aims to evoke in its readers the sense that passionate love is a force as relentless as death and strong enough to survive the onslaughts of the disintegrating forces of death.

The dissolution of self that happens in the loss of control in romantic love is an experience of ecstasy rather than anguish. In some cases the prospect of such loss of control creates so much anxiety for some lovers that they will flee to the ends of the earth to escape the dying to self required for the communion constitutive of love. But the desire for the other that involves forgetfulness of self can lead to a communion that shows that love is stronger than death. This transcendence of death through love is illustrated in the desire that drove Odysseus to return to Penelope when he might have lived a trouble-free existence filled with the pleasures of lovemaking with Calypso in the paradise-like environment of Ogygia. But his experience of human love in his relationship with Penelope convinced him of the enduring character of that love. The communion experienced in authentic love transcends the forces of dissolution that constitute death. This communion is an experience charged with significance that far exceeds the *carpe diem* philosophy Shiduri offered to Gilgamesh. It is this communion experience that the Song extols when it says of love that "its flashes are flashes of fire, the flame of YHWH" (8:6). Human erotic experience has the potential to be a participation in God's love. Carnal love can become sacramental love.

Comparative Summary of Factors Giving Rise to Celibacy and Related Forms of Sexual Renunciation in Ancient Israel, Mesopotamia, and Greece

Chapter 1: Sexual Restraint Within the Context of a Cosmic Household

Collective Existence Personified as a Woman in a Patriarchal Culture

Sexual desire is a powerful natural force that takes on a personal character when it is channeled into a network of committed human relationships. Woman Jerusalem is a metaphor for the collective existence of the people of Jerusalem. Their commitment to one another is situated within the context of their covenantal relationship with Yhwh. This vertical relationship with Yhwh puts constraints on Woman Jerusalem's relationships with other humans. Ezekiel describes Woman Jerusalem's relationship to Yhwh as a marriage in which Woman Jerusalem must not enter into erotic sexual relationships with any human. Just as Woman Jerusalem is a metaphor, so also are her adulterous relationships with other humans. Literally such relationships take the form of worship of other deities and the forging of alliances with other nations. To refrain from such relationships makes Jerusalem appear to be alone and separate from its neighbors. Jerusalem is portrayed as unmarried to a human partner. On this level of horizontal relationships one might say that Jerusalem, personified as a collective entity, is called to a life of celibate chastity.

The personification of a city as a woman is illustrated in the Mesopotamian tradition where the patron of a city is a goddess. Just as Woman Jerusalem embodied the people of Jerusalem in their interrelationships, so did the goddess Inanna for the people of Ur. But Inanna celebrated the sacred marriage ritual with the king of Ur. However, the genders of the divine and human partners in the marriage relationship in Ur are inverted vis-à-vis those in Jerusalem. The patriarchal model of marriage is not operative in Ur because the superior partner is the goddess; thus the exclusivity of relationship required of the woman in the patriarchal model is not applicable to Inanna.

The collective existence of Athens is personified as a woman in terms of Athena's patronage. Her statue in the Parthenon embodies the collective identity of the Athenians. Yet the feminine imagery for the collective existence of Athens is not limited to Athena. Solon refers to *Dikē* as the goddess integral to the collective bonds of this polis. Also the androgynous Dionysus has an important role to play in sustaining the vitality of Athens's collective existence, particularly in the sacral performance of the tragedies.

The origin of the collective existence of the citizens can be captured in the imagery of birth and maturation. Ezekiel portrays the Jerusalemites as embodied in the infant girl Jerusalem who is cast off by her Amorite father and Hittite mother. YHWH adopts and raises the girl Jerusalem and marries her when she has reached the age of puberty. In Mesopotamia the collective existence of the people of a city can be seen as arising out of its soil, as shown in "The Song of the Hoe." The masculine role of Enlil and Enki in providing the form for this growth co-opts the primacy of the womb of the mother goddess in the people's birth; such co-opting of the feminine role is countered by the rise of the "androgynous" goddess Inanna/Ishtar, who embodies the powers of sex and war, which are indispensable for the life of a city. The Athenians cultivated their links to their homeland by claiming to have been born from the soil. When the virgin Athena cast off from her leg the sperm of Hephaestus who had tried to rape her, Erichthonius was conceived and born from the soil; he was then given over to Athena to be raised. In the fifth-century Athenian funeral orations the Athenians as a whole are regarded as born from mother earth.[48] These examples illustrate the larger development in these three cultures of a pattern of male hierarchical rule, which sidelined a partnership model of male and female rule. However, the feminine power of fertility could not be channeled into the patriarchal model without resistance.

Erōs Out of Control: *Erōs* Without the Context of the Cosmic Household

Sexual desire is a physical and cultural power that is pervasive, persistent, and indispensable to human life. If the generation of erotic desire is the primary focus of one's life, one will be driven to take rather than to give to others. The cultivation of a desire that is a "lack" keeps one in a constant state of neediness. Erotic desire is open to others but is predisposed to take rather than to give. Ezekiel takes this state of neediness to an extreme in his characterization of Woman Jerusalem as a nymphomaniac queen. Her spiraling desire for sexual relations is rooted in her narcissism, which separated her from YHWH. Her self-understanding lost its context within the covenant relationship and so

48. Robert Parker, *Athenian Religion: A History* (Oxford: Clarendon Press, 1996), 138.

abandoned the cosmic household under YHWH's authority. Her adulterous promiscuity goes beyond that of a prostitute. She does everything imaginable to keep erotic desire alive, but she derives no satisfaction from these activities that are outside the context of the household—the privileged place in which sexual relations can lead to authentic communion with others. Raw, unhindered erotic desire is self-destructive because it is self-absorbed and operates without commitment to others. Such self-absorption reaches the extreme of child sacrifice in which children are offered not only to local deities but also to YHWH (Ezek 16:20; 20:25; cf. Jer 7:31).

In Mesopotamia laws against adultery were similar to those in Israel. Even though child sacrifice is not attested in Mesopotamia, there is evidence that abortion was practiced. Unwanted children were also exposed. The story of Sargon's birth is a rags-to-riches account in which his mother, an *entu*-priestess who was not supposed to have children, deposited him in a basket on the river. She is not censured for this in the story; perhaps she had become pregnant through a sacred marriage ritual and so was driven to expose her son. The practice of extramarital sex was recognized as a reality for men not only through prostitution but also by Ishtar's role as patroness of diverse forms of sexual expression, including homosexuality and bestiality. If Woman Jerusalem had been in Mesopotamia she could have appealed to Ishtar as the divine power to support her promiscuous behavior.

In Athens the laws against adultery were also similar to those in the Israelite tradition. An instance of child sacrifice is attributed to Erechtheus. In a war against the Eleusinians he was called upon by an oracle to sacrifice one of his daughters to save Athens.[49] His daughter Aglauros offered herself, but the other daughter Creusa was spared. Euripides created a tragedy (*Ion*) in which Creusa is the mother of Ion (the progenitor of the Ionians) by the god Apollo. She exposes her son in such a way that Apollo is challenged to rescue him and raise him. Thus Ion was raised in Apollo's sanctuary at Delphi by a priestess.

Ezekiel charges that Woman Jerusalem went astray when she became enamored of her own beauty and forgot how she had been adopted and raised by YHWH. By ignoring all that she had been given she began to act as if she were autonomous. Such an attitude quickly led to sexually addictive behavior that destroyed her life. She was unfavorably compared to Samaria and Sodom, the latter notorious for its low ethical

49. Jon D. Mikalson, "Erechtheus and the Panathaneia," *American Journal of Philology* 97 (1976): 141–53, at 143.

standards. Ezekiel states that the scandalous behavior of Woman Jerusalem was a consequence of her being like her mother, an indication that this family resemblance was due at least in part to a genetic factor.

Sargon's forgetfulness or hubris led to the demise of the first Akkadian empire, according to the *Curse of Agade*. He wished to renovate the Ekur, Enlil's temple in Nippur; however, Enlil refused to give him permission. When Sargon forged ahead on his own, Enlil became enraged and Ishtar withdrew from protecting Sargon, which meant that Akkad was doomed. Even though Sargon introduced military and administrative practices that subsequent Mesopotamian kings imitated, they avoided attributing these accomplishments to him because of the curse adhering to him.

In Sophocles' *Oedipus Tyrannus*, Oedipus tries to find the cause of a plague besetting the kingdom of Thebes. He discovers that unwittingly he not only has killed his father but also has had sexual relations with his mother. These abominations lead to his loss of the throne and eventual exile. When he is about to discover his identity and previous history his wife/mother Jocasta urges him to ignore the ominous oracles about himself, as if they had merely been fabricated (*OT* 711-24). The ancestral curse adhering to the house of Laius had afflicted Oedipus despite his attentiveness to oracles and his best efforts to circumvent their dire predictions.

Impurity and the Experience of the Irrational

In the Israelite tradition sexual substances were incompatible with the holy. In the priestly regulations for the tabernacle great care was taken to keep the impure separate from the holy. Ezekiel implies that when Woman Jerusalem acted promiscuously she defiled the temple. Her own body was an analogue to the temple. When Oedipus committed incest—even though it was without his knowledge—he objectively defiled the boundaries foundational to the integrity of the household. He blinded himself so that he did not have to look upon himself and his offspring. When the temple servant defiled the sanctuary of Ishtar the goddess immediately had the servant cast headlong to her death—not only a form of capital punishment but also a purging.

The irruption of the irrational into the life of a city triggers anger and confusion. If no one can be blamed, this experience of bad luck is attributed to a flaw in the workings of the cosmos. But Ezekiel does not hesitate to blame Jerusalem for its misfortunes. He claims that collective Jerusalem was guilty of narcissism that led to her withdrawal from Yhwh and turning to false sources of support that only made Jerusalem more needy. The challenge for Jerusalem was to commit to YHWH alone as its God. In Mesopotamia the goddess Ishtar was depicted as encompassing opposites in her person: love/death, sex/war, male/female. Although the clash of these opposites brought chaos and tension to the life of an individual or group the ongoing tension between them was believed to be a dynamic inherent in the cosmic structure. In Greece, Dionysus plays a role similar to that of Ishtar in Mesopotamia. He invades the consciousness of individuals in order to induce chaos into the established institutions in the polis to make them more attuned to the life-force: the tension between *nomos* (convention) and *physis* (nature). The monotheistic system of Israel regarded creation as good and was not ready to allow the people to claim to be victims of unethical or amoral cosmic processes. Celibacy for Jeremiah would be a sign of the lengths to which monotheism would go in defending the ethical character of the created order. But the polytheistic system entertained speculation about the activity of chaos within the cosmos and was ready to claim that humans were tragic victims of the unfairness of life.

Chapter 2: Intermarriage: A Threat to the Household as the Enduring Matrix of Personal Identity?

Maintenance of the Intergenerational Web of Relationships Within the Patriarchal Household

The alewife Shiduri advised Gilgamesh to abandon his quest for individual immortality and embrace the pleasures, rewards, and sense of enduring identity granted by life in the household. The father symbolized the household and exercised authority over its members and activities. He would oversee the transfer of his property to his sons, with particular emphasis on the eldest son who was charged with providing offerings for the ancestors and clan deities on a regular basis. The deified ancestors were different from the clan deities, who were symbolized by the blood line and regarded as embodying the distinguishing characteristics of the clan through the generations.

In ancient Greece a longstanding theory linked the attention given to the hearth in the Greek household with the honor given to the ancestors; this theory of Fustel de Coulanges emphasized the blood relationships in the identity of the household and how these were sustained by the domestic cult. Such a theory has been strongly criticized as lacking data; in its place the identity and integrity of the ancient Greek household are seen to lie primarily within its matrix of relationships, which was sustained by domestic arrangements, inheritance practices, and rituals.

A fundamental act of the father was to arrange the marriages of his daughters—and sometimes those of his sons. Marriage was understood as the process of transferring a woman from her father's household to that of her husband. The primary purpose of marriage in ancient Israel, Mesopotamia, and Greece was procreation. The woman played a pivotal role in the reproduction of the household by giving birth to children and socializing them. The wife-mother was the culture-bearer. Since she married young she could be a member of her husband's household for three generations and thus an important source of continuity in its relationships and culture. She also was unique in that she belonged to two households—her natal household and that of her husband.

Communal Identity in the Face of Diversity and Competition for Resources

In these three cultures an individual was virtually without an identity if he or she did not belong to a household. Therefore the identity of the household was the status marker. Competition among households can be seen in each of the cultures: in Yehud aristocratic families would marry up in order to advance their interests relative to other households. In fifth-century Mesopotamia under Persian rule households engaged in entrepreneurial activities in order to increase their wealth, power, and status. In fifth-century Athens the aristocratic households vied with one another and the rising middle class over status. Violence directed toward the household would typically draw a strong collective response: for example, the sons of Jacob retaliated against the Shechemites for Shechem's forcing Dinah to have sexual relations with him (Genesis 34). Sexual transgressions against the women of the household, especially adultery, posed serious threats to the honor of a household in all three cultures. Preventing such boundary violations was a collective concern of the community and not just of individual households. In all three cultures defilement was regarded as an objective reality that needed to be addressed regardless of the subjective intention of the violators.

The state or the community at large challenged the individual households to adapt to the common good. This intrusion into the affairs of the clans and households became contentious around the issue of intermarriage. In the fifth century Ezra lamented the presence of foreign wives in Yehudite households and tried to engage the entire community to join him in lamenting this situation and confessing their collective sin. With the assistance of his advisers he implemented a plan in which the foreign wives and their children would be dismissed from these households. He expanded upon the newly promulgated Torah to create an argument for their dismissal. In Mesopotamia a point at which intermarriage became an issue was the marriage of a herder with a city-dweller. Such a marriage was often perceived as a clash between two cultures even though the herders and city-dwellers were economically interrelated. The marriages of Babylonians with Persians commonly occurred in the fifth century according to the onomastica but do not seem to have triggered culture wars such as those in fifth-century Israel. In Athens in 451 BCE, Pericles was involved in the assembly's promulgation of a law requiring that for one to be an Athenian at birth both of the newborn's parents had to be Athenian citizens. The influx of immigrants threatened to dilute the representation of the autochthonous Athenians. Ironically, the funds that facilitated the participation of the middle class in public institutions were provided by imperial taxes and tributes. Greeks from other cities were funding the development of democratic practices in Athens. Despite the Athenians' predilection for endogamy they were known for finding ways to incorporate immigrants into their households and public institutions. Thus in Sophocles' *Oedipus Colonus*, Oedipus appeals to this sense of Athenian openness when he seeks domicile at Colonus.

Immortality in the Continuity of the Patriarchal Line

The household from which one's identity arose would live on after one's death. This awareness of the quasi-immortality of the family offered a way of domesticating death. This strategy for dealing with death was the primary one in ancient Israel; it seems to have been implemented through offerings to ancestors within the household but probably shifted in light of Deuteronomic polemics (Deut 13:6-11; 18:10-14) to a more biological understanding of living on in one's descendants (cf. Gen 15:1-6). In the Mesopotamian tradition the individual heroic quest of Gilgamesh for immortality reveals a way of confronting the terror of death. Reflection on this story within royal or wisdom circles would have allowed individuals to monitor their investment in efforts aimed at escaping death. In early-sixth-century Greece mystery cults evolving from agricultural cults such as that of the Eleusinian mysteries centered on the grain goddess Demeter began to offer individuals an avenue for hoping in a meaningful afterlife—other than that offered by the prospect of living on in one's progeny.[50]

Chapter 3: Sex and the Holy: Erotic Synergy or Warfare?

The Janus-character of *Erōs* as a Defining Issue in the Divine-Human Relationship

The positive side of *erōs* as a lack or need within a person is that one is moved to search outside him- or herself. The negative side of *erōs* is the danger of disregarding the face of the other and relating to the other only to fulfill one's own needs. This Janus-character of *erōs* raises questions about the right way to go about responding to the call to enter into an intimate relationship with a spiritual being. Israel stumbled in its efforts to love YHWH. The Mesopotamians often angered a god because they neglected this god in the midst of three thousand other deities. The Greeks also felt the burden of maintaining adequate coverage for a pantheon with multiple deities, although the identification of the twelve Olympian gods simplified this task somewhat. In each culture one would look for guideposts from the tradition to depict what a god was like, what this god expected, and what this god could provide.

Israel's major transgression in its worship of YHWH was to transfer worship practices from Baalism or other neighboring cults and apply them to YHWH. Since YHWH was the only God to whom an Israelite could be devoted according to a strict monotheism, the tendency would be to synthesize baalistic rituals with Yahwistic ones by simply changing the name of the deity. But the difference between YHWH and Baal needed to go beyond names to defining characteristics. Here Baal's patronage of hierarchical, socially stratifying political figures would distinguish Baal from YHWH, who had allotted land to the Israelites that they were to maintain in perpetuity. If the worship practices were indistinguishable, the consequence would seem to be that the sociopolitical practices of Yahwistic worshipers would merge with those of Baal worshipers. Hosea condemned Israelites for worshiping on the heights and engaging in promiscuous sexual activity at these sanctuaries (Hos 2:7, 11). He also condemned the Israelite priests for not teaching the *tōrōt* of YHWH.

50. Walter Burkert, "Athenian Cults and Festivals," CAH, 2d ed., vol. 5, *The Fifth Century B.C.*, ed. by D. M. Lewis, John Boardman, and J. K. Davies, 245–67 (Cambridge: Cambridge University Press, 1992), at 264–65.

In Mesopotamia the sacred marriage ritual as practiced from 2100 to 1800 BCE seems to have included sexual intercourse between the king and a priestess. This sacramental form of fertility worship was replaced thereafter with a more abstract or symbolic form of the ritual in which the statues of the deities Dumuzi and Inanna were regarded as having intercourse. The anxiety over fertility in an agricultural economy would be sufficient reason to account for the creation of rituals to address this deeply felt need. In this vein, then, it would seem that the more concrete the ritual the more effective it would be in giving the community the sense that it had done what it could to intercede for favorable growing conditions. The situation in which famine and barrenness beset the land underlies the story of *The Descent of Inanna to the Netherworld*. Her eventual release by the stratagems of the androgynous cult figure Asushunamir illustrates the awe Mesopotamians had for these figures with both masculine and feminine characteristics. They seemed capable of passing into the netherworld and returning, a kind of transcendence of death to which no other human could lay claim.

In Greece, Aphrodite was acknowledged as the goddess of love. The Homeric epics speak of how she interacts with humans, often besetting them with passions they would rather not have at that moment. In Plato's *Symposium* the question of "getting it right" with the gods over the act of loving is focused on the question of what *erōs* is like. Thus the goal of the speakers at this banquet was to describe *erōs* in a way that praised him. One speaker refers to Hesiod's *Theogony*, where *erōs* is regarded as a cosmic force or as an assistant to Aphrodite. So for Plato the intellectual task of properly conceptualizing *erōs* is the proper procedure for rightly relating to this divine reality of love. Three speakers regard *erōs* as a god; Diotima refers to *erōs* as an intermediary between gods and humans; Erixymachus and Socrates regard *erōs* as a cosmic force that binds all things together. This dialogue illustrates Plato's innovation of transforming the issue of worship of the gods into one of intellectual engagement with dynamic ideas.

Transmuting Sexual *Erōs* into Human-Divine Erotic Energy

The question of right worship of YHWH demands a faithful interpretation of the Yahwistic tradition. It appears that the priests condemned by Hosea had become mechanistic in their rituals and were interested primarily in gaining the foodstuffs from sacrifices rather than fostering a relationship between the worshipers and YHWH. For Hosea, attentiveness to this divine-human relationship calls one to imitate the exclusive, intimate relationship a wife has with her husband. So YHWH says that he will allure Israel into the wilderness. What kind of *erōs* is involved here? Is it something that is spiritualized so that it is a conceptual matter that engages a Platonic soul? Or is it rather an embodied kind of love in which sexual feelings are exchanged—a kind of crossing of the flesh between the two parties? Perhaps YHWH is to be conceived in this marital relationship less in a spiritualized form and more in anthropomorphic terms. Hosea's criticism of sexual rites at the hilltop shrines indicates that a proper ritual is one that fosters a personal, erotic relationship between Israel and YHWH rather than an anonymous sexual exchange where the purpose of the human partner is simply to have a pleasurable experience rather than a committed relationship as in married love. If a sexual way of relating to YHWH is inappropriate for Israel, how should the erotic language in Hosea describing the divine-human marriage relationship be transmuted? Erotic love has the potential to bring a new level of communion to personal relationships even if one of the partners is human and the other divine.

The communication between sexual partners can impart new knowledge to them. In Mesopotamia the erotic relationship between Nergal and Ereshkigal brought love even into the realm of death. Shamhat's initiation of Enkidu into human culture through intense lovemaking over the course of a week brought him an understanding of *erōs* that moved him to stop Gilgamesh from carrying out abusive, anonymous sexual acts on young women about to be married. There was a sense that proper sexual relations brought one a kind of knowledge that was civilizing. Gilgamesh's relationship to Enkidu indicates that their love had assumed such a meaningful part in Gilgamesh's life that a major part of him seemed to descend to Sheol with Enkidu. The transcendent character of an eroticized personal relationship seems to be the element that makes love as strong as or stronger than death.

In Plato's *Symposium*, Diotima describes *erōs* as an intermediary between gods and humans. *Erōs* is a means of transcending the confines of the human condition. But in Plato's *Republic*, *erōs* as passion is regarded as a hindrance to reason in its quest for transcendence. In the *Symposium*, although Socrates describes *erōs* as the undying desire for the beautiful, true, and good, the role of reason (*nous*) is privileged. However, in the *Phaedrus* passion for the beautiful is given a significant complementary role to reason because the feeling of attraction to the beautiful is vital to the ascent to the truth. The restoration of passion to the lover of wisdom who wishes to ascend to the transcendent makes this person's relationship to the beautiful more holistic than the highly rational relationship described in the *Republic*.

The proper way to relate to YHWH so as not to turn the relationship into one resembling that to Baal rests on a passionate, trusting commitment to YHWH in which the Israelites relinquish their claims on YHWH and allow YHWH to be God. In Plato's ascent, the receptivity of the *nous* to the form of the Good is foundational to the communion with the Good. Such receptivity is an active form of beholding. In Hosea the sense of hearing is more prominent than sight. Thus the receptive listening that actively yearns for YHWH's presence is what YHWH is asking of Wife Israel. The yearning for YHWH seems to have a physical component. It is not simply a matter of intellect and will. Yet the physical joining of god and human symbolized by the Mesopotamian sacred marriage violates YHWH's transcendence. In the Israelite tradition the mixture of impure sexual substances with the holy rule out this ritual. Thus, in Ezek 16:8, YHWH's passing his cloak over the young woman who is to become Woman Jerusalem is a figurative rather than a physical joining of YHWH with Woman Jerusalem. The question remains as to the shape erotic experience assumes when mediating the divine presence to the human person as a force of integration.

Chapter 4: Virginity and Chastity: Feminine Ideals Integral to the Patriarchal Household

Collective Responsibility for the Integrity of Family Relationships

The virginal status of a daughter assures a future husband that any offspring born from this woman in the first year of their marriage will be his sons or daughters, unless he himself has not monitored his wife's behavior. As Tikva Frymer-Kensky has noted, this concern of the future husband could have been managed by simply agreeing that offspring born from a woman in the first year of her marriage belong to her natal household.[51] However, concern of the father's household for the virginity of its daughters extends beyond their capacity to preserve the purity of the patrilineal line of their future husbands. The bond between father

51. Tikva Frymer-Kensky, "Virginity in the Bible," in *Gender and Law in the Hebrew Bible and the Ancient Near East*, *JSOTSup* 262, ed. Victor H. Matthews, Bernard M. Levinson, and Tikva Frymer-Kensky, 79–96 (Sheffield: Sheffield Academic Press, 1998), at 81.

and daughter is intact if she has not received the seed of any other man within her. The integrity of family relationships is an issue that concerned not only the father but all the other members of the household. This obligation to respond to breaches in the family's boundaries is narrated in the story of the "forcing of Dinah" in Genesis 34. The violent retaliation by Dinah's brothers indicates that their collective identity as sons of Jacob has been challenged when Shechem the Canaanite has relations with their sister Dinah without first negotiating with Jacob. The honor of the patriarchal household was diminished by such an action. Slander spread by a husband that his wife was not a virgin at the time of their marriage was another way in which the household could be dishonored. Deuteronomy 22:13-18 and the *Laws of Lipit-Ishtar* legislate against such slander. In Solon's laws in sixth-century Greece any young woman who became pregnant prior to marriage was to be dismissed from her father's household.

The definition of an intact virgin as one whose hymen has not been breached is a modern invention.[52] Nevertheless, in the first millennium BCE tests were concocted to try to determine the virginal status of a bride such as the examination of the bloody sheets in Deut 22:13-18, the taking of oaths by the bride-to-be as attested in OB times, and the use of ritual ordeals or divination in Ephesus and other parts of ancient Greece. The expectation of premarital virginity was well established in Israel and Greece and probably in Mesopotamia, although the available Mesopotamian data leaves room for debate. These cultures regarded the deflowering of a virgin as having physical consequences, which they indicated by means of the language of impurity.[53]

Special measures by the household for safeguarding the virginity of daughters and the fidelity of wives were not generally implemented in these three cultures. There were women's quarters within the household, but these areas were not designed to restrict the women's movement. In terms of distinctive dress, the only regulation in these three cultures was that married women in Assyria (and probably in Babylonia) were required to be veiled in public. This sign would have been important for men in this culture, who were restricted from making advances only

52. Giulia Sissa, *Greek Virginity*, trans. Arthur Goldhammer (Cambridge, MA: Harvard University Press, 1990), 106, 111; Londa Schiebinger, *Nature's Body* (Boston: Beacon Press, 1993), 93–94.

53. Genesis 34:13, 27; Sissa, *Greek Virginity*, 87; Sophie Lafont, *Femmes, Droit et Justice dans l'Antiquité orientale: Contribution à l'étude du droit pénal au Proche-Orient ancien*, OBO 165 (Fribourg: Universitätsverlag; Göttingen: Vandenhoeck & Ruprecht, 1999), 97–98.

upon married women; their own married status did not prohibit extramarital liaisons. In Greece the veil played an important symbolic role in the part of the marriage ritual known as the *anakalyptēria* ("unveiling"): the bride's lifting of her veil at the banquet was portrayed as the first time that the eyes of the bride and groom met and was to be a preview in the sight of the assembled guests of the sexual consummation of the marriage to take place later. In Assyria and Greece the veil was a sign of the woman's status as a wife. In Israel a woman's veil is mentioned in Gen 38:14 as part of Tamar's attire as she poses as a prostitute at the roadside; otherwise a symbolic function for the woman's veil is not made explicit in the Hebrew Scriptures.[54]

Safeguards for the Integrity of Personal and Communal Bodies

In light of the high value placed on female virginity and bodily wholeness, attention was paid not only to guarding the portals of the body against unwanted entry but also to monitoring the emission of genital fluids. Leviticus 15 legislates for both males and females the steps that are to be taken so that the impurity associated with normal and abnormal genital emissions is not allowed to come into contact with *sancta*. Such preventive measures were intrusive in the daily lives of women and men and seemed designed to fend off death from the community by calling for the containment of reproductive fluids in the body so as to maximize the body's reproductive potential; however, there also seems to be an anxiety about the fluidity of boundaries that is not sufficiently explained by referring to genital emissions as a diminishment of the life-force and thus as a manifestation of death. An analogous system for regulating bodily fluids is not in evidence in Mesopotamia, but there were omens that regarded the loss of genital fluids as portentous. The discomfort or sense of defilement that came with such a loss was present in folk beliefs in the ancient Near East. Also in Mesopotamia the expectation that sexual substances should be kept out of sanctuaries was a matter of etiquette toward the deity. Even though these regulations tended to support male dominance, they appear to have arisen more from the family's concern for safeguarding the bodies of its members

54. Karel van der Toorn, "The Significance of the Veil in the Ancient Near East," in *Pomegranates and Golden Bells*, ed. David P. Wright, David Noel Freedman, and Avi Hurvitz, 327–339 (Winona Lake, IN: Eisenbrauns, 1995), at 330, proposes that on the basis of *rĕʿālâ* in Isa 3:18-23 the veil was simply a regular part of the attire of upper class Israelite women.

than from the patriarch's desire to maintain the hierarchical structure of the household. The ancient Greeks were attentive to the defiling character of birth, death, and sex but did not regard genital emissions as contaminating.

Male Sexual Constraint: A Stepping-Stone to a Higher Goal

Male virginity was countercultural in all three of these ancient cultures. Even though the main burden of maintaining the purity of the patriline fell upon women, men were not without constraints in their sexual expression. In Genesis 38–39, Judah compares unfavorably with Joseph. The restraint Joseph exercised in resisting the adulterous advances of Potiphar's wife portray him as wiser than Judah, who fathered twins by his daughter-in-law Tamar, whom he mistook for a "veiled" prostitute. Judah's having sexual relations with a prostitute was permitted, but the story brands such an action as carrying a high risk of defilement of the bodies of the individual and the household. By contrast, the sexual discipline of Joseph reveals his mindfulness of his indebtedness to his master and his responsibility to God. Joseph's circumspectness eventually leads to his promotion to a national position.

In the Greek tradition, Euripides' character Hippolytus is also victimized by another man's wife (his stepmother Phaedra) who frames him with a false charge of adultery after he has resisted her advances. Euripides develops the characters of Hippolytus and Phaedra in a plot that brings to life the tensions and ambiguities in times of temptation when the power of *erōs* may be believed to overpower even the most virtuous. The portrayal of Hippolytus as one who slighted Aphrodite emphasizes that virginity is a way of life that runs counter to the normal order of things and so tempts fate.

The discipline required, on the one hand, to resist adultery and, on the other, to live as a virgin seems to consist of the same skills, with the important exception that the virgin has no sexual outlet. How then does the virgin respond to the sexual drive? In Proverbs 7 the pursuit of wisdom offers an avenue for transmuting sexual energies from a physical to a more spiritualized plane. The invitation by Woman Wisdom to listen to her and gain her assistance lends a spiritual concreteness to this form of eroticism that parallels the erotic discipline promoted by Socrates in the pursuit of knowledge of the beautiful and the good.

The Voice of Women on Virginity and Their Status in a Patriarchal Society

Regarding the expectation of premarital virginity and chastity, the voice of women is expressed only indirectly in the tradition. The protest of young women in Judges 11 is indirect, yet vigorous in this text of terror. Jephthah's sacrifice of his daughter in response to a vow that slipped from his lips as he was heading into battle places the question of the sacrifice of virginity in a mysterious context: did God will that Jephthah make this vow? Did Jephthah literally sacrifice his daughter, or is the story making the point that the daughter's loss of virginity in an arranged marriage is equivalent to a death experience? She must pass out of her natal household at an early age and face the alien environment of a new household where she will soon encounter the dangers of childbirth and the responsibility of raising children.

How the patriarchal structure of the household deals with the dilemmas of human existence surfaces poignantly in the story of the rape and death of the Levite's concubine in Judges 19. The householder's turning of the Levite's concubine over to sexually abusive men from Gibeah emphasizes the gender hierarchy in Israelite society. The householder's decision to defend his Levite guest from homosexual rape by offering his virgin daughter or the Levite's concubine to appease the criminals in Gibeah shows that the consequences of homosexual rape were more feared in Israelite society than those of heterosexual rape. In light of the strictures of Lev 19:18 against a man assuming the position of a woman in sexual relations, homosexual rape would have constituted an inversion of roles that would have shaken the self-understanding of the Israelite male shaped by priestly teachings.[55]

The indirect expression of women's protest against patriarchal power is evident in a Greek festival such as the Thesmophoria in which the women withdrew to commune with nature and with one another. This time of escaping from the routine of the household provided women with a chance to regenerate; however, the goal of these rituals was not to overthrow the patriarchal household but to return to it and bring new energy to life within it.

The *nadiātum* in OB Mesopotamia were probably designated for this cloistered way of life by their fathers and families. Their entrepreneurial enterprises established them as a significant social force in Sippar and

55. Cf. Tamar Kamionkowski, *Gender Reversal and Cosmic Chaos: A Study of the Book of Ezekiel*, *JSOTSup* 368 (Sheffield: Sheffield Acadmic Press, 2003), 7–8.

Nippur, particularly in their capacity as brokers of real estate transactions across tribal lineages. Their membership in their natal households and in the household of the cloister gave them the capacity to negotiate transactions between lineages that would otherwise have been resisted by those committed more to the tribal customs than to the opportunities offered by the state. Their religious role as intercessors for the family is underreported in the extant tablets, which are largely devoted to contracts and matters of property. However, this intercessory—not priestly—role offers an explanation of why these women were dedicated to a temple and cloistered. In the OB lexical list *Proto Lu*, the *nadītum* is identified with the *qadištum*. If the *qadištum* is regarded as one who engaged in prostitution, this seems to have been a development after the OB period. Against the identification of the *nadiātum* as engaged in prostitution, Benno Landsberger contends[56] that the *nadiātum* were not only unmarried and cloistered but also followers of a chaste way of life—a view that seems more likely.

Chapter 5: Composite Guardian Figures: Tension at the Cosmic Junctures

The Imaginative Interplay of Polarities of Sex and Gender: An Exercise in Pragmatic World Construction

If the intensity of sexual desire functions like the tension of a bowstring, efforts to eliminate it will only make it more obstinate, whereas exercising an appropriate amount of repression will make this desire orderly and life-giving. As a reality that reaches out beyond individual bodies to connect with other bodies, sexuality is a force not only in physical bodies but also in those collective entities we figuratively refer to as bodies, such as the body politic. This body politic can be identified as feminine (Mother Zion, Wife Jerusalem) or masculine (the king's two bodies: the physical and the metaphorical). The attribution of gender to a personified, metaphoric entity discloses significant aspects of the way the collective entity functions; nevertheless, the collective entity does not literally possess gender.

When a human being, a mythical figure, or a god is described as an androgyne (i.e., possessing male and female sex and masculine and femi-

56. Benno Landsberger, "Jungfräulichkeit: Ein Beitrag zum Thema 'Beilage und Eheschliessung,'" in *Symbolae Iuridicae et Historicae Martino David Dedicatae*, 2 vols., ed. J. A. Ankum, Robert Feenstra, and William F. Leemans, 2:41–105 (Leiden: Brill, 1968).

nine gender simultaneously), it contains fundamental polarities within its being that are usually kept separate. This being possessing dual sex and gender has overcome the distinction between sex and gender because these two sexes and two genders have been sufficiently unified to form a new entity (i.e., an androgyne), which is a third sex and a third gender. Dionysus is an androgynous deity who is ritually symbolized as the god of the phallus but acts as if he is unconcerned about sex. In ancient Mesopotamia and Greece a divine androgyne was viewed as propitious, but a human androgyne as a threatening omen. A human androgyne concretely presents its dual, contradictory nature as a fact, whereas a divine androgyne cannot be seen or touched and so the presence of contradictory features can be treated as a work of the imagination. In other words, literal androgyny is more threatening than figurative androgyny.

A strong benefit gained from a divine or human androgyne is the presence of a being capable of mediating between the earth and the netherworld. Threatening forces that invade a community are often seen as issuing from the netherworld. If an androgyne can dispatch this threatening force, the presumption is that this being has connections with the netherworld—a viewpoint found in ancient Mesopotamia and Greece and probably in ancient Israel. Calling on the services of these androgynes when there is an eruption of the irrational in the social or national life places them at points of vulnerability within the collective body to see if they can restore balance. The power of an androgynous figure was ambiguous: it could heal or harm. The androgynous officials of the Ishtar cult known as the *kurgarrû* and *assinnū* were both ridiculed and revered for their wild cultic behavior, which testified to an abundance of divine erotic power in them. A few sex omens of *Šumma ālu* regard sexual relations with one of these androgynous figures as propitious; however, the intent of such omens is to provoke reflection in the one who receives the omen rather than to provide an absolute directive. The capacity of the *kurgarrû* and *assinnū* to bless was matched by their capacity to curse. Thus in the *Maqlû* ritual's measures for protecting against sorcerers, androgynous figures are named as potential threats (IV: 83; VII: 92).

Other imaginative composite figures were also called upon to be guardians. The cherub figure in the garden of Eden in Ezekiel 28 is pictured as having the potential to strengthen the kingdom of Tyre and Jerusalem, but instead it brings about its downfall by ruling as if it were the sovereign rather than the throne-bearer. The sages of Mesopotamia—the fish-men (*apkallū*)—similarly had this potential to bring healing and harmony to the earthly kingdom. Because they were believed to have participated in the creation of basic human institutions by their wisdom, they were expected to be in a position to fix them. Seven heroic wisdom figures in Greece came to be known as "the seven sages" by analogy to the *apkallū* in Mesopotamia. One of these figures, Epimetheus, was called upon to heal the plague in Athens associated with the Cylonian affair at the end of the seventh century BCE. Thus composite wisdom figures like androgynous officials were shrouded in ambiguity because their excess of power could become destructive if they became focused on their own self-interests and used their power for self-aggrandizement rather than for service.

Servants on the Margin: Eunuchs as Protectors of the Common Good

Eunuchs functioned in the palace households in Israel and Mesopotamia. According to Deut 23:1 they were not to be part of the Israelite assembly. In postexilic Judah the Isaianic circles tried to override this distinction, claiming that Sabbath observance was a more authentic sign of being in covenant with YHWH than bodily wholeness. In Assyria eunuchs served throughout the ranks of the palace from the royal bodyguard to the lowliest of household servants. In Persia they were the overseers of the royal harem and became the chief communication link of these "cloistered" royal women with the public outside. Eunuchs were present with the royal offspring in their upbringing and so were well connected with those who held power in the empire. In both Assyria and Persia eunuchs held important posts in the provincial administration. Many eunuchs had been recruited from among prisoners of war. They were brought to the capital of the empire and indoctrinated with Assyrian or Persian culture. Then, as members of two cultures, they could more effectively bring about mediation and change. Their status as eunuchs rendered them outsiders to both cultures, and so they developed their own "eunuch-culture," characterized by loyalty to the monarch. In the eighth through the seventh centuries BCE in Assyria the power of the eunuchs grew in the midst of political crises in which they emerged as a stable group allied with the monarchy.

The Challenge of Negotiating Rather Than Eliminating Boundaries

Cross-dressing was forbidden in Israel according to Deut 22:5. Androgynous officials of the Ishtar cult practiced it as a mark of their identity. In Euripides' play *The Bacchae*, Pentheus, who functions as the sacral king of Thebes, becomes possessed by the god Dionysus and is persuaded to dress as a maenad—a disguise necessary for spying on the secret rituals of the women in the mountains. Cross-dressing becomes a metatragic symbol for Pentheus. It captures his anxiety about the presence of the feminine in his own person. As king he tries to keep women within the conventions of the household. Their retreat to the mountains under Dionysus's influence threatens such containment. He is prepared to send out his military to return the women to the city, but Dionysus warns him that this will be disastrous. These supernaturally empowered women will easily overpower the soldiers of Thebes. Every effort Pentheus makes to suppress the presence of the feminine is counterproductive: every action produces an equal or stronger reaction from the feminine. The androgynous character of Dionysus symbolizes for Pentheus the mixture of feminine and masculine traits he wants to remove from Thebes. But as Pentheus fights against Dionysus he finds that he is fighting against himself. Thus the scene in which Pentheus parades to the mountain dressed as a maenad symbolizes his alignment with Dionysus: instead of banishing androgyny, Pentheus reveals it in his own person. Dionysus grins as he looks on the tragic demise of Pentheus; Dionysus represents the amoral life-force, which is extinguished only in death. Pentheus's mother, raving as a maenad under Dionysus's influence, tears Pentheus to pieces; the mother who bore him shreds him as a consequence of his efforts to banish Dionysus from Thebes and from his life. The simultaneous presence of the bestial and divine in the god Dionysus distinguishes him from other deities.

Composite boundary-keepers must be mindful of their binary character and their position in the cosmic hierarchy. The narcissism of the king of Tyre and the blasphemy of Pentheus resulted in their destruction. The divinized perfect Mesopotamian king in the Ur III period was celebrated for his capacity as a builder of civilization; he was portrayed as having masculine and feminine traits in these efforts. Although the balance between masculine and feminine traits of the king of Tyre is not the focus of Ezekiel 28, his identification with the cherub in 28:14 suggests that he needed to be mindful of the tension between the human and the divine and between the human and bestial in his role as boundary-keeper. The crossing of forces from the spheres of the animal, human, and divine intensifies in the figure of the composite boundary-keeper. The polarities of myth identify these crossing forces and try to bring intelligibility to them as they irrupt in human experience. The strategies in ritual for maintaining equilibrium between these competing life-forces differ radically from those in tragedy: ritual seeks to reconcile these polarities whereas tragedy tries to explode them. In tragedy the individual characters die but the life-force continues; their individual identities dissolve into the natural elements only to be reconfigured in new forms that once again struggle for equilibrium. The grinning Dionysus reflects this polymorphous, timeless life-force. The polytheistic mindset demands that humans be respectful of this divine force. However, a monotheistic mindset calls humans to a purity of heart in which they see YHWH as the creator of this life. The way to deal with the powers of disintegration and alienation from this force of life is to reestablish one's focus through wholehearted devotion to YHWH. Passionate, focused love of YHWH will overcome the forces of death.

Chapter 6: Celibacy as a Proleptic Death and a Quest for Transcendence

Radical Self-Denial and Truth Telling as Measures for Combating the Amorphous Power of Death

Celibacy is an extreme response to the brokenness of the human condition. Foregoing the pleasures and satisfactions of domestic life is itself a strong measure of self-imposed suffering, but even more challenging was the fact that not having offspring in these ancient cultures meant that one was cutting off a primary form of life after death. This belief that one lived on in one's offspring was of central importance in the Israelite tradition. Factors that might consciously or subconsciously have moved someone in these ancient cultures to opt to forgo marriage would be homosexuality, a diminished sex drive, opportunities for social advancement for individuals such as eunuchs, the security and power of the cloistered life of the *nadiātum*, resonance with the lifestyle of androgynous officials of the cult of Ishtar, or similar reasons that would have made some individuals resist heterosexual marriage, the difficulties of childbirth, and the responsibility of raising children. The factor that led to Jeremiah's adoption of a celibate way of life—a death-dealing crisis—is more compelling. Jeremiah's forgoing of wife and children was to be a sign of the destruction that would bring an end to the kingdom of Judah. Facing death before it actually took possession of him, Jeremiah confirmed that a transcendent power was working in his life, urging him to look beyond death to some new, not-yet-visible possibility. In his fifth confession he expresses trust that YHWH will save him; the abrupt reversal of mood characteristic of individual laments shapes Jeremiah's response here, yet it shows that the key content of his statement is the expression of trust in YHWH.

The crisis in which death was near also characterized the trouble that beset the sufferer in the Babylonian poem *Ludlul bēl nēmeqi*. His physical illness provoked rejection from his community rather than compassion. Apparently his illness generated fear with which his family and community did not know how to cope, so they chose to shun him and look for ways to distance him from their collective existence lest his troubles devolve on them. Social rejection was also the problem faced by Socrates in the last years of his life. As a gadfly whose conversations tended to make his interlocutors feel quite uncomfortable, Socrates created enemies in Athens through his commitment to inculcating virtue. In the social and political unrest in Athens during the final decade of the fifth century generated by the defeat of Athens by Sparta in the Peloponnesian War and the brief rule of a tyrannical oligarchy (the rule of the Thirty, 405–404 BCE), individuals who challenged the democratic process in light of values claiming a closer approximation to transcendent truth were vulnerable to the whims of the city assembly. In Plato's *Apology*, Socrates does not refrain from provoking the hostility of the assembly members; on a number of occasions he tries to elicit an emotional response from them. Socrates has reached the point in his life at which he feels joined with the transcendent sphere and is convinced that no human can harm him or put him (i.e., his soul) to death. He will not flee from Athens to preserve his life, for that would compromise his integrity.

A sharp confrontation with death can trample one's defenses underfoot. Jeremiah engages in radical truth telling in his confessions. He does not hold back his confusion and anger, but unleashes these strong emotions against Yhwh and his Judahite oppressors. He criticizes the Judahites' fasting and collective confession of sin as gestures that do not acknowledge the necessary connection between deeds and consequences (Jer 14:10-11). Yhwh will not lightly turn back punishment for sins; justice demands that consequences of some form be visited on even the repentant sinner. As a member of the Judahite community Jeremiah also resists his share in the punishment being visited on Judah and Jerusalem (Jer 12:1-4; 15:10-18). The truth telling in which Jeremiah engages in his confessions is paralleled by the anguish the sufferer in *Ludlul bēl nēmeqi* expresses toward the gods in his lamentations. He reaches the point at which he not only finds the ways of the gods inscrutable but also contends that the gods have set a high standard of behavior for humans that they have not revealed to humans but for which they nevertheless hold humans accountable. Socrates was put on trial for his radical honesty in dealing with others, particularly his fostering of habits of critical thinking in the youth with whom he dialogued. His view of the divine realm transmuted the traditional and civic gods into rational principles—a move his opponents judged to be dangerous to the common good. So they charged him with promoting impiety and corrupting the youth.

Self-Denial and the Search for the Divine

The acceptance of a life of celibacy creates an empty space in one's life that cries out to be filled. Jeremiah's call to celibacy is narrated in 16:1-4. Shortly thereafter the text speaks of how the tree planted next to a flowing stream never withers (17:8). This text echoes that of Psalm 1 in extolling the life-giving character of the torah. Psalm 19 proclaims that the torah not only instructs humans but also nourishes them. Jeremiah and the Judahites are urged to meditate on the torah so that they might connect with a source of life that will sustain them even in the most trying times.

The sufferer in *Ludlul bēl nēmeqi* is at the point of death and is given up for lost when he receives three dreams. In the second dream he recognizes a man who recites incantations; in the third dream this same man holds a tablet in his hand. This figure appears to have been an *āšipu*, "a healer of mind and body, an exorcist." Such a person was not only a scholar but also a practitioner. His scholarly art was to heal mind and body. Although one element of his healing may have been turning away the sorceries directed by foes against a client, this battle with evil spirits was not his primary focus. The *āšipu*'s form of holistic medicine differed from that of the *asu*, a physician whose remedies consisted of pharmaceutical substances. The *āšipu* studied the omen tradition to assess the symptoms of a client and make a prognosis, but then employed apotropaic rituals to try to change an ominous fate. Language, particularly the performative language of incantation and prayer, was the primary tool with which the *āšipu* sought to bring healing to a sufferer. The art of the *āšipu* was a major component of the written theological traditions that took shape at the beginning of the first millennium BCE and aimed to create a sacred canopy over the Mesopotamian communities. Mesopotamian scholars tried to bring a measure of intelligibility to the course of events by attending to traditions they regarded as revealed in primordial times by Ea to the sages (*apkallū*). These traditions were put in written form and handed on by master scribes known as *ummanû*. This written tradition contributed stability to the tradition and so helped to create from within it an aura of divine wisdom. Divination and prophecy continued to provide a communication link with the divine world, but this vertical form of communication was complemented by the horizontal one anchored in written texts.

In the *Republic*, Socrates explained how reason (*nous*) is the capacity within humans that enables them to behold the beautiful, the true, and the good. By means of this beholding, humans are given knowledge (*epistēmē*) of the transcendent realm. This knowledge is unchanging. That which does not change is free from the reality of death. Socrates used three metaphors to describe how such knowledge is imparted to humans: the sun, the divided line, and the allegory of the cave. The eye cannot perceive without light, which he identifies as imparted by the sun. The divided line illustrates how humans are prone to find their way in the world by means of pictures of things rather than knowing the essences of things. To discover what things truly are, a person must move to the upper portion of the divided line where one thinks first in a mathematical way and then dialectically. This final form of dialectical thinking pushes a thinker to examine radically his or her assumptions and thereby come to the transcendent sphere of unchanging essences. This movement from imagistic thinking to dialectical thinking is illustrated by the allegory of the cave. A human imprisoned from birth and able to see only the shadows of things projected against the wall of a cave is set free and taken by the hand to look at the actual images that were projected and then invited to go up the ramp from the cave to the upper world where the sun shines. This ascent from the cave is enlightenment by means of education; the freed prisoner moves from the lower world of shifting shadows to the upper world of unchanging Forms where the blinding light of the sun shows how human beholders are not capable of looking directly upon the Good. The Good or transcendent principle that suffuses all of reality is beyond the capacity of reason to comprehend. For Socrates death is not to be feared because reason is not subject to death. The form of death that impedes reason is the shifting data communicated by the senses. Unlike reason, the senses do not take the step of discovering the essence of a thing within a sensuous image.

Salvation Through Contemplation of Transcendent Truth

Jeremiah was able to see beyond his severe crisis and have hope because Yhwh communicated his saving presence to him. This communication took on a more enduring form than that of an oracle of salvation in the written instructions of the torah. Meditation on the torah became the means for bringing a sense of wholeness and well-being to his fractured person. For the sufferer in *Ludlul bēl nēmeqi* the healing arts of the *āšipu* as predicted in a dream allow him to gain hope and start on the road to recovery. He attributes this oracle and the promised healing to Marduk, a deity he now proclaims to be sovereign over cosmic events. This new Marduk religion—a kind of Marduk monotheism—operated on the level of personal protection as well as on the macro-level of nature and history. In the Greek world Socrates domesticated death by appealing to unchanging knowledge. In his view the rational was true reality. Plato fought with the poets—the tragedians—who allowed their audiences to feel that life was unfair, that there was something out of synch in the cosmos and humans often experienced the unfortunate consequences of this disorder. Plato claimed that the poets were appealing to the lower part of the human soul and thus impeding their hearers from taking responsibility for their actions and trying to free themselves from the ignorance that had brought them this suffering. To live as Socrates did, with one's rational soul in control of the appetitive and spirited parts of the soul, would allow one to accept the passing away of the body and the things of the visible world and to anchor oneself in the world of truth, of unchanging essences. Aristotle was also dedicated to the life of reason, but as a biologist he was committed to the particularity of individual organisms and their environments. Therefore he did not allow the essence of a thing to be separated from the matter in which it had become manifest. For Aristotle, death was part of nature. He did not exchange the visible world for the invisible as Plato did. He tried to find the form of equilibrium and integration for specific beings according to their particular essences and circumstances. Therefore a radical response to death that would call for renouncing sexual relations and the option of having offspring would seem out of balance for Aristotle. Aristotle revered the life of theoretic reason in which a person contemplated the eternal verities. Such an activity imparted harmony to the person that came as close to the goal of being as happy as one could expect. Yet for Aristotle such contemplation was not meant to lift one out of embodied existence but rather to bring together reason and emotion for a citizen of a state. For Aristotle, celibacy would be an exercise in disintegration.

Desire is the movement within animals and plants that makes them reach out to the environment on which they depend. This reality of desire (*orexis*) is a principle of movement within animate things that is goal-oriented. For Aristotle such desire is channeled by practical reason, a form of discernment that is attuned to the particularities at hand. Therefore asceticism of the Aristotelian variety would not endorse a Stoic program of silencing the passions. Rather, the passions should be channeled. In this regard Aristotle agrees with the tragedians and with the later views of Plato expressed in the *Phaedrus* that the passions communicate vitality and a cognitive content of their own that is vital for human flourishing.

Conclusion. Celibacy Within the Cosmic Household: A Journey Beyond Death Through Love

Occurring at strategic points in the traditions of pre-Hellenistic Israel, Mesopotamia, and Greece, celibate practice reveals essential ways that the sex drive was channeled for the well-being of the patriarchal household. Celibacy emerges from the patriarchal household in these three cultures in times of crisis as a way of responding to the threat of death. As the locus of immortality, the natal household is the matrix of relationships within which the childless celibate finds her or his place and function. But in a crisis situation in which even the existence of the natal household is called into question the celibate must take his or her place in the divine cosmic household within which death is domesticated.

Jeremiah undertook the celibate way of life to prefigure the destruction of Judah and Jerusalem and to symbolize the conviction that the life of the people of Judah would triumph over death (16:1-4). In the Old Testament no other Israelite or Judahite was commanded to be celibate. As sketched out in the book of Jeremiah, the literary *persona* Jeremiah suffers intense inner conflict over the way he is treated by YHWH and the community. However, this alienation shows how celibacy paradoxically becomes a way of life that provides meaning beyond death. Jeremiah renounces wife and family under the conviction that YHWH will bring a new future. This advent of YHWH will occur not simply in an end-time cataclysm but more important in the heart of the devoted one. Thus, essential to the practice of celibacy is wholehearted devotion to YHWH (Jer 17:7-8). Parallels to aspects of Jeremiah's celibate way of transcending death can be found in Mesopotamian texts such as the *Myth of Adapa* and the *Epic of Gilgamesh* and in Greek texts such as Plato's *Republic* and *Phaedrus*, in which the quest for wisdom situates human life in a cosmic context reaching beyond the appearances perceived by the senses.

The sexual renunciation constitutive of celibacy is continuous with the avoidance of adultery and incest essential to the integrity of a household. Premarital virginity for women is defended as a practice required for maintaining patrilineal descent. This limited time of total abstinence from sex suggests that if lifelong celibacy is to find a rationale it must do so within the context of its contribution to the integrity of household relationships. To exist outside a household in these three ancient cultures was to be virtually nonexistent. The sexual renunciation of the celibate must provide ways for the transcendent to be at work within the earthly household. In other words, the celibate must become a living symbol for connecting the earthly with the cosmic household, which spans the spheres of heaven, earth, and the netherworld. Examples of these living celibate symbols that link the cosmic spheres in each of the three cultures are the following: (1) Jeremiah aims to become like a tree planted near living water (Jer 17:8); (2) the cloistered *nadītum*-women of Old Babylonian Mesopotamia refrain from marriage and regularly make intercession to the gods for their families at the temples of Shamash in Sippar and of Ninurta in Nippur; (3) the tragic character Antigone renounces marriage and terrestrial life in order to serve and uphold the honor of her ancestral household. The ideal and the practice of celibacy intersect in the efforts of family members to maintain their bonds within the matrix of relationships that spans heaven, earth, and the netherworld.

The alienation from family and neighbors experienced by Jeremiah forces him to greater openness to YHWH. The initial diminishment of horizontal (human-to-human) relationships issues in a deepening of vertical (divine-to-human) relationships that in turn strengthens horizontal relationships. The literary *persona* of Jeremiah sketched out in the book of Jeremiah finds a symbolic analogue in the figure of Wife Jerusalem in Ezekiel 16 who is expected to be exclusively faithful to YHWH. Wife Jerusalem and the literary *persona* Jeremiah are prohibited from marrying or having sexual relations with human partners. Within the books of Jeremiah and Ezekiel, Jeremiah and the Wife Jerusalem are symbolic figures whose historical impact arises most significantly from the extent to which the individuals in the community imitate their profile and thus embody their personae in the historical experience of the Israelite people. As illustrated by these two symbolic figures, the ideal of exclusive fidelity to YHWH lies at the heart of the covenant relationship and is constitutive of the integrity of the relationships within YHWH's cosmic household.

Jeremiah's renunciation of human marriage in favor of exclusive fidelity to YHWH means that, in terms of the marital metaphor, he takes on the role of the wife in the divine-human relationship and does so as a symbol of the collective existence of the Israelites. His wholehearted devotion to YHWH may appear to be a withdrawal from normal family relationships, but the long-term aim of his celibate practice is to strengthen those family relationships by directing them toward right relationship with YHWH. Wife Jerusalem, however, is portrayed as a counterexample to the faithful wife and thus instructs by showing those attitudes and behaviors that should be avoided in order to relate properly to YHWH. As a collective symbol for the Jerusalemite community, Wife Jerusalem is to refrain from sexual relations and marriage with human partners; she is called to be celibate on the horizontal plane. Within the Mesopotamian and Greek traditions, mythical and legendary portraits of the mother of Sargon of Akkad and of Sophocles' Antigone form symbolic analogues to the literary figures of Jeremiah and wife Jerusalem by illustrating how the ideal and the practice of refraining from marriage are formative of the collective life of the people.

Long-term renunciation of sexual relations calls for a creative reconfiguration of one's erotic energies. Even within the experience of a sexually active individual, vital sexual desire demands discipline and a measure of repression. These two countervailing forces of desire and repression play off one another like the forces that keep a bowstring taut. For the celibate to strive for the elimination of sexual desire would be to diminish life. The alternative is to transmute direct sexual expression into forms in which erotic desire is operative but is incorporated into aesthetics, friendship, altruism, or other activities that enhance the common good and the quality of life. The prophet Hosea exhorts Israel to focus its erotic energies on YHWH and condemns Israel for diverting this erotic impulse into illicit cultic and political activities. When YHWH tries to restore his relationship with Israel he "allures" her into the wilderness (Hos 2:7). The tone of YHWH's entreaty indicates that the erotic dimension of experience has a vital role to play in the human-divine relationship. To dismiss erotic approaches to God by labeling them as "pagan" reads more into prophetic denunciations of Israel's relations with foreign gods than the texts allow. Instead of eliminating erotic desire from Israel's way of relating to YHWH, Hosea exhorts the Israelites to channel this vital human energy constructively. In Mesopotamian and Greek literature erotic relationships among the gods as well as between a deity and a human are attested (e.g., Inanna and Ishulannu; Apollo and Creusa). In Plato's *Symposium* the speakers praise the divine character of erotic desire that brings humans into contact with beauty and truth and fuels the pursuit of realities that extend beyond appearances.

As an extreme form of sexual renunciation, celibacy nevertheless stands in continuity with the discipline of sexual renunciation in premarital virginity for women and in the avoidance of adultery, incest, and other violations of familial and household relationships. Shechem's relationship to Dinah in Genesis 34 and Jephthah's relationship to his daughter in Judges 11 illustrate the importance of female virginity for the integrity of the relationships constituting the patriarchal household. Similar emphases on premarital virginity can be found in law and omen collections, literature, and letters from Mesopotamia and from literary and philosophical works in Greece. An engaging treatment of the theme of virginity is found in Euripides' *Hippolytus*, where the male protagonist of the same name champions the ideal of virginity until the goddess Aphrodite finds an indirect way to subvert his idealism.

The sexual pair male/female is matched by the gendered pair masculine/feminine within the human person. The overlap and interplay between the categories of sex and gender is intensified in the person of the androgyne who embodies all four opposites of these two polarities simultaneously. The anomalous figure of the androgyne evoked both fascination and fear in human communities. In the tradition of ancient Israel the mixing of categories in sex and gender was prohibited. Such transgressions were regarded as defiling. However, in Ezek 28:11-18 and Genesis 2 the primal human may well have been an androgyne. Since Gen 1:26-28 refers to humankind—the communion of male and female—as made in God's image, some scholars dare to describe God as androgynous. But such literalization of metaphorical language creates an anomalous picture of Yhwh, who is usually regarded as transcending sex and gender. In Mesopotamia the cultic figures of the *kurgarrû* and *assinnu* are depicted as androgynes. Also eunuchs—whose male sexual potential has been neutered—are depicted sometimes as androgynes. In Greece, Euripides created the androgynous figure Pentheus in his play *The Bacchae* as an unwilling manifestation of the androgynous deity Dionysus. Typically, human androgynes are ominous, while divine androgynes are propitious. The potent character of human androgynes in cultic roles is often explained as their uncanny ability to enter the netherworld and return from there, which for the typical human is the land of no return.

The Hebrew Bible foregrounds the heterosexual model of Genesis 1–3 focused on procreation. This same concern for populating and forming the household is dominant in ancient Mesopotamia and Greece. In Gen 1:26-28 humans symbolize God. Their activities of creating or initiating something new reflect the way the communion of the human couple brings them into communion with God. The difference from the God who transcends sex and gender is evident in the humans' begetting or giving birth while God creates (*bārāʾ*). Yet the sacramentality of their union for the sake of procreation is one of the ways in which their exchange of love builds up both the human and the cosmic households. Their work in sustaining the material basis of the household and their love in cultivating the relationships of the household are also vital ways in which they symbolize God. Analogous ways of promoting the matrix of relationships in the household are evident in ancient Mesopotamia and Greece.

The matrix of relationships in the particular human households extends into the matrix of relationships in the cosmic household. The primal human in Genesis 2 and Ezek 28:11-12 functioned within this matrix of relationships in the cosmic household spanning heaven and earth. The primal human prefigures the celibate boundary-keeper who tries to sustain this connection between the human and cosmic households. The celibate is an intermediary between the visible and invisible spheres who fosters the vision of household life enduring beyond death.

Abbreviations

AbB	*Altbabylonische Briefe*
ABD	*Anchor Bible Dictionary*
AHw	Wolfram von Soden, *Akkadisches Handwörterbuch*
ANET	J. B. Pritchard, ed., *Ancient Near Eastern Texts*
ARM	*Archives royales de Mari*
ASOR	American Schools of Oriental Research
BASOR	*Bulletin of the American Schools of Oriental Research*
BAL	Riekele Borger, *Babylonische-assyrische Lesestücke*
BDB	Francis Brown, Samuel R. Driver, Charles A.Briggs, *Hebrew and English Lexicon of the Old Testament (Oxford, 1951)*
BE	*Babylonian Expedition of the University of Pennsylvania, Series A: Cuneiform Texts*
Bib	*Biblica*
BIN	*Babylonian Inscriptions in the Collection of J. B. Nies*
BWL	Wilfred G. Lambert, *Babylonian Wisdom Literature* (Oxford: Clarendon Press, 1960)
BO	*Bibliotheca Orientalis*
CAD	*The Assyrian Dictionary of the Oriental Institute of the University of Chicago*. Editor-in-charge, Martha T. Roth; editorial board, Robert D. Biggs et al. 15 vols. (Chicago: Oriental Institute, 1956–2009)
CAG	Commentaria Aristotelem Graeca

CAH	Cambridge Ancient History
CANE	*Civilizations of the Ancient Near East*, 2 vols., ed. Jack Sasson et al. (Peabody, MA: Hendrickson, 2000)
CBQ	*Catholic Biblical Quarterly*
CH	*Code of Hammurapi*
COS	*The Context of Scripture*, 3 vols., ed. William W. Hallo and K. Lawson Younger, Jr. (Leiden: Brill, 1997)
CP	*Classical Philology*
CRRAI	Comptes rendu, Rencontre Assyriologique Internationale
CT	*Cuneiform Texts from Babylonian Tablets in the British Museum*
DDD	*Dictionary of Deities and Demons*, ed. Karel van der Toorn, Bob Becking, and Pieter van der Horst (Leiden: Brill, 1995)
DK	Hermann Diels, *Die Fragmente der Vorsokratiker: griechisch und deutsch*, 3 vols., 9th ed., ed. Walther Kranz (Berlin: Weidmann, 1959–1960)
EE	*The Standard Babylonian Creation Myth: Enūma Eliš*, SAA 4, ed. Pilippe Talon (Helsinki: The Neo-Assyrian Text Corpus Project, 2005)
HALAT	W. Baumgartner et al., *Hebräisches und aramäisches Lexikon zum Alten Testament* (Leiden, 1967-90)
HAR	*Hebrew Annual Review*
HTR	*Harvard Theological Review*
HUCA	*Hebrew Union College Annual*
JANES	*Journal of the Ancient Near Eastern Society*
JAOS	*Journal of the American Oriental Society*
JBL	*Journal of Biblical Literature*
JCS	*Journal of Cuneiform Studies*
JESHO	*Journal of the Economic and Social History of the Orient*
JETS	*Journal of the Evangelical Theological Society*
JHS	*Journal of Hellenic Studies*
JNES	*Journal of Near Eastern Studies*

JNSL	*Journal of Northwest Semitic Languages*
JQR	*Jewish Quarterly Review*
JSOT	*Journal for the Study of the Old Testament*
KAR	*Keilschrifttexte aus Assur religiösen Inhalts*
KTU	Manfred Dietrich, Oswald Loretz, and Joaqín Sanmartín, *The Cuneiform Alphabetic Texts from Ugarit, Ras Ibn Hani and Other Places* (2d, enlarged edition; Münster, 1991)
MA	Middle Assyrian
NA	Neo-Assyrian
NB	Neo-Babylonian
OB	Old Babylonian
OLP	*Orientalia Louvaniensia Periodica*
Op	Hesiod's *Works and Days*
Or	*Orientalia*
OTL	Old Testament Library
RA	*Revue d'assyriologie et d'archéologie orientale*
RIME	The Royal Inscriptions of Mesopotamia, Early Periods
RLA (or *RlA*)	*Reallexikon der Assyriologie*
SAA	State Archives of Assyria Cuneiform Texts
TAPA	*Transactions of the American Philosophical Society*
UET	*Ur Excavation Texts*
VAT	Tablets in the collections of the Staatliche Museen, Berlin
VT	*Vetus Testamentum*
WO	*Die Welt des Orients*
ZA	*Zeitschrift für Assyriologie*
ZAW	*Zeitschrift für die alttestamentliche Wissenschaft*

For additional abbreviations see the *Chicago Assyrian Dictionary* or the journal *Orientalia* for topics on ancient Mesopotamia and *Old Testament Abstracts* or *Elenchus Bibliographicus Biblicus* for biblical Israel.

Bibliography

Primary Texts

Ancient Israel

Biblia Hebraica Stuttgartensia. Edited by Kurt Elliger et al. Stuttgart: Deutsche Bibelstiftung, 1966–77.

Mesopotamia

Borger, Riekele. *Die Inschriften Asarhaddons, Königs von Assyrien*. AfO Beiheft 9. Graz: by the author, 1956.

———. *Babylonisch-assyrische Lësestücke*. 2 volumes. AnOr 54. Rome: Pontifical Biblical Institute, 1979.

Cagni, Luigi. *L'epopea di Erra*. Studi Semitici 34. Rome: Istituto di Studi del Vicino Oriente, University of Rome, 1969.

Charpin, Dominique, et al., eds. *Archives epistolaires de Mari II/2*. [*ARM*] 26. Paris: Editions Recherche sur les Civilisations, 1988.

Cohen, Mark E. *The Canonical Lamentations of Ancient Mesopotamia*. 2 volumes. Potomac, MD: Capital Decisions Limited, 1988.

Cooper, Jerrold S. *The Curse of Agade*. Baltimore and London: Johns Hopkins University Press, 1983.

Driver, Godfrey R., and John C. Miles. *The Babylonian Laws*. Volume I: *Legal Commentary*. Oxford: Clarendon Press, 1952.

———. *The Assyrian Laws*. Oxford: Clarendon Press, 1935.

Farber, Walter. *Beschwörungsrituale an Ištar und Dumuzi*. Akademie der Wissenschaften und der Literatur 30. Wiesbaden: Franz Steiner Verlag, 1977.

Foster, Benjamin. *Before the Muses: An Anthology of Akkadian Literature*. 3d edition. Bethesda, MD: Capital Decisions Limited, 2005.

Frayne, Douglas. *Sargonic and Gutian Periods (2334–2113 BC)*. *RIME* 2. Toronto: University of Toronto Press, 1993.

———. *The Royal Inscriptions of Mesopotamia. Early Periods: Volume 4. Old Babylonian Period (2003–1595 BC)*. [*RIME*] 4. Toronto: University of Toronto Press, 1990.

George, A. R. *The Babylonian Gilgamesh Epic*. 2 volumes. Oxford and New York: Oxford University Press, 2003.

———. "Babylonian Texts from the Folios of Sidney Smith, Part Three: A Commentary on a Ritual of the Month Nisan." In *If a Man Builds a Joyful House: Assyriological Studies in Honor of Erle Verdun Leichty*. Edited by Ann Kessler Guinan et al., 173–85. Leiden: Brill, 2006.

———, and F. N. H. Al-Rawi. "Tablets from the Sippar Library. VII. Three Wisdom Texts." *Iraq* 60 (1998): 187–206.

Gurney, O. R. "The Sultantepe Tablets (Continued): VII: The Myth of Nergal and Ereshkigal." *Anatolian Studies* 10 (1960): 105–31.

Izre'el, Shlomo. *Adapa and the South Wind: Language Has the Power of Life and Death*. Winona Lake, IN: Eisenbrauns, 2001.

Jacobsen, Thorkild. *The Harps That Once . . . Sumerian Poetry in Translation*. New Haven: Yale University Press, 1987.

Kataja, Laura, and Robert M. Whiting. *Grants, Decrees and Gifts of the Neo-Assyrian Period*. SAA XII. Helsinki: Helsinki University Press, 1995.

Kramer, Samuel Noah. "The Marriage of Martu." In *Bar-Ilan Studies in Assyriology: Dedicated to Pinhas Artzi*. Edited by Jacob Klein and Aaron Skaist, 11–27. Ramat Gan: Bar-Ilan University Press, 1990.

Kraus, Fritz R. *Altbabylonische Briefe in Umschrift und Übersetzung*. Volume 1. Leiden: Brill, 1964.

Lambert, Wilfred G. *Babylonian Wisdom Literature*. Oxford: Clarendon Press, 1960.

———, and Alan R. Millard. *Atraḫasīs: The Babylonian Story of the Flood*. Winona Lake, IN: Eisenbrauns, 1999.

Lewis, Brian. *The Sargon Legend: A Study of the Akkadian Text and the Tale of the Hero Who Was Exposed at Birth*. ASOR Dissertation Series 4. Cambridge, MA: American Schools of Oriental Research, 1980.

Livingstone, Alasdair. *Mystical and Mythological Explanatory Works of Assyrian and Babylonian Scholars*. Oxford: Clarendon Press, 1986.

Mayer, Werner. *Untersuchungen zur Formensprache der babylonischen "Gebetsbeschwörungen."* Studia Pohl: Series Maior 5. Rome: Pontifical Biblical Institute, 1976.

Meier, Gerhard. *Die assyrische Beschwörungssammlung Maqlû*. AfO Beiheft 2. Osnabrück: Biblio-Verlag, 1967.

Parpola, Simo. *Letters from Assyrian and Babylonian Scholars*. SAA 10. Helsinki: Helsinki University Press, 1993.

Römer, Willem H. P. "Hymne an Inanna-Dilibad. Heilige Hochzeit Iddindagāns mit der Göttin." In idem, *Sumerische 'Königshymnen' der Isin-Zeit*, 128–208. Leiden: Brill, 1965.

Roth, Martha T. *Law Collections from Mesopotamia and Asia Minor*. 2d edition. SBL Writings from the Ancient World Series 6. Atlanta: Scholars Press, 1995.

Schroeder, Otto. *Keilschrifttexte aus Assur verschiedenen Inhalts*. Wissenschaftliche Veröffentlichungen der Deutschen Orient-Gesellschaft in Assur 35. Leipzig: J. C. Hinrichs, 1920.

Sefati, Yitschak. "An Oath of Chastity in a Sumerian Love Song (SRT 31)?" In *Bar-Ilan Studies Dedicated to Pinḥas Artzi*. Edited by Jacob Klein and Aaron Skaist, 45–63. Ramat Gan: Bar-Ilan University Press, 1990.

———. *Love Songs in Sumerian Literature: Critical Edition of the Dumuzi-Inanna Songs*. Ramat Gan: Bar-Ilan University Press, 1998.

Stolper, Matthew W. "Fifth Century Nippur: Texts of the Murašûs and from Their Surroundings." *JCS* 53 (2001): 83–132.

Talon, Philippe. *The Standard Babylonian Creation Myth Enūma Eliš*. SAA 4. Helsinki: Neo-Assyrian Text Corpus Project, 2005.

Van Soldt, Wilfred H. *Solar Omens of Enuma Anu Enlil: Tablets 23 (24)–29 (30)*. Leiden: Nederlands Historisch-Archaeologisch Institut, 1995.

Volk, Konrad. *Die Balag-Komposition Uru-Àm-ma-ir-ra-bi: Rekonstruktion und Bearbeitung der Tafeln 18 (19'ff), 19, 20 und 21 der späten, kanonischen Version*. Freiburger Altorientalische Studien 18. Stuttgart: Franz Steiner Verlag, 1989.

Weidner, Ernst. "Hof- und Harems Erlasse assyrische Könige aus dem 2. Jahrtausend v. Chr." *Archiv für Orientforschung* 17 (1954–56): 257–93.

Ancient Greece

Campbell, David. *Greek Lyric*. 4 volumes. Cambridge, MA: Harvard University Press, 1982.

———. *The Golden Lyre: The Themes of the Greek Lyric Poets*. London: Duckworth, 1983.

Diels, Hermann. *Fragmente der Vorsokratiker*. 3 volumes. 9th edition, Walther Kranz. Berlin: Weidmann, 1959–60.

Fowler, Harold N. *Euthyphro, Apology, Crito, Phaedo, Phaedrus* by Plato. LCL. New York: G. P. Putnam's Sons, 1923.

Kovacs, David. *Euripides II*. LCL 484. Cambridge, MA: Harvard University Press, 1995.

———. *Euripides IV*. LCL 10. Cambridge, MA: Harvard University Press, 1999.

———. *Euripides VI*. LCL 495. Cambridge, MA: Harvard University Press, 2002.

Lloyd-Jones, Hugh, and N. G. Wilson. *Sophoclis Fabulae*. Oxford: Clarendon Press, 1990.

Murray, A. T., and William F. Wyatt. *Iliad I–II* by Homer. LCL 170, 171. Cambridge, MA: Harvard University Press, 1999.

———, and George E. Dimock. *Odyssey I–II* by Homer. LCL 104, 105. Cambridge, MA: Harvard University Press, 1998.

Rackham, Harris. *The Nicomachean Ethics* by Aristotle. LCL 19. Cambridge, MA: Harvard University Press, 1934.

———. *The Politics* by Aristotle. LCL. New York: G. P. Putnam's Sons, 1932.

Shorey, Paul. *Plato, The Republic*. Cambridge, MA: Harvard University Press, 1935.

Smyth, Herbert Weir. *Aeschylus*. LCL 146. Cambridge, MA: Harvard University Press, 2006.

West, Martin L., ed. *Theogony* by Hesiod. Oxford: Clarendon Press, 1966.

———. *Iambi et Elegi Graeci ante Alexandrum Cantati*. Oxford: Clarendon Press, 1972.

———. *Works and Days* by Hesiod. Oxford: Clarendon Press, 1978.

Theory, Hermeneutics, and General Background

Adams, Robert McCormick. *The Evolution of Urban Society: Early Mesopotamia and Prehispanic Mexico*. Chicago: Aldine, 1966.

Arendt, Hannah. *The Life of the Mind*. Volume 1: *Thinking*. New York: Harcourt, 1977.

———. *The Human Condition*. Chicago: University of Chicago Press, 1958.

Benko, Stephen. *The Virgin Goddess: Studies in the Pagan and Christian Roots of Mariology*. Studies in the History of Religions 59. Leiden and New York: Brill, 1993.

Bloch, Maurice. *Prey into Hunter: The Politics of Religious Experience*. Cambridge and New York: Cambridge University Press, 1992.

Bourdieu, Pierre. "The Production and Reproduction of Legitimate Language." In *Language and Symbolic Power*. Edited by John B.Thompson. Cambridge, MA: Harvard University Press, 1991.

Buchan, Thomas. "Paradise as the Landscape of Salvation." In *Partakers of the Divine Nature: The History and Development of Deification in the Christian Traditions*. Edited by Michael J. Christensen and Jeffrey A. Wittung, 146–59. Madison, NJ: Fairleigh Dickinson University Press, 2007.

Bullough, Vern L. "Eunuchs in History and Society." In *Eunuchs in Antiquity and Beyond*. Edited by Shaun Tougher, 1–17. London: Classical Press of Wales and Duckworth, 2002.

Butler, Judith. *Gender Trouble: Feminism and the Subversion of Identity*. New York: Routledge, 1990.

Clement, Catherine, and Julia Kristeva. *The Feminine and the Sacred*. New York: Columbia University Press, 2001.

Culler, Jonathan. *The Pursuit of Signs*. Ithaca, NY: Cornell University Press, 1987.

Delaney, Carol. "Seeds of Honor and Fields of Shame." In *Honor and Shame and the Unity of the Mediterranean*. Edited by David D. Gilmore, 35–48. Washington, DC: American Anthropological Association, 1987.

Eliade, Mircea. *Mephistopheles and the Androgyne*. New York: Sheed & Ward, 1965.

Faraone, Christopher A., and Laura McClure. *Prostitutes and Courtesans in the Ancient World*. Madison: University of Wisconsin Press, 2006.

Fink, Bruce. *The Lacanian Subject: Between Language and Jouissance*. Princeton: Princeton University Press, 1997.

Foucault, Michel. *The History of Sexuality*: Volume 1: *An Introduction*. Translated by Robert Hurley. New York: Pantheon, 1978.

———. *The History of Sexuality*: Volume 2: *The Use of Pleasure*. Translated by Robert Hurley. New York: Pantheon, 1985.

Giddens, Anthony. *The Transformation of Intimacy: Sexuality, Love and Eroticism in Modern Societies*. Stanford, CA: Stanford University Press, 1992.

Gill, Christopher. "The Human Being as an Ethical Norm." In *The Person and the Human Mind: Issues in Ancient and Modern Philosophy*. Edited by Christopher Gill, 139–61. Oxford: Clarendon Press, 1990.

Graver, Margaret R. *Stoicism and Emotion*. Chicago: University of Chicago Press, 2007.

Habermas, Jürgen. "Comments on John Searle's 'Meaning, Communication, and Representation' (1998)." In idem, *On the Pragmatics of Communication*. Edited by Maeve Cooke, 215–55. Cambridge, MA: MIT Press, 1998.

Harpham, Geoffrey Galt. *The Ascetic Imperative in Culture and Criticism*. Chicago and London: University of Chicago Press, 1987.

Hart, Jonathan. *Northrop Frye: The Theoretical Imagination*. New York: Routledge, 1994.

Hegel, Georg W. F. *The Encyclopaedia Logic (with the Zusätze)*. Part I of the *Encyclopaedia of Philosophical Sciences with the Zusätze*. Translated by T. F. Geraets, W. A. Suchting, and H. S. Harris. Indianapolis: Hackett, 1991.

Henaff, Marcel. *Claude Levi-Strauss and the Making of Structural Anthropology*. Minneapolis: University of Minnesota Press, 1998.

Jameson, Fredric. *The Political Unconscious: Narrative as a Socially Symbolic Act*. Ithaca, NY: Cornell University Press, 1981.

———. *The Seeds of Time*. New York: Columbia University Press, 1994.

Jaspers, Karl. *The Origin and Goal of History*. Translated by Michael Bullock. London: Routledge & Kegan Paul, 1953.

Jones, Peter. "Androgyny: The Pagan Sexual Ideal." *JETS* 43 (2000): 443–69.

Kantorowitz, Ernst. *The King's Two Bodies: A Study in Mediaeval Political Theology*. Princeton: Princeton University Press, 1957.

Kitchen, John. "Cassian, Nocturnal Emissions, and the Sexuality of Jesus." In *The Seven Deadly Sins: From Communities to Individuals*. Studies in Medieval and Reformation Traditions 123. Edited by Richard Newhauser, 73–94. Leiden and Boston: Brill, 2007.

Kristeva, Julia. *Hannah Arendt*. New York: Columbia University Press, 2001.

Lacan, Jacques. "The Mirror Stage as Formative of the Function of the I as Revealed in Psychoanalytic Experience." In idem, *Écrits: A Selection*, 1–7. New York and London: W. W. Norton & Company, 1977.

———. "The Signification of the Phallus." In idem, *Écrits: A Selection*, 281–91. New York and London: W. W. Norton & Company, 1977.

Laqueur, Thomas. *Making Sex: Body and Gender from the Greeks to Freud*. Cambridge, MA: Harvard University Press, 1990.

Leupin, Alexandre. *Lacan Today: Psychoanalysis, Science, Religion*. New York: Other Press, 2004.

Lyon, M. L., and J. M. Barbalet. "Society's Body: Emotion and the 'Somatization' of Social Theory." In *Embodiment and Experience: The Existential Ground of Culture and Self*. Edited by Thomas J. Csordas, 48–66. Cambridge: Cambridge University Press, 1994.

Mach, Zdzislaw. *Symbols, Conflict, and Identity: Essays in Political Anthropology*. New York: SUNY Press, 1993.

MacIntyre, Alasdair. *After Virtue*. Notre Dame, IN: University of Notre Dame Press, 1981.

Mandarossian, Carine M. "Laboring Women, Coaching Men: Masculinity and Childbirth Education in the Contemporary United States." *Hypatia* 18 (2003): 113–34.

Marion, Jean-Luc. *The Erotic Phenomenon*. Translated by Stephen Lewis; Chicago: University of Chicago Press, 2007.

Meeks, Wayne A. "The Image of the Androgyne: Some Uses of a Symbol in Earliest Christianity." *History of Religions* 13 (1974): 165–208.

Midgley, Mary. "The Soul's Successors: Philosophy and the 'Body.'" In *Religion and the Body*. Edited by Sarah Coakley, 53–68. Cambridge: Cambridge University Press, 1997.

Needham, Rodney. "Introduction." In *Right & Left: Essays on Dual Symbolic Classification*. Edited by Rodney Needham, xi–xxxix. Chicago: University of Chicago Press, 1973.

Nietzsche, Friedrich. *Beyond Good and Evil*. Translated by Marianne Cowan. Chicago: Henry Regnery, 1955.

———. "Genealogy of Morals." In *Birth of Tragedy and the Genealogy of Morals*. Translated by Francis Golffing. Garden City, NY: Doubleday, 1956. 165–66.

———. *Twilight of the Idols*. Translated by Duncan Large. Oxford: Oxford University Press, 1998.

Nissinen, Martti, and Risto Uro, eds. *Sacred Marriages: The Divine-Human Sexual Metaphor from Sumer to Early Christianity*. Winona Lake, IN: Eisenbrauns, 2008.

Parpola, Simo, and Robert M. Whiting, eds. *Sex and Gender in the Ancient Near East: Proceedings of the 47th Rencontre Assyriologique Internationale, Helsinki, July 2–6, 2001*. 2 volumes. CRRAI 47. Helsinki: Neo-Assyrian Text Corpus Project, 2002.

Rappaport, Roy. *Ritual and Religion in the Making of Humanity*. Cambridge: Cambridge University Press, 1999.

Reginster, Bernard. *The Affirmation of Life: Nietzsche on Overcoming Nihilism*. Cambridge, MA: Harvard University Press, 2006.

Ricoeur, Paul. *The Symbolism of Evil*. Boston: Beacon Press, 1969.

Searle, John R. *Mind, Language and Society. Philosophy in the Real World*. New York: Basic Books, 1998.

Smith, Steven G. *Appeal and Attitude: Prospects for Ultimate Meaning*. Bloomington: Indiana University Press, 2005.

Soler, Colette. *What Lacan Said About Women: A Psychoanalytic Study*. Translated by John Holland. New York: Other Press, 2006.

Strauss, Leo. *Natural Right and History*. Chicago: University of Chicago Press, 1953.

Taylor, Charles. *A Secular Age*. Cambridge, MA: Belknap Press, 2007.

Tiefer, Leonore. "The Medicalization of Impotence: The Normalizing of Phallocentrism." *Gender and Society* 8 (1994): 363–77.

Turner, Terence. "Bodies and Anti-bodies: Flesh and Fetish in Contemporary Social Theory." In *Embodiment and Experience: The Existential Ground of Culture and Self*. Edited by Thomas J. Csordas, 27–47. Cambridge and New York: Cambridge University Press, 1994.

Turner, Victor. *The Ritual Process: Structure and Anti-Structure*. New York: Aldine de Gruyter, 1969.

Ancient Israel

Ackerman, Susan. "The Personal Is Political: Covenantal and Affectionate Love (ʾAHĒB, ʾAHABÂ) in the Hebrew Bible." *VT* 52 (2002): 437–58.

———. *When Heroes Love: The Ambiguity of Eros in the Stories of Gilgamesh and David*. New York: Columbia University Press, 2005.

Albertz, Rainer. *A History of Israelite Religion in the Old Testament Period*. 2 volumes. OTL. Louisville: Westminster John Knox, 1994.

———. "The Thwarted Restoration." In *Yahwism After the Exile: Perspectives on Israelite Religion in the Persian Era*. Edited by Rainer Albertz and Bob Becking, 1–17. Assen: Van Gorcum, 2003.

———. "Family Religion in Ancient Israel and its Surroundings." In *Household and Family Religion in Antiquity*. Edited by John Bodel and Saul M. Olyan, 89–112. Malden, MA: Blackwell, 2008.

———, and Bob Becking, eds. *Yahwism After the Exile: Perspectives on Israelite Religion in the Persian Era*. Assen: Van Gorcum, 2003.

Allen, Leslie C. *Jeremiah*. OTL. Louisville: Westminster John Knox, 2008.

Anderson, Francis I., and David Noel Freedman. *Hosea*. AB 24. Garden City, NY: Doubleday, 1980.

Anderson, Gary A. "Celibacy or Consummation in the Garden? Reflections on Early Jewish and Christian Interpretations of the Garden of Eden." *HTR* 82 (1989): 121–48.

———. "The Cosmic Mountain: Eden and Its Early Interpreters in Syriac Christianity." In *Genesis 1–3 in the History of Exegesis: Intrigue in the Garden*. Edited by Gregory A. Robbins, 187–224. Lewiston, NY: Edwin Mellen, 1998.

———. *The Genesis of Perfection: Adam and Eve in Jewish and Christian Imagination*. Louisville: Westminster John Knox, 2001.

Arnold, Bill T. *Genesis*. Cambridge: Cambridge University Press, 2009.

Bal, Mieke. *Death & Dissymmetry: The Politics of Coherence in the Book of Judges*. Chicago: University of Chicago Press, 1988.

Balentine, Samuel. *The Torah's Vision of Worship*. Minneapolis: Fortress Press, 1999.

Barr, James. "'Thou Art the Cherub': Ezekiel 28.14 and the Post-Ezekiel Understanding of Genesis 2–3." In *Priests, Prophets and Scribes: Essays on the Formation and Heritage of Second Temple Judaism in Honour of Joseph Blenkinsopp. JSOTSup* 149. Edited by Eugene Ulrich, et al., 213–23. Sheffield: JSOT Press, 1992.

Batto, Bernard. "The Institution of Marriage in Genesis 2 and Atrahasis." *CBQ* 62 (2000): 621–31.

Bautch, Richard J. *Developments in Genre between Post-Exilic Penitential Prayers and the Psalms of Communal Lament*. SBL Academia Biblica 7. Atlanta: Society of Biblical Literature, 2003.

Becking, Bob. "Law as Expression of Religion (Ezra 7–10)." In *Yahwism After the Exile* (2003), 18–31.

———. "Continuity and Community: The Belief System of the Book of Ezra." In *The Crisis of Israelite Religion: Transformation of Religious Tradition in Exilic and Post-Exilic Times*. Edited by Bob Becking and Marjo Korpel, 256–75. Leiden: Brill, 1999.

Berlinerblau, Jacques. *The Vow and the 'Popular Religious Groups' of Ancient Israel: A Philological and Sociological Inquiry. JSOTSup* 210. Sheffield: Sheffield Academic Press, 1996.

Berquist, Jon. *Judaism in Persia's Shadow*. Minneapolis: Fortress Press, 1995.

———. *Controlling Corporeality*. New Brunswick, NJ: Rutgers University Press, 2002.

Biddle, Mark. "The Figure of Lady Jerusalem: Identification, Deification and Personification of Cities in the Ancient Near East." In *The Biblical Canon in Comparative Perspective: Scripture in Context IV*. Ancient Near Eastern Texts and Studies 11. Edited by K. Lawson Younger, Jr., William W. Hallo, and Bernard F. Batto, 173–94. Lewiston, NY: Edwin Mellen, 1991.

Bird, Phyllis. "To Play the Harlot: An Inquiry into an Old Testament Metaphor." In *Gender and Difference in Ancient Israel*. Edited by Peggy Day, 21–38. Minneapolis: Fortress Press, 1989.

———. "Prostitution in the Social World and the Religious Rhetoric of Ancient Israel." In *Prostitutes and Courtesans in the Ancient World* (2006), 40–58.

Blenkinsopp, Joseph. *Ezra–Nehemiah*. OTL. Philadelphia: Westminster, 1988.

———. *Ezekiel*. Louisville: John Knox, 1990.

———. "A Jewish Sect of the Persian Period." *CBQ* 52 (1990): 5–20.

———. "Deuteronomy and the Politics of Post-Mortem Existence." *VT* 45 (1995): 1–16.

———. *Isaiah 56–66*. AB 19B. New York: Doubleday, 2003.

Block, Daniel I. *The Book of Ezekiel: Chapters 1–24*. Grand Rapids: Eerdmans, 1997.

———. *The Book of Ezekiel:Chapters 25–48*. Grand Rapids: Eerdmans, 1998.

———. "Marriage and Family in Ancient Israel." In *Marriage and Family in the Biblical World*. Edited by Ken M. Campbell, 33–102. Downers Grove, IL: InterVarsity Press, 2003.

———. *The Gods of the Nations: Studies in Ancient Near Eastern National Theology*. 2d edition. Grand Rapids: Baker, 2000.

Boadt, Lawrence. *Ezekiel's Oracles against Egypt: A Literary and Philological Study of Ezekiel 29–32*. BibOr 37. Rome: Pontifical Biblical Institute, 1980.

———. "Rhetorical Strategies in Ezekiel's Oracles of Judgment." In *Ezekiel and His Book: Textual and Literary Criticism and Their Interrelation*. Edited by Johan Lust, et al., 182–200. BETL 74. Leuven: Leuven University/Peeters, 1986.

Boda, Mark J. "From Complaint to Contrition: Peering through the Liturgical Window of Jer 14,1–15,4." *ZAW* 113 (2001): 186–97.

Bodi, Daniel. *The Book of Ezekiel and the Poem of Erra*. OBO 104. Fribourg: Universitätsverlag, 1991.

Bouzard, Walter C. Jr. *We Have Heard With Our Ears, O God: Sources of the Communal Laments in the Psalms*. SBLDS 159. Atlanta: Scholars Press, 1997.

Boyarin, Daniel. *Carnal Israel: Reading Sex in Talmudic Culture*. Berkeley: University of California Press, 1993.

———. "Are There Any Jews in 'The History of Sexuality'?" *Journal of the History of Sexuality* 5 (1995): 333–55.

Braaten, Laurie J. "God Sows: Hosea's Land Theme in the Book of the Twelve." In *Thematic Threads in the Book of the Twelve*. BZAW 325. Edited by Paul L. Redditt and Aaron Schart, 104–32. New York: Walter de Gruyter, 2003.

Brenner, Athalya, ed. *A Feminist Companion to the Latter Prophets*. Sheffield: Sheffield Academic Press, 1995.

———. "On Prophetic Propaganda and the Politics of 'Love': The Case of Jeremiah." In *A Feminist Companion to the Latter Prophets* (1995), 256–74.

———. *The Intercourse of Knowledge: On Gendering Desire and 'Sexuality' in the Hebrew Bible*. Biblical Interpretation Series 26. Leiden: Brill, 1997.

Brown, William P. *Seeing the Psalms*. Grand Rapids: Eerdmans, 2002.

Brueggemann, Walter. *Genesis*. Atlanta: John Knox, 1982.

Bultmann, Christoph. "A Prophet in Desperation? The Confessions of Jeremiah." In *The Elusive Prophet*. Edited by Johannes C. de Moor, 83–93. OtSt 45. Leiden: Brill, 2001.

Callender, Dexter Jr. *Adam in Myth and History: Ancient Israelite Perspectives on the Primal Human*. HSM 48. Atlanta: Scholars Press, 2000.

———. "The Primal Human in Ezekiel and the Image of God." In *The Book of Ezekiel: Theological and Anthropological Perspectives*. SBL Symposium Series 9. Edited by Margaret Odell and John Strong, 175–93. Atlanta: Scholars Press, 2000.

Campbell, Ken M., ed. *Marriage and Family in the Biblical World*. Downers Grove, IL: InterVarsity Press, 2003.

Carley, Keith W. *The Book of the Prophet Ezekiel*. London and New York: Cambridge University Press, 1974.

Carmichael, Calum M. *Laws of Deuteronomy*. Ithaca, NY, and London: Cornell University Press, 1974.

Carr, David M. "Gender and the Shaping of Desire in the Song of Songs and its Interpretation." *JBL* 119 (2000): 233–48.

———. *The Erotic Word: Sexuality, Spirituality, and the Bible*. New York: Oxford University Press, 2003.

———. *Writing on the Tablet of the Heart: Origins of Scripture and Literature*. New York: Oxford University Press, 2005.

Carr, David M., and Colleen M. Conway. "The Divine-Human Marriage Matrix and Constructions of Gender and 'Bodies' in the Christian Bible." In *Sacred Marriages: The Divine-Human Sexual Metaphor from Sumer to Early Christianity*. Edited by by Martti Nissinen and Risto Uro, 275–303. Winona Lake, IN: Eisenbrauns, 2008.

Carroll, Robert. *Jeremiah: A Commentary*. OTL. Philadelphia: Westminster, 1986.

———. "Desire Under the Terebinths: On Pornographic Representation in the Prophets: A Response." In *A Feminist Companion to the Latter Prophets* (1995), 275–307.

———. "Whorusalamin: A Tale of Three Cities As Three Sisters." In *On Reading Prophetic Texts: Gender-Specific and Related Studies in Memory of Fokklien Van Dijk-Hemmes*. BibIntSer 18. Edited by Bob Becking and Meindert Dijkstra, 62–82. Leiden: Brill, 1996.

Carter, Charles E. "The Province of Yehud in the Post-Exilic Period: Soundings in Site Distribution and Demography." In *Second Temple Studies. 2. Temple and Community in the Persian Period. JSOTSup* 175. Edited by Tamara C. Eskenazi and Kent H. Richards, 106–45. Sheffield: Sheffield Academic Press, 1994.

Childs, Brevard. *Exodus*. Louisville: Westminster, 1976.

Clements, Ronald E. "Jeremiah's Message of Hope: Public Faith and Private Anguish." In *Reading the Book of Jeremiah: A Search for Coherence*. Edited by Martin Kessler, 135–47. Winona Lake, IN: Eisenbrauns, 2004.

Clifford, Richard J. *Proverbs*. OTL. Louisville: Westminster John Knox, 1999.

———. *Psalms 1–72*. Nashville: Abingdon, 2002.

———. *Psalms 73–150*. Nashville: Abingdon, 2003.

Cody, Aelred. *Ezekiel*. Wilmington, DE: Michael Glazier, 1984.

Cook, Stephen L. "Cosmos, Kabod, and Cherub: Ontological and Epistemological Hierarchy in Ezekiel." In *Ezekiel's Hierarchical World*. Edited by Stephen Cook and Corrine Patton, 179–97. Atlanta: Society of Biblical Literature, 2004.

Craigie, Peter. *Psalms 1–50*. WBC 19. Waco, TX: Word Books, 1983.

Crenshaw, James. "Deceitful Minds and Theological Dogma: Jer 17:5-11." In *Utopia and Dystopia in Prophetic Literature*. Publications of the Finnish Exegetical Society 92. Edited by Ehud Ben Zvi, 105–21. Helsinki: The Finnish Exegetical Society; Göttingen: Vandenhoeck & Ruprecht, 2006.

Crüsemann, Frank. *The Torah: Theology and Social History of Old Testament Law*. Translated by A. W. Mahnke. Minneapolis: Fortress Press, 1996.

Davidson, Richard M. *Flame of Yahweh: Sexuality in the Old Testament*. Peabody, MA: Hendrickson, 2007.

Davies, Graham I. *Hosea*. Grand Rapids: Eerdmans, 1995.

Davies, Philip R. "The Wilderness Years: Utopia and Dystopia in the Book of Hosea." In *Utopia and Dystopia in Prophetic Literature*, 160–74.

Day, John. *Molech: A God of Human Sacrifice in the Old Testament*. Cambridge: Cambridge University Press, 1989.

———. "Yahweh and the Gods and Goddesses of Canaan." In *Ein Gott allein? JHWH-Verehrung und biblischer Monotheismus im Kontext der Israelitischen und altorientalischen Religionsgeschichte*. Edited by Walter Dietrich and Martin A. Klopfenstein, 181–96. OBO 139. Göttingen: Vandenhoeck & Ruprecht, 1994.

Day, Peggy L., ed. *Gender and Difference in Ancient Israel*. Minneapolis: Fortress Press, 1989.

———. "From the Child Is Born the Woman: The Story of Jephthah's Daughter." In *Gender and Difference in Ancient Israel* (1989), 58–74.

———. "The Personification of Cities as Female in the Hebrew Bible: The Thesis of Aloysius Fitzgerald, F.S.C." In *Reading from this Place*. Volume 2: *Social Location and Biblical Interpretation in Global Perspective*. Edited by Fernando F. Segovia and Mary Ann Tolbert, 283–302. Minneapolis: Fortress Press, 1995.

———. "Yahweh's Broken Marriages as Metaphoric Vehicle." In *Sacred Marriages* (2008), 219–41.

De Moor, Johannes C. "The Duality in God and Man: Gen 1:26-27 as P's Interpretation of the Yahwistic Creation Account." In *Intertextuality in Ugarit and Israel*. Edited by Johannes C. de Moor, 112–25. OTS 40. Leiden and Boston: Brill, 1998.

Dempsey, Carol. "The 'Whore' of Ezekiel 16: The Impact and Ramifications of Gender-Specific Metaphors in Light of Biblical Law and Divine Judgment." In *Gender and Law in the Hebrew Bible and the Ancient Near East*. Edited by Victor Matthews, Bernard Levinson, and Tikva Frymer-Kensky, 57–78. *JSOTSup* 262. Sheffield: Sheffield Academic Press, 1998.

Diamond, A. R. *Confessions of Jeremiah in Context: Scenes of Prophetic Drama*. *JSOTSup* 45. Sheffield: JSOT Press, 1987.

Dijkstra, Meindert. "The Law of Moses: The Memory of Mosaic Religion In and after the Exile." In *Yahwism After the Exile* (2003), 70–98.

Dobbs-Allsopp, F. W. *Weep, O Daughter of Zion: A Study of the City–Lament Genre in the Hebrew Bible*. Biblica et Orientalia 44. Rome: Pontifical Biblical Institute, 1993.

Dolansky, Shawna, ed. *Sacred History, Sacred Literature: Essays on Ancient Israel, the Bible, and Religion in Honor of R. E. Friedman on His Sixtieth Birthday*. Winona Lake, IN: Eisenbrauns, 2008.

Dor, Yonina. "The Composition of the Episode of the Foreign Women in Ezra IX–X." *VT* 53 (2003): 26–47.

Douglas, Mary. *Purity and Danger: An Analysis of the Concepts of Pollution and Taboo*. London: Routledge & Kegan Paul, 1966.

———. *Leviticus as Literature*. New York: Oxford University Press, 1999.

———. "Responding to Ezra: The Priests and the Foreign Wives." *Biblical Interpretation* 10 (2002): 1–23.

Eilberg-Schwartz, Howard. *Savage Judaism: An Anthropology of Israelite Religion and Ancient Judaism*. Bloomington: Indiana University Press, 1990.

Ellens, Deborah L. *Women in the Sex Texts of Leviticus and Deuteronomy: A Comparative Conceptual Analysis*. Library of Hebrew Bible/Old Testament Studies 458. New York and London: T & T Clark, 2008.

Elon, Menachem. "Bigamy and Polygamy." *Encyclopedia Judaica*, 2d edition, 691–94.

Eskenazi, Tamara. "Out of the Shadows: Biblical Women in the Postexilic Era." *JSOT* 54 (1992): 25–43.

Exum, J. Cheryl. *Song of Songs*. OTL. Louisville: Westminster John Knox, 2005.

———. *Tragedy and Biblical Narrative: Arrows of the Almighty*. Cambridge: Cambridge University Press, 1992.

Fitzgerald, Aloysius. "The Mythological Background for the Presentation of Jerusalem as a Queen and False Worship as Adultery in the OT." *CBQ* 34 (1972): 403–16.

Fleishman, Joseph. "Why Did Simeon and Levi Rebuke Their Father in Genesis 34:31?" *JNSL* 26 (2000): 101–16.

Fontaine, Carole R. "Hosea." In *A Feminist Companion to the Latter Prophets* (1995), 40–59.

Freedman, David Noel. *Psalm 119: The Exaltation of the Torah*. Winona Lake, IN: Eisenbrauns, 1999.

———. "The Real Formal Full Personal Name of the God of Israel." In *Sacred History, Sacred Literature* (2008), 81–89.

Fretheim, Terence. *Abraham: Trials of Family and Faith*. Columbia, SC: University of South Carolina Press, 2007.

Frymer-Kensky, Tikva. "Virginity in the Bible." In *Gender and Law in the Hebrew Bible and the Ancient Near East* (1998), 79–96.

Galambush, Julie. *Jerusalem in the Book of Ezekiel*. SBLDS 130. Atlanta: Scholars Press, 1992.

Galling, Kurt. "Das Gemeindegesetz in Deuteronomium 23." In *Festschrift Alfred Bertholet zum 80. Geburtstag*. Edited by Walter Baumgartner, 176–91. Tübingen: Mohr, 1950.

Gerstenberger, Erhard S. *Psalms, Part 2, and Lamentations*. FOTL 15. Grand Rapids: Eerdmans, 2001.

Gnuse, Robert. *No Other Gods: Emergent Monotheism in Israel*. *JSOTSup* 241. Sheffield: Sheffield Academic Press, 1997.

Goldingay, John. "Hosea 1–3, Genesis 1–4 and Masculist Interpretation." In *A Feminist Companion to the Latter Prophets* (1993), 161–68.

Grabbe, Lester. *Ezra–Nehemiah*. London: Routledge, 1998.

Graetz, Naomi. "God Is To Israel as Husband Is To Wife: The Metaphoric Battering of Hosea's Wife." In *A Feminist Companion to the Latter Prophets* (1995), 126–45.

Greenberg, Moshe. *Ezekiel 1–20*. AB 22. Garden City, NY: Doubleday, 1983.

———. *Ezekiel 21–37*. AB 22A. New York: Doubleday, 1997.

Gruber, Mayer I. "The Hebrew *qĕdēšāh* and Her Canaanite and Akkadian Cognates." In idem, *The Motherhood of God and Other Studies*, 17–47. South Florida Studies in the History of Judaism 57. Atlanta: Scholars Press, 1992.

Halpern, Baruch. "The Assyrian Astronomy of Genesis 1 and the Birth of Milesian Philosophy." In *Hayim and Miriam Tadmor Memorial Volume. Eretz Israel* 27. Edited by Israel Eph'al, Amnon Ben–Tor, and Peter Machinist, 74–83. Jerusalem: Israel Exploration Society, 2003.

Hamilton, Victor P. "Marriage (OT and ANE)." *ABD* 4: 559–69.

Handy, Lowell K. *Among the Host of Heaven: The Syro-Palestinian Pantheon as Bureaucracy*. Winona Lake, IN: Eisenbrauns, 1994.

Hayes, Katherine M. *"The Earth Mourns." Prophetic Metaphor and Oral Aesthetic*. Academia Biblica. Boston and Leiden: Brill, 2002.

Hess, Richard S. *Song of Songs*. Grand Rapids: Baker, 2005.

Hill, Andrew E. *Malachi*. AB 25D. New York: Doubleday, 1998.

Hillers, Delbert. "Analyzing the Abominable: Our Understanding of Canaanite Religion." *JQR* 75 (1985): 253–69.

Holladay, William L. *Jeremiah 1: A Commentary on the Book of the Prophet Jeremiah Chapters 1–25*. Edited by Paul D. Hanson. Hermeneia. Philadelpia: Fortress Press, 1986.

———. *Jeremiah 2: A Commentary on the Book of the Prophet Jeremiah Chapters* 26–52. Edited by Paul D. Hanson. Hermeneia. Minneapolis: Fortress Press, 1989.

Hollis, Susan Tower. "The Woman in Ancient Examples of the Potiphar's Wife Motif, K2111." In *Gender and Difference in Ancient Israel* (1989), 28–42.

Horbury, William. "Extirpation and Excommunication." *VT* 35 (1985): 13–38.

Houtman, Cornelis. *Exodus*. Volume 3, *Chapters 20–40*. Leuven: Peeters, 2000.

Huffmon, Herbert. "Gender Subversion in the Book of Jeremiah." In *Sex and Gender in the Ancient Near East* (2002), 245–53.

Humphreys, W. Lee. *Joseph and His Family: A Literary Study*. Columbia, SC: University of South Carolina Press, 1988.

Hunt, Patrick. *Poetry in the Song of Songs: A Literary Analysis*. Studies in Biblical Literature 96. New York: Peter Lang, 2008.

Japhet, Sara. "People and Land in the Restoration Period." In *From the Rivers of Babylon to the Highlands of Judah: Collected Studies on the Restoration Period*. Winona Lake, IN: Eisenbrauns, 2006. 96–116.

———. "Composition and Chronology in the Book of Ezra–Nehemiah." In *From the Rivers of Babylon to the Highlands of Judah* (2006), 245–67.

Jarrell, Robin H. "The Birth Narrative as Female Counterpart to Covenant." *JSOT* 97 (2002): 3–18.

Jennings, Theodore. *Jacob's Wound: Homoerotic Narrative in the Literature of Ancient Israel*. New York: Continuum, 2006.

Jobling, David. "The Quest of the Historical Jeremiah: Hermeneutical Implications of Recent Literature." USQR 34 (1978): 3–12.

Joosten, Jan. *People and Land in the Holiness Code: An Exegetical Study of the Ideational Framework of the Law in Leviticus 17–26. VTSup* 67. Leiden: Brill, 1996.

Joyce, Paul. *Divine Initiative and Human Response in Ezekiel. JSOTSup* 51. Sheffield: JSOT Press, 1989.

Kakkanattu, Joy Philip. *God's Enduring Love in the Book of Hosea*. FAT 14, 2d series. Tübingen: Mohr Siebeck, 2006.

Kaminsky, Joel S. *Corporate Responsibility in the Hebrew Bible*. *JSOTSup* 196. Sheffield: Sheffield Academic Press, 1995.

Kamionkowski, S. Tamar. *Gender Reversal and Cosmic Chaos: A Study of the Book of Ezekiel*. *JSOTSup* 368. Sheffield: Sheffield Academic Press, 2003.

Kaufmann, Yehezkel. *The Religion of Israel: From Its Beginnings to the Babylonian Exile*. Translated by Moshe Greenberg. Chicago: University of Chicago Press, 1960.

Keefe, Alice A. *Woman's Body and the Social Body in Hosea*. *JSOTSup* 338. Sheffield: Sheffield Academic Press, 2001.

Keel, Othmar. *Song of Songs*. Minneapolis: Fortress Press, 1994.

———, and Christoph Uehlinger. *Gods, Goddesses, and Images of God in Ancient Israel*. Translated by Thomas Trapp. Minneapolis: Fortress Press, 1992.

Kelle, Brad E. *Hosea 2: Metaphor and Rhetoric in Historical Perspective*. Atlanta: Society of Biblical Literature, 2005.

Klawans, Jonathan. "Pure Violence: Sacrifice and Defilement in Ancient Israel." *HTR* 94 (2001): 133–55.

———. *Purity, Sacrifice, and the Temple: Symbolism and Supersessionism in the Study of Ancient Judaism*. Oxford and New York: Oxford University Press, 2006.

Knoppers, Gary N. "Sex, Religion, and Politics: The Deuteronomist on Intermarriage," *HAR* 14 (1994): 121–41.

———. "An Achaemenid Imperial Authorization of Torah in Yehud." In *Persia and Torah: The Theory of Imperial Authorization of the Pentateuch*. SBL Symposium 17. Edited by James W. Watts, 116–34. Atlanta: Society of Biblical Literature, 2001.

Kutsko, John. *Between Heaven and Earth: Divine Presence and Absence in the Book of Ezekiel*. Biblical and Judaic Studies 7. Winona Lake, IN: Eisenbrauns, 2000.

Labahn, Antje. "Antitheocratic Tendencies in Chronicles." In *Yahwism After the Exile* (2003), 115–35.

Landy, Francis. "Fantasy and Displacement of Pleasure: Hosea 2:4-17." In *A Feminist Companion to the Latter Prophets* (1995), 146–60.

Lang, Bernhard. *Monotheism and the Prophetic Minority*. Sheffield: Almond Press, 1983.

Lapsley, Jacqueline. *Can These Bones Live? The Problem of the Moral Self in the Book of Ezekiel*. BZAW 301. Berlin and New York: de Gruyter, 2000.

———. "Shame and Self-Knowledge: The Positive Role of Shame in Ezekiel's View of the Moral Self." In *The Book of Ezekiel: Theological and Anthropological Perspectives* (2000), 143–73.

Launderville, Dale. *Piety and Politics: The Dynamics of Royal Authority in Homeric Greece, Biblical Israel, and Old Babylonian Mesopotamia*. Grand Rapids: Eerdmans, 2003.

———. "Ezekiel's Cherub: A Promising Symbol or a Dangerous Idol?" *CBQ* 65 (2003): 165–83.

———. *Spirit and Reason: The Embodied Character of Ezekiel's Symbolic Thinking*. Waco, TX: Baylor University Press, 2007.

Levenson, Jon D. *The Death and Resurrection of the Beloved Son: The Transformation of Child Sacrifice in Judaism and Christianity*. New Haven: Yale University Press, 1993.

———. *Resurrection and the Restoration of Israel: The Ultimate Victory of the God of Life*. New Haven: Yale University Press, 2006.

Levine, Baruch A. *Numbers 1–20*. AB 4A. New York: Doubleday, 1993.

———. "'Seed' versus 'Womb': Expressions of Male Dominance in Biblical Israel." In *Sex and Gender in the Ancient Near East* (2002), 337–43.

———, and Jean-Michel de Terragon. "Dead Kings and Rephaim: Patrons of the Ugaritic Dynasty." *JAOS* 104 (1984): 649–59.

Levine, Étan. "Biblical Women's Marital Rights." *Proceedings of the American Academy for Jewish Research* 63 (1997–2001): 87–135.

Levinson, Bernard M. "The Reconceptualization of Kingship in Deuteronomy and the Deuteronomistic Historian's Reconceptualization of Torah." *VT* 51 (2001): 511–34.

Lewis, Theodore. "The Ancestral Estate (*naḥălat ʾelōhîm*) in 2 Samuel 14:16." *JBL* 110 (1991): 597–612.

———. "CT 13.33-34 and Ezekiel 32: Lion-Dragon Myths." *JAOS* 116 (1996): 28–47.

Lundbom, Jack R. *Jeremiah 1–20*. AB 21A. New York: Doubleday, 1999.

———. *Jeremiah 37–52*. AB 21C. New York: Doubleday, 2004.

Lyke, Larry. "The Song of Songs, Proverbs, and the Theology of Love." In *Theological Exegesis: Essays in Honor of Brevard S. Childs*. Edited by Christopher Seitz and Kathryn Greene-McCreight, 208–23. Grand Rapids: Eerdmans, 1999.

Macintosh, A. A. *Hosea*. Edinburgh: T & T Clark, 1997.

Malul, Meir. "Adoption of Foundlings in the Bible and Mesopotamian Documents: A Study of Some Legal Metaphors in Ezekiel 16.1-7." *JSOT* 46 (1990): 97–126.

———. *Knowledge, Control, and Sex: Studies in Biblical Thought, Culture, and Worldview*. Tel-Aviv and Jaffa: Archaeological Center Publications, 2002.

Marbury, Herbert. "The Strange Woman in Persian Yehud: A Reading of Proverbs 7." In *Approaching Yehud: New Approaches to the Study of the Persian Period*. Edited by Jon L. Berquist, 167–82. Atlanta: Society of Biblical Literature, 2007.

Marcus, David. *Jephthah and His Vow*. Lubbock, TX: Texas Tech University Press, 1985.

Marks, John H., and Robert M. Good. *Love and Death in the Ancient Near East: Essays in Honor of Marvin H. Pope*. Guilford, CT: Four Quarters Publishing, 1987.

Matthews, Victor. "Marriage and Family in the Ancient Near East." In *Marriage and Family in the Biblical World* (2003), 1–32.

Matties, Gordon. *Ezekiel 18 and the Rhetoric of Moral Discourse*. SBLDS 126. Atlanta: Scholars Press, 1990.

Mayes, A. H. D. *Deuteronomy*. Grand Rapids: Eerdmans, 1981.

Mays, James Luther. *Hosea*. OTL. London: SCM, 1969.

McConville, J. G. *Judgment and Promise: An Interpretation of the Book of Jeremiah*. Winona Lake, IN: Eisenbrauns, 1993.

McKane, William. *Jeremiah: Introduction and Commentary on Jeremiah I–XXV*. Edinburgh: T & T Clark, 1986.

———. *A Critical and Exegetical Commentary on Jeremiah XXVI–LII*. Edinburgh: T & T Clark, 1986.

McKenzie, Steven. *1–2 Chronicles*. Nashville: Abingdon, 2004.

Mettinger, Tryggve N. D. *The Dethronement of Sabaoth: Studies in the Shem and Kabod Theologies*. ConBOT 18. Lund: Gleerup, 1982.

———. *The Riddle of Resurrection: "Dying and Rising Gods" in the Ancient Near East*. ConBib OT 50. Stockholm: Almqvist & Wiksell International, 2001.

Meyers, Carol. *Discovering Eve: Ancient Israelite Women in Context*. Oxford and New York: Oxford University Press, 1988.

———. *Exodus*. Cambridge: Cambridge University Press, 2005.

———. "Daughters of the Inhabitants of the Land as Marriage Partners (Exod 34:16; Gen 24:3; 27:46; 28:1, 6, 8; Deut 7:3; Josh 23:12-13; Judg 3:5-6)." In *Women in Scripture*. Edited by Carol Meyers, 200–1. Boston: Houghton Mifflin, 2000.

Milgrom, Jacob. *Leviticus 1–16*. AB 3. New York: Doubleday, 1994.

———. "Law and Narrative and the Exegesis of Leviticus XIX 19." *VT* 46 (1996): 544–48.

———. "The Nature and Extent of Idolatry in Eighth-Seventh Century Judah." *HUCA* 69 (1998): 1–13.

———. *Leviticus 17–22*. AB 3A. New York: Doubleday, 2000.

———. *Leviticus: A Book of Ritual and Ethics*. Minneapolis: Fortress Press, 2004.

Murphy, Roland. "Dance and Death in the Song of Songs." In *Love and Death in the Ancient Near East* (1987), 117–19.

———. *The Song of Songs*. Hermeneia. Minneapolis: Fortress Press, 1990.

Nakhai, Beth Alpert. "Female Infanticide in Iron II Israel and Judah." In *Sacred History, Sacred Literature* (2008), 257–72.

Nardelli, Jean-Fabrice. *Homosexuality and Liminality in the Gilgameš and Samuel*. Classical and Byzantine Monographs 64. Amsterdam: Adolf M. Hakkert, 2007.

Neef, Heintz-Dieter. "Jephta und seine Tochter (JDC. XI 29-40)." *VT* 49 (1999): 206–17.

Nelson, Richard. *First and Second Kings*. Louisville: John Knox, 1987.

———. *Deuteronomy*. OTL. Louisville: Westminster John Knox, 2002.

Newsom, Carol A. "Woman and the Discourse of Patriarchal Wisdom: A Study of Proverbs 1–9." In *Gender and Difference in Ancient Israel* (1989), 142–60.

Niditch, Susan. *Judges*. OTL. Louisville: Westminster John Knox, 2008.

Niehr, Herbert. "In Search of YHWH's Cult Statue in the First Temple." In *The Image and the Book: Iconic Cults, Aniconism, and the Rise of Book Religion in Israel and the Ancient Near East*. Biblical Exegesis and Theology 21. Edited by Karel van der Toorn, 73–95. Leuven: Peeters, 1997.

Nissinen, Martti. *Homoeroticism in the Biblical World*. Translated by Kirsi Stjerna. Minneapolis: Fortress Press, 1998.

———. "Song of Songs and Sacred Marriage." In *Sacred Marriages* (2008), 173–218.

Noort, Ed. "The Creation of Man and Woman in Biblical and Ancient Near Eastern Traditions." In *The Creation of Man and Woman: Interpretations of the Biblical Narratives in Jewish and Christian Traditions*. Themes in Biblical Narrative 3. Edited by Gerald P. Luttikhuizen, 1–18. Leiden and Boston: Brill, 2000.

Noth, Martin. *Exodus*. Philadelphia: Westminster, 1962.

Novick, Tzvi. "*ʿqb hlb mkl wʾnš hûʾ mî ʿmû* (JEREMIAH 17:9)." *JBL* 123 (2004): 531–535.

O'Connor, Kathleen M. *The Confessions of Jeremiah: Their Interpretation and Their Role in Chapters 1–25*. SBLDS 94. Atlanta: Scholars Press, 1987.

———. "The Book of Jeremiah: Reconstructing Community after Disaster." In *Character Ethics and the Old Testament: Moral Dimensions of Scripture*. Edited by M. Daniel Carroll R. and Jacqueline E. Lapsley, 81–92. Louisville: Westminster John Knox, 2007.

Odell, Margaret. "An Exploratory Study of Shame and Dependence in the Bible and Selected Near Eastern Parallels." In *The Biblical Canon in Comparative Perspective* (1991), 217–29.

———. "I Will Destroy Your Mother: The Obliteration of a Cultic Role in Hosea 4.4-6." In *A Feminist Companion to the Latter Prophets* (1995), 180–93.

———. "The City of Hamonah in Ezekiel 39:11-16: The Tumultuous City of Jerusalem." *CBQ* 56 (1994): 479–89.

Odell, Margaret, and John Strong, eds. *The Book of Ezekiel: Theological and Anthropological Perspectives*. SBL Symposium Series 9. Atlanta: Scholars Press, 2000.

Olyan, Saul M. "'And with a Male You Shall Not Lie the Lying Down of a Woman': On the Meaning and Significance of Leviticus 18:22 and 20:13." *Journal of the History of Sexuality* 5 (1994): 179–206.

———. *Rites and Rank: Hierarchy in Biblical Representations of Cult*. Princeton: Princeton University Press, 2000.

———. *Biblical Mourning: Ritual and Social Dimensions*. New York: Oxford University Press, 2004.

Page, Hugh R. Jr. *The Myth of Cosmic Rebellion: A Study of Its Reflexes in Ugaritic and Biblical Literature*. VTSup 65. Leiden: Brill, 1996.

Patton, Corrine. "'I Myself Gave Them Laws That Were Not Good': Ezekiel 20 and the Exodus Traditions." *JSOT* 69 (1996): 73–90.

———. "Pan-Deuteronomism and the Book of Ezekiel." In *Those Elusive Deuteronomists: The Phenomenon of Pan-Deuteronomism*. *JSOTSup* 268. Edited by Linda

Schearing and Steven McKenzie, 200–15. Sheffield: Sheffield Academic Press, 1999.

———. "Layers of Meaning: Priesthood in Jeremiah MT." In *The Priests in the Prophets*. *JSOTSup* 408. Edited by Lester Grabbe and Alice Ogden Bellis, 149–76. London and New York: T & T Clark, 2004.

Perdue, Leo, and Joseph Blenkinsopp, John J. Collins, and Carol Meyers. *Families in Ancient Israel*. Louisville: Westminster John Knox, 1997.

Poorthuis, Marcel J. H. M. "Introduction." In *Purity and Holiness: The Heritage of Leviticus*. Edited by Marcel Poorthuis and Joshua Schwartz, 3–26. Leiden: Brill, 2000.

Pope, Marvin. "Mixed Marriage Metaphor in Ezekiel 16." In *Fortunate the Eyes That See: Essays in Honor of David Noel Freedman in Celebration of His Seventieth Birthday*. Edited by Astrid Beck et al., 384–99. Grand Rapids: Eerdmans, 1995.

———. *Song of Songs*. AB 7C. New York: Doubleday, 1977.

Pressler, Carolyn. *The View of Women Found in the Deuteronomic Family Laws*. BZAW 216. Berlin and New York: de Gruyter, 1993.

Quell, Gottfried. "*ἀγαπάω, agapaō*." *TDNT* 1:21–35.

Rad, Gerhard von. *Genesis*. OTL. Translated by J. H. Marks. Rev. ed. Philadelphia: Westminster, 1972.

Renz, Thomas. *The Rhetorical Function of the Book of Ezekiel*. *VTSup* 76. Leiden: Brill, 1999.

Römer, Thomas. "Why Would the Deuteronomists Tell About the Sacrifice of Jephthah's Daughter?" *JSOT* 77 (1998): 27–38.

Sarna, Nahum. *Genesis*. Philadelphia: Jewish Publication Society, 1989.

Schenker, Adrian. "Kinder der Prostitution, Kinder ohne Familie und ohne soziale Stellung: Ein freundschaftliches Sed contra für Lothar Ruppert und eine These zu Hos 1." In *"Ich bewirke das Heil und erschaffe das Unheil (Jesaja 45,7): Studien zur Botschaft der Propheten: Festschrift für Lothar Ruppert zum 65. Geburtstag*. FzB 88. Edited by Friedrich Diedrich and Bernd Willmes, 355–69. Würzburg: Echter Verlag, 1998.

Schloen, J. David. *The House of the Father as Fact and Symbol: Patrimonialism in Ugarit and the Ancient Near East*. Studies in the Archaeology and History of the Levant, 2. Winona Lake, IN: Eisenbrauns, 2001.

Schmid, Konrad. "The Persian Authorization as a Historical Problem and as a Biblical Construct: A Plea for Distinctions in the Current Debate." In *The Pentateuch as Torah: New Models for Understanding Its Promulgation and Acceptance*. Edited by Gary N. Knoppers and Bernard M. Levinson, 23–38. Winona Lake, IN: Eisenbrauns, 2007.

Schmidt, Brian. *Israel's Beneficent Dead: Ancestor Cult and Necromancy in Ancient Israelite Religion and Tradition*. Winona Lake, IN: Eisenbrauns, 1996.

———. "Afterlife Beliefs: Memory as Immortality." *Near Eastern Archaeology* 63 (2000): 236–39.

Schniedewind, William M. *How the Bible Became a Book: The Textualization of Ancient Israel*. Cambridge: Cambridge University Press, 2004.

———. "The Textualization of Torah in Jeremiah 8:8." In *Was ist ein Text? Alttestamentliche, ägyptologische und altorientalische Perspektiven*. BZAW 362. Edited by Ludwig Morenz and Stefan Schorch, 93–107. Berlin: de Gruyter, 2007.

Schüngel-Straumann, Helen. "God as Mother in Hosea 11." In *A Feminist Companion to the Latter Prophets* (1995), 194–218.

Schwartz, Baruch. "Israel's Holiness: The Torah Traditions." In *Purity and Holiness* (2000), 47–59.

Sherwood, Yvonne. "Boxing Gomer: Controlling the Deviant Woman in Hosea 1–3." In *A Feminist Companion to the Latter Prophets* (1995), 101–25.

Sjöberg, Mikael. *Wrestling with Textual Violence: The Jephthah Narrative in Antiquity and Modernity*. Sheffield: Phoenix Press, 2006.

Smith, Daniel L. *The Religion of the Landless: The Social Context of the Babylonian Exile*. Bloomington, IN: Meyer-Stone Books, 1989.

Smith, Mark S. *The Origins of Biblical Monotheism: Israel's Polytheistic Background and the Ugaritic Texts*. New York: Oxford University Press, 2001.

Smith-Christopher, Daniel. "The Mixed Marriage Crisis in Ezra 9–10 and Nehemiah 13: A Study of the Sociology of the Post-Exilic Judaean Community." In *Second Temple Studies*. 2 (1994), 243–65.

Soll, Will. *Psalm 119: Matrix, Form, and Setting*. CBQMS 23. Washington, DC: Catholic Biblical Association of America, 1991.

Stager, Lawrence. "The Archaeology of the Family in Ancient Israel." *BASOR* 260 (1985): 1–35.

———. "Jerusalem and the Garden of Eden." *Eretz-Israel* 26 (1999): 183–94.

Stählin, Gustav. "φίλος, *philos*." *TDNT* 9:152–53.

Stauffer, Ethelbert. "ἀγαπάω, *agapaō*." *TDNT* 1:35–55.

Steinberg, Naomi. "The Problem of Human Sacrifice in War: An Analysis of Judges 11." In *On the Way to Nineveh: Studies in Honor of George M. Landes*. Edited by Stephen L. Cook and S. C. Winter, 114–35. Atlanta: Scholars Press, 1999.

Stone, Ken. "Gender and Homosexuality in Judges 19: Subject–Honor, Object–Shame?" *JSOT* 67 (1995): 87–107.

Stulman, Louis. *Jeremiah*. Nashville: Abingdon, 2005.

Sweeney, Marvin. *King Josiah of Judah: The Lost Messiah of Israel*. New York: Oxford University Press, 2001.

———. *I & II Kings*. OTL. Louisville: Westminster John Knox, 2007.

Talmon, Shemaryahu. "The Emergence of Jewish Sectarianism in the Early Second Temple Period." In idem, *King, Cult and Calendar in Ancient Israel: Collected Studies*, 165–201. Jerusalem: Magnes Press, 1986.

Terrien, Samuel. "The Omphalos Myth and Hebrew Religion." *VT* 20 (1970): 315–38.

Tigay, Jeffrey. *You Shall Have No Other Gods: Israelite Religion in the Light of Hebrew Inscriptions*. HSS 31. Atlanta: Scholars Press, 1986.

Trible, Phyllis. *God and The Rhetoric of Sexuality*. Philadelphia: Fortress Press, 1978.

———. *Texts of Terror: Literary-Feminist Readings of Biblical Narratives*. Philadelphia: Fortress Press, 1984.

Trotter, James M. *Reading Hosea in Achaemenid Yehud*. *JSOTSup* 328. Sheffield: Sheffield Academic Press, 2001.

Tuell, Steven. "The Priesthood of the 'Foreigner': Evidence of Competing Polities in Ezekiel 44:1-14 and Isaiah 56:1-8." In *Constituting the Community: Studies on the Polity of Ancient Israel in Honor of S. Dean McBride*. Edited by John T. Strong and Steven S. Tuell, 183–204. Winona Lake, IN: Eisenbrauns, 2005.

Uehlinger, Christoph. "Anthropomorphic Cult Statuary in Iron Age Palestine and the Search for Yahweh's Cult Images." In *The Image and the Book* (1997), 97–156.

Uehlinger, Christoph, and Susan Müller Trufaut. "Ezekiel 1, Babylonian Cosmological Scholarship and Iconography: Attempts at Further Refinement." *TZ* 57 (2001): 140–71.

Van der Toorn, Karel. *Sin and Sanction in Israel and Mesopotamia*. Assen and Maastricht: Van Gorcum, 1985.

———. "The Nature of the Biblical Teraphim in the Light of the Cuneiform Evidence." *CBQ* 52 (1990): 203–22.

———. "Cultic Prostitution." *ABD* 5:510–13.

———, ed. *The Image and the Book: Iconic Cults, Aniconism, and the Rise of Book Religion in Israel and the Ancient Near East*. Biblical Exegesis and Theology 21. Leuven: Peeters, 1997.

———. "The Iconic Book Analogies Between the Babylonian Cult of Images and the Veneration of the Torah." In *The Image and the Book* (1997), 229–48.

———. *Scribal Culture and the Making of the Hebrew Bible*. Cambridge, MA: Harvard University Press, 2007.

Van Leeuwen, Raymond C. "Liminality and Worldview in Proverbs 1–9." *Semeia* 50 (1990): 111–44.

Vaux, Roland de. *Ancient Israel*. 2 volumes. New York: McGraw-Hill, 1965.

Wallis, Gerhard. אָהֵב, *ʾāhēb*, "love." *TDOT* 1:101–18.

Walsh, Jerome T. "Leviticus 18:22 and 20:13: Who Is Doing What to Whom." *JBL* 120 (2001): 201–9.

Wenham, Gordon. "*Bĕtûlāh* 'A Girl of Marriageable Age.'" *VT* 22 (1972): 326–48.

Westermann, Claus. *Genesis 1–11*. Translated by John J. Scullion. Minneapolis: Augsburg, 1984.

———. *Genesis 12–36*. Translated by John J. Scullion; Minneapolis: Augsburg, 1985.

Williamson, H. G. M. *The Book Called Isaiah: Deutero-Isaiah's Role in Composition and Redaction*. Oxford: Clarendon Press, 1994.

Wilson, Gerald Henry. *The Editing of the Hebrew Psalter*. SBLDS 76. Chico, CA: Scholars Press, 1985.

Wilson, Robert. "The Death of the King of Tyre: The Editorial History of Ezekiel 28." In *Love and Death in the Ancient Near East* (1987), 211–18.

Wright, David P. "Holiness, Sex, and Death in the Garden of Eden." *Bib* 77 (1996): 305–29.

Wyatt, Nicholas. "The Story of Dinah and Shechem." *UF* 22 (1990): 433–58.

______. "Androgyny in the Levantine World." In idem, *The Mythic Mind: Essays on Cosmology and Religion in Ugaritic and Old Testament Literature*, 238–55. London and Oakville, CT: Equinox, 2005.

Yee, Gale. "'She Is Not My Wife and I Am Not Her Husband': A Materialist Analysis of Hosea 1–2." *Biblical Interpretation* 9 (2001): 345–83.

———. *Poor Banished Children of Eve: Woman as Evil in the Hebrew Bible*. Minneapolis: Fortress Press, 2003.

Zimmerli, Walther. *Ezekiel 1: A Commentary on the Book of the Prophet Ezekiel, Chapters 1–24*. Philadelphia: Fortress Press, 1979.

Zlotnick-Sivan, Helena [Hagith Sarah Sivan]. "The Silent Women of Yehud: Notes on Ezra 9–10." *Journal of Jewish Studies* 51 (2000): 3–18.

Zvi, Ehud ben. *Hosea*. FOTL 21A/1. Grand Rapids: Eerdmans, 2005.

———. "What Is New in Yehud? Some Considerations." In *Yahwism After the Exile* (2003), 32–48.

Ancient Mesopotamia

Abusch, Tzvi. "Ishtar's Proposal and Gilgamesh's Refusal: An Interpretation of *The Gilgamesh Epic*, Tablet 6, Lines 1-79." *History of Religions* 26 (1986): 143–87.

———. "Gilgamesh's Request and Siduri's Denial: Part I, The Meaning of the Dialogue and its Implications for the History of the Epic." In *The Tablet and the Scroll: Near Eastern Studies in Honor of William W. Hallo*. Edited by Mark E. Cohen, Daniel C. Snell, and David B. Weisberg, 1–14. Bethesda, MD: Capital Decisions Limited, 1993.

———. "Sacrifice in Mesopotamia." In *Sacrifice in Religious Experience*. Studies in the History of Religions 97. Edited by Albert I. Baumgarten, 39–48. Leiden: Brill, 2002.

———. "Ishtar." *DDD*, 452–56.

———. "Etemmu." *DDD*, 309–12.

Adams, Robert McCormick. *Heartland of Cities: Surveys of Ancient Settlement and Land Use on the Central Floodplain of the Euphrates*. Chicago: University of Chicago Press, 1981.

Alster, Bendt, ed. *Proverbs of Ancient Sumer: The World's Earliest Proverb Collections*. Bethesda, MD: Capital Decisions Limited, 1997.

Ankum, J. A., Robert Feenstra, and William F. Leemans, eds. *Symbolae iuridicae et historicae Martino David dedicatae*. 2 volumes. Leiden: Brill, 1968.

Asher-Greve, Julia. "Decisive Sex, Essential Gender." In *Sex and Gender in the Ancient Near East* (2002), 11–26.

Assante, Julia. "From Whores to Hierodules: The Historiographic Invention of Mesopotamian Female Sex Professionals." In *Ancient Art and Its Historiography*.

Edited by A. A. Donohue and Mark D. Fullerton, 13–47. Cambridge: Cambridge University Press, 2003.

Bahrani, Zainab. *Women of Babylon: Gender and Representation in Mesopotamia.* London: Routledge, 2001.

Batto, Bernard. *Studies on Women at Mari.* Baltimore: Johns Hopkins University Press, 1974.

Beaulieu, Paul-Alain. "King Nabonidus and the Neo-Babylonian Empire." *CANE* 1:969–79.

———. "A Finger in Every Pie: The Institutional Connections of a Family of Entrepreneurs in Neo-Babylonian Larsa." In *Interdependency of Institutions and Private Entrepreneurs.* MOS Studies 2. Edited by A. C. V. M. Bongenaar, 43–72. Leiden and Istanbul: Nederlands Historisch-Archaeologisch Instituut te Istanbul, 2000.

———. The Setting of Babylonian Wisdom Literature." In *Wisdom Literature in Mesopotamia and Israel.* SBL Symposium 36. Edited by Richard J. Clifford, 3–19. Atlanta: Society of Biblical Literature, 2007.

Bedford, Peter. "The Economy of the Near East in the First Millennium." In *Trade and Finance in Ancient Mesopotamia.* MOS Studies 1. Edited by Jan G. Dercksen, 58–88. Leiden: Nederlands Historisch-Archaeologisch Instituut, 1999.

Behrens, Hermann, Darlene Loding, and Martha T. Roth, eds. *DUMU-E$_2$-DUB-BA-A: Studies in Honor of Åke W. Sjöberg.* Occasional Publications of the Samuel Noah Kramer Fund 11. Philadelphia: University Museum, 1989.

Berger, Paul-Richard. "Der Kyros-Zylinder mit dem Zusatzfragment BIN II Nr. 32 und die akkadischen Personennamen im Danielbuch." *ZA* 64 (1975): 192–234.

Berlejung, Angelika. "Washing the Mouth: The Consecration of Divine Images in Mesopotamia." In *The Image and the Book* (1997), 45–72.

Bidmead, Julye. *The Akītu Festival: Religious Continuity and Royal Legitimation in Mesopotamia.* Piscataway, NJ: Gorgias, 2002.

Biggs, Robert D. "Conception, Contraception, and Abortion in Ancient Mesopotamia." In *Wisdom, Gods, and Literature: Studies in Assyriology in Honour of W. G. Lambert.* Edited by A. R. George and Irving L. Finkel, 1–13. Winona Lake, IN: Eisenbrauns, 2000.

Binsbergen, Wim van, and Frans Wiggermann. "Magic in History: A Theoretical Perspective, and Its Application to Ancient Mesopotamia." In *Mesopotamian Magic: Textual, Historical, and Interpretative Perspectives.* Ancient Magic and Divination 1. Edited by Tzvi Abusch and Karel van der Toorn, 3–34. Groningen: Styx, 1999.

Black, Jeremy, and Anthony Green. *Gods, Demons and Symbols of Ancient Mesopotamia.* Austin: University of Texas Press, 1992.

Böck, Barbara. *Die babylonisch-assyrische Morphoskopie.* AfO Beiheft 27. Vienna: Institut für Orientalistik der Universität Wien, 2000.

———. "Überlegungen zu einem Kultfest der altmesopotamischen Göttin Inanna." *Numen* 51 (2004): 20–46.

Bodel, John, and Saul M. Olyan, eds. *Household and Family Religion in Antiquity*. Malden, MA: Blackwell, 2008.

Bottéro, Jean. *Mesopotamia: Writing, Reasoning, and the Gods*. Translated by Zainab Bahrani and Marc van de Mieroop. Chicago: University of Chicago Press, 1992.

———. *Religion in Ancient Mesopotamia*. Translated by Teresa Fagan. Chicago: University of Chicago Press, 2001.

Briant, Pierre. *From Cyrus to Alexander: A History of the Persian Empire*. Translated by Peter T. Daniels. Winona Lake, IN: Eisenbrauns, 2002.

Brinkman, John A. *Prelude to Empire: Babylonian Society and Politics, 747–726 B.C.* Philadelphia: University Museum, 1984.

Burnstein, Stanley. *The Babyloniaca of Berossus*. Malibu, CA: Undena Publications, 1978.

Clifford, Richard J. *Creation Accounts in the Ancient Near East and in the Bible*. CBQMS 26. Washington, DC: Catholic Biblical Association of America, 1994.

Cohen, Mark E. *Cultic Calendars*. Bethesda, Md.: Capital Decisions Limited, 1993.

Cooper, Jerrold S. "Enki's Member: Eros and Irrigation in Mesopotamian Literature." In *DUMU-E$_2$-DUB-BA-A* (1989), 87–89.

———. "The Fate of Mankind: Death and Afterlife in Ancient Mesopotamia." In *Death and Afterlife: Perspectives of World Religions*. Edited by Hiroshi Obayashi, 19–33. New York: Greenwood Press, 1992.

———. "Sacred Marriage and Popular Cult in Early Mesopotamia." In *Official Cult and Popular Religion in the Ancient Near East*. Edited by Eiko Matsushima, 81–96. Heidelberg: C. Winter, 1993.

———. "Paradigm and Propaganda: The Dynasty of Akkade in the 21st Century." In *Akkad: The First World Empire: Structure, Ideology, Traditions*. History of the Ancient Near East 5. Edited by Mario Liverani, 11–23. Padova: Tipografia Poligrafica Moderna, 1993.

———. "Buddies in Babylonia: Gilgamesh, Enkidu, and Mesopotamian Homosexuality." In *Riches Hidden in Secret Places: Ancient Near Eastern Studies in Memory of Thorkild Jacobsen*. Edited by Tzvi Abusch, 73–85. Winona Lake, IN: Eisenbrauns, 2002.

———. "Prostitution." *RlA* 11 (2006): 12–21.

———. "Virginity in Ancient Mesopotamia." In *Sex and Gender in the Ancient Near East* (2002), 91–112.

———. "Genre, Gender, and the Sumerian Lamentation." *JCS* 58 (2006): 39–47.

Dalley, Stephanie. "The Hanging Gardens of Babylon at Nineveh." In *Assyrien im Wandel der Zeit: XXXIXe Rencontre Assyriologique Internationale, Heidelberg 6.–10. Juli 1992*. CRRAI 39. Heidelberger Studien zum Alten Orient 6. Edited by Hartmut Waetzoldt and Harald Hauptmann, 19–24. Heidelberg: Heidelberger Orientverlag, 1997.

———. "The Influence of Mesopotamia on Israel." In *The Legacy of Mesopotamia*. Edited by Stephanie Dalley, 57–83. Oxford: Oxford University Press, 1998.

———. "Occasions and Opportunities: 1. To the Persian Conquest." In *The Legacy of Mesopotamia* (1998), 9–33.

———. "Review of R. Mattila, *The King's Magnates*, SAAS 11. Helsinki: State Archives of Assyria Project, 2000." *Bibliotheca Orientalis* 58 (2001): 197–206.

———. "Evolution of Gender in Mesopotamian Mythology and Iconography with a Possible Explanation of *ša rēšēn*, 'the man with two heads.'" In *Sex and Gender in the Ancient Near East* (2002), 117–22.

Dandamaev, Muhammed A. *Slavery in Babylonia: From Nabopolassar to Alexander the Great (626–331 BC)*. Translated by Victoria Powell. Edited by Marvin Powell and David Weisberg. Revised edition. DeKalb, IL: Northern Illinois University Press, 1984.

———. "An Age of Privatization in Ancient Mesopotamia." In *Privatization in the Ancient Near East and Classical World*. Edited by Michael Hudson and Baruch A. Levine, 197–210. Cambridge, MA: Peabody Museum of Archaeology and Ethnology, Harvard University, 1996.

———. "Neo-Babylonian and Achaemenid State Administration in Mesopotamia." In *Judah and the Judeans in the Persian Period*. Edited by Oded Lipschits and Manfred Oeming, 373–98. Winona Lake, IN: Eisenbrauns, 2006.

Deller, Karlheinz. "The Assyrian Eunuchs and Their Predecessors." In *Priests and Officials in the Ancient Near East*. Edited by Kazuko Watanabe, 303–11. Heidelberg: C. Winter, 1996.

Dempsky, Aaron. "The Education of Canaanite Scribes in the Mesopotamian Cuneiform Tradition." In *Bar-Ilan Studies in Assyriology Dedicated to Pinhas Artzi*. Edited by Jacob Klein and Aaron Skaist, 157–70. Ramat Gan: Bar-Ilan University Press, 1990.

Dobbs-Allsopp, F. W. "Darwinism, Genre Theory, and City Laments." *JAOS* 120 (2000): 625–30.

Driel, G. van. "The Murašûs in Context." *JESHO* 32 (1989): 203–29.

———. "Landless and Hungry? An Assessment." In *Landless and Hungry? Access to Land in Early and Traditional Societies. Proceedings of a Seminar held in Leiden, 20 and 21 June, 1966*. Edited by Bernhard Häring and R. de Maaijer, 190–98. Leiden: Research School CNWS, School of Asian, African, and Amerindian Studies, 1998.

Driver, Godfrey R., and John C. Miles. *The Babylonian Laws*. Volume I: *Legal Commentary*. Oxford: Clarendon Press, 1952.

———. *The Assyrian Laws*. Oxford: Clarendon Press, 1935.

Edzard, D. O. "Review of Manfred Hutter, *Altorientalische Vorstellungen von der Unterwelt*." *ZA* 79 (1989): 124–27.

Ehrenberg, Erica. "Persian Conquerors, Babylonian Captivators." In *Regime Change in the Ancient Near East and Egypt*. Proceedings of the British Academy 136. Edited by Harriet Crawford, 95–103. Oxford: Clarendon Press, 2007.

Ellis, Maria DeJong. "An Old Babylonian *kusarikku*." In *DUMU-E$_2$-DUB-BA-A* (1989), 121–35.

Eyre, Christopher J. "The Agricultural Cycle, Farming, and Water Management in the Ancient Near East." *CANE*, 175–89.

Farber Flügge, Gertrud. *Der Mythos "Inanna und Enki" unter besonderer Berücksichtigung der Liste der me*. Studia Pohl 10. Rome: Pontifical Biblical Institute, 1973.

Farber, Walter. "Lamaštu." *RlA* 6 (1980–83): 439–46.

Finkelstein, Jacob J. "On Some Recent Studies in Cuneiform Law." *JAOS* 90 (1970): 243–56.

Fleming, Daniel E. "Job: The Tale of Patient Faith and the Book of God's Dilemma." *VT* 44 (1994): 469–82.

———. "The Integration of Household and Community Religion in Ancient Syria." In *Household and Family Religion in Antiquity* (2008), 37–59.

Foster, Benjamin. "Gilgamesh: Sex, Love and the Ascent of Knowledge." In *Love and Death in the Ancient Near East* (1987), 21–42.

Frame, Grant. *Babylonia 689–627 B.C.: A Political History*. Istanbul: Nederlands Historisch-Archaeologisch Instituut te Istanbul, 1992.

Franke, Sabina. *Königsinschriften und Königsideologie: Die Könige von Akkade zwischen Tradition und Neuerung*. Münster: LIT Verlag, 1995.

———. "Kings of Akkad: Sargon and Naram-Sin." CANE, 831–41.

Frankfort, Henri. *Kingship and the Gods*. Chicago: University of Chicago Press, 1948.

Frayne, Douglas. "Notes on the Sacred Marriage Rite." *Bibliotheca Orientalis* 42 (1985): 5–22.

Frymer-Kensky, Tikva. *In the Wake of the Goddesses: Women, Culture, and the Biblical Transformation of Pagan Myth*. New York: The Free Press, 1992.

Grayson, A. K. "Assyria: Sennacherib and Esarhaddon (704–669 BC)." CAH, Volume 3, Part 2, *The Assyrian and Babylonian Empires and Other States of the Near East, from the Eighth to the Sixth Centuries B.C.* Edited by John Boardman, et al., 103–41. Cambridge: Cambridge University Press, 1982.

———. "Eunuchs in Power: Their Role in the Assyrian Bureaucracy." In *Vom Alten Orient zum Alten Testament. Festschrift für Wolfram Freiherrn von Soden zum 85. Geburtstag am 19. Juni 1993*. AOAT 240. Edited by Manfried Dietrich and Oswald Loretz, 85–97. Neukirchen: Neukirchener Verlag, 1995.

———. "The Struggle for Power: Challenge to Absolute Monarchy in the Ninth and Eighth Centuries." In *Priests and Officials in the Ancient Near East* (1999), 253–70.

———. *Assyrian and Babylonian Chronicles*. Texts from Cuneiform Sources 5. Winona Lake, IN: Eisenbrauns, 2000.

Greenfield, J. C. "Apkallu." *DDD*, 72–74.

Greengus, Samuel. "The Old Babylonian Marriage Contract." *JAOS* 89 (1969): 505–32.

———. "Legal and Social Institutions of Ancient Mesopotamia." *CANE*, 469–84.

Groneberg, Brigitte. "Der sumerisch-akkadische Inanna/Ištar: Hermaphroditos?" *WO* 17 (1986): 25–46.

———. "Toward a Definition of Literariness as Applied to Akkadian Literature." In *Mesopotamian Poetic Language: Sumerian and Akkadian*. Cuneiform Monographs 6. Edited by Marianna E. Vogelzang and Herman L. J. Vanstiphout, 59–84. Groningen: Styx, 1996.

Guinan, Ann Kessler. "Erotomancy: Scripting the Erotic." In *Sex and Gender in the Ancient Near East* (2002), 185–201.

———. "Auguries of Hegemony: The Sex Omens of Mesopotamia." In *Gender and Body in the Ancient Mediterranean*. Edited by Maria Wyke, 38–55. Malden, MA: Blackwell, 1998.

Haas, Volkert, ed. *Aussenseiter und Randgruppen: Beiträge zu einer Sozialgeschichte des Alten Orients*. Konstanz: Universitätsverlag, 1992.

Hallo, William W. *Early Mesopotamian Royal Titles, A Philologic and Historical Analysis*. AOS 43. New Haven: Yale University Press, 1957.

———. "The Birth of Kings." In *Love and Death in the Ancient Near East* (1987), 42–52.

———. Origins: *The Ancient Near Eastern Background of Some Modern Western Institutions*. Leiden and New York: Brill, 1996.

———. "Sumerian Religion." In *Kinattūtu ša darāti*. Edited by A. F. Rainey, 15–35. Tel Aviv: University of Tel Aviv, 1993.

———. "Adapa Reconsidered: Life and Death in Contextual Perspective." *Scriptura* 87 (2004): 267–77.

Harris, Rivkah. "The *Nadītu* Woman." In *Studies Presented to A. Leo Oppenheim, June 7, 1964*, 106–35. Chicago: The Oriental Institute of the University of Chicago, 1964.

———. *Ancient Sippar: a Demographic Study of an Old-Babylonian City (1894–1595 B.C.)*. Istanbul: Nederlands Historisch-Archaeologisch Instituut te Istanbul, 1975.

———. "Inanna-Ishtar as Paradox and a Coincidence of Opposites." *History of Religions* 30 (1991): 261–78.

———. "The Conflict of Generations in Ancient Mesopotamian Myths." *Comparative Studies in Society and History* 34 (1992): 621–35.

———. *Gender and Aging in Mesopotamia*. Norman: University of Oklahoma Press, 2000.

Henshaw, Richard A. *Female and Male: The Cultic Personnel, The Bible and the Rest of the Ancient Near East*. Princeton Theological Monograph Series 31. Allison Park, PA: Pickwick, 1994.

Jacobsen, Thorkild. *Treasures of Darkness*. New Haven: Yale University Press, 1976.

———. "The lil$_2$ of ^{d}En-lil$_2$." In *DUMU-E$_2$-DUB-BA-A* (1989), 267–76.

———. "The Graven Image." In *Ancient Israelite Religion: Essays in Honor of Frank Moore Cross*. Edited by Patrick D. Miller Jr., Paul S. Hanson, and S. Dean McBride, 15–32. Philadelphia: Fortress Press, 1987.

Jean, Cynthia. *La magie néo-assyrienne en contexte: recherche sur le métier d'exorciste et le concept d'āšipūtu*. SAAS 17. Helsinki: Neo-Assyrian Text Corpus Project, 2006.

Jeyes, Ulla. "The *Nadītu* Women of Sippar." In *Images of Women in Antiquity*. Edited by Averil Cameron and Amélie Kuhrt, 260–72. Detroit: Wayne State University Press, 1983.

Joannès, Francis. "Private Commerce and Banking in Achaemenid Babylon." *CANE*, 1475–85.

Jursa, Michael. *Neo-Babylonian Legal and Administrative Documents: Typology, Contents and Archives*. Guides to the Mesopotamia Textual Record, 1. Münster: Ugarit-Verlag, 2005.

———. "The Babylonian Economy in the First Millennium BC." In The *Babylonian World*. Edited by Gwendolyn Leick, 224–35. London and New York: Routledge, 2007.

———. "The Transition of Babylonia from the Neo-Babylonian Empire to Achaemenid Rule." In *Regime Change in the Ancient Near East and Egypt* (2007), 73–94.

Katz, Dina. "Enki and Ninhursaga, Part Two: The Story of Enki and Ninhursaga." *Bibliotheca Orientalis* 65 (2008): 320–42.

Kilmer, A. D. "The First Tablet of *Malku* = *Šarru* Together With Its Explict Version." *JAOS* 83 (1963): 421–46.

———. "How Was Queen Ereshkigal Tricked? A New Interpretation of the Descent of Ishtar." *UF* 3 (1971): 299–309.

———. "A Note on an Overlooked Word-play in the Akkadian Gilgamesh." In *Zikir Šumim: Assyriological Studies Presented to F. R. Kraus on the Occasion of his Seventieth Birthday*. Edited by G. van Driel, et al., 128–29. Leiden: Brill, 1982.

———. "The Investiture of Enkidu in the Epic of Gilgamesh." In *Sex and Gender in the Ancient Near East* (2002), 283–88.

Klein, Jacob. "Sacred Marriage." *ABD* 5:867–68.

———. "Akitu," *ABD* 1:138–39.

Kramer, Samuel Noah. *The Sumerians: Their History, Culture, and Character*. Chicago: University of Chicago Press, 1963.

———, and John Maier. *Myths of Enki, the Crafty God*. New York: Oxford University Press, 1989.

Kuhrt, Amélie. "Nabonidus and the Babylonian Priesthood." In *Pagan Priests: Religion and Power in the Ancient World*. Edited by Mary Beard and John North, 119–55. Ithaca, NY: Cornell University Press, 1990.

Lafont, Sophie. *Femmes, Droit et Justice dans l'Antiquité orientale: Contribution à l'étude du droit pénal au Proche-Orient ancien*. OBO 165. Fribourg: Editions Universitaires; Göttingen: Vandenhoeck & Ruprecht, 1999.

Lambert, Wilfred G. "The Gula Hymn of Bullutsa-rabi." *Or* n.s. 36 (1967): 105–32.

———. "The Historical Development of the Mesopotamian Pantheon: A Study in Sophisticated Polytheism." In *Unity and Diversity: Essays in the History, Literature, and Religion of the Ancient Near East*. Edited by Hans Goedicke and J. J. M. Roberts, 191–99. Baltimore: Johns Hopkins University Press, 1975.

———. "The Theology of Death." In *Death in Mesopotamia: XXVIe Rencontre Assyriologique Internationale*. Mesopotamia 8. Copenhagen: Akademisk Forlag, 1980. 53–66.

———. "Kosmogonie." *RlA* 6 (1980/83): 218–22.

———. "Studies in Marduk." *Bulletin of the School of Oriental and African Studies* 47 (1984): 1–9.

———. "The Pantheon of Mari." *MARI* 4 (1985): 525–39.

———. "Ancient Mesopotamian Gods: Superstition, Philosophy, Theology." *Revue de l'Histoire des Religions* 207 (1990): 115–30.

———. "Prostitution." In *Aussenseiter und Randgruppen* (1992), 127–57.

———. "Some New Babylonian Wisdom Literature." In *Wisdom in Ancient Israel*. Edited by John Day, Robert P. Gordon, and H. G. M. Williamson, 30–42. Cambridge: Cambridge University Press, 1995.

———. "Ištar of Nineveh." In *Nineveh: Papers of the XLIXe Rencontre Assyriologique Internationale London, 7–11 July 2003*. 2 volumes. Edited by Dominique Collon and Andrew George, 1:35-39. London: British School of Archaeology in Iraq, 2005.

Landsberger, Benno. "Jungfräulichkeit: Ein Beitrag zum Thema 'Beilage und Eheschliessung.'" In *Symbolae Iuridicae et Historicae Martino David Dedicatae*. 2 volumes. Edited by J. A. Ankum, Robert Feenstra, and William F. Leemans, 2:41–105. Leiden: Brill, 1968.

Lapinkivi, Pirjo. *The Sumerian Sacred Marriage in Light of the Comparative Evidence*. SAAS 15. Helsinki: Neo-Assyrian Text Corpus Project, 2004.

Lawson, Jack. "The Sumerian Sacred Marriage and Its Aftermath." In *Sacred Marriages* (2008), 7–41.

———. *The Concept of Fate in Ancient Mesopotamia of the First Millennium: Toward an Understanding of Šimtu*. Wiesbaden: Harrassowitz, 1994.

Leichty, Earl. "Esarhaddon, King of Assyria." *CANE*, 949–58.

Leick, Gwendolyn. *Sex and Eroticism in Mesopotamian Literature*. London and New York: Routledge, 1994.

———, ed. *The Babylonian World*. London and New York: Routledge, 2007.

Lenzi, Alan. *Secrecy and the Gods: Secret Knowledge in Ancient Mesopotamia and Biblical Israel*. SAAS 19. Helsinki: Neo-Assyrian Corpus Project, 2008.

Lipschits, Oded, and Manfred Oeming, eds. *Judah and the Judeans in the Persian Period*. Winona Lake, IN: Eisenbrauns, 2006.

Llewellyn-Jones, Lloyd. "Eunuchs and the Royal Harem in Achaemenid Persia (559–331)." In *Eunuchs in Antiquity and Beyond*. Edited by Shaun Tougher, 19–49. London: Classical Press of Wales and Duckworth, 2002.

Longman, Tremper III. *Fictional Akkadian Autobiography: A Generic and Comparative Study*. Winona Lake, IN: Eisenbrauns, 1991.

Maier, John. "Gender Differences in the First Millennium: Additions to a Canonical Lamentation." In *Sex and Gender in the Ancient Near East* (2002), 345–54.

Makaewa, Kazuya. "Animal and Human Castration in Sumer, Part II: Human Castration in the Ur III Period." *Zinbun* 16 (1980): 1–55.

Malul, Meir. "The Mesopotamian *Susapinnu*: The Mesopotamian Paranymph and His Role." *JESHO* 32 (1989): 241–78.

Maul, Stefan M. "*kurgarrû* and *assinnu* und ihr Stand in der babylonischen Gesellschaft." In *Aussenseiter und Randgruppen* (1992), 159–71.

Melville, Sarah C. *The Role of Naqia/Zakutu in Sargonid Politics*. SAAS 9. Helsinki: Neo-Assyrian Text Corpus Project, 1999.

Metzler, Kai Alexander. "Tod, Weiblichkeit und Ästhetik im Mesopotamischen Weltschöpfungsepos *Enūma elîš*." In *Sex and Gender in the Ancient Near East* (2002), 47, 393–411.

Michalowski, Piotr. "Adapa and the Ritual Process." *Rocznik Orientalistyczny* 51 (1980): 77–82.

———. "Memory and Deed: The Historiography of the Political Expansion of the Akkad State." In *Akkad: The First World Empire: Structure, Ideology, Traditions*. History of the Ancient Near East 5. Edited by Mario Liverani, 69–90. Padova: Tipografia Poligrafica Moderna, 1993.

———. "The Cyrus Cylinder." In *The Ancient Near East: Historical Sources in Translation*. Edited by Mark Chavalas, 426–30. Malden, MA: Blackwell, 2006.

Mieroop, Marc van de. *The Ancient Mesopotamian City*. Oxford and New York: Oxford University Press, 1999.

———. *A History of the Ancient Near East, ca. 3000–323 BC*. Malden, MA: Blackwell, 2004.

Moran, William. "New Evidence from Mari on the History of Prophecy." *Bib* 51 (1969): 15–56.

———. "The Creation of Man in Atrahasis I 192–248." In *The Most Magic Word*. CBQMS 35. Edited by Ronald S. Hendel, 75–86. Washington, DC: Catholic Biblical Association, 2002.

———. "The Babylonian Job." In *The Most Magic Word* (2002), 182–200.

Nemet-Nejat, Karen Rhea. *Daily Life in Ancient Mesopotamia*. Peabody, MA: Hendrickson, 1998.

Nissen, Hans. *The Early History of the Ancient Near East, 9000–2000 B.C.* Chicago: University of Chicago Press, 1988.

Nissinen, Martti. *References to Prophecy in Neo-Assyrian Sources*. SAAS 7. Helsinki: Neo-Assyrian Text Corpus Project, 1998.

———. "Love Lyrics of Nabû and Tašmetu: An Assyrian Song of Songs?" In *"Und Mose schrieb dieses Lied auf." Studien zum Alten Testament und zum Alten Orient: Festschrift für Oswald Loretz zur Vollendung seines 70. Lebensjahres mit Beiträgen von Freunden, Schülern und Kollegen*. AOAT 250. Edited by Manfried Dietrich and Ingo Kottsieper, 585–634. Münster: Ugarit-Verlag, 1998.

———. "The Socioreligious Role of the Neo-Assyrian Prophets." In *Prophecy in Its Ancient Near Eastern Context: Mesopotamian, Biblical, and Arabian Perspectives*. SBL SymS 13. Edited by Martti Nissinen, 89–114. Atlanta: Society of Biblical Literature, 2000.

Novák, Mirko. "The Artificial Paradise: Programme and Ideology of Royal Gardens." In *Sex and Gender in the Ancient Near East* (2002), 443–60.

Oppenheim, A. Leo. "Akkadian *pul(u) ḫ (t)u* and *melammu*." *JAOS* 63 (1943): 31–34.

———. *Ancient Mesopotamia: A Portrait of a Dead Civilization*. Chicago: University of Chicago Press, 1964.

Pearce, Laurie E. "Statements of Purpose: Why the Scribes Wrote." In *The Tablet and The Scroll* (1993), 185–93.

———. "The Scribes and Scholars of Ancient Mesopotamia." *CANE*, 2265–78.

Pongratz-Leisten, Beate. *Ina Šulmi Irub: Die kulttopographische und ideologische Programmatik der akītu-Prozession in Babylonien und Assyrien im 1. Jahrtausend v. Chr*. Mainz: Verlag Philipp von Zabern, 1994.

———. "Sacred Marriage and the Transfer of Divine Knowledge." In *Sacred Marriages* (2008), 43–73.

Porter, Anne. "The Dynamics of Death: Ancestors, Pastoralism, and the Origins of a Third-Millennium City in Syria." *BASOR* 325 (2002): 1–36.

Powell, Marvin. "Wir müssen alle unsere Nische nutzen: Monies, Motives, and Methods in Babylonian Economics." In *Trade and Finance in Ancient Mesopotamia* (1999), 5–23.

Postgate, J. N. *Early Mesopotamia: Society and Economy at the Dawn of History*. London: Routledge, 1992.

Potts, Daniel T. *Mesopotamian Civilization: The Material Foundations*. Ithaca, NY: Cornell University Press, 1997.

Radner, Karen. "Neo-Assyrian Period." In *A History of Ancient Near Eastern Law*. 2 volumes. Edited by Raymond Westbrook, 883–910. Leiden: Brill, 2003.

Reiner, Erica. "Nergal and Ereshkigal: Epic into Romance." In eadem, *Your Thwarts in Pieces, Your Mooring Rope Cut: Poetry from Babylonia and Assyria*, 50–60. Ann Arbor: Horace H. Rackham School of Graduate Studies at the University of Michigan, 1985.

———. *Astral Magic in Babylonia*. TAPA 85, Part 4. Philadelphia: American Philosophical Association, 1995.

Renger, Johannes. "Heilige Hochzeit. A. Philologisch." *RlA* 4 (1972–75): 251–59.

———. "Institutional, Communal, and Individual Ownership or Possession of Arable Land in Ancient Mesopotamia From the End of the Fourth to the End of the First Millennium B.C." *Chicago-Kent Law Review* 71 (1995): 269–319.

Richardson, Seth. "The World of Babylonian Countrysides." In *The Babylonian World* (2007), 13–38.

Roller, Lynn E. "The Ideology of the Eunuch Priest." In *Gender and Body in the Ancient Mediterranean* (1998), 118–35.

Röllig, Wolfgang. "Aktion oder Reaktion? Politisches Handeln assyrischer Könige." In *Anfänge politischen Denkens in der Antike: Die nahöstlichen Kulturen und die Griechen*. Edited by Kurt Raaflaub and Elisabeth Müller-Luckner, 105–13. Munich: Oldenbourg, 1993.

Roscoe, Will. "Priests of the Goddess: Gender Transgression in Ancient Religion." *History of Religions* 35 (1996): 195–230.

Roth, Martha T. "Age at Marriage and the Household: A Study of Neo-Babylonian and Neo-Assyrian Forms." *Comparative Studies in Society and History* 29 (1987): 715–47.

Rowton, Michael B. "Enclosed Nomadism." *JESHO* 17 (1974): 1–30.

———. "Urban Autonomy in a Nomadic Environment." *JNES* 32 (1973): 201–15.

Sallaberger, Walther. "Ur-III Zeit." In Walther Sallaberger and Aage Westenholz, *Mesopotamien. Akkade-Zeit und Ur-III Zeit*, 121–414. OBO 160/3. Fribourg: Universitätsverlag, 1999.

Scurlock, Jo Ann. "Baby-Snatching Demons, Restless Souls and the Dangers of Childbirth: Medico-Magical Means of Dealing with Some of the Perils of Motherhood in Ancient Mesopotamia." *Incognita* 2 (1991): 135–83.

———. "Death and the Afterlife in Ancient Mesopotamian Thought." *CANE*, 1883–93.

Snell, Daniel. "Methods of Exchange and Coinage in Ancient Western Asia." *CANE*, 1487–97.

Soden, Wolfram von. *The Ancient Orient: An Introduction to the Study of the Ancient Near East*. Grand Rapids: Eerdmans, 1994.

Solvang, Elna K. "Another Look 'Inside': Harems and the Interpretation of Women." In *Orientalism, Assyriology and the Bible*. Edited by Steven W. Holloway, 374–98. Sheffield: Phoenix Press, 2007.

Stol, Marten. "Women in Mesopotamia." *JESHO* 38 (1995): 123–44.

———. "Private Life in Ancient Mesopotamia." *CANE*, 485–501.

———. *Birth in Babylonia and the Bible: Its Mediterranean Setting*. Cuneiform Monographs 14. Groningen: Styx, 2000.

Stolper, Matthew W. *Entrepreneurs and Empire: The Murašû Archive, the Murašû Firm, and Persian Rule in Babylonia*. Leiden and Istanbul: Nederlands Historisch-Archaeologisch Instituut te Istanbul, 1985.

———. "Archive of Murashû." *ABD* 4:927–28.

Stone, Elizabeth C. "The Social Role of the *Nadītu* Women in Old Babylonian Nippur." *JESHO* 25 (1982): 50–70.

———. "Adoption in Old Babylonian Nippur." In Elizabeth C. Stone and David I. Owen, *Adoption in Old Babylonian Nippur and the Archive of Mannum*-mešu-*liṣṣur*, 1–33. Winona Lake, IN: Eisenbrauns, 1991.

Tadmor, Hayim. "The Role of the Chief Eunuch and the Place of Eunuchs in the Assyrian Empire." In *Sex and Gender in the Ancient Near East* (2002), 603–11.

Teppo, Saana. "Sacred Marriage and the Devotees of Ištar." In *Sacred Marriages* (2008), 75–92.

Tetlow, Elizabeth Meier. *Women, Crime, and Punishment in Ancient Law and Society*. New York: Continuum, 2004.

Vanderhooft, David. "Cyrus II, Liberator or Conqueror? Ancient Historiography Concerning Cyrus in Babylon." In *Judah and the Judeans in the Persian Period* (2006), 351–72.

Van der Toorn, Karel. *From Her Cradle to Her Grave: The Role of Religion in the Life of the Israelite and the Babylonian Woman*. Translated by Sara J. Denning-Bolle. Sheffield: JSOT Press, 1994.

———. "The Significance of the Veil in the Ancient Near East." In *Pomegranates and Golden Bells*. Edited by David P. Wright, David Noel Freedman, and Avi Hurvitz, 327–39. Winona Lake, IN: Eisenbrauns, 1995.

———. *Family Religion in Babylonia, Syria and Israel: Continuity and Change in the Forms of Religious Life*. Studies in the History and Culture of the Ancient Near East 7. Leiden: Brill, 1996.

———. "The Domestic Cult at Emar." *JCS* 47 (1995): 35–49.

———. "Family Religion in Second Millennium West Asia (Mesopotamia, Emar, Nuzi)." In *Household and Family Religion in Antiquity* (2008), 20–36.

Veldhuis, Niek. "Kurigalzu's Statue Inscription." *JCS* 60 (2008): 25–51.

Vogelzang, Marianna E. "Repetition as a Poetic Device in Akkadian." In *Mesopotamian Poetic Language: Sumerian and Akkadian*. Cuneiform Monographs 6. Edited by Marianna E. Vogelzang and Herman L. J. Vanstiphout, 167–82. Groningen: Styx, 1996.

Walker, Christopher, and Michael Dick. *The Induction of the Cult Image in Ancient Mesopotamia: The Mesopotamian Mīs Pî Ritual*. SAALT 1. Helsinki: Neo-Assyrian Text Corpus Project, 2001.

Walls, Neil. *Desire, Discord, and Death: Approaches to Ancient Near Eastern Myth*. Boston: American Schools of Oriental Research, 2001.

Watanabe, Chikako E. *Animal Symbolism in Mesopotamia: A Contextual Approach*. WOO 1. Vienna: Institut für Orientalistik, 2002.

Weisberg, David B. "Polytheism and Politics: Some Comments on Nabonidus' Foreign Policy." In *Crossing Boundaries and Linking Horizons: Studies in Honor of Michael C. Astour on His 80th Birthday*. Edited by Gordon D. Young, Mark W. Chavalas, and Richard E. Averbeck, 547–56. Bethesda, MD: Capital Decisions Limited, 1997.

Weissert, Elnathan. "Royal Hunt and Royal Triumph in a Prism Fragment of Ashurbanipal (82–5–22,2)." In *Assyria 1995: Proceedings of the 10th Anniversary Symposium of the Neo-Assyrian Text Corpus Project, Helsinki September 7–11, 1995*. Edited by Simo Parpola and Robert M. Whiting, 339–58. Helsinki: Neo-Assyrian Text Corpus Project, 1997.

Westbrook, Raymond. "The Enforcement of Morals in Mesopotamian Law." *JAOS* 104 (1984): 753–56.

______. *Old Babylonian Marriage Law*. AfO Beiheft 23. Horn, Austria: F. Berger, 1988.

———, ed. *A History of Ancient Near Eastern Law*. Two volumes. Leiden: Brill, 2003.

Westenholz, Joan Goodnick. "Heroes of Akkad," *Studies in Literature from the Ancient Near East by Members of the American Oriental Society Dedicated to Samuel Noah Kramer*. AOS 65. Edited by Jack M. Sasson, 327–36. New Haven: American Oriental Society, 1984.

———. "Tamar, *Qĕdēšā*, *Qadištu*, and Sacred Prostitution in Mesopotamia." *HTR* 82 (1989): 245–65.

———. *Legends of the Kings of Akkade*. Winona Lake, IN: Eisenbrauns, 1997.

Wiesehöfer, Josef. "The Achaemenid Empire in the Fourth Century B.C.E.: A Period of Decline?" In *Judah and the Judeans in the Fourth Century B.C.E.* Edited by Oded Lipschits, Gary N. Knoppers, and Rainer Albertz, 11–29. Winona Lake, IN: Eisenbrauns, 2007.

Wiggermann, Frans A. M. "Theologies, Priests, and Worship in Ancient Mesopotamia." *CANE*, 1857–70.

———. *Mesopotamian Protective Spirits: The Ritual Texts*. Cuneiform Monographs 1. Groningen: Styx & PP Publications, 1992.

Wilcke, Claus. "Politik im Spiegel der Literatur, Literatur als Mittel der Politik im älteren Babylonien." In *Anfänge politischen Denkens in der Antike* (1993), 29–75.

Wilson, E. Jan. *"Holiness" and "Purity" in Mesopotamia*. AOAT 237. Kevelaer: Butzon & Bercker; Neukirchen: Neukirchener Verlag, 1994.

Winter, Irene J. "The Body of the Able Ruler: Toward an Understanding of the Statues of Gudea." In *DUMU-E$_2$-DUB-BA-A* (1989), 573–83.

Wiseman, Donald J. *The Vassal-Treaties of Esarhaddon*. London: The British School of Archaeology in Iraq, 1958.

———. "A New Text of the Babylonian Poem of the Righteous Sufferer." *Anatolian Studies* 30 (1980): 101–7.

Wunsch, Cornelia. "The Egibi Family." In *The Babylonian World* (2007), 236–47.

Ancient Greece

Adcock, Frank E. "The Breakdown of the Thirty Years Peace B.C. 445–431." CAH, 1st edition. Volume 5, *Athens, 478–401 B.C.* Edited by J. B. Bury, S. A. Cook, and F. E. Adcock, 165–92. Cambridge: Cambridge University Press, 1927.

Allen, Diogenes, and Eric O. Springstead. *Philosophy for Understanding Theology*. 2d edition. Louisville: Westminster John Knox, 2007.

Almeida, Joseph. *Justice as an Aspect of the Polis Idea in Solon's Political Poems*. Leiden: Brill, 2003.

Andrewes, Antony. "The Spartan Resurgence." CAH, 2d edition. Volume 5, *The Fifth Century B.C.* Edited by D. M. Lewis, John Boardman, and J. K. Davies, 464–98. Cambridge: Cambridge University Press, 1992.

Annas, Julia. *An Introduction to Plato's Republic*. Oxford: Clarendon Press, 1981.

———. "Plato." In *Greek Thought: A Guide to Classical Knowledge*. Translated by Catherine Porter. Edited by Jacques Brunschwig and Geoffrey E. R. Lloyd, 672–92. Cambridge, MA: Belknap Press, 2000.

Arrowsmith, William. "Introduction to the Bacchae." In *The Complete Greek Tragedies*. Volume 3: *Euripides*. Edited by David Grene and Richmond Lattimore, 530–41. Chicago: University of Chicago Press, 1955.

Avagianou, Aphrodite A. *Sacred Marriage in the Rituals of Greek Religion*. European University Studies, Classics XV. New York: Peter Lang, 1991.

———. "*Hieros Gamos* in Ancient Greek Religion: The Human Aspect of a Sacralized Ritual." In *Sacred Marriages* (2008), 145–71.

Bernadette, Seth. *The Tragedy and Comedy of Life: Plato's Philebus*. Chicago: University of Chicago Press, 1993.

Blyth, Douglas. "The Ever-Moving Soul in Plato's 'Phaedrus.'" *American Journal of Philology* 118 (1997): 185–217.

Brisson, Luc. *Plato the Myth Maker*. Chicago: University of Chicago Press, 1998.

———. *Sexual Ambivalence: Androgyny and Hermaphroditism in Graeco-Roman Antiquity*. Translated by Janet Lloyd. Berkeley: University of California Press, 2002.

———. "Agathon, Pausanias, and Diotima in Plato's *Symposium: Paiderastia* and *Philosophia*." In *Plato's Symposium: Issues in Interpretation and Reception*. Edited by James H. Lesher, Debra Nails, and Frisbee C. C. Sheffield, 229–51. Cambridge, MA: Center for Hellenic Studies of Harvard University Press, 2006.

Brown, John Pairman. *Israel and Hellas*. 3 volumes. BZAW 231, 276, 299. Berlin: de Gruyer, 1995–2001.

Blundell, Sue. "Clutching at Clothes." In *Women's Dress in the Ancient Greek World*. Edited by Lloyd Llewellyn-Jones, 143–69. London: Duckworth and the Classical Press of Wales, 2002.

———. "Marriage and the Maiden: Narratives on the Parthenon." In *The Sacred and the Feminine in Ancient Greece*. Edited by Sue Blundell and Margaret Williamson, 47–70. London and New York: Routledge, 1998.

Bremmer, Jan. "Adolescents, *Symposion*, and Pederasty." In *Sympotica: A Symposium on the Symposion*. Edited by Oswyn Murray, 135–48. Oxford: Clarendon Press, 1990.

Brunschwig, Jacques, and Geoffrey E. R. Lloyd, eds. *Greek Thought: A Guide to Classical Knowledge*. Translated by Catherine Porter. Cambridge, MA: Belknap Press, 2000.

Buchan, Morag. *Women in Plato's Political Theory*. London and New York: Routledge, 1999.

Budin, Stephanie. *The Origin of Aphrodite*. Bethesda, MD: Capital Decisions Limited, 2003.

———. *The Myth of Sacred Prostitution in Antiquity*. Cambridge: Cambridge University Press, 2008.

Burkert, Walter. *Greek Religion*. Cambridge, MA: Harvard University Press, 1985.

———. "Athenian Cults and Festivals." CAH, 2d edition. Volume 5, *The Fifth Century B.C.* (1992), 245–67.

Canto-Sperber, Monique. "Socrates." In *Greek Thought* (2000), 745–62.

Carone, Gabriela Roxana. "The Virtues of Platonic Love." In *Plato's Symposium* (2006), 208–26.

Carpenter, Thomas H., and Christopher A. Faraone, eds. *Masks of Dionysus*. Ithaca, NY: Cornell University Press, 1993.

Carson, Anne. "Dirt and Desire: The Phenomenology of Female Pollution in Antiquity." In *Constructions of the Classical Body*. Edited by James I. Porter, 77–100. Ann Arbor: University of Michigan Press, 1999.

Clay, Jenny Strauss. *Hesiod's Cosmos*. Cambridge: Cambridge University Press, 2003.

———. "The Generation of Monsters in Hesiod." *CP* 88 (1993): 105–16.

Cohen, David. *Law, Sexuality, and Society: The Enforcement of Morals in Classical Athens*. Cambridge: Cambridge University Press, 1994.

Cohen, Edward E. "Free and Unfree Sexual Work: An Economic Analysis of Athenian Prostitution." In *Prostitutes and Courtesans in the Ancient World* (2006), 95–124.

Cole, Susan Guettel. "Domesticating Artemis." In *The Sacred and the Feminine in Ancient Greece* (1998), 27–43.

———. *Landscapes, Gender, and Ritual Space: The Ancient Greek Experience*. Berkeley: University of California Press, 2004.

Cooper, John M. *Reason and Emotion: Essays on Ancient Moral Psychology and Ethical Theory*. Princeton: Princeton University Press, 1999.

———. "Plato's Theory of Human Motivation." In *Essays on Plato's Psychology*. Edited by Ellen Wagner, 91–114. Lanham, MD: Lexington Books, 2001.

Copleston, Frederick. *History of Philosophy:* Volume 1. *Greece and Rome*. Westminster, MD: Newman Press, 1960.

Cox, Cheryl Ann. *Household Interests: Property, Marriage Strategies, and Family Dynamics in Ancient Athens*. Princeton: Princeton University Press, 1998.

Crane, Gregory. "Creon and the 'Ode to Man' in Sophocles' *Antigone*." *Harvard Studies in Classical Philology* 92 (1989): 103–16.

Crudden, Michael, trans. *The Homeric Hymns*. Oxford: Oxford University Press, 2001.

Davies, J. K. "Economy and Society." CAH, 2d edition. Volume 5, *The Fifth Century B.C.* (1992), 287–305.

———. "Athenian Citizenship: The Descent Group and the Alternatives." *Classical Journal* 73 (1978): 105–21.

Despland, Michel. *The Education of Desire: Plato and the Philosophy of Religion*. Toronto: University of Toronto Press, 1985.

Detienne, Marcel. "Forgetting Delphi between Apollo and Dionysus." *Classical Philology* 96 (2001): 147–58.

———. *The Writing of Orpheus: Greek Myth in Cultural Contact*. Translated by Janet Lloyd. Baltimore: Johns Hopkins University Press, 2002.

Debnar, Paula. "Fifth-Century Athenian History and Tragedy." In *A Companion to Greek Tragedy*. Edited by Justina Gregory, 3–37. Malden, MA: Blackwell, 2005.

Dobbs, Darrell. "The Piety of Thought in Plato's *Republic*, Book 1." *American Political Science Review* 88 (1994): 668–83.

Dodds, Eric Robertson. *Euripides' Bacchae*. Oxford: Clarendon Press, 1944.

Donlan, Walter. "Reciprocities in Homer." *Classical World* 75 (1982): 137–75.

Dowden, Ken. *Death and the Maiden: Girls' Initiation Rites in Greek Mythology*. London: Routledge, 1989.

Euben, J. Peter, ed. *Greek Tragedy and Political Theory*. Berkeley: University of California Press, 1986.

Everson, Steven. "Psychology." In *The Cambridge Companion to Aristotle*. Edited by Jonathan Barnes, 168–94. Cambridge: Cambridge University Press, 1995.

Faraone, Christopher A. *Ancient Greek Love Magic*. Cambridge, MA: Harvard University Press, 1999.

———. "Household Religion in Ancient Greece." In *Household and Family Religion in Antiquity* (2008), 210–28.

Finley, Moses I. *The World of Odysseus*. New York: Viking, 1965.

———. "The Ancient City: From Fustel de Coulanges to Max Weber and Beyond." *Comparative Studies in Society and History* 19 (1977): 305–27.

Foley, Helene P. *Ritual Irony: Poetry and Sacrifice in Euripides*. Ithaca, NY, and London: Cornell University Press, 1985.

———. *Homeric Hymn to Demeter*. Princeton: Princeton University Press, 1994.

———. "'The Mother of the Argument': *Eros* and the Body in Sappho and Plato's *Phaedrus*." In *Parchments of Gender: Deciphering the Bodies of Antiquity*. Edited by Maria Wyke, 39–70. Oxford: Clarendon Press, 1998.

Fornara, Charles W., and Loren J. Samons II. *Athens from Cleisthenes to Pericles*. Berkeley: University of California Press, 1991.

Foxhall, Lynn. "Pandora Unbound: A Feminist Critique of Foucault's History of Sexuality." In *Rethinking Sexuality: Foucault and Classical Antiquity*. Edited by David Larmour et al., 122–37. Princeton: Princeton University Press, 1998.

Frede, Dorothea. "Disintegration and Restoration: Pleasure and Pain in Plato's *Philebus*." In *The Cambridge Companion to Plato*. Edited by Richard Kraut, 425–63. Cambridge: Cambridge University Press, 1992.

Furley, William D. *Studies in the Use of Fire in Ancient Greek Religion*. New York: Arno Press, 1981.

Fustel de Coulanges, Numa Denis. *The Ancient City*. New York: Doubleday, 1956 [first published 1864].

Gantz, Timothy. *Early Greek Myth: A Guide to Literary and Artistic Sources*. Baltimore: Johns Hopkins University Press, 1993.

Gerson, Lloyd P. "A Platonic Reading of Plato's *Symposium*." In *Plato's Symposium* (2006), 47–67.

Gould, Thomas. *The Ancient Quarrel between Poetry and Philosophy*. Princeton: Princeton University Press, 1990.

Grene, David. "Introduction, Euripides, *Hippolytus*." In *Three Greek Tragedies in Translation*, 155–68. Chicago: University of Chicago Press, 1942.

Griswold, Charles L. Jr. *Self-Knowledge in Plato's Phaedrus*. New Haven: Yale University Press, 1986.

Guthrie, W. K. C. *A History of Greek Philosophy*. 4 volumes. Cambridge: Cambridge University Press, 1962.

Hague, Rebecca. "Ancient Greek Wedding Songs: The Tradition of Praise." *Journal of Folklore Research* 20 (1983): 131–43.

Halperin, David, John Winkler, and Froma Zeitlin, eds. *Before Sexuality: The Construction of Erotic Experience in the Ancient Greek World*. Princeton: Princeton University Press, 1990.

Hanson, Ann Ellis. "The Hippocratic *Parthenos* in Sickness and Health." In *Virginity Revisited: Configurations of the Unpossessed Body*. Edited by Bonnie MacLachlan and Judith Fletcher, 40–65. Toronto: University of Toronto Press, 2007.

Henrichs, Albert. "'He Has a God in Him': Human and Divine in the Modern Perception of Dionysus." In *Masks of Dionysus* (1993), 13–43.

Hobbs, Angela. "Female Imagery in Plato." In *Plato's Symposium* (2006), 252–71.

Hoffer, Stanley. "Violence, Culture, and the Workings of Ideology in Euripides' 'Ion.'" *Classical Antiquity* 15 (1996): 289–318.

Hornblower, Simon. "Greece: History of the Classical Period." In *The Oxford History of the Classical World*. Edited by John Boardman et al., 124–55. Oxford and New York: Oxford University Press, 1986.

Humphreys, Sarah C. *Anthropology and the Greeks*. London: Routledge & Kegan Paul, 1978.

———. "Family Tombs and Tomb Cult in Ancient Athens." *JHS* 100 (1980): 96–126.

Hunter, Richard. *Plato's Symposium*. New York: Oxford University Press, 2004.

Irigaray, Luce. "Sorcerer Love: A Reading of Plato's *Symposium*, 'Diotima's Speech.'" In *Feminism and the History of Philosophy*. Edited by Genevieve Lloyd, 68–78. New York: Oxford, 2002.

Irwin, Eleanor. "The Invention of Virginity on Olympus." In *Virginity Revisited* (2007), 13–23.

Irwin, Elizabeth. *Solon and Early Greek Poetry*. Cambridge: Cambridge University Press, 2005.

Irwin, T. H. "Plato: The Intellectual Background." In *The Cambridge Companion to Plato* (1992), 51–89.

Jaeger, Werner. *Paideia*. 2 volumes. New York: Oxford University Press, 1939.

Jameson, Michael. "The Asexuality of Dionysus." In *Masks of Dionysus* (1993), 44–64.

Janko, Richard. *The Iliad: A Commentary*. Volume 4: *Books 13–16*. Cambridge: Cambridge University Press, 1992.

Kahn, Charles. *Anaximander and the Origins of Greek Cosmology*. New York: Columbia University Press, 1960.

———. *Plato and the Socratic Dialogue: The Philosophical Use of a Literary Form*. Cambridge: Cambridge University Press, 1996.

Karageorghis, Jacqueline and Vassos. "The Great Goddess of Cyprus or the Genesis of Aphrodite in Cyprus." In *Sex and Gender in the Ancient Near East* (2002), 263–82.

Kirk, Geoffrey S. *The Iliad: A Commentary*. Volume 1: *Books 1–4*. Cambridge: Cambridge University Press, 1985.

Kirk, Geoffrey S., John E. Raven, and Malcolm Schofield. *The Presocratic Philosophers*. 2d edition. Cambridge: Cambridge University Press, 1983.

Kofman, Sarah. "Socrates and His Twins (The Socrates[es] of Plato's *Symposium*)." In *Feminism and the History of Philosophy* (2002), 41–67.

Kraut, Richard. "The Defense of Justice in Plato's *Republic*." In *The Cambridge Companion to Plato* (1992), 311–37.

Lacey, Walter K. *The Family in Classical Greece*. London: Thames and Hudson, 1968.

Lapatin, Kenneth. "The Statue of Athena and Other Treasures in the Parthenon." In *The Parthenon: From Antiquity to the Present*. Edited by Jenifer Neils, 261–91. Cambridge: Cambridge University Press, 2005.

Lear, Jonathan. "Inside and Outside the *Republic*." In *Essays on Plato's Psychology* (2001), 169–201.

Lesher, James H., Debra Nails, and Frisbee C. C. Sheffield. *Plato's Symposium: Issues in Interpretation and Reception*. Cambridge, MA: Center for Hellenic Studies of Harvard University Press, 2006.

Loraux, Nicole. *Born of the Earth: Myth and Politics in Athens*. Trans. Selina Stewart. Ithaca, NY: Cornell University Press, 2000.

Lord, Carnes. "Aristotle's Anthropology." In *Essays on the Foundations of Aristotelian Political Science*. Edited by Carnes Lord and David K. O'Connor, 49–73. Berkeley: University of California Press, 1991.

Ludwig, Paul W. *Eros and Polis: Desire and Community in Greek Political Theory*. Cambridge: Cambridge University Press, 2002.

Manville, Philip Brook. "Toward a New Paradigm of Athenian Citizenship." In *Athenian Identity and Civic Ideology*. Edited by Alan L. Boegehold and Adele C. Scafuro, 21–33. Baltimore: Johns Hopkins University Press, 1994.

Marcovich, Miroslav. "From Ishtar to Aphrodite." *Journal of Aesthetic Education* 30 (1996): 43–59.

Marinatos, Nanno. "The Cosmic Journey of Odysseus." *Numen* 43 (2001): 381–416.

Marrou, Henri I. *A History of Education in Antiquity*. Translated by George Lamb. New York: Sheed and Ward, 1956.

McGahey, Robert. *The Orphic Moment: From Shaman to Poet-Thinker in Plato, Nietzsche, and Mallarmé*. Albany, NY: SUNY Press, 1994.

Mikalson, Jon D. "Erechtheus and the Panathaneia." *American Journal of Philology* 97 (1976): 141–53.

Miller, Margaret C. *Athens and Persia in the Fifth Century BC: A Study in Cultural Receptivity*. Cambridge: Cambridge University Press, 1997.

Mills, Sophie. *Theseus, Tragedy, and Athenian Empire*. Oxford: Clarendon Press, 1997.

Mitchel-Boyask, Robin. "Euripides' *Hippolytus* and the Trials of Manhood (The Ephebia?)." In *Rites of Passage in Ancient Greece: Literature, Religion, Society*.

Edited by Mark W. Padilla, 42–66. Lewisburg, PA: Bucknell University Press, 1999.

Morris, Ian. "The Use and Abuse of Homer." *Classical Antiquity* 5 (1986): 81–138.

———. *Archaeology as Cultural History*. Oxford: Blackwell, 2000.

Murray, Oswyn. *Early Greece*. Atlantic Heights, NJ: Humanities Press, 1980.

———. "The Affair of the Mysteries: Democracy and the Drinking Group." In *Sympotica* (1990), 149–61.

Neils, Jenifer. "'With Noblest Images on All Sides': The Ionic Frieze of the Parthenon." In *The Parthenon: From Antiquity to the Present* (2005), 199–223.

Nussbaum, Martha. *The Fragility of Goodness: Luck and Ethics in Greek Tragedy and Philosophy*. Cambridge: Cambridge University Press, 2001.

Obbink, Dirk. "Dionysus Poured Out: Ancient and Modern Theories of Sacrifice and Cultural Formation." In *Masks of Dionysus* (1993), 65–86.

Ober, Josiah. *Political Dissent in Democratic Athens: Intellectual Critics of Popular Rule*. Princeton: Princeton University Press, 1998.

Ogden, Daniel. *Greek Bastardy in the Classical and Hellenistic Periods*. Oxford: Clarendon Press, 1996.

———. "Binding Spells: Curse Tablets and Voodoo Dolls in the Greek and Roman Worlds." In *Witchcraft and Magic in Europe: Greece and Rome*. Edited by Bengt Ankarloo and Stuart Clark, 1–90. Philadelphia: University of Pennsylvania, 1999.

Orwin, Clifford. "Feminine Justice: The End of the Seven against Thebes." *Classical Philology* 75 (1980): 187–96.

Osborne, Robin. "Law, the Democratic Citizen and the Representation of Women in Classical Athens." *Past and Present* 155 (1997): 3–33.

Ostwald, Martin. "Athens as a Cultural Centre." CAH, 2d edition. Volume 5: *The Fifth Century B.C.* (1992), 306–69.

Parker, Robert. *Miasma: Pollution and Purification in Early Greek Religion*. Oxford: Clarendon Press, 1983.

______. *Athenian Religion: A History*. Oxford: Clarendon Press, 1996.

———. *Polytheism and Society at Athens*. Oxford: Oxford University Press, 2005.

Patterson, Cynthia B. *The Family in Greek History*. Cambridge, MA: Harvard University Press, 1998.

Pieper, Josef. *Enthusiasm and Divine Madness: On the Platonic Dialogue Phaedrus*. Translated by Richard and Clara Winston. South Bend, IN: St. Augustine's Press, 2000.

Pomeroy, Sarah B. *Families in Classical and Hellenistic Greece: Representations and Realities*. Oxford: Clarendon Press, 1997.

Randall, John Hermann. *Aristotle*. New York: Columbia University Press, 1960.

Rehm, Rush. *Marriage to Death: The Conflation of Wedding and Funeral Rituals in Greek Tragedy*. Princeton: Princeton University Press, 1994.

Rhodes, P. J. "The Athenian Revolution." CAH, 2d edition. Volume 5: *The Fifth Century B.C.* (1992), 62–95.

———. *A History of the Classical Greek World, 478–323 BC*. Malden, MA: Blackwell, 2006.

Robertson, Noel. "Orphic Mysteries and Dionysiac Ritual." In *Greek Mysteries: The Archaeology and Ritual of Ancient Greek Secret Cults*. Edited by Michael B. Cosmopoulos, 218–40. London and New York: Routledge, 2003.

Roisman, Hanna M. *Nothing Is As It Seems: The Tragedy of the Implicit in Euripides' Hippolytus*. Lanham, MD: Rowman & Littlefield, 1999.

Roochnik, David. *Beautiful City: The Dialectical Character of Plato's Republic*. Ithaca, NY: Cornell University Press, 2003.

———. *Retrieving the Ancients*. Malden, MA: Blackwell, 2004.

Rose, H. J. "The Bride of Hades." *Classical Philology* 25 (1925): 238–42.

Rosen, Stanley. *Plato's Symposium*. 2d edition. New Haven: Yale University Press, 1987.

Rosivach, Vincent J. "Autochthony and the Athenians." *Classical Quarterly* n.s. 37 (1987): 294–306.

Roth, Paul. "Teresias as *Mantis* and Intellectual in Euripides' *Bacchae*." *Transactions of the American Philological Association* 114 (1984): 59–69.

Rowe, Christopher. "The *Symposium* as a Socratic Dialogue." In *Plato's Symposium* (2006), 11–22.

Saxonhouse, Arlene W. *Fear of Diversity: The Birth of Political Science in Ancient Greek Thought*. Chicago: University of Chicago Press, 1992.

———. "Myths and the Origins of Cities: Reflections on the Autochtony Theme in Euripides' *Ion*." In *Greek Tragedy and Political Theory* (1986), 252–73.

Seaford, Richard. "Dionysus as Destroyer of the Household: Homer, Tragedy, and the Polis." In *Masks of Dionysus* (1993), 115–46.

Schlesier, Renate. "Mixtures of Masks: Maenads as Tragic Models." In *Masks of Dionysus* (1993), 89–114.

Schwab, Katherine A. "Celebrations of Victory: The Metopes of the Parthenon." In *The Parthenon: From Antiquity to the Present* (2005), 159–97.

Schwartz, Joel D. "Human Action and Political Action in *Oedipus Tyrannos*." In *Greek Tragedy and Political Theory* (1986), 183–209.

Scodel, Ruth. "Sophoclean Tragedy." In *A Companion to Greek Tragedy* (2005), 233–50.

Segal, Charles. "Trachiniae." In idem, *Tragedy and Civilization: An Interpretation of Sophocles*, 60–108. Cambridge, MA: Published for Oberlin College by Harvard University Press, 1981.

———. *Dionysiac Poetics and Euripides' Bacchae*. Princeton: Princeton University Press, 1982.

———. "Theatre, Ritual and Commemoration in Euripides' *Hippolytus*." *Ramus* 17 (1988): 52–74.

———. "Greek Tragedy and Society: A Structuralist Perspective." In *Greek Tragedy and Political Theory* (1986), 43–75.

———. *Oedipus Tyrannus: Tragic Heroism and the Limits of Knowledge*. New York: Twayne Publishers, 1993.

———. *Singers, Heroes, and Gods in the Odyssey*. Ithaca, NY: Cornell University Press, 1994.

Sheffield, Frisbee C. C. *Plato's Symposium: The Ethics of Desire*. Oxford: Oxford University Press, 2006.

Sissa, Guilia. *Greek Virginity*. Translated by Arthur Goldhammer. Cambridge, MA: Harvard University Press, 1990.

———. "Sexual Bodybuilding: Aeschines against Timarchus." In *Constructions of the Classical Body* (1999), 147–68.

Slatkin, Laura. "*Oedipus at Colonus*: Exile and Integration." In *Greek Tragedy and Political Theory* (1986), 210–21.

Sourvinou-Inwood, Christiane. "Festivals and Mysteries: Aspects of the Eleusinian Cult." In *Greek Mysteries* (2003), 25–49.

Strauss, Barry S. "On Aristotle's Critique of Athenian Democracy." In *Essays on the Foundations of Aristotelian Political Science* (1991), 212–33.

Strauss, Leo. *On Plato's Symposium*. Chicago: University of Chicago Press, 2001.

Tandy, David W. *Warriors into Traders: The Power of the Market in Early Greece*. Berkeley: University of California Press, 1997.

Taylor, A. E. *Plato: The Man and His Work*. New York: Meridian Books, 1957.

Thalmann, William. *The Swineherd and the Bow: Representations of Class in the Odyssey*. Ithaca, NY: Cornell University Press, 1998.

———. "Review of Carol Dougherty, *The Raft of Odysseus: Ethnographic Imagination of Homer's Odyssey*." *Classical Journal* 98 (2002): 221–24.

Vernant, Jean-Pierre. *The Origins of Greek Thought*. Ithaca, NY: Cornell University Press, 1982.

———. *Myth and Thought among the Greeks*. London: Routledge & Kegan Paul, 1983.

———. "A General Theory of Sacrifice and the Slaying of the Victim in the Greek *Thusia*." In idem, *Mortals and Immortals: Collected Essays*. Edited by Froma Zeitlin, 290–302. Princeton: Princeton University Press, 1991.

Vernant, Jean-Pierre, and Pierre Vidal-Naquet. *Myth and Tragedy in Ancient Greece*. New York: Zone Books, 1988.

Vidal-Naquet, Pierre. *The Black Hunter: The Forms of Thought and the Forms of Society in the Greek World*. Translated by Andrew Szegedy-Maszak. Baltimore: Johns Hopkins University Press, 1986.

Wagner, Ellen. "Introduction." In *Essays on Plato's Psychology*. Edited by Ellen Wagner, 1–32. Lanham, MD: Lexington Books, 2001.

Walker, E. M. "The Periclean Democracy." In CAH, 1st edition. Volume 5: *Athens 478–401 B.C.* (1927), 98–112.

West, Martin L. *The Orphic Poems*. Oxford: Clarendon Press, 1983.

———. *East Face of Helicon: West Asiatic Elements in Greek Poetry and Myth*. Oxford: Clarendon Press, 1997.

White, David A. *Rhetoric and Reality in Plato's Phaedrus*. Albany, NY: SUNY Press, 1993.

Wider, Kathleen. "Women Philosophers in the Greek World: Donning the Mantle." *Hypatia* 1 (1986): 21–62.

Williams, Charles K. *The Bacchae of Euripides: A New Version*. Introduction by Martha Nussbaum, vii–xliv. New York: Farrar, Strauss & Giroux, 1990.

Winkler, John. *Constraints of Desire: The Anthropology of Sex and Gender in Ancient Greece*. New York: Routledge, 1990.

———. "Laying Down the Law: The Oversight of Men's Sexual Behavior in Classical Athens." In *Before Sexuality* (1990), 171–209.

Zaidman, Louise Bruit, and Pauline Schmitt Pantel. *Religion in the Ancient Greek City*. Cambridge: Cambridge University Press, 1989.

Zeitlin, Froma. "Thebes: Theater of Self and Society in Athenian Drama." In *Greek Tragedy and Political Theory* (1986), 101–41.

———. "Staging Dionysus between Athens and Thebes." In *Masks of Dionysus* (1993), 147–82.

———. *Playing the Other: Gender and Society in Classical Greek Literature*. Chicago: University of Chicago Press, 1996.

Zimmermann, Bernhard. *Greek Tragedy: An Introduction*. Baltimore and London: Johns Hopkins University Press, 1991.

Subject Index

Index of Biblical Texts

Greek Texts